Bookplate ink

*Shirin Dastur Patel*

*A LIFE OF OUR TIMES*

# A Life of Our Times

RAJESHWAR DAYAL

*Orient Longman*

ORIENT LONGMAN LIMITED

*Registered Office*
3-6- 272 Himayatnagar, Hyderabad 500 029 (A.P.), India

*Other Offices*
Bangalore, Bhopal, Bhubaneshwar, Calcutta, Chennai, Ernakulam,
Guwahati, Hyderabad, Jaipur, Lucknow, Mumbai, New Delhi, Patna

© Orient Longman Limited 1998
First Published 1998

ISBN 81 250 1546 9

*Typeset by*
Scribe Consultants
New Delhi 110 029

*Printed in India at*
Baba Barkha Nath Printers
New Delhi 110 015

*Published by*
Orient Longman Limited
1/24 Asaf Ali Road
New Delhi 110 002

*To my wife*
*Susheela*

My guide, and mine own familiar friend,
We took sweet counsel together; and walked
in the house of God as friends.

after Psalm 55: 13–14

# Contents

# *Preface*

This is a record of some of the author's experiences and impressions during a lifetime which has spanned the best part of the twentieth century. It is episodic in character, dealing with separate events and periods of time.

An attempt has been made to recount events as objectively and dispassionately as possible and to avoid any undue obtrusion of the subjective and personal factor. But any piece of writing is, in a sense, autobiographical as it must perforce reflect the personality of the writer. In this sense this writing can be considered autobiographical, although it can hardly qualify as such in the classical sense.

To the contemporary reader the state of Indian society in the early years of the twentieth century seems remote and almost inconceivable. And memories of British administration, about which myths and legends abound, have receded into the tenebrous and distant shadows of the past. Having been privileged to work directly under three Prime Ministers, an impression is here recorded of their ideas, working habits and personalities. On the Simla Agreement to which India attaches much importance, a critical analysis, based on new material, including the Pakistani perception of its relevance, has been appended.

Certain international peacekeeping operations which are as of special political significance and on which new light is here being cast, have been dealt with in some detail, although they were of comparatively short duration.

This is therefore neither a historical record nor an autobiography, but a series of vignettes of events and personalities.

An attempt has been made, when dealing with complicated political issues, to present them in a readable and non-technical manner. If the author has been able to convey a glimpse of the panorama of the passing decades of the century of which he has been a witness, he shall feel amply rewarded.

It was to the insistence of those who felt that there was a story to tell, that this book owes its origin. It was a task undertaken at an age long after most have withdrawn into comfortable retirement or senility.

I am grateful to those who looked at parts of the manuscript and made useful suggestions, especially my nephew, Ravi and my wife, Susheela. To Mr T.G. Jayaraman of Orient Longman I am deeply obliged for deciphering my hand-written scrawl and typing out the text. I am obliged to Ashok Chib for his valuable comments on the Simla Agreement. The publishers, Orient Longman have been very patient and indulgent and I owe them deep appreciation.

# ONE

# *Early Years*

If you were to climb up the steep gradient to Cheena peak or the forested hillside to Larya-Kanta or up the grassy slopes of Sher-ka-Danda in Naini Tal, you would see wave after wave of green mountains, shading into blue and paling to a light purple in the far distance. And towering above them all, raising their dazzling white summits majestically towards the azure sky, you would see the great Himalayan range of eternal snow-clad peaks and mountains. Overlooking the glorious array, stands the presiding deity, with arms outstretched, the stately massif of Nanda Devi, the consort of the great God Shiva.

Framing Nanda Devi are her attendant peaks, Nanda Ghunti and Nanda Kot, and the Panch Pandavas of the Mahabharata, while standing proudly alongside is Trishul, Shiva's trident. From these immense ramparts issue the great rivers that give life and sustenance to the vast and populous plains below. One cannot but be awe-struck by a spectacle so stupendous. Young and old alike must carry away with them something of the glory, the exaltation of these mountains.

The resort town of Naini Tal, named after Naina Devi, its

presiding deity, is set in a green bowl of hills formed by the oak covered Ayarpatta to the west, Deopatta clothed in giant cypresses to the north, and Sher-ka-danda, with mixed vegetation to the east. A great landslide had brought down the northern hillside and swept away the old settlement; the debris formed a natural amphitheatre at the lake's edge. The scars have healed and are shaded by tall trees. The hillsides are dotted by the charming red-roofed bungalows of the new settlement.

The jewel of the town is the emerald-green lake which lies cradled by the surrounding hills. Lined by swaying willows, its waters ripple in the sunlight, and sail boats flit on its surface like butterflies. A temple dedicated to the goddess stands protectively on its shore.

Such were the surroundings in which I was born and brought up. They shaped my youth and have left a lasting imprint on my mind. Growing up here, I became attuned to the varying moods of nature, sensitive to the gold of the morning sun or to the purple shadows of the evening as they etched out every crease and fold in the hill; to the soughing of the wind in oak and pine; to the flower-perfumed air; to the orchestra of Himalayan bird song; to the distant sound of the shepherd's flute from across the deep valley; to the simple hill folk who dwell on the lower slopes amidst their terraced fields. I still turn to these sights and sounds for respite and renewal from the toil and tumult of life. I was the sixth child in a family of eight. Watched over and guided with loving care by a devoted mother, under the protection of a proud and affectionate father, we grew up in an atmosphere of security and harmony. Trying to live up to older brothers and a sister, I began to emulate their ways, to benefit from their conversation or their poetry recitations, to take part in their games or their riding expeditions into the hills. The house was always full of relatives and friends come for the summer, providing us with older company and a glimpse of the wider world below.

Vivid in my memory is the warm feeling of happiness and

pride, when, holding Father's hand, with my older brothers accompanying, we went to the club along the Mall. Well remembered too, is the morning when I was taken up the hill to be admitted to the kindergarten at St Mary's Convent. I remember the treasury guard saluting Father as we passed him. The smell of the rose creeper forming the hedge of Mother Florian Weir's garden, the Virgin Mary's grotto and Sister Theresa's bare classroom. The cleanly-scrubbed air of the surroundings, the silence and orderliness of the chapel—all these often come up in memory. But of these two early school years, little else lingers in my memory except the tiny garden patch which each of the children was given to tend, and my joy when the first shoots burst from the dark soil. Less pleasurable, but as vividly recalled is the sharp smack of the edge of Sister Theresa's ruler on my knuckles for some minor misdemeanour.

Before the winter winds blew and the snows fell, the courts and schools closed, and my family moved down to Haldwani, our orchard home in the foothills. Here, Father could be seen surrounded by clients as he sat at his table under a tree. A bag of silver rupees and gold coins would later be carried into the house and emptied into a tin trunk in the bedroom.

The annual return move to Naini Tal—sixteen miles by cart road and another three up a steep bridle-path—was a major operation. Preparations would start a day or two before the appointed time, when large numbers of tin trunks, crates, baskets and bundles would start piling up. On the morning of departure, a great to-do would start well before sunrise; mountains of food—fried puris, minced meat, vegetables and condiments— would be packed into baskets. The whole family and some essential luggage would be piled on to horse-driven two-wheeled tongas or ekkas, while the heavy stuff would be loaded high on bullock-carts. There were a couple of staging posts on the way up the hill, where one could rest and picnic at a mountain spring under shady trees while fresh horses were yoked in. Arriving at the staging post known as the Brewery in the late afternoon, the children would be sorted out, the youngest sitting with Mother in her dandy, a light palanquin carried by four men. The next one would be in a basket strapped to a coolie's back, or would be perched on his shoulder, strumming happily on his greasy cloth cap which had acquired the texture of leather. The older children either rode or walked. Our arrival at the shuttered house provided further excitement as doors and windows were flung open, the faithful cook got busy with his kitchen, tradesmen began arriving to replenish the larder and, after an early dinner, the whole household would be deep in slumber.

The morning's awakening made us rub our eyes in wonder: the once familiar surroundings of three months earlier seemed strangely new and different. The cool mountain air on one's face, the song of the Himalayan thrush as it hopped about on the tin roof, the croak of the raven. Nature awakening to new life after its winter slumber had a dream-like quality. It took days for the old familiar feeling to return.

But we were happy to return. We children sorted out our school things, looking forward to moving up one step to a higher class with new books and new subjects. Our eldest brother, Bhagwat, had done brilliantly at the Senior Cambridge examination and was preparing to join Allahabad University; Kishen was going to the higher classes at Philander Smith College, a fine school on the very crest of the hill with enormous views of the Great Himalaya range; Bishumber had moved up to the same school a year or two earlier.

One such home-coming stands out in my memory. The school term had just commenced when a crushing blow fell on the young household. It had the suddenness and devastation of a bolt of lightning which strikes a giant oak, incinerating it instantaneously and shrivelling up the life sap of the young trees sheltering under its protective shade. Some events have such a powerful impact that they forever cause pain when recalled, and even the solace of forgetfulness is denied. Father's sudden death of heart failure on an April morning of 1916 was such an event.

I was sitting at my kindergarten desk at school when Bishumber, who should himself have been at school, appeared at the classroom door. Sister Theresa got up to enquire of his business and after a few whispered words, came over to me and, holding me gently by the hand, said I should go home. Puzzled, I asked Bishumber as we were walking down past Reverend Mother's garden with the scent of roses filling the air, what the matter was. I listened with total incomprehension when he said Father had died. When I asked what that meant, he said: 'Who will now look after us and feed us?' I still did not understand. But then we reached the house and saw a great throng of people assembled there. A ripple of sad murmuring passed through it as we arrived.

Behind a drawn curtain, on a bed, lay Father, fully clothed in a grey suit with his eyes open, staring sightlessly at the sky. On the threshold sat Mother, distraught, with her hair undone while other ladies beside her were weeping piteously. An aunt was trying to console Mother, and as we entered, she implored Father to open his eyes at least to see his little ones who had just arrived.

The rest in my mind is a blur, except that our faithful Ayah quietly led us to the road behind the house where we would be away from it all. But we did see on the far hill a long procession hurrying behind a bier covered in red. Even our brother Mahesh, barely four at the time, noticed it and remembers. Late that afternoon we were brought back to a home now deep in gloom.

Everything seemed to have become unusually quiet; talk was in whispers, the silence being broken only by an occasional sob. A dark and portentous shadow had fallen over the home. It was to linger and leave a mark on the hearts of young and old alike.

Long after, I learnt that Father had had a heart problem which, in the state of medical knowledge at the time, had not been thought serious enough for him to settle at a lower altitude. It had been his intention to shift his law practice to the High Court at Allahabad when the children were a little older. But as time went by and he prospered and acquired substantial properties, he deferred a decision. Besides, there were Naini Tal's healthy climate and excellent educational facilities which also encouraged him to stay on.

On the morning of his death, Father had taken our little sister, hardly two and a half years old, to the Crosthwaite Hospital to show her eye to the doctor, as a small mote, noticed some weeks earlier, appeared to be growing. The diagnosis was shattering. The child had a galloping form of cancer which was possibly invading the brain. Returning to the waiting room, Father collapsed on a bench and passed away almost instantly.

A terrible ordeal now began for Mother as tragedy was to follow tragedy. The lovely little child's condition worsened and the doctor advised that she be taken to Delhi to be treated by the highly reputed Dr Harish Chandra. Mother observed strict purdah. Nevertheless she undertook the journey to Delhi with the sick child and three of the younger children, including myself. Accompanying us were a cousin and servants.

One morning the child returned from the hospital with a heavy bandage where her eye had been. After the operation, Mother was advised to return home with the little invalid. But the removal of the eye did not stop the spread of the disease, and her condition rapidly worsened. My sister was the gentlest and sweetest of God's creatures, a happy child, never crying or complaining. Although she must have endured intense pain, never a moan or cry escaped her parched lips. One night she was quietly relieved of her suffering.

The lifelong love and companionship between Mother and our sister-in-law helped to sustain both through the difficult years ahead. Bhabi, who was the wife of our step-brother, was only a few years younger than Mother. She was a rare being, with no sense of self, wholly dedicated to serving others, and even at the grimmest moments, smiling and bravely trying to restore everyone's drooping spirits.

Mother, who had led such a sheltered and secure life, now determined to be the father of the family as well. She had never been to school but had been taught in the traditional way at her modest home. She wrote and spoke beautiful Urdu; she read Hindi books and had a good knowledge of Persian. Spoken English and Western ways she learnt from a warm-hearted Anglo-Indian lady who became a close family friend. Mother taught herself to copy Father's very regular English handwriting as well as to read English. She took up the management of our properties and resources and set about organising the life of the household without cutting down on anything. We continued to retain our two or three horses, the same complement of servants and to attend the same expensive schools, as well as to receive house guests who still came but now in diminishing number. She had the greatest influence on our lives, and though secluded from the outside world, she had remarkably sound and accurate judgement about people and things and the advice she gave was almost infallible. Her unseen presence was felt by the tradesmen and local officials with whom we had to deal and she dealt with the family's affairs—domestic and business—with a sure hand. She had extremely progressive views. Though in purdah herself, a practice which she later gave up, she felt strongly about the general backwardness of women and their absence from the professions and other activities outside the home. In another day and age she would have been an active social reformer; but she died of cancer at the early age of forty-nine.

Mother was widowed at the age of thirty-four; our step-brother being only about ten years younger. He had the utmost difficulty in passing any examination and his repeated failures at the law examination caused Mother deep disappointment. By contrast, Bhagwat was an outstandingly clever young man, brilliant at his studies, bright in conversation and with a fine presence. He had excelled himself at the Senior Cambridge examination and great things were expected of him as he went down to the plains to join Allahabad University. Kishen was to follow two or three years later. Our step-brother at long last qualified to practice law, but he was too timid to make an appearance in court, even though implored to accept their briefs by Father's old clients, who were still loyal to him. Instead, he too descended to the plains, ostensibly to learn the work, a process which seemed to have been without result. So Bishumber and I, a couple of years younger, were left to help Mother with her concerns.

It was a good, though unusual training for us. We learnt to deal with banks, tradesmen and municipal authorities. A couple of years later when Bhagwat went to England for his further studies and to take the ICS examination (as no lesser employment was considered suitable for him), we also learnt how to deal with bank drafts in pounds sterling. Meanwhile, our regular studies continued at the same boys' school at which I was for nine long years, spending nine months each year at school, riding or walking up at 7.15 in the morning, rain, hail or shine, spring, summer and autumn after which we dispersed for the winter. There were always two of us—sometimes three—continuously at the same school for twenty-one years from 1909–1930.

Bhagwat was the first Indian boy to be admitted in Naini Tal to a European school, and the Principal, a Reverend Hyde, was so impressed by him that he broke convention by accepting him. But he advised that Bhagwat should call himself Bertram Doyle—advice that was disregarded!

Our schoolmasters were devoted to their tasks and took an interest in each one's progress. School education was on English lines—poetry and literature, the Old and New Testaments and even French and Latin figured in the curriculum. We were intensely loyal to our school and to some of the masters who encouraged us with our work and whose handwriting we even emulated. The Principal, a Territorial Force Colonel, R.C. Busher (Dick), was a stern disciplinarian who kept the unruly boys in fear of his corrective whip. Many ingenious devices were invented by the habitual offenders to soften the sharp cracks of the cane on their posteriors. 'Ma' Brandon was the Urdu teacher, a language which she could hardly speak. Kenneth Macintosh, who ostensibly taught French, was wholly innocent of any knowledge of the language. He ascribed our lack of progress to our lack of knowledge of English, as in his view most of the words were shared by the two languages but mispronounced by the French!

School was both a pleasure and a penance; a penance during the fierce three-month-long monsoon when the sun could not be seen for days. Rising early at dawn with the rain cascading down and beating a deafening tattoo on the tin roof, we would dress hurriedly and unwillingly gulp down breakfast and venture out on horse or foot to our distant school. Umbrellas and raincoats provided only minimal shelter, we arrived at school with dripping legs and squelching shoes. Coughs and colds, not surprisingly, were our frequent lot. But though an equally good school lay hardly ten minutes away from our house, we would not dream of changing one for the other. Our old school shut its doors at the start of the second world war. The building was later taken over to become the Birla Vidya Mandir.

At home, we lived in Indian style, picking up Urdu from Mother, observing all the festivals and regularly visiting the temple of Naina Devi. Our training and upbringing seemed to run on parallel lines. Mother laid the greatest emphasis on character-formation; she abhorred lying or deceit and, while inspiring us to give of our best, laid greater stress on honour, dignity and self-reliance.

We were an isolated family, perforce dependent upon our own resources. The hill gentry lived in the rabbit-warren of the bazaars in their traditional ways to which people from the plains were foreign. There were few other middle-class resident Indian families in the town. The Indians who did come up but only to summer in the hills, belonged mostly to the landed gentry who largely consorted with each other in their own fashion. The Anglo-Indians, too, mixed only with each other and had their own interests. As for the British, they were remote beings and could well have come from some distant planet—tall, red-faced men and tall, sour-faced women, striding along with long steps or riding big horses or being carried royally in dandies with liveried jhampanies, servants and chaprasis in resplendent red and gold uniforms. Never a word was uttered in one's direction, never a smile; they even seemed to avert their eyes as one passed by them. Their haughtiness and aloofness was matched by that of their flunkeys and servants. One could see them twice a week at the Flats, playing polo ferociously, their ladies watching from their exclusive pavilion. Polo over, they would repair to their exclusive boat-club near by, followed by a hundred pairs of dark eyes. They would also be sailing in their yachts, that being their privileged sport. Sometimes they were glimpsed from a window of the club as they gyrated on the dance floor.

The greatest fault of the British was their exclusiveness and indifference towards Indians and their ancient culture and religion. The self-imposed 'apartheid' which the British practised, was reflected in the exclusive residential areas which they favoured. The villas where these celestial beings dwelt were dotted along the most secluded parts of the wooded hills and bore nostalgic names such as 'Windermere', 'Snowdon', 'Braemar', 'Woodstock', 'Suffolk Hall', 'Killarney', etc. The houses were over-hung with wisteria or honeysuckle creepers and the gardens were imitations of English gardens. At their gate-posts were hung little black boxes marked "Not at Home", to receive visiting cards from new arrivals of their kind. Indians, but only those of impeccable credentials, could be admitted beyond those gates at prescribed hours, strictly on official business or to render homage.

These rather awesome childish impressions were imparted to us by the servants and interview-seekers who came up to seek some favour or promotion and who looked upon the burra sahibs with fear and awe. Because of their rigid exclusiveness, whatever may have been the better traits in their character were obscured by their evident failings. Years later when we too joined the senior services and, to some extent, shared the privileged position of the British officials, we discovered their admirable qualities of devotion to duty, sense of humour, and innate kindliness and fair-mindedness, concealed beneath a natural shyness and reserve. Our early impressions, we realised, were the result of ignorance and a lack of contact with the British. But at that time it was difficult to overcome the resentment one felt at belonging to a subject people while they represented the ruling race.

Naini Tal was the summer capital of the Government of the United Provinces (as Uttar Pradesh then was), and also the headquarters of the military's Eastern Command. Between April and October therefore all officials and administrators came up to Naini Tal. All the high officials with a few notable exceptions, were British. The administration, from the all-powerful Governor down to the lower Secretariat officials, as well as the administrators in the districts, each ruling over a million people or more were also mostly British. Even the higher judiciary, including the High Court, was manned by ICS men. The absolute rule of the mandarins was untrammeled by responsibility to any elective Indian assembly or politicians, and ICS men could not be removed by the Governor or even the Governor General of India, but only by the Secretary of State for India in distant Whitehall, with whom they were under contract. After World War I, however, entry to the all-India services including the ICS was made in India itself by examination. No wonder that the greatest ambition of a fond mother was for her son to enter the 'heaven-born' service. Entry into the service involved qualifying at the very top at a gruelling examination held both in London and New Delhi.

With Bhagwat's return from England in 1924, a new dimension entered our lives. We greatly admired him for his fine mind, personality, literary tastes and culture and owed him much for the broadening of our horizons. He inspired in us a taste for English literature; he introduced us to classical western music, and brought some western influences into our predominantly Indian way of life.

At home we heard and spoke only in Urdu or Hindustani to our elders but in English to each other. While our Hindustani pronunciation and syntax was being constantly corrected, English manners and language were not discouraged provided we did not foresake our own. We thus lived in two worlds, not belonging wholly to either. But it certainly widened our horizons and created a greater awareness of and sensitivity to cultural influences from different sources.

We did quite well at school and our teachers who expected much of us were not often disappointed. In my case, it all began when I was in the third standard, aged eight or nine. I had stood second in class and proudly announced the fact at home. But instead of the expected 'Shabash' ('well done'), Mother quietly said that someone must have come first and why was it not me? This greatly hurt my self-esteem and I sulked, but something must have registered, as thereafter there were few occasions for a similar reproach. We managed to win merit scholarships both in the Junior and Senior Cambridge examinations which helped comfortably to meet our fees up to the University level. As I had secured a high position in the school-leaving examination with distinctions in Mathematics, English and Urdu with a handsome scholarship, it was thought that I should take up a science course, which the brighter students were expected to do. It was also decided that I could telescope a two year course in one year; I was soon to prove how mistaken these assumptions were. The Intermediate College at Allahabad—the Kayastha Pathshala—which I joined was a devastating experience from the start. An untidy jumble of buildings, the place had a shoddy and unkempt appearance. There was an air of languor and neglect about everything. The classrooms were laden with dust and a large pankha swished overhead trying unsuccessfully to stir the torpid air. The students were of a piece with the surroundings, hailing mostly from villages and regarded me with not a little curiosity. For my part I found their habits of sitting cross-legged on the benches, scratching themselves, and behaving in a generally uncouth fashion rather obnoxious. The teachers seemed to share in the general apathy and were an uninspiring and dispirited lot. They rattled off their lectures without much regard for their audience and left. The English teacher, a venerable Bengali gentleman in pince-nez spectacles, had a totally unintelligible pronunciation. The authorship of the only essay I wrote which was on Charles Dickens was questioned by him as having been plagiarised. The portly and turbaned physics and chemistry teacher was more interested in the shop that he ran in Katra bazaar than in his students. Soon, I too began to be infected by the general lassitude and, to make matters worse, I was completely at sea with the science and mathematics I was reading.

Dr Tara Chand, the Principal, tried valiantly to dispel the listless air of the institution by prescribing uniformity in dress which would smarten up the students and staff, everyone was required to wear khaki shorts and white shirt. The result was bizarre. The Principal himself set the example and other teachers and students had to conform, despite their protests. The science teacher's outfit was crowned by his familiar bulky turban, but his legs, used to squatting, hardly seemed able to sustain his weight. The students looked a motley crowd, their newly-exposed and little-exercised legs hardly providing an aesthetic sight. To further activate students and staff, there was compulsory parade in the afternoons, and we were formed into platoons. Our drill-master was none other than the science teacher. He and the other teachers had been given some instruction in elementary drill. All we could do was to stand to attention and form fours, or to about turn and march (generally out of step). The different platoons would snake around the limited grounds, intersecting each other. After half an hour of this ordeal in the sun, we were too hot and bothered to pay much attention at class.

In the intermediate examination I barely scraped through with a second class. That made me decide to take up arts at the university, which I looked forward even more eagerly to joining. The impressive buildings, the quality of the professors and their teaching fully justified the high reputation of Allahabad University as one of the very best in the country. Many of the teachers were eminent scholars and authors of considerable distinction and some of their original research had won wide acclaim.

The new K.P. University College, which I now joined, faced the grand University Senate Hall; it pioneered the holding of tutorials on Oxbridge lines. Forsaking the rough and tumble of the Bar, my brother Bhagwat had joined it as the Warden, his heart being more in education than in law. Dr Tara Chand had moved over to be the head of the college. The new college attracted good students and athletes and soon acquired a fine reputation. As some form of sport at the university and college was obligatory, and not being an athlete, I plumped for the University Training Corps.

A British Staff Sergeant who had a particularly salty vocabulary and was a martinet for discipline was in charge of our training. The recruits assembled at the armoury at the dot of 6.30 a.m. and were issued used uniforms and equipment, evidently leftovers of World War I. The uniforms were hopelessly oversized, but somehow, with belts and braces, we managed to defy gravity. Woollen stockings, puttees, heavy hob-nailed and well-worn ammunition boots, webbing belts and straps which were our harness, completed our outfit. Before parade, there would be much polishing of brass buttons and buckles and much effort to coax some shine out of the old boots whose tough leather often needed softening with oil. After being put through our preliminary paces with much bantering and hectoring in his strong Yorkshire accent, Staff Sergeant Giles would ultimately pronounce us as no longer being a total rabble. In due course we were issued dummy rifles and later qualified in the use of bayonets against stuffed gunny-bags. Our drill and marching reached a point when, with bayonets flashing and to the accompaniment of our own bagpipe band and with much energetic drumming, we were thought fit for public exposure and taken for long route marches.

The two week winter camp in bitter cold and rain was, however, a rough and rugged experience. There was much parading, night and day marches, sundry exercises and games which occupied all our days. Sentry duty at night was a particularly unpleasant chore. We slept crowded, eight to a small tent, on the damp ground on thin tarpaulins and blankets. The food was execrable, always gritty, the lavatory arrangements were nauseous, while only the hardiest would dare a shower in the open in icy cold water. Despite four years in the training corps, I could never rise above the rank of lance-corporal and it was no consolation that Napoleon made all his great conquests rising from that lowly rank.

There was a strange sequel to my none too glorious soldierly career. There had been a great agitation in the Indian Central Assembly and press about the almost total exclusion of Indians from the officer ranks of the Indian Army. A Royal Commission was accordingly appointed to enquire into the matter under General Sir Andrew Skeen. On one particularly torpid and humid afternoon while a lecture on some dull branch of economics was in progress and I sat drowsily at the back of the classroom, there was a sudden flurry of activity which jolted me to wakefulness. General Skeen and members of his Commission walked in and after some conversation with Professor Rudra and between themselves, started peering at the students. Suddenly I heard my name called out; when I stood up, I was asked to see the General in the Professor's ante-room. I followed doubtfully, wondering what it was all about. The General, after eyeing me, asked what career I intended to follow; I replied hesitantly that I supposed I would take one of the competitive examinations. What if I did not succeed, asked the General. I said I had not thought about that. I was then asked whether I would like to join the Army. Quite taken aback, I stammered that I had not thought of that either. The General said reassuringly that if I would like to be considered, I should let him know at next morning's parade which he would be inspecting. I made no further contact with him nor he with me. I was certainly not cut out to be a soldier and I shudder to think what could have became of me—or of our Army—had I said 'yes' to the General.

The Indian Army was officered entirely by British Officers, from subalterns upwards, a sort of 'apartheid' being practiced in it. It was put out that no British officer would condescend to serve under a superior Indian Officer; accordingly an 'Indianised' unit, the 4/19 Hyderabad Regiment was assigned for the appointment of Indian officers which they joined as Second-Lieutenants, the senior officers still being British. Those who managed to survive the gruelling training course at Sandhurst which was beset with discriminatory hurdles, had a rough run when they joined their segregated regiment in India, then posted at Allahabad. There were many casualties among our friends, some having been sent down from Sandhurst, others cashiered and sacked later. Two of the great soldiers of the Indian Army—Field Marshal Cariappa and General Thimayya—were junior officers in Allahabad at the time and we used to hear from them of their harsh treatment. All this offered little encouragement for a military career even for those who had an aptitude for it.

When the B.A. results came out, I acquired an entirely meretricious reputation for scholarship. Having wasted much of my time during the year, I was assailed by pangs of conscience a couple of months before the examination. I then got down to leafing through the yet unread prescribed volumes, working from dawn to midnight, keeping at hand some classic textbooks for the essential facts. I thus managed, before each paper, to refresh my memory and to regurgitate all that I had ingested the previous day. This technique, born of sheer panic, stood me in good stead at the examinations. I got a high position in the B.A., winning the history and economics prizes, medals and a merit scholarship. In the M.A. in history I also managed to pull off a surprise by standing first in the University. I do not consider that these feats made me a good student as I took no part in debates or dramatics and was indifferent at sports and games.

The Civil Disobedience Movement was raging and there was a great ferment among the students, many of whom were torn between joining the agitation and abandoning their studies, or trying to qualify for a living.

Many great political leaders came to address the students. We were thrilled by the eloquence of Sarojini Naidu, greatly excited by the stirring words of Netaji Subash Chandra Bose, whom I drove in my brother's car from one meeting to another. Jawaharlal Nehru was the spoilt darling of the students, who accepted anything from him. On one occasion, trying to leave the Senata Hall he was mobbed by the adoring students; in a display of his famous temper and petulance, he lashed out to left and right with his baton. His sister, Krishna, was adopted as a sort of mascot and half the students seemed to have fallen in love with her. Also some of the revolutionaries who believed in the cult of violence were much admired.

The student community watched with fascination and

sympathy the frequent protest meetings and processions led largely by the Nehru family, but not many joined the movement. The call to abandon schools and colleges, law courts and offices, etc. and to offer civil disobedience, largely fell on dèaf ears at the university. The students were more preoccupied with the need to qualify for earning a livelihood than with anything else. Nor were they disposed to burn foreign goods or clothes as they could not possibly afford a second wardrobe. Since not many avenues of employment were open to educated young men at the time, the scramble for government jobs continued unabated. Also, the prospect of being submerged in an anonymous mass of processionists and braving police beating, and spells in prison, was less than alluring. Therefore, while the students were greatly moved by the swelling mass agitation, they were unwilling to become insignificant drops in an ocean of faceless humanity. There were, of course exceptions, sometimes even among non-Indians. A young Ceylonese freshly returned from Oxford who was staying with us, was so taken up by what he witnessed that he decided to join the movement forthwith. Clad precariously in an unfamiliar khadi dhoti, he made a bundle of his Oxford suits and blazers to which he added his English tennis racquet for good measure, and flung the lot into the smouldering bonfire of foreign things. After this purificatory sacrifice, he joined the processionists led by Krishna Nehru and shared in their daily travails. After some months of this and considerable personal experience of the attentions of the Indian police, his enthusiasm waned and he took off for his own country. It was said that his devotion to the cause was exceeded only by that to the enchanting Krishna.

What really thrilled the students was the cold courage and self-sacrifice of the revolutionaries, the votaries of violence. At the very gates of the University a great drama took place when an epic battle was fought to the death between an intrepid revolutionary, Chandrashekhar Azad, and the British

Superintendent of Police which ended only when Azad, his ammunition exhausted, was shot down. Stories of political assassination attempts, mostly in Bengal, some successful, received much attention and applause. The Communists attracted a certain following but not many continued with the movement on leaving the University.

Yet another political tendency which found favour chiefly among the educated and professional and propertied classes, was represented by such patriotic figures as Sir Tej Bahadur Sapru, M.R. Jayakar, Hriday Nath Kunzru, Rt.Hon. Srinivasa Sastry, Sir Surendra Nath Banerji, Sir Feroze Shah Mehta, to name a few. They believed in a policy of constructive cooperation, the establishment of a parliamentary system of government responsible to the people, and independence within the Commonwealth. They advocated the entry of Indians in increasing numbers into the senior administrative services and the armed forces. Their methods were constitutional with due respect for the law, and they believed in achieving their objectives by a process of peaceful negotiation. They were skilled negotiators and constitutional and legal experts of eminence. By these means, Indians could be enabled to penetrate the citadel of power from within rather than attempt to assail the impregnable fortress from without. They joined issue with the Congress on boycotting educational institutions and resigning from government jobs and professions as this would only deprive the country of talent and experience which it sorely needed. They also cautioned against the breaking of laws, civil disobedience and jail-filling, as this would breed habits of lawlessness and indiscipline which would indubitably endure even after independence and make the country ungovernable. All other political movements were, however, eventually swamped out by the Congress flood.

After doing my M.A. I applied to take the forthcoming examination for the Indian Civil Service (ICS) in January 1931 and was asked to appear before a Medical Board at Lucknow in

August. Its Chairman was a Colonel Townsend, the Civil Surgeon there. As the candidates were numerous, they were divided into batches, I falling in a group headed by a Major Salamatullah, a man of enormous proportions who was the Jail Superintendent. To my dismay, I was declared to be anaemic and therefore medically unfit. This caused much disappointment among family and friends and plans began to be discussed about my taking the London examination which, incidentally, offered many more vacancies and was regarded as easier than the Delhi examination which had only three or four places. To avoid a similar mishap, I went for a medical examination to the Civil Surgeon of Allahabad, who, unknown to us and by a stroke of fortune, turned out to be none other than Colonel Townsend, recently transferred there. He found me one hundred per cent fit. When told that only a couple of months previously his Board had rejected me, he was shocked and indignant, and fair-minded man that he was, he immediately sent a strong letter to the head of his department in Lucknow demanding a rectification of the mistake. The wheels of Government thus being set in motion, I heard after some time that I would be permitted to appear again before a Board set up for the benefit of the half a dozen failed candidates from London who were returning to take the Delhi examination. When I again appeared before Major Salamatullah, who had obviously received a reprimand, he was all smiles and remarked how well I now looked. I was passed, and in early December, informed that I could appear at the January examination.

In the doubt and confusion of the previous few months, I had abandoned whatever preparations I had begun and felt most diffident about taking a gruelling test with such little preparation as the limited time would permit. But Mother, with her unerring instinct, gave me heart to make the attempt, which would at least, provide useful experience. The examination, held in the stately Metcalfe House, was abuzz with candidates from all parts of India engaged in animated discussion. Many of them, smartly turned out, seemed very knowledgeable and confident. After the paper, they again engaged in an animated post-mortem. I had offered many papers in Indian, British and European history, besides political organisation and political theory, all of which required much study. The examination stretched over three weeks, and the frequent gaps of half a day to a whole day between papers provided some opportunity for preparation. When the ordeal at last ended, it left me exhausted and without hope as I returned home to Allahabad.

I soon went on holiday to Jamshedpur where I received an urgent letter from Allahabad asking me to return as the U.P. Government had asked for a certificate of vaccination. I paid no attention to it since I had already had a successful medical examination. But a telegram from my brother followed to say that the certificate had positively to be furnished by a certain date. My brother-in-law Prem Narain Mathur, with whom I was staying, said that this clearly meant that I had got into the ICS and I was packed was off home, still doubting my luck. A few days later the newspapers came out with a list of candidates in order of merit. There were four vacancies and I was fifth. I began receiving letters of sympathy from friends and relations for so narrow a miss.

The suspense was, however, short-lived as a spate of official letters began arriving asking about my choice of university and college in England for my training, my preference in regard to the province of posting, etc. It transpired that by a stroke of luck, Muslim candidates had obtained the second and fourth places against their reserved quota for the year of five or six. That enabled not only me to get in but also my colleague, Vidya Shankar, who stood eighth.

I had seldom been out of my home state and was hugely impressed by the great metropolis of Bombay, when I soon went there to begin the voyage to Britain as an ICS probationer. I found the immensity of the sea overwhelming, while the enormous bulk of the ocean-going vessel, the P&O *SS Maloja* seemed unbelievable. I explored the ship's great public rooms, treaded the broad promenade decks and revelled in the wide choice offered at each meal in the cavernous dining hall. My two colleagues from Allahabad with whom I shared a table were absolutely terrified of the daily knife and fork drill which they performed most inexpertly, while we all found the rather supercilious British table steward most daunting. After a couple of exciting days, the old tub of 11,000 tons began rolling and pitching as the Arabian Sea became somewhat boisterous. For the next couple of days I lay tossing uncomfortably in my heaving bunk while my companions in the second-class cabin moved around merrily, much to my envy and annoyance. Gradually emerging unsteadily for some fresh air to get away from the constant odour of food and ship's paint, the agony began to abate as we approached Aden, a coaling station. The Red Sea was hot and airless and it was a relief to arrive at Port Said. The entire ship-load disgorged itself at Port Said and made for the vast store of Simon Artz, full of miscellaneous goods. The Mediterranean was cool and drizzly and, as we passed through the Straits of Messina, the silhouette of Stromboli appeared in eruption. Arrived at Marseilles, we disembarked to take the boat train to Calais. Completely lost, we clung to the uniformed and English-speaking Thomas Cook's guide who led us to the train.

Reaching Paris at night we piled into a taxi with our voluminous baggage (consisting in my case of an enormous cabin trunk of buffalo hide inherited from my brother Bhagwat) and made for the modest Hotel du Nord. I had been advised by Bhagwat to do so as the Gare du Nord railway station, where we were to entrain for Calais, lay just across the square. To our dismay, there was not a room vacant and after a fruitless dash from hotel to hotel, we landed up at the Grand Hotel d'Angleterre, where, after much pleading, two rooms were found for the three of us. The great Paris Exhibition was on and every hotel was full to the rafters. It was well past midnight and we looked forward to a few hours rest before catching our early morning train. The Grand Hotel was indeed grand and we had been warned by the receptionist about the cost. After getting installed in our rooms, I looked in next door to see my companions, inadvertently locking myself out. Much of the rest of the short night was spent in going up and down in my pyjamas looking for the night watchman with the master-key. Bleary-eyed, we caught the early morning train to Calais where we boarded a ferry which plied to Dover across the turbulent English Channel. The twenty-two miles across was sheer agony for the passengers who had all been doled out basins as a matter of routine. It was a relief to detrain at Victoria Station, our final destination after a voyage of ten days followed by a train journey of almost two. We were met by a friend who seemed to know his way around and were taken to the Indian Students Hostel on Cromwell Road. It was a crummy kind of place, noisy and reeking pungently of half-cooked spices, while the dormitory to which we were assigned was none too clean. That was to be our base until we got to our respective colleges.

Our first duty was to call on the Indian High Commissioner at Aldwych, where we received our first cheque for £75. That seemed an opulent amount and I was thrilled to receive my first renumeration. We set about equipping ourselves enthusiastically with what were almost regulation clothes, at Hector Powe's on Regent Street. There we opened a running account, as Oxbridge students were apparently considered creditworthy, a confidence not always deserved. The pound sterling went a long way those days and, although our allowance could have met our purchases, we had to make do with it for three months. It was then not *de rigeur* to wear clothes off the peg and we were measured for a full dress suit (twelve guineas), dinner jacket (nine guineas), blue and grey suits (eight and six guineas), riding breeches (three guineas) and, most functional of all, a Norfolk jacket (three and a half guineas) and grey flannels (one and half pounds each). Stiff and plain shirts, butterfly collars, ties, woollen underwear and overcoat, completed the wardrobe.

We were awestruck by the size and opulence of London with its meticulously dressed men in bowler hats and rolled umbrellas, its dazzling shop displays, its great museums and monuments and the majesty of the great city. Our first visit to a music-hall left us dazzled, as also the museums and art galleries with the profusion they contained.

Oxford was a retreat in time to the Middle Ages about which one had read in history books. Its spires, domes and steeples, its weathered college buildings, its quaint streets, all invoking the past, contrasted vividly with the youthful undergraduate population which inhabited it. I had been admitted to New College (new when founded in A.D. 1379), one of the three largest and oldest colleges. It had an 'old' quad, a 'garden' quad and a 'new' quad, and was approached through a narrow twisting lane from under an arched bridge linking two wings of an adjacent college. The Warden's Lodge was above the main entrance and my first call was on its occupant, the Right Honourable H.A.L. Fisher, a noted historian whose classic work *Bonapartism* I had read. Fisher received me in kindly manner and, after informing me (as he did all new entrants), that he had been a Cabinet Minister, spoke of the career which awaited me in the ICS. In conversation he remarked that three of the finest orators in the English language were from my country, namely Sarojini Naidu, Srinivasa Sastry and the Maharaja of Alwar.

I had been given rooms in an ancient cottage in a depression in the 'new' quad which had somehow escaped the builder's attention when the new wing was built. It was overshadowed by the huge bell tower and the old city wall which ran through the college grounds. It had a low plinth, and was damp and dark. Whatever sunshine could have trickled through was obscured by an overhanging willow. My rooms were on the ground floor. The largish sitting-room was furnished with a fireplace, but the dark and dingy bedroom had none. The baths were in a basement of the new building across the quad. Adding to the general air of gloom and menace was the tolling every quarter of an hour of the huge bell in the bell tower. My rooms were so cold and damp that I soon caught a bad chill and had to be taken to an expensive nursing home and then to the Radcliffe infirmary.

I was assigned to two tutors, one for history and the other whose designation and function I then did not know. I later discovered that he was to keep an avuncular eye on his ward, to look after his welfare and help with advice when asked and discreetly to watch his behaviour and morals. He was known as the Moral Tutor. This designation has since changed to something less inquisitorial. Some forty-five years later when I returned to Oxford as a Visiting Fellow, I looked at the name plate at the entrance of the staircase where he had lived all those years ago. To my astonishment, his name was still there! I climbed up to the third floor to see him, he recognised me and said he had been following my career, but had lost track during a certain period. When I tried to fill in the gap, he pulled out a writing pad to complete his record. I was moved by his genuine interest and concern which were almost parental.

Our main scholastic business was to receive instruction in Indian laws, history and languages. The Indian Institute was beautifully located right in the heart of Oxford in the midst of a number of colleges and adjacent to the Sheldonian Theatre and Bodleian Library, as well as the famous Macmillan Publishers. It was in a fine building built with funds collected from Indian princes, but after independence, it was unfortunately allowed to be taken over by the university authorities. I wish instead that the Indian Government had claimed it by right and set up a Centre for Indian Studies, making it also a repository for the vast store of Indian books and manuscripts, paintings and sculptures, now scattered and obscurely housed.

At the Institute the lecturers were all long-retired British members of the Indian Civil Service whose lectures were of uniform dullness. The history tutorials with Mr Williams at the college were, however, quite another matter. An essay would be set and studiously written and discussed in depth in front of a blazing fire over a glass of sherry, every assertion or loose statement being minutely dissected. It helped to sharpen one's analytical faculties and to breathe life into the subject under discussion. These sessions, which meant much reading in the excellent college library and careful presentation, were most rewarding. However, because of the daily toll on one's time at the Institute, the history tutorials had unfortunately to be abandoned.

New College was not a very friendly place; the students mostly hailed from Winchester or Eton. There was a good deal of snobbishness about those hailing from lesser schools, the lowly grammar schools were quite beyond the pale, and there was snobbishness about 'colonials' too. The 'natural' shyness and insularity of the British could hardly explain the absence of any attempt on their part to make the few Indians and students of other nationalities, understandably diffident at finding themselves amongst unfamiliar faces and surroundings, feel more at ease and not unwelcome. Even in the dining hall or common room, those who were 'not one of us' would be ignored, which created a feeling of neglect and, among the subjects of the British empire, a consciousness of their subject status.

However, I found friends in other colleges. They were of different nationalities and had varied interests, and were neither 'hearties' nor 'intellectuals', but of wide outlook and sensibility. I attended Union debates, the Indian Majlis and Labour Club meetings, browsed in the Bodleian, took long walks to explore the charming surroundings, tried my hand at punting on the Isis and fell into it; not being a swimmer, I was lucky to haul myself to safety. In the golden summer afternoons, tennis on the velvety lawns was a delight, as also horse-riding in Port Meadow. Later, I shared with my friends an ancient two-seater Morris car acquired for some thirteen pounds in which we toured from Spain to France, Italy, and, via Austria and Germany, back to Oxford. We drove some 1,000 miles surprisingly without mishap, except for the paucity of funds which we tried to eke out by sleeping out of doors in fields or under trees and free-wheeling down inclines to save on fuel. The contraption, still feebly running, was finally abandoned in an empty field.

It was the 'done thing' to go abroad on vacations and our allowance of £350 a year was just about enough, if carefully nursed, to see one through college and inexpensive vacations. We three companions of the initial voyage to Britain took a long trip to Spain in the Easter vacation of 1932 which, including the return trip to Gibralter by P&O, cost us only £13 each! This included hotels, long train journeys, bull-fights, etc. King Alphonso XIII was still on his tottering throne and there was a strong Republican movement among the students whom we met, countered by an equally strong Monarchist one. On a train, we met a Jesuit priest who had been teaching for years at Loyola College in Madras and was now back in Seville. He was delighted to see Indians—there were few Indians in Spain then—and he introduced us to the student community. Thereafter we were passed on from one university to another, which made our stay pleasant and instructive. The smattering of Spanish we had acquired from Hugo's *Spanish Simplified*, came in very handy. The evidences of Arab culture were present everywhere in the great monuments of Cordoba, Granada and Seville and even in the language, food and song. That helped to reduce our nostalgia for home.

On a later visit to the Rhine valley, an Indian friend and I went over to witness a mammoth Nazi rally at Coblenz. It was an awe-inspiring show with serried ranks of brown-shirts and black-shirts in their thousands, often breaking into thunderous applause or shouting slogans. They were being harangued from a vast podium by a uniformed figure (presumably Hitler). While we were innocently taking snapshots, we found ourselves surrounded by half a dozen SS toughs in black who, shouting unintelligibly and ferociously at us, made as if to arrest us. Luckily, a little man in the audience, evidently a Jew, urged us in English to show our British-Indian passports. On seeing these and hearing us repeat the incantation 'Oxford', the mood of the bullies changed and with grunts and salutes they disappeared. As advised by our little protector, we hid our cameras and made off from the scene, hoping that would be the last we would see of the Nazis. But though the bookshops in England were awash with Nazi literature, and Hitler's testament *Mein Kampf* was prominently displayed in shop-windows, nobody took Hitler's fulminations at all seriously—not the British establishment, newspapers, Oxford dons or students.

A famous debate on the question of war took place at the Oxford Union, the subject being: 'Resolved that this House will not, under any circumstances, fight for King and Country'. In typical Oxford fashion, such debates, however provocative the title, were hardly taken seriously and generated general merriment and good-natured banter and repartee. The present debate, despite its portentous theme, was no exception. G.D.H. Cole, the famous economist whose books were then widely read, was an ardent pacifist and he had been invited as the guest speaker. In the course of the debate he had been asked what he would do if a German tried to rape his wife; pat came the answer: 'I would try to get in between'! This brought the House down. When the vote was taken, the motion was carried by a thumping majority.

The Conservative establishment, the Empire loyalists and flag-wavers and even the serious newspapers took alarm at the apparent decadence of the flower of British youth: in such hands the future of the Empire would be in peril. Yet only a few years later, the same young men sacrificed their lives on the blood-sodden battlefields of France and Belgium and the beaches of Dunkirk and Normandy.

Undergraduates were treated like monks under vows of chastity and austerity. No woman was permitted in the precincts of a male college after 7 o'clock in the evening. The colleges were enclosed within high walls and their great gates were locked at half-past nine at night; thereafter there were fines rising progressively by the half-hour until midnight. Any arrival after then would be regarded as a major misdemeanor to be visited by a fine and a stern reprimand from the head of the college himself. Late entry for the third time would result in the offender being 'sent down' in disgrace. No wonder that agile and adventurous students developed remarkable skills at climbing up high walls, evading iron spikes or sprinting away from 'bull-dogs' or monitors.

Every morning there was roll-call in the dining hall for which undergraduates hurriedly dressed, dashed up the stairs in their short gowns and thereafter returned to bed. The system of 'scouts' or room-servants was very much in vogue, while the hall-porters, a class by themselves, seemed endowed with encyclopaedic memories.

Dinner in the vast panelled hall with portraits of lugubrious-looking notables looking down, was served with much fanfare by a clutch of cooks in chef's high hats whose appalling productions hardly merited such ceremony. What was served to the dons at the upper end at High Table with candlelight and glittering silver, was very different.

In the Hilary (or winter) term I received a shattering blow when I heard of Mother passing away, she who had made such sacrifices for us and on whom we were so dependent. I felt quite disconsolate and bereft and could find little to comfort me. The gloomy weather with looming skies and rain did little to raise my downcast mood. It was only with the advent of spring and summer when the fruit trees burst into blossom, the crocuses raised their heads from the sodden earth and the trees sprouted new leaves, that my drooping spirits uplifted.

The summer or Trinity term and my last at Oxford, brought glorious weather when the countryside was transformed, the beautiful college gardens burst forth into colour and nature appeared in full panoply. All examinations over, there was a festive mood all around and young and old alike gloried in the weather and the end of another scholastic year.

From a callow youth when I went up to Oxford two years earlier, I had attained maturity and a certain measure of self-confidence. Our final examination concluded, we received Covenants from the Secretary-of-State for India appointing us to the Indian Civil Service. Not even the Viceroy had the power to appoint or dismiss ICS officers. The last few carefree weeks passed in a round of gaiety before one plunged into the serious business of life while the undergraduates looked forward to the long vacation. Sharing in the prevailing mood, I was at that time much taken up with an attractive young lady, whose family had greatly befriended me on Mother's passing away. We spent many pleasant hours together, punting on the river, attending college dances or just walking about the college gardens. Once, driving in the countryside a policeman stopped us at Abingdon and demanded our driving-licenses. The lady, still a beginner, had none and we were fined £1 each at the local magistrate's court! After my departure, the lady married one of our colleagues who became a University Professor and Fellow of All Souls, and a renowned philosopher.

It was the season of Commemoration Balls, elegant affairs in great marquees raised on college lawns, with sprung floors, where champagne was provided *ad liberum*, and the tables groaned with choice foods. Lively music filled the air and young men in formal wear and young women in long gowns and gloves, usually danced until dawn. In the cold light of dawn the revellers a would pile into a car and drive off, still in their festive attire, for breakfast at a distant inn. I had returned early from one such occasion when the fatal hour of midnight began to strike in the great bell-tower just as I was entering New College Lane, but I could not make it before the last stroke. Next morning I received a polite note from the Warden inviting me to see him that evening. Dr Fisher was all smiles, spoke of the great traditions of the service which I was entering and asked me how I had enjoyed my stay at Oxford. He then added, almost as an aside, that I was late the previous night as I had no doubt lost count of time in the pleasant ambience of the evening, and concluded reassuringly, that he was sure it would not happen again. I offered my apologies and, after wishing him goodbye, I took my leave, fairly certain that my transgression would be forgiven. Next morning I received a note from the Warden fining me £1.

And with that I said farewell to Oxford.

*TWO*

# Going Through the Paces

O n arrival in Bombay, we were required to report at the
Secretariat to receive our orders of posting. Our voyage
by the P&O *S.S Narkunda*, this time by first class, had
been uneventful. The reputed transformation of British people
travelling east at Suez was no myth at all but a glaring reality;
ordinary British people, fundamentally decent, would at Suez be
metamorphosed into arrogant stand-offish colonials who
imagined that their manifest destiny was to rule over the 'lesser'
races. After Suez, even college colleagues became nodding
acquaintances.

My homecoming was received joyously by the family, but
without the glow of Mother's loving presence, there seemed a
great emptiness about the house. She had kept writing to me to
the last, interested in every detail of my life. I now had to join
duty in a small place called Etawah. After the purchase of
necessary equipment and the recruitment of a personal valet, I
took the train to Etawah. On arrival, my boss William Waters
Finlay, the Collector and District Magistrate invited me to stay
with him. For accommodation I had a large tent held up by a

huge central pole, with galleries all around, the whole contraption resembling a pyramid. I was to pay my host the princely sum of just Rs. 100 per month, all found, from which a proportionate deduction would be made for any absences during holidays and week-ends. Finlay was a competent and fair-minded Scotsman in his late thirties. He had just returned from leave in Scotland newly married to a "bonnie Hieland lassie", Lorna by name. Lorna, hardly twenty, was overwhelmed by her surroundings— the huge house, the hordes of servants and orderlies and the scale of life generally. Another inmate was 'Joey' Fordham, who had been in acting charge but had to revert on Finlay's arrival, marking time for his next posting. Fordham was a Londoner, a cockney, who, despite his poor health, had a bubbling sense of humour which did not forsake him from breakfast until bed-time. Finlay, on the other hand, was rather dour and serious-minded and refused to be amused by Fordham's wit, which I thought rather funny. Soon a coolness began to develop towards the joker. The only work assigned to Fordham was the training of the Assistant Magistrate, namely myself, which consisted of going shooting partridge every afternoon in a nearby forest.

The real training, however, was imparted by Finlay himself. I would accompany him to the Kutcherry (court) while he made his inspections. In the treasury huge piles of silver rupees would be emptied on to huge scales and weighed, the expert treasurer unfailingly identifying spurious coins which had no ring when sounded. Currency notes in bundles would be counted and the lumpy and smelly opium weighed. Trade in opium was a government monopoly and opium was issued in minute quantities to buyers from licensed shops. Eating opium in small quantities was permissible but smoking it was prohibited by law. Opium had long been eaten in India for medicinal purposes. It was also said to give one strength and energy and therefore would be taken by warriors before battle. On the other hand, it was believed that smoking opium was harmful, and that opium-smokers became pale, listless, cadaverous, and died. The armoury was often inspected and the Nazir's department and record room as well. The Nazir was a sort of general factotum who looked after petty purchases and held charge of government property. After these inspections made at random, the Collector would attend his court to hear appeals while I would attend to mine.

I had been invested with the powers of a Third Class Magistrate which empowered me to impose a fine of up to Rs. 50 and imprisonment of one month. The pettiest cases would go to Third Class Magistrates, the commonest being under the Municipal laws such as 'committing a nuisance' in a public place; sometimes cases of causing simple hurt or brawling would come up. My first case, which caused me much anxious thought, was a complaint by some half a dozen villagers against another half a dozen of assault over a land dispute. The accused in one case had simultaneously filed a counter-complaint on an identical charge against the first party. Both produced a dozen witnesses, each on oath, who could not be broken in cross-examination. At the end, the lawyers on each side argued vehemently, and to me, convincingly, on behalf of their respective clients. Since I could not believe both parties, I mentioned my predicament to Finlay. Giving Solomon's judgement, he said both sides had had a good fight and had now brought their dispute to court and both should be fined Rs. 50 each to teach them a lesson.

When the Finlay went into camp, I accompanied them. We first crossed the Jamuna by ferry. At Chakranagar, the Jamuna was broad, deep and blue and her waters were renowned for their medicinal properties. Between the Jamuna and the equally impressive Chambal lay a broken tongue of land, celebrated for its partridge-shooting which attracted the Viceroy himself annually. There we filled our own larder. At the confluence of the two great rivers was a sandspit and the river-banks were broad and sandy. There lay, basking in the sun, a huge concourse of alligators and crocodiles, some of enormous size. But Finlay, unlike most Englishmen, did not care for blood sports and was not interested in acquiring a prize trophy.

After ferrying across the river, we had hardly sat down to a picnic lunch on a high knoll, when Lorna exclaimed that she could hear a rumbling noise. Her husband tried to reassure her that it was nothing but the wind and the waves. Soon Lorna cried out in alarm that the sound was getting louder and sounded like a railway train. The rumble indeed kept increasing and the knoll began heaving like an elephant in flight. We held ourselves down with our hands and saw the waters of the Chambal churning furiously and large waves lapping at the shores. This went on for a considerable time causing even Finlay much alarm, while poor Lorna became hysterical. There was no wireless at the time and it was only the next day that we learnt, when the newspapers arrived in camp, of the terrible Bihar earthquake which caused enormous devastation and loss of life in northern India.

One day I received a letter from the Military Secretary to the Governor inviting me on behalf of His Excellency and Lady Hailey to be their guest for ten days. Though couched in the polite language of an invitation, it was an order: on the due date I presented myself at Government House, Lucknow. The Governor, Sir Malcolm Hailey (later Lord Hailey of Raipur), was in every inch of his over six foot frame, proconsular both in appearance and attributes. He was known to be of outstanding ability and industry and had come to Lucknow after a very successful term as Governor of the Punjab. He later became a renowned expert on Africa and produced a voluminous tome which was a mine of information on that continent.

Among fellow guests were three other young ICS officers, two of them Indian, and a couple of police officers. We took our meals at the Governor's table and found ourselves seated alongside him or Lady Hailey at every meal in rotation, our host and hostess engaging us in conversation. Sometimes His Excellency would ask us to take a brisk walk with him in the park and, pointing to trees and birds, would ask casually if we liked the outdoors and knew the names of the various plants or the names and habits of the birds which abounded in the park. Sometimes there would be a vigorous game of tennis. His Excellency had been carefully sizing up each one of us and getting to know all about our background, education, aptitudes and interests and meticulously recording his impressions in a big black book. These character-sketches were to govern future postings and promotions.

With the approach of the hot weather Finlay was moved out of Etawah, while I was moved on to another small district—Pilibhit. This was a sub-montane, humid and very green area, in contrast to the dryness of Etawah. A segment of the great Terai and Bhabar forests passed through Pilibhit which abutted on Nepal. The District Magistrate and Collector, Ronald Symons invited me to stay with him. He was a Cambridge Wrangler, much younger than Finlay, very hard-working and able, and very congenial company.

I had a bedroom-cum-study on the ground floor of the Collector's house. Life and work was very much the same as in Etawah with some minor variations. The day began at 6.30 a.m. when we rode out, cantering and strolling across the fields, while Symons, who was also most knowledgeable about the flora and fauna of the area, indicated the various types of soils, cropping patterns, etc. After an hour's brisk ride, bath and breakfast, we repaired to our respective offices, he, to receive a stream of visitors and I, the left-overs. We then drove to the Kutcherry in his dimunitive Baby Austin to attend to out respective duties. I now had Second Class criminal powers and was empowered to award a six months' sentence of imprisonment and a fine of up to Rs. 200. I was also given charge of the Collectorate offices and excise. Work at the office went on until four when we changed and drove to the gardens of the local Raja for tennis and billiards. After dinner we sat out on the lawn under a tent made of mosquito-netting (because of the malarial nature of the place) and read or did our work.

The grounds harboured rats and snakes which infested the numerous rat-holes in the mound. My bed would be put out under the net tent, and every morning a snake would be found under the durrie, presumably in pursuit of the frogs which had made for the insects and moths attracted by the petro-max lamp. One evening as I was dressing for dinner on my bare feet, my servant standing behind me cried out "Snake, Snake!" I jumped on to a chair, and saw a large banded krait, the most poisonous of the species, glide past it. An alarm being raised, the reptile doubled back and slid between the thick coir matting of the bedroom and the wall. The sentry on guard was called in and he crushed the reptile with his rifle-butt. Next night the mate of the snake appeared outside my door and was soon dispatched. Thereafter snake-boards were put up on all doors around the house. These boards, a foot high, their tops nailed with strips of toothed tin, were an effective safeguard against snakes. Their one defect was the visitors, raising the bamboo chick to enter and bowing politely, would sometimes fail to see them and come down heavily on their faces. I did not see very many snakes during my ten years in districts, and as they hibernated during winter, camping in that season was perfectly safe.

With the approach of winter, Symons was shifted to Lucknow, his place being taken by a very senior Indian officer with a large family, just returned from "home leave" for whom a post of sufficient seniority was not available at the time. With his long experience, he was a stickler for rules and regulations.

I had gone into camp in the sub-division of which I was in charge, and was camping with my brother Maheshwar in a heavily-forested area teeming with game of every variety. One night, according to the usual practice, my staff had set out with my baggage, in bullock carts for the next camp so as to arrive there by dawn and to have everything ready before our arrival.

We camped in inspection bungalows set up at 8 or 10 mile intervals when the great Sarda Canal irrigation system, whose headwaters were near by was built. Next morning when we arrived at the next camp, we found the staff and servants in a state of shock and terror. It appeared that my horse had been tethered to the last cart and a large and hungry tiger, attracted by it, had followed behind. The people piled up on the carts where they would normally have slept peacefully, kept awake all night beating tin cans and pots and pans and lighting lamps in a vain attempt to scare the tiger away. It was only towards dawn when the convoy entered the gates of the dak bungalow that the tiger reluctantly slunk away.

A rather pleasant duty, normally performed by the Collector himself, was inspection of the boundary with Nepal. This entailed over a week's camping in the forest with a dozen elephants and ambling along the border to see if the high grass and bushes which had come up during the monsoon had been cleared and the boundary pillars in proper repair. The contract for the job was annually awarded to one Sher Ali, a noted guide and hunter, who ensured that the Collector bagged a tiger or two during his inspection. As the present Collector was not interested, I was entrusted with this duty, to the evident disappointment of Sher Ali. A mere half a dozen elephants were mustered and although I set out hopefully every morning on my heaving mount, no tiger appeared. As we were returning from our expedition, we encountered an enormous procession of elephants plodding along towards the same area. Sher Ali broke off from us to join the shoot of the Maharaja whose elephants they were. His party bagged several tigers which Sher Ali had craftily protected from our much less profitable and inexpert attention.

But the nights in my solitary tent, isolated by a dry watercourse from the rest of the camp, were made hideous by the roaring of tigers from all directions during what was their mating season. I originally mistook them for the bellowing of buffaloes, whose herds would be brought there to graze by the hardy Gujars, even at the cost of risking sacrificial offerings to the tigers. Buffaloes are large-hearted and courageous animals, who form a tight ring facing outwards and, with horns lowered, are ready to challenge any predator. Although I heard but saw no tigers, a large leopard cornered by the elephants swam gracefully across a stream and disappeared in a cane thicket. Once we stumbled upon a sleeping bear in a tuft of grass, much to his own and our surprise. Deer and antelope there were in plentiful variety and herds of the graceful and stately swamp deer, now rare, would be encountered in great number, and when they stampeded, clouds of dust would arise before they plunged into the broad Sarda river and swam across to safety. Practically every dip sheltered a hog-deer or barking-deer, and there was always enough game to satisfy the voracious and carnivorous appetites of the mahouts and camp staff. The beautiful spotted-deer and black buck lived in herds nearer cultivation and the large antelope, the nilgai, was also frequently seen there.

A more serious business of the Sub-Divisional Officer was the inspection of the land records maintained by village officials known as 'patwaris'. These documents recorded in detail, with maps, the contours of each field, their ownership, the names of the cultivators and the nature of the tenancies, the crop pattern, etc. One day when on 'partal' of a village ravaged by wild animals where the cultivators were exceptionally poor, I found the entries in the records of the patwari extremely incorrect and apparently deliberately so. I upbraided the patwari who replied insolently, sneering at my youth and inexperience. My anger with the patwari was matched by my sympathy for his victims. It was clear that his object was to foment disputes and litigation among the poor villagers from which he alone would profit. At that point something possessed me and I, not prone to violence, gave the startled patwari a resounding slap. As he turned around to flee,

I administered a kick which sent him sprawling, scattering his records.

I felt ashamed and aghast at what I had done and I still cannot recall the incident without a pang of shame and regret. I was soon recalled by the Collector to receive a well-deserved reproof which could have been stronger but for the nature of my motives. As good sometimes flows out of wrong, all the patwaris of the sub-division immediately set about correcting their forged records, which as subsequent partals showed, were faultless. At the same time I found myself looked upon with a new admiration and respect by the village folk.

A startling but highly efficacious method of dealing with errant patwaris was adopted by the Commissioner of the Division in which Pilibhit district lay. The Commissioner was a very exalted personage who oversaw five or six districts and was the final court of appeal in revenue cases next only to the Board of Revenue. The Commissioner, a Mr Rawlinson, a tall, gaunt figure with beetling eyebrows and lowering countenance, was on a visit of inspection to the district. He suddenly announced his decision to partal a certain village, to the consternation of his staff at such an unusual order on the part of so exalted an authority. He strode off to the village and, as expected, found the patwari's records full of wrong entries. At the end of the partal, he commanded the trembling patwari in a gruff voice to follow him, while he marched rapidly ahead to his camp. He ordered his office table to be placed under a tall shisham tree and calmly sat down to receive petitions and hear appeals. Commanding the patwari to approach, he directed him to climb up the tree. Not being very agile, the frightened patwari somehow managed to clamber up a branch, but was ordered to go higher still and higher until he reached the very top with his bundle of papers. There he sat to the astonishment and delight of the assembled village folk, the litigants and their lawyers. He became a figure of fun in the district. His work completed, Rawlinson retired to his quarters.

As night fell, and the patwari, paralysed with fear, held on to his precarious perch, the Commissioner's personal orderly alone had the courage to approach him to obtain the release of the offender. It was said that the patwari thereafter became a paragon of integrity, while all the land records of the whole area were speedily rectified.

Another episode involving a senior British District Officer which caused much comment and hilarity was about his highly innovative method of dealing with a communal dispute. A Hindu religious occasion and a Muslim one fell on the same day and both parties proposed to take out their respective processions at precisely the same time. To avoid a head-on clash, negotiations had been going on with both parties to get them to agree to slight alterations in their schedules. Lesser authorities having failed to get them to agree, the matter was referred to the District Magistrate himself. But neither cajolery nor threats could prevail. A riotous collision seemed inevitable. The District Magistrate thereupon issued invitations to the leaders and instigators of both parties to a reception at his residence shortly before the processions were due to start. The recipients, feeling greatly flattered, readily accepted the invitations. They were received in two shamianas, one for each community, where they happily quaffed generous quantities of the 'Burra Sahib's' lemonade. But, thereafter, instead of going on to lead their opposing processions as planned, they hurried back to their respective homes. There they remained confined indoors all evening. The time for the processions passed and the mobs having waited in vain for their leaders, melted away. The crisis was over. The lemonade, it turned out, had been heavily laced with Epsom Salts!

I had been one year in Pilibhit when I was transferred to Jhansi at the onset of summer. Jhansi was a much bigger district, the headquarters of the Commissioner of the Bundelkhand Division, an important military base and the hub of a railway network. Jhansi was a large district, rocky and undulating, inhabited by the militant Bundela Rajputs and the last of the Maratha rulers whom the British had ousted. It lay on the direct route to the Deccan plateau and had seen turbulent times. It was the capital of the heroic young Rani of Jhansi who rose to such fame in the uprising of 1857 and whose memory remains evergreen in the district. I had received a warm letter from the officiating Collector and District Magistrate to stay with him. Bernard Cook was an admirable senior and a pleasant companion, very conscientious and able.

With winter came the customary round of transfers and postings. The substantive Collector, G.L. Vivian, a man diminutive in size but not in reputation or experience, on return from long leave in England, resumed his post while Bernard Cook reverted to his post of Joint Magistrate of Lalitpur, an independent sub-division of the district. I moved into a chummery with a young colleague, Robert Saner, who had joined the ICS, and a young policeman named Ingram. I had been given charge of the headquarters' sub-division and, with the arrival of winter, set out to camp along with Saner, whose training had been entrusted to my inexpert care. Over three decades later, I ran into Robert Saner in Harare (then Salisbury) when I was Chairman of the Commonwealth Commission for the supervision and monitoring of the Independence elections of Rhodesia (now Zimbabwe). He had joined the British diplomatic service, risen to become an Ambassador, been knighted, and sprouted a beard; he had come to Harare as an observer of the elections.

Summer was another season for a reshuffle of the official pack of cards. Cook was posted outside the district and I was appointed in his place in Lalitpur. Along with this appointment I was also given First Class powers as a magistrate.

Lalitpur had a salubrious climate. Degrees cooler than Jhansi, it was a much coveted post. I now had independent charge of a huge area with all the powers of the Collector and with a sumptuous allowance to boot. It was an exhilarating experience indeed. The official residence at Lalitpur, my very first own home, was charming and quite spacious. Though yet bare of furniture, it gave me a thrill of satisfaction. The house had an extensive, well-kept lawn and an orchard of citric fruits of all kinds. Beyond, the vast compound harboured small game among the wild trees and shrubs. All government departments were represented in Lalitpur but at a low key. There was a sub-jail and a sub-hospital, a junior police officer and a sub-government counsel. The SDO had no supporting staff, not even an honourary magistrate to take up the pettiest cases. All day I laboured in court, painfully taking down evidence as there was no stenographer. Court orders and judgements as well as reports had all to be written out by hand.

The sub-division, despite its rugged and forested nature and the warrior Bundelas who formed the core of its inhabitants, was not particularly crime-infested, though there were some murders over the classic causes of 'Zan, Zar, Zamin' (women, money, land), some dacoities and some petty crime, but no road-robberies. The revenue litigation, however, was particularly vexatious. There were various types of land ownership coming down from previous rulers and the jagirdars, who were mostly small-holders with fractional shares but proud of their status, would contest fiercely over every rupee or fraction thereof.

An important duty, scrupulously performed by all magistrates from the District Magistrate downwards, was inspection of the jail. The prisoners and undertrials would be lined up in separate rows, all holding sheets indicating, in the case of the former, the crime for which convicted, the sentence and date; in the case of the latter, the offence, the date of arrest and dates of court appearance. The grievances of the prisoners, if any, would be looked into and dealt with, the cleanliness of the barracks and the quality and quantity of the food inspected. There were strict governmental injunctions about the maximum period that an undertrial could be held before being produced in court and the period within which the case against him must be decided. Any dereliction in the matter on the part of the dilatory magistrate would merit severe censure; the High Courts too would pull up judges for any unconscionable delay in the disposal of cases. What a contrast to the present situation when undertrials languish in prison in their thousands, often for petty offences, without once having a court hearing and long after their maximum sentence, even if they had been convicted, would have expired!

It betokened enormous confidence in the order of things that a young magistrate in his twenties could administer such a vast trust in all its branches almost single-handedly with only a miniscule staff and police force. It was the prestige of the government and respect for authority and belief in its sense of fairness and justice that could sustain so highly personalised a form of administration. The magistrate's word was law and the slightest gesture of disapproval of any action would lead to its immediate rectification by the offender. A petition was once filed in my court by a poor tenant complaining of high-handedness on the part of his powerful jagirdar. The issue of a mere 'parwana' or message written on a scrap of brown paper brought the offender to my house forthwith in penitence. He was a distinguished-looking and venerable Rajput, with a fine white beard parted in the middle. He came riding a white steed, wearing a turban and spotless white clothes and held his sword out to me in a gesture of submission. After admonishing him, I touched his sword signifying that he had been pardoned.

A government runs on its prestige and acceptability, not on the power of bayonets. Peace and order are maintained not by the policeman's rifle or baton, but by confidence in the government's sense of justice and its readiness and ability to correct wrongdoing. But if justice is denied, wrongdoing condoned and the canons of law and public morality flouted by their very guardians, public confidence is extinguished and the prestige of the government and its agents destroyed. Neither force nor blandishments can then restore what has thus been squandered.

Like most such places, Lalitpur boasted of a tennis club where a foursome could generally be formed. An enclosed pool was available for the exclusive use of the SDO. But what was most striking about Lalitpur was its surrounding forests and fields that abounded in game of every variety. A casual stroll with a shotgun in the nearby fields would yield a brace of partridge or a covey of quail. British army officers would frequently appear, even at the height of summer with only a personal bearer, festooned with sporting rifles and carrying the wisp of a tent, a mosquito net and stores on their backs. They would disappear into the deep forest, and resurface a week or ten days later, laden with trophies of tigers, leopards, and bears. I myself did not generally avail of the opportunities for shikar, nevertheless I often found myself against leopards, notorious in the area as cattle-lifters. Frequently a breathless villager would burst into my court and implore me to destroy a leopard which was causing havoc to the livestock. I would dismiss the court, get my horse saddled, and with a shotgun strapped to my back, gallop to the village. The village folk would have made a low hide-out overlooking the leopard's kill of the previous day. As the sun dipped, the leopard would emerge slyly from his cave and scrutinise every inch of the ground below with his piercing eyes. He would then descend a few steps to another crag where he would repeat his scrutiny. Finally, he would descend to the ground and resume his watch. Meanwhile, I, in my uncomfortable perch, would sit stock-still, my gun at the ready. One shot at the leopard as he made for the kill would enter the skull, the nine large grape shots slumping him to the ground. The joyous villagers, delivered of their oppressor, would carry the beast triumphantly to my house. Once, when thus seated over a kill, waiting for the expected leopard to appear, I heard behind me the sound of approaching padded footsteps. Turning around in alarm, I saw a big black head with yellow eyes, that started at me with even greater alarm. The hyena, for that was what it was, then swung around and disappeared the way it had come.

Only once did we go after big game for sport when two of my brothers were on a visit and news arrived that a tiger had taken up residence in the wooded part of a deep and wide ravine in a nearby forest. We set our on a burning summer day, accompanied by a coolie, carrying on his head a forty kilogram slab of ice, perfunctorily covered by a piece of sacking, which, no doubt, kept him cool from the head downwards and provided us with iced drinks throughout the parched day. For bait we had a piglet, form a herd of wild pig. Reaching the ravine, we took our positions on opposite sides of it and the beaters threw rocks from the top to flush out the tiger. But instead of any tiger, a bear came out and as it rolled along the far edge of the ravine, a shot deflected it in my direction. I had no intention of shooting it and had it not been making straight in my direction would not have done so. But now a couple of rifle shots through its thick fur and fat, disposed of it. An enormous beast, lashed to a stout pole, it needed eight men to carry it.

We camped at a delightful bungalow near the beautiful Deogarh temples; bits of stone and broken figures lay scattered but none touched these out of reverence. It was a balmy moonlit evening. We laid our tired and fevered limbs on the smooth pebbles of a fast flowing shallow river flowing nearby and let the cool water soothe us. Refreshed, we repaired to camp and a delectable meal of the piglet, roasted over the spit by our skilled cook! It was a day to remember.

During my ten years' of service in districts only two could boast of electricity, but not one of running water. Touring officers kept a large array of kerosene lights: there were the ubiquitous hurricane lanterns, table-lamps and a 'Petromax' or two. The last-named gave out a strong incandescent light when not sputtering or throwing up a flame, but it kept up a constant hiss and needed frequent pumping and priming. Every evening the lamps would be cleaned, filled with kerosene, cracked chimneys or mantles were changed, wicks were trimmed, and the lamps would then be conveyed to the various rooms. As snakes were not uncommon, one had to move warily both in and outside the house, always with a light.

An episode which occurred to disturb the normal tranquility of the sub-division led to my transfer. At the end of Muharram the customary tazias were to be taken out in procession for subsequent burial. On the appointed route lay a pipal tree, one of whose branches had so sagged as to impede the passage of the tazias. The highest tazia was measured and found to be of the customary height, and while negotiations were on to resolve the stalemate, tempers began to rise, especially on the Muslims side which felt wronged. The police officers and tahsildar, all Hindus, urged the lopping off of the obstructing branch and to avoid a riotous situation, I agreed, especially as the Hindus of the town were not much involved except for a few trouble-makers. That having been done quietly at night the tazias were duly taken out and buried. That seemed to be the end of the matter. But not so, as sometime later a full report on the affair was demanded by Government, no less. A Congress Ministry had taken over under the Montague-Chelmsford Reforms of 1935 and a highly garbled version of the incident had been conveyed to it by some Congress followers, hitherto unknown and unseen. We had tried every alternative, viz., digging up the road a foot or two or creating a diversion, but nothing was found practicable within the limited time. Our explanations notwithstanding, and without any further word from Lucknow, I found myself transferred to another independent sub-division at the other extreme of the Division.

Karwi was a desolate place, at the back of beyond, approachable only by two trains, one from east to west and the other from west to east, both arriving at dead of night within an hour of each other. I was met at the dimly-lit railway station by a few sleepy officials and led with the aid of a smoky lantern into the presence of an oldish gentleman in a dressing-gown and unshaven face, from whom I was to take over. Papers signed in the dim light of a lantern in a cavernous room, Mr. Niblett regaled me with a dismal account of life and work in the place, and then shuffled off in his slippers to catch the east-bound train.

Fortunately, my servants and baggage had arrived and my bed, having been put out in the back verandah of the house, I fell into a deep sleep. I was awakened early in the morning by a loud chattering above and around me and on opening my eyes, saw a number of monkeys perched on the bed-frame, peering curiously through the mosquito curtain. I tried vainly to shoo them off, but instead, they only grimaced and held their ground. I was extricated from my predicament only with the arrival of the servants.

The house had been built by the Marathas, presumably for their princes coming on pilgrimage to nearby Chitrakut, where Sri Rama was said to have dwelt in the course of his banishment. It was an enormous stone structure; its massive stone beams supporting the soaring roof were of single blocks of stone. Half the house was occupied by the Magistrate's offices, treasury, etc. and a string of quarters by lawyers, clerks and litigants. A mango grove of ancient trees filled the front of the compound. Monkeys, had made their abode among the trees and they wandered about freely everywhere, though fortunately, not entering the house. Because they were regarded as part of Sri Rama's army and therefore sacred, they took full advantage of their privileged status. My predecessor had invented an ingenious way of dealing with them when they became particularly unruly. A narrow-mouthed earthen pot would be dug into the ground and gram placed in it. This would lure a monkey to thrust his hand into the pot to grab a handful of gram. But the narrow month would not permit him to pull out his clenched fist. The trapped monkey's red face and posterior would be coated with tar and he would be released, by smashing the pot, to rejoin the herd. But on seeing the strange black-faced creature the rest would panic and disappear for some considerable time.

Karwi was a very dry and arid sub-division and there was absolutely no diversion of any kind except for an occasional and very rough trip on horse- or elephant-back to Chitrakut. The only company was the occasional visit of a learned and saintly sadhu, which I greatly welcomed. Karwi had just one very rough metalled road, seventeen miles in length, blocked on one side by an unbridged river and on the other by the main railway line from Bombay to Calcutta. Touring was a dreary business. With no canals and little well-irrigation, the parched fields were entirely dependent on a capricious monsoon.

Serious crime was almost endemic, and dacoities being common. I would step from my living quarters directly into the court-room to the clanging of fetters and irons as dacoits and murderers would be led in for trial. There was a memorable case when seven persons were charged with the murder of a particularly obnoxious and usurious money lender. They were said to have ambushed him at a lonely spot at dusk and, after killing him, carrying his body to a deep pool which harboured two large crocodiles. There they chopped up the body into small pieces and flung them to the hungry reptiles. Not a person came forward to depose against the accused and there was not a shred of evidence except for the money-lender's riderless pony. Even the victim's clothing had been burnt. There being no direct or even circumstantial evidence, although the facts of the case were widely known, the accused were discharged to the jubilation of the assembled villagers. At Chitrakut, the mahants who were in charge of the temples and their considerable endowments, were not always men of religion. There were often feuds amongst them and some were notorious for their licentiousness and criminality.

In one particularly gruesome case, a murder was discovered by a pilgrim while on a devotional round of a sacred hill. A trickle of blood from the water-spout revealed the hacked body of the mahant of the temple.

Sometimes accused persons would want to make a confession of guilt on oath before a magistrate, a statement to a police officer being inadmissible in evidence. Under the law, the prisoner would be brought from jail. No policeman or spectator would be allowed to enter the court. After cautioning the prisoner that he could be convicted, possibly to death, on the strength of his confession, and if he still insisted on making it, his statement on oath would be recorded. The magistrate would have to certify that he was fully satisfied that the confession was voluntarily made and not under duress. The reasons given by prisoners were generally that they were deeply repentant for their crime or that they were haunted by the spirit of the murdered person or that they feared divine retribution. The confessions, often of a blood-curdling nature, left one aghast.

By now I had been through my paces and in a year or two would be considered sufficiently experienced and senior as to be in line for promotion to the senior scale and independent charge of a district. I had to put in more time in Karwi, but it could be endured by the prospect of an ultimate release from my solitary existence and, hopefully, to a more agreeable place.

# THREE

# Clodhopping Collector

There was soon to be a marked change in my way of life as my state of solitude was about to end. It all began at a dinner *en famille* at Sir J.P. and Lady Kailash Srivastava's where I met their daughter Susheela, who was about to go up to Cambridge to read for her B.A. (Hons.) Tripos in History, having spent some years at a finishing school for young ladies in London. Susheela was beautiful, intelligent, well-read and vivacious and I felt greatly attracted to her. She, too, in a way, seemed interested. Thereafter began some delicate exchanges between the two families which led to an undeclared understanding. I wrote tentatively to Susheela at Cambridge to which she replied rather formally. An exchange of letters followed, although in desultory and stilted fashion; after a while even this sporadic correspondence came to an end. But on her return to India, the broken strands were restored.

We were married on 28 March 1938, soon after which Susheela arrived at her new home in Karwi. I was apprehensive about how she, with her sophistication and background, would be able to put up with so desolate and cheerless a place. But to my infinite relief and admiration there was not a word of complaint, only puzzled interest and curiosity. The ubiquitous presence of the monkey population did not alarm but merely amused her. Nor was she scared by the clanging irons and fetters of the dacoits and murderers as they were led into the court-room on the other side of the door. In the evenings we would take a walk along the ankle-deep dust of the road or along the railway track, ending up, when Susheela felt tired, with me carrying her piggy-back, much to the surprise and embarrassment of a railway linesman who would dutifully salaam his resident magistrate! Our occasional drives in our new car along the bumpy seventeen-mile stretch ended at the Manikpur railway station; we would watch the Bombay Mail clatter past, lights blazing and its dining car festive with diners, leaving in its wake, a great silence and darkness.

I was glad when a few months later we were able to shake off the dust of Karwi. I was selected for land-settlement work in the district of Aligarh. This related to the re-assessment, due every forty years, of the land revenue to be paid by the zamindars and proprietors to the Government. It was based upon the productivity of each class of holding and required at least four months hard touring. Data was collected by personal inspection, an intricate formula was applied to arrive at crop values. The land revenue would then be calculated as a percentage (about forty per cent) of the crop value. Thereafter, all the patwaris would assemble at 'headquarters' under a huge shamiana and set to work to apply the formula to the inspection results.

It was a very gruelling business but valuable experience for a revenue official. Early every morning I would ride out on my horse, with assorted officials in tow, to the different groups of villages. The local patwaris, a horde of villagers, and I would pore over a map of the village in which each field would be demarcated, and the soil classified according to productivity. There were five or six broad categories of loam, clay, sand and combinations thereof. At harvest time a large hoop of measured area would be cast at random in the middle of a field and the crop within its circumference cut and threshed and the grain carefully weighed. This provided another index of the productivity of each type of soil. The villagers would be loud in their protestations about how poor the soil was, how erratic the canal irrigation and how low the yield, hoping thereby that their rents would be reduced. Rental assessments of tenants also accompanied the assessment of land revenue.

Returning to camp, I would deal with the numerous official papers that had snowballed and commit to paper my findings of the morning. The tehsil (revenue sub-division) covered some two hundred villages, large and small. The land-revenue system in U.P. closely followed the pattern set by Raja Todar Mal, the able Finance Minister of the Emperor Akbar and the Persian terminology was still in use. Certain modifications had no doubt been made, but the essentials remained basically the same. As the results of the patwaris' calculations came churning out, they were found to be widely divergent when, according to the formula, they should have yielded a fair average of the crop value. These anomalies left me in a quandary: the Office Superintendent, who had seen many settlements and Settlement Officers, kept asking what sort of figure I thought would be reasonable. This would have violated the principles underlying the formula, but when the Office Superintendent assured me that was invariably done, I reluctantly agreed. Basing myself largely on the random sampling, I gave a figure which the Office Superintendent accepted approvingly. Thereafter the patwaris' calculations began almost miraculously to approximate closely to the given figure. So much for statistics!

From there on, the work proceeded at a steady pace and the assessments were accepted without question both by the zamindars—whose land revenue had been substantially raised— and by the cultivators, and there were hardly any appeals against them. Now began the much more agreeable task of writing the settlement report of Tehsil Sikandra Rao. These reports were a mine of information, dealing not only with land tenure and agriculture. They included an account of the area's history, its castes and communities, their habits and traditions, religions, festivals, archaeological monuments, etc. The information contained in them is accepted by courts as irrefutable evidence. According to a pleasant tradition, the report could be written in Naini Tal. The report completed, the final results were submitted to the Government, and a welcome commendation followed. Having done a year of strenuous settlement work, I was now due for promotion as a District Officer.

Three or four months of the winter until a district charge was available were spent camping in Hardoi, a very dusty district, but rich in agriculture and taluqdars. It was full of marshy jheels and lakes and abounded in every species of waterfowl which provided excellent sport. From Hardoi, I was moved back to Jhansi as District Officer. I had hardly been there a few weeks when the Chief Secretary, Francis Mudie (later 'Sir'), telephoned to say that I should move to Mathura. I reminded him that my elder brother, Bishumber, was the Superintendent of Police there, and it might not be proper for two brothers to be running the same district. The Chief Secretary said that should not matter but he would confirm the posting after speaking to the Governor, Sir Maurice Hallett. A few minutes later he rang up to say that the Governor saw no objection and I should proceed to Mathura. My brother, however, felt very concerned and insisted that he would ask for a transfer, but was ultimately persuaded to wait and see how matters worked out.

The District Magistrate, as head of the district, is ultimately responsible for law and order and to that extent the Superintendent of Police is answerable to him in the first instance. But the police force is under the Superintendent whose responsibility it is to suppress crime and apprehend and prosecute criminals. Between these two leading officials, there is danger of one or other overstepping the limits of his authority. The relationship therefore calls for the exercise of tact and restraint on both sides and the development of mutual confidence and trust. Actually, Bishumber and I got on extremely well in our work and whenever we rode out together into the city for inspection of the municipal services and to settle any local problems or grievances on the spot, we were received most warmly by the citizens. Nor was there a word of complaint on the part of the public about 'collusion' between the magistracy and the police.

The District Magistrate was also known as the Collector, with reference to his duties as collector of land revenue and other government dues, as well as the District Officer, since he, as head of the district, oversaw the work of all other departments. The title 'District Magistrate' referred to his capacity as the chief magistrate with appellate powers, there being a combination of executive and judicial functions in the same official. This was much criticised in theory, but it worked well enough in practice in the given conditions, and although the severance of the two functions has since been effected, the results hardly justify the exaggerated expectations.

The District Officer's functions were many and varied. A primary function was to ensure security of life and property and a measure of stability—preconditions for any kind of progress or development. The District Officer was expected to oversee and, if necessary, guide all the 'nation-building' departments and to keep a close eye on the working of the Municipal and District Boards. No activity of any governmental or semi-governmental agency was beyond his ken. Another duty of considerable responsibility was management of the estates under the Court of Wards. These consisted of estates, large and small, some very large indeed, whose management had been taken over because of gross mismanagement, chronic indebtedness, or on behalf of a minor, etc. There was a local manager who functioned under the direct supervision of the District Officer.

Safeguarding the interests of the cultivators was of special concern and there were numerous legislative enactments protecting them against arbitrary eviction and conferring various types of rights from hereditary occupancy but not alienation, to statutory rights, etc. There were also provisions to safeguard against usurious loans and land alienation in default. The cooperative movement had been started long before. But because of the propensity of the kulak class to grab control and to help themselves to generous loans while purloining the rest of the funds, it did not inspire any more confidence than it does today. A department recently started was Rural Development under a senior Indian ICS officer at headquarters, the District Officers being responsible for the work of implementation in their own districts.

Within a few months of my joining the service, I was designated the Rural Development Officer in Pilibhit, and also later in Jhansi. Full of youthful enthusiasm, I acquainted myself with the work being done elsewhere and, guided by the writings of Sir Malcolm Darling and F.L. Brayne, pioneers of the movement for rural uplift, I launched out somewhat inexpertly into a number of what I felt were beneficial activities. But because of my as yet perfunctory knowledge of village conditions and psychology, some of these activities proved unsuccessful. I introduced a pneumatic-tyred improved bullock cart, but this proved too heavy for the small local bullocks; when a tyre got punctured, the cart's short life came to an untimely end. Similarly, the large bulls and buffaloes from what is now known as Haryana intended to improve local breeds, did not take kindly to the local cows nor the latter to them. The same fate of enforced celibacy met the imported Merino ram. Trench-pattern latrines were introduced, but while one may take the horse to water, how does one make it drink? Improved seeds wilted for lack of sufficient and timely irrigation. All these consistent failures left me a sadder but no wiser man until I realised that changes in ingrained habits of hoary antiquity could not be expected if imposed from the top (and especially by inexperienced hands); they had to come up from the ground.

The District Officer was expected to be versatile, an all-rounder who could apply himself to almost any task. It was said that barring being a midwife or a Field Marshal, he could be anything else.

Mathura was a very agreeable charge. It was an important centre of pilgrimage, it had a dry and healthy climate, no communal problem, and it was not very criminal or litigious. The majority of the population comprised Jats and Gujars, very good cultivators and herdsmen. The Collector's house was a mansion of noble proportions and, once more, was the legacy of Maratha princes who used to visit Mathura on pilgrimage. Thanks to my predecessors, it had a large and well-kept lawn and garden and an enclosed swimming pool whose water irrigated the grounds. And what is more, it had electricity, though no running water.

A British artillery brigade was stationed in Mathura during the War. We got on well with the Commanding Officer and when polo was revived, my brother and I took full advantage of it, he playing the game with much panache and I with more effort than skill. The sole Indian officer, in charge of a small unit of the Service Corps, was a young Indian captain, Mohammad Ayub Khan. He felt rather isolated and lonely and had little in common with the British Officers or they with him. Almost every evening he would be at our house and with my brother and his wife, my Joint Magistrate and house guests, we would relax on the lawn. Ayub Khan had great charm and all of us developed a warm friendship with him. He could tell a good tale, especially after refreshing himself with a few drinks, and was excellent company always. His wife was in his native Abbotabad; and he had left her there as she spoke no English, only Punjabi and some Pashtu.

But our wives persuaded him to send for her and when she arrived, a shy girl who felt lost in the wide world, Susheela made her feel at home and helped her to set up house, a kindness which she never forgot.

My sister came to stay with us as she had just lost her husband, Prem Narain Mathur, a top executive of the Tata Iron and Steel Company at Jamshedpur. Prem Narain was a remarkable man: at a young age he had taken off for the United States where he qualified as a Metallurgical Engineer and joined the Ford Motor Company. There he invented a process which, while lowering costs, improved the quality of the finished steel. This brought him to the notice of Henry Ford himself and thereafter his rapid rise in the company was assured. News of his abilities reached Jamshedpur and the management, under criticism for employing only Americans and Englishmen in the senior-most positions, persuaded Prem Narain to join Tatas. He became Tata's top steel-maker and was in charge of the Open Hearth and Bessemer processes. His fame spread in India and Pandit Nehru invited him to join the National Planning Commission set up by the Congress party, and he became Chairman of the Committee on Heavy Industry. It was on a visit to Bombay to attend a meeting of the Commission that he contracted double pneumonia and, disregarding his doctors' advice, insisted on returning home, but died on the way. It was a great tragedy for the family as my sister was only 34, and a loss to the country of a man of singular vision, drive and ability.

With the approach of winter, orders arrived transferring me to the district of Barabanki, near Lucknow. In the meantime, Bishumber too had been transferred. Barabanki, situated in the area known as Oudh, was an important taluqdari district, and unlike Mathura was noted for its big landowners, some owning several score villages. In Oudh and the hill divisions of Kumaon and Garhwal, the District Officers were known as Deputy Commissioners; but their powers and functions were the same as those of Collectors. The difference in designation was due to the fact that these areas had been annexed more recently and were administered by mixed civil-military commissions. Only some of the laws in force in settled areas had been applied there and some new or modified ones adopted.

The taluqdars derived their titles from 'sanads' or title-deeds granted by the new sovereign power, for services performed during the 1857 uprising and in some cases to those who had enjoyed the status and possessions under the rule of the deposed Kings of Oudh, but had not opposed the annexation. As the rulers of Oudh were known as the Nawab-Wazirs in their original capacity as viceroys of the Mughal Emperor, the nobles of Oudh were not permitted to use the title of 'Nawab'. Most therefore were designated 'Raja' and one even enjoyed the title of Maharaja. The taluqdars were generally people of great wealth and sophistication, brought up in the ways of the Oudh court. They were served by managers who were a smooth-spoken and witty lot. Some of the great estates were well enough managed but many others were wrack-rented and all kinds of illegal exactions were levied to satisfy the taluqdars' profligate needs. The taluqdars built great palaces on their estates which seemed incongruous amidst villages of mud and thatch. Many of the estates were moreover indebted, some heavily. The taluqdars were ostentatiously loyal to the British, but some of the smaller landholders—not the taluqdars—were involved in the Congress movement.

Barabanki thus presented a very different appearance to Mathura; the town itself was small and nondescript, the Collector's house, a ramshackle old structure with gloomy rooms and a neglected garden, looked far from inviting. My predecessor, an old gentleman, promoted from the provincial service and ready for superannuation, was a picture of despondency and frustration when I met him. A widower, he lived most austerely with hardly a stick of furniture in the empty rooms beyond a cot and a few chairs borrowed from the Collectorate. Almost tearfully, he told us of the miserable time he had spent there due to the machinations and wickedness of the taluqdars and their minions. They would come, he lamented, asking for some favour in contravention of the rules and when politely refused would threaten to take up the matter with the officers in the secretariat on their next visit to Lucknow. Another visitor, no doubt acting in collusion, would then go through the same exercise and follow up with more specific complaints against the district administration. A third would follow suit, and soon the ears of the powers that be would be thoroughly poisoned against the long-suffering Deputy Commissioner. He warned me that, so early in my career, I would be ruined by the machinations of the evil men who had engineered his downfall and that I should try and get out of the posting before I too was snared. Leaving the poor man to his gloomy thoughts, I went away determined to face whatever problems I encountered.

Susheela was more than depressed to see the house, but its owner, the Maharaja, gave us carte blanche to have it put into shape and make it habitable. This was done while we were away on our long winter tour and the place became not uninviting, especially after it had been curtained, carpeted and furnished.

The countryside of Oudh is uniquely beautiful with its rich fields of wheat, peas or mustard, its deep and shady mango groves, its lakes and jheels adorned with lotuses and alive with wildfowl.

We were fortunate to experience this beauty on our winter camps. The itinerary would have been worked out in advance, friendly groves having been selected for the camp sites and the officials along the way notified in advance. Comfortably housed in our three or four spacious 'Swiss Cottage' tents, heated against the winter chill by stoves, we would set out every morning on our waiting horses. It was exhilarating riding through the fields with the morning air scented by pea blossom and the perfume of water on dry earth, the morning mist rising over lake and marsh, the dewdrops still shining on the young blades of wheat and to the honking of high-flying geese and the squawking of waterbirds near by.

The camp resembled a Mughal encampment, for besides the Deputy Commissioner's tents, there was a whole range of lesser tents pitched at a discreet distance, which sheltered the accompanying officials, court staff, numerous orderlies, domestic staff, etc. As most of the tracks in the interior were fit only for bullock-carts, the motor-car had to be left on the nearest metalled road, mobility of an assorted variety being provided by horse, elephant and bullock-cart. The whole camp, barring only the D.C's bedroom tent, would move at night when, after going to bed, we would hear the sound of wooden hammer against tent-peg and the swish of falling tents. On arising in the morning, there would just be our bedroom tent and no more, with breakfast neatly laid out under a tree and our horses waiting impatiently to be off. The last tent and the remaining staff would follow by bullock-cart. The normal complement was four or five carts, which in some of the drier districts could be supplemented or replaced by camels.

On arrival at the next camp, the whole entourage would be in position, appearing as though it had long been there. In the wake of our long ride, the lunch prepared by the cook tasted especially delicious. After a brief rest, court would be laid out in the sun if the weather was particularly chilly, or under a shady tree or in the office tent. There, petitions would be received and dealt with, appeals argued by lawyers from headquarters, reports of the morning's inspections dictated. In the evening villagers would be waiting eagerly to lead us to a nearby jheel for a shot at duck or geese. Returning in the gloaming, tired after a full day's exertions, our sitting-room tent, kept warm by a glowing fire in the 'Moradabad' stove, would greet us as lights and wood-fires began to appear in camp. After a day's halt when other areas would be inspected, the camp would again move to the next stage.

The grandees of the district were the 'first' class of taluqdars who owned enormous estates, some covering thirty or forty whole villages. They lived in palaces of different degrees of opulence, with domes and marbled halls and provided with such unheard of luxuries as electric generators, modern plumbing and elevators, etc. These buildings were visible for miles around as they stood out high above the surrounding extensive gardens and orchards, and fields and villages. But their owners were often absentees, preferring the varied delights of Lucknow to isolated splendour in the countryside. There were very strict government rules and conventions about hospitality; there was no question of the D.C ever making a sojourn—however brief—in one of these mansions, even if his tents in a nearby grove, were damp and drenched in winter rain. But he could accept a dinner invitation at the palace, and what a dinner it could be! The taluqdars of the 'second' class were to be allowed the privilege of partaking of their own dinner with the D.C. in his tent, while the taluqdars of the 'third' degree had to be satisfied with sending cooked and raw food to the camp as their expression of hospitality.

Most parts of Oudh, especially the great houses, were famed for the superb quality of their Mughlai cuisine. A procession of impressively uniformed flunkeys and orderlies, in turbans and sashes, led by a major domo, would turn up in camp holding aloft enormous salvers of the most delectable dishes. The standard fare would be mountains of biryani rich in saffron, several 'murgh mussalam' (whole chicken, butter-soft and subtly flavoured), a hundred quail, a dozen partridge, assorted kababs and curries.... A great speciality was 'rasawal', a cloyingly sweet pudding of rice cooked in fresh sugarcane juice over a smoky fire in an earthen pot, to be eaten with 'balai' or cream skimmed off boiling milk. We could hardly stomach such opulent food day after day and it would be passed on to the camp staff, to their enormous delight. Milk and the horses' feed was also, by custom, supplied by the local landowner and occasionally an enormous fish or two, freshly caught, would be presented to us. Our whole staff, from the junior magistrate and revenue officials down to the humblest, waxed fat and shiny as the camp progressed and it was no wonder that they so welcomed the onset of the cold season.

Very occasionally, I would interrupt camp for a day or two to attend to urgent business at headquarters. Susheela had joined Lucknow University as an honorary lecturer to teach European history to post-graduate classes twice or three times a week. She would make for the waiting car on elephant-back or bullock-cart, drive down to our house in Barabanki and on from there to Lucknow, returning in the evening. When we were encamped across the Sarju river, she had to cross over by boat; often when she returned in the evening, the weather would be stormy and the great river turbulent. She obviously enjoyed her lectures, as did her students, to undergo the hazards of the journey.

The following year from November 1941 onwards was a period of personal tragedy and official strain. My brother, Bishumber, while on a brief leave in Naini Tal, suddenly passed away leaving a young wife and two little boys. He was just 34 and although only two years older than me, I looked up to him as an elder. We had been inseparable companions in our childhood and youth and had shared a great deal together and it took me long to recover from the blow.

Political clouds had begun to gather on the hitherto calm and peaceful horizon of Barabanki as the Independence Movement gathered strength and urgency. The district was home to a Muslim family of medium landholders who were prominent in Congress politics, one of whose number, Rafi Ahmad Kidwai, rose to all-India stature. The local organisation, headed by a cousin of his, was not particularly active in the district, perhaps because of the counteracting influence of the big landowners who generally kept away from politics. I had previously warned the

Congress leaders that in the event of any major trouble, the heavily-armed British troops could react violently (especially if it involved their installations) without reference to me, as they were not within my jurisdiction or control.

The Governor, Sir Maurice Hallett, a rather uncharismatic character, had been on an official visit to Barabanki where he was greeted with flags, buntings and welcoming arches, and at a well-attended public meeting, had been presented with a handsome purse for the war effort. He had previously been our house-guest in Mathura on a similar mission, where there had been even more flags and arches, but a much leaner purse.

The war situation was disastrous for Britain at the time, for with the collapse of France and before Hitler marched against Russia and the Japanese attacked Pearl Harbour, Britain doggedly fought on alone to resist a threatened Nazi invasion. In the eastern theatre the Japanese seem irresistible as they overran all the countries of south-east Asia and, after taking Burma, threatened the eastern frontier of India. Vast numbers of Indian refugees were fleeing ahead of the Japanese advance through the trackless jungles of Upper Burma into India. In sleepy little Barabanki a British Captain of Engineers with a platoon of his regiment arrived and set to work to instal enormous tanks to hold a million gallons of petrol. The Captain was quartered on us and his platoon in tents not far behind our house along the railway track where the work was going on with the added employment of local labour. I had been given no official word about all this presumably for reasons of security, although the whole town came to know about it at once. I had no authority over the troops, and not long after, Berlin radio made an announcement warning the residents of Barabanki to keep away from attacks by their bombers. There was much speculation in the Secretariat about the source of the leak but it was never discovered. The Captain turned out to be pleasant and very discreet, taking his meals in his own room near the entrance and not disturbing us except when asked. He never spoke about the War situation nor did any of the high British Officials at Lucknow, although they must have been consumed with anxiety as one military disaster followed another.

To try and beat back the Japanese onslaught, a South-East Asia Command had been established under Lord Mountbatten who had set up his headquarters in the comparative safety at Kandy in Ceylon. British and American soldiers and airmen began pouring into the country. India was to be the main base for the counter-offensive after the defence of India itself had been secured, and was also to be the main source of supply.

The country, however, was seething with discontent and all shades of opinion were in an angry and sullen mood. India had been dragged into the War like a lackey without the least reference to its leaders and people. With some sensitivity on the part of the governments in Whitehall and New Delhi, India, which was no less opposed to Nazism and Fascism, could have been a willing partner in the War. But nothing was done to seek the cooperation of the Indian leaders; and a deaf ear was turned to their modest demands and even to their enquiries as to the extent to which the brave declarations made regarding war aims would apply to India. Had Indian leaders been invited to share in the responsibility of government together with a firm promise of Dominian Status at the end of the War, the story may well have been different. But with a stolid and obtuse Viceroy, Lord Linlithgow, in Delhi and an obdurate and overbearing Prime Minister, Winston Churchill, in London, nothing could have been expected. Instead of willing cooperation, therefore, there was only frustration and a bitterness in the country. True, India contributed over two million men and vast resources to the War effort, but most of the recruits joined for economic reasons. The valour and sacrifices of the Indian armies in many theatres of war were seldom openly acknowledged, and only grudgingly so when they were.

The political situation in India was heading towards a climax, which came on 8 August 1942 when the Quit India movement was launched nation-wide. The programme of direct action, as passed down to party cadres, enjoined the severance of rail and road traffic and telecommunications, attacks on government offices and public utilities like post offices, police stations, etc. and acts of sabotage and defiance of administrative authority generally. The Mahatma had insisted on the avoidance of any violence. But it proved impossible to ensure that aroused multitudes could be made to conform to the Mahatma's exacting standards. In any case, it is arguable whether the instructions issued and the programme of action did not exclude the possibility of violence as the institutions to be attacked were manned by human beings who would naturally react. Responding to the call, there was much destruction of public property, dislocation of rail and road traffic and telecommunications and seizure by force of police stations, etc. and there was considerable loss of life both of police and other official functionaries, but much more of the agitators. Enormous hardship was caused to the general public and the war effort too suffered for a while. It has been said that the movement would not have gone out of hand but for the precipitate action of the government in arresting the leaders in advance of the movement being launched. Be that as it may, the British authorities were taking no chances as they were engaged in a desperate life-and-death struggle and felt that they were being unfairly stabbed in the back.

The great effort deployed and the enormous sacrifices made by countless Indians did little to hasten the advent of independence. If anything, it made the ruling power even more unbending and relentless and the country still more sullen and angry. At the same time the political rift between the Congress and the Muslim League began to widen, as taking advantage of the incarceration of the Congress leaders, the Muslim leaders began to ingratiate themselves with the British. On the part of the authorities in both London and New Delhi there was an egregious misreading of the situation in India and an utter lack of statesmanship and vision. If the demands of the national leaders had been met even partially instead of being conceded under the pressure of circumstances a bare half a dozen years later, the course of the history of Indo-British relations may well have been changed.

While these portentious events were taking place in a vast arena, little Barabanki could not have remained immune from their impact. Some routine arrests had been made, there were some processions and some slogan-shouting. But we were spared any of the more violent manifestations of the movement except for the cutting of telegraph wires from time to time. The damage was speedily repaired and no particular harm was done. But I was called upon to explain why collective fines had not been imposed. Investigation had shown that our villagers were dutifully patrolling telegraph lines, the canals and railway tracks, and were in no way implicated. It was easy for agitators to bicycle up from Lucknow a few miles distant and to cut the lines quietly in the dark and disappear. If innocent villagers were punished with a collective fine, they would turn against us. The nuisance soon died out and no further questions were asked. It was, however, a trying time as one was torn between the demands of official duty and sympathy for the movement for independence, if not always for the methods employed. The British Government, for its part, refrained from imposing any demands on its Indian officers which would have created serious problems of conscience for them.

During those troubled times we had staying with us for a prolonged period as a house guest, besides the British Captain, an Indian writer, Raja Rao, who habitually wore a khaddar kurta and dhoti and kept long hair. The two made an incongruous pair and whenever they happened to meet, they eyed each other with much curiosity and distaste. Raja Rao, an emotional and somewhat erratic figure, was in a state of great excitement at the stirring events taking place in the country. Every now and then he would disappear to Lucknow to meet various leftists and Congress workers (some of them 'underground') and would resurface after such meetings to the sanctuary of the Deputy Commissioner's house! He was fired by the call of the Congress leaders for all government servants to resign, and he urged that a beginning be made by Susheela's father, then a Member of the Viceroy's Executive Council. Susheela's sisters came to be infected by his enthusiasm and they pestered their father with frantic telephone calls to resign. Even Susheela advised that I should thereafter follow suit. All these goings-on were certainly not unknown to the authorities at Lucknow, but the matter was never so much as hinted at when I met them.

My colleague, the Superintendent of Police, was a college acquaintance and we got on quite well together. As was usual, he would report to me from time to time and discuss law and order matters. One morning he turned up in camp and I thought he had some urgent problem which had occasioned so long a journey. But he talked only of routine matters, and instead of leaving thereafter, he sat on so we invited him to share our lunch. But after lunch he still continued to sit. I therefore asked if he had anything on his mind; in reply he handed me in some embarrassment an official envelope. It contained an enquiry from the CID for particulars about a certain Mrs Susheela Dayal who had been sending leftist literature to a political detenu lodged in the Kanpur Central Jail. My offer to dictate a reply on behalf of the SP was gratefully received by him; it was to the effect that the said lady was the wife of so-and-so, Deputy Commissioner and daughter of so-and-so, who had been awarded a Knighthood, was a Member of the Viceroy's Executive Council and an important industrialist of Kanpur. The detenu was a trade union leader whom Mrs Dayal had met at her father's house and, in response to his request from jail for political literature, had, as a humane gesture, sent him leftist literature acquired by her at Cambridge. The SP, after thanking me profusely and looking much relieved, took his leave. Nothing further was heard of the matter!

I had been two years in Barabanki and it was now time for a move according to the prevalent practice. In anticipation, we had begun a process of winding up. There were a number of estates under the management of the Court of Wards, the biggest being that of the Rajas of Surajpur comprising some sixteen canal-irrigated villages. The estate had fallen heavily in debt due largely to the Raja's prolonged absence, but by careful management, its fortunes had been restored and it was with considerable satisfaction that I signed a cheque for a huge sum in liquidation of the last outstanding debt. Susheela and I had gone over to Surajpur to return some borrowed books and to have a last look at the place before our departure from the district.

The late Raja was a strange character whose life-story read like a fairy tale in reverse. Unlike almost all his peers, he had a university degree and had built up a fine library of serious works, many on religion and philosophy which were well-thumbed and underlined and not kept merely for decoration. He had fallen desperately in love with a Naik girl from the hills, a dancing girl and courtesan and he, a Rajput, had shocked everyone by marrying her. Her portraits depicted her as a rather earthy beauty, laden with jewellery, and were displayed in every room of the vast palace. She had clearly longed for offspring as creches, swings, cupboards crammed with infants' clothes, and toys of all descriptions were to be found in the bedrooms. The Raja's guru was a tantrik of fearsome expression whose oil portrait dominated a large room set aside for pooja; large photographs of him were prominent everywhere. Sadly, the lady contracted tuberculosis and nothing could be done to save her. Her body was taken to Nasik, the tantrik's ashram, where it was placed seated on a platform in all its wedding finery and jewellery, then set alight and floated down the Narbada river. The Raja, distraught, took up residence as a mendicant in a hut at the feet of his guru and lived a life of the severest austerity, which led him also to contract tuberculosis. But he refused all treatment, and when at death's door, returned to Surajpur, sleeping on a rope cot under the grand staircase. There he died. But before his death, he had adopted as his heir a youth of twelve who was now under the guardianship of the Deputy Commissioner. The Raja had left a bizarre will according to which, if the estate were to be left without an heir, all its income was to be used for the feeding of birds. We hoped that such an awful contingency would never arise. I had appointed a British tutor for the boy, who was later sent to the Taluqdar's College at Lucknow. Every care was lavished on him, but unfortunately he contracted typhoid and had to be sent to hospital.

Susheela and I reached the palace at dusk when, according to the late Raja's instructions, the daily pooja to the tantrik was in progress. There was a great clanging of bells and cymbals and blowing of conches, while 'arati' was being offered in the big pooja room dimly lighted by 'diyas'. Ghoulish shadows danced on the bare walls, while the rest of the great house lay in tenebrous darkness. Looking down from his portrait his bloodshot eyes in an angry scowl, was the tantrik. Susheela and I stood transfixed at the scene with a sense of fear and foreboding. Suddenly, a courier burst in with an urgent message: it was to announce that the young Raja had just died.

# FOUR

# Changing of the Guard

T he War situation was getting worse and worse, with the
seemingly invincible Japanese thrusting their way across
the eastern frontier to Assam. Calcutta had come within
range of Japanese bombers and some raids had already taken
place. Lucknow, further west, had become like a garrison town
with British and American soldiers and airmen to be seen all over
the town, swarming in the cinemas, dance-halls, restaurants and
shops. In this situation, I found myself in Lucknow, in the Civil
Defence Department.

Arrangements to meet the menace of air raids were being
discussed and devised with more energy and zeal than skill or
the availability of resources. Home guards were being set up in
townships, their uniforms were being designed, the preferred
colour being grey; their funding and training were being planned.
Zig-zag air-raid shelters were to be dug in empty lots or in lawns
and gardens, air-raid sirens were being set up and to deal with
fires caused by incendiary bombs, stirrup pumps and fire buckets
were to be provided. Detailed instructions poured out to District

Magistrates who were the Chief Air-Raid Wardens in their districts.

These often somewhat amateurish efforts did little to reassure the public; if anything, they made it even more apprehensive and nervous. But that may well have been the intention. There was perhaps the hope that fear of the unknown might impel a rather sullen and perverse people to seek the protection of the government and to offer its active cooperation.

After the epic battle of Kohima when the Japanese advance was stemmed, the invaders were steadily pushed back through Burma. The relevance of the Department of Civil Defence began to abate. As the Allied counter-offensive continued, the Department became quite redundant and was soon abolished, leaving behind only dug-up gardens, mountains of water buckets and stirrup pumps and reams of paper as memorials to its two years of devoted labour.

From being very much in the air in Civil Defence, the next transition for me to Civil Supplies was like coming down to earth with a bang. Nothing could have been more earthy than to function, almost literally, as a trader or wholesaler—but without the profit motive. India was the main supply base for the entire South-East Asia Command and its gathering legions. The appetite of the vast war machine had to be satisfied and there was no limit to its demands. At the same time the huge urban populations of the cities and towns had to be kept supplied with their basic needs. Purchases by government agents in the open markets of enormous quantities of foodstuffs had the effect of pushing up prices and encouraging hoarding in the hope of yet higher profits.

In U.P. the movement outside its borders of a large variety of articles, especially food-grains, had been prohibited. An elaborate system of rationing was introduced in the main cities and fair-price shops designated. Petrol was severely rationed and weird charcoal-burning contraptions were invented which were attached to the rear of trucks and motor-cars, the coal gas fuelling—and ruining—the engines. A huge network of official and private agencies had been set up to administer the rules and ordinances which poured out from the Civil Supplies Department. Regional Food Controllers—all ICS men—were appointed to ensure the implementation of government policies and the procurement of the food requirements of the Government. In U.P. pure wheat atta and flour disappeared and the mills were enjoined to mill only a mixture of wheat, barley and maize or sorghum.

I was assigned the responsibility for controlling the movement of coarse grains and pulses, oils and oilseeds, 'gur' and molasses and some residuary articles, including even pigs and sheep guts which were used for making sausages for the British troops. It was an educative experience, as I had little idea about these esoteric matters, but not one that I particularly relished. The rationing scheme was largely devised on the British model and its minutae in the province were dealt with by a junior British officer. We all depended heavily for statistical information and the vagaries of the market on our Chief Marketing Officer, a canny Jat who seemed to have the most detailed information readily available at his fingertips. The British Secretary to Government was in overall charge, and presiding over the entire network and determining policy was a very senior British ICS officer, Sir Archibald Ibbotson.

The worst part of the job was the importunity of wholesalers and exporters who crowded the corridors of the Secretariat. Although we enjoyed a great deal of autonomy, when there was a particularly large demand to be fulfilled or when there were competitive bids, etc., there would be a quick consultation between us and a decision taken. It was a very clean 'licence-permit raj' under the British, poles apart from what it was to become under the people's representatives soon after Independence. Indeed, there was not a whisper of complaint among the public about any wrongdoing or misuse of authority on the part of the Regional Food Controllers or their officers, and not a word of accusation or innuendo reached the vigilant eyes and ears at the Secretariat.

In July/August 1943 I found myself in New Delhi as the U.P. representative on the first Royal Commission ever to have been set up to review the entire food situation. The country had always been assumed to be surplus in food, yet that year had seen the terrible Bengal famine which took a frightful toll of some three million lives, many on the streets of Calcutta, and was a great blot on British rule. A Royal Commission on Foodgrains Policy under the Chairmanship of the economist Sir Theodore Gregory was set up to probe into the matter and to come out with concrete recommendations. The Commission had an impressive representation and I felt wholly inadequate to the task, especially as its main concern was with wheat and rice, with which I had not directly dealt.

The Commission met for some six weeks and examined at length representatives from all the provinces. The deficit provinces generally tended to exaggerate their shortages while the surplus ones concealed their surpluses. The Bengal Chief Minister, Shaheed Suhrawardy, was examined at length and torn to shreds in the cross-examination. It was strongly rumoured that he had a prominent hand in the hoarding of rice at the time. The Punjab representative argued a losing case with skill but was overruled. I presented my case as best I could against disclosing any surpluses, as I had been instructed to do, but failed to carry any conviction. To compensate for my performance I appended a Minute of Dissent to the report.

The enquiry revealed that the famine was essentially manmade and not due to any natural causes. It suggested that the main factors causing it were the loss of the one million tons of rice normally imported from Burma and the failure of the means of distribution of the indigenous stocks. The fear of a Japanese incursion into Bengal had caused the authorities to destroy the rivercraft which provided the principal mode of transport in Bengal. The enquiry also revealed that when there is an overall shortage of food, it is not the entire population that reduces its intake, but the poorest who are totally deprived. An urgent recommendation of the Commission was that, to compensate for the loss of the one million tons of Burmese rice, a fertiliser factory producing one-third of a million tons of urea be set up with all possible speed, the assumption being that one ton of fertiliser would produce three additional tons of rice. All the findings and recommendations of the Commission were accepted by the Government and the first fertiliser plant was set up at Rishra.

To ensure procurement of wheat at a stable price, the U.P. government decided to introduce compulsory procurement at all the great wholesale market centres. Farmers were prohibited from selling their wheat to private parties and all the purchases made by the wholesalers were to be strictly on government account. The price fixed was eight maunds to the rupee, then a fairly generous price. The whole machinery was geared into action and on the appointed day when the wheat harvest would normally be expected to flood the mandis (wholesale markets), the wireless reports, as they came, revealed a dismal picture. For example, if at a particular centre the normal daily arrivals were ten thousand cartloads, hardly one hundred came in. The whole scheme, on which much time and ingenuity had been invested, had turned into a fiasco, threatening even the rationing network. Before matters could get out of hand, the Adviser to the Government asked some half a dozen of us to meet at his house in the evening for a drink, when the situation was thoroughly discussed. Each person present, however junior, was asked in turn to express his views with the utmost candour. The British officers were frank enough to admit that such a scheme of total mobilisation of supplies needed the willing support of the people, which only a grass-roots political organisation could provide. But all agreed, without question, that the whole scheme should be scrapped forthwith. After securing the Governor's approval every person present received his instructions for action. The first task next morning was to inform the Regional Food Controllers, who in their turn would spread the word to the wholesale markets and the countryside. At the same time, a notification cancelling the Ordinance under which the scheme was launched was issued in a Gazette Extraordinary. It took under twenty-four hours after the momentous decision was taken to implement it throughout the province. Another officer sent out wireless messages to the Regional Food Controllers and District Magistrates informing them of the decision, so that in a matter of hours all that had to be done was done.

This method of taking decisions in a thoroughly relaxed manner even on the gravest issues was typical of the British. Each one would be encouraged to speak out his mind with the utmost candour. Team-spirit was an essential element in the British way of administration, and virtuoso performances were severely frowned upon. Everyone, even the lowest, was expected to state his views frankly and without looking over his shoulder. A senior official in putting up a paper to the Governor would not merely say that he agreed with his junior's opinion, but would be required to state why he agreed. At the conclusion of informal meetings when everyone present had had their say, the upshot of the discussion would be summed up by the presiding officer, which would be binding upon all, and especially the dissenters. Action would then be promptly taken. Meetings never dragged on, the participants being expected to be well prepared with their briefs and able to give cogent reasons for their views. How different this approach is from the one where officials sit formally at a conference table, with each participant trying to show off at the expense of his fellows and with little regard for the issues at hand: this can only lead to delays and distorted decisions.

The tide of war was at last beginning to turn. Burma was

cleared of the Japanese and as the land war progressed, great naval battles fought in the eastern seas ousted the enemy from island after island. With the horrendous atomic bombing of Hiroshima and Nagasaki, came Japan's total surrender. The War having at last ended, the process of unwinding began with the progressive withdrawal of the British and American forces from India and the demobilisation of the wartime Indian army. This greatly eased the problem of supply, and government procurement for the war-effort came to an end. As work in the Department of Civil Supplies diminished rapidly, the process of paring down the staff began.

At a cocktail party early in 1946, the Chief Secretary told me almost casually that I was to be the next Home Secretary of U.P. I was both surprised and elated at this sudden elevation to a rather senior position from my modest standing in Civil Supplies. I happened to be the first Indian officer named to the former post, which had hitherto apparently been reserved for British officers. Conditions in the province were fairly calm at the time but with the spread of vicious sectarian propaganda by the Muslim League, ominous clouds of communal violence had begun to appear, first in the Punjab. I went to Lahore to meet the top officials there and to see things for myself, and was much disturbed by what I saw and heard.

In the winter of 1945–46 countrywide elections had been held and in the Hindu majority provinces, the Congress had swept the board; in the reserved Muslim seats it was the Muslim League that had won. Soon a Congress Government took office at Lucknow. The senior British Officers began to depart on retirement, followed in a steady stream by officers of middle and junior rank. N.B. Bonarjee, some eight years my senior, took over as Chief Secretary and other Indian colleagues as Finance Secretary and Secretary to the Governor, all of them key posts. Many senior Indian officers also departed in quest of greener pastures to the Central government. The election had been held under the Government of India Act of 1935, according to which the provincial governments constituted thereunder enjoyed limited powers, the final authority still vesting legally in the Governor.

The new government, under the leadership of Pandit Gobind Ballabh Pant (who liked to be known as Hon'ble Premier, or H.P.) included such redoubtable figures of cabinet rank as Rafi Ahmad Kidwai, Dr Kailas Nath Katju, Hafiz Muhammad Ibrahim and Vijayalakshmi Pandit. Among the Parliamentary Secretaries attached to the Premier were Lal Bahadur Shastri and Charan Singh who later became Prime Ministers of India. Many of the other Ministers, although less prominent, were also persons of character and integrity, a far cry indeed from their latter-day successors. The new government came in in a rather belligerent mood, determined to stretch the Constitution to the limit and beyond, and to show the remaining British officials their place in the new order of things.

The change that came over the Secretariat was almost unbelievable. The orderly and silent corridors with officers and staff moving purposefully about their business were transformed into babels of noise. Every now and then someone from the throng in the corridors would barge in with a complaint or request, generally of a personal nature and highly motivated. The Minister's rooms were generally inundated with favour-seekers or just hangers-on, and it was sometimes difficult to discuss official matters with them, especially of a confidential nature. The Ministers kept very irregular hours, having often been delayed at their residences by importunate constituents or simply because they were unused to observing regular working hours. They would then be around until far into the evening, sometimes even after nightfall. All this hardly made for the speedy and orderly disposal of business.

We were middle-rank ICS officers who had taken over the key departments from the former senior British incumbents and we put in our best to ensure as orderly and effective working of government as was possible in the circumstances. To give well-considered advice to the Ministers, three or four of us would meet at home every evening to review the day's happenings and to hammer out the next day's problems. We were thus, from the Chief Secretary down, able to give uniform advice and so made the task of the Ministers easier. Most of them were new to office and the qualities which enabled them to win an election did not necessarily qualify them to be skilled in the art of governance.

There had been a change of Governor, Sir Francis Wylie having replaced the unimaginative and dull Sir Maurice Hallett. Wylie was very different from his predecessor; he had a warm and outgoing personality, and considerable tact and ability. He insisted on all social constraints and barriers between the British officials and Indians being removed, but the change in attitude came too late. There was much scepticism about when Independence would come as hopes had so often been blighted. When Wylie told me that within six months' there would be an Indian governor in his seat, I could hardly believe him.

From the outset of his advent in Lucknow, Wylie began acting as a constitutional head of government and refraining from exercising his considerable powers under the Government of India Act of 1935. The Instrument of Instructions, however, enjoined that certain matters had to be referred to him, as in law he could still veto or alter decisions taken by his cabinet or refer them back for reconsideration. I therefore had at least one interview with him every week when he spoke with considerable candour and understanding of the problems facing the new government, towards which he showed a liberal attitude. Some of the Ministers, however, were needlessly discourteous and abrasive in their notings and at their interviews with him. Wylie was too suave and sophisticated a man to allow himself to be needled by such uncouth behaviour. But he often lamented to me that he had heard of the U.P.'s culture, elegance and courtesy and wondered how his Ministers could be thought to represent those celebrated values. As Home Secretary I had to deal with no less than five ministers. Pandit Pant had overall charge of law and order, Rafi Ahmed Kidwai was Police (later Home) Minister, Dr Katju, the Law Minister, dealt with Criminal Justice, Thakur Hukam Singh with Transport and a Parliamentary Secretary functioning under Kidwai, with Jails. It was quite a merry-go-round for the files, but to reduce the time lag I would personally see Pantji and Kidwai. Pantji was inclined to be rather prolix and he would invariably note at length on a file in his spidery scrawl, writing on the margins and wherever a few spare inches could be found. Kidwai was just the opposite as he seldom noted on any file. Pantji always had a crowd of party members and others in his room and even the most confidential matters were discussed, after some waste of time, in their presence. Kidwai on the other hand had few hangers-on in his room, and when matters had to be discussed, they were asked to clear out. His desk too was clear of files and he was always most relaxed.

Because of Kidwai's allergy to files, I would take an armful to his room, tell him briefly in Urdu about each problem and my proposal, and the business would be done in a few minutes, he almost invariably giving his assent in every case. In his hurry to get things done and sometimes under pressure from his constituents, Kidwai would often ride roughshod over the rules. He would sometimes telephone orders directly to police officers. In one celebrated instance, the police official concerned forwarded his report through his official superior to the Inspector-General of Police, Sir Philip Measures. Measures, a rather proud man, took strong exception to being bypassed and forwarded to me a protest to the Minister, couched in strong and intemperate language, at the Minister's breach of rules and discipline of the force. To avoid a head-on clash, I sent for Measures and tried to prevail upon him to moderate the language of his letter while still making his point. But Measures, a stubborn man, refused to agree. I therefore had no choice but to forward the offending letter to the Minister. As feared, Kidwai shot through the roof on its receipt. He had been straining for a fight and what could be more exciting and eye-catching than an unequal duel with the seniormost British police officer, the very epitome of British rule? Some acrid exchanges between the Minister and the Governor followed, the latter using all his diplomatic skill to pour oil on troubled waters. But Kidwai would have none of it and demanded nothing less than the Inspector-General's head. The Governor then referred the matter to the Central Government which, in turn, forwarded it to Whitehall. The British Government, in view of impending events, took a political view of the dispute and strongly advised Measures' resignation. Measures thereupon left, leaving Kidwai triumphant. I then managed to persuade Sir George Pearce, the next in line and a man of a very different stamp, not to follow his chief, but to stay on as his successor and help the police force to tide over the difficult period of the transfer of power. Pearce gallantly agreed and was of the greatest help in dealing with the critical situation which accompanied Partiton.

Dr Katju, the Law Minister, was a personal friend of mine and a very amiable gentleman. He was a highly successful High Court lawyer and had made his mark in the profession. It was through him that mercy petitions from condemned prisoners to the Governor had to be forwarded. Both the Sessions Courts which tried cases for the more heinous offences and the High Court which heard the appeals, were generally averse to awarding death sentences. Yet, in a large province like U.P. a fairly large number of capital sentences were awarded. These were cases of a particularly gruesome nature which even our lenient courts could hardly treat with their usual clemency. The mercy petitions which almost invariably followed, came to the Home Department and they, along with the bulky files of the case, were examined in great detail and with much competence by one of my deputies who would then forward them to me with his recommendations. After a quick scrutiny I would pass on the case to the Minister with my remarks. Dr Katju, deeply religious and compassionate, would note at very great length on the file, stretching every possible argument to the limit and seizing upon the flimsiest bit of evidence to come to only one conclusion. That conclusion was invariably one of clemency, and the commutation of the death sentence to life imprisonment or only a few years of imprisonment. The Governor, clearly disagreeing with the Minister, would not overrule him, but note 'I must concur'. This became almost routine, to the despair of my able deputy and of the guardians of the law.

A date for the transfer of power had by now been announced as June 1948, but the Governor-General, Lord Mountbatten who had taken over from Field Marshal Lord Wavell, was a man in a hurry. He advanced the date to 15 August 1947. As the time approached, there was a palpable increase of tension in the province. Highly respected Muslim citizens of Lucknow whose families had lived in the city for generations and who were most prominent in society, began leaving for the new state; Muslim officers, senior and junior, also began opting out in large numbers in the hope of bettering their prospects. The U.P. police force, however, was affected only marginally as only the officers were leaving. U.P. had been the epicentre of the separatist movement, and the precipitate departure of their leaders and notables began greatly to agitate the Muslim population.

The U.P. police force had till hitherto enjoyed a practically unsullied reputation and in its functioning, even in the case of communal riots, had displayed no communal bias. But in the new situation one could hardly be sure how a section of the force would acquit itself if faced with a difficult choice. The force was heavily weighted in favour of Muslims in practically every branch, while in some ranks and functions Muslims had a near-monopoly. At the rank of Inspector, Muslims constituted some 80 per cent, at Sub-Inspector, about 50 per cent and among the constabulary some 33 per cent. Since in most of U.P. Urdu was the official language, the person who took down first information reports at police stations was almost invariably a Muslim. This was a crucial function as much depended on these reports in the course of a criminal prosecution. In the armed police too, the Muslim element was considerable.

Another problem of primordial importance was that, in the not unlikely event of major upheavals in large parts of the province, the police force would be grossly insufficient to deal with them. The civil police were armed only with lathis and numbered a bare 20,000 or so in a state with 49 districts and a population of about 75 million. The armed police was a small force, equipped only with ancient muskets whose range was less than 100 yards, and was mostly engaged in static duties such as keeping guard over armouries and treasuries, with a small reserve. Of particular concern was the fact that little or nothing could be expected from the army in aid of the civil power as the armed forces were themselves in the process of being partitioned.

In fact, the British Major-General commanding the area informed me to my dismay that the regiments destined for India were locked up in the North-West Frontier, while those for Pakistan were in U.P. For example, the Rajputana Rifles was still in the north-west while the Baluchis and Pathans were in Lucknow and Bareilly. The General was genuinely apprehensive that, in case of major trouble, it would be difficult to hold down the Muslim regiments and he even thought of keeping them behind barbed wire. Any aid from the army being thus ruled out, it became a matter of greater urgency to have an alternative in a mobile force with considerable hitting power to deal effectively with major disturbances.

The possibility of raising such a para-military force within the given time of only a few months was worked out in detail with the concerned officials. The demobilisation of Rajput regiments was then going on in Fatehgarh and of Kumaonis, Garhwalis and Gurkhas, in Almora. The jawans had been through years of war, fighting in North Africa, Palestine, Italy and Burma and were tough and highly disciplined. It would be easy at the demobilisation centres to recruit them into the proposed force by simply replacing their military badges on their military fatigues with police badges. Their officers too could be recruited simultaneously. A few months training in Police Regulations and in police duties would equip them for the tasks we had in mind for them. They had to remember, however, that in the police the minimum force was to be used to gain a given objective, whereas in the military the maximum was used.

The next question, a particularly tricky one, was how we were to equip the new force. Here the contacts of the British Deputy Inspector-General of Police (Supplies) with the British Colonel in charge of the growing dump of war surplus equipment at Bamrauli, near Allahabad, was most useful. With Pearce's help, our requirements were worked out in detail and referred to the Colonel who was himself anxious to get rid of as much as he could, price being no consideration. We had planned on not less than twelve companies of 100 men each, fully armed with the latest rifles, light and heavy machine-guns, with plenty of ammunition, light trucks for mobility and, most important of all, a very large number of wireless sets of different kinds. Surplus uniforms, etc. were thrown in for good measure. The price was adjusted to fall within our capacity to pay, and for each company's full equipment it was well under two lakhs of rupees—an incredibly low figure. The annual salary bill of a company would be one lakh.

On the setting up of the new force, our own group of officials had fully covered the ground; our colleague the Finance Secretary had agreed to find the funds while the Chief Secretary was fully in line with the plan and strategy. An unspoken advantage was that at the two military demobilisation centres, the jawans were almost entirely Hindu, so without breaching the general principle of maintaining an equal field for all communities in the matter of recruitment, a corrective step to reduce the imbalance would be taken.

Among the Ministers there was, surprisingly, an air of supreme unconcern about the dangers to peace and stability that might lie ahead; matters of secondary or tertiary importance seemed to be engaging their attention. The problem was how to alert the Government and secure its agreement to the emergency measures that had been worked out.

I accordingly saw the Premier and told him at length of our various concerns and the kind of measures which would be required to deal with them. Pantji, after listening to my urgent presentation, said to my surprise that there was no reason to expect any trouble. Hoping that it would be so, I pointed out that, as a student of history, whenever in India any dynasty or empire had given place to another, there were big upheavals, and it was to guard against such a contingency that the proposals had been made. Pantji asked why I was so panicky and lacking in faith; to this I could only reply that I believed with Cromwell in trusting in God but keeping my powder dry. To have the last word, Pantji said that I did not seem to show much trust in God either!

When I returned to the charge with some persistence, Pantji doubted if in the short time ahead it would be possible to make the proposed arrangements. I then came out with the scheme in detail, explaining how the force would be recruited, equipped, trained and funded and at what little cost. It would be a very cheap insurance policy against a serious contingency. The scheme would also take effective care of the internal communal aspect of the problem. With all objections answered, Pantji finally gave his assent.

With the greatest relief I informed my colleagues of the outcome and gave the go-ahead signal to the Inspector-General of Police. Thereafter, the whole scheme was set in full motion and it went like clockwork. Despite my insufficient knowledge of Hindi, I christened the new force the 'Prantiya Rakshak Dal', or the 'Provincial Armed Constabulary'. We were able to raise thirteen fully equipped and mobile companies. It was a fine body of men, battle hardened, skilled in the use of modern weaponry and highly disciplined. As events were soon to prove, they became our sword-arm and shield at the same time and because of their efficiency and mobility could be widely deployed and were able to prevent the spread of the conflagration attending Partition. Of particular utility also were the wireless sets with which the force was equipped. Furthermore, to guard against the cutting off of communications, wireless sets were provided to all the districts and even to the Central Home Ministry and the Chief Commissioner of Delhi. Instant communication was thus ensured over the whole province and with the Centre, which was invaluable during the crucial months that followed. One could hardly have imagined that a force that rendered such great and impartial service during those critical days, should have fallen into such evil favour today.

Sardar Patel, greatly concerned about the possible impact of Partition on U.P., had earlier flown down to Lucknow to take stock of the situation. He sent for me to give him a detailed report and the steps we had taken to deal with possible large-scale disturbances. He seemed particularly concerned about the communal composition of the police force. Fortunately, I was able to inform him about the PAC which was then in the process of formation, and would incidentally also take care of any communal inequalities within the force. He expressed approval of the proposed arrangements and did not ask for any additional measures.

We were ready to the extent of our limited resources to face the impact of Partition on our western borders. But the rest of the province would have only a thin security cover. It was therefore of the utmost importance to contain the shock, when it came, to the western districts.

When Independence day dawned, there was great rejoicing when the old order changed, giving place to the new. The previous night there was a farewell banquet by the retiring Governor, Sir Francis Wylie, a very formal affair with men in full evening dress, while the British ladies wore long gowns and gloves. Last toasts were drunk in champagne, and the Governor, gracious and courteous as ever, said farewell to all the guests. The British guests, most of whom were also leaving, said farewell to their Indian colleagues. In the morning we all trooped to the red-carpeted railway station to say our final farewell to the Governor as he departed in his special train. That was the requiem of the British Raj in U.P.

The new Governor, Sarojini Naidu, later arrived at the same platform. The scene, however, was very different from what it had been only hours earlier. A vast and miscellaneous crowd swarmed all over the platform, the Premier and Ministers were pushed around and the smiling Mrs Naidu, almost smothered in garlands, was extricated from the pandemonium with difficulty. The evening's function at Government House was a veritable nightmare. Invitations had been issued in Hindi on the familiar Government House stationery, but now prescribing the official dress and dhoti-kurta. The Indian officers were in a quandary as most did not know how to tie a dhoti, so we decided to appear in our own native dress. I had no problem as I had an achkan and churidars. But the general sartorial turn-out of the top officials was hilarious. Our Tamil colleagues came in mundus but were dissuaded from appearing bare-chested and bare-footed. Others came in bedroom pyjamas and shirts with a waistcoat from a three-piece suit for effect, and still others, in whatever they could devise for the occasion. We need not, however, have worried. The gates of Government House, hitherto kept inviolate, had been thrown open, and the mohallas had seemingly emptied themselves out into the reception rooms and halls of the palace, the overflow flooding the lawns. All restraint and decorum had been thrown to the winds and the Indian sweets and delicacies laid out for the invited guests disappeared as soon as they were replenished. It was truly a day to remember!

The euphoria of Independence had hardly subsided when the stricken and divided Punjab succumbed to violent communal upheavals of volcanic proportions. The shock waves of the horrific events soon assailed U.P. with increasing intensity. It was not long before multitudes of ragged Punjabi refugees, men, women and children, consumed by fear and anger, began pouring into the western districts. Their heartbreaking tales of murder, rapine and loot of which they had been the victims, greatly inflamed an already excited population. Led by the Jats who preponderated in many of the western districts, huge mobs began to assemble, thirsting for revenge which they sought to wreak on the hapless Muslims of the area. Armed with whatever weapons were at hand, they fell upon village after village, filling the wells with corpses.

The local police force was woefully inadequate to stem the rising tide of violence and, despite the gallant intervention of the newly-raised Provincial Armed Constabulary, the security forces were themselves in danger of being overwhelmed. At dead of night, the Commissioner of Meerut Division telephoned in a state of great alarm to say that the situation had gone quite out of control and begged for more reinforcements. But reinforcements there were none. When I asked him to call out the military, he said the only military formation there was a tank regiment. There was no option but to ask him to take out the tanks and quell the violence at whatever cost. Taken aback, the Commissioner, a very senior ICS officer, asked if those were the orders of Government and demanded written confirmation of them. This I did by wireless the first thing the following morning. The Commissioner and his District Officers took immediate and stern action and managed to quench the conflagration before it could spread and overwhelm the whole province.

The political fall-out, however, was not long in coming. Legislators and 'netas' (a term for leader, now largely used pejoratively), most of them Jats from the western districts, began to arrive in a state of alarm, complaining bitterly about the high-handed and draconian actions of the local officials. They were particularly incensed at the fact that Hindus had been mowed down in such numbers. Their lamentations made even Pantji lose his habitual calm, especially as he was until then in the dark about the events of the night before.

When asked to explain, I described to Pantji the perilous situation in the western district, when even the Commissioner, a highly experienced and intrepid Jat Sikh officer was himself in such desperate straits. The hordes of rioters numbering tens of thousands, bent upon murder and arson, had already taken a terrible toll of hundreds of innocent lives. They were nothing but criminals, arsonists and murderers and had to be treated as such. If the communal frenzy was not stamped out on the province's western border, there was nothing to prevent it from spreading like wildfire throughout the province. And it would not stop at the border, but would engulf the adjoining state of Bihar and spread to West Bengal as well. There was a sizeable Muslim population in this vast area and the consequences would be too horrendous for words. It was probably true that as many rioters had been shot down as the number of their victims, but they had only got their just deserts. It was to be hoped that what had been done would have a deterrent effect and convey a warning to all lawless elements that the Government would act resolutely to maintain peace and order in the province. Despite some lingering doubts, this explanation was ultimately accepted, and fortunately, violence on such a massive scale did not recur.

Over most of the province comparative calm prevailed, but the occurrence of minor incidents here and there kept the police and magistracy in a state of high alert. The police force performed its duties impartially and the ready availability of the PAC helped to strengthen its confidence and morale. The blood-letting in the Punjab continued almost uncontrollably and soon spread perilously near to Delhi as well. News from the capital became increasingly ominous, of uncontrollable mobs bent upon murder and arson, roaming about the city creating havoc.

Late one night I received a most immediate telephone call from the Chief Commissioner of Delhi, Khurshid Ahmad Khan, a distinguished member of the ICS and an old and respected friend. He was clearly in a state of great stress and anxiety. He said the situation in Delhi was desperate and the administration had come to the end of its resources; he urged me to send urgently whatever help was possible. Otherwise there would be a total collapse of authority there. We were ourselves very hard-pressed, but I persuaded our Commissioner of the Meerut division to dispatch a couple of companies of the PAC immediately for the succour of the Delhi administration. A few days later, gratefully acknowledging our help, Khurshid Ahmad Khan said our two PAC companies' timely arrival had saved the day and helped to turn the tide against the frenzied mobs.

Soon, trouble of another variety began brewing at our very doorstep. The students of Lucknow University were up in arms against some real or imaginary grievances and were daily taking out slogan-shouting processions. These became increasingly noisy and unruly and occasionally violent. The hard-pressed district authorities asked for instructions from the Government about how to deal with the students, since the latter thought of themselves as privileged beings and were also so regarded by the general run of politicians. The district authorities were hesitant to apply the usual drastic police methods of breaking up unruly mobs lest they were themselves taken to task for doing so by the political masters. Earlier, in the case of Aligarh Muslim

University students who had behaved in similar fashion, Rafi Ahmad Kidwai had no hesitation in ordering that the ring-leaders be arrested. On the present occasion, too, he had no compunction in telling the harassed District Magistrate to break up the processions and to arrest the main culprits. Soon the local jail began filling up with students.

The students then turned their attention towards U.P. Secretariat itself, at first gathering in the square opposite and shouting slogans mostly against Premier Pant himself. The Council House then had no walls or gates and nothing to protect it beyond a sentry at the entrance. One day I decided to walk down to the square to talk to the student leaders. But before I could get into their midst, I was suddenly gripped firmly by the arm. Taken by surprise I turned to face a young police constable who began pulling me towards a waiting "black maria" already full of arrested students. I thought of prying myself loose from the iron grip of my captor and making for shelter in the 'Darul Shafa' across the square where resided the Chief Secretary. But perceiving the constable's lathi poised menacingly, I tried to break our progress towards the awaiting vehicle, aware that once in, it would take days to sort me out in jail from the rest of its student occupants. Resigning myself to what seemed inevitable, my weak remonstrances notwithstanding, the distance between us and the police van was shortening by the second. At that moment, a Secretariat orderly, resplendent in red, perceived the Home Secretary being dragged into custody and rushed to his rescue just in time. After much persuasion and upbraiding, the constable released his grip most reluctantly. I lost no time dallying and made as fast as I could to the sanctuary of 'Darul Shafa'. I could hardly blame the young constable who was only doing his duty, for there was nothing to distinguish me from the students since I too was dressed like them, and looked rather young. The newspapers got hold of the story and the next morning it appeared prominently, to the great amusement of the public and much to my embarrassment.

The students soon extended their activities by trying to storm into the Council House shouting 'Down with Pant' and were held back with difficulty. Pantji was much disturbed by these developments and kept enquiring after the Home Minister. But the Home Minister was nowhere to be found: he had disappeared four days ago. When he did reappear quite unconcernedly, he feigned surprise at Pantji's agitation about the students. He then stepped out of the building and scolded the agitators for their behaviour and was greeted with shouts of 'Long Live Rafi'. The students promptly dispersed. Kidwai then went to the jail where again he was applauded by the arrested students who he released at once. The shrewd operator that he was, Kidwai had stolen a march over Pantji whom he loved to tease: he had won the hearts of the students by feeding them in jail with pulao and kababs and then letting them out!

Typical of Kidwai's manner of cutting corners was his peremptory release of all those whom he regarded as political detenues. So that people could feel the 'thrill of Independence', he asked for the immediate release of all such prisoners. I pointed out that they would have to be sorted out in the jails all over the province from others who had been jailed for criminal offences, and that, as the numbers involved ran into thousands, the process would take time. Kidwai, however, said that he would be able to do the sorting out personally from the lists of all those detained under the Defence of India Act and other wartime measures. All the jails were accordingly notified and wads of lists began snowballing in. Those were passed on to the Minister who wrote one word, 'Release', on all of them without exception. Release orders to the jails were thereupon issued for every prisoner in the lists. But that was not the end of the matter. It was not long before protests began pouring in from District Magistrates against the release of dacoits, arsonists, forgerers and all manner of criminals who had been detained. The police authorities had been in the habit of misusing wartime legislation by simply detaining criminals and suspects and saving themselves the trouble of a long investigation and trial in court. When I told Kidwai of the consequences of his omnibus release orders, he promptly said that all such criminals should be rearrested!

I must record an episode of a very grave nature when the procrastination and indecision of the U.P. Cabinet led to dire consequences. When communal tension was still at fever-pitch, the Deputy Inspector-General of Police of the Western Range, a very seasoned and capable officer, B.B.L Jaitley, arrived at my house in great secrecy. He was accompanied by two of his officers who brought with them two large steel trunks securely locked. When the trunks were opened, they revealed incontrovertible evidence of a dastardly conspiracy to create a communal holocaust throughout the western districts of the province. The trunks were crammed with blueprints of great accuracy and professionalism of every town and village in that vast area, prominently marking out the Muslim localities and habitations. There were also detailed instructions regarding access to the various locations, and other matters which amply revealed their sinister purport.

Greatly alarmed by those revelations, I immediately took the police party to the Premier's house. There, in a closed room, Jaitley gave a full report of his discovery, backed by all the evidence contained in the steel trunks. Timely raids conducted on the premises of the RSS (Rashtriya Swayam Sevak Sangh) had brought the massive conspiracy to light. The whole plot had been concerted under the direction and supervision of the Supremo of the organisation himself. Both Jaitley and I pressed for the immediate arrest of the prime accused, Shri Golwalkar, who was still in the area.

Pantji could not but accept the evidence of his eyes and ears and expressed deep concern. But instead of agreeing to the immediate arrest of the ring leader as we had hoped, and as

Kidwai would have done, he asked for the matter to be placed for consideration by the Cabinet at its next meeting. It was no doubt a matter of political delicacy as the roots of the RSS had gone deep into the body politic. There were also other political compulsions as RSS sympathisers, both covert and overt, were to be found in the Congress party itself and even in the Cabinet. It was no secret that the presiding officer of the Upper House, Atma Govind Kher, was himself an adherent and his sons were openly members of the RSS.

At the Cabinet meeting there was the usual procrastination and much irrelevant talk. The fact that the police had unearthed a conspiracy which would have set the whole province in flames and that the officers concerned deserved warm commendation hardly seemed to figure in the discussion. What ultimately emerged was that a letter should be issued to Shri Golwalkar pointing out the contents and nature of the evidence which had been gathered and demanding an explanation thereof. At my insistence, such a letter if it were to be sent, should be issued by the Premier himself to carry greater weight. Pantiji asked me to prepare a draft, which I did in imitation of his own characteristic style. The letter was to be delivered forthwith and two police officers were assigned for the purpose.

Golwalkar, however, had been tipped off and he was nowhere to be found in the area. He was tracked down southwards but he managed to elude the couriers in pursuit. This infructuous chase continued from place to place and weeks passed.

Came January 30, 1948 when the Mahatma, that supreme apostle of peace, fell to a bullet fired by an RSS fanatic. The whole tragic episode left me sick at heart.

The time was approaching when I was to leave Lucknow, never to return for any length of time. The Prime Minister of India was setting up a new diplomatic service and I was soon to join it as one of the pioneers. It would be a leap in the dark, but a change would not be unwelcome. The decision had its origin at a banquet given by the Governor, Sarojini Naidu, in honour of the visiting Governor-General, Lord Mountbatten and Lady Mountbatten. Mrs Naidu was well-known to Susheela's family and she often asked us over for an evening's relaxation, when she loved to hear Susheela sing. When we moved to the salon after the banquet, Mrs Naidu insisted that Susheela sing, having quickly sent her ADC to collect the tamboura from our house. Susheela reluctantly sat down with her tamboura and the Mountbattens led all the guests to join her on the floor. Later, Mountbatten tried to persuade us to join the new diplomatic service. Not long afterwards, when a demand came from Delhi asking for my services, I suspected the hand of Mountbatten in the decision. Pantji, however, strongly demurred and it was only when Pandit Nehru came to Allahabad for the immersion of the Mahatma's ashes in the Sangam where Pantji met him, did the latter finally agree. He informed me of his agreement, and said he had insisted that I should return after six months—but the time never came.

Lucknow in the brief span of a year or two had completely changed its character. The great houses of the landed gentry closed down one after another as their owners retreated to their estates. They soon had to abandon their country mansions as well as the Zamindari Abolition Act at one fell swoop deprived them of their ancestral lands. Their city mansions were given over to Punjabi refugees. Gone were the sumptuous entertainments, the music and dance, and social life dwindled. The elegance, culture and etiquette for which Lucknow was justly famed all but vanished, and even the graceful Urdu language was imperilled. Thus, while British style and decorum disappeared almost without trace, the long-celebrated Urdu culture of the city was on the retreat. The pattern—if there was any—was now to be set by the new governing class. Barring some notable exceptions, they were in a category by themselves. The majority had a rural or small-town background, many of the kulak class, some were petty lawyers or schoolmasters and the like, few of whom had particularly distinguished themselves in their professions or even in public life. True, they had taken part in meetings and processions and had gone to prison during the freedom movement. They were dazzled by their new standing to which they were totally unaccustomed and made a virtue of their plebeian and bucolic ways. The composite culture of Lucknow was regarded as decadent and 'nawabi', while orderly and polite middle-class ways were discredited as those of the now reviled 'Sahibs'. Even elegance of dress was thought to smack of the old order.

The passport to acceptability were now the dhoti and kurta of homespun cotton, and flapping sandals. Politeness of speech gave place to raucousness. Not only was the Urdu language frowned upon, but the Devanagari script was sought to be imposed. Words in common parlance came to be substituted by newly contrived expressions never heard before. The Urdu script in current use throughout the province was substituted by the Devanagari. Even in the Secretariat some Ministers began noting in Hindi, to the dismay of the permanent officials, high and low. In my own case, Lal Bahadu Shastri, who had taken over from Rafi Ahmad Kidwai when the latter joined the Central Cabinet, suddenly began noting in Hindi and expected me to do the same. But when I explained that I was quite incapable of doing so, he was considerate enough merely to ask me to sign my name in Hindi or Urdu!

A new phenomenon was the propensity of rank-and-file Congressmen to interfere in district administration and even to try and usurp the functions of the District Officer, without however carrying any of the responsibility. This became not only a nuisance but a growing menace, and District Officers were hard put to fend off these intruders. To the latter, election to the Assembly meant little unless they could throw their weight about in their own districts and exercise executive power to further their own interest and those of their friends and relations. The essence of democracy is the separation of powers between the legislative, judicial and executive branches, for while party governments may come and go, the administration must go on without interruption. In pre de Gaulle France, for example, while a series of Ministers came and went as through a revolving door, the administration was not affected. In fact, the French Prefects created by Napoleon enjoy great power and prestige to this day, unaffected by the changing fortunes of the country and the political system. When I protested strongly to Pantji about this pernicious development, he agreed to issue, as party President, a strong letter to district Congress Committees, enjoining them to desist from interfering with the administration. As usual, I was asked to draft the letter, which I did gladly, advisedly sending copies to the beleaguered districts officers. This had a very salutary effect.

Of social contact between Ministers and senior officials there were none, perhaps not even between the Ministers themselves. While they had made it clear that they would not accept any invitation from Government House when there was a British Governor, even Mrs Naidu's invitations were accepted reluctantly. On one occasion when the Cabinet Ministers did respond, there was hardly any public conversation and not sooner was dinner over than the whole lot trooped out without ceremony, which led Mrs Naidu to explain 'There go my ministers like a cloud of mosquitoes!' Most of the ministers perhaps kept aloof because they were unused to moving in polite society and had no particular cultural, social or intellectual interests. (A shining exception, of course, was Vijayalakshmi Pandit.) And their mode of dress also distinguished them as a class apart. Their wives presumably observed strict purdah as they were never seen.

Besides bringing about a vast political transformation, Independence had also ushered in deep social changes whose direction was till then uncertain. The so-called Congress culture seemed to be harking back atavistically towards the past, while the general trend was towards modernity.

The Governor, Mrs Naidu, stood poles apart from her ministers. She was most sociable and loved to savour the best of Lucknow culture. Government House became a focus of social gatherings where the embattled Lucknow society assembled to be treated lavishly to evenings of good conversation, good fare and good music. But in vivid contrast to her predecessor, she was kept insulated from official concerns to such an extent that she once innocently enquired what I did as Home Secretary, and was surprised to learn of the nature and extent of my responsibilities.

With the departure of the British, the changes, both political and social, that had taken place practically overnight, inevitably invited a review of their nature and extent. The incubus of foreign rule had been removed and national self-respect restored. The evil system of colonialism based upon the sordid instincts of greed, exploitation and domination over other races had been extirpated from India. Indeed, it has been condemned by the United Nations as a massive form of racial discrimination and has now happily all but disappeared from the face of the earth. Colonialism was imperial policy at the time and was determined in London, and even if the young Englishmen who came out to serve in the Indian administration had little to do with it, they nevertheless came as a part of the British mystique of imperialism which professed an almost messianic inspiration and role.

The Congress rulers who followed had other motivations. As servants of the people, their mission was to promote the people's hopes and aspirations as followers of the Mahatma's principles and ideals. The Congress pledge therefore enjoined on them observance of the Gandhian principles of simplicity, poverty, abstinence and self-sacrifice. We young Indian officers, for our part, had long determined that with the departure of the foreigners, we would strain every nerve and resource to help build our country in association with the elected leaders. This we all tried our best to do in conditions that were not always congenial, and which were frequently disappointing.

Govind Ballabh Pant's ministry comprised many members of all-India renown; it was one of the ablest in the country, and infinitely superior to anything that followed. While it inherited what was widely regarded as the best administered province in India, Pantji had great respect for law and procedure and for the parliamentary system, and we did try to maintain acceptable standards of governance. But certain contradictions between precept and practice became increasingly apparent even then.

The Congress governments were expected to observe the highest standards of probity and service of the people and to take the path of austerity and self-sacrifice. But while they fixed their salaries at a mere Rs 500 a month, a quarter of those of senior secretaries to governments, they compensated themselves lavishly in other ways. The ministers moved into the largest and best official residences and had them furnished expensively. A fleet of new American cars was acquired, the vehicles being used with such abandon as to require extensive repairs or replacement within months. Petrol, which was still rationed, was allowed without limit, while telephones and electricity were used without restraint. The khadi apparel surmounted by a Gandhi cap became almost the regulation outfit of the new ruling class and set it apart from the rest of the people. Public money began to be squandered in many profligate ways. It was difficult to believe that the big bungalows and the life-style of their occupants could be maintained on the meagre salary of ministers. Hordes of followers and hangers-on infested ministers' premises and were being daily fed. Already the nexus between the politicians and corrupt businessmen was becoming evident. Security guards and armed sentries also began to appear, but on nothing like the scale being witnessed today when every ministerial bungalow has become an armed camp, surrounded by iron railings and barbed wire with search lights blazing and roads being closed for over an hour for the safe passage of VVIPs.

We, the Indian officers, who were accustomed to a different order of things until only the other day, found the new order distasteful and hypocritical. In the first place, every official from the highest to the lowest received a salary on the basis of a time-scale with no perquisites whatsoever. Official residences were no doubt provided, but we had to pay a rent equivalent to ten per cent of our salaries, the houses were totally unfurnished and electricity and telephones had to be paid for, except when used for strictly official business. No official transport was provided, and from the beginning of the War until well after its end, the strictest petrol rationing was enforced. The main mode of transport was the bicycle and every morning a procession of the highest among the 'burra sahibs' could be seen cycling along to the Secretariat in shirt and shorts, followed by chaprasis in red with official dispatch black boxes strapped behind. There were no armed guards at residences and no barbed wire or any other security arrangements. Even Government House had no special security arrangements, apart from the ceremonial sentries at the gates. And this was the state of affairs at the height of the national movement and Quit India upheavals. In the matter of public expenditure, the pre-Independence government was positively parsimonious, with a vigilant finance department freely axing proposals which it considered unnecessary or expensive. The standard of integrity was of the highest, although vast purchases were being made to feed the voracious War machine; and while controls covered a wide penumbra, there was never a whiff of scandal. Permits and licenses were being issued to exporters and to manufacturers of commodities such as sugar, hydrogenated oil, etc. But the thought never crossed one's mind that such favours were marketable. What a contrast to today, when the way to untold riches is via the ballot box and a ministerial chair!

To point to certain incontrovertible facts about the manner of functioning of the pre-Independence system is not necessarily to laud it, for it assuredly was far from being perfect. But it was not, at the same time, all evil and brutal. It has been dubbed as a 'law and order' government and even derisively as 'police raj'. That is a travesty of the facts. It is certainly true that the maintenance of peace and tranquility was among the primary duties of the administration, but it was by no means the only duty. And surely any government worth the name must assure to all its citizens safety of life and property. It must suppress crime and criminals, ensure the safety of communications and the provisions of basic civic necessities such as water, electricity and sanitation. Without these basic needs how can any nation-building activity flourish? There can then be no progress in education, improvement in public health or economic development. The present condition of U.P. and Bihar, steeped in misery and squalor, amply bear out this fact.

It is also not true to say that the former administration was indifferent to activities designed for the welfare and progress of the people. Most of the so-called development departments had long been in place and had much to show for themselves. The vast network of irrigation canals and tubewells, of roads and railways, of schools and colleges, of hospitals and rural clinics, of agricultural and forestry services, to name a few, had proved their worth. But there was much, much more to be done and a foreign power had its own limitations in persuading the common people to change or reform their ancient ways. But we see that, in spite of the expenditure of astronomical sums during a series of Five Year Plans, there has been little alleviation in the grinding poverty of the villages, while some ministers, corrupt officials and kulaks have been greatly enriched. Basic civic amenities which were formerly taken for granted have now almost become a rarity, which only the privileged may enjoy.

A great and tragic failure has been in a matter of primordial importance, viz., national integration. The British, as was the case with imperial powers throughout history, practised policies of 'divide and rule', the reservation of seats for Muslims and separate electorates eventually leading to the partition of the country. But half a century after Independence we are witness to policies which not only widen the Hindu-Muslim sectarian gap, but fracture the entire national fabric along caste lines. The egregious policy is creating minority communities where there were none before, and destroying the cohesion of society. Such a policy of division, far from its professed aim of social justice, has been cynically devised merely to garner votes for purposes of self-aggrandisement. The danger is that it might lead not to one, but to many Pakistans. Instead of the occasional communal riot of the past, generally put down with a firm hand, we now have violent communal explosions, caste wars and massacres on a scale and for a duration undreamt of before despite a greatly enhanced police force—a Director-General, some twenty Inspectors-General, countless Deputy Inspectors-General and a force of at least 100,000, as against the earlier force of one Inspector-General, seven Deputy Inspectors-General and a constabulary of some 25,000. There are, besides, all kinds of para-military forces, including the Provincial Armed Constabulary whose thirteen companies had rendered such splendid service in 1947. Now greatly swollen, the PAC has become more a menace than a protector of the law-abiding.

With the departure of the British, the burden of running the administration throughout the country fell on some six hundred Indian ICS officers. The districts were mostly manned by them and it was they who headed the various ministries at the centre and in the provinces. They also took on many unfamiliar tasks as, for example, in the new international organisations, and it was they who pioneered the newly set up Foreign Service and provided its backbone. If at Independence there was no administrative collapse and a certain measure of continuity was maintained, some credit is due to the unremitting labour of this small band of ICS officials. It was well known that Pandit Nehru had an aversion to the ICS and had declared more than once that, with the advent of Independence, the Service would be disbanded. The Indian members, having been thus put on notice, had already began to condition themselves to the uncertain prospect of a change in circumstances. It was Sardar Patel, however, who stood out firmly in favour of the services so that the contingency that had been feared never came to pass. The Sardar had insisted that the country could not possibly afford to deprive itself of the assistance of a disciplined and highly experienced group of officers whose patriotism and love of the country were beyond reproach. Pandit Nehru's change of attitude became immediately apparent when he hand-picked members of the ICS to set up the new Foreign Service on which he had set his heart, and to select an officer of the same service as his first Private Secretary, my younger brother, Harishwar.

# FIVE

# *In Stalin's Realm*

The lend-lease Soviet Dakota droned on and on over the frozen black and white expanse below. We were the only passengers on that plane, which was devoid of any vestige of comfort or safety, including seat-belts. A peasant woman in rubber boots and a head scarf, with steel bands for teeth, served as the hostess. As a concession to propriety, the toilet cubicle was screened off by a flapping curtain. Our thirteen items of miscellaneous baggage, comprising suitcases, trunks, holdalls, crates, etc., were placed on the seats around us.

We had made an early start from Stockholm after a hurried cup of tea, hoping to find some refreshment on the way. But the Soviet plane at Helsinki was already awaiting our arrival, with engines running, and we were bundled off at a smart pace across the frozen tarmac, our baggage following behind. But of refreshments on the Soviet plane there were none, not even drinking water. When the plane touched down on a snow-covered, wind-swept expanse, there was no sign of any airport; what was visible was the gaunt skeleton in the far distance of what presumably had been the Leningrad terminal. While the plane was being refuelled from a tanker, the crew wandered off behind various snow-drifts, and on comprehending their intentions, we followed suit. After a few official-looking passengers with a large number of crates had boarded the aircraft, we took off over the vast empty landscape.

Our departure from New Delhi on a March morning of 1948 was the start of an adventure into the unknown from the comparative security of life in Lucknow. The Pan American Constellation, which bore us aloft, was to us the height of luxury. The twenty-four hour flight to London with stopovers at Karachi, Damascus, Istanbul, Rome and Geneva, seemed incredibly swift. In London we were treated sumptuously by the High Commissioner, V.K. Krishna Menon, who lodged us in a suite at the Dorchester Hotel with a chauffeur-driven Daimler at our disposal. Krishna Menon had fixed appointments for me with some Communist missions, including that of the Soviet Union, whose Ambassador, Jacob Malik, was later to be my counterpart at the United Nations. The only impression of these encounters which survives is the sense of secrecy and reticence which surrounded them.

London in the spring of 1948 was a sad place, showing the scars of war, with gaping holes where apartment blocks or stately homes once stood. The City area was the worst affected, and St Paul's alone stood out untarnished in the desolation. The shops had only goods of inferior quality to offer, and food, even at the Dorchester, was spartan and indifferent. Two incidents particularly stand out in memory. The first concerned breakfast one morning. The *maitre d' hôtel* announced with great ceremony that it was 'Egg Day', and asked how we would like the rarity to be served! The second incident was about shoes. I had put out a pair in the corridor for cleaning, as used to be the practice once. When the shoes did not turn up for days, I complained to the management, who, to my surprise, advised that I should have known better. Needless to say, I never saw those shoes again.

It was originally thought that we would fly to Moscow via Prague, but as Czechoslovakia had just fallen into the Soviet orbit, we were diverted via Stockholm and Helsinki. Foreign airlines, except those of Finland, were not permitted to fly into Soviet airspace. Stockholm presented a great contrast to down-at-heel London as Sweden, having kept out of both World Wars, had prospered exceedingly. The shops were bursting with goods and food was in abundance, the people appeared well-dressed and well-nourished and there was a general air of prosperity and well-being. Sweden claimed to have created a truly socialist society and was justifiably proud of its achievements. We were soon to see another, much vaunted but very different, socialist state, that created by Stalin.

As we flew on, dusk fell and, tired and hungry, our spirits matched the twilight gloom. Presently, pale lights began to appear below, and by nightfall the lights of Moscow glowed in the distance. When the plane came to a bumping halt, it was with a sense of infinite relief that we staggered across the tarmac to the terminal building.

On entering the arrival hall, which had the aspect of an Indian railway waiting-room crowded with men and women in padded coats carrying packages of every description, we were accosted by a representative of our Embassy, a Dr Ghoshal, a humourless man of mournful aspect, who recounted the rigours of life which lay ahead of us. Our spirits, already low, sank deeper.

If in London the scars of war were painfully evident, in Moscow the deep wounds were still raw and all-pervasive. As we drove from the airport we could discern, even in the half-light, row upon row of trenches and barbed-wire defences. More formidable were the row upon serried row of tank traps of crossed steel girders and deep ditches that bore testimony to the hard-fought battles against the Nazi invaders.

Human suffering was poignantly visible on the streets of Moscow as one frequently encountered young men, and sometimes women, without an arm or a leg or sometimes without both legs. The supply of artificial limbs being quite insufficient to meet the enormous demand, countless young men and women were condemned for years to lead handicapped lives. The number of casualties of the war were computed at the staggering figure of twenty-five million, almost half of them civilian. The cost to the long-suffering Soviet people of even such basic necessities as food, shelter and clothing, was incalculable.

We were to stay initially at the Hotel Metropole. It had obviously seen better days, but now black marble figures at its entrance dolefully eyed visitors as though, like Cerberus, they guarded the gates of the underworld. At the shabby reception counter of the Hotel Metropole, Ghoshal engaged in what seemed a long argument, at the conclusion of which we were led up a staircase to the accommodation assigned to us by Soviet Protocol. It comprised a sitting-room with a threadbare carpet and sparse furniture, while the small bedroom was almost fully occupied by two enormous beds and a huge wardrobe. The bathroom was of a piece with the rest of the accommodation. A peculiar smell assailed our nostrils at the very moment of entering the hotel, which was all-pervasive except in the bathroom, where the cracked toilet made its own malodorous contribution. We did not know how long this was to be our abode.

Our first experience of the ways of Soviet bureaucracy was when, famished and exhausted, and ignorant of a single word of Russian, we asked Ghoshal to order a meal for us. After much ringing of the call bell, a rather unkempt waiter appeared with a greasy menu card. It took time for Ghoshal to explain what we wanted. Finally a cabbage soup, a fish dish and a sweet were selected and duly entered by the waiter in his well-thumbed order book. After much delay, the waiter showed up with a tray, but the food looked, smelt and tasted so unappetising that, ravenous though we were, we left it practically untouched.

Next morning, after a sleep of exhaustion, we dolefully

surveyed our surroundings. The Metropole stood at one end of a spacious square with the great Bolshoi Theatre opposite, while at a higher level lay the vast Red Square housing Lenin's mausoleum and the enormous 'GUM' department store. The crenellated walls of the Kremlin and the golden domes of the cathedrals and palaces within crowned the scene.

Soon, T.N. Kaul, the First Secretary, bounced in, ebullient as ever, with an all-knowing air. 'Tikki', as Kaul was universally known, had a solution for everything, although frequently with a catch. Yes, the food was awful but we could employ a Russian cook-cum-maid. No, we could not change our rooms as they had been allotted by 'Burobin' according to rank. All our needs, even the most trivial, had to be referred to 'Burobin', the organisation which dealt with the requirements of foreign diplomats. An Embassy car had been assigned to us, the driver having been chosen by 'Burobin'. There was not much to be had in the department stores; we could place orders with the firm of Nordiska in Stockholm, but the goods would take some two weeks to arrive and had to be cleared by customs. There was no chancery—though we had been promised a building—and no official papers, and we were expected to function from our own rooms. Our diplomatic bag was sent out every week and for want of any other arrangement, it was handed over to the British Embassy for dispatch to Delhi via their Foreign Office.

Susheela and I were happy to renew our friendship with Mrs Vijayalakshmi Pandit, the Ambassador. She was sorely disappointed with her mission, as what she encountered was vastly different from what she, and indeed the Prime Minister, Nehru, had imagined. She found the harsh living conditions and austerities of life intolerable. She was full of complaint of the total lack of all the finer things of life, barring the ballet, opera and music, and she deplored the general drabness of the place. She had arrived in Moscow, one of our first missions to be set up after Independence, with a large and hand-picked entourage, including a Minister as her deputy, an eminent economist as Commercial Counsellor, a couple of First Secretaries, a Political Secretary and a host of non-diplomatic personnel. But, one by one the staff was pruned down, largely for lack of anything useful to do and sometimes even for personal reasons.

Being entirely new to the ways of diplomatic protocol, the First Secretary had armed himself with a classic and ponderous work on the subject known as May's *Diplomatic Practice*. This compendium was meant to guide one through the labyrinthine ways of protocol. Sometimes reference had to be made to the British Embassy on intricate points of protocol, not adequately covered by May. Thus we learnt such esoteric matters as on whom to drop our visiting cards, and when to mark them with the letters p.p (*pour presenter*), and how one corner had to be turned down to indicate their presentation in person, etc. As the numbers of missions in such a large capital as Moscow were numerous, this function took up a lot of time. Another job, somewhat more demanding on one's intelligence, was to call on one's opposite numbers or heads of missions (if they would condescend to receive one of lower rank). These visits were occasionally found useful, when the interlocutor was a serious and experienced diplomat. By this means one gathered some useful information as well as some understanding of what the process of gathering and analysing information entailed, which, after all, was one of the basic tasks of a diplomatic mission.

Some of the major embassies were headed by distinguished War leaders. General Walter Bedell Smith, who said that there was no such thing as knowledge about the Soviet Union but only degrees of ignorance, was the American Ambassador. Another War-time leader was General Catroux who headed the French Embassy. The British Embassy had as its head Sir Maurice Peterson, a real old-timer, very set in his ways. He held weekly meetings of the heads of Commonwealth missions which Mrs Pandit had long ceased to attend, as she found them utterly boring, passing on this weekly penance to her deputy. So rigid in his views was Peterson, that when the young Canadian Charge d' Affaires, John Holmes, pointed out that he had observed from numerous indications that a serious rift was developing between Stalin and Tito (in whose capital, Belgrade, the Cominform had its headquarters), Peterson ridiculed poor Holmes. Not long afterwards, the rift came out into the open and was the first serious breach in the much-proclaimed 'monolithic unity of the Soviet block'. Peterson, of course, never acknowledged John Holmes' perspicacity.

It was not until the early summer that the promised accommodation was made available to us. It was an 'L'-shaped building, situated on a wide boulevard known as Smomlenskaya Sadovaya. The Ambassador's apartment occupied the entire first floor, while five rooms on the ground floor housed the chancery. A corridor led to a number of small rooms which housed members of the non-diplomatic staff. Each floor was served by only one bathroom-cum-toilet, each equipped with an ancient geyser to provide hot water. The Ambassador's apartment had just two bedrooms, one large sitting cum-dining room and a vast ballroom. The whole establishment needed various types of furnishing and Mrs Pandit gallantly set out for Stockholm to purchase it within our limited budget. It was all rather spartan. The furnishing was in great contrast to the comparative lavishness of other missions, yet Mrs Pandit's 'extravagance' was criticised in Parliament. One member chivalrously rose to her defense, explaining that the furnishing was in fact, 'swadeshi' (not being aware of the word 'Swedish').

The sheer business of daily living to which one had never given a thought before, seemed to have become a constant preoccupation. The smallest request had to be referred in the most formal terms, along with a Russian translation to the 'Burobin' in the Protocol office of the Soviet Ministry of Foreign Affairs. The missive began with: 'The Embassy of India presents its compliments to the Ministry of Foreign Affairs of the Union of Soviet Socialist Republics and has the honour to request it kindly to provide the services of a plumber to repair a leaking toilet in the Chancery', and ended 'With the assurances of the Embassy's highest consideration.' A lot of time and energy went into the preparation of such inconsequential letters, and their follow-up. Mr. Molochkov was the Chief of Protocol, a very smooth-spoken individual, never lacking in sympathy or attentiveness, but equally, never committing himself to anything. The only other officials with whom we had any contact were the Head of the Asia Division, Ambassador Mikhailov, a seasoned bureaucrat full of craftiness, concealed under a kindly demeanour. His deputy was somewhat more accessible, but equally evasive and noncommittal.

Nehru, the architect of India's foreign policy, had maintained that the country would seek and offer friendship to all nations regardless of their ideology. While the western world was not unfamiliar to Indians, little or no contact had been permitted by the imperial power with the Soviet Union and even China and Japan. The new India was therefore eager to get to know its immediate neighbours, and the Soviet Union was a towering neighbour to the north.

During the years of the Indian freedom movement Nehru had visited Moscow and, like most nationalist leaders of the time, felt warmly towards the Soviet Union. Socialism seemed to provide the answer to many of the problems of economic and social backwardness which beset the colonised countries. Soviet propaganda had sought to nurture the belief that they were creating a more just and equitable society. The feeling of friendship towards the Soviet Union was also a reaction to the exploitation and backwardness resulting from long years under imperialism. Also, as the United Nations was subsequently to proclaim, colonialism was a form of racism; the Soviets, in contrast, never tired of proclaiming the equality of all peoples, irrespective of race, colour or country.

The attitude and expectations on the part of the Soviet leaders towards India were, however, of a different order—that India would move into the Soviet orbit. Thus Mrs Pandit's arrival in Moscow had initially been welcomed by the Soviet leadership. She was, after all, Nehru's favourite sister and had played a prominent role in the political life of the country. Accordingly, Madame Kollontai, an associate of Lenin, a highly respected lady and the first woman Ambassador in the world, had been assigned to woo Mrs Pandit so that she could influence her brother to propel India towards the Soviet orbit.

Perhaps Stalin was confident of this outcome because he could never understand how India, which had ostensibly gained independence, could possibly remain in the Commonwealth under the British Crown, and with Lord Mountbatten as Governor-General. It was during this time that full encouragement was given by the Russians to the Indian Communist Party, and the rebellion in Telengana was fomented. But when neither Kollontai's wooing, nor blandishments and pressures had any effect on India's political orientation, further attempts to influence Mrs Pandit were given up. All contacts with the Indian mission at the cultural and social level were severed and it was also put under the same rigorous quarantine as other non-Communist missions. Throughout our two years in Moscow we never exchanged a word, even with our smattering of the language, with any Russian, apart from our domestic staff and interpreter or the music or language teachers assigned to us through 'Burobin'. This we greatly regretted, as the Russian people are naturally warm-hearted and friendly, and they seemed curious to know us, as India was a legendary country to them.

Partly to compensate for the absence of any contact with the Russian people, the foreign diplomats had perforce to fall back upon each other for company and relaxation. A great consolation and support were the deep friendships that developed and which have continued to this day. Very special friends were the Chargé d' Affaires of Switzerland, Felix Schnyder and his charming wife, Sigrid, with whom we often spent agreeable evenings, listening to music. We also found charming friends in the American and French embassies. At these social evenings, we sometimes picked up interesting snippets of information as in the midst of conviviality there was also much political talk.

What was particularly irksome was the almost ubiquitous presence of the Soviet 'militia', or police, who seemed to trail our every movement. We had only to step out to find ourselves being followed by a plainclothes man whom it was difficult to shed, even by slipping into a side street. There was a pleasant tree-lined, paved walk around the towering walls of the Kremlin, but no sooner had we stepped on it for an evening stroll, than a shrill whistle would blow and a uniformed militiaman materialise almost from nowhere and utter the word *nilzia*, meaning 'forbidden'. For a brief respite from the greyness of Moscow, we would sometimes venture out on a fine spring day to the lush countryside for a picnic in the pine or birch forests. But suddenly our spirits would be dampened by the forbidding whistle announcing that we were out of bounds: we had exceeded the 25 km limit from the centre of Moscow prescribed by state security for diplomats.

It was proudly claimed that the Soviet system had made available the highest form of cultural expression to the broad masses of the people and that it was no longer the preserve of any particular class or condition of society. This was true only up to a point. Some art forms flourished and were unsurpassed in excellence, but others came under strict party and bureaucratic scrutiny and restriction. Poetry and literature suffered greatly at the hands of the philistine censors and many great writers were proscribed, persecuted or penalised, some ending up in the wastes of Siberia.

The cultural czar at the time was Zhdanov whose ukases issuing from time to time prescribed the strait-jackets within which artists, writers and musicians could perform. Only what conformed to the tenets of 'Socialist realism' was permitted. Those writers whose work was philosophical or imaginative were termed 'homeless-cosmopolitans'. Thus writers and poets such as Pasternak, Solzhenytsin, Alexander Bloch, Akhmetova, etc. were *personae non grata*, their works only circulating clandestinely. The Russian people however are avid readers, and everywhere, at bus stops, on park benches or even while waiting in queues, we saw people, especially the young, reading well-thumbed paperbacks. The public libraries were always full. Approved books were published cheaply and abundantly by the state publishing houses. Some books by foreign writers of a leftist bent or fellow-travellers were permissible, but not much else, although Shakespeare was acceptable.

While the great literary tradition of the country was kept under severe constraint, musical expression was allowed greater freedom, although Stalin's prescription was that it should be so melodious that the listener would go home whistling it. But some great composers managed to break out and gave to the world a wealth of fine music, the names of Prokofief, Shoshtakovich, Khatchaturien particularly coming to mind. Folk music and dance from the far-flung regions was also encouraged. The Moscow orchestra was excellent and performances of the great classics, Russian and western, were frequently given. There was a galaxy of celebrated musicians such as the Oistrakhs, father and son.

The opera, much appreciated by Soviet audiences, provided another feast for ear and eye. Great operas by Russians and some by western composers, especially Mozart, were frequently to be seen at the Bolshoi. Magnificent were the male voices and the choreography was breathtaking: so were the sets—in *Boris Goudinov*, cathedrals with their bells tolling would appear, and horse-drawn carts would move across the stage, while in *Prince Igor* the Tartar camp on the battlefield was striking in its realism. The ballet—and reportedly a certain prima ballerina as well—were beloved of Stalin and therefore allowed full rein. The imperial tradition not only continued, but flowered, the Bolshoi and Kirov ballets being unequalled anywhere. Such legendary ballet dancers as Semyenova, Ulanova, Lepeshinskaya and Plasetskaya were constantly on the stage, as also male dancers like Chabukiyani, whose stupendous leaps almost suspended in mid-air could be emulated decades later only by Nureyev. The ballet was a constant delight, an escape from the tedium and dreariness of life, especially during the long dark winters. Great ballets such as *Romeo and Juliet, Swan Lake, Giselle, The Fountain of Bakshi-Sarai, Sheherezade*, etc. were often performed and we attended them regularly.

Moscow also provided first rate theatrical performances at the Mali and Mkhat theatres, some of which we enjoyed despite our very elementary knowledge of the language, by reading their scripts earlier in translation. Chekhov and Gogol seemed to be the popular favourites. The theme of the Mongols frequently recurred in opera and ballet, the Khans being generally depicted as noble and gallant personages. In *The Fountain of Bakshi-Sarai* the Khan tries unsuccessfully to win the favours of a captured Polish princess and is distraught when she is stabbed to death by a jealous wife, who is tried by a court of mullahs and flung to her death from the battlements. A fountain springs up where the princess is buried, over which the Khan builds a marble pavilion at which he mourns his loss. In *Prince Igor* the Khan shows much generosity to his captive Russian prince. The Mongol followers, however, are depicted as a barbarous horde sweeping down on palace and town, burning and pillaging. In contemporary Moscow, we constantly encountered Mongol and Tartar, Kalmuck, Kirghiz, Uzbek and other Far-Eastern and Central Asian peoples, often in their distinctive costumes.

Presiding benignly over the Soviet scene, the prophet of the future, was Josef Vissarionovich Stalin, whose status and portraits in different poses met one everywhere, sometimes standing with an arm uplifted in exhortation, sometimes as a massive monolith, in busts of various sizes and in innumerable photographs and paintings. No public institution or place seemed to lack a reminder of 'Big Brother' and the saviour watching over one. He was lauded as a universal father, the true successor of the dethroned deity. This belief, like religious dogma, was drilled into old and young alike.

This fact was vividly brought home to us by the four-year old daughter of one of our attachés, who was attending a Soviet primary school. One day her mother, in great alarm, reported to Susheela that the little child was insisting that Stalin and not the gentleman behind the typewriter was her father, and cited the authority of her teacher. Her mother, a virtuous Hindu wife, felt deeply offended and scandalised. Susheela tried to correct the girl's belief, and for a while her authority prevailed. But next day it was the turn of the child to be indignant as she accused her mother and Susheela of lying, the teacher having asked her to convey to them that Stalin was 'everybody's father'.

The broad purpose of our mission was to observe and report on what was going on and to establish greater mutual understanding between our countries. At a deeper level, we were to try and analyse the extent to which the proclaimed aims of the socialist state were being realised. But even the task of daily reporting was reduced to pure guess-work. Not much information could be gleaned from the state-controlled newspapers. Of the two principal dailies, *Izvestiya* and *Pravda*, it was said that there was no news in the former and no truth in the latter. (*Izvestiya* in Russian means 'news', and *Pravda*, 'truth'.) There was a journal in English called *New Times*, meant for circulation abroad, which contained long and critical articles about other countries and laudatory ones about the Soviet Union. Particular attention was devoted to the United States and its 'military-industrial complex', where the most inhuman forms of racial discrimination and merciless exploitation by the rich and powerful were alleged to be rampant. Western societies were described as utterly decadent and destined to be supplanted by progressive socialism, while the newly independent countries were decried as being steeped in superstition, poverty and ignorance where the elite exploited the 'toiling masses'.

However, some basic information could be garnered from the daily news-sheet which the British and American Embassies had teamed up to produce in translation from the Soviet press. There was sometimes a trickle of news from some far-flung republic when a few lines would appear in an inconspicuous corner, whose significance only a discerning eye could detect. Even natural disasters or accidents were not reported, leave alone any news of political import. One learnt almost by accident much later that a state of rebellion had prevailed in the Central Asian region, which probably accounted for the frustration of our attempt to travel there. When names of high officials or party members were blocked out, it was assumed that they had fallen from grace. There was of course no mention of the movements of Stalin or even of members of the Politburo. The arrival of Stalin from his country retreat was signalled by the clearing of a street named Arbat: after nightfall, a fleet of large black Zis limousines with blackened windows would glide swiftly down this street.

In such an atmosphere of almost pathological secrecy, the western powers relied heavily on their secret agents and spies. But such information, for what it was worth, was available only to the larger missions, which had such organisations as the American CIA, the French Deuxieme Bureau and the British M.I. 5 and 6. The Soviets, with their NKVD, later the KGB, were by no means lacking in this regard. In this clash of giants, with their conflicting ideologies, countries like ours had to tread a wary path.

During our two years in Moscow we were not once asked over to the foreign office for any business, but we ourselves made it a practice to call every few weeks to meet the official at the Asia desk to try and draw him out, but with little success. Most of the visits, however, related to making strong protests against slanderous attacks on India and Indian leaders appearing in the Soviet press, but particularly in the *New Times*. While we took every opportunity to assure the Soviets of our desire for friendly relations, they were engaged in trying to undermine, if they could, the foundations of the Indian state and to create a situation ripe for violent uprisings. Soviet doctrine was that the road to Europe lay through the Far East and India. 'Fraternal contacts' were therefore being assiduously cultivated with the Communist Party of India. Indian party-members and fellow-travellers came to Moscow off and on, but they generally gave a wide berth to the Indian mission, no doubt for fear of forfeiting future invitations and other favours.

While Mrs Pandit gave tea and sympathy to Madame Kollontai in full measure, she was able to offer little hope of India joining the Soviet camp, or, indeed, any other camp. A lingering hope still seemed to remain, the approach being not by offering political blandishments, but by playing the cultural card.

An Indo-Soviet cultural evening had been arranged at which the Indian mission was to display its talent. A galaxy of Soviet dancers and musicians was present on the occasion, including the ballerina Ulanova and two leading composers, Shaporin and Belayev. The only talent that we could muster was Susheela's; she had been trained in classical Indian music and could still sing well despite the interruption caused by her years at Cambridge. Her singing seemed greatly to interest the composers, who requested her to visit the music academy for a rendering as they would like to orchestrate the melodies. This she did on successive days, but we never heard the results. It was only eight years later, in 1956, when Prime Minister Nehru was on a week's official visit to the Soviet Union, that the orchestrated rendering was heard for the first, and perhaps the last, time. It was in Tashkent when, at a musical concert given in honour of the visitors, the Prime Minister was astonished to see on the programme: 'Indian melodies—by Susheela Dayal'. A week or so later, when he came to Yugoslavia where we were then posted the mystery was unravelled!

After this last attempt at weaning India over to their side, the Soviets gave up and we came to be treated as objects of suspicion, to be kept at arms length. This, however, was the rule, not the exception, unless one belonged to a 'fraternal', i.e., Communist, country. Indeed, it was embedded in the Russian psyche to regard all foreigners save those from a 'fraternal' or Communist country with extreme suspicion, and officials and diplomats with near paranoia. This was no doubt a result of Russia's historical experience, for she had been repeatedly ravaged by Mongol and other tribes from across the eastern steppes and by the Scandinavian and Germanic tribes from the west. For centuries the country had been under the yoke of the Golden Horde. When the foreign intruders ultimately fell back or were expelled, leaving pockets of settlers behind, the Russians shut themselves in until Peter the Great opened a window to the west.

The secretiveness of the Russian state and distrust of foreigners has been vividly recounted by a late eighteenth-century Ambassador of France who, with his large entourage, was held up at the frontier for months in extreme discomfort before being allowed entry to the soil of Mother Russia; and it took more months before he was granted permission to present his credentials to His Imperial Majesty the Czar of All the Russias. The feudal tradition practically survived until the Revolution and serfdom continued until late into the nineteenth century. There was never any experience of democracy; the country was an absolute monarchy, a 'despotism tempered only by assassination'. The rulers lived in constant fear of the furtive dagger or bullet, an obsession inherited by their revolutionary successors.

Ignorant of the ways of dictatorships, we slowly realised, with some disbelief, that our telephones were tapped, that the entire premises were 'bugged', that the Russian staff were either trained spies or were obliged to report on our every movement, that our comings and goings were immediately reported from the telephone at the corner of our premises by the militiamen on constant vigil outside, that we would be tailed by a police car when we ventured out of Moscow. Travel within the vast country was prohibited, except by rail or air to Leningrad and by air to Tblisi. Even to visit Tolstoy's estate and grass-covered grave at Yasnaya Polyana, about an hour's distance from Moscow, one had to seek permission, which we were granted as a special case, presumably because of Tolstoy's close links with Mahatma Gandhi. We could also visit, with permission, the splendid cluster of churches and monasteries at Zagorsk, some 40 kilometres from Moscow. It became quite a game to dodge the inevitable black police car following behind, by quickly slipping into a side lane undetected around a bend and to watch the sleuths dash past in futile pursuit. Even to carry a camera was a risky business for fear of being accused of spying. No foreigner that we knew drove his own car, as not even the American motor engineer in charge of the Embassy's fleet of cars was able to pass the driving test! The only exception was our own First Secretary, T.N. Kaul, who drove around without a Soviet licence in the face of repeated warnings and protests by the Protocol office that he was violating Soviet laws.

Soviet citizens were not allowed to have anything to do with foreigners, nor were they permitted to travel abroad. If a Soviet citizen was intercepted trying to escape, the general direction of escapees being to the west, he would inevitably land up east in Siberia. There was a particularly poignant case of a young Chilean diplomat who fell in love with—and married—a lovely Russian girl. The young couple were virtual prisoners, watched over night and day by two dour-faced KGB men. The two finally tried to escape by hiding in large cabin trunks, but were discovered at the airport. What happened to the young bride we never knew, but could only imagine.

A particularly sordid incident concerned a KGB agent who was planted to seduce the wife of the military attaché of a West European mission. Incriminating photographs were taken, and used to blackmail the officer into revealing military secrets. The officer shot himself.

Another episode often recounted, but no doubt apocryphal, related to the Ambassador of Afghanistan, whose Russian maid had disappeared. When the police came to enquire about her whereabouts, the Ambassador led them into the garden and pointed to a mound. In his country, he explained, the penalty for spying was death and on Embassy territory Afghan laws prevailed.

In our own Embassy a cypher assistant was hospitalised for a gall-bladder operation and a Russian lady visitor was observed daily at his bedside. As we could not take any risks with our cypher, we were compelled to ask for the operator's recall. Another incident concerned T.N. Kaul who kept frequent rendezvous with a Russian lady whom he took out for drives. Soviet Protocol authorities protested more than once against this breach of Soviet legality. Eventually the lady broke off contact and Kaul himself asked for a change of posting. Some two decades later, a Soviet KGB defector in his testimony before a US Senate Committee, confirmed the agency's hand in breaking up the affair.

As the long dark winter turned into a cheerless spring, the carpeting of snow in the streets and pavements gave way to grey slush, and snowflakes to hail, sleet and rain. As a diversion from the inclemencies of the weather and the monotony of life in Moscow, as well as to see something of the fabled lands of Central Asia, Mrs Pandit suggested that we go on a tour of that area. We accordingly drew up an ambitious plan which would have taken us to Tblisi, Samarkand, Bokhara and Alma Ata, and we looked forward to the prospect of an adventurous journey.

The project was accordingly presented by me to Mr Molochkov, who presided over our destinies. He lent an attentive ear to our request but explained politely that the agency which made travel arrangements was really Intourist and not Protocol, and advised a visit to them. The next morning found me at the Intourist office where a young woman at the counter noted the details of our requirements, to which she seemed to give affirmative nods. While poring over airplane schedules, etc. she was approached by a colleague, and after a whispered conversation she enquired if we were foreign diplomats. On receiving our answer, she explained that Intourist could not arrange for the travel of diplomats, and said that it was the responsibility of the Protocol department. A further visit to Mr Molochkov elicited only mild surprise on his part and another polite explanation that Intourist were mistaken and that they should be approached again. Armed with this information about departmental responsibilities, a second visit to Intourist met with a firm and decisive refusal. Frustrated by these infructuous efforts, the court of last appeal, viz., Ambassador Mikhailov who presided over the Asia desk, was approached. He paid kind attention to our request for redressal, but said neither yes nor no. That clearly clinched matters and, after this Kafkaesque experience of the Soviet system, a useful lesson in diplomacy was learnt.

The newspapers frequently reported on the great successes achieved by Soviet science and research and their successful application, to which the regime attached particular importance.

These we duly reported to New Delhi. One such achievement was the claim that coloured cotton—red and khaki—had been evolved in place of the common white. New Delhi was much interested in this achievement and asked for some seeds for trial. A formal request was therefore addressed to the Ministry of Foreign Affairs. When no reply was received, a reminder was duly issued. The Agriculture Ministry in New Delhi was meanwhile getting impatient and pressing us to send the samples early. So a personal visit to Ambassador Mikhailov followed. As usual, he was most courteous and offered the information that the matter really related to the Soviet Ministry of Agriculture, but he would nevertheless pass on our request to them. Again, after a long delay and more enquiries from New Delhi and still no response from the Soviet side despite reminders, the last resort was again Ambassador Mikhailov. In the name of friendship and the Soviet Union's concern for and sympathy with the poorer countries of Asia, he was approached to use his good offices to meet our modest request. Again Mr. Mikhailov was the picture of solicitude and, after listening patiently and with what appeared to be a tinge of sympathy, said: 'Please understand that no reply is sometimes itself a reply.' This was my second lesson in Soviet diplomacy. Red and khaki cotton has, however, not appeared on the fields of Uzbekistan to this day.

Similarly, it was proudly announced that Soviet ophthalmologists has made a remarkable breakthrough in developing procedures for transplanting the cornea of cadavers to people suffering from blindness or chronic cornea problems. This achievement drew the attention of eye surgeons in India, who requested information on the subject. Pleading the chronic problem of blindness in India and the enormous benefits that would flow from the adoption of the fine results achieved by Soviet surgeons, a request was addressed to the Soviet authorities in the name of suffering humanity. A repetition of previous such approaches followed, with no different results.

After the first atomic test conducted by the Soviets which, it was tirelessly emphasised, was not for destructive but for constructive purposes, newspaper articles began to appear about how atomic power would be used to reverse the course of the Siberian rivers. These vast rivers flowing from south to north into the Arctic Sea were frozen solid in winter. In spring the upper reaches would thaw much earlier than the lower, causing extensive floods. By blocking them by means of atomic power, their direction would be reversed, all of them would be inter-linked by a mighty canal system, their combined flow falling into the salt-water Aral Sea which lay below sea level, transforming it into a fresh-water lake. A vast network of canals would provide both navigation and irrigation to the whole Siberian and Central Asian regions. The entire concept was grandiose indeed, but after some time nothing further was heard of it.

At the time a great controversy was raging among geneticists about the relative influence of heredity and environment on the species. The Soviet press was loud in its condemnation of what it described as 'reactionary Mendelism' which championed heredity. The high priests of 'progressive' environmentalism were Michurin and Lysenko. Indeed, Lysenko claimed to have evolved new strains of fruits and coloured posters were to be seen of rosy-cheeked and buxom girls smiling happily as they plucked over-sized rosy apples from overladen trees. We, however, never tasted or saw these fine apples in Moscow. Lysenko also claimed that he had succeeded in growing oranges in the steppe regions by evolving a strain of runners which crept along the bottom of a trench which could be covered with plastic sheets to protect them from the harsh winter with its −25°C or lower temperatures. One would have thought it would be cheaper to import oranges from abroad. New Delhi, however, made no enquiry about this singular achievement as there was presumably no intention of growing oranges in Ladakh or Aksaichin! The heredity versus environment controversy was jocularly commented upon as follows: If a child is born to Ivan who resembles his father, it is a case of reactionary Mendelism; but if he resembles Pyotr, the next-door neighbour, it is progressive Lysenkoism!

There was constant reference in the papers and speeches of Soviet leaders to the creation of what was described as 'Soviet man', a creature very different from the general run of humanity. He would be endowed with all the qualities making for perfection—cheerfulness, optimism, efficiency, patriotism, selflessness, honesty, goodness, loyalty, courage, etc. Presumably such paragons of virtue existed somewhere, but we never had the good fortune to meet them. What we encountered were naturally warm-hearted people, patriotic, patient and long-suffering; but cowed down by a harsh regime and whose natural talents were not allowed to find free or full expression.

One startling piece of information created quite a stir among the diplomatic corps. It appeared that the Soviet government, in view of the announced abundance of food-grains which its vast lands were producing, was considering making the supply of bread free, fulfilling the Communist ideal of 'to each according to his need'. If such a feat could have been performed, it would indeed have had an electrifying effect throughout the world. The poor countries and the famished masses would have turned towards the Soviet Union as to a saviour. But soon after, we learnt that the Soviet Union was having to import wheat from the United States of all countries.

The Soviet Union undoubtedly had great scientists, but greater importance seemed to be given to applied science as being socially correct. Scientists were a privileged community, but they functioned in great secrecy and isolation, with little or no contact with their peers abroad. There were also some charlatans, who, because of the tall claims they made, earned the favour of the regime but only the ridicule of scientists abroad.

While we were still struggling with the problems of protocol, we found ourselves put to a practical test. On arrival at the Chancery one morning, I was accosted by the sad faces of colleagues who said the Ambassador wished to see me urgently. I dashed up to the Ambassador's residence to find her looking similarly distressed. She told me that the tragic news had been conveyed to the mission a little earlier that the Iranian Minister-Councellor had passed away that night. Only the previous evening she and we had been dining with the Hekmats; he was in excellent health and cheerful form and now this sad blow had suddenly fallen. We though of his poor wife, a charming lady and mused on the mutability of human life. The mission would of course be represented at the funeral by an officer of equivalent rank.

At the chancery, we consulted Dr Ghoshal who claimed to be knowledgeable about the right protocol in Slav countries on such occasions. I had first to wear a black tie with a dark suit or a more formal morning suit and I should take a wreath to place on the casket. As the time of the funeral was given as 4 p.m., I was advised to be there half an hour earlier to be able to join the funeral procession. Dr Ghoshal was dispatched to procure a suitable wreath, while I made my preparations.

The wreath, when it arrived, was of enormous size, mounted on a wooden trapeze which filled the full length of the carrier on the roof of the American staff car. On reaching the Iranian mission there was neither sight nor sound of mourners, and as I was driven in I wondered if a ghastly mistake had been made in sending me to the wrong embassy; perhaps the bereavement had taken place at the Iraqi Embassy and the name of the country had, typically, been misheard. I wished to make an immediate retreat, but being ignorant of a single word of Russian at the time I remained tongue-tied. Before I could recover my wits, the chauffeur had rung the bell and a doorman ushered me in, while the chauffeur began undoing the wreath. Gesturing to him to keep it back, I slowly walked up the stairs, wondering how to account for my presence at the Embassy at that hour. On reaching the landing, still deep in thought, to my intense surprise I found Mr Hekmat himself there to receive me, brimming with good health. In friendly manner he led me into the vast reception room, where he left me. My confusion was great as I studied the pattern of the magnificent Persian carpet covering the floor and the huge portrait of the Shah which adorned the wall opposite, wondering how I could make good my escape without further embarrassment. After what seemed a very long wait, the Ambassador, clad in formal attire, blew in and, uttering in French 'that for him it was a misfortune' withdrew without further ado. His brief remark revived my drooping spirits as I felt reassured that some mournful occurrence had, in fact, taken place. At 4 p.m., the appointed hour of the funeral, another counsellor was ushered in who, after having also been received by Mr Hekmat, sought light on the situation from me, which I was unable to provide. At intervals, other mourners began to arrive and there was much puzzled whispering all along the lengthening line. It was only with the arrival of the dean of the diplomatic corps, Ambassador Fou of Nationalist China, that we hoped for the enlightenment which we avidly sought. Saying that we should leave the matter to him, he went into a brief huddle with his Iranian counterpart and, beaming with smiles, returned to announce that we could all leave as a wreath would be laid on behalf of the corps on the deceased Economic Counsellor, who had been ill since his arrival and had now unfortunately passed away. We all trooped down to our cars, with my chauffeur making one more unsuccessful bid to hand me Dr Ghoshal's wreath.

In many ways, the two opposing super-powers, the USA and the USSR were very similar to each other, though they would have been deeply offended to be told so. Both aimed to spread their influence over the entire globe by various means—by entering into alliances with countries far and wide, by the lavish supply of weapons to their client states, and through economic aid. Both touted their own antithetical ideologies with equal fervour as the solution to humanity's problems. And both ideologies were essentially materialistic though clad in idealistic garb.

Towards the end of the summer, Mrs Pandit left Moscow with her family and private staff, to return some six or seven months later only to say her farewells before taking up her post in Washington. Her term in Moscow had been one of great frustration as neither could anything useful be accomplished, nor were the life and living conditions at all congenial.

The strain of living in an atmosphere of fear and suspicion begins to tell on one, and we too felt the need for a respite. We flew to Geneva, via Prague, a city once known for its beauty and elegance, but now looking sad and run-down. Particularly pathetic were the still well-dressed men and women who approached us furtively in the streets to offer a family heirloom or some other cherished object against foreign exchange.

Arriving in Geneva, where Susheela's parents had come on holiday, we felt like inmates of a concentration camp on parole in paradise. The high Alps, to which we proceeded, the glorious scenery, the bracing mountain air and the unbelievable luxury of the hotels revived one in body and mind. The return to Moscow for me seemed to come all too soon. Susheela, who stayed on with her parents, followed later but found herself stranded overnight in a miserable hotel in Lwow; the ancient Soviet plane developed engine trouble and she would have missed the connection but for the help of a fellow-passenger hastening to Moscow to be with his dying wife.

My term in Moscow as Charge'd' Affairés was prolonged until Dr Sarvepalli Radhakrishnan took up residence in January 1950. When Mrs Pandit returned for a month, we had to revert to a worse purgatory in the Metropole. The bedroom was small and nauseous, the trickle from the malodorous bathroom flowing into the bedroom. The sitting room lay across the corridor and the rooms had to be locked on going from one to the other.

Any further requests from New Delhi for information about Soviet research dried up after the earlier experiences. Nevertheless, I made it a practice to call every few weeks at the India desk for scraps of information, which, however, were never forthcoming. The papers, and especially the *New Times*, used to come out with extremely disparaging and slanderous articles about India, describing Nehru as the Chiang-Kai-Shek of India, which in the Soviet lexicon was a term of abuse and contempt. India was described as the 'running dog of British Imperialism'. As for the Mahatma, he was no more than a 'Hindu social reformer'. To my energetic and repeated protests against these scandalous writings, Mikhailov invariably gave the reply that I should know that the Soviet press was free and the papers could write as they wished and perhaps they reflected the opinions of the trade unions or the 'broad masses' of the people. It seems almost incredible now that such a gross misjudgement of India and its respected leaders could have been made and was no doubt responsible for the aberrations in Stalin's policies towards the Indian subcontinent.

An interesting article appeared some time in 1949 by a Professor Dyakov, who seemed to specialise in matters concerning Asia, making out a detailed case for redrawing the boundaries of Indian provinces, as they then were, on linguistic lines. That was well before K.M. Pannikar's States' Reorganisation Commission recommended the division of India into linguistic states. That decision, as experience seems to prove, has led to the encouragement of fissiparous tendencies—regional, linguistic and sectarian. As if to compensate for the spate of negative writings about India, a Professor Barrenikov published a brilliant translation of Tulsidas's *Ramayana* in verse.

The Cold War was getting increasingly menacing and the setting up of the NATO alliance provoked much vituperation.

The Soviet denial of road and rail access to Berlin, then under the joint occupation of the Soviet Union, the United States, Britain and France, raised antagonisms to near boiling point. The rapid organisation of the massive allied air-lift, which took the Soviets by surprise, did little to reduce the tension; in reply to NATO, the Soviets began organising the Warsaw Pact, both sides intensifying the propaganda war.

While these portentous events were taking place in the west, in the eastern firmament a bright red star had risen. In 1949 a vast convulsion was caused by the ousting of the Kuomintang by the victorious Red Army and the forced flight of the former's remnants. The red flag now fluttered from Berlin to Canton. Mao-tse-Tung, the leader of the new China arrived in Moscow in triumph and it was thought that it was to pay homage at the 'fount of World Communism.' But the visit, which was enveloped in secrecy, dragged on and on, despite the urgent tasks awaiting the new leadership at home. It became evident that something was amiss. Acute doctrinal differences had developed, the Chinese were strongly resistant to acknowledging the hegemony of the Soviet Union over world Communism, and refusing to kowtow to Stalin as the presiding deity of the world movement. The Chinese Revolution was purely indigenous and owed nothing to Moscow, not even moral support, for had not Stalin sent two of his envoys, Borodin and M.N. Roy, to dissuade the Chinese Communist leaders from continuing their fruitless struggle against the supposedly invincible Kuomintang? They had advised coming to a settlement with their opponents. Stalin was convinced that China was by no means ripe for revolution; indeed, it was accepted wisdom as proclaimed by Lenin, that it was only the awakened industrial proletariat of Europe and not the inert and backward peasant masses of Asia that would rise in revolt against the capitalist order. The prolonged wrangling between the rival Communist leadership also related to Chinese demands for massive economic and technological assistance.

This Stalin was not prepared to accord, not only because the demands were excessive, but also because the proud Chinese were not prepared to pay the price of subservience which was expected.

On these developments, of great significance to India, I sent a detailed report from various scraps of information available, along with conjecture and deduction, ending with the conclusion that the Chinese tail may well wag the Soviet dog. I also sent a long dispatch on the comparative attitudes of the two opposing blocs towards India. At the time, India was being hard-pressed on the Kashmir issue in the United Nations Security Council, where the tables had been turned against the Indian complainant in favour of the Pakistani aggressor largely as a result of western machinations. There was also resentment against India among the colonial powers for opening the flood-gates against colonialism, thus leading to its ultimate demise. My conclusion was that neither group could be relied upon as neither wished to see a strong and resurgent India not open to manipulation. We should therefore depend upon our intrinsic strength and resources and build ourselves up by our own efforts so as to become a significant power in the world. I felt greatly encouraged when Prime Minister Nehru recorded a two-page minutes on each report, basically agreeing with the conclusions.

In the summer of 1949, the American Minister-Counsellor, Brewster Morris, and his wife invited me to join them on a boat trip down the Volga. Accordingly, we took cabins on the top deck of an antique paddle-steamer at the Moscow river port, and soon entered the mighty Volga, with its deep green waters. Our vessel slowly churned downstream, stopping at wooden jetties along its stately course to pick up and disembark passengers, peasants all, with their bags and bundles and, occasionally, livestock. After two very interesting days and not uncomfortable nights, and depending entirely on the provisions brought by our companions, we left the boat before it reached the town of Gorki, entry to which was prohibited to foreigners. The village fair was in progress in a muddy field and there was much buying and selling of agricultural produce from trestle tables and horse-drawn carts. The men generally wore beards, some black, some red, and had long hair; they were dressed in smocks and knee-high felt boots held together by crossed ropes, while the women were in traditional attire. The whole scene seem to come straight out of the pages of Tolstoy. Our return to Moscow was, unromantically, by train.

My next attempt to break out of Moscow was, however, less of a success. Encouraged by the fact that a party of foreign diplomats had been able to visit Tblisi by taking the Georgian military highway, I felt that we comparatively innocuous Indians could do the same. Accordingly, accompanied by a member of our staff, I flew down to a place called Mineralnye Voda (or Mineral Water). From there we proceeded by train, seated on wooden benches with friendly peasant families as companions, to the foothills of the great Carpathian mountains. Arriving at a resort called Vladi Kafkaz ('Queen of the Caucasus'), we were housed in a pleasant-looking inn with much greenery around, including a large garden with sweet-scented flowering creepers and arbours. The manager, a rather oily and unctuous Armenian, showed us much deference and was most solicitous about our every need, even proposing menus of Georgian dishes. For our onward journey by road, we approached the manager who also served as a travel agent. He promised to make enquiries and to try and arrange matters for the following day; meanwhile, he advised that we have a look at the town and relax in the garden. The next day we were told that due to heavy landslides the mountain road was blocked and closed to all traffic. The following day and for three or four days thereafter we were similarly fobbed off with much shrugging of shoulders.

Meanwhile, a young couple who had taken up residence next to us, accosted us in very friendly fashion and soon became our inseparable companions. We welcomed their company, as such an opportunity had been denied to us in Moscow, and gave us a chance to exercise our limping knowledge of Russian. They said they were students on holiday, bound for the same destination, and felt equally frustrated by the delay. Becoming sceptical about the road being closed for so long, my colleague went to the bus terminal at dawn, the time when the buses left on their long journey. He found that buses were in fact leaving one after another. Enquiring at the counter about the landslide, his query was received with surprise and he was offered two seats. But on becoming aware that we were foreign diplomats, he advised my colleague to obtain our tickets at the inn.

At last it dawned on us that it was a repetition of our experience of the year before, although played more theatrically. And our pleasant companions, we recollected wryly, who always kept their door open and were ready to accompany us no sooner did we leave our rooms, had been planted on us. We later learnt that there was an institute for training intelligence agents near by and we had unwittingly provided excellent practical training. Realising that there was no way to beat the system, we asked if we could reach our destination by air; that too was not possible and we were advised to return to Moscow and, from there, to fly down direct to Tblisi. By now we were running out of funds and so had to wire the Embassy for money, which fortunately arrived promptly. The obliging manager had no problem in arranging a small aircraft, free of charge, to fly us to the airfield of Mineralnye Voda from where we took a regular flight back to Moscow. What was puzzling was how western diplomats, including Americans and a military attaché, were able to make the road trip to Tblisi while we Indians were not. Perhaps it was a case of oversight; the lapse on the part of security seemed to have been corrected at our cost.

I had my revenge two decades later on the occasion of a week's state visit to the Soviet Union by the President of India,

Dr Zakir Hussian, whom I accompanied as Foreign Secretary. Sending for the Soviet Ambassador in New Delhi, I told him to arrange visits to Tblisi, Tashkent, Samarkand, Bokhara and Dushanbe. These visits were duly arranged, with red carpet and all.

Conditions in Moscow compelled a certain measure of improvisation to overcome the monotony of life and a feeling of claustrophobia, especially during the long winters. In the summer one could always take a walk along the river esplanade or in Gorki Park near by. But in the winter, when temperatures fell to −30°C, we could hardly stay out of doors for even half an hour, without our breath freezing on our coat fronts and our feet, despite being encased in fur-lined boots, becoming numb. What seemed to warm pedestrians, surprisingly enough, was ice-cream, which was sold by hawkers from open trays.

The large ballroom in the chancery, a kind of no-mans' land stretching between the dining room and kitchen, was so large as to accommodate comfortably a full-sized badminton court. Our evenings were enjoyably and healthily devoted to much-needed exercise in which the whole Embassy staff joined enthusiastically. Thereafter, other foreign missions joined in and tea and badminton evenings, somewhat reminiscent of the tennis-teas in India, became a regular feature of our lives. The only other mission with a ballroom comparable to ours in size was at Spaso House, the residence of the American Ambassador, where our example was followed, and tournaments came to be arranged at the two venues.

Despite the labelling of religion as the opiate of the people, visits to the Moscow cathedral to attend the midnight mass on Christmas, and Easter Sunday at the cathedral at Zagorsk impressed us greatly, not only for the stately ritual, but more so for the vast attendance of young and old alike. The intensity of religious fervour was evident from the fact that the congregation at the midnight mass which filled to capacity the vast cathedral, spilled over into the enormous snow-covered square outside, with people on their knees in a temperature of –30°C. No doubt the immense suffering of the people during and after the War had compelled a return to religion and no official persecution could stifle the natural yearning for solace from the travails of daily life and bereavements of the past.

Vijayalakshmi Pandit was an easy enough person to work with if one struck the right chord with her. She was quick and intelligent and made up for her lack of academic learning by her ready wit and sturdy commonsense. She had her share of vanity and expected the homage of others, which she received in full measure. Elegant to the finger-tips, she expected style and elegance in others and could not abide the shabby or boorish. She loved good company and sparkling conversation, to which she contributed with her lively sense of humour and her gift as racontour. Her tastes were of a piece with her personality— expensive and exacting, but she could not always satisfy them because of poor financial management. She liked to live life to the full and was scornful of the hypocrisy practised by many of her party colleagues, and was therefore indulgent towards the foibles and peccadilloes of others. But she was inclined to be capricious and wayward and could make hasty judgements.

As an envoy of India, Mrs Pandit was a remarkable success in more than one capital. Among the very first of the Ambassadors of India, she took up her unfamiliar assignment in Moscow with remarkable self-confidence and grace, as though long experienced in the practice of international politics and diplomacy. She won instant popularity and the respect of her colleagues. Excellent at public speaking, she was the epitome of womanly grace, combined with the more robust quality of holding her own in a world of men.

She had qualities of leadership, and instilled in our Moscow mission a sense of purpose and pride in their country. To many foreign countries, India and Indians were unfamiliar, and their envoys could not suppress their astonishment at the fact that a country which could nurture personalities of such quality and distinction as Mrs Pandit, and had such intelligent and gifted people, should have been under colonial rule for so long.

While Mrs Pandit could engage in discussion with highly experienced envoys with facility and without a trace of diffidence, she could not suffer pomposity or obtuseness and would betray her impatience. On one occasion when receiving a call from the envoy of Mongolia who evidently lacked much knowledge of the outside world, the visitor opened the interview by enquiring in his obscure language if there were camels in India. This was duty translated into Russian by the envoy's interpreter. Our interpreter thereupon translated the question into English and Mrs Pandit's affirmative reply was duly conveyed back in like manner. Then followed other similar questions about buffaloes, cattle, sheep, etc., until it came to horses. At this point, with ennui rising, Mrs Pandit interjected: 'Please tell His Excellency that there are donkeys also in India.' That concluding piece of information was apparently received with satisfaction, probably because that animal is much respected in some countries, including the visitor's.

I would see the Ambassador every morning to brief her on current developments for half an hour or so, after which her interest would begin to flag. With a cup of coffee to refresh us, we would then converse in lighter vein, when Mrs Pandit would regale us with anecdotes in her inimitable style, ending with light-hearted gossip. This was a daily and rather pleasant routine. She was content to leave official reporting to the Counsellor: her own 'official' despatches to the Prime Minister, addressed to 'My dear Bhai', began with some information and analyses of a political nature, generally concluding with complaints about living conditions and other minutiae of a personal nature. They did not find their way into the chancery archives, and not much action seemed to have been taken on them.

In the autumn of 1949, Professor Sarvepalli Radhakrishnan, a world-renowned philosopher, was appointed to succeed Mrs Pandit. At the time he was holding the chair of Spalding Professor of Eastern Religions and Ethics at All Souls' College, Oxford and was the current President of the General Conference of the United Nations Educational and Scientific Organisation (UNESCO). He came on a brief preliminary visit to present his credentials before proceeding to Paris and Oxford to fulfil his other responsibilities. He was received at the airport by the Chief of Protocol, some press correspondents and representatives of the Commonwealth missions. As he emerged from the plane, noticing the book in his hand, I hurried forward to seize it in order to conceal its title. It was *I Chose Freedom* by Kravchenko, a KGB defector, which had attracted much attention in the west and was naturally anathema to the Soviet Union.

The new Ambassador made an arresting figure, tall and lean and with smiling countenance, dressed austerely in a knee-length achkan. He exuded friendliness and understanding but in a distant way. Those who met him could not but be struck by his unusual personality.

The delicate irony of Dr Radhakrishnan's appointment to Moscow attracted much curiosity, for here was an idealist Hindu philosopher and a man of religion accredited to a country whose ideology was materialism and a total rejection of religion. The foreign missions, and indeed we at the Indian Embassy, were agog to see how he would be received by the Soviet leadership.

The new Ambassador had brought his own South Indian cook to look after his simple needs and he insisted that we stay on at the residence as he needed only his bedroom. For the rest, he said he had accepted the appointment at the request of the Prime Minister who assured him that Moscow was an ideal place for him to complete his monumental commentary on the Upanishads on which he was currently engaged. He wanted us to carry on exactly as before with the official entertainment and other concerns in running the Embassy. As he was new to diplomacy, reporting to the Ministry should continue as before while keeping him in touch with developments.

Katya, our Soviet cook, an estimable woman who by now had greatly improved her performance and had also learnt some quite passable Indian cooking, was left to preside over the vast kitchen. Like the ancient central heating system whose radiators hissed and crackled incessantly, the kitchen oven was also fired by wood fuel. A pair of wood-cutters would be active from dawn to dusk out in the snow, sawing or chopping logs to feed the ravenous boilers. On one occasion in mid-winter the ancient contraption went out of commission, mercifully when the Ambassador was away, and for a couple of freezing days and nights we went about from room to room clad in our warmest gear from head to foot.

Dr Radhakrishnan followed more or less the same routine as he did in India, winter or summer. He would be up very early and, after his bath in the only bathroom of which the residence boasted, to the accompaniment of much chanting of Sanskrit shlokas, he would return to bed where, after a frugal breakfast of porridge, he would attend to his academic work, the adjacent bed being littered with books. There he stayed all morning until the stroke of twelve when he emerged for a walk. I would accompany him on these walks, reporting on the day's developments. The promenade, which lasted one hour initially, became briefer and briefer as the temperature dropped. The latter part of the conversation was invariably a most illuminating discourse on Vedanta and the *Bhagavad Gita*. At precisely one o'clock we sat down at table, Dr Radhakrishnan to a simple meal of rice, lentils and boiled vegetables, followed by yoghurt, and we to our usual fare. He would again retire to his room, coming out in the evening. Often, at the request of all of us, he would give lectures on the *Gita*. Sometimes we would listen to records of Subbulakshmi's music, or Susheela would sing bhajans.

Dinner at 7.30 p.m. was for Dr Radhakrishnan a very spare and simple affair and before 9.00p.m. he would retire for the night.

The Ambassador conducted whatever business had to be done within the mission from his room. But when a foreign envoy came to call, he was received in the sitting room, the Ambassador hurriedly donning his achkan for the occasion. His own calls on his colleagues did not exceed some quarter of an hour and those that he took were also of the same brief duration.

The Ambassador's protocol calls on Soviet officials began with the Chief, followed by the Foreign Minister who, in the absence of the redoubtable Molotov, was the well-known Vyshinsky. The presentation of credentials to the nominal Head of State was arranged at unusually short notice. I had suggested to the Ambassador that he make a formal request to the Foreign Minister for an interview with Generalissimo Stalin, which would no doubt be refused as was the case with Mrs Pandit, as Stalin was known to receive only Ambassadors of the Great Powers. Vyshinsky's cryptic reply was: 'The possibility of that is not excluded,' leaving us wondering what precisely he meant. Soon after, the Ambassador left for Paris, returning only in early January, 1950.

On Dr Radhakrishnan's return, we were relaxing after dinner when the telephone rang. It was Mr Molochkov on the line who, in a tone of urgency, insisted that he wished to speak to the Ambassador himself. Dr Radhakrishnan took up the phone somewhat reluctantly when the following conversation ensued. In the manner of Soviet bureaucracy, Mr Molochkov asked if the Ambassador on a certain date had asked Mr. Andrei Y. Vyshinsky, Acting Minister of Foreign Affairs, if he, the Ambassador, could pay a call on Generalissimo Stalin. On receiving an affirmative reply, Mr Molochkov enquired if the Ambassador could come on the following day at 9.30 p.m. Again, on receiving confirmation, I was asked to take over the call.

Mr Molochkov, assuming that I would accompanying the

Ambassador, provided details of the gate by which we should reach the Kremlin, where an officer would meet us and escort us inside. The number of the car and the name of the Soviet chauffeur were asked for; meanwhile, we should keep the matter confidential. The comparatively early hour of 9.30 p.m. for the meeting was no doubt a concession to the Professor's early habits. Stalin kept a nocturnal schedule, working all night till dawn, and his interviews to western envoys and delegations were generally given in the small hours of the morning.

We were naturally quite elated at the prospect, and even Dr Radhakrishnan could not conceal his pleasure. We discussed the reasons for this unusual courtesy which had been denied to Mrs Pandit. The Ambassador asked what he should say at the interview. I advised that, apart from the usual courtesies, he was entirely at liberty to converse as he thought fit and not be inhibited by any official view. I did, however, remind him that Stalin fancied the title of 'Generalissimo' by which he should be addressed.

As we were setting out for the Kremlin, Susheela reminded me that perhaps I would be able to take notes, and for want of anything quickly at hand, thrust her laundry-book into my pocket. When I finally disclosed our destination to Alexei, our driver, he was visibly scared and with trembling hands took the steering wheel. It was a blisteringly cold night. The deserted streets glistened under a carpet of sand-like ice-particles. We drove silently through the empty streets, immersed in our own thoughts. Arriving at the towering Spassky gate, we were met by a Colonel who, after glancing at us, flashed his torch at the chauffeur, demanding his papers, which he briefly scrutinised, and then beckoned us to follow him. The great gates swung open and we drove into the heart of the citadel to a porch where, on alighting, another Colonel met us. We followed him up the stairs and along endless, empty corridors until we were ushered into a room where a number of officers in uniform were seated at a long table. Hardly had we taken our seats when an adjacent door opened and Mr Pavlov, an interpreter (whom we often had occasion to meet subsequently) said: 'The Generalissimo is waiting'.

We entered through the adjacent door to be confronted by a second thickly-padded door, which, fumblingly we pushed open to enter a large brightly-lit room. At the far end we espied Stalin emerging from a desk; advancing, he met us under the vast chandelier which brightly lit the room, clicked his heels, bowed a little and shook hands, uttering the name 'Stalin'. We were then ushered to a long green baize-covered table at the rear corner, when Vyshinsky emerged. Stalin, with Vyshinsky at his side, sat opposite the Ambassador and me, while Pavlov sat at the end of the table between us.

Stalin was quite short, much shorter than portrayed in his innumerable pictures and statues. He had a heavy moustache tinged with grey and a heavy mouth on a pock-marked face. Dressed in a powder-blue uniform with no decorations apart from the insignia of rank on his epaulettes, his manner was brusque. His hard countenance belied the encomiastic description of him by an American envoy as a benevolent 'Uncle Joe on whose knee a child would love to be dandled'. He exuded an aura of authority and ruthlessness which brooked no challenge or deviation.

As the interview began, Vyshinsky took up a writing pad to scribble notes in clerk-like fashion, uttering not a word throughout. Stalin lit a papyrus (a Russian cigarette only half-filled with tobacco) and chain-smoked all the time. I took out my 'dhobi book' and began scribbling. Stalin spoke a simple and direct Russian with a broad accent and it was not too difficult to follow him, even without the benefit of the interpreter.

The Ambassador opened the interview by addressing the Generalissimo as 'Mr Stalin', which made me wince. He spoke of India's desire to establish and develop friendly relations with her great northern neighbour. India's foreign policy was one of peace and friendship towards all in consonance with her own traditions. India followed an independent path free of foreign entanglements or alliances. She was engaged in the gigantic task of providing a better life for her people and overcoming the ravages of long years of colonial exploitation. It was natural therefore for India to seek the friendship and understanding of the Soviet Union which had always championed the cause of the suppressed nations of the world and had given full support to their freedom struggles.

Stalin did not react to this opening gambit, and without wasting words abruptly said he had heard that the condition of the Indian peasantry was 'wretched' and asked why nothing was being done about it. The Ambassador replied with legislative, if not factual, accuracy saying that we had abolished landlordism and the land was now with the tiller. This was received with some scepticism. Stalin exclaiming 'Really?' The next question related to the problem of illiteracy in India, Stalin enquiring if the Indian language was hieroglyphic or alphabetical: he was informed that the ancient Devanagiri script was alphabetical and highly developed. Stalin probably had in mind the discussions then going on with the Chinese leaders on the subject. Stalin then asked if the Indian army was still under British command and was told that it was under the Indian government and had its own Indian Commander-in-Chief (General Cariappa had only recently taken over from the last British incumbent). Did India have a navy? was the next question, which also received an affirmative answer (the few hulks left over after the War could perhaps be so described). The Ambassador then proffered the information that India also had an air-force (the left-overs of the War-time air armada).

Another surprising question followed, which was why Ceylon was not a part of India, to which no explanation could be offered beyond saying that it was and had been a separate country. To the enquiry as to whether the Maldives belonged to

India, I recall with some regret that we were both stumped; to evade the issue we mumbled disingenuously that the Laccadives were part of India. Fortunately Stalin did not pursue the subject.

The interrogation continued. Did India have any influence in the South-east Asian region? This was easily answered by reference to the very names of countries such as Indo-China, Indonesia, etc., emphasising that Indian influence was purely cultural as evidenced by existing historical monuments of Indian inspiration.

His curiosity apparently satisfied, Stalin stated that he had no more questions and enquired if the Ambassador had any. Responding, Dr Radhakrishnan observed that the Soviet Union was a great peace-loving country; Stalin interjected to say with passion that his country had made unequalled sacrifices during the War in the cause of world peace and to defeat the forces of Fascism, which had wrought untold havoc and had tried to enslave the world. Expressing agreement, the Ambassador deplored the existence of the Cold War and suggested that the Soviet Union, in consonance with its own fine tradition, should try to stop it. At this Stalin visibly bristled and asked what about the others who were responsible for it? Raising his hand, the Ambassador suggested that as a peace-loving country, the Soviet Union could withdraw its own hand as it takes two hands to clap. Now it was Stalin's turn to fumble for an answer, but answer there came none. At this stage Dr Radhakrishanan said he had no more questions and so the interview came to an end. Stalin again shook hands and clicked his heels; we were led out by Pavlov and handed over to a Colonel who escorted us back to our car. We drove home in silence, mystified by our recent encounter.

Next morning, elated at having been able to encounter the fabled and inaccessible Stalin, but rather perplexed at the purport of his interrogation and the general impact of the interview, we tried to recapitulate the event in detail. In the first place, why did

Stalin condescend to grant the interview when Mrs Pandit had been cold-shouldered? Perhaps the realisation was beginning to dawn that India was truly independent, a conclusion emphasised by the decision of India's Constituent Assembly to declare India a Republic on 26 January 1950. At a personal level, perhaps Stalin was intrigued by reports of the new Ambassador's unusual personality and was curious to meet an Indian philosopher of renown. Perhaps the real reason was a hard-headed political assessment of India's present and potential geo-political role in the Indian Ocean region and her influence further afield in South-east Asia. Because of the sharp differences which had developed with the new Chinese leadership, Mao-tse-Tung being still held up in Moscow wrangling with his hosts, Stalin may have considered India as a possible counterbalancing force in case the Chinese proved to be too recalcitrant and aggressive. Be that as it may, it seemed possible that a new chapter might be opening in relations between our two countries. The constant press attacks might cease and the encouragement of Communist activists to violence in India become restrained. As later events showed, these expectations were to be realised to some degree. The apparent naivete of Stalin's questions was puzzling as he must have been fully briefed beforehand, or was it shrewdness on his part? He was believed to weigh a country's significance in terms of military power, the query, no doubt apocryphal, 'How many divisions has the Pope?' being attributed to him.

Different from each other in every conceivable way, there was, however, one respect in which Stalin and Radhakrishnan matched each other; both were men of few words, and those were spoken plainly and directly. The test of Stalin's reactions to the interview was to follow a few days later on the occasion of the celebration of our first Republic Day. The accepted criterion of the estimation of a particular country in Soviet eyes was the level and extent of the Soviet official hierarchy attending official functions. Attendance by only the Chief of Protocol, or worse still, his deputy, was the lowest watermark. We therefore awaited with some uncertainty the forthcoming Republic Day to gauge where we stood.

On the appointed day, while the Ambassador and I waited at the head of the stairs to receive our guests, at the stroke of the hour, a galaxy of Soviet officialdom, civil and military, glittering in their uniforms, was observed being ushered in. There was the Acting Foreign Minister, Andrei Vyshinsky, the Chief of Protocol and the whole Asia desk, two Soviet Marshals with their ample chests covered in medals and decorations, and other lesser functionaries. As members of the diplomatic corps trooped in, there was a current of surprise, as not even the larger missions were so generously graced by high Soviet officialdom.

Presently, Pavlov the interpreter, arrived and excitedly asked what we thought of the interview; when the Ambassador and I genuinely expressed ignorance, Pavlov exclaimed; 'Didn't you see? The Generalissimo was pleased.' That both surprised and gratified us, and the function, despite our offered beverages of orange juice and lemonade on a freezing Arctic evening, seemed to assume a warm and roseate hue. Even Dr Radhakrishanan was not too fatigued at the end of it.

Stalin's personal satisfaction at the interview was no doubt due to the startlingly unorthodox nature of his visitor and his direct and uninhibited questions and answers. He may also have felt that India's leaders had broken away decisively from their former colonial moorings and must indeed be pursuing an independent path, as they claimed.

At a social level, with Susheela leading, our staff were seen to be conversing happily with our Soviet guests. Susheela's rudimentary Russian was learnt at her music lessons under a very earnest and exacting music master from the Conservatoire, and in dealing with Katya, the cook, and the maidservants. The staff members had picked up a working knowledge of the language while shopping or moving around in the city. This proved to be quite an asset on such occasions. Our depleted diplomatic staff, which now consisted of just three officers, had been reinforced by two bright young probationers under training, whose prescribed task was, first and foremost, to acquire a sound knowledge of Russian. I had been making a plodding attempt at learning something of the language and had a martinet of a woman teacher who figuratively (literally, if she could) gave me a spanking at each mistake I made, and they were numerous. I found the prescribed book rather impractical, as it contained phrases such as 'How is your grandmother's toothache today?' which would hardly be of much use in polite conversation with Soviet officials. But I did manage to be able to read and write the Cyrillic script and even to understand the broad gist of newspaper articles. What, however, we found particularly galling after all our painstaking efforts, was Vyshinsky's parting observation that Madame Dayal spoke the best and most comprehensible Russian! On the question of language, the serious lesson one learnt was how important it is for all members of our diplomatic missions, wherever stationed, to acquire at least a working knowledge of the language.

We were returning from a walk on a particularly freezing day, when, seeing us at the door, the cleaning woman rushed out with a cry of alarm and, picking up a handful of snow, began vigorously rubbing Dr Radhakrishnan's nose. We were taken aback by what seemed rather impudent behaviour on the part of a normally inoffensive woman until we learnt that the tip of the Ambassador's nose was getting frost-bitten, and she had applied the recognised Russian treatment in the nick of time to prevent a catastrophe. The nose was saved, but the tip remained discoloured for months afterwards.

Dr Radhakrishnan had few possessions that he cherished more than an ancient clothes-brush, a valued companion of may a summer. After being washed, Katiya put it in her oven for quick drying but forgot it there; the later recovery of a charred and unidentifiable object caused great lamentation. But Katya's soups were much relished by the Professor, until Susheela happened to look closely into the ingredients and received a shock. Katya had been given very strict injunctions about the Ambassador's dietary taboos, but she thought the 'reverend gentleman' (referring to Dr Radhakrishnan's apparently ecclesiastical garb) was too weak and needed strengthening nourishment.

Our two-year assignment was drawing to a close, but Dr Radhakrishnan insisted that we continue for another year after our home leave. To this we agreed. But despite our assurance we were not to return, as other totally unexpected duties were assigned to me on reaching India even before the commencement of my leave, followed by much confusion and dithering in the Ministry regarding my next posting.

The insights gained in those two years in Moscow were invaluable to me in my life as a pioneer of India's diplomatic service and, later, its head. I realised how inadvisable it was to start with a large mission and then to have to pare it down according to needs; far better to start in a modest way and to build up in relation to the business to be done. Some knowledge of the language of the place is essential and each mission should have some personnel who can speak and read it fluently. Language specialisation, especially for new entrants, is very necessary and even their seniors should make a serious attempt to learn something of the language. In making postings, the language factor must be kept in mind. As one is expected to acquire a sound grasp of the situation in the country of posting in very limited time, a study of the history, culture, politics and economics of different countries should be encouraged to enable one to get down to serious work from the start instead of floundering about trying to acquire even an elementary knowledge of things. To maintain even the smallest mission abroad is a very expensive business, the humblest functionary costing more in terms of rupees—in view of the exchange factor—than the most exalted official at home. Every mission, irrespective of its size, should be required to generate at least enough economic activity so as to pay its way. Economic strength in the present-day world counts for more than military capability, besides being essential for a country's own progress and welfare. The foremost business of our foreign missions should be to promote trade and collaboration in various fields of economic activity. Our diplomatic personnel should therefore receive some grounding in matters of international commerce and finance.

Looking back over the years, it seems incredible that the Soviet leadership should have so egregiously misread the situation as to imagine that the newly-liberated India was still an appendage of the fast disintegrating British Empire, or that having overthrown one colonial domination it would put itself under the yoke of another. Such a glaring misconception could hardly have been the result of any lack of detailed information about the new India. There was a heavily-staffed Soviet Embassy in New Delhi, an extensive KGB network and an Indian Communist party owing allegiance to Moscow. Stalin's astonishing questions to Dr Radhakrishnan at the famous interview would suggest that either he had not been adequately briefed about India or that he had not cared to study the brief, since he was far too shrewd a man and was hardly likely to have put such questions out of sheer naivete. Those questions did reveal, however, how Stalin's mind worked: he sized up a country in terms of its armed might and influence, with little regard to its declared or applied foreign policy. Even the fact that Nehru had sent his own sister as India's first envoy was evidently not considered by him sufficient proof of India's genuine independence and sincere desire for friendship with his country. True, the efforts made to subvert the independence of the newly-liberated country by promoting a Communist-led rebellion in Telengana and violence and disorder elsewhere had met with frustration. And the persuasion and pressure exercised by Madame Kollontai on behalf of the Soviet leadership on Mrs Pandit, to use her influence with her brother to draw India into the Communist orbit, had been rebuffed. To a dictator as absolute as Stalin, it was beyond his comprehension that friendly relations between sovereign states particularly those following different political and social systems, should be based on principles of equality, mutual respect, and non-interference. In his own country he had amply demonstrated his brutal intolerance of the slightest shade of dissent. How could he then admit that a state still struggling to its feet would presume to be regarded as an equal? He looked at the world in black or white, and believed that those who were not with him were against him. It was only after Tito's defiant breakaway from the Soviet orbit and Stalin's own death that his successors began to realise that there could be peaceful, even cooperative, co-existence between states with different social and political systems.

After anathematising Tito for his apostasy, Stalin spared no effort in isolating him and attempting to bring about his liquidation for propagating the pernicious doctrine of 'different roads to socialism' which could have undermined the hegemony of the Soviet Union and destroyed the myth of Stalin's infallibility. But having failed in his efforts, it was left to Stalin's successors to go as penitents in sackcloth and ashes to Tito in Belgrade. Having been in Moscow at the time of the momentous break, when the Yugoslavia Ambassador, Vladimir Popovu, quietly slipped away before the full wrath of Stalin descended on Tito, the wheel had turned full circle. I was present in Belgrade to witness the drama when a contrite Khrushchev accompanied by Bulganin paid court to a reluctant Tito. Not only was Tito's heretical doctrine acknowledged, but so too was the genuineness of the non-aligned movement among states of different political hues.

By a curious parallelism at the other end of the pole, the proselytising zeal of which John Foster Dulles was the apostle, had begun to abate with his demise. His rejection of non-alignment was even more absolute than Stalin's, being pronounced by him in theological terms as 'sinful'. But while non-alignment as a growing political force came to be reluctantly accepted, its genuine impartiality was weighed in a tilted balance to its detriment.

In conclusion, it must be said that despite the tergiversations in Soviet policies, Pandit Nehru continued to pursue a consistent line towards that country. The early euphoria had given place to a more realistic and mature attitude, shaped by experience. At this distance of time, which encompasses an era when Indo-Soviet relations prospered to the point of cordiality and mutual esteem, and when close economic ties were forged, it is difficult to imagine that they had their origins in such hostile beginnings. On the Kashmir issue the Soviet stand in the UN Security Council was to abstain although Pakistan since its very creation was a western favourite. But after Stalin's death in 1953 and especially after it was revealed that the Kahuta air-base had been given over to the United States to enable it to overfly the Soviet Union, and with Pakistan's adherence to the Baghdad Pact, Soviet eyes were opened to the existing realities. Thereafter Soviet support was invaluable help in thwarting all attempts to browbeat India on the vital issue of Kashmir. Economic relations between the two countries prospered to their mutual advantage. Whatever may have been the drawbacks of the rupee trade agreement, it did provide an outlet for India's manufactures, especially in consumer goods, when the markets of the affluent countries of the west were virtually closed to them or restricted by quotas and controls.

With the massive American military aid to Pakistan ostensbily as a bulwark against the spread of communism, but in Pakistani calculations as a means to fulfil its aims in Kashmir, India was forced to strengthen its own defences. It was the supply of Soviet arms on favourable terms that helped correct the balance. Politically, the steady Soviet connection was useful when relations with the other super-power were subject to seasonal variations. After the Chinese incursion into India in 1962, it was the United States that provided a shield. But with its relations with China deteriorating rapidly, the Soviet Union found India's support even more invaluable. These developments, which were the outcome of the new perceptions of the post-Stalin leadership and the changing world situation, could not possibly have been foreseen in 1948–50. With the demise of the Soviet Union the foundations of Indo-Soviet relations remain, but the superstructure can no longer be the same.

# SIX

# Eyeless in Assam

e had barely landed in Bombay after a long, slow flight from Moscow when a frantic search began for me in New Delhi. What accounted for our disappearance was our decision to fly straight down to Trivandrum to pay homage to the great Vendantic sage, Shri Atmananda, whom Susheela had visited before.

I had never travelled south of Bombay before and was captivated by the verdant beauty of Kerala, with its rich green rice fields, stately palms, lush plantations of banana and rubber and the abundant lakes and waterways. The people, clad in spotless white, the women adorned with jasmine garlands in their lustrous hair, the children going in orderly rows to school were a pleasure to behold. Striking also were the villages, clean and neat, the houses well-built with their curving tiled roofs. What a contrast the scene presented to the vast flat, dry plains of the north, the dust-laden clothing of the people, the mud huts, the villages reeking of squalor and dirt.

Of this first pilgrimage to the sage, it is difficult to speak except to say that it was the first of a never-ending series, and indeed, life itself became a lifelong pilgrimage. It opened up the portals of the head and heart to endless vistas, stretching into the beyond.

On arriving back in Delhi, I was immediately sent for by the Prime Minister. The government of Assam was in a great mess, the tribesmen were burning villages in the valley, refugees from East Pakistan were pouring in and the administration seemed quite unable or unwilling to deal with the situation. I was to go there as soon as possible to see what could be done to restore peace and order. A Minister of State, Mohanlal Saksena, had been sent to Assam earlier, but the Centre was not satisfied with his performance as he was able to do little or nothing. Nehru said I should see the Sardar (the Home Minister, Sardar Vallabhbhai Patel) for fuller instructions, and also the Secretary-General of the Ministry of External Affairs.

I was dismayed at this peremptory and unwelcome diversion from what was to have been a brief holiday before our return to Moscow. I called on Sir Girija Shankar Bajpai, the distinguished head of the Ministry of External Affairs to voice my doubts and discontent. I pleaded that I knew nothing about Assam or Indo-Pakistani affairs, that the assignment seemed so vague and indeterminate that I hardly knew where to begin. Besides, I had made a promise to return to Moscow, but now both my return and our much needed holiday would be in doubt. If a Minister of State had been unsuccessful in dealing with an elected Congress government, what hope would an unknown official have to influence it?

Bajpai listened sympathetically, but saying that he was afraid I had no choice in the matter, handed me a sheet from a file containing a Cabinet decision. After referring to the very difficult situation in Assam and the non-performance of the provincial government, it had been decided to send a central government officer with full powers to deal with the situation. It went on to say that the Special Commissioner should be me and, as if to seal my fate, there were complimentary references about my suitability for the job.

Accepting the inevitable, I replied with feeble humour that I could always refer to the testimonial contained in the Cabinet decision in case I got into trouble, as I feared I would. I then set about studying the *Gazetteer* on Assam and meeting Assam officials to gain some elementary knowledge about the place of my future labours.

The Sardar gave me an appointment for 6.30 a.m. When I showed up at his residence, I was ushered into a bedroom where he was seated facing the wall, a masseur working on his back and shoulders. While I sipped a cup of coffee, the Sardar, in precise terms, gave his instructions. He said the Assam government of Chief Minister Bardaloi was weak and ineffective and the situation in the border state was becoming increasingly dangerous and getting out of control. Refugees were pouring in from East Pakistan and the hill tribes were sweeping down into the plains, killing and burning. The administration was not functioning, and the directives of the Centre were being disregarded. Unless matters were firmly controlled now, there would be complete anarchy. As Special Commissioner of the Government of India I would be given all the powers necessary to deal with the situation; in case the provincial government refused to comply with Central directives or to heed my advice, I was empowered to recommend its supersession under section 93A of the Government of India Act. He assured me that I would have the full support of the central government.

The message over, the Sardar donned his shirt and turned around to ask me a few personal questions. He then very courteously escorted me to my car.

This was my second meeting with the Sardar; the first was just before Partition when he had come to Lucknow to review the arrangements to ensure tranquility in U.P., that hotbed of Muslim League secessionist agitation.

I was much impressed by the Sardar at that first and very down-to-earth meeting. In a few crisp sentences, he had summed up his concerns; his responses were brief and decisive. It did not take him long to get to the very core of a problem, a great contrast to most of the U.P. ministers who would waffle endlessly without coming to a decision. At this second meeting my respect and admiration for the Sardar was greatly enhanced. He had an air of command and could inspire strong loyalties.

I felt quite overwhelmed by the portentious nature of the task I was now expected to fulfil and reported to the Ministry to seek some comfort and enlightenment, especially from S. Dutt, a senior and very capable official of the Assam cadre. India and Pakistan had almost gone to war over the perilous situation of Hindus in East Pakistan who were being harshly persecuted and were fleeing in droves, mostly into Assam. To prevent an armed clash the two Prime Ministers had met and had come to an agreement known as the Nehru-Liaquat Pact, according to which certain corrective measures were to be taken urgently by both governments. The implementation of that crucial agreement was being jeopardised by the cavalier attitude of the Assam government.

I collected some tropical gear, a mosquito net and bedding roll and took off for Shillong via Calcutta, leaving Susheela behind with her family. From Calcutta I took a bumpy Dakota flight over the Garo Hills to Guwahati, peering anxiously through the thick cloud cover at the tree-tops which we barely skimmed over. After the beautiful drive up from Guwahati, the vegetation changing from bamboo to pine, I checked in at a hotel. Strolling out to enjoy the cool of the evening and to explore my surroundings, I happened to notice the signboard of an ICS officer and, seeing lights in the house, I walked up the driveway and knocked at the door to be met by a surprised young couple. After introducing myself, I was invited to accompany them to the Club. The Club seemed to be a convivial and relaxed place, beautifully housed, with the members at the bar engaged in indoor games. I was introduced to the Chief Secretary and other senior officers as a visitor on holiday from New Delhi and, after the interruption, they resumed their game of bridge or billiards. They all seemed a leisurely and contented lot, brimming with well-being, as well they might in those charming and salubrious surroundings.

On my return to the hotel, I was met by a messenger from the Governor, Sri Prakasa; I was to be collected and be the Governor's guest. Sri Prakasa was an amiable and cultured gentleman, cast in a Victorian mould. He was different to the general run of Congressmen: he was a Cambridge graduate, a good public speaker, had courteous ways and, surprisingly, was fond of riding. He was in the front rank of Congressmen, and had been associated with most of the great leaders of the Independence Movement in which he himself had been an active participant.

Sri Prakasa was curious to know what precisely was the nature of my mission, as a long telegram from Sardar Patel, which he showed me, did not disclose any details. The message was mostly a strong recommendation that he should have full confidence in me and give me all possible help. I told him of the anxiety which prevailed in New Delhi about the situation in the border state and the apathy of the local government which did not seem to realise its gravity. I was to see things for myself and advise the Assam authorities on the measures required to deal with the situation and to offer the full support of the central government, as the situation was perceived to be a matter of national and not merely provincial importance. I tried to reassure the Governor that I was there only to be of the maximum possible help to him and to his government and not to spy on them. I suggested that he call a meeting of the Cabinet forthwith, when I could convey the central government's views to them.

Accordingly, an emergency meeting of the Cabinet was

called for the same evening; when the ministers trooped in, they looked puzzled and not a little suspicious on seeing me. The Governor, after introducing me, spoke of the central government's concerns which accounted for my presence there. I was then asked to address the meeting. I spoke in some detail on how the situation was perceived in New Delhi, emphasising the need for urgent action. On enquiring, I found that nothing had been done to address the problems. To my suggestion to appoint a Relief and Rehabilitation Commissioner forthwith, the bland response was that no officer could be spared from the important work on which everyone was currently engaged. When I pressed the point, I, a stranger, was asked to suggest a name. I could only think of my host of the previous evening, Balachandran, the Transport Commissioner. Overriding all objections, the Governor agreed that the crisis situation must take priority over routine functions and Balachandran was immediately summoned to the meeting. After a search, he turned up rather breathlessly in tennis gear, racquet in hand, to be told to his bewilderment that he had been appointed Commissioner for Relief and Rehabilitation. His protests that he was about to go home on leave to Trivandrum were over-ruled.

The Governor seemed satisfied at the outcome of the meeting, but later asked what should be done if the ministry continued to stall. I said in that case my instructions were to recommend the supersession of the government and the imposition of Governor's rule. Alarmed, Sri Prakasa said he could not possibly be party to the summary removal of a duly elected government. I tried to reassure him, hoping that the contingency would never arise.

Next morning Balachandran was duly installed in his new office and, at my request, was given full powers to direct the police, handle forest supplies and the medical or public works departments, to render all material or other assistance that may be required of him. I paid calls on the Chief Minister and the

Finance Minister, the latter being markedly unhelpful and evasive. The Chief Secretary, a very senior Gujarati ICS officer, seemed particularly provincial in his outlook and regarded me with the utmost distrust, as well he might, considering that my very presence in Assam was an indictment of the local officials. I learnt that not a single officer or Minister had taken the trouble to go down to the hot and humid plains to study the situation at first hand. I decided to do so myself.

I first drove towards the border with East Pakistan and found swarms of refugees in makeshift or no shelters, unfed and uncared for by any government agency. Only monks of the Ramakrishna order and their disciples were rendering what succour they could within their limited resources. On my return I reported this to the Governor and asked Balachandran to take matters in hand without delay and before epidemics broke out or deaths occurred due to starvation.

At brief intervals, I made tours of the valley, visiting one district after another, with my bedding roll and mosquito net, subsisting on the way to district headquarters on tea and bananas. The newly appointed district magistrates were a young, callous and lazy lot. Driving through their districts, I saw village after village burnt to ashes, with only the black stumps of timber still standing, while cattle grazed unchecked in the rice fields, with not a human being in sight. Nothing had been done to prevent such wholesale destruction, to take punitive action or to resettle the fugitive villagers cowering in fear on the banks of the Brahmaputra. Everywhere I insisted on stern punitive action against the miscreants, the apprehension and trial of the criminals, the imposition of collective fines, the rehabilitation of those evicted, and the provision of armed protection for them, including the provision of licensed weapons.

The refugee problem in the district of Karimganj, cut off from the rest of Assam by the district of Sylhet in East Pakistan, of which it formerly was a part, needed urgent attention. Access to it by road through Indian territory was a long and tedious business, involving a long detour over the hills; the direct route was through Sylhet. Mohan Lal Saksena, the Minister from Delhi, had flown back to Calcutta from Shillong, from where he had taken another plane to Karimagnj. I knew the Governor of East Bengal, Sir Feroze Khan Noon, and telephoned him for permission to motor down via Sylhet to Karimganj. Noon was most cordial and readily agreed to provide safe conduct through Sylhet.

My drive down to Sylhet and beyond was interrupted at Sylhet by an unplanned diversion to the Circuit House where a large throng of Sylheti dignitaries awaited me and, despite my protestations, insisted on my partaking of a sumptuous repast which they had hospitably arranged. I noticed that Sylhet had been rechristened 'Jalalabad' and the new name was printed all over in Urdu lettering, which gave the impression that Urdu had gained popularity there. But my attempts to start up a conversation in that language only led to much embarrassment among my hosts. After this gesture of goodwill I proceeded on my way to Karimganj.

But now I had visited, sometimes on my own, and sometimes with the Commissioner for Relief and Rehabilitation, almost all the districts from Goalpara to Tezpur which had been wracked by disturbances. Summary instructions were given to the local authorities of the measures to be taken, and arrangements made where required for additional assistance from headquarters. Fortunately, the disturbances had not spread to upper Assam and were mostly confined to districts north of the Brahmaputra. The state machinery had been set in motion and all departments were by now making their contribution towards the mitigation of the problem. It was a question of time before things settled down. The main task remaining was to monitor the progress.

As neither the Governor nor the Centre would agree to my recall, insisting on my continuing there to see matters through,

Susheela now joined me in Shillong. We visited the reputedly wettest place on earth, Cherrapunji, which we found to be rather dry and sunny on that day. A most interesting tour we made was by road to Dimapur and up the Naga Hills to Kohima and onwards to Manipur. The luxuriance of nature was everywhere apparent. The main highway, arcaded by tall trees in mauve bloom and with sprays of multi-coloured orchids festooning their branches, were a sight to behold. And occasionally, we would see an irridescent carpet of blue spread on the highway itself. As we approached the carpet would rise up in the air—a myriad butterflies. The whole area seemed peaceful as people went about their daily concerns and it was difficult to imagine that Kohima, the point at which the Japanese advance was stemmed, had seen such desperate resistance just a few years ago. The cemetery was the only sad reminder of those events. Manipur, set in a bowl between green mountains, presented a picture of rural tranquility where bejewelled women with elegant coiffeurs did brisk trade in farm produce, while their menfolk sat idly by or smoked under trees. What struck a visitor to Assam was the large number of tribes, with their varied customs, dress and languages which inhabited the hilly areas north of the Brahmaputra and along the eastern rim of the country. By and large, they lived in a state of peaceful co-existence, with only occasional flare-ups, as between the warlike Nagas and Kukis.

But, as I reported to New Delhi, the situation in Assam was not only the result of the influx both of Hindu refugees fleeing from Pakistani oppression, and also of Muslim infiltrators in search of land, but also of domestic politics as well. The population of Assam was almost evenly divided between the Assam valley Hindus, the tribals and the Bengalis, Muslims and others. The Assam Congress was composed almost entirely of Hindus; they formed the government and tried to dominate over the other two segments. There was a marked bias against the Bengalis. The Bardaloi government of Assam was dominated by

Finance Minister B.N. Mehdi, a man of strongly parochial views who was trying to enforce a policy of 'Assam for the Assamese'. Senior Bengali officials had been got rid of by deputation or otherwise and young and inexperienced Assamese put in their places. A propaganda campaign had been launched to the effect that there was a conspiracy to create a 'Greater Bengal' by including in it Assam, eastern Bihar and much of Orissa. A Calcutta newspaper, *Jugantar*, was cited as its principal and most articulate crusader. In fact, this argument was urged by the Finance Minister when he claimed that the Hindu refugees were not victims of religious persecution, but were actually voluntary arrivals, part of the plan to raise the Bengali ratio of the population. That was also why nothing had been done for the refugees; it had been hoped that their sorry plight would force them to return to where they had come from. A further proof of this anti-Bengali bias was the widely believed circumstance that no serious attempt had been made at the time of Partition to retain the district of Sylhet within the boundaries of Assam. The population of the district, which geographically and ethnically fell in Bengal, was fairly evenly divided between Hindus and Muslims. Only the tehsil of Karimganj, now a district, was allotted to Assam. The Sylhet Hindus were known for their ability and acumen and they had dominated the public services and professions in Assam. They were now cut off from India and their talents lost to the country.

The Congress politicians of Assam, disregarding the province's vulnerable situation, had been playing a reckless game of politics, alienating different sections of the population for their own aggrandisement. Unless they were made to view the situation from a wider national perspective and temper their actions accordingly, the problems besetting the province would keep recurring with increasing virulence. The sturdy tribal people had no respect for the weak and narrow-minded Congress government which was unable to maintain even a semblance of order. The tribal belt had been directly administered through the North-East Frontier Agency (NEFA) by a central government officer—generally young and energetic—who mixed freely with the tribal people and won their confidence by attending to their needs and grievances. The Governor had a direct responsibility for the area, but the system which had kept the tribes pacified, was beginning to falter.

The position of the Muslim population was particularly complex. They were almost entirely rural, working as tenants on lands belonging to absentee landowners, many of whom were Congress politicians. In addition to the indigenous Muslims, there was a steady and practically unchecked infiltration from across the border of poor Muslims in search of land. The valley still had surplus land awaiting the plough, and the landowners welcomed the new arrivals who were only too grateful to find work even for a pittance. They were reputed to be excellent cultivators, who were prepared to take up the most back-breaking and unrewarding labour such as working waist-deep in the flood waters of the Brahmaputra or on 'char' lands, planting rice or jute seedlings. The Muslims were at the bottom of the economic and social scale and constituted an unfailing source of votes for their landlords.

In my reports to the Centre, I emphasised the fact that the Assam situation had many ramifications. It was a political problem with heavy ethnic overtones, and both had cast their shadow on the administration. There was, in addition, an economic aspect as well. The monopoly of power by the valley Hindus had alienated the other two groups and the fear of being outclassed by Hindu Bengalis had led not only to the unattended refugees problem but also to the weakening of the administration. The unhindered and perhaps welcome influx of the East Pakistani Muslims had infuriated the tribesmen, which in turn led to killings and destruction.

To stem the administrative collapse, I urged that a firm and efficient Chief Secretary, assisted by a handful of capable officers, be deputed by the Centre to take charge of the government machinery and activate it from top to bottom and give it tone and direction. The Assamee ministers would hesitate to defy the advice of officers deputed by the Centre or to hamper their activities. At the same time, firm political action by the Congress High Command was essential to bring the errant provincial leaders in line, for unless they were disciplined, other corrective measures would be difficult.

Soon, the Sardar had flown down to Calcutta, summoned the Chief Minister and the Finance Minister to meet him there and he took them firmly to task.

I felt that I had done what I could and it was now time to close the chapter and return to resume my interrupted holiday. In my closing report I could not refrain from saying that 'Assam is eloquently represented by its state symbol—the rhinoceros—an animal noted for its short-sightedness, the thickness of its hide and its incapacity for survival unless artificially protected.'

On my return to New Delhi, I learned with alarm that the Prime Minister had been passing on copies of my confidential reports to the Assam government! No wonder that the attitudes of the ministers towards me remained less than cordial, and that they were glad to see the last of me. My administrative proposals had been accepted by the Home Ministry, especially regarding the deputation of a Chief Secretary. To my horror, I learnt that their choice had fallen on me, which, considering the fact that my outspoken opinions about the ministers had been communicated to them, would have been a hazardous enterprise. Fortunately, the Prime Minister turned down the proposal.

Looking back over the years, it is saddening to think that the problems of Assam are no better than they were forty-seven years ago. In some respects they are worse. Refugees and infiltrators continue to enter the state and the clamour for their expulsion has assumed all-India dimensions. The Bodo insurgency raging in upper Assam has required from time to time the intervention of the Army. The aims of this movement seem to be to expel not only infiltrators but even all non-Assamese from Assam. Kidnappings of senior executives of the tea industry (the biggest industry in Assam) for ransom have almost become routine. The burning and looting of villages and the massacre of the fleeing inhabitants have become all too frequent. The political situation, which the Congress government at the Centre by its interference and manoeuvring has frequently exacerbated, has been highly unstable. The carving out of miniature hill states has hardly contributed to the contentment and progress of their inhabitants. There is a general sense of grievance against Delhi, a sense of neglect and a feeling that the oil, tea and natural resources of the region are being exploited for the benefit of others. Only the rigorous pursuit of a well-planned overall policy for the development of the area's considerable resources, in which the people themselves are closely involved, would help to stem the tide of disaffection. An Assamese government, freely and fairly elected and enjoying the confidence of all sections of the people, could lead them to more constructive activity.

On vacation in Naini Tal, I enquired from the Foreign Secretary, K.P.S.Menon, about my next posting and I was told that it was to be at headquarters. Shortly after, in reply to my acknowledgement, the Foreign Secretary informed me that I was instead to go to New York as Consul-General. While we were conditioning ourselves to the prospect, came another missive to say that I would be required in the Ministry at headquarters after all!

I duly reported to the Foreign Secretary on the date of the expiry of my leave. He seemed surprised and not a little embarrassed to see me as no decision had apparently been taken about my duties. I was later told to take over as Joint Secretary (West) to deal with Europe, the Americas and the United Nations. When I went over to my colleague, Y.D. Gundevia, to take over from him, he exploded at his sudden dislodgement. Gundevia had an irascible manner and a droll sense of wit which often found vivid expression in his official notes. When he had calmed down, he went to see Menon in protest. He had evidently had another explosion when Menon told him that he would take my place at our Moscow Embassy, not a pleasing prospect at the beginning of a long and dreary Russian winter.

After a few weeks, another colleague, Khub Chand, turned up to report at the Ministry prior to his departure for Pakistan as Deputy High Commissioner. The Foreign Secretary asked him to defer his plans for Karachi as he had other plans for him. It transpired that he would be taking my place in the Ministry, although I was told nothing about it. To my embarrassment and some dislocation in my work, Khub Chand occupied part of my room and began dictating long personal letters to my secretary informing all and sundry of his new appointment.

Meanwhile, another drama was being enacted. Ex-Colonel Inder Chopra, who had been Chief of Protocol, on the expiry of his term, got the Foreign Secretary to agree to post him as Political Officer to Gangtok, a rather coveted post which covered Sikkim, Bhutan and Tibet. Chopra had the letter of credentials signed by the President and, to clinch matters, had an announcement made by All India Radio. My brother, Harishwar, who had been the first Private Secretary to the Prime Minister in his capacity as Foreign Minister, had been posted to Gangtok less than a year before, succeeding the last British Political Officer, Sir Hugh Richardson. He happened to be dining with the Maharaja (as he was then called) when they together heard the radio broadcast of the announcement. Harishwar carried little credence with the Maharaja when he tried to assure him that that was also the first he was hearing about the matter. Harishwar naturally sent a strong protest to the Ministry at this peremptory decision, especially when he was in the midst of the delicate business of negotiating new treaties with the durbars of Sikkim and Bhutan. At this stage the Prime Minister intervened and forthwith rescinded the transfer orders. Harishwar stayed on to complete the treaties to the satisfaction of the two durbars and of New Delhi, and also to pay a six-month visit to Lhasa with a large entourage to attend the installation of the Dalai Lama.

Soon after, Chopra arrived from Kashmir where he had equipped himself with heavy tweeds, woollens, mountaineering gear, alpenstocks, etc. in preparation for trekking in the mountains of Sikkim and Bhutan. The news of a change in plans came as a shock to him and he especially regretted the waste of his mountaineering equipment. A few days later, he entered my room to announce that he was now to take over from me. This came as another surprise to me and also to Khub Chand who was greatly agitated. There followed a long squabble between the two aspirants, which remained unresolved until my own future was decided.

The Secretary-General, Sir Girija Shankar Bajpai, told me that it had been decided to send me to New York as Deputy Chief of Mission to assist our Permanent Representative to the United Nations, as our mission there was weakly staffed with only one First Secretary. I was to see the Prime Minister to get fuller instructions and I would be accompanied for public relations work by B.L. Sharma, the Principal Information Officer. Recalling the warning that Harishwar had given about avoiding at all costs any involvement in delegation work because of the propensity of Indian delegates to squabble and work at cross-purposes, and also to eschew anything to do with Indo-Pakistan affairs which were a bottomless pit, I expressed some misgivings. But Bajpai advised me not to refuse, as the post was one 'of great opportunity'. The confusion in regard to the occupancy of the chair which I was about to vacate was resolved by Chopra getting the better of Khub Chand who was sent packing to Karachi, his original place of posting.

*SEVEN*

# The Disunited Nations

The United Nations was yet in its infancy in the September of 1950 when its Fifth Session took place. After the bitter suffering of World War II, mankind yearned for peace and security. The United Nations was the Parliament of the world where nations, large and small, could meet together in sovereign equality to concert measures to establish justice and respect for the human person and the promotion of social and economic progress of all mankind. The small and weak and newly-independent countries looked upon the United Nations as their shield and protector, while those not yet free, looked up to it as their emancipator.

Before leaving Delhi, along with Principal Information Officer of the Government of India (who was accompanying the delegation for the duration of the session), I met Pandit Nehru, who pointed out that the Kashmir question would soon be coming up in the Security Council but, our Delegation there was weak and needed strengthening. The Pakistan delegation led by Zafrullah Khan was already in New York and very active. After a pause he added that our Permanent Representative, Benegal

Narsingh Rau, was a sick man and was unduly influenced by his brother, Shiva Rau, who was, in turn, much influenced by his Austrian wife. With that, the interview ended, leaving us wondering what the significance of the personal references was. But ours was not to reason why.

Our flight from Delhi to New York had taken the best part of two days, the flight to London with half a dozen stops en-route, being followed after an interval by a twelve-hour flight to New York.

Arriving in New York, we were housed, along with the rest of the delegation, in Essex House, an enormous high-class hotel on Central Park South. The leader of the delegation lived in a small but elegant penthouse apartment within walking distance on Fifth Avenue and 63rd Street, while New India House, the sumptuous office of the delegation, lay next door on 64th Street. There was a daily morning meeting in Sir B.N. Rau's apartment when the day's agenda would be discussed, then a quick visit to the office to collect papers and telegrams to supplement those already delivered early that morning, followed by a forty-minute drive to Lake Success on Long Island. Meetings of the Security Council or the various Committees began at 10.30 a.m., and gave over well after 6 p.m. We would then drive back in the dark straight to the office, where cables and reports would be prepared and dispatched to New Delhi. Each day was long and tiring, the work and surroundings unfamiliar and members of the delegation were comparative strangers to each other.

By a strange irony, the United Nations, which was dedicated to the cause of peace, was then housed in Lake Success in a building built for war production. Half the building was still occupied by the Sperry Company that produced war-plane parts. The General Assembly, which needed a large area, was accommodated in a skating rink at Flushing Meadow where, presumably, delegates would be able to skate on thin ice to their heart's content.

The Indian delegation was a formidable one, brimming with prima donnas. There was the Maharaja Jam Sahib of Nawanagar, of enormous girth and *savoir-faire*, who habitually wore bejewelled buttons on his Jodhpur jacket. He had rented a duplex apartment on Park Avenue and was served by a couple of his own retainers supplemented by sundry local staff, and moved around in his chauffeured Lincoln limousine. He entertained, as was appropriate, in princely style, and was immensely popular in UN circles and especially with the ladies. He had been elected Chairman of the Fifth or Administrative and Budgetary Committee whose meetings he conducted in true princely fashion, invoking the sporting spirit of members when the discussion became particularly heated or a tricky legal or procedural problem arose.

Then there were two Ministers of State, Kelkar from Information and Broadcasting and Lakshmi Menon from External Affairs. The former was obsessed with protocol and thought he had been downgraded by not being named leader of the delegation. Nobody treated him seriously, however, and he was distinctly unpopular. Lakshmi Menon we had known well from Lucknow where she had been active in the women's movement and where her husband was a professor at the University. She functioned in the Third or Social and Cultural Committee of which she was a very active member, especially in regard to matters concerning women's rights and status. She was naturally very popular with women's organisations, but occasionally, because of an excess of zeal, she would nettle other delegates, especially from the more conservative Arab countries. Once she created a diplomatic incident when, in responding to the claim of the Saudi Arabian delegate that women in his country enjoyed equal rights with men, she expressed full agreement since men in that country also enjoyed no rights at all. Shiva Rau was the star of the Fourth or Trusteeship Committee, an acknowledged champion of non-self-governing territories and a fervent anti-colonialist. Nawab Ali Yawar Jung, formerly a minister of the Nizam of Hyderabad, looked after the Second or Economic and Financial Committee. As a former Hyderabadi courtier, he was suave, discreet and polished and performed competently in his committee. Later, R. Venkataraman (who became President of India) attended many UN sessions and also served on the Administrative Tribunal. Another new entrant was Gopal Swarup Pathak, a prosperous lawyer and Member of Parliament who later became Vice-President of India. Two or three officials came from Delhi to assist the delegation, but there were no miscellaneous MP's or party hacks out on a jaunt. Presiding over it all was the gentle and self-effacing Sir B.N. Rau.

Sharma and I were at first completely at sea about the items under discussion and, indeed, with UN jargon, and it took time and study to catch up with things. The leader of the delegation, Sir B.N. Rau, under whom we were to work, received us with cold formality but gave us no instructions and assigned us no work. The delegation staff comprised just one First Secretary, an over-age entrant of unknown antecedents and pedestrian ability, but he enjoyed the confidence of the leader. There was a small Indian Office staff consisting of a Research Assistant, a couple of clerks and a stenographer or two and a Cypher Superintendent. The rest of the staff were American, including my secretary. Some Indian students had been taken on board for the duration as messengers. For transport, it was the practice to purchase three or four Chevrolet cars and to sell them at the end of the session; there was a good deal of bickering in the delegation about their use.

In the Security Council a fierce debate was raging over the question of Korea. The problem had its genesis in the surrender of the occupying Japanese army to the Soviets north of the 38th parallel and to the United States in the south. Under the Moscow Agreement a joint commission had been established to set a provisional democratic government, but the commission was soon deadlocked. The United States thereupon referred the matter to the United Nations. The General Assembly created a nine-member UN Commission on Korea charged with conducting elections throughout the country and setting up a unified democratic government. But while the South was able to hold elections and to constitute a government, access was denied by the North to the UN Commission. The North set up its own government, and thus Korea was partitioned into two ideologically antagonistic entities, a condition which persists to this day. The UN Commission reported the withdrawal of US forces from the South but could not verify the reputed withdrawal of Soviet forces from the North.

In June 1950, the UN Commission on Korea, whose Chairman was K.P.S. Menon, reported to the Secretary-General that North Korean forces had invaded the South and attacked all along the 38th parallel. The Security Council met forthwith and determined by a majority vote that the North had committed a breach of the peace and demanded the immediate cessation of hostilities and withdrawal of the invading forces. However, no heed was paid to the call; thereupon the United States introduced a resolution asking members to furnish necessary assistance to repel the attack, which was passed, India voting for it. The Soviet Union had rather unwisely been boycotting the Council since January in protest against the continued occupancy of China's permanent seat by the representative of the ousted Kuomintang. India's response to the call for assistance was to provide an ambulance team. The Soviet Union in the General Assembly denounced the resolution as illegal as it had been adopted in the absence of two permanent members, viz., the Soviet Union and the rightful government of the People's Republic of China. Instead, it charged the South with having committed aggression against the North. On the same day the United States announced that it had ordered a naval blockade of the North and the deployment of US troops in aid of the beleaguered South Korean army.

The United States followed with yet another resolution in the Council calling upon member states to place their forces under a Unified Command set up by it, of which General MacArthur had been designated the Commanding General. As the United States appeared to be trying to draw members states deeper into the conflict with one resolution following another in rapid succession, there were serious misgivings among many delegations about the wisdom of thus intensifying the conflict.

The Indian delegation found itself in a difficult position as it was under double pressure. At the United Nations there was intense lobbying by the American delegation for support; they argued that the fact of aggression having been acknowledged by India's positive vote in the Council, it would be only logical to take follow-up action. But New Delhi seemed to be regretting in retrospect the delegation's acknowledgement of the invasion in the first instance, although it could hardly have repudiated the findings of the UN Commission chaired by its own K.P.S. Menon, an eminent and highly esteemed diplomat. The exchange of telegrams between the Ministry and the delegation became increasingly acrimonious and contentious, much to the distress of Sir B.N. Rau.

Because of the return after over six months' boycott of the Security Council by the Soviet representative, Jakob Malik, the sword of a Soviet veto could now frustrate further American moves. To circumvent the Council's jurisdiction a resolution had been passed entitled 'Uniting for Peace' which empowered the General Assembly to take up a matter involving peace and security should the Council be deadlocked by exercise of the veto. The American Secretary of State, Dean Acheson, frequently led his delegation to give added weight to the American presence. His oratory was counterbalanced by the vitriolic tongue of Vyshinsky, Vice-Foreign Minister of the Soviet Union.

With the pouring in of American reinforcements in Korea, marginally supported by contingents from some other countries, the Northern forces which had succeeded in overrunning the whole peninsula down to its very tip were pushed back. Soon they were forced to withdraw behind the 38th parallel. The further military intentions of the swashbuckling and arrogant General MacArthur were unclear. Sir B.N. Rau pleaded that the forces operating under the UN flag should not, by transgressing the 38th parallel, themselves do what they had intervened to repel. The Americans and their allies, as well as the Military Command, were, however, in no mood to listen to the voice of moderation. In the euphoria of what appeared to be a glorious victory, MacArthur continued to advance deep into the North. The Chinese then began making warning noises against any approach towards their border, but these were ignored. MacArthur, highly elated with his successes, confidently proclaimed that 'the boys would be back home by Christmas'.

The Indian Ambassador in Peking, Sardar K.M. Panikkar, reported that the Chinese government had informed him that they could not stand idly by if the Americans advanced to the Yalu river, their border with Korea. They had important hydro-electric and other industrial installations in the area for whose safety they feared. Sir B.N. Rau communicated these ominous messages to the American and British delegations, but they only scoffed at them, Sardar Panikkar being dubbed 'Sardar Panicky'. *Time* magazine even came out with Panikkar's portrait on its cover under the caption 'The Red Face of Nehru'. All that Sir B.N. Rau's urgings did was to reinforce the western charge that India was a communist sympathiser. Even repeated warnings sent directly by Premier Chou-en-Lai through Panikkar were dismissed and MacArthur continued his reckless advance right up to the Yalu.

Then the Chinese avalanche struck and, with devastating force, swept all before it. With the sudden reversal in the fortunes of war, the euphoric mood among the Americans and their allies turned with equal abruptness into one of alarm and panic. There followed much scurrying to and fro in search of a means to bring about a ceasefire. The Americans and British and four other delegations tabled a resolution appealing for a ceasefire, the withdrawal of all forces on both sides of the 38th parallel, an assurance that the interests of China and North Korea would be fully respected and inviting the Chinese to participate in meetings of the Council. The resolution was promptly vetoed by the Soviet Union, while China rejected the invitation outright. The problem now was how to establish some means of contact with the Chinese since American policy continued to exclude the Peoples' Republic of China from the United Nations. India's views were no longer taken lightly and Sir B.N. Rau's advice came to be much sought after. A slight opening seemed to present itself when the Peking government made a complaint to the Security Council charging the United States with aggression against it by invading Formosa (as Taiwan was then known). A Chinese delegation led by General Wu Hsiu-Chuan arrived in New York to prosecute China's case.

Meanwhile, the military situation was worsening by the hour from the American viewpoint as the Chinese flood swept down irresistibly. President Truman now abruptly sacked the errant and headstrong General MacArthur who had landed the United States in such a desperate situation. The General Assembly, for its part, appointed a three-member Ceasefire Committee charged with exploring every means of putting a stop to the bloodshed. Known as the 'Three Wise Men' it comprised Nasrollah Entezam, President of the General Assembly, a suave and respected Iranian statesman; Lester Pearson, Foreign Minister of Canada, who enjoyed enormous esteem internationally; and Sir B.N. Rau, greatly respected for his wisdom and devotion to the cause of peace. But despite their best efforts, Peking was not prepared even to recognize them.

At this point US Ambassador Ernest Gross, and British

Ambassador Sir Gladwyn Jebb called on Sir B.N. Rau in his apartment. They pleaded with him that, as a leading Asian country with close relations with Peking, an appeal by India along with other Asian countries to Peking for a ceasefire would surely be heeded. Sir B.N. Rau, anxious to leave nothing undone to stop the bloodshed, agreed. I thereupon telephoned the heads of the Asian delegations with an invitation to attend a meeting at Sir B.N. Rau's apartment. Some ten heads of delegations responded and a carefully drafted appeal was drawn up and duly cabled through the United Nations to Peking, a copy being also presented to General Wu.

When Sir B.N. Rau, accompanied by me, called on General Wu in his sumptuous suite in the Waldorf Astoria, we were received most courteously. To the joint Asian appeal, Sir B.N. Rau added his own. He explained that the situation now greatly favoured Peking in regard to all pending issues, including admission to the United Nations and diplomatic recognition by the United States, and urged that at the coming meeting of the Security Council on China's complaint against the United States, he should exercise moderation. General Wu was all smiles, but made no commitment. When the Council met, General Wu's speech, made in a sharp staccato tone and replete with invective and vituperation, was extremely bellicose and uncompromising. We were dismayed to see that it was read out from a printed booklet in Chinese. General Wu was clearly not a free agent.

About this time information of sinister portent came to light. The British Prime Minister, Clement Attlee, sent word to Sir B.N. Rau to meet him when he made a brief stopover at the New York airport on his way to Washington. On his return from the interview at which some other Commonwealth heads of delegation were also present, Sir B.N. Rau recounted with a sense of deep shock and alarm what Attlee had to impart. The British government, it appeared, had got wind of some information that President Truman had been contemplating the use of atomic weapons in Korea, evidently with his experience of Hiroshima and Nagasaki in mind. Attlee's mission was to use the strongest possible dissuasion against any such abhorrent step which would have disastrous world-wide consequences. One has to be infinitely grateful that he succeeded in his mission of sanity and mercy.

Meanwhile, the Chinese delegation remained practically incommunicado to all but a very select few. General Wu invited some members of the Indian delegation to dinner at his hotel, but while there was considerable bonhomie, not a word about the serious issues at stake was uttered by him or his guests to spoil the ambience of the evening.

As the war took its relentless course there was increasing impatience about Peking's reply to the Asian appeal and we were constantly button-holed by the Americans and British about word from Peking either directly or through the no longer discredited Panikkar, or New Delhi. But General Wu, without awaiting further developments even on China's own complaint, was determined to return home, so Sir B.N. Rau and I went to pay him a farewell visit. When we reminded him about a reply and urged that delay was daily costing a heavy toll of lives, he replied: 'You will see what you will see.' We came away wondering what that laconic reply meant in Chinese since it made little sense in English. Needless to say, it provided cold comfort to our anxious western friends and much disappointment to us.

Various ideas were then floated, especially by India, for a ceasefire, which involved concessions on the question of China's representation at the United Nations and the problem of Formosa, but they were unacceptable to the United States even as a basis for negotiation. The war, however, was now stalemated along the 38th parallel.

Finally, one year after hostilities began, the North's willingness at last to discuss a ceasefire was declared indirectly through a remark make by the Soviet representative at a press conference. The talks eventually began aboard a hospital ship but they dragged on for two long years.

There was a dramatic interlude from preoccupation with Korea when the question of the nationalisation of the Anglo-Iranian Oil Company came up before the Security Council as a matter threatening international peace and security. It was announced that the new Prime Minister of Iran would himself appear to represent his country. A powerful popular movement had gripped Iran which compelled the Shah to reform the archaic land system and power structure. The leader of the ferment, Dr Mossadeq, was appointed as head of government to replace the old royalist and feudal oligarchies. Mossadeq, on arrival, requested Sir B. N. Rau, the then President of the Council, to meet him at his hotel, when he demanded a postponement of the date of the meeting. When Sir B.N. Rau said it would be difficult, Mossadeq threatened that he would go into hospital to compel an adjournment! When the Council, conceding the visitor's demand, eventually met on the appointed day, there was a stir of expectation. To the whirring of television cameras, Mossadeq staggered in, propped up on one side by his Ambassador, Nasrollah Entezam, and on the other by Secretary-General Trygve Lie. The British delegation gnashed its teeth in anger at their opponent's dramatic entry which would invite widespread sympathy for the frail and stricken old man. Unshaven and tie-less, Mossadeq began his speech in a trembling voice to plead that he had been compelled to arise from a bed of sickness to travel all the way to New York to defend the honour and protect the interests of his weak and impoverished country from the rapacity and oppression of an imperial power. Then, breaking down with emotion, he craved permission for his Ambassador to read out his speech. By his performance, Mossadeq had won much sympathy for Iran's case and the British reply only served to confirm his accusations. Sir B.N. Rau, who had been a distinguished judge, was unused to the wiles of politicians and was most amused and wonder-struck at Mossadeq's unusual tactics.

The Sixth Session of the General Assembly was held in Paris on the bizarre notion that, as the American Presidential election was due in November, it would be inadvisable for the UN Assembly to be in session in New York at the same time. The Palais de Chaillot was ingeniously and expensively converted with extensive scaffolding and partitioning to accommodate the General Assembly and the various councils and committees. All the delegations, with supporting staffs and even transport, moved at great expense to Paris for the session. Our Ambassador in Paris, Sardar Hardit Singh Malik, a very senior and distinguished member of the ICS, a reputed golfer and a popular figure in Paris, had arranged accommodation for our delegation and its offices. His choice had fallen on the Hotel Palais d'Orsay on the left bank of the river Seine. It was an old structure built over an underground railway station, with creaky floors and draughty corridors and there was the constant rumble of trains below. The American secretaries promptly named the corridor 'Pneumonia Alley'. What with the fluff flying around the Palais de Chaillot, the draughty and cold corridors and rooms of the hotel, and the damp chill from the river, half the delegation began suffering from chronic throat ailments and fevers which took weeks to shake off. There was much grumbling in the delegation about the choice of hotel and members began seeking other accommodation. We too later shifted to Claridges on the Champs Elysées, then not at all cluttered with parked vehicles or gawking tourists. Paris, in 1951, still suffering from the ignominy of defeat in the war, had a depressed and run-down appearance.

The General Assembly plodded on with its ponderous agenda and the various committees got into slow motion. The US delegation was now led by the gracious and earnest Eleanor Roosevelt, who was particularly active in the Human Rights Commission of which I was a member at the time.

Sir B.N. Rau had set his heart on becoming a judge of the International Court of Justice, a post for which he had the right aptitude and temperament, and which would have provided an escape both from the rough-and-tumble of United Nations work as well as the hectoring of the Ministry. A vacancy had arisen in the Court which would be filled on the basis of simultaneous voting in both the Security Council and General Assembly. It was confidently expected that Sir B.N. Rau, with his great reputation, would be elected unopposed. For the election I took India's chair at the Council table. After some preliminaries, the name of a Latin American candidate was suddenly proposed by a Latin member. Taken aback, I tried hard to play for time by raising one procedural objection after another. Eventually, I pressed for and obtained half an hour's adjournment for private consultations among the members. However, we could not persuade the Latin caucus to withdraw despite the breach of the convention of fair geographical representation and the presence already of a Latin American on the Court's bench. Meanwhile, Sir B.N. Rau, obviously very worried, had hurried over from his hotel. My hope was that the General Assembly, which was at that moment engaged in voting, would decide in favour of Sir B.N. Rau. When, to our delight, news came that the Assembly had in fact so decided, we quietly passed the word around to all the Council members. That clinched the issue, as there would have been a deadlock had the Council taken a contrary decision. Sir B.N. Rau, delighted, lost no time in assuming his new functions.

With his departure, the delegation was left orphaned and rudderless. The gentlest and most modest of men, he carried in his frail body an indomitable spirit; for clarity of thought and incisiveness of expression, he had few equals. He shunned fame and publicity, but fame sought him out. His very quietude inspired attention and respect. His leadership of the delegation was effortless and unquestioned. He was known as the saint of the United Nations and in his aura the whole delegation was described by Alastair Cooke in the London *Times* as messengers of peace casting sweetness and light around.

After an initial period of reserve, Sir B.N. Rau bestowed his confidence on me, which seemed almost boundless. I drafted and sent all the cables to the Prime Minister on his behalf even before he saw them and I accompanied him at all crucial meetings and interviews. He prepared his statements with meticulous care and discussed them word by word, changing a phrase here and a word there to ensure the right nuance. He believed that words should be soft and facts hard in order to carry the greatest conviction. His statement on Kashmir in the Security Council was so finely chiselled and the argument so devastating that in a forty-minute presentation he wiped our Sir Zafrullah Khan's highly polemical and laboured oration of over three hours. His interventions in the Council and Assembly, always brief and compelling, invariably received extensive coverage in the newspapers, along with his photograph. Once, two Latin American delegates approached him by common consent of their governments to arbitrate on a boundary dispute of long standing between them. With some reluctance he agreed in his personal capacity and his award was accepted by both sides without question, ending years of conflict, frequently accompanied by bloodshed.

Sir B.N. Rau served his country and the cause of peace with unflinching devotion and ability. He was an acknowledged constitutional expert who made a signal contribution by his erudition and drafting skill in the framing of the Indian Constitution. He was a hero of the early days of India's emergence on the world scene, but sadly he has not received due recognition by the nation which he served with such fidelity and distinction.

The General Assembly had convened late to allow the Government of France time for preparing the venue in Paris and it adjourned for ten days or so for Christmas and the New Year of 1952. Susheela and I went to Crans-sur-Sierre up in the snow-clad Swiss mountains to clear our lungs and breathe the fresh mountain air. We gave ourselves up to the joy which the high mountains can give and revelled in the exhileration of the sparkling environment, the toil and turmoil of the United Nations quite forgotten. Towards the end of December, I happened to pick up an old edition of a British newspaper and, turning idly over the pages, my eye caught a brief report in a middle page to the effect that Sir B.N. Rau, a known international figure, on his election to the World Court, was withdrawing from the Indian delegation and that his place as Permanent Representative would be taken by me. Our surprise was as great as our scepticism as we had received no word from the delegation office or from New Delhi. It was only on our return to Paris that we had confirmation of the report. I had certainly not expected that my first independent charge at the age of 42 would be to a major mission like the United Nations. I later learnt that the decision was the Prime Minister's, strongly backed by Sir B.N. Rau. But the appointment was apparently not favoured by senior officials in New Delhi—that became evident by the denial of the rank that went with the post. What national purpose was served by underplaying India's voice in the world forum one could not tell.

The delegation under the new leadership of Sardar H.S. Malik found it difficult to settle down. Malik's temperament was very different from that of his predecessor, and his blunt and somewhat abrasive manner created unnecessary tension and dissension in the delegation. Matters came to a head when he and the Secretary-General of the delegation, R.K. Nehru, India's Foreign Secretary, ceased even speaking to each other. The Permanent Representative whose job was to keep the wheels moving smoothly found himself faced with the unenviable task of trying to keep the peace between two key figures within the delegation.

The Kashmir question, like a noxious weed, had again flared up. A weighty delegation had arrived from India led by the

Attorney-General, Mr Chimanlal Setalvad, a lawyer of great eminence. It included Sir Girija Shankar Bajpai, the distinguished Secretary-General of the Ministry of External Affairs who had been a member of the Viceroy's Executive Council and whose ability and industry were phenomenal. A third member was Sheikh Mohammad Abdullah, Prime Minister of the state of Jammu and Kashmir, known as the 'Sher-i-Kashmir', a man of strong personality and strong convictions and prejudices. Two senior military officers had also arrived to assist the delegation; they were the gallant General K.S. Thimayya and the sharp-witted Brigadier (later Field Marshal) Sam Maneckshaw. Each of the three members had his preference of hotel: Sir Girija Shankar, a man of meticulous and expensive tastes, took up residence in a suite in the Ritz; Sheikh Abdullah and his brother-in-law, Harry Nedou in the Meurice, while Setalvad was in a third. This did not make for facility of physical communication even had there been a meeting of minds between them. Mr Setalvad unfortunately was laid low from the very moment of arrival with a painful and chronic back condition. The equation between Bajpai and Abdullah, it soon became apparent, could hardly have been worse. Since they would not even see or talk to each other it fell to me to shuttle from one to the other, to hear their diatribes and invectives against each other. A speech had to be prepared and Bajpai, a superb draftsman, set about the task. Early every morning he would summon me to his hotel where he would be fuming and fulminating against Abdullah. We would go carefully over the speech and he would ask me to show it to the Sheikh. The latter would flare up on seeing it, taking exception to every sentence and word. A redraft would meet with no less explosive an outburst. And so it went on until Bajpai decided to cable the whole speech in cypher to the Prime Minister whose approval promptly arrived, thus bypassing the Sheikh who was left gnashing his teeth in impotent rage. All this was not a very propitious beginning for the forthcoming gladiatorial contest.

We had been trying to persuade delegations, particularly that of the Soviet Union, to take an objective view of the matter. Many were under strong western pressure while the Soviet attitude had been to keep aloof, and to abstain in the voting. Even the growing evidence of Pakistan's accession to anti-Soviet military pacts did not seem to move them. About this time an item appeared in a British paper that Pakistan had leased an air base near Peshawar to the Americans; it was from this base that American spy planes would overfly Soviet air space. When the newspaper was shown to Ambassador Yakob Malik, he was greatly concerned and took a clipping of the item.

On the day of the Council meeting, Setalvad just about managed to pull himself out of bed with some help and to take his seat at the Council table. Bajpai had geared himself to read out the speech which he himself had written and was resentful about Setalvad now stealing the show. The British and American delegates had already assumed predetermined positions, and however cogent and pertinent India's case was, it could not change their closed minds. These bulldozing tactics, intended to give aid and comfort to Pakistan, unexpectedly failed in their purpose, however. The Soviet representative, much to the consternation of the western representatives, instead of the usual non-committal attitude of the past, made a strong statement indicating disagreement with the western position. After many whispered confabulations, an adjournment was asked for and obtained. Greatly sobered, the western representatives subsequently contented themselves with an anodyne statement by the President of the Council, the upshot being that the Kashmir question was to be referred to an impartial person for the exercise of good offices. Accordingly, Dr Frank Graham, a kindly old gentleman of a high academic background who had occupied a temporary vacancy as Senator from South Carolina, was appointed. The unfair pressure on India was henceforth staved off for years to come for fear of a Soviet veto. Our high-powered delegation, after all the internal bickering, departed for home, neither victorious nor vanquished.

Sir Zafrullah Khan was to represent Pakistan in the talks with Dr Graham; I suggested that New Delhi depute a senior politician or minister to face so formidable an opponent as a Foreign Minister. To my dismay, however, I was asked almost casually to deal with the matter. At the first meeting which took place in Paris, there were arrayed on the opposite side Zafrullah Khan, flanked by Ambassador A.S. Bokhari, the Pakistani Permanent Representative, followed by Lieut-General Khalid Sheikh from military headquarters and sundry political and military advisers in diminishing order of rank. I was assisted by my First Secretary; fortunately, I had managed to hold on to General Thimayya and Brigadier Sam Manekshaw to maintain some sort of balance, however, uneven. Dr Graham, a former Princeton Professor and a Quaker, was essentially a scholar, mild and trusting, and without the wiles of a politician. He began by reading out a homily on peace and good neighbourliness and all but refrained from calling upon both sides to settle their differences in true Christian spirit!

The main question at issue was the creation of the proper conditions for ascertaining the wishes of the people of the state. The essential condition was for the soil to be cleared of the invader and the restoration of normal conditions. U.S. Admiral Nimitz, a distinguished wartime leader, who had been designated as Plebiscite Administrator, had been cooling his heels in the corridors of the UN Secretariat. Zafrullah Khan made a harangue on the usual lines, insisting that conditions were quite normal in the area under Pakistani occupation and that no invaders or Pakistani military were there, only local elements for internal security purposes. Our line was that the Pakistan held area was in fact under the countrol of the Pakistani army units and the bloated so-called Azad Kashmir force was nothing but an offshoot of the regular army. Besides, normal conditions demanded a return of Pakistan-held territory to the Indian administration as an essential prerequisite. In reply, Zafrullah Khan argued that all Indian armed forces must simultaneously withdraw from the state's territory. This was countered by our assertion that India had the sovereign right to deploy its armed forces anywhere on its territory for the protection of its borders. The nature and numerical strength of the armed forces on Pakistan-held territory was repeatedly questioned, the phrase-coined by Bajpai, 'the quality and quantum', being freely bandied about by us.

Day after day the argument would go on, back and forth, with minor variations on the theme. Every evening Maneckshaw and I would prepare a new argument for the morrow to get the better of our opponents and to add to the bewilderment of the good Dr Graham. As General Thimayya was too blunt and outspoken for a situation which called for subtlety and dexterity, we asked him to keep silent, leaving the talking on military matters to his glib and ingenious junior. Manekshaw had the shrewdness and smoothness of a Parsi trader and could wriggle or wheedle his way out of any situation as occasion demanded. Dr Graham, quite confused by the arguments, had appointed a Colonel Deevers to assist him out of the thicket, but Deevers would himself often get lost in it. When Zafrullah tried a new tack, I would ask for time, much to his annoyance, on the plea that I would have to obtain instructions from New Delhi whereas he, as Foreign Minister, gave himself his own instructions. One day Zafrullah accosted me to ask if we were serious or were only playing games, and threatened: 'You know, we Pakistani Muslims would burn our own house in order to destroy our enemy's'. All that I could say was to ask him to refrain from doing any such desperate thing and to keep his own house in order. Not many years later, the Ahmediyas, Zafrullah Khan's community in Pakistan, were dubbed heretical and anathematised, forbidden from calling themselves Muslim and barred entry into mosques. There was bitter anti-Ahmaediya rioting with much loss of life and property. Members of the sect were debarred from holding public office. Zafrullah Khan had been elected to the International Court of Justice in the vacancy caused by the premature and sad demise of Sir B.N. Rau and found escape in the Hague.

In New York, Dr Graham found himself in a small room somewhere in the bowels of the vast UN skyscraper. Some more talks took place under his auspices with A.S. Bokhari on the other side, while I was left bereft without my two army friends. Bokhari, however, had other fish to fry and was rather lackadaisical about continuing the verbal skirmishing, and so Dr Graham's pathetic but well-meaning efforts petered out, no doubt to his great relief. I used to visit the old Professor in his den from time to time, a forlorn and lonely figure who would talk about a variety of things—notably not Kashmir—and would ask for books on Indian history, art and philosophy which I was glad to supply in generous measure. This would keep him happily occupied until my next visit with another armful of volumes. He remained at the UN for a goodly time, as did Admiral Nimitz as *functus officio*, then both quietly faded away.

The headquarters of the United Nations had shifted to the new but yet unfinished thirty-eight floor glass and steel skyscraper on Turtle Bay in the summer of 1951. The cement floors were still bare and the unwary were in constant danger of tripping over loose wires which lay in great profusion along the floors. Early committee meetings were held there to the accompaniment of much hammering and banging as assorted workmen carrying ladders and other paraphernalia of their respective trades scurried busily about the place. But it was a welcome relief from the long and dreary drives to Lake Success. The site of the UN building had been a very run-down part of town, a maze of slaughter-houses and slum dwellings on First Avenue and 48th Street. The land was acquired with a grant of eight and a half million dollars from the Rockefeller family, cleared and beautified by the City administration at a cost of some twenty-five million, and the building was constructed at a cost of some sixty-five million, on an interest free loan from the US government. Its location in the United States had been insisted upon by the Soviet Union to ensure US participation in the United Nations, unlike its abstention from the League of Nations, the brainchild of President Woodrow Wilson. Later, the Soviets and some others were to regret their choice because of the constant pressure on delegates by the American media and public and the general ambience of the place.

Indians in New York were still a rarity and on National Day we could hardly muster, incredible through it may seem today, three or four individuals besides members of the delegation and consulate and the evergreen J.J. Singh. J.J. as he was called, was an affluent version in New York of what Krishna Menon had been impecuniously in London. He too ran an 'India League' and had built up quite a clientele whom he entertained lavishly in his comfortable apartment. Indians, perhaps because of their scarcity value and the fame of the Mahatma and the peaceful nature of the freedom struggle, were rather popular and members of the delegation were socially much sought after. While blacks were nowhere to be seen in midtown New York and could not even enter shops, hotels or restaurants, in the matter of housing in some localities there was prejudice even against Jews, Indians seemed to be welcomed everywhere. When Susheela contacted a house-agent on the phone about an apartment, the unseen woman who was most obliging and seemed to have taken to Susheela simply because of her voice, said she had found a very suitable apartment in a 'reserved locality'. Having heard of racial prejudice in America, Susheela naturally assumed that it would be out of bounds for us, but the lady assured her that the restriction applied only to Jews, blacks of course being quite outside the pale. However, we took on temporary lease an apartment from Jewish friends. The house agent, disappointed, asked if there was anything else she could possibly do. When Susheela rather ingenuously asked for tickets for a popular musical, *South Pacific*, the woman said that was a difficult one, but some days later she miraculously produced two tickets for the show. We later learnt that seats had been booked in advance for months and tickets were selling at a heavy premium and even the ticket stubs carried a price! Among other non-white friends was Dr Max Yergan, an eminent black leader close to the U.S. Administration, who was married to a wealthy Jewish woman doctor and lived in upstate New York in a fine house on a beautiful garden estate whose week-end guests we sometimes were. I had asked Max over to a hotel for lunch on several occasions, but he declined each time. When I asked him why, he said to my amazement and distress that he would not have been allowed entry. Things began to change only with Dr Martin Luther King's advent and his mass awakening of the oppressed community; but official policy and laws notwithstanding, prejudice dies hard, especially in the South. Such aberrations apart, we found the American people warm and friendly, and all doors open to us, however high. The friendships made then and since have endured and ripened over the years and we greatly cherish and value them.

At the United Nations in New York—in the Palace of Peace—the atmosphere could hardly have been more charged with contention and controversy, the acrimony aroused by the Korean War not having abated a whit. An ugly controversy was raging over the position of the Secretary-General, Trygve Lie, which was paralysing the Secretariat. A hysterical witch-hunt for Communists which had been sweeping across the United States had now invaded the UN Secretariat; and Cold War manoeuvrings were shaking the very foundations of the organisation.

The first Secretary-General, Trygve Lie's initial five-year

term had ended in 1950 and he was re-elected for a further three years. But soon after, with the outbreak of the Korean War, he fell foul of the Soviets, because of what they regarded as his partisan and over-enthusiastic support of American military action against North Korea. Their animosity against Lie seemed to know no bounds; they studiously ignored him, referring to him as the person occupying the Secretary-General's chair, and lost no opportunity of slighting him. Lie found his position becoming increasingly untenable, while the effect on the Secretariat was devastating. A tussle developed over the issue between the gladiators of the Cold War. Names of possible successors to Lie were proposed and promptly shot down by one side or the other. Compromise proposals failed to take off. Among the names that came up were those of Lester Pearson of Canada, Nasrollah Entezam of Iran, Padilla Nervo (Foreign Minister of Mexico), and Sir B.N. Rau, but none could command acceptance. Even Mrs Vijayalakshmi Pandit's name was heard but not taken seriously, with the Pakistani Representative who had now replaced India on the Security Council, going about saying 'The Lady's Not for Burning'.

In the midst of the stalemate, a surprise was sprung by the French representative, Ambassador Hoppenot, who circulated a proposal for the appointment of an unknown Mr Hammarskjold to the post of Secretary-General. The biographical data sent around indicated that the said gentleman was in his eighties. When I telephoned Mr Hoppenot to enquire if the proposal was serious, he replied with some embarrassment that the bio data sent in error was that of a former Prime Minister of Sweden who happened to be the candidate's father! Dag Hammarskjold was then a Vice Minister in the Swedish government who at European Economic conferences had favourably impressed the French but was otherwise little known, while his father had been eminent in the public life of his country. When the Security Council again wearily took up the long-deadlocked issue, no objection could be raised for the reason that none knew the candidate, and from sheer ennui let the nomination pass. The unusual appointment came as a complete surprise to all the delegations, not least to the designated incumbent himself!

Dag Hammarkjold was lean and youthful in appearance, unlike his portly predecessor, brisk and courteous in manner, sharp in intellect and independent in action. At what was intended by me as a mere courtesy call, the new Secretary-General sought an exchange of views on the numerous internal and external problems besetting the organization. With Trygve Lie, my vists lasted only a few minutes as he seemed to have time only for the big powers. I used to receive telephone calls from Hammarskjold himself: 'If you are around this building at about, say, 3 p.m. could you please drop by as there is something interesting to discuss?' To this polite summons the response would be immediate and the problems for discussion turned out to be related to matters such as Secretariat reorganisation, the Palestine situation, the Indo-China situation, disarmament questions and so on; nothing was raised about matters of purely Indian concern. The only negotiation with the Secretary-General on a problem affecting India was concerning a demand by New Delhi that, following the adherence of Pakistan to American-sponsored anti-Soviet military pacts, American military observers in Kashmir must be withdrawn as they could no longer be regarded as impartial. This view was refuted by Hammarskjold on the principle that those serving under the UN flag were bound only by Charter principles and not by their national policies; besides, the Secretary-General alone had the right to hire and fire UN employees. Changing the argument, I said that from a practical point of view the observers would not be able to function if denied the necessary facilities by the host government. After a few days of reflection Hammarskjold found a solution: the terms of the American observers would not be renewed and they would all be withdrawn successively within two or three months. This solution our Prime Minister accepted and a confrontation both with the Secretary-General and the United States was avoided.

The frenzied anti-Communist drive led by the rabid Senator Joseph McCarthy who was searching for 'a red under every bed' (as the saying went) was knocking at the portals of the United Nations itself. Trygve Lie had succumbed to the pressure by allowing the McCarthy inquisitors to investigate American members of the Secretariat and even to enter the international premises, breaching their inviolability, in search of incriminating material against them. Trygve Lie had sacked a number of American staff members who had chosen to exercise their constitutional right under the Fifth Amendment to decline answering questions of a self-incriminatory nature. An outstanding official who was the Secretary-General's principal legal adviser and had been seconded by the State Department, a man of unimpeachable credentials, Abraham Feller, was so humiliated and distressed by the grilling he received at the hands of the investigators, that he threw himself to his death from the UN building to the shock and horror of delegates and staff. Throughout the United States the inquisition pursued its merciless and unscrupulous course, ruining the lives and reputations of countless honourable and patriotic citizens. What amazed and alarmed one was that not a voice was raised either by the Eisenhower or Truman administrations or by any responsible public figure to denounce the McCarthy terror.

With a turbulent international situation and a fractured Secretariat, Dag Hammarskjold had succeeded to a *damnosa hereditas*. The morale of the staff was in a state of near collapse and even the day-to-day functioning of the Organisation was becoming difficult. He immediately set about restoring the broken fabric of the Secretariat, the very instrument without which he was powerless to function. With the support of most delegations he tactfully and firmly devised practical solutions for the various problems paralysing the Secretariat. His proposals on personnel policy received strong endorsement by the General Assembly; the independence and impartiality of the international staff was reaffirmed and the Secretary-General's right to employ and remove staff without outside interference was fully recognised. In the debates in the Assembly and committees, India gave the Secretary-General strong support, which he greatly valued.

The Sixth Session of the General Assembly saw a different constellation of delegates from India led by Mrs Vijayalakshmi Pandit. The most striking figure was Krishna Menon who had recently been stripped of the office of High Commissioner in London because of what was known as the 'Jeep Scandal'. A very welcome addition was R. Venkataraman, a very able and effective Minister of Industries from Madras. Ali Yawar Jung and Lakshmi Menon were also back again.

The Korean question was a dominant item on the agenda, but with a difference. Feelers had been received through indirect channels that the Chinese and North Koreans were prepared to discuss the terms of an armistice. The great stumbling block to an agreement now was the question of the exchange of prisoners of war. While China and North Korea demanded the repatriation of all prisoners regardless of their wishes, the United States insisted that they must be allowed free choice. Krishna Menon, who was in the Special Political Committee which was seized of this item, did a great deal of footwork among delegations and the burning of midnight oil to find a solution. He had a unique way of functioning as he played his cards very close to his chest, leaving the leader and the delegation totally in the dark about his activities. Although we had deputed a junior officer to assist him, he preferred to entrust his papers to a young Canadian research student. The only manner in which I could get wind of what was brewing was from the Canadian Foreign Minister, Lester Pearson. Pearson, who had become a good friend, would frequently ask me if what 'Krishna' was doing was in consultation with the mission's leader; he also asked if Menon could possibly be persuaded not to telephone him at two o'clock in the morning as it disturbed Mrs Pearson's sleep; besides, she had to serve him endless cups of tea when he showed up. Eventually, a resolution emerged and was tabled on behalf of India to the effect that the prisoners should be repatriated after ascertaining their wishes under the supervision of a Neutral Nations' Commission. It was shot down summarily by the Soviet representative, Vyshinsky, in a bitter attack, describing it as 'rotten'. The Soviet rejection provided the cue to the Americans, normally suspicious of anything emanating from Menon, to praise it to the skies, much to the latter's embarrassment.

Some months later, the Chinese seemed to have had a change of mind and heart and proposed that all prisoners who did not wish to be repatriated should be turned over to a neutral authority. This was in essence the Indian proposal dished up in somewhat different form. Earlier, the Chinese had tried to avoid the embarrassment of it being disclosed that the majority of prisoners did not want to return to China or North Korea. They now proposed the setting up of a Repatriation Commission of five 'neutral' nations which, though substantially similar to that suggested by India, they now usurped as their own. Be that as it may, the end of the Korean War was now well within sight. But another hiccup was yet to come. News arrived that thousands of prisoners of war held mostly in American-guarded camps had suddenly and simultaneously made good their escape. The Chinese were aroused to fury, and accused the Americans of engineering or conniving at this mass escape. Realising that trying to shut the stable door after the horse had fled would be a pointless exercise, the Chinese, with their North Korean partners, finally returned to sign the long-delayed armistice agreement.

India had been named Chairman of the Neutral Nations' Repatriation Commission and assumed custodial charge of the prisoners—some 22,000 held by the UN Command and 350 or so by the North. It was a most exacting and delicate task to sort out such a multitude of prisoners according to their preferences, but it was performed with exemplary tact and efficiency by General K.M. Thimayya and Brigadier (later General) Thorat, which won universal praise and the warm compliments of President Eisenhower.

Mrs Pandit's leadership endowed the Indian delegation with style and distinction. She was an arresting figure at the United Nations, graceful and elegant with her silver-grey hair and air of distinction. She bore herself well in committees and employed the commonsense with which she was richly gifted, to the best possible advantage. Her speeches were well delivered but crafted in a manner uniquely her own. The Prime Minister and Sir B.N. Rau prepared their own speeches as a matter of course. Mrs Pandit would be given a draft which she would quietly pass on to one person to review and then to another, after which she would make a few cosmetic changes before delivery, leaving the various contributors wondering where it all came from as they recognised a sentence here and there of their own authorship but little of the whole. This was also Indira Gandhi's way of doing things.

Mrs Pandit was not always punctilious about attending committee meetings, but it would not be difficult to find a delegate to read out her prepared speech, especially if it seemed likely to attract publicity at home. Occasionally, she would cancel a television interview or speaking engagement at short notice. Sometimes she would pass these engagements on to Susheela, who had a way with American audiences; but on one occasion at a television interview, instead of questions about India or the UN, Susheela was asked about Indian spices and cookery about which she knew little, but Mrs Pandit knew much. On another occasion, Mrs Pandit had accepted an invitation from the US Representative, Henry Cabot Lodge, to a speaking engagement in Boston before a distinguished audience, but at the last minute she wished to cancel it. When this was conveyed to Cabot Lodge he said: 'Please tell Mrs Pandit that there are also Brahmins in Boston.' Mrs Pandit got the message and kept the engagement.

When the next session of the General Assembly approached, the question of the Presidency came under informal discussion. I felt that it would be a crowning achievement to her distinguished association with the United Nations were Vijayalakshmi Pandit to be elected to adorn the Presidential chair. It would also be a tribute to Indian womanhood and, indeed, to women the world over; she would be the first woman to preside over the world body. When I mooted the proposal to New Delhi, the Prime Minister accepted it with the injunction that no canvassing should be done. Some footwork in matters of elections done in a dignified and restrained manner was necessary even then, unlike the blatant and tasteless canvassing that goes on now unashamedly on their own behalf by candidates themselves. In the result, other potential candidates were persuaded to stand down and Mrs Pandit was elected unopposed. It filled us with pride to see her grace the Presidential chair with such poise and dignity.

A word about the Permanent Mission. There was just one First Secretary and a research assistant on the staff. On being pressed for more staff the Ministry posted a young Second Secretary and another research assistant. With this skimpy staff we managed to look after the Economic and Social and Trusteeship Councils of which we were members, almost all the principal committees and bodies like the Disarmament Commission of Twelve, the Commission for The Relief and Rehabilitation of Korea, UNICEF, the Afro-Asian Group, liaison with the press, public speaking engagements, etc. I often felt like a conjuror keeping several balls in the air at the same time.

It was a matter of no small pride that India's voice was listened to with respect in the councils of the world and no decision was taken at the United Nations on any issue, big or small, without India being consulted by member states or the Secretary-General. India was still barely recovering from the grievous wounds of Partition and lacked both military and economic strength, yet it enjoyed a certain moral magistracy as the aura of the Mahatma still shone with undiminished radiance. Nehru's persuasive voice urging peace and conciliation articulated the Mahatma's noble teachings and was heard by the world with attention and respect.

The United Nations was conceived in order to promote and maintain world peace and develop friendly relations among the nations. Prime Minister Nehru, the architect of India's world view, an ardent crusader for peace, freedom and equality among nations, reflected the very aims and objectives of the United Nations. Peace, he insisted, was not only good in itself—but essential for mankind's progress and development. But those who strive for peace must speak in the accents of peace. Not only was the substance of importance, but equally the style as well. This accorded fully with Sir B.N. Rau's sentiments, style and temperament.

Mrs Pandit, too, earned wide respect as a messenger of peace. But with the advent of Krishna Menon, a certain stridency was imparted to India's voice. And in the delegation itself, a marked abrasiveness made its appearance.

Menon arrived in New York broken in body and spirit, having been recently demitted from his post in London. His protege, Arthur Lal, whom Menon's patronage had brought to the New York Consulate-General, came to plead with me to do something for Menon, who was not only out of a job but also physically shattered. Menon had been very kind to us when we were on our way to Moscow in 1948, so along with Ali Yawar Jung we hurried to see Menon in his hotel. There we found him slumped in a chair, moaning and groaning; to our anxious enquiries, he complained that he was stiff all over as he had been knocked down by a taxi in London the day before. We counselled a hot bath, but he said he could not move or undress, whereupon I proceeded to divest him of his upper garments and Ali his lower ones and shoes, and we then carried him and laid him in his bath. Meanwhile, I sent for a young officer from New India House to minister to Menon's needs thereafter. But we were not able to detect any abrasions or other physical signs of the accident. Next morning Menon, duly revived, appeared at the United Nations, limping slightly, with his famous walking stick which, however, he seemed to use more as a rudder to propel himself in any desired direction than as a means of support. But he had succeeded in attracting public attention to himself and sympathy for his physical condition. We could only marvel at the ingenuity which marked his entry into a new career, a dramatic example of consummate political adroitness.

It did not take long to discover that Menon was a solo performer; at delegation meetings he seemed to doze off and, when listening, would make caustic interjections without himself disclosing developments in his own Committee. His manner of functioning was rather secretive and in the opinion of the leader of the delegation and others almost conspiratorial. His propensity for cronyism among the permanent staff tended to undermine discipline and loyalty, although towards the head of the permanent mission his attitude was correct if not confiding. Mrs Pandit began to feel increasingly sidelined as the leader, and remained apprehensive about what Menon was up to both at the United Nations and outside.

An episode which could have undermined her prestige and acclaim as President of the General Assembly strengthened her antipathy towards Menon. On the opening day of the Assembly, I learnt to my dismay that Mrs Pandit would make some excuse to absent herself as she had been advised that Zafrullah Khan of Pakistan, the third speaker on the list, would make a highly insulting and derogatory speech in which he would severely criticise Nehru and attack India in vituperative terms. It would therefore be unseemly and embarrassing for her to sit through such a vicious tirade. I could hardly believe my ears and so rushed to the President's chamber behind the podium just as Mrs Pandit was preparing to leave on the excuse that she had a bad cold. When questioned, she disclosed that it was the Secretary-General himself who had advised her about Zafrullah Khan's intentions. I then burst into Hammarskjold's chamber next door and was shocked to learn that his informant was none other than Krishna Menon. Thereupon, staking my own reputation, I pleaded with Mrs Pandit to take the chair as I was confident that Zafrullah Khan would not do such an unchivalrous and contemptible thing, for it would only redound to his eternal shame. Reluctantly, Mrs Pandit agreed. I then rushed to take my place next to Menon in the Assembly hall when Mrs Pandit walked on to the podium to assume the chair. Menon, aghast, angrily demanded to know who had advised her to do so and, when told, showed extreme doubt and displeasure. Mrs Pandit made a most gracious appearance and, as she entered, the entire Assembly rose to it feet in a spontaneous burst of applause.

The first speaker was the representative of Indonesia who, in his faltering English, read out a long speech addressed exclusively to the President, praising her in fulsome language. The next speech was by a Latin American in an even more extravagant vein. Then came Sir Zafrullah Khan's turn and I waited with bated breath for him to begin. His half an hour's oration was a paean of praise of the 'great and gracious' lady who adorned the chair and honoured not only the United Nations but all of Asia. In most extravagant and glowing terms he lavished praise on Mrs Pandit's father and brother whom he called 'a great world statesman'. There was almost a surfeit of compliments. Most of the opening day's session was devoted to delegates speaking in praise of the President, but Zafrullah Khan's oration surpassed all the rest in effusiveness. I could not refrain from saying rather churlishly to Menon: 'I told you so'. The Secretary-General was too sensitive a man to fail to draw an appropriate conclusion from the sorry episode. In the delegation itself and in the mind of the leader, there was much puzzlement as to its motivation and what national purpose it was expected to serve.

Krishna Menon was without doubt very agile and inventive in devising intricate formulae for intractable problems. Although he enjoyed the Prime Minister's trust and confidence, he lost no opportunity of strengthening the latter's regard for him. An example of this occurred on the conclusion in July 1954 of the Nine-Power Geneva Conference on Indo-China which ended France's nine-year colonial war to regain its lost colony. The French army had been surrounded at Dienbienphu and, in desperation, the French government appealed to its western allies for help. Only the United States was inclined to do so, obsessed as it was with the fallacious 'domino theory' of John Foster Dulles which held that if one country in the region was to espouse Communism, it would have a multiplier effect over the greater part of South-east and South Asia. The American military even began talking about the use of atomic weapons. It was a very dangerous situation which Nehru's vigorous intercession with the parties concerned helped to mitigate. A conference was called at Geneva with the participation of the warring parties and the United States and United Kingdom, as well as the Soviet Union and China. India was not a participant, yet Krishna Menon, on his way to New York, turned up at Geneva as an unofficial observer and stayed on for the whole length of the long-drawn-out conference. He did a great deal of footwork between mutually hostile delegations—the French and British on one side and the Chinese and Soviets on the other. On arrival in New York after the conclusion of the conference he sent a cable to Anthony Eden, the British Foreign Secretary, in most effusive terms, lauding his wise statesmanship which led to the success of the conference, adding that if he had been of any assistance he would deem it a great privilege. Promptly came Eden's reply thanking Menon profusely for his invaluable contribution. Thereupon Menon, in a fawning message replied that Prime Minister Nehru would be pleased to hear from Eden in the matter. In return, Eden sent a commendatory message to Nehru with a copy to Menon. All these messages passed through the delegation office and left us amused and impressed by Menon's ingenuity.

Menon's interventions in committees, often the despair of the keeper of briefs from the Ministry, were prolix and involved and delivered extempore with much shuffling of papers and incomplete sentences. The United Nations is not a forum for the exercise of oratorical skills, as delegates represent states and are expected to make statements precisely on their government's position. Almost every delegate, including Foreign Ministers, but with the exception of some Latin Americans who spoke more to their political constituents at home, relied on written statements. Menon trended to stray into irrelevance and the verbatim record of his speeches had always to be extensively edited before going into print. He was often provocative and even overbearing in his speeches, which caused unnecessary offence to those at whom his barbs were aimed, especially the Americans who were his favourite target. It was a great change after Sir B.N. Rau, during whose tenure differences with the United States on issues of critical importance were real and serious, but not a word uttered by Rau caused umbrage to anyone and the delegation enjoyed universal respect for moderation and reasonableness. Now, there were few real differences on pending issues, yet India came to acquire a strong anti-Western and, especially, anti-American image and reputation. And this was at a time when we were sorely in need of food and financial aid from America. When I remonstrated with Menon for exceeding briefs, he would quieten down, but soon his eloquence would get the better of him. Incidentally, he was very indulgent towards the Indian correspondents so as to ensure a good press and coverage for himself in India.

Menon was a complex character, an inveterate bachelor who spent years of penurious living in London where, with no resources, he had set up an 'India League'. He had the eccentricities and prejudices of the Bloomsbury intellectuals with whom and with left-wing circles he consorted, and was scornful of opinions other than his own. As High Commissioner in London he continued to observe rather bohemian ways, contenting himself with occupying an anteroom in India House, denying himself the lush comforts of the sumptuous official residence on Kensington Palace Gardens. His diet was of a piece with his way of life as he seemed to live on tomato soup, toast and endless cups of sugared tea, but he was not averse to an occasional meal of rice and spicy dishes. Although he was often entertained in our apartment in New York, he was not known to offer hospitality to anyone. We used to exchange a good deal of friendly banter, sometimes barbed but seldom offensive. Those who stood up to him, he treated correctly; but the deferential or obsequious, he treated as doormats. This I witnessed when, on visiting him in his hotel, I found the Consul-General and another officer crawling around the floor on all fours; when asked what they were up to they said that Krishna was in the habit of throwing his shoes and socks around and they were searching for them under sofas and chairs!

As leader of the delegation to the General Assembly in place of Mrs Pandit, Menon became insufferable and very unpopular with the other delegates from India. I felt that it was time, after four years at the United Nations, for me to leave before my fairly good relations with Menon soured. When I asked for a move, the Foreign Secretary pressed me to continue, but I finally had my way. But I did not realise that my total association with the United Nations would, with some interruptions and in various capacities, continue until 1980, thirty years since my first appearance.

Between Hammarskjold and Menon there was hardly any rapport; they were of opposite temperaments and Menon, strongly anti-establishment, regarded the Secretary-General as just another civil servant and resented his authority.

Krishna Menon was always impeccably dressed in elegant London suits of superb cut stitched by a rather Dickensian character who looked more like a left-wing intellectual than a tailor. Once when my brother Harishwar and I converged on London, Menon kindly gave us an obscure London address and asked us to get our suits tailored there with a personal recommendation from him. With some difficulty we located the address somewhere in High Holborn, up a narrow, creaky staircase leading into a dingy little room littered with cloth clippings, samples and other evidence of the tailor's profession. A slim figure of Menon's age emerged from a cloud of cigarette smoke and exclaimed, 'Ah, I see that my friend Krishna has sent you; time was when I helped him; now he helps me'. Cloths of excellent quality were chosen from samples and measurements taken and a fitting was promised for the next day. Then, to our surprise, the tailor asked for an advance for the cloth and, when handed the money, he dashed out and returned triumphantly with the chosen suit length. The end result was superb, revealing the secret of Krishna's elegance. His friend did piecework for expensive Saville-Row tailors who charged three or four times as much from their customers. In India, when Menon affected a South Indian 'mundu' he looked strangely out of place, a misfit among the homespun crowd of politicians. Indeed, they spoke different languages in more senses than one—the inward-looking, mostly rural party hacks, and the left-wing intellectual with his roots abroad.

For all his cleverness and subtlety, Menon lacked finesse, nor did he show good judgement. His needling of the Americans was petulant and his open denigration of the leadership of Mrs Pandit damaged India's reputation at the UN. His disdain of the Afro-Asian group betrayed a failure to appreciate its potential. His animus towards Pakistan blinded him towards the possibility of at least attempting to establish relations of peaceful co-existence with it. A disastrous result of this perverse attitude was when, a few weeks before the Chinese struck across the border in 1962, Menon was looking in the other direction towards Pakistan as the source of impending danger. His subsequent conduct as Defence Minister during the border row with China was catastrophic and led to India's humiliation.

Menon's propensity to create cliques and divisions within organisations and his strong prejudices created havoc in the armed forces. Inept officers were pushed up and efficient ones pulled down on the basis of whims and fancies. All these faults betrayed a serious lack of judgement and leadership qualities, which was to cost the country dear and proved to be Menon's own Waterloo.

Speculation about how and why Menon had such a hold on Nehru has never ceased. But the fact remains that more than any of his Congress colleagues, Menon could talk on matters about which others had little knowledge or interest. Nehru had a wide-ranging world-view and a vision of the future, while his homespun party colleagues' interests were strictly parochial and narrow and they were more inclined to hark back to the past than to look to the future. Menon, by contrast, had little knowledge of or interest in domestic politics and politicians and was more at home in the wider field of international affairs. Menon was on easy terms with the Prime Minister, unlike most of the other politicians who had little or no social contact with him. On the many occasions when I was in New Delhi for consultations, I would be asked to lunch at Teenmurti House. Menon was often there, also Vijayalakshmi Pandit when in town, and occasionally

Padmaja Naidu. Mrs Pandit kept up a lively and witty conversation, while Indira, the hostess, sat mostly silent.

After the debacle of the 1962 India-China war, Nehru was most reluctant to part with Menon, and only when his own position was threatened did he submit to the nation-wide clamour for Menon's head. Thereafter, Menon, who had been riding high, suddenly collapsed like a deflated balloon. Such is the fate of discredited politicians: he was shunned and cold-shouldered by those who only the other day had fawned on him. He became a forlorn figure who often dropped in to see me for a friendly chat and a cup of tea. *Sil transit tempora gloria mundi!*

I had worked closely with the Secretary-General of the UN. I happened to be one of his regular consultants, through whom he kept in touch not only with Indian views but also those of the Afro-Asian Group which had now gained recognition as a regular feature, almost like the Latin American caucus or the Atlantic Pact countries.

The Group, initially known as the Arab-Asian Group, came almost spontaneously into being during the heated debates on the Korean War. The first meeting of Asian and Arab members was not as an organised group but called in response to the earnest pleas of the western powers for the intercession of Asian states with the Chinese for a ceasefire and withdrawal north of the 38th parallel in Korea. Unwittingly and ironically, the Americans and British were the prime movers of this—it led to the formation of what later became the Afro-Asian Group and, finally, the Non-Aligned Group, whose unified approach to world problems and voting strength in the United Nations they were so greatly to resent. As the Americans brought in resolution after resolution during the Korean debates and the weaker countries were under great pressure to go along with them against their own better judgement, they found safety in numbers in casting votes of abstention.

Until 1955, when there was a sort of general amnesty and a

large number of states which had been knocking at the doors of the United Nations but whose entry had been blocked because of the Cold War, took their rightful places in the Organisation, the voting strength in the General Assembly lay with the western powers. With progressive decolonisation, the voting pattern changed accordingly and the Non-Aligned Group acquired an almost dominant position. But even earlier, its forerunner, the Afro-Asian Group, had taken up vigorously in the Security Council the questions of the independence of Tunisia and then of Morocco, and a more unified stand on questions of racial discrimination, human rights, economic and technological development, etc.

Surprising though it may now seem, the only two black African states in the UN before that time, namely Ethiopia and Liberia, and Thailand and sometimes the Philippines from Asia, would go along with the western countries on such issues, contrary to their own interests. Their participation in meetings of the Afro-Asian Group helped to wean them away from so unnatural a stand. As India was by far the largest and most influential member of the Group, it came to be regarded in the popular perception as the leader. We certainly made every effort to strengthen it by convening regular meetings and thrashing out a common and independent stand on contentious issues. By throwing its full weight on softening the acerbities of the Cold War antagonists, it helped to limit the area of discord. Since both sides seemed to believe that those who were not with them were against them, the Group's role was not appreciated by either side. In taking an independent line we were not alone; Yugoslavia, most notably, voted along with us, and often Sweden and occasionally a Latin-American country or two, such as Mexico. In course of time, I had began to feel that India was too big and consequential an international power to be confined to the somewhat limited context of the Group, which concerned itself with race and anticolonialism rather than wider global political issues. However, for the time being, the Group was serving a useful purpose; the time for it to be subsumed in the wider context of the Non-Aligned Movement was to come later.

Trygve Lie had little time for countries other than the permanent members or western powers. Dag Hammarskjold, however, was in complete empathy with the Afro-Asian Group as he felt its policies and attitudes were more in conformity with the letter and spirit of the United Nations' charter. The Organisation had, so to speak, no ideology and in that sense was non-aligned. While the big powers could look after themselves, the United Nations was the shield and protector of the security and interests of the smaller and weaker powers. It was not fortuitous that for peace-keeping and mediatory roles, Hammarskjold turned to the non-aligned and neutral countries. None of the big powers or members of military alliances were associated with any of the field operations undertaken during his tenure. Personnel from countries adhering to opposing military and ideological blocs could not possibly be expected to work together harmoniously in a peace-keeping operation. In return for the reliance he placed on them, the non-aligned countries extended their full support to the Secretary-General, especially when he came under direct and open attack from the Communist side and furtive and underhand opposition from the western camp.

The two rival blocs used the United Nations not in accordance with the lofty purposes and principles of the Charter to which they had solemnly subscribed, but as a forum for the pursuit at their conflicting aims and interests. Far from practising tolerance and living together as good neighbours and uniting their strength to maintain international peace and security, they relentlessly did just the opposite. As for achieving international cooperation in solving international problems of an economic, social, cultural, or humanitarian character, and for harmonising the actions of nations for the attainment of these common ends, they were the most divisive and discordant factors which almost wrecked the Organisation. So much for Charter principles. On the other hand, the weaker states adhered more closely to Charter principles in their pronouncements and actions. This was not necessarily because they were more moral or faithful to their pledges, but because it accorded with their own interests. They had no global or ideological interests to promote and the Charter provided a sheet-anchor for their security and integrity.

The United States seemed to regard the United Nations as a means for securing legitimacy and international acceptance of its policies designed to further its own global interests and political rivalries in the context of the Cold War. Its main concern was to combat the spectre of Communism which it perceived as a universal threat. For this it was prepared to abandon the very principles on which it was founded. It, therefore, gave unstinting support to the colonial powers in recovering their lost colonies (as to the French in Vietnam), to opposing movements for decolonisation, to supporting the racist regime of South Africa and in opposing demands for greater economic justice and equity. True, some programmes were undertaken by the United States and its partners to extend economic and technological assistance to the poorer countries, but these efforts were wholly inadequate considering the scale of the problems. Nothing like the Marshall Plan, which revived a war-stricken Europe, was ever contemplated. Nor did the US pay heed to the insistent demand to divert a mere one per cent from military budgets of the affluent nations towards amelioration of the lot of the poorest. In their perception, the piling up of weapons of mass destruction—matched equally by their opponents—was the surest means to international security and stability, rather than its greatest menace. They failed to recognise that the vast and growing gap between the affluent and the impoverished was, in fact, the greatest danger to world stability.

The Soviets and their allies, though no less obdurate than

their opponents in their perception of their own infallibility, took full advantage of the dissatisfaction aroused among the non-aligned nations by the unsympathetic western attitude towards their basic concerns. They supported almost all the issues which agitated the developing countries and they championed the cause of the oppressed and subject peoples of the world. There was more than an element of hypocrisy in this as the true nature of the Soviet empire which embraced vast tracts of land in Central and Eastern Asia and myriad races and peoples, revealed its true nature as a disguised form of colonialism only with the collapse of the Soviet Union and the Communist system. Nevertheless, in the Cold War context, the Soviet attitude served as a balancing factor. On economic questions, however, it was as unbending as the western powers, no doubt because it was in no position to extend help to the developing countries despite its roseate propaganda.

Towards Indo-Pakistani problems, the Soviet attitude served Indian interests well, but also its own. The Soviets recognised the obvious fact of India's significance, by reason of its size, population, resources, geographical location and leadership of the non-aligned movement as the dominant power in the Indian Ocean area. The United States, however, with an obsessive fear of the spread of Communism in Asia, could conceive of military means alone to contain it, discounting its own faith in the democratic way of life as the most effective counter to the alien ideology of Communism. It thus placed all its faith in setting up military alliances of the weak countries of West Asia and Pakistan to contain the mighty Soviet military machine and to provide a physical shield against its ideology. India, on the other hand, felt secure in its democratic structures grafted on to its own ancient values and way of life, confident that it was impervious to alien and unwelcome ideologies imposed from outside. America also failed to perceive that the non-aligned movement of which it strongly disapproved, with its growing number of adherents, was a powerful bulwark against the spread of foreign ideologies, whether of the west or the east, including Communism. It therefore spurned the friendship of a democratic and potentially strong sub-continental power, India, in favour of a weak and fractured dependent country. In lavishing military paraphernalia on a tottering dictatorship, it attempted, in defiance of the laws of logic and in the face of facts, to balance the one with the other in a spurious equation. This only helped to sow the seeds of conflict in the area without serving any useful purpose for the western alliance. It was only with the advent of the Kennedy administration and the change in America's policies more in conformity with its own history and traditions, that some degree of mutual comprehension began to dawn. The so-called immoderation of the non-aligned countries, especially on questions concerning Palestine, South Africa and colonisation, about which the western powers complained, were the result of the latter's consistent failure to take a fair and equitable stand on them, which led to a sense of futility and frustration.

But it was not all Cold War politics at the United Nations at the time. There were the beginnings of the involvement of the Organisation in social and developmental projects. Aid projects were generally bilateral and in order to introduce an element of multilaterism a scheme was launched to associate the United Nations in a triangular arrangement in such programmes. Perhaps the earliest such instance concerned Norway and India. Sometime in 1952, I was approached by my Norwegian colleague who said that there was much admiration in his country for India, and the common people were anxious to help in any way they could in a development project of India's choosing. Norway was a small country, barely recovering from the ravages of war, and it could hardly presume to attempt anything on a scale commensurate to India's needs. Would I, the Ambassador asked, be prepared to receive informally a delegation from his country to discuss the matter? I was very moved by this generous gesture and readily agreed. A couple of days later a party of three distinguished Norwegians engaged in the reconstruction of their own devastated country arrived, led by a Dr Lund who was head of his own country's reconstruction programme. I had informed the Prime Minister of the proposal and he promptly accepted the offer with much warmth. I suggested various possibilities to the Norwegians in the field of forestry, power generation and fisheries and a visit to India to see matters for themselves. After visiting different sites in India, they chose to start a fisheries project in Kerala. A tripartite agreement was duly drawn up and signed by Ambassador Hans Engan of Norway, Secretary-General Trygve Lie and myself.

That winter when we came home on leave, we visited the Norwegians in their camp on the sands near Quilon, where a number of families under the kind Dr Lund had settled down to work. They had already begun providing motors to the country fishing boats to increase their range, to organise the training of the fisherfolk and to set up a cold storage and ice plant in Quilon. It was they who discovered the vast and almost inexhaustible extent of the shrimp beds all along the coast which the local fishermen had not been able to exploit. Despite trouble from local unions, red-flag strikes and agitations for higher educational allowances, etc., and the proclivity of young fishermen to yearn for clerical jobs, the gallant Norwegians, men and women, struggled for years in the sand and sun, and left behind the lasting legacy of a lucrative industry.

About that time Maurice Pate, a bachelor who loved children, started a modest programme with voluntary donations on an emergency basis to help children orphaned by the War. Little did he realise what world-wide scope his brainchild, UNICEF, would attain. We took active interest in the programme and chaired the Executive Board of the young organisation.

The United Nations' Development Programme also had its beginnings in those early years. Its first Director, Mr Hoffanaw, built it up energetically until it became an integral and highly beneficial part of the UN system. Its beneficial activities have spread world-wide and are much appreciated by developing countries.

During the half century of its existence, the United Nations has passed through many vicissitudes, weathered many a storm and survived many a shipwreck. But it has emerged with renewed strength from every ordeal, testifying to its indispensability as an essential fact of international life. The organisation is more than a collective of its members, although it is from them that it derives its legitimacy. Its moral strength and acclaim derive from the high purposes and principles enshrined in its Charter, that noble instrument all member states are pledged to strengthen and uphold.

The long years of the Cold War claimed the full attention and energies of the United Nations to the problems of global war and peace, to stanching local or regional conflicts, and to combating colonialism as a threat to international peace and security. The parallel aims of the Organisation—to solve by international cooperation, problems of an economic, social, cultural or humanitarian nature and to promote respect for human rights and fundamental freedoms for all—consequently suffered by neglect or lukewarm support.

But even in its peacekeeping role the United Nations has been hamstrung by Cold War rivalries. The great powers were the supposed policemen of the world whose primary responsibility was to keep the peace. But when they themselves were at daggers drawn, the task fell to the Secretary-General. He therefore counted on the assistance of the non-aligned powers in fulfilling the task, hoping that the big powers, in the absence of their active support, would at least refrain from unwanted interference. But more often than not, they would assume partisan attitudes favouring one party or another, to the extent of inciting opposing parties to resort to violence against each other, or even against the United Nations peacekeepers. The task of international peacekeeping, never an easy one, was made infinitely more difficult as it involved not only keeping the contending factions apart; it also required exposing or side-stepping the intrigues of the big powers and contending with their rivalries in the midst of a volatile situation. Indeed, one of the major concerns of the United Nations, voiced vigorously and persistently by the medium and smaller powers unconnected with rival military pacts, was to prevent the two superpowers from unleashing a nuclear war which would have destroyed both, and the rest of the world with them.

Because the big powers, having virtually pre-empted themselves from initiating action for maintaining international peace, the slogan 'Leave it to Dag' came into UN parlance. The technique of what broadly falls under the rubric of 'peacekeeping' was developed by Hammarskjold under the stress of Cold War compulsions. The methods adopted took ingenious and varied shapes and forms, depending upon each situation.

The most unobtrusive was a single-man UN 'presence' in an area of tension as the ears and eyes of the United Nations, to give advance warning of developments likely to lead to a breach of the peace, or to act as a mediator or good officer. Such a 'presence' was, for example, sent to Laos to watch over events in that part of the world. Military personnel came to be used in unarmed 'Observer' missions, when by means of making the UN's active presence felt and preventing or interrupting armed clashes by force of moral persuasion, peace could be restored and the way paved for peaceful negotiations. Such an operation with unarmed military personnel under civilian leadership was mounted in Lebanon in 1958 with conspicuous success. The mission would of course need the sanction of the Security Council and be acceptable to the parties concerned.

Under the Charter, the Secretary-General could himself bring a situation threatening international peace and security to the notice of the Security Council and propose appropriate action. Action under Article 99 of the Charter was taken by Hammarskjold in the case of the Congo and a massive armed operation was launched to safeguard the country's independence and to assist in restoring public order there.

It may well be asked how UN 'peacekeeping' operations conducted in Cold War conditions could have, by and large, been so successful. This was all the more remarkable as Hammarskjold, relying almost religiously on the power of moral over brute force, was strongly averse to the use of force, except as a last resort, and then only in self-defence. Force was in no case to be used to gain a political objective or to favour one side or another in a conflict. The role of the United Nations was to make peace, not war, and if it had to suffer unjust criticism or even to sacrifice lives in a righteous cause, it was part of its function.

Operationally, Hammarskjold turned almost exclusively to the non-aligned and medium powers for military and civilian personnel. For logistical support, the United States, Canada and Italy were the principal sources. Politically, it was the Afro-Asian Group on which he counted. Despite the difficulties, the fact that so many peacekeeping missions managed to succeed was due largely to the dogged persistence of the Secretary-General and the unyielding support of the non-aligned countries. Besides, the consequences of failure would have been very dangerous for world peace, a fact which, in the ultimate analysis, imposed some degree of restraint on all states. It is a tribute to the participating countries in peacekeeping operations that, despite suffering heavy casualties in the field and unjustified criticism, they did not waver in their support. Contrast this with the withdrawal from Somalia of the United States contingent following some casualties suffered by it and its disinclination to participate in the United Nations mission to Yugoslavia. It is significant that in peacekeeping missions Russian troops are still not to be seen alongside western ones, which signifies a continuing conflict of perceptions and interests. While earlier missions rigorously excluded the intervention by any outside agency in parallel action with or in conflict with an ongoing UN operation, American warships and warplanes have been operating independently of the UN mission in Somalia and NATO warplanes in Yugoslavia. This inevitably complicates the task of the United Nations in fulfilling its mandate in the spirit of the Charter.

# Tito's Yugoslavia That Was

A rift had been brewing between Tito and Stalin over doctrinal matters. Tito prided himself on the fact that he and his 'Partisans' as they were called, had fought the Nazi invaders for four bitter years and had immobilised no less than seventeen Nazi divisions, inflicting heavy casualties and damage on them. Unlike the other East European countries who had ridden to power on the bandwagon of the victorious Soviet armies, Tito's revolution was entirely indigenous, owing nothing to the Soviet Union. Furthermore, Tito's stubborn insistence on his doctrine of 'different roads to Socialism', would have destroyed the Stalinist myth of 'the monolithic unity of the Communist party'. Stalin, who regarded himself as the supreme pontiff of the faith, could not possibly countenance a rival Pope presiding over a schismatic church. He pronounced anathema on the renegade Tito and vowed to destroy him and all his works. His extreme animosity took the form of an almost personal vendetta.

Given the fact of the Cold War, this revolt in the Soviet system came as a gift to the west. From its former comparative obscurity, Yugoslavia became a significant factor on the world stage, attracting international attention. But Tito found himself isolated. He could not, as an avowed Communist, openly seek the protection of the west without abjuring his faith, though he was not averse to taking the arms and aid proffered by the west or seeking a security alliance with his non-Communist neighbours, Greece and Turkey. Fences were repaired with Greece where a guerrilla war was being fought to instal a Communist regime, and friendly approaches made to Turkey, both members of the NATO alliance. A security treaty, known as the Balkan Pact, was entered into to break out of the country's isolation. Tito had, however, set his sights wider, and he tried to build friendships with countries outside the opposing blocs. The first such country whose friendship he sought was India.

I had been posted to Belgrade as India's first resident Ambassador. We took the Cunard Line's *Queen Mary* to sail from New York to Southampton, and onward via Paris to Belgrade. We had been seen off by a large assortment of American friends from different walks of life and by sundry colleagues and officials, including surprisingly, Andrei Vyshinsky, my Soviet colleague, who burst into our room with a bottle of vodka to raise our spirits! We were due to leave by rail from Paris, but were held up as Yugoslavia and Italy, who had been embroiled in a bitter dispute over their rival claims to the Free Territory of Trieste, were about to resort to the arbitrament of arms. The arrival of a new envoy in Belgrade at such a time would hardly have been appropriate. We had, therefore, to mark time in Paris. Meanwhile, international mediators had got busy, and, at the last moment, a 'Provisional Agreement' was negotiated, which enabled the two armies to disengage. The city was assigned to Italy: the hinterland, which provisioned the city and provided much of its work-force, fell to Yugoslavia. Neither country was required to renounce its formal claim to the whole. The arrangement has proved remarkably durable and has worked without friction.

We were set to travel to Belgrade by the famed Orient Express. On the appointed day, our major domo, Sardar Nanhe Khan, who had long been in our service, was sent on ahead to the Gare Montparnasse with our heavy baggage. We followed a little later, but found our progress impeded by an enormous traffic jam. When we reached the railway platform, we were mortified to see the Orient Express steaming away. However, we made it the next day. The train had retained its old-fashioned aspect, with red plush seats and brass fittings, but it rattled and swayed abominably and, after leaving Italy, even the dining car vanished and it began to display signs of general fatigue. We worried about the fate of Nanhe Khan, with no knowledge of any European language, not even English, with little money but plenty of luggage. On arrival in Belgrade we were accosted by a distraught Nanhe Khan who, poor man, had been without food or water for thirty hours. His odd assortment of currency could, at best, have bought him a sandwich, but as a devout Muslim, anything but kosher meat was forbidden. He did not know the name of the town for which he was headed, or even that of the country, which he insisted on calling 'Yugoslovakia'. He might have landed up in Athens, the train's final destination, had he not been discovered by our mission staff which had come to receive us.

After four years in New York, a world capital, with its opulence, glitter and infinite variety, provincial and impoverished Belgrade, so drab and dismal, came as a sad anti-climax. A totally undistinguished city, except for its location at the confluence of the Danube and Sava, it carried the scars of war and a decade of socialism contributed visibly to its depressed condition. The shops were empty, the people ill-dressed, there were no amenities and even the feeble street lights added to the prevailing gloom. The hostelry where the whole mission, including the office and staff, was accommodated was as down-at-heel as everything else. The Balkan was said to be the best hotel in town, and as we were told that suitable housing was unavailable, we wondered ruefully how we could possibly endure our three or four years there.

I presented my credentials with my sole diplomatic officer, the First Secretary, K.P. Lukose, in tow, to President Joseph Broz Tito at the Bieli Dvor (White Palace) and began making calls on my diplomatic colleagues. It all seemed very dull and leisurely after the hectic years at the United Nations. Although Yugoslavia had opened a resident mission in New Delhi years ago headed by very senior and experienced persons, by a bizarre arrangement, India was hitherto represented by our Ambassador in Rome, who was also accredited to Stalinist Albania. As the three countries were not on speaking terms with each other, our Ambassador, B.R. Sen, during his occasional forays, would visit one enemy country and then another and return by the same route. The Yugoslavs had been pressing for a resident mission, and one had the impression that it would be little more than an *acte de presence* to establish a sort of diplomatic equilibrium. But it turned out to be a cornerstone of Yugoslavia's foreign policy and of much significance to India as well. Tito, excommunicated by one bloc and opposed to conversion to the other, was searching for a partner to relieve his loneliness and to deter a threatened Soviet invasion.

One of the earliest Yugoslav Ambassadors to India was Jose Vilfan, an extremely able and far-sighted diplomat, who was now the Secretary-General to the President, whose full confidence he enjoyed. Vilfan had a great deal to do with influencing Tito regarding cultivating India's friendship and understanding. Rather like an Indian marriage proposal, tentative approaches began regarding a presidential visit to India, to which equally cautious replies were recieved. I found myself in the role of the traditional Indian barber, who smoothens the way to a satisfactory outcome. When at the United Nations, I had noticed that on contentious issues India and Yugoslavia independently took a similar view and cast their votes invariably in an identical manner. Both were stepping cautiously between the rival blocs and were equally consistent in their advocacy of peaceful settlements of disputes. Besides, India was too large and significant a country to be confined to the Afro-Asian group, a group held together largely by shared colonial experiences, under-development and racial considerations. Association with a European country on the basis of policy would open new horizons. Tito would be the first European Head of State to visit India.

The delicate diplomatic dance ended satisfactorily and dates were set and programmes arranged. Tito, with an entourage of some forty persons was to travel by sea in his yacht, the *Jadranka*, as he was averse to flying for some reason. I flew on ahead to report to our Prime Minister.

Nehru kindly asked me over to lunch to be briefed: among the guests were Krishna Menon, Vijayalakshmi Pandit and Padmaja Naidu. The first question I was asked was why Tito was coming. Krishna Menon interjected that he was nothing but an American stooge. There was much laughter when he likened Tito's light blue uniform of a Marshal to Goering's. It was obvious that little was known about the country, its leader or its international significance. All that I succeeded in conveying was the information that Tito had been proclaiming principles of international relations over a period of time, which corresponded closely to our own Panchsheel or Five Principles of Peaceful Co-existence. I said he would almost certainly publicly subscribe to them in the joint communique to be issued. Nehru seemed sceptical and Menon cynical, until I said I had brought copies of Tito's speeches which would bear out the point. When I presented myself at the Prime Minister's office to show him the speeches, underlining the relevant portions, he studied them carefully. Menon, meanwhile, disregarding the draft communique prepared by the Ministry, insisted on drafting one himself, clearly intending to test the genuineness of Tito's protestations.

I had been assured by ex-Colonel Inder Chopra, the Chief of Protocol, that all arrangements for the prolonged visit had been made in meticulous detail and would be found impeccable. The finest food and wines would be served on board the special trains conveying the visitors. Chopra was indeed as good as his word and everything went like clockwork. When Tito's special train steamed on to the ceremonial platform at the New Delhi railway station, the red carpet had been laid, the band ready to play the national anthems, the flags and buntings were out, and, most surprisingly, the Ministers had turned out in correct attire and were lined up in orderly rows, with Chopra acting as Sergeant-Major.

The Yugoslavs seemed to know as little about India as the Indians knew about them. They were awestruck by the magnificence of Delhi, the splendour of the President's House, the grandeur of the old monuments, the luxuriousness of their accommodation. Tito's party consisted of Vice-President Rankovic, held in fear in his country as head of the interior ministry and the secret service; the Foreign Minister, Koca Popovic, witty, astute and Sorbonne-educated; the Commanders-in-Chief of the Army and Navy, the President of Croatia, assorted officials, led by Vilfan, and a clutch of journalists. The composition of the party showed that Tito was taking no chances.

The talks between Nehru and Tito went smoothly, beginning tentatively while each leader tried to probe the other's mind, but ended cordially. It was evident that Nehru had taken to Tito for his clear exposition of Soviet policies, the ramifications of the Cold War and his own adherence to a policy of non-alignment. When the two draft communiques were exchanged for discussion, Tito found himself in full agreement with the Indian

(Krishna Menon's) draft which went well beyond what his own Foreign Minister had cautiously produced. Nehru found that an inside view of the closed Soviet system would be opened up by one who was formerly part of the system and had a rare knowledge and insight into its intricacies. It was therefore decided that the two leaders would consult each other over international developments and maintain a regular exchange of letters. It became my pleasant duty to act as a messenger in Belgrade, conveying the Prime Minister's letters to the President who was then at his favourite resort of Brioni.

The official business in Delhi done, the Yugoslav party embarked on its long tour of the country. I accompanied them throughout while Surendra Singh of Alirajpur, Deputy Chief of Protocol and his staff, looked after all the arrangements en route. I naturally found myself constantly in the company of the President and prominent members of his delegation and got to know them well. Tito had a commanding presence and exuded an air of authority. Thoroughly self-possessed and a man of few words, he commanded great respect and adulation. His relations with his colleagues were informal and he did not expect nor receive subservience. His eyes bespoke the man: steely grey, they seemed to penetrate through one. Though he was addressed by all as 'Drug' or 'Comrade', no one would take liberties with him. The Yugoslavs were generally a cheerful lot, enjoying every moment of their journey, often bursting into song. The odyssey took us from one end of the country to the other, from Simla and Chandigarh down to Bangalore, Madras and Cochin, and from Agra, Gwalior and Bombay to Calcutta. A planned tiger shoot in Gwalior was converted into a photography session at the last moment, as the Yugoslav's feared that the western press would scoff at a Communist leader shooting tigers with a feudal Maharaja. Tito caught up with Nehru towards the end of the tour at Madras where the famous Avadi session of the All-India National Congress was being held which Tito was invited to witness. A great open air stadium, festooned with flags, had been set up at a high, canopied platform provided for the leaders. Seated in front were a hundred thousand party members in dazzling white. It was indeed an awe-inspiring spectacle. As the party speeches were going on, Nehru asked me to make discreet soundings if Tito would like to address the audience. Tito had no hesitation in agreeing, with Vilfan acting as interpreter. In his long speech made in Serbo-Croatian, he pronounced India to be a country well and truly embarked on the task of building up a genuinely socialist society. The Yugoslavs were quite dazzled not only by the scale of the occasion, but also by Tito's warm words of appreciation of what he had learnt and observed in India. The Yugoslavs finally sailed away from Cochin while I flew back to Belgrade.

When I called on Tito after his triumphal return to Yugoslavia, he expressed great satisfaction over his visit and showed me much kindness. He asked if we had found a house and immediately ordered that the state guest house be allotted to us. This turned out to be a beautiful Italianate villa which had been built by a former Prime Minister's corrupt and extravagant son, Rade Pasic, who was now living in penury and had been expropriated of his wealth. The main salon had fine old panelling, a splendidly patterned parquet floor in many-coloured woods, a ceiling painted by Italian artists with cherubs and Renoir-style nudes. The latter was a great distraction to visitors from India, whose eyes turned skywards as if in deep meditation. The dining room was panelled in carved oak. The house was fully furnished, with Aubousson tapestries, covered period furniture in the salon, gilt tableware for twelve, and Limoges crockery. Fully carpeted and curtained, with three bedrooms and a guest wing, the accommodation was quite luxurious. The paved courtyard and rose-creepered patio with water channels and a swimming pool adorned the house. The garden was a constant source of delight where I could indulge my hobby of gardening to the full. I added many varieties of perennials to it and planted an orchard of different fruits. We even managed to grow Indian vegetables during the hot season, much to the astonishment of the gardener. The house had been the residence of the Soviet Ambassador until the break in relations. The Yugoslavs used to remind me that the valuable old French tapestries which hung in the library had been purloined by the former tenant. To ensure that nothing of value was lost I had the tableware and china returned as soon as our official replacements arrived.

Thanks to President Tito, all doors had been thrown open to us. I was always welcomed when I called on ministers and senior officials, and Yugoslav officials and others had no inhibitions in coming over to us. After our experience of Moscow, this was indeed a most welcome change in a professedly Communist country. Yugoslav ministers and other officials responded gladly to our invitations, but they asked that no foreigners, especially western diplomats, be invited. Our guests loved to burst into song, in which Susheela joined. She had acquired a wide repertoire of Yugoslav songs from the different regions of the country, her teacher being a delightful old lady who later became the Director of the National Academy of Music.We had become the envy of our western colleagues because of our proximity to the top leadership. As both India and Yugoslavia had an equal interest in developing the greatest common degree of understanding in political matters and close cooperation in the cultural and economic fields, the work by the mission was pleasant and constructive.

Yugoslavia had been cobbled together from the ruins of the Austro-Hungarian Empire after the First World War and comprised six states, viz., Slovenia, Croatia, Serbia, Bosnia-Herzigovina, Montenegro and Macedonia. They had varied backgrounds and were at different stages of development. Slovenia and Croatia were Catholic and had been part of the Austro-Hungarian Empire, they were the most developed and had a mixed Slavo-Germanic culture. Serbia, the largest, was Orthodox and mainly agricultural; as part of the Ottoman Empire for some six centuries, traces of Turkish influence were still evident. Bosnia-Herzigovina had a mixed Muslim and Serb population, was largely mountainous and backward economically, the Muslim population being rather conservative and traditional. Montenegro, also mountainous, was the smallest and most obscure, with affinities with the Serbs and a history of sturdy independence. Macedonia, with a very mixed population, was the most backward, economically and culturally. There had been bitter enmity between Croatia and Serbia, and during the Second World War a bloody civil war had raged between the two, the Yugoslavs asserting that it claimed as many victims as the Nazi invasion.

Although every state spoke Serbo-Croat with local variations, because of the mixed population and different historical backgrounds, certain foreign languages were also understood in different regions. It was Tito's powerful personality and political creed that welded the disparate republics into a coherent whole. The Yugoslavs used to say proudly that they were one state and had two scripts—Roman and Cyrillic; three religions, viz., Roman Catholism, Russian Orthodox, Islam; four races, viz., Slovenian, Serbian, Hungarian and Turkish; five languages— Serbian, Slovenian, Hungarian, Turkish, German, Italian; and six republics. Every republic enjoyed a certain measure of autonomy with its own executive and legislature. What held the country together ideologically was its communist underpinning; economically, it was the Central Bank, the sole banking institution in the country. To this should be added a certain natural pride, enhanced by the valiant struggle against the Nazi hordes. It was a very confident country, proud of itself and looking forward with hope to a future of prosperity and increasing international importance under its prestigious leadership.

The alienation from the Soviet regime necessitated a new interpretation of Communist doctrine. But more importantly, it required the support of the people who had not taken kindly to an imported creed. To win the adherence of the peasantry, especially of the sturdy and independent Serbs, collectivisation, which had converted one million tons of foodgrains into an equal deficit, had to be abandoned. To win over the industrial workers, a system of workers' management of enterprises was introduced. A certain degree of freedom of speech and expression was allowed. Under an umbrella organisation known as the Socialist Alliance, non-Communists could also take part in the political process, although in fact few actually did so.

But freedom of speech had its limitations, and a book which received world-wide attention, entitled *The New Class* written by a former Vice-President and senior party member who had broken away from Tito, was anathematised and Milovan Djilas the author, excommunicated. Despite being reduced to a non-person and undergoing jail sentences, Djilas did not retract. He bitterly criticised the life-styles of the leading lights of the party, of whom he had been one; they had replaced the old aristocracy and plutocracy, whom in Djilas' eyes they now emulated. The secret police was around, but not nearly as all-pervasive as in Moscow.

I was always struck by the animated and free discussions of the top leadership with Tito about ideological and governmental matters. These seemed to seek new and innovative methods to break out of the circle of poverty and backwardness. They had great faith in rapid industrialisation, regardless of the paucity of resources and technical know-how. The peasantry was left much to its own devices as Communist theology had proclaimed it to be a drag on progress. There were state farms intended to be models, whose equipment and methods were beyond the reach of the farmers with their small holdings. Some cooperatives too had been set up, which partially negatived their description by imposing a measure of compulsion.

I visited a large number of factories in different parts of the country and attended the meetings of their self-management boards. In the technically and educationally advanced republics of the north, the industries were well run and the elected workman-chairman seemed equal to his responsibilities. But in the backward areas of the south, the workman-chairman was often ill at ease and relied heavily on the professional manager. The theory was that an enterprise belonged to its workers who would distribute the profits, in cash or by way of amenities, between themselves, after meeting all taxes due to the central government. There was, of course, no question of labour disputes since there was no outside management to agitate against. The higher the profits, the better-off would be the workers. This provided the incentive for greater productivity and efficiency. Extravagance was curbed by the denial of funds by the Central Bank and party discipline did the rest. There were, of course, exceptions. In a modern arms factory near Sarajevo, the substantial profits were squandered on setting up a huge and opulent complex with restaurants, a dance hall, theatre, swimming pool and other such luxuries. I had reported on the Yugoslav economic system to New Delhi, which attracted the attention of the Prime Minister who dispatched the Labour Secretary to study its application to the Indian context. The worker-management system was tried desultorily in one or two state-run enterprises. But it never got off the ground.

An over-riding concern of the Yugoslav leadership was how to fend off the constant threats of assassination and invasion from the north. The country shared common borders with Hungary, Romania and Bulgaria, all totally subservient to Moscow. The threats could not be taken lightly. Tito was building a defence force, some quarter of a million strong, which could repel at least the first impact of an invasion. For this he needed modern weaponry, which the United States and the western powers were ready to supply. But he was adamantly opposed to being lured into their Cold War camp. Through astute diplomacy, he succeeded in his efforts and could build up a modern defence system. He also entered into the Balkan Alliance for mutual security with the two NATO powers to the east, again without sacrificing his non-aligned policy.

Tito had built up around him a galaxy of men of talent, courage and vision whom any country would have been glad to have had. His choice of envoys to serve abroad was made with meticulous care, and in every capital of the world the Yugoslav envoy could be counted upon to be very well informed, alert and active.

I had been accredited to Romania and Bulgaria; the first problem was how to get to their capitals to present my credentials. All communication between Yugoslavia and the East European countries had been severed and the borders sealed off by eight-foot high barbed wire fencing with watch-towers and, in places, minefields. I called on the envoys concerned to discuss dates and routes. They were an uninspiring lot, party apparatchiks, who kept mostly to themselves, shunned by the Yugoslavs and westerners alike, and, living in a hostile country, afraid of their own shadows. The Bulgarian advised a roundabout route via Moscow, but I insisted on going by road. The road was bad, I was told, but ultimately he gave in to my insistence, and I was able to set off. Susheela and a secretary accompanied me. The unmetalled road on both sides of the border was indeed terrible, but we made it without breaking the axle. At the border post, which was heavily guarded, the wired gates slowly opened after a detailed scrutiny of our passports and a commendatory letter from the Bulgarian Ambassador, the Yugoslav chauffeur's passport attracting particular attention. We were installed at a modest hotel, our American car, parked in the street below, mesmerising the throng that gathered around it.

Bulgarian protocol demanded that, before reviewing the guard of honour lined up before him, a new envoy should ask in a loud voice in Bulgarian how the soldiers were and if they were being well looked after. I complied as best I could. The reply, which came in a great roar from a hundred young throats, nearly bowled me over. Susheela and I and our lone official were led up to the presidential presence in the adjacent government building. We were received most cordially, and invited by the President to a banquet which turned out to be a grand affair in the palace of the former king. Toasts were drunk, and then, after the elaborate banquet, a band appeared; the Bulgarians burst into song and began dancing in a great chain, holding hands and snaking through the state room. It seemed a most original way of welcoming a new envoy!

We paid our respects to the first President, Donitrov, who lay embalmed in a glass case in his mausoleum in the central square. This strictly and obsequiously followed the Soviet pattern. In fact, it was said that when it rained in Moscow, the umbrellas went up in Sophia. The city was Germanic in architecture. The main avenues were wide and lined with flowering roses, which in summer cast their perfume far and wide. The country was rich in agricultural produce. Its fruits and vegetables were unsurpassed and it had a near monopoly in Europe of the essence or attar of roses which were cultivated in great quantities.

My first visit to Romania to present my credentials was even more adventurous. Driving to the border, the road seemed to come to an abrubt end. Ahead lay only a great stretch of tall grass. The barrier too was a forbidding and heavily wired gate. This was reluctantly opened, we ploughed slowly through the tall grass towards some trees in the distance where a car and some people were visible. It was the Romanian Chief of Protocol who had come all the way from Bucharest to receive us. With him joining us in our car we climbed up the Carpathian mountains, encountering ethnic Germans, long settled there, in their national costume. We spent the night at Sibiu at an old inn. Making an early start, we were coasting along at speed along an empty road raised some fifteen feet above the low-lying pasture land where buffaloes were grazing. A truck appeared in the distance and it was only when it approached that we noticed that it was swaying from side to side on the narrow road. A frightful head-on collision seemed inevitable, but Asim, our driver, with great presence of mind and skill, swerved suddenly to the grassy verge, avoiding both a fall and a large stone marker. The truck stopped. Asim got out in a towering rage and made as if to batter the errant driver to death. The Romanian sat transfixed with fear, quivering like an aspen and blabbering incoherently. My Indian assistant and I sat stoically, exclaiming that it was only providence that had saved us. Restraining Asim from doing violence to the driver, I made the Romanian Chief of Protocol seize the offender's driving licence, of which he was permanently deprived, as I learnt later. The man was dead drunk.

Bucharest, the 'Paris of East', must have been a fine city in its day. But now its avenues and luxurious villas and gardens showed signs of neglect. The once famous hotel which gloried in the name of Palais Athene, celebrated for its comfort and cuisine, now unfortunately had neither. The people who shuffled along the vast square opposite seemed ill-fed and ill-clothed. The shops, as expected, were empty and the whole place had a dispirited air. Romania, known earlier as Dacia, had been the eastern outpost of the Roman empire. Its inhabitants were thus largely of Roman origin and its language resembled Italian, with a slight admixture of Slavic and even some Turkish terms. It was an island of Latin culture in the midst of a sea of Slav tribes.

After presenting my credentials to the titular President who described himself as a banker by profession, I was received by the Supreme leader, Georgin Georgin-Desh, who exercised absolute power, tempered only by subservience to Moscow. He had built himself a huge mausoleum which he hoped to occupy in embalmed form in a glass case when the time came. So abject was the subordination to Moscow that Stalin, in effigy and portrait, dominated all government offices and public places. One of the biggest statues of Stalin stood with arm upraised in benediction, or warning, in a park named after him. Indeed, even Marx and Lenin were crowded out by the Generalissimo.

I was taken on a weary round of factories where incomprehensible statistics were rattled off mechanically by the managers and officials. Charts and graphs, equally meaningless, were proudly displayed. Canteens of the happy workers at their meals were visited. One of the penalties of serving in East European People's Democracies was the almost obligatory duty of trudging around factories and farms and trying to show intelligent interest. The only visit which had any positive outcome was to the Ploesti oilfields, which I later learnt were beginning to run out, and the negotiation of a team of oil experts going to India with an oil rig to make some preliminary borings.

I determined to drive back to Belgrade via Sophia, an unheard of enterprise. I was told there were no petrol pumps en route until Sophia; besides, there were problems of payment in an appropriate currency. I again had recourse to my Yugoslav colleague in Bucharest, who helped me out with jerry cans of petrol which, along with a full tank, would just about get me across to Sophia. Having got over the paper formalities, especially concerning the car and the Yugoslav chauffeur, we finally set off.

To reach Bulgaria we had to cross the so-called Bridge of Friendship across the Danube. The road was unmetalled and there was hardly any motor traffic as we drove along. But in Dobruja we encountered parties of cheerful Turks in tarbooshes and gowns or bulging Turkish trousers resembling salwars. They were gaudily clad and in high spirits as they trotted along in their carts with their womenfolk. Curious as to our identity, they responded heartily to our salutations of 'Salaam-aleikum'.

In both countries there was much interest in Indian culture and an irrepressible desire to regale us with glimpses of their own. A frequent topic of conversation was about the Indian film *Awara* and its star, Raj Kapoor, and there was much disappointment when we said we had never seen it. Resisting offers for a special showing of the film, we succumbed to witnessing performances of traditional and peasant dances in costume. These have a certain fascination of their own, but after opt-repeated performances, they began to pall. But Romanian gipsy music, of which we were presented with an album of gramophone records, has a peculiar enchantment.

Cultural exchanges began with the arrival from India of assorted dancers, vocalists and instrumentalists, described as a 'Cultural Delegation' under the leadership of a Minister of State, Anil Chanda, and his wife. It had come via Moscow where it had had a rough passage. Apparently one member had fallen ill of some stomach complaint and was taken to hospital, where a general examination revealed that he was also suffering from what the Soviets politely described as a 'social disease'. Greatly perturbed lest the pure Soviet society be infected, the unfortunate man was bundled off to India. It also transpired that the secretary of the delegation, an unmarried woman, was pregnant, so she too had to take the next plane home. The Soviet authorities now insisted that the whole delegation undergo a medical examination to ensure that they were not carriers of unnamed diseases. With difficulty the Chandas obtained an exemption for themselves, but the rest had to submit. As Soviet ideas of modesty differed from Indian, they required all members of the delegation, male and female, old and young, to line up in the nude. After much negotiation, the sexes were separated. But as the doctors and attendants were mostly female, the Indian males felt added embarrassment at their exposure. The examination revealed no more than half a dozen cases of piles and one of hydrocele, which were allowed to pass, the last mentioned being left to carry his own burden.

When the party, some thirty strong, arrived in Bucharest, they greeted me almost as a saviour. Recounting their sad Moscow experience, they were much worried by the indiscipline and waywardness of their very disparate group. They were particularly watchful about their wards—young girl singers from Shantiniketan—whose virginal purity they zealously guarded against the more predatory members of the delegation and the unknown perils of foreign lands. Implored to discipline the particularly recalcitrant members, I exhorted them, in the name of the mother country, with a mixture of appeals and threats, to behave. This worked for a while, but it needed repetition at the next two capitals visited by the party.

There were many *prima donnas* among the members, and some neophytes and, along with the usual bickering about precedence, there was much dissatisfaction about the time allotted to each. There were celebrities like Ustad Vilayat Khan, the eminent sitarist, Samta Prasad, the tabla wizard, Sitara Devi the dazzling Kathak dancer, a troupe of Manipuri dancers, a Baul singer from Bengal, the Shantiniketan chorus, a vocalist and numerous accompanists. But the wisdom of trying to compress a dozen or more items of classical Indian music and dance into the space of two hours did not allow enough time to the performers either to tune in or to warm up. The returns from so much expenditure, talent and trouble were minimal, leaving audiences perplexed and disappointed. Far better to have a few short items instead.

This happened once when Susheela's mother, two of her daughters and a daughter-in-law came on a visit. Discovering that Sarala, Susheela's sister, was an accomplished Bharata Natyam dance, and, already aware of Susheela's musical talent, there was much insistence on a concert being given to introduce Yugoslav audiences to Indian dance and song. The ladies agreed. Belgrade was soon plastered with posters, and on the appointed day the largest theatre hall was filled to capacity and more. Sarala, who had fortunately brought her costumes and taped music, danced superbly, the other three, with Susheela singing solo as well as in the chorus, could hardly restrain their own merriment, which infected the rapturous audience. In their gorgeous sarees and their grace, the ladies provided a dazzling spectacle. The performance concluded to thunderous applause. Leading Yugoslav functionaries and a host of diplomats had turned up and were effusive in their praises. Bowing to consistent demand, a repeat performance did not satisfy the clamour for more. The sizeable funds collected were donated to set up a village medical centre. The concert was long remembered and we were often told that its spontaneity, charm and grace had made a deep and lasting impression, far exceeding anything that the large official delegation had been able to achieve.

There was a distant echo of the occasion some fifteen years later when we were attending a United Nations' sponsored conference in Yugoslavia; it was held on the shores of the fabulous Lake Ohrid in a delightful hotel. The lake was very large and very deep, with crystal-clear water and noted for its unique variety of trout, about which it was said that the Ottoman Sultan had runners carry it to his table at Istanbul, everyday.

Our Yugoslav hosts had organised a picnic on a charming verdant island where a band was in attendance. The Yugoslav Protocol officer and others came over to our table, proudly displaying the day's newspaper which carried a long interview by the Director of the National Conservatory of Music on the occasion of its fiftieth anniversary. Displaying a full-length photograph of Susheela, the Director said that her last pupil was Susheela Dayal. The Director was none other than Madame Stomatovic, with whom Susheela had spent many happy afternoons years earlier. The Yugoslavs thought it was my daughter's photograph, but when they realised who it was, they begged Susheela to sing. The orchestra was in raptures when she joined it and sang one song after another with perfect confidence and mastery. All the delegates were astonished to see an Indian lady in a saree so thoroughly familiar with Yugoslav melodies, singing away with evident enjoyment.

Susheela was gifted with a beautiful, silvery voice and could take the notes up and down the scale with ease. Recognising her talent her parents had an Ustad of the Lucknow gharana to teach her from the age of four or five. But she was also gifted with a quick and highly intelligent mind, and so was sent to school in England after which she decided to go to Cambridge where she obtained a good history tripos. When she spent some months in Vienna with her parents, the leading soprano of the Vienna Opera tried to prevail upon her to take up a career with the opera, something which her parents would not hear of. Her quick ear enabled her to pick up foreign languages and their pronunciation quite easily and she could hold her own in French, Russian and even Serbo-Croat. In Moscow, while we were studying Russian with a teacher and worrying about the syntax and grammar, Susheela would converse easily with Soviet officials. The Acting Foreign Minister declared to our discomfiture that she spoke the best Russian in the Embassy!

Pandit Nehru paid his first official visit to Yugoslavia in the summer and took the place by storm. The city was festooned with flags and buntings and huge crowds lined the streets strewing rose petals. There was a huge banquet at the White Palace and a return luncheon by Pandit Nehru at the embassy residence. Our cook Rashid rose to the occasion, while Nanhe Khan, as a mark of special respect, served President Tito and Pandit Nehru on his knees! The luncheon was served in the beautiful Italianate garden, which was gay with summer flowers. There was a special session of the Skuptshiva or Parliament at which Nehru, to one's surprise, made a disclosure of his belief, describing himself as an agnostic. I noticed, sitting just behind Nehru, that his speech had been written in English and copies distributed: but he began rendering a rough and ready translation of it in Hindustani! This expression of linguistic nationalism delighted the Hindi journalists accompanying the party. A visit had been arranged to the medieval fortified port city of Dubrovnik, and a large convoy set out across the whole width of the Republic of Bosnia-Herzigovina up hill and down dale along a winding, untarred and dusty road. Visiting a new well dug by the state on our way (of which our hosts were inordinately proud), we hurtled on to Sarajevo, that epicentre of conflict. Passing through the lonely old city of Moster and the famous Roman bridge, we began descending towards the Adriatic coast. Nehru was housed in a blue-domed villa overlooking the sea and the rest of the party in an adjacent hotel, within walking distance of the southern gate of the great citadel. Dubrovnik seemed to have been caught in the web of time; nothing had changed since its apogee of power and wealth when it rivalled the other Adriatic city state of Venice. formerly known as Argusa, it lent its name to the word 'argosy', meaning a large merchant ship no doubt laden with precious merchandise. The main street, paved and with beautiful Renaissance houses situated on it, came straight out of bygone days. The old churches and alleys, the crenellated battlements with the sea lapping at their feet, the enclosed harbour, the absence of any modern construction and all vehicular traffic gave the city its unique character. A concert on period instruments held in the fine old courtyard of a grand mansion, contributed to the illusion. A visit to the delectable island of Brioni, reputedly beloved of the ancient Romans, whose architectural traces it still bore, and later of European glitterati, was a favourite resort of Tito and seemed almost obligatory. Nehru's discovery of Yugoslavia after Tito's discovery of India set the seal for the intimate relations of mutual confidence and interest that became a keynote in their foreign policies.

The visit of Khrushchev and Bulganin was of a very different nature. After years of bitter enmity, the new Soviet leadership suddenly decided to mend fences with the defiant Tito. The two Soviet leaders arrived, almost penitentially, in sackcloth and ashes, to ask that bygones be bygones. Standing in line on the tarmac, I watched with particular curiosity the arrival of the Soviet party, having been witness in Moscow to the rupture. Tito received his visitors with cold formality. Khrushchev delivered an offensive speech. Tito, ignoring protocol, made no reply. Tito then escorted his self-invited guests through practically empty streets to their place of residence. There were no flags or buntings, no flowers, no cheering crowds. That evening there was the usual reception for the visitors when the Chief of Protocol sought me out to lead me to the room where Tito sat with his guests. Khrushchev, who had been drinking solidly, greeted me as though I was a long-lost friend, and raising his glass toasted 'Great India', saying the prefix no longer suited Britain. In reply, I said with mock modesty: 'Not yet, but will be.' By the time the evening ended, Khrushchev was roaring drunk and almost took a headlong toss coming down the steps as visitors came and went, leaving the Yugoslavs proud of their defiance and highly amused as tales of Khrushchev's behaviour freely circulated.

Despite his oafish behaviour, Khrushchev was trying to pursue a very different foreign policy to Stalin's, who had imposed on his vast country a rigid quarantine. He wanted his country, as a superpower, to take its due place in the comity of nations and to establish friendly, or at least normal, relations with other countries, except those in open enmity with the Soviet State.

He was realistic enough to recognise that the Soviet system could no longer be imposed on the unwilling, and that different countries would wish to pursue policies suited to their own interests and conditions. He had also realised the growing significance of the non-aligned movement which tried to maintain a balance between the two hostile blocs. He had been wooing India as a leader of the movement and now sought Yugoslavia's friendship as another influential member of the group.

Khrushchev had debunked Stalin and all his works in his epoch-making speech at the Tenth Party Congress. Within the Soviet Union itself, although the basic policies remained unchanged, the Stalinist rigours of the system were somewhat relaxed. But Khrushchev had his personal reasons too; he had bitter complaints about Stalin's insulting behaviour towards his senior party colleagues and his arbitrary and capricious nature. Khrushchev had recounted how Stalin ordered him to dance the Kazachok, which he forced himself to do, fearing death if he failed to obey. This is a particularly energetic Cossack dance in which the dancer squats on his toes and, with arms akimbo, flings out one leg after another and goes round in circles in ever-rising tempo. For Khrushchev, with his pot belly and pudgy legs, it must have been sheer torture; to the onlookers it must have provided rare entertainment.

In the summer of 1956 a particularly significant event took place which attracted world-wide attention. It was the celebrated Brioni meeting between Tito, Nehru and Nasser. Nehru arrived in Yugoslavia after a long tour of the Soviet Union, looking fresh and full of energy. Nasser flew over direct from Cairo. A record number of journalists of every hue gathered on the mainland. Expectations ran high that some far-reaching pronouncements would emerge from a meeting of the three foremost leaders of the non-aligned movement. The western correspondents feared a deep-seated conspiracy to undermine the western position in the Cold War. Others hoped that a far-reaching programme would emerge for bringing about a more just and equitable world order in conditions of international peace and security. Nothing that we could say or do did anything to allay these fanciful fears or dispel the extravagant hopes.

Nasser had arrived with a formidable accompanying cast; Nehru, much more modestly, with just two officials. The leaders were housed in separate villas and met in Tito's splendid seaside mansion. There was a very elaborate programme of concerts, music and banquets, with private talks between the leaders. There was to be a great naval review on the last day. The visit would conclude with a full session of all three delegations, when a joint communique would be issued.

While all these diversions were taking place, I kept reminding the Yugoslavs to show us the draft communique so that we could hammer it into shape in good time before it was presented to our principals. In accordance with the usual custom, the host country was to provide the first draft. The Yugoslavs kept assuring us that the draft was ready in translation and that it would not take long to go over the document. The leaders were to meet at half-past nine on the morning of departure to have a preliminary look at it, before the elaborate naval review. After a farewell luncheon the departure of both visitors was scheduled for 2 o'clock in the afternoon. Nehru was due to go to Cairo after Nasser's departure, the aim being to reach there before dark.

There was a lengthy programme of folk dances from the different regions of Yugoslavia and a formal banquet thereafter at President Tito's residence on the last evening. The dance went on and on; when they at last finished, the banquet began, punctuated by long speeches and accompanying toasts. As course after course was served, my impatience to see the draft communique increased. At last I managed to persuade the Yugoslavs to break away from the table and, along with the Egyptian Secretary-General, we proceeded to my hotel suite to study the draft.

When we saw the draft, our hearts fell. Instead of the concise and tightly-packed document that is usually issued on such occasions, the Yugoslav effusion ran into a score of pages and more of loosely-phrased and ungrammatical prose. Even a first glance showed that not only was it prolix, but also highly repetitive and otiose, and covered items of a most controversial nature, tendentiously worded. The Egyptians shared our concern and it was decided that we should go over it page by page and line by line. We began hacking the draft to pieces, omitting whole paragraphs and later whole pages, and redrafting much of what was retained. At three o'clock in the morning I sent for my sleepy secretary to type it all out and have it ready by seven-thirty when we would have a fresh look at the clean draft. When we met again, it still needed some changes. The time for its submission to the principals had already arrived and messages began coming in exhorting us to turn up. The final document was not more than two and a half pages and with this we hurried to Tito's residence.

There we found the three leaders either strumming their fingers on the table or looking out of the window, the very picture of boredom. When Nasser saw the draft, he exclaimed: 'There is nothing in it about Palestine and Israel. What will my enemies say.' Tito looked at it and said: 'It is a mountain in labour producing a mouse.' Nehru asked them what was wrong with it, and after a brief discussion it was decided that all three delegations should produce their own drafts which would then be jointly discussed. Thereupon the visitors hurried to their residences. Accompanying Nehru in his carriage to his villa, I began the laborious task of redrafting the communique, while Nehru went into his room. Every now and then he would come out and ask how I was getting on. When I was more than half-way through, he came out holding a couple of typed sheets which he had been dictating to his secretary. He looked at my efforts and, making a few changes in his draft, asked that the two should be married. He asked that a dozen fair copies be prepared and brought over to Tito's residence as soon as possible. He then hurried off to attend the farewell luncheon while I organised the typing.

The luncheon over, we were taken to another little island

beyond Brioni called Vanga, with Tito at the wheel of a speed-boat. A path, hacked through the brambles, led to an open space where a large deal table and benches had been placed. In this rural setting, we sat down to the business of issuing a joint communique. Tito and Nasser had been joined by their delegations, Tito's occupying one side of the table. On the near side, sat Nehru with Raghavan Pillai and me, and Nasser with his delegation.

Nehru began by asking Tito if his draft was ready. Tito turned to Vice-President Kardely, Kardely to Foreign Minister Koca Popovic. Popovic replied in the affirmative, but added that it was in Serbo-Croatian! Nehru next turned to Nasser to ask the same question. Nasser turned to Vice-President Al-Baghdadi, Baghdadi to Foreign Minister Mahmood Fauzi, who too replied in the affirmative but said it was in Arabic!

Nehru then asked me to distribute copies of our draft. Tito had it studied, but asked no questions and raised no objections. Nasser began examing it line by line and, apologising for his poor knowledge of English, asked what a particular word meant. When he showed some hesitation in accepting it, Nehru would ask me for synonyms, which I would hastily note down and pass on to him. Nasser would nod his head in approval of one of them and continue his reading. This exercise was repeated some half a dozen times, after which the draft communique was declared adopted by all three leaders.

I was full of admiration for the superb diplomatic skill and adroitness with which Nehru had managed what could have become a very awkward situation. The communique, rather anodyne in character, was received with a mixture of incredulity and disappointment. The western journalists thought there was more to it than met the eye, having convinced themselves that there was a secret protocol where the real teeth lay. The Asian journalists accepted it at face value, contenting themselves with the thought that the meeting had furthered the cause of non-alignment.

After the successful conclusion of the Vanga meeting, one could relax and enjoy the short cruise in Tito's yacht, the *Yadranka*. Madame Jovanka Tito was on board and so was Indira Gandhi, who had accompanied her father and had remained very much in the background. Susheela, who was also in the party, decided to take a snapshot of the three leaders together. They chivalrously obliged, standing together on the poop. But Susheela was no expert with the camera: the picture came out very clearly, only the heads were missing!

The hour of departure had been considerably delayed, but it was still light. Nehru had come in a brand new Viscount turbo-jet aircraft of which he seemed rather proud. He had earlier asked me to try and arrange for Nasser to travel to Cairo with him. I spoke to my old friend Mahmood Fauzi to put it to his President, not failing to mention the comfortable new plane in which he was being invited to travel. Mahmood Fauzi however said that, as a matter of fact, his President had brought two Viscounts and invited Nehru to travel with him. So it was with Nasser that Nehru went. The psychological advantage of Nehru, the guest, arriving in Nasser's own capital with his host as his guest passenger was thus lost!

After the departure of the eminent visitors, Tito and his colleagues were in a very relaxed and jovial mood. Tito invited Susheela and me to accompany him for an impromptu supper. He again drove his speed-boat, racing past both Brioni and Vanga, to a still smaller and unspoilt little island. Its sole structure, to which we went, was a stone hut, rather like an igloo; it had a counter and a small wooden table with benches. We were a small party of eight, including Vice President and Madame Kardely, Foreign Minister Popovic, the Yugoslav Ambassador to India and ourselves. Tito and his wife donned aprons and got behind the counter, Tito expertly mixing cocktails which he passed around. There was plenty of Zilarka, Tito's favourite white wine. The whole party burst into song, Susheela joining in to the appreciation of all. Jovanka turned out sausages and eggs at the grill. It was a thoroughly relaxed and enjoyable occasion and we parted contentedly, to a well deserved rest.

Tito's views regarding India's naval defence strategy were offered on the occasion of the call of the newly-refitted cruiser, INS *Vikrant*, at the port of Split. The Captain, B.R. Nanda (later Admiral), was to call on Tito at Brioni and I was to present him after visiting the fine ship myself. It was a nightmare drive all along the narrow untarred road which hugged the coast and, as it was high-tide, it was often lashed by the sea and, in places, inundated.

When Tito received us, he asked about our coastal defence strategy and explained his own. India was rather like an island because of its long coast-line and the coast could best be defended from land by air power combined with high-speed patrol boats. Airstrips along the coast for fighter aircraft could wreak havoc on a hostile naval force. Speed-boats armed with two torpedoes could do the rest. Yugoslavia was producing the latter by the score; they were cheap and expendable. He questioned the utility of expensive aircraft carriers for coastal defence as they themselves needed heavy naval protection without which they were sitting ducks, like the British carriers *Prince of Wales* and *Republic* which were sent to the bottom by Japanese fighter planes. He was sure India could also turn out torpedo boats by the score. Tito's wise counsel, however, had little impact on Defence Minister Krishna Menon's thinking; he remained enamoured of the dinosaurs which the British were anxious to get rid of.

Brioni was very much Tito's private domain and we were often invited to that exclusive island paradise. There, the top leaders and high officials would disport themselves on the beach and, in between excursions into the crystal clear water, I would settle whatever business there was on hand. Never before or after have I had occasion to do diplomatic business at the highest level in swimming trunks!

Tito often showed us special consideration, thanks to the growing relations between our countries, which earned me the sobriquet of 'the favourite son' among my colleagues. Susheela and I had driven the 250 kilometres to Zagreb from Belgrade to attend a large international trade fair where India, for the first time, had a stall. Although the stall was on a rather parsimonious scale, Tito and Jovanka lingered on, showing their appreciation. As he was leaving, Tito invited Susheela and me to accompany him back in his special train. Our car was loaded on to the train and we were ushered into our compartment. As soon as the train started, the Military Secretary said the President and Madame Broz were awaiting us in their carriage. We were received by them at a dinner table and we four sat facing each other. Tito's favourite Zilarka was poured out and the glasses constantly replenished. Susheela, who was practically a teetotaller, had to be persuaded to keep pace with the rest. In this pleasant ambience, Tito began putting a volley of questions with surprising openness. Even President Ayub Khan of Pakistan, with whom I was on much closer personal terms, never asked us questions with such frankness about his own country. Tito asked me to give my opinion about the Yugoslav economy. With my tongue loosened, I said that Yugoslavia was basically an agricultural country and that, while it used to have an exportable surplus of a million tons of wheat, it had now to import an equivalent quantity. Although compulsory collectivisation had been scrapped after the break with the Soviet Union, the damage it had done had not been righted and, unless the agricultural base of the economy was strengthened, the economy would not improve. Tito asked what I thought of the state farms and cooperatives. I said that by their very definition, cooperatives should be free and voluntary, but there was a considerable degree of compulsion in them; as for the state farms, they were bureaucratically run and inefficient. In the towns there were chronic shortages due both to paucity of supplies and inefficient distribution. The conversation continued in this vein. Tito also posed questions about how India was tackling its numerous problems.

In the midst of this, a loud noise which sounded like an explosion or gunshot, rang out. Before our startled eyes, Tito ducked like lightening under the table, with Jovanka on top of him for his protection. We sat transfixed in our places until our host and hostess re-emerged. They had, no doubt, developed such quick reflexes from their long experience of war and the Balkan tradition of political assassination. Thereafter, the conversation continued as if nothing had happened. There was no interpreter and the language problem was overcome by using scraps of whichever language came in handy. Tito's German was excellent; but we had none. But both he and his wife had been learning English, of which they had acquired a smattering. Jovanka knew a little French.We had picked up some Russian and had a passable knowledge of French. So our conversation which lasted two or three hours, if not elegant, was at least mutually comprehensible.

Jovanka had been taking a lively interest in the conversation, sometimes asking a question or seeking clarification and also helping Tito in interpreting from English. A large, kindly woman—Susheela likened her to an Earth Goddess—Jovanka had been a redoubtable warrior in the fight against the Nazis. Her's and Tito's was a comradeship that was welded in the fires of that life-and-death struggle. An intelligent woman, she had begun taking increasing interest in affairs of state and expanding her influence and contacts. As the President grew older and needed more rest, Jovanka became correspondingly more active and interfering. But then she went too far. She began setting herself up as a power centre, screening visitors to Tito and even making access to him difficult for old party colleagues and high officials. Matters reached such a pass that complaints began to reach Tito's ears. Warnings proved ineffective. Eventually, in a sad end to their relationship, Tito banished her from his residence and forbade all communication with her.

In the autumn of 1956, Hungary, under the leadership of Imre Nagy, suddenly broke out in revolt against Soviet overlordship. The Soviet army of occupation was forced to withdraw, but as the new regime began dismantling the communist structure with the enthusiastic support of the population, Moscow took alarm lest the infection spread to its other client states. The Red Army then backtracked and, rumbling into Budapest, crushed the movement with great savagery. A hard-line puppet was installed and Imre Nagy was tried by a kangaroo court and executed.

The Yugoslav authorities at first welcomed the revolt as a hostile government had been ousted, and especially as their exposed northern border had been freed of the lowering presence of the Red Army. But they were less enthusiastic when the new Hungarian regime began moving fast towards being a free and open democracy as they (the Yugoslavs) were not prepared to make any changes in their own system. Very little news of the dire happenings had been allowed to percolate through when the Soviets returned. The Yugoslav Foreign Office, however, had hourly information from its Ambassador in Budapest with whom it was in direct wireless connection. This was freely and fully imparted to me on my daily visits to the Foreign Office. The information was detailed and accurate and I sent daily cables to South Block in Delhi to relay it, knowing of the news blackout. Our Ambassador to Hungary, K.P.S. Menon, was based in Moscow; the young Chargé d' Affaires, Ishi Rahman, was holed up in Budapest, cut off from all communication with the outside world. But he diligently maintained a daily diary which kept piling up, until he had an opportunity to have it surreptitiously taken out to Vienna, from where the Indian mission forwarded it to New Delhi. But that was much later. My reports were the first to reach New Delhi, but they were discounted as not being first-hand. In fact, Krishna Menon had expressed considerable annoyance at my temerity in poking my nose into something with which I was not directly concerned. He had earlier brushed off a questioner when asked to comment on the Hungarian uprising by playing it down as nothing but a riot which had to be put down. Krishna Menon had considerable clout in South Block and, because of his deliberate obfuscation of inconvenient facts, conditioned India's public reaction to the Hungarian revolt.

While the whole world condemned the brutal suppression of a popular revolt to replace the existing system by a democratic one, India's response was weak and almost apologetic. The reason put out that India was not in possession of the full facts from its envoy was perhaps technically correct, as Menon was away in Moscow. But whatever information was available to other countries was also available to us, even if the Yugoslav reports were discounted. This was an unfortunate lapse on India's part, which received much international criticism.

When the Soviet hold was re-established, we had occasion to spend a day in Budapest on our way to Vienna by road. Rahman fully confirmed all that the Yugoslavs had passed on to me and the evidence of our own eyes did the rest. Whole streets were just a heap of rubble in process of being cleared by bulldozers. Apartment blocks and houses had gaping shell-holes or were pitted with deep bullet marks. There was broken glass everywhere. Soviet tanks stood menacingly at street corners and intersections and in front of public buildings and the parliament. The streets were still partially deserted and pedestrians silently hurried by. Normally a city full of animation and gaiety, Budapest now wore a funereal appearance. While Susheela and I were standing on the high bank on the southern side of the Danube looking at the once-stately city, a couple of ladies, obviously of high estate, sided up to us and in English invited us to their house near by saying that they were relatives of the eminent artist Amrita Shergil. We accompanied them into a small room of a mansion, once theirs but now taken over, leaving them with two or three rooms on the ground floor. They talked *sotto voce* of their hardships and recent experiences and begged us to buy some valuables from them, which we had to decline. It was a saddening chance encounter as it typified how an entire proud nation had been cowed down into abject submission.

Life for us in Belgrade was varied and agreeable except during two or three months in midwinter when one was holed in by heavy snow and a fierce wind called the Kosh-hava, a Turkish name. In winter the main diversions were music concerts and opera when they took place, and wining and dining among the diplomatic crops. On one winter's week-end, Tito invited many ambassadors to join him and his party at a hunt at the former royal hunting lodge in the reserved forest of Karageorgero (known after the former Karageorge dynasty). We assembled in the evening and were up betimes when we were each assigned to a beautiful phaeton drawn by a pair of the famed Serbian horses. I had brought only a shotgun, thinking that our quarry would be pheasants which abounded in the wilds, having been out before on such errands with Yugoslav friends. But the president's Military Secretary insisted that I go after a stag and he pressed a Mannlicker rifle of ·275 bore into my hands. Choosing my partner, the Burmese Ambassador, we set off in the open phaeton with a forester sitting up with the groom. The gallant horses, snorting in the freezing air and pulling the phaeton axle-deep in snow, ploughed on into the forest, dodging trees and sudden dips in the snow. After some time we reached a clearing ·at the far end from where we espied a herd of some twenty does with a few stags. The forester, pointing at them, urged me to fire, but I refused to take a random shot and certainly not from a carriage. To the forester's dismay, I dismounted, and entering the forest cover, stalked the animals, working my way through the snow, which drowned my footfall, upwind, so that the animals would not get my scent. Getting within some twenty-five yards of them, I chose the biggest antlers. The shot crackled in the cold air, the herd vanished and the stag stumbled a few yards and fell into a snow drift.

When the carriage came up, the forester was full of admiration at the trophy, a huge stag, the size of a horse with enormous antlers of fourteen points. It was far too heavy to lift and, marking the spot for it to be collected later, we moved on to the rendezvous place where we were all expected to assemble for an al-fresco lunch with the President. But my companion, seeing how easy it was, also wished to collect a trophy. We therefore tracked the herd and, after a long time, came upon it again. I instructed my companion on what to do but, when he fired, the herd disappeared without a trace. Not satisfied, he insisted on another try, but the herd could not be found. Meanwhile, the hour for the rendezvous had passed and our high boots were full of melting snow which froze our feet. We stopped by a forester's hut in the middle of the woods and, after drying ourselves, proceeded in search of some nourishment and a hot drink. We arrived to find the guests gone and the waiters packing up. When we eventually returned to the hunting lodge, our colleagues had been debating among themselves as to our fate. Many of our western colleagues had stereotypical, if contradictory, images of Indians—Maharajas on the one hand, and Gandhian non-violence on the other, and therefore did not expect me to display any skill as a huntsman. One who prided himself as a hunter had even said tauntingly that my hunting partner and I may have shot each other. I was put to much questioning which turned to astonishment when the stag arrived in a cart. The Yugoslavs were of course delighted. Moreover, the day's picking had not been good. Throughout the day, the forest had resounded to the sound of firing as in a battlefield, but all there was to show for it was a few birds, which too had been shot by Tito and other Yugoslavs. At this point, the stag arrived in a cart to be met with astonishment and delight. Stereotypes of Indians obviously did not take into consideration the fact that in India in my generation, hunting, especially of big game as I had done, was regarded with approval as a manly sport.

At dinner that evening, I was given the place of honour at Tito's right and before we rose from the table, the antlers, duly mounted, were presented to me. As venison was an export commodity, I was allowed, by special dispensation, to keep a leg, which came in handy for our Republic Day reception the following day.

There was a particularly agreeable tradition in Yugoslavia to treat the month of August as a virtual holiday. While Tito and his entourage withdrew to Brioni, the heads of diplomatic missions were expected to go to the delightful resort of Bled up north at the foot of the Alps. The mountain lake of Bled, with its clear, limpid water, was some four miles in circumference. In the middle of the lake was a small island. A church stood on this island, its steeple reflected in the shimmering waters. On the far side was a tree-covered hill, some thousand metres high, surmounted by an abbey. There were plenty of agreeable walks and rowing and swimming. On week-ends one could drive up a steep winding road to a mountain pass which led into Austria, which we occasionally did with our close friends, Walter and Erna Wodak. He later became the Secretary-General of the Austrian foreign office. We were housed in a hotel on the lake, with the balcony jutting out over the water. It was an altogether delightful interlude to be in those lovely surroundings.

A wonderful experience, which remains fresh in my memory, was an eighteen-day cruise along the Adriatic coast as the guests of the Yugoslav naval Commander-in-Chief, Admiral Mate Jerkovic and his wife. Fellow-guests were General Papo, a good friend, and his Russian wife. Papo was a celebrated surgeon, one of the pioneers of open-heart surgery. He had been allowed to accept an English knighthood. It was he who looked after our medical needs and those of the Indian missions for years. The yacht in which we sailed was a beautiful, sleek vessel, captured from the Italians. It was manned by eleven sailors and a captain. We had a fine bedroom below deck, with bath and hot and cold water, but, apart from sleeping there, all our time was spent on deck in bathing costume. Leaving Opatigi in the north, we made for the small island of Mjlet where the inbred inhabitants, still in medieval costume, were regarded as mentally deficient, but they could still make good wine. We bought two huge casks of red and white wine for a song, and then sailed down the coast from one beautiful island to another. The islands were of all sizes, many uninhabited, but the larger ones had some communities of fisherfolk and growers of grapes and olives. Whenever there was a naval presence, the Admiral's yacht with flag flying, the Admiral himself turned out in starched uniform and the sailors in theirs, would sail in to dock, to the admiration of tourists and residents. A naval guard of honour would be lined up with a band in attendance and we would follow appropriately clad. After some sight-seeing, the evening would end at an inviting seaside restaurant or terrace where the excellent sea food of the area, washed down with the local wine, would be served to the accompaniment of the haunting music of the Adriatic coast. We generally cast anchor at dusk in some secluded cove or bay without sight of man or habitation. The clear water, so clean that even the bottom, forty feet down, and the marine life there, could be clearly seen, would tempt one for a swim before supper. Often we would cast anchor en route for a swim in the hot daytime. The sea abounded in fish of every variety and our diligent sailors caught enough to keep us well provided. Between a cluster of islands known as Kornati, the sea is over two hundred feet deep, and is noted for the plentifulness of a deep-sea fish called 'Red Snapper' or 'Zubitsa' in the local tongue and 'Rouget' in French. We let down the jolly boats and line with three hooks baited with sardines. Almost immediately, the line was pulled up; all three hooks had shimmering fish. In an hour or two, we caught over one hundred fish, which kept us well provided for days. For fruit we would send out to one of the islands and the sailors would return with baskets full of sweet red and white grapes and delicious figs which grew in wild profusion.

We could seldom use the sails—there was little wind—and travelled instead on the engines. The weather had remained perfect, but on the last day it became stormy. We were to visit an island off Split, our last port of call, a short distance away. We got badly caught in the storm and the yacht began tossing and pitching wildly. Susheela was so sick that she had to be given first aid by Papo, and I too felt miserable. Our companions' high spirits did nothing to improve matters. The moment we touched land, after what seemed an eternity, we felt quite normal, as though nothing had happened. The 'blue grotto' could be entered by boat only at low tide, and only when the setting sun entered it. Everything inside was blue, the water, the fishes, the walls, ourselves, and when we jumped into the sea, our bodies were phosphorescent. That was the last episode of our never-to-be forgotten cruise. No wonder that Edward VIII lost both his heart as well as his throne during an Adriatic cruise!

We had been over three and a half years in Yugoslavia and the time for departure was near. It was with a pang that we were leaving the colourful and varied life that Yugoslavia provided and the warm relationships that had been established with the Yugoslav government and people. We were, moreover, leaving a country with which our relations could not have been better, for Pakistan—with which they could not have been worse. Unknown to our policy-makers when we came to Yugoslavia, it had become a staunch friend, central to our policy of non-alignment. As Yugoslavia bestrode the great divide between East and West, it was in a unique position to interpret their policies towards each other and towards the non-aligned movement which it epitomised. Having been an insider of the communist block, then an inveterate enemy and now a reluctant friend, its information and analysis of Soviet policies was of exceptional interest. The association of Yugoslavia as a key member of the non-aligned group of countries gave the movement a global complexion, no longer confined to Asian and African countries and extending beyond racial or colonial limitations.

When the nation emerged from its fiery ordeal after the War, Josip Broz Tito stood out as its unchallenged leader. With his redoubtable 'Partisans' he had held the Nazi invaders at bay; no foreign 'liberators' had intervened to bring about the expulsion of the enemy. Tales were proudly recounted of the heroic battles fought by the 'Partisans' against great odds. Tito's dominating personality was a powerful force for unity. The socialist alliance, its ideology and organisation, were another cementing factor. The harsh reality of the Soviet threat and the country's isolation kept the different areas together in the face of a common danger. The divisive effects of different sects and religions were offset by Marxist ideology and the economic and social imbalance between north and south was partly compensated by the five-year plans.

Tito was aware of the problem of succession and, had Vice-President Kardelj lived, the transition might have been smoothly effected. But Kardelj predeceased Tito. A new constitution was accordingly drawn up which provided for a rotating presidency on a yearly basis between the six republics. This worked well enough for a while, but latent animosities, hitherto held in check, began surfacing. The weakening state and party structure, along with a depressed economy, gave rise to increasing public dissatisfaction.

The first outbreak was between the Serbs and the Croats. During the War, many Croats had turned quislings and their fascist organisation—the 'Ustashi'—had launched a reign of terror against the Serbs and the resistance movement. Along with the war against the invader, a bitter civil war was also being fought; the Yugoslavs estimated that the two wars claimed no less than one and half million victims each. The bitter memories of the civil war had continued to fester and led to a renewed outburst of fighting between Serbs and Croats.

The spark was lit when the turn of a Croat as President of the Federation came up by rotation. The Serbian President happened to be an ambitious, parochial and narrow-minded man—Milosevic—who dreamt of a Greater Serbia. A pro-forma election on the basis of unanimity by the presidents of the six republics as electors was normally a formality. But Milosevic voted against the Croat candidate, thus breaching both the constitution and convention. Thereupon, the Croats, deeply outraged, declared they could not co-exist with the Serbs and proclaimed their independence. Slovenia followed suit. Alarmed at the prospect of the Balkan tinder-box igniting, mediators from the European community began scurrying about, trying to calm down passions and to prevent the disintegration of the country. These efforts continued for some time, raising hopes and dashing them again. Meanwhile, the German foreign office under Genscher, presumably in expectation of widening the area of German influence, became restive at the delay and threw out an ultimatum setting a date for the mediators to show results, failing which they would unilaterally recognise the independence of both Slovenia and Croatia. That act of crowning stupidity blew up all efforts at reconciliation, and with it the integrity of Yugoslavia. Serbs and Croats fought each other with renewed ferocity, until a ceasefire was brought about with UN intervention, but not before much blood had been shed, thousands made refugees and towns and villages reduced to charred ruins.

Bosnia-Herzigovina, unwilling to fall under Serb hegemony, likewise declared its independence and was recognised by the international community. Macedonia followed suit, only little Montenegro remained with Serbia, the rump still calling itself

Yugoslavia. The breakup of the once proud Yugoslavia was nearly complete. But not quite. Serbia determined to extend its boundaries further. The Bosnian Serbs were incited to rise against their predominantly Muslim government to wrest areas where they were in a majority and to oust the others, Muslims and Croats, from yet more territory. They were heavily armed by Serbia while their opponents had to depend on light arms. Years of fractricidal war have followed which has brought terrible suffering and bloodshed to the civilian population. As Bosnia has mixed populations of Muslims, Serbs and Croats spread all over the towns and countryside, the battle-lines have shifted like desert sands. Serbs have fought Muslims, Muslims have fought Croats and both have joined to fight the Serbs. With their superior military equipment and numbers, the Serbs have captured almost two-thirds of the territory.

The term 'ethnic cleansing', which has been freely used, is a misnomer, as all three groups are Slav and belong to the same ethnic family. The Bosnian Muslims are not Turks or Arabs: they are Slav converts. A distinct ethnic group in Serbia are the Albanians (or Shiptars as they are sometimes called) who inhabit the Kosovo region. There was a small Turkish community in the Macedonian Republic, but it migrated to Turkey in the nineteen-fifties and there were no Turks in Bosnia.

Despite the efforts of the United Nations and the European Community, peace has not been restored in Bosnia. Ceasefires have been made and almost immediately unmade. Millions have been uprooted from their homes and, like flotsam, move from place to place as the tide of battle ebbs and flows. Amidst all the destruction, the most grievous has been that of the great historic port city of Dubrovnik, a veritable jewel of the Adriatic, which once vied with Venice in power and wealth and glory. Its ruthless bombardment by the Serbs was an act of sheer vandalism as it was far removed from any strategic or military involvement. Whenever and however the fires of hatred, greed and violence are quenched, one thing is clear. Tito's Yugoslavia, once a force for peace and harmony among nations, will be buried deep. Instead, the tinder-box of the Balkans will continue to smoulder, posing a recurrent threat to the peace of Europe.

It is saddening to see today the shattered remains of that once proud and happy country. Yugoslavia (meaning 'Southern Slav') was created from the dismemberment of the Ottoman and Austro-Hungarian empires after World War II. The present-day republics of Serbia, Bosnia-Herzigovina and Macedonia were part of the Ottoman Empire. In the fifteenth-century the last Serbian prince, Lazar, along with the flower of Serbian nobility, was slain on the blood-soaked battlefield of Kosovo; since then the land had been the western outpost of the Ottomans. The two northern republics of Slovenia and Croatia were for centuries part of the Austro-Hungarian Empire. Over the centuries, the two areas under their respective overlords developed very differently. The north was essentially Germanic in culture, Catholic in religion, socially and economically advanced, sharing in the prosperity of the Empire. In contrast, the southern lands were much influenced by Turkish ways; they were culturally and economically backward and followed the Orthodox faith—while the Serbs resisted the onslaught of Islam, large numbers were converted in Bosnia-Herzigovina. While the Hapsburgs made little difference between the subjects of their more cohesive Empire, the Ottomans gave preference to Turks and converts. They set up the corps of 'janisseries', young boys taken from their parents, converted them to Islam and put them through a course of rigorous military discipline. They formed a Praetorian guard around the Sultan, multiplied greatly and came to exercise considerable power and influence in the affairs of the Empire. Any attempt at revolt was suppressed with great brutality. A Serbian uprising in the nineteenth century was crushed savagely and the heads of the leaders embedded in a tower of skulls. They still gape reproachfully at one, as a grim reminder of the past.

# NINE

# Pakistan—The Perennial Problem

My arrival in Pakistan was due in June 1958. I had received a cordial message from the Prime Minister, Sir Firoze Khan Noon, whom I had known fairly well before, welcoming my assignment and requesting my early arrival. But I was delayed by six months as, while on a few weeks home leave, I was called to Lebanon by the UN Secretary General, Dag Hammarskjold, with Prime Minister Nehru's approval, to deal with the first civil war in that troubled country.

When I arrived in Karachi in the middle of November, the situation there had undergone a complete somersault. Just a month earlier, the government had been overthrown by a military coup. The President, Iskander Mirza, had been exiled, the Prime Minister and his cabinet sacked. An inquisition had been launched into the antecedents and activities of businessmen, politicians and senior government servants. Many leading businessmen found themselves in prison and many senior officials who had been riding high were summarily dismissed for corruption or inefficiency, or both. Politicians were barred from holding public office. Military officers at all levels had replaced heads of departments and ministries. A Council of Ministers, hand-picked from among army generals with a sprinkling of civilians, had been set up.

An atmosphere of fear and suspicion prevailed and stories were told in hushed voices of the high-handedness of military officers suddenly catapulted into positions of command. In the Secretariat, senior civil functionaries, unaccustomed to much physical exertion, were punished by being made to sprint, panting almost to the point of collapse for petty peccadilloes, such as being late for office. It was even rumoured that errant officials were being caned by young subalterns.

In Delhi there was natural alarm at the coup, as those who had hurled threats against India now also had the means to carry them out. Mr Nehru, when asked in Parliament for India's reaction to events in Pakistan, described the new dispensation, with some justification, as 'naked military dictatorship'. There could hardly have been a more inauspicious moment for a new envoy to take charge of the Indian mission in Pakistan.

Relations between India and Pakistan, because of the entangled nature of the problems between them and their emotional colouring, were difficult enough at the best of times, but they had become even more intractable with the rapid turnover of Pakistani regimes. No sooner were contacts established with one group, than it would be toppled and another with different perceptions and capabilities would take its place. Both countries at Independence had inherited the 1935 Constitution of British India which envisaged a parliamentary form of government. But with the early demise of Mohammad Ali Jinnah, himself brought up in the parliamentary tradition, and the assassination of Liaquat Ali Khan, the first Prime Minister, the shaky democratic structure in Pakistan began rapidly to crumble.

After Liaquat Ali's death, the officials leap-frogged over the Muslim League politicians who had already discredited themselves by their seamy intrigues and reckless self-serving manoeuvres. Ghulam Muhammad, who had served in the accounts service in India and was then Finance Minister, took over as the Governor-General after Jinnah. Defying his constitutional status, he began to function as a dictator, changing Prime Ministers at will. He, in turn, was made to abdicate by General Iskander Mirza who, if anything, was even more autocratic and capricious. Prime Ministers came and went as through a revolving door.

Meanwhile, the administration had reached the point of collapse while popular discontent increased by the day. Mirza set up a hand-picked Constituent Assembly, having dismissed the one appointed by his predecessor, which produced a constitution in 1956 tailor-made to Mirza's specifications. It provided for a presidential form of government with the President enjoying extensive powers, and was speedily adopted by a tame Assembly which also elected Mirza as President.

Mirza pursued his unbridled exercise of power, which only accelerated the process of national disintegration. The government, without national elections, lacked a representative character, but Mirza and his entourage were determined to avoid elections. In the 1954 elections in East Pakistan the Muslim League had been wiped out and a similar fate would have overtaken the party in the west had national elections been held. From the start, Mirza had been plotting a take-over. But without the support of the army, the ultimate repository of state power in Pakistan, he was powerless to act.

General Ayub Khan had been content to pursue a military career during his term as Army Commander in the east wing. But with his promotion as Commander-in-Chief and his return to West Pakistan he felt alarmed at the low morale of the army, which the rival political factions were trying to infiltrate. He set about with determination to insulate the army from politics and politicians and to build it up into an efficient force. Mirza and he were the architects of the American connection in 1954 on the strength of their proclaimed anti-communism, which went straight to the heart of John Foster Dulles, the Secretary of State, and the Pentagon. Thereafter, a supply of modern American arms began to flow into Pakistan in generous measure.

Ayub Khan had been granted a two years' extension in service by Mirza which, the latter hoped, would firmly rivet him to his side in support of whatever action he may choose to take. There were indeed some close similarities in their political views. Although in 1954 Ayub Khan still seemed committed to a parliamentary form of government and the subordination of the military to the civil power, he had, like Mirza, come round to the conviction that the politicians and the existing system of governance were responsible for the country's ills. The two had persuaded themselves that Pakistan needed a strong government and a firm hand at the controls, which only the military could provide. Therefore the corrupt politicians were to be ousted, the venal bureaucracy purged and rapacious businessmen curbed.

Mirza, confident that having prepared the ground meticulously and with the support of the army, was now prepared to deliver the *coup de grace*. On 7 October 1958, the central and provincial governments were summarily dismissed, the legislature abrogated, the constitution of 1956, of which he was the architect and to which he had sworn allegiance, revoked. Martial Law was declared in both wings and a Presidential proclamation in justification of the measure carried a strong denunciation of the politicians for their 'shameful exploitation' of the simple masses, their ruthless struggle for power and 'the prostitution of Islam for political purpose'.

Not a dog barked at this turn of events; the elimination of the venal politicians was welcomed by the people with relief. Indeed, responsible people had for some time been urging desperate remedies for a desperate situation. After the coup, Iskander Mirza, elated at the success of his plan, appointed his co-conspirator, General Ayub Khan, as Chief Martial Law Administrator. But little did he realise that the prop on which he had built his strategy would be suddenly pulled away from under him and the same ladder used by Ayub Khan to climb to the top.

Ayub Khan had been biding his time, cautiously pursuing his objective silently and resolutely, without arousing in Mirza an inkling of suspicion. He refrained from taking action until the time was ripe and the ground thoroughly prepared; not by him, but by Mirza, on whom would fall the onus if anything went wrong. True, he had been offered the reins of government by Ghulam Muhammad, whose faltering hands could no longer hold them. Others, such as Fatima Jinnah and the Aga Khan, too, had been pressing him to take the destiny of the country into his hands. But he had declined as he felt the situation was not then ripe nor the time propitious.

On 27 October 1958, with the full support of the army, Mirza was ousted as President in the quiet of the night. Effective power was already in Ayub Khan's hands; all that he needed was his formal designation as President. Mirza was peremptorily bundled out of the President's house and Ayub Khan stepped into it. It was all very smoothly managed and went like clockwork. Mirza, stunned and helpless, had perforce to resign himself to his fate and to accept exile from the country.

Soon after this, in November 1958 I arrived in Pakistan. There was not a single passenger on the usually crowded Dakota flight as I set out for Karachi. This was far from reassuring and I wondered what awaited me at the other end. I had enough time during the slow four-hour flight for rumination as we skimmed over the desert landscape. During the decade since Partition my predecessors had been able to accomplish very little to improve relations which had soured from the very moment of Pakistan's birth. Would my tenure be as barren as the endless Thar desert below?

It had been thought that when the wounds of Partition were still raw, Indo-Pak relations extremely tense, and innumerable vexed problems, both political and psychological, constantly threatening to erupt in an explosion, a dialogue with the Muslim League rulers of Pakistan could best be conducted by senior political figures as High Commissioners. They would be acquainted with Pakistani leaders from before Partition. Accordingly, the first envoy was Shri Prakasa, a front-line Congress leader of Cabinet rank. He was followed by Sir Sita Ram, who had been President of the UP Legislative Council when Liaquat Ali Khan, still in his political novitiate, was his deputy. Then came a well-known educationist who had been a senior minister in the state of Udaipur, Dr Mohan Singh Mehta. C.C. Desai, a very senior ICS officer who later entered Parliament and had a very successful business career, was then appointed, largely on the strength of his friendship at Cambridge with Iskander Mirza, the then all-powerful President of Pakistan. If so little could be accomplished by such experienced men with comparitively democratic governments, the chances of my achieving anything with an unknown and untried military dictatorship seemed highly unpromising.

Karachi had the appearance of a city under siege. But the traffic was orderly, people moved about in a business-like way, and the streets were swept clean. The very air seemed as sanitised as a military cantonment. While policemen were often seen, there was little evidence of any obtrusive military presence. Unlike any city in the subcontinent, there was remarkably little noise or the cacophony of human voices, and even the numerous Indian mission staff that had assembled at the airport appeared rather quiet and subdued.

President Ayub Khan, whom I had known in Mathura in 1940, was good enough to grant an early date for the presentation of credentials. The protocol prescribed for the credentials ceremony was elaborate and was spelt out in a printed booklet; it involved proceeding towards the centre of the durbar hall followed by the senior officers of the High Commission, advancing and bowing every few paces. The President would appear from the far end and await the envoy, who would then make his speech and present his letters of credence. After the President's reply, the President would lead the envoy to an ante-chamber for a private conversation.

When I alighted at the President's house from the horse-drawn coach with a mounted escort of the President's bodyguard (accoutred much like our own), I wondered if the President would recall our past association, now some eighteen years past, since previous friendships had not been of any advantage to any of my predecessors. However, a very pleasant surprise awaited me.

I had hardly entered the durbar hall and, as instructed by the Chief of Protocol, was trying to recall the prescribed drill, when the President advanced rapidly towards me with outstretched hand. All protocol forgotten, and smiling profusely, he said how happy he was to see me, asked about my family in detail, recalling each of their names. I had to remind him that I had a speech to make to which he was expected to reply. Stepping back, I delivered my piece and he, his, consisting of the usual platitudes on both sides. The subsequent interview was not devoted to affairs of state, but to complete the enquiries about families and friends. My return to the residence, accompanied by a rather bewildered Chief of Protocol, was in a mood of considerable relief.

I proceeded to make the usual calls on central ministers and senior officials, and generally met with a cool reception almost everywhere. Only the Foreign Minister, a distinguished and highly cultured lawyer, received me with courtesy, reminding me that he was completing his last year at Cambridge when my wife,

Susheela, had joined Newnham College as an undergraduate. His father, Sir Abdul Qadir, a member of the India Council in London, was a friend of Susheela's father and had been asked to be her local guardian. I was glad to have found a friend at court, particularly as my experience with the then Foreign Secretary, Sikander Baig, formerly of my service, whose brother Rashid was a distinguished Indian diplomat, had been frigid to the point of unpleasantness. I returned to New Delhi shortly after to report to the Prime Minister on the new situation in Pakistan and to seek his instructions.

After a hurried visit to Beirut to complete the work of the UN peace-keeping mission on which I had been engaged for the previous six months, I returned to my post with a certain degree of confidence aroused by the unexpected success at resolving the 1958 civil war—the first of many—in Lebanon.

The main problems dividing India and Pakistan were part of the unfinished business of Partition. These were the undemarcated border, the division of the waters of the Indus basin, the question of evacuee property, the settlement of the public debt of undivided India, and the disposition of the India Office Library in London. There was also the hardy annual of the Kashmir question, over which wordy battles had been fought for years at the United Nations and which was straining the rhetoric of vituperation on both sides. Overhanging all these problems, a poisonous psychological atmosphere prevailed, the result of which was an almost total stoppage of trade, severe restrictions on travel, and unbridled press propaganda. My instructions from the Prime Minister, as indeed were my own predilections, were to try and work towards the reduction of the state of tension between the two countries and to promote the solution of the more manageable problems. The question, however, was how and where to start.

While still floundering around for a way through the thicket, a faint gap, which could perhaps be exploited, fortuitously presented itself. Our Republic Day was approaching and a large number of invitations had, as usual, been addressed to ministers, notables, high officials and other figures. Their replies were pouring in, almost all regretting their inability to attend 'due to previous engagements'. I had enquired of the wise-acres at the High Commission, some of whom had been there for years, whether we should also invite the Head of State, as was the normal custom everywhere. The reply was emphatically in the negative, the previous years' experience being cited. The facts as reported to me, and confirmed by my predecessor's graphic reporting, were as follows.

C.C. Desai had asked for a formal interview with President Iskander Mirza whose constant bridge partner he was, which was speedily granted. Ushered into the Presidential presence, the High Commissioner solemnly said: 'Mr President, I have come to invite you to be good enough to attend our Republic Day function on January 26th.' To this the President thus made reply: 'Mr High Commissioner, I would indeed be a hypocrite, considering the state of relations between our two countries, were I to accept your invitation.' The High Commissioner responded: 'Mr President, in that case, I have nothing more to say', and, turning on his heels, he withdrew. Such a direct plunge without a preliminary testing of the waters seemed to me to invite a sharp rebuff.

A way out of the dilemma was provided by the receipt of an invitation from my neighbour, the High Commissioner of Ceylon (as it then was) to their National Day (which followed shortly after our own) in which it was announced that the President would be arriving at a certain time and asking the guests to be present a quarter of an hour earlier. That provided the cue for my seeking an interview with the Foreign Minister the following day.

I told Manzur Qadir that I had come to seek his advice and guidance on a matter of some delicacy. Should I or should I not approach the President to request him to honour us by attending our Republic Day function? If I did not, it would appear discourteous to him since he would be attending a similar function at my neighbour's a few days later. But if I did and got a refusal, it would cause needless embarrassment on both sides, especially at the start of my mission. Manzur Quadir asked if the President's acceptance would indeed be well received in India, and I assured him it would. He said he would take up the matter with the President the next day as a cabinet meeting was then due. He asked me to await his phone call at lunch-time and, if the President agreed, he would simply say 'It is all right', otherwise 'not'.

Next day, with a couple of senior officers, we awaited the promised call, while the clock ticked away past the hour. It was some forty-five minutes after one o'clock when the phone rang and the Foreign Minister's voice came through to say it was all right! Thereupon notices announcing the arrival of the President were promptly issued to all the invitees. Our telephones began ringing incessantly and messages now began arriving to say that the other Pakistani invitees were not so busy after all, and would be delighted to come, notwithstanding their 'previous engagements'!

On the fateful day, a record crowd began assembling on the spacious lawns of the Clifton residence. All necks were craned to catch a glimpse of the unfamiliar sight of President Ayub Khan at the official Indian residence. The two national anthems duly played, the President took his seat between Susheela and me on the large terrace overlooking the lawns. He was wreathed in smiles and chatted away with Susheela and me animatedly and with much laughter. Great was the curiosity among the assemblage at the evident bonhomie, to which they were witness. Word quickly spread around that the President and we were close friends of long standing. The function concluded very pleasantly, and from that moment I felt assured of the personal goodwill of the President and his desire to improve relations, with the confident support of his Foreign Minister.

The whole atmosphere surrounding us seemed to lighten up palpably. The officers and staff who had been living in virtual quarantine, suddenly found Pakistanis no longer shying away from them, but actually inviting them over to their homes. At government offices, greater understanding became evident at all levels. Invitations sent out by us were eagerly accepted and we could resume contacts with all our UP friends, most of whom were delighted to renew old ties without having to look over their shoulders. Old politicians like Chaudhuri Khaliquzzaman, the Raja of Mahmudabad, and friends like Colonel M.A. Rahman, Dr Abdus Samad, Ishat Habibullah, Faridi, Shamim to name only a few, were our frequent guests. At functions, Urdu-speaking migrants would cluster around us, provoking *Dawn* to comment that the Indian High Commissioner had been observed hobnobbing in high-falutin Urdu with his 'UP cronies'.

To further lighten the atmosphere, Susheela and I set about reordering arrangements at the residence. The feeling of being embattled, and that dangers lurked all around one, had to give place to more relaxed conditions. C.C. Desai had kept the two gates of the residence closed with armed security guards in khaki, brandishing rifles, posted at each gate. All other security guards at the chancery and blocks of flats occupied by the officers and staff were similarly ostentatiously protected. At the residence, a red light on a high flagstaff, as at the President's house, would proclaim when the High Commissioner was in residence. The house itself, rather large and awkwardly planned, was in a run-down state as my predecessor had made extensive changes for the worse, enclosing verandahs and dividing bathrooms. Susheela undertook the task, within the budget for annual repairs, to restore and improve the interior, to ferret out from the musty storeroom silver candelabra and tableware, etc. The neglected garden became our pride and joy as we converted an ugly dump of rubble into a fine rockery, with a tea house, an ornamental pool and water-chute, all under a spreading acacia tree which could be lighted up. It became a favourite part of the garden for tea and cocktail parties. The unusual feat of growing roses in the sandy and salty Karachi soil was also successfully performed, much to the delight of visitors. With further changes in the interior decorations and the addition of our own paintings and silver, etc., the residence began to look attractive and dignified. We had a superb Mugh-cook, who had been with us for several years, and with the addition of a skilled cook in Mughalai food, and a well-stocked cellar, we were ready to meet the exacting culinary tastes of the Pakistani gentry and our diplomatic colleagues.

At one of my early meetings with President Ayub Khan, he discussed with remarkable candour the problems besetting our two countries, adding disarmingly that he hoped I trusted him. I replied that I hoped that he too felt the same about me. We then discussed our mutual relations and the problems facing us. I repeated my view that the pending problems constituted the unfinished business of Partition and it was for the successor states to resolve them one by one in order to fulfil the intentions of their respective leaders. The two neighbours should, in their own interests, try to live together peacefully, and if possible harmoniously, but certainly not in a perpetual state of tension and conflict.

The very first problem was to fix on the ground where India ended and Pakistan began. The Radcliffe Line was a hasty and ill-defined line, drawn up by Sir Cyril Radcliffe, who never left Viceroy's House during the four months he spent on the task. It made no pretence of observing any geographical contours or landmarks and relied entirely on census reports, allotting areas and villages, however tenuous their communal proportions, to one side or the other. It was nothing more than a blue pencil line drawn on a map, which cut villages and even houses in two. The brief description accompanying the Radcliffe Award provided little accurate guidance. Also, while the Suleimanki and Husseiniwala headworks lay in India, the canals ran into Pakistan: on this matter protracted and acrimonious negotiations had been dragging on for eight long years in Washington under the aegis of the World Bank. Meanwhile, there were daily disputes about water, with much vituperation and violence on both sides. Tension between villages ran high along the undemarcated border, farmers being shot by border guards if they strayed unwittingly on the wrong side in search of a missing cow or for some other trifling reason. There were also many enclaves, scattered pockets containing one or more villages, left stranded on the wrong side. The primary task therefore was to define the border.

Ayub Khan reacted positively to the suggestion. Both our countries were large enough and necessary adjustment of the boundaries could be made along more rational lines. The respective Home Ministers could meet to discuss the proposal and come to an agreement regarding the modalities and to give it practical effect.

Armed with this proposal, I flew to Delhi to obtain the Prime Minister's approval. Pandit Nehru welcomed the idea and I was asked to discuss it with the Home Minister, Pandit Gobind Ballabh Pant. Pantji, in his cautious manner, examined it from every angle, trying to weigh, with his sharp political antennae, the chances of success or failure. This was not unnatural as few negotiations between the two countries had hitherto yielded any positive results. I assured him that the negotiations could not but succeed as Ayub Khan had given his nod, and especially as the Pakistani team would be led by General Khalid Sheikh. Sheikh was an ambitious man, regarded as the number two in the hierarchy and a prospective successor to Ayub, who, for the sake of his own reputation, would ensure success. Pantji too sensed the political advantage of leading a successful negotiation with

Pakistan, but eventually decided against it. He enjoyed great prestige in the government and was averse to taking the slightest risk of failure. Also, his health was deteriorating. The Prime Minister's choice then fell on Sardar Swaran Singh, an experienced politician, skilled in the art of survival, who had been in governments of the undivided Punjab before Independence and continued at the centre almost without a break ever since. Thus came into existence what were to be known as the Sheikh-Swaran Singh talks.

I had deliberately short-circuited our Ministry, as the Commonwealth Secretary, M.J. Desai, had highly-coloured views about Pakistan and an almost pathological aversion to it. He poured cold water over any suggestion to try and do business with Pakistan. He was skilled in the practice of sophistry and could obfuscate any issue, however simple and straightforward it might be. In this as in other respects, he was strongly under the influence of V.K. Krishna Menon, who was then riding high and throwing his weight around, first as Minister without Portfolio and then as Defence Minister, in which capacity he was later to meet his nemesis.

The very first meeting on the border question was accompanied by much bonhomie and back-slapping on both sides. The Punjabi members of the rival delegations met as long-lost friends, conversing eagerly in their own language and asking anxious questions about mutual friends. One could not but wonder at the spectacle, considering that not so many years ago the Punjabis were at each other's throats, causing such turmoil and upheaval as to rock both fledgling countries to their very foundations.

The talks proceeded remarkably smoothly, the venue alternating between the two capitals. The exchange of enclaves, and rationalising the western Indo-Pak boundary-line along thousands of kilometres was first taken up, as it was there that violent incidents were of dangerously frequent occurrence. The eastern boundary was then demarcated and agreements arrived at without much difficulty, although some enclaves yet remained. The land surveyors who had attended the talks which lasted some two years then got down to the laborious task of surveying and erecting boundary pillars.

There has been no problem along much of the border since, except in regard to an enclave or two in the east. But one glaring omission, which was to lead to an armed conflict soon thereafter, was the Sindh-Kutch border. I pressed Desai before the talks finally ended to get that question settled too, while the momentum lasted and the two Ministers were still involved in the task and had developed a commendable rapport with each other. But for reasons which were not clear, Desai adamantly refused, saying that the matter could be taken up later. It was, indeed; but not by peaceful discussion, for a war erupted and international arbitration became necessary.

The boundary settlement was received with great satisfaction in both countries and raised hopes of better things to come. The Indian mood of suspicion and hostility towards the military regime in Pakistan began to soften with the prospect of better relations in the future.

At one of our meetings, the Foreign Minister of Pakistan Manzur Qadir, informed me that the President would be flying to Dacca shortly and asked how a brief stop-over at Delhi for him to pay a courtesy call on Mr Nehru would be viewed in India. It was an imaginative suggestion and could help greatly in facilitating future negotiations. I accordingly sent a carefully worded cable to the Prime Minister, adding that we could hardly refuse a request for a courtesy-call from the Pakistan President who would be overflying Indian territory. Prompt came a reply, welcoming the proposal. The date, time and other modalities were soon arranged. News of the visit created quite a stir and there was a considerable press turnout at Palam airport in Delhi to catch a glimpse of the unusual visitor and to garner what information could be had about the outcome of the meeting. A smiling Ayub strode into the VIP lounge to be greeted by Nehru, and the two were ensconced together for the best part of two hours. At the conclusion of the meeting, a communique couched in conciliatory terms was issued. Nehru, normally allergic to dictators, especially those of the military variety, was not impervious to Ayub's courtesy and charm and apparent goodwill.

With the further lifting of the miasma of fear and mistrust between the two countries, the flood of visa-seekers for India, which had previously nearly dried up, resumed fully. We had more counters opened at the mission and speedier procedures enforced. One bottleneck was the reference required in each case to a thick volume containing the names of undesirable characters. This list had remained unverified and uncorrected for years, and common names such as Mohammad Ali occupied dozens of pages and, from the security point of view, they were meaningless and time-consuming. Regrettably, corrupt practices were detected on the part of some of the consular staff, including an officer who was much addicted to betting at the race-course. A process of cleansing was undertaken and the guilty officer was recalled and punished.

The flow of Pakistani visitors to India, who returned laden with purchases, created much goodwill as they could discount the disparaging anti-Indian propaganda from their personal experiences. The reverse flow from India also increased, and many notable musicians and distinguished visitors came to Karachi. We took the opportunity of holding concerts in the chancery hall or at the residence; such eminent musicians as Vilayat Khan, Bismillah Khan, and Munawwar Ali Khan gave recitals which were much appreciated in culture-starved Karachi. The flow of visitors to India became so great that the Pakistani Foreign Office politely hinted that it should be slowed down.

Commerce, too, which had dwindled to a mere trickle, began to pick up quite rapidly, much to the satisfaction of the respective business communities and consumers. Pakistani industrialists were, however, a little worried, as Pakistan's nascent industries, mostly light-and medium, were hardly in a position to compete with the vast number of long-established and technologically more advanced industries of India. However, a leading businessman, Ghulam Farouqui, who had long been an associate of a leading Calcutta-based business house and had a distinguished career in the Indian Railways, was more concerned with the economic progress of his adopted country than with its convoluted politics. As Pakistan would find it difficult to balance its trade with India, various ideas were advanced to make the exchanges more even. Pakistan lacked coal, but it could pipe gas to western India from its ample supplies and in return import coal from India rather than from as far afield as Poland and China. It could also export high-grade cotton to India against machinery and other industrial goods. As a former railwayman, Farouqui saw the advantage of importing railway rolling-stock along the existing tracks from next door rather than from Europe at dollar prices and heavy freight charges.

Pakistan had ambitious plans to set up a steel industry and a well-known Indian firm, Dustoor & Co., had been invited to prepare a project report. Since Pakistan lacked practically all the basic raw materials for such an industry, a long-term agreement could be arrived at for the supply of iron ore from Goa. When Farouqui became Governor of East Pakistan, he found the possibilities of economic development there very limited as a result of Partition. Undivided Bengal was one economic unit, with the east providing the raw materials to feed the industries in the west. Also, communications were mostly dependent on the vast complex of waterways, the rivers flowing from north to south and converging on the Calcutta area which provided the main entrepot. The railways also ran north to south and few spanned the great rivers. Therefore, unless East Bengal could cooperate with West Bengal in developing its economy, future prospects for it were unpromising.

These ideas made sound economic sense, but their implementation was contingent on the state of mutual relations. Pakistan seemed to be prepared to suffer severe economic and technological deprivation rather than entertain even a business relationship with India. The fears heard in Pakistan were that, if the two economies did get enmeshed together in what might appear to be mutually beneficial arrangements, the Pakistani economy could be easily paralysed if India were to turn off the tap. Another inhibiting factor was the unequal strength of the two economies and the fear that Pakistan would be swamped with Indian goods. These almost pathological fears frustrated attempts to develop closer relations in the economic field. But even in regard to cultural matters, a similar complex prevailed, that Indian dance, music cinema and even literature would take over and stifle whatever there was of these arts in Pakistan. At a deeper level, it was feared that the sense of separateness, which the Establishment was trying to inculcate, would be diluted and that Pakistan, as a separate national entity, would lose its individuality and character.

Pakistan was suffering severely from a crisis of identity. As a separate state, all that could be said was that it was not India, but that alone would not define its character. Did it have a distinctive ethos and ideals? It could hardly claim to be the true homeland of the Muslims of India, as even after Partition India had a greater population of Muslims than Pakistan. Besides, had not the Quaid-i-Azam proclaimed that, after the creation of Pakistan, the two-nation theory would no longer apply and that all citizens were to be treated alike, regardless of caste or creed? It was the homeland of all its citizens regardless of religious distinctions. Also, where did Pakistan's history commence—since its creation in 1947, or since the first Muslim (Arab) invader, Mohammad bin Qasim, landed in Sindh? Should Pakistan repudiate the ancient historical and cultural legacy it shared with India? The facts of geography could not be denied;

Pakistan was not a part of the Arab mainland, but an inextricable part of the sub-continent. It was watered by rivers which rose in or flowed from the Himalaya and its shores were washed by the same seas that bounded India. Ethnically, the polyglot peoples of the two wings could hardly claim to be Arabs, Persians, or Central Asians: the Muslim population of India comprised some 90 per cent of converts and even the remainder was very mixed. Culturally too Pakistan was a part of the sub-continent. The classical music of ragas and raginis was a shared tradition of ancient Indian origin and mostly devotional in theme and inspiration. What was proclaimed as 'Pakistani' classical dance and described as 'Pak-raks' was Bharata Natyam in another form. The Urdu language, which the Pakistani rulers proclaimed as their national language and which they attempted to foist on the Bengalis who had a rich and vibrant language of their own, had its origin and was spoken in the northern Indian cities, but was alien to the Punjabis, Sindhis, Pathans and Baluchis, who had dialects of their own. Even the founder of Pakistan, Mohammad Ali Jinnah, could hardly speak Urdu, his own language being Gujarati. The hard fact is that in the sub-continent, which embraces a large variety of peoples, religions and languages, diversity is based more on regional than on religious considerations. For example, in Bengal all communities speak Bengali, in Tamil Nadu, Tamil, in Kerala, Malayalam, in Andhra, Telugu, etc., and they share the same regional cultures. The absurd proposition that Indian Muslims constitute a separate nation within a nation would imply that all religions groups in India should equally be considered distinctive nationalities. This theory was buried by Jinnah himself when he said on 14th August, 1947 to Pakistan Constituent Assembly:

> If you change your past and work together in a spirit that every one of you, no matter to what community he belongs, no matter what relations he had with you in the past, no

matter what his colour, caste or creed, is first, second and last a citizen of this state with equal rights, privileges and obligations.

He went on in this vein, adding that if the above ideal was followed, in course of time Hindus would cease to be Hindus and Muslims would cease to be Muslims, not in the religious sense as that was a private affair, but as equal citizens of the state.

On the attainment of Pakistan, Jinnah had rejected both the 'two nation' falsehood but also the concept of a theocratic state. If today Pakistan describes itself as the 'Islamic' Republic of Pakistan, harps on its Muslim character and calls incessantly on the name of Allah, it is betraying the express wishes and ideals of its creater.

These unorthodox pronouncements of Jinnah, which advocated a secular state and society, caused dismay and alarm among the conservative and orthodox elements. They also undermined the very basis on which Pakistan was created. Accordingly the Mullahs and their supporters soon started an agitation demanding a truly 'Islamic' state, one fit only for Muslims to live in.

To try and resolve these evident contradictions and to evolve a distinctive national ethos, various seminars and conferences were held, some attended by scholars from abroad. But nothing came out of their deliberations. To meet the promises held out by the founding father of Pakistan the question arose as to what the attributes were of an Islamic state. What were its governing principles, its laws and institutions? Much controversy raged on the subject, the Mullahs and the orthodox claiming that the *Quran*, the *Sunna* and *Hadith* represented ultimate divine wisdom and embraced every aspect of the life of the Muslim, his state and society. No amendments, adaptation or interpretation whatsoever were permissible, and the texts and fatwas of the Mullahs were final and must be strictly observed and obeyed.

The modernists, with equal fervour argued that such a complete reversal to what may have been relevant centuries ago would set back the clock of progress forever and the country would remain weak and retarded. But the Mullahs equated modernism with Westernism, which in their eyes was utterly corrupt and decadent. So the argument went on, ending only in stultification and confusion.

The Mullahs, however, kept returning to the charge with demands such as the establishment of Muslim courts. They were then asked to define what exactly a Muslim was. A conclave of Mullahs representing various sects met and after much disputation and controversy, failed to find an acceptable definition! All that they were able to accomplish was to get the Ahmadiyya community, of which Sir Zafrullah Khan was the most distinguished among many prominent members, declared heretics and non-Muslims. They were to be debarred from mosques and Muslim religious celebrations and even from calling themselves Muslims. They were also to be ineligible for the public services or the professions, and in fact were literally denied their rights as citizens, in violation of Jinnah's pledge. No greater violation of the most elementary human rights solely on narrow sectarian grounds can be imagined. Intolerance breeds intolerance, and in the predominantly Sunni country, the Shias began to be persecuted. The Christians and the few remaining Hindus were reduced to the status of second-class citizens.

To carry the inherent contradictions to the point of absurdity, theories are now being propounded that the Punjabis of Pakistan, who constitute about two thirds of its total population, are a race apart from the general run of Muslims of the sub-continent, and they pretend to affiliate themselves to the Afghans and Persians and even Tajiks and Uzbeks of Central Asia. The fact of course is that the Punjabi Muslims are mostly converts and it is common to find in the same clan or even family, Hindus, Muslims and Sikhs. This is borne out by the fact that many Punjabi Muslim families continue to use their former Hindu clan or caste names such as Rathor or Sehgal. With the demise of the 'two nation' theory and the separation of Bangladesh, psychological and territorial compensation is being sought in Kashmir. Pakistan could then hope to repudiate its Indian origins and culture and look westwards towards the Muslim world and turn its back on its own history, culture and origin.

The penalty of straining to equate itself with its giant Indian neighbour, over five times its size in area and population and far more advanced in industrialisation, has led the ruling elite of Pakistan to suffer schizophrenically from both an inferiority complex as well as delusions of grandeur. There is also the contradictory obsession about India waiting to pounce upon an innocent Pakistan to undo Partition, as if it did not have enough problems of its own to wish to take on those of Pakistan as well!

In pursuing a policy of confrontation and conflict with India, it is the common people of Pakistan who are the worst sufferers. Unwilling to cooperate and unable to compete, Pakistan tries to equate itself with India by attempting to build up a vast military machine incommensurate with its resources and size, but more especially its needs. With an over-developed military arm, the rest of the body politic is doomed to atrophy. Pakistan's short history bears testimony to the ascendancy of the military over all other institutions, political and governmental. Hence the succession of swash-buckling military dictators. Even when there is a civilian government of sorts, the real power rests in the armed forces, who, like a scowling presence, are overseeing and monitoring every act and antic of the politicians.

Another constricting factor is the ubiquitous presence of the Mullahs who weigh every law and governmental policy against their narrow interpretation of the principles of Islam. They are a constituency that cannot be ignored, for besides the considerable influence which they command over the trusting masses, the very relevance of Pakistan is dependent upon its apparently Islamic character. This also, like the undeclared rivalry between the politicians and the military, generates considerable friction.

In stark contrast, India has built up and sustained despite many vicissitudes a secular democratic polity founded upon a succession of national and state elections in a multi-party system. Such basic differences in regard to their respective ideologies, state structures, societies, perceptions and aspirations have made the conduct of negotiations unusually difficult. These dissonant factors cast their shadow over relations between the two countries at a higher level of policy-making.

At official-level talks, both sides speak to tight briefs which allow little or no room for flexibility. Also, both sides are tempted to display their virtuosity in argument rather than to seek solutions. And the only solutions sought are to take all and to concede nothing. No wonder that they invariably end in complete deadlock. It is only when the political leaders themselves enter the arena or permit a range of options to their official negotiators that any progress becomes possible.

A consummate practitioner of the art of political negotiation was Dag Hammarskjold, Secretary-General of the United Nations. He had said: 'The other's face is more important than your own.' It followed therefore that 'you can only hope to find a lasting solution to a conflict if you have learned to see the other objectively, but at the same time to experience his difficulties subjectively.' How similar was Mahatma Gandhi's approach when he said, 'We must measure people with their own measure and see how far they come up to it.' Both began with a complete mastery of the facts and then allowed themselves full scope for flexibility and mobility.

Experience has shown that access to the very apex of power would enable an envoy to avoid getting lost in the labyrinthine maze of officialdom were he to approach a serious problem at that level. I had found this to be the most productive of results in the personal rapport built up with Secretary-General

Hammarskjold at the United Nations, with President Tito and his Vice-Presidents and cabinet ministers in Yugoslavia, with the heads of state and government in Bulgaria and Romania, and now with President Ayub Khan and his ministers in Pakistan. Prime Minister Nehru also gave very general instructions, permitting a sufficient degree of flexibility.

Whatever may have been the change in Ayub Khan's perceptions since his transformation from an Indian patriot during our Mathura days in 1940 to a Pakistani zealot, he took an encouragingly pragmatic view of the situation and saw the advantage of coming to political settlements with India, starting with the more immediate problems. On economic matters, however, his attitude was more ambiguous. Nevertheless, he no doubt sensed that the reduction of tensions would be generally welcomed by the masses and make his dictatorship appear less onerous.

The presidential cabinet comprised, among others, Generals Khalid Sheikh, Azam Khan and Burki. They were powerful figures in the government whose word would go a long way. The two civilian ministers who carried considerable weight were Manzur Qadir, the Foreign Minister and Shoaib, the Finance Minister. Qadir, an eminent lawyer, was a man of integrity and refinement, and of enlightened views, free from any complexes about India. Shoaib had held a senior position in the World Bank and had considerable skill as a financier.

A new star, hitherto practically unknown, had appeared on the political horizon, thanks to Ayub Khan's patronage. That was Zulfiqar Ali Bhutto, a playboy of wealth with an Oxford and Harvard education. His inclusion in the cabinet provided an element of youthfulness and sophistication among the senior and not particularly erudite Generals. He was entrusted with the portfolio of Commerce which he used to good effect to get into the limelight. His advent was at a low key, his soaring ambition having yet to reveal itself, but he carefully negotiated his subsequent entry into the inner corridors of power. He was of a gregarious nature, entertaining lavishly, and was known to have a roving eye. Bhutto was born in Bombay and had his early education and upbringing there. His wife, Nusrat, then a quiet and unassuming lady, reputedly of Persian-Indian extraction, was believed to be rather neglected; she was certainly completely overshadowed by her domineering husband. Bhutto's father, Shah Nawaz, was the Dewan of Junagadh State whom Jinnah needed in order to embarrass India by getting the Nawab to accede to Pakistan. His wife, Zulfiqar Ali's mother, was said to be a Hindu. The Bhutto family, like others of their class in Sindh, were considerable landlords, frequently absentee, whose estates had been skilfully managed by their Hindu Amils or managers, who had since fled the country.

Bhutto's residence was close to ours in the Clifton area of Karachi and he frequently strolled across to borrow a book or two from our personal library and to have a chat. He was an interesting talker with an inquisitive mind and wide literary interests. But what he showed particular interest in was international politics and, in particular, the policy of non-alignment.

When Ayub Khan moved the capital to Rawalpindi, we, like other missions, set up a temporary summer residence and a small office at the nearby hill-station of Murree. Whenever I sought an interview with Bhutto he would invariably reply that it was too hot in Rawalpindi and that he would himself drive up the twenty-two miles or so with his family to have lunch with us, adding that he hoped the champagne would be cooled for the occasion! I naturally welcomed this way of combining business with conviviality. The business part completed, Bhutto would start discussing international affairs in a wider framework. He was particularly interested in understanding how India, with its policy of distancing itself from the power blocs, was yet able to maintain friendly relations with the United States, the Soviet Union as well as China.

At that time, India's relations with China were in the 'Bhai-Bhai' phase, and at our frequent meetings the Chinese Ambassador spoke very disparagingly about Pakistan. The Soviet Ambassador, Kapitsa, and his East European colleagues were similarly outspoken in their denunciation of the Pakistani regime. Kapitsa, who was the brother of a noted Soviet nuclear scientist, was a fine linguist who conversed freely and in precise English—an unusual kind of Soviet diplomat of that period, and in the relaxed atmosphere of Murree we frequently exchanged visits and Kapitsa confided to me that Bhutto had been visiting him frequently and was trying to cultivate him. About the same time the Chinese Ambassador was observed to have become more reticent and cautious in his conversation with us. Bhutto's cultivation of the communist envoys was quite contrary to Ayub Khan's policy and predilections, as he was paranoid about 'godless communism' and regarded it as the greatest menace to the sub-continent. Indeed, his stock-in trade with Washington, and especially with the Pentagon, was his oft declared hatred of communism. It was he who in 1954, as Commander-in-Chief, led Pakistan to join the US sponsored Baghdad Pact and the South-East Asia Treaty Organisation, both set up to threaten what was described as the 'soft under-belly' of the communist bloc, including China. That opened the floodgates for the massive arming of Pakistan by the United States: behind the anti-communist facade, Pakistan's real intention of course was to try and get even with India.

On the welcome departure of Sikander Ali Baig, M. Ikramullah took over as Foreign Secretary of Pakistan. He was a very senior member of the old ICS and did not suffer from the complexes that one frequently encountered among Pakistani officials. He agreed that it was both necessary and possible to sort out the problems between the two countries by peaceful negotiations in order to establish good-neighbourly relations. Ikramullah's family hailed from Nagpur and his brother, Hidayatullah, was then the distinguished Chief Justice of the Bombay High Court who was to become Chief Justice of the Supreme Court and was then elected Vice-President of India. Ikramullah's wife, Soghra, had been a close friend of Susheela's since long before Partition, when her husband was posted in Delhi.

There was thus a fortunate conjunction for India in the Foreign Office of Pakistan. Further, Manzur Qadir was Foreign Minister; his wife, Asghari, was the sister of Azim Husain, a distinguished senior Ambassador of India, and with the warm rapport between our three families, it became possible to discuss Indo-Pak problems in a rational and constructive manner. This congenial atmosphere was a new experience; though the leading politicians and officials of both countries in those early years were well acquainted with each other, this did not seem to help at all in their arriving at mutual understanding. Instead, the fact that the parties knew each other so well only enabled them to exploit to the full, each other's preferences, prejudices and weaknesses.

In discussions at the Foreign Office it was agreed that a piece-by-piece approach offered the best prospect of progress, the more pressing and practical questions being taken up first. With each settlement, the momentum generated would prepare the ground for the more intractable issues. Emotional questions should be held over until the last, by which time it was hoped the temperature would have appreciably lowered for constructive negotiations.

The question was whether the President would accept such a methodical and pragmatic approach or would wish to go all out on all fronts at the same time. Qadir and Ikramullah undertook to take up the matter with Ayub Khan and I to follow it up. The President's reaction was cautious but not negative. At that point

I moved in and fortunately found the President, who had had time to ponder over the suggestion, quite receptive. Ayub Khan no doubt had his own reasons too; he wanted, as Pakistan's first military dictator, to win over his people's loyalty and to gain legitimacy for his regime. As events were to prove, the comings and goings of delegations from both countries raised hopes of a more relaxed atmosphere for which the people longed, and each settlement was received with relief and applause.

To put an end to needless irritants, the Pakistani press was directed by the authorities to exercise restraint and to avoid vituperative and abusive language against India, a practice which had become second nature to it. The worst offender in this respect was Altaf Husain, a muhajir, Editor of the widely-read *Dawn* whose pen was habitually dipped in venom. He always referred to India as 'Bharat'. When asked about our reactions to this by a Pakistani journalist, I said that Altaf Husain might regard us as chauvinists if he knew that the spread of what was known of old as 'Bharat' embraced the whole of the present Pakistan and extended right up to the Hindu Kush. By a Presidential order Altaf Husain, and the press generally, were enjoined to refer to India as India. The Indian press, for the most part, was more responsible and restrained, and observed greater caution so as not to impede the process of healing.

The question of evacuee property which had caused much bad blood was earnestly taken up. Exaggerated claims of properties left behind in the forced exchanges of populations had been filed with both governments which, however, were almost impossible to verify. What was obvious was that the Hindu and Sikh communities evicted from their farms, factories and businesses in Pakistan had been far more prosperous than the Muslims who had left India. Most of the Partition troubles were in the Pubjab area, of which the eastern part was sandy and less fertile, while the fertile canal-fed areas, which the sturdy Sikh farmers had greatly developed, lay in the west. In the cities, the industrialists, merchants and professional classes were mostly Hindu or Sikh and few Muslims went into commerce or industry, the wealthy among them were mostly feudal landlords belonging to powerful clans. Pakistan was naturally reluctant to concede that it owed more than it received. Reference to how the problem was handled in Europe after World War II, where many national borders had altered causing much movement of population, revealed that the only practicable principle was for each side to hold what it had and to compensate its citizens as best it could. Accordingly, it was tacitly accepted that the status-quo should remain. In India a ceiling was fixed on claims and a fraction of proven claims met from evacuee property or otherwise. Somewhat similar procedures were adopted in Pakistan, although some people benefited greatly because of their political pull or influence, suddenly finding themselves owners of industries which they had no idea of how to run. It often happens that tacit understandings which are based on practical considerations are more binding than a form of words in a written document reluctantly arrived at, which could subsequently be variously interpreted and could itself be a cause of further dispute. The question of evacuee property thus left to itself, has to all intents been finally buried and has not been heard of since.

The division of the fabulous India Office Library in London was another contentious issue. The India Office had a vast collection of historical records, manuscripts, art objects, etc., collected by one means or another over the centuries of Britain's connection with India from the earliest days of the East India Company. To divide the contents of a library without breaking its cohesion would need the judgement of a Solomon. The matter was further complicated by the claims of a third and vital party which held physical possession of the library. Britain wished to retain those documents, etc., which were of historical and antiquarian interest to her, and Pakistan those of an Islamic character. After much discussion in which scholars, archivists and librarians participated, an arrangement was arrived at on the basis of microfilming documents and manuscripts, etc., to complete, as far as possible, the records in which each country was interested. This matter, once the division on agreed lines was completed, was then struck off the agenda.

Encouraged by the success achieved on these matters which had been hanging fire, the atmosphere now seemed propitious for taking up still more contentious issues. The burden of the public debt of undivided India was being borne entirely by Indian shoulders and India was anxious that part of the burden should be shared by Pakistan according to the prescribed formula for the division of assets, which was 82.5 per cent and 12.5 per cent between India and Pakistan. Meetings were arranged between the respective Finance Ministers, Morarji Desai and Shoaib, to sort out the issue. The opening gambit took place in New Delhi where the experts on both sides excelled each other in the production of copious accounts and intricate calculating and, especially, in argumentation. When no progress was being made at the level of financial experts, the Ministers took up the matter themselves. Morarji Desai came to Rawalpindi, which had then become the temporary capital. The meetings took place in a company guest house, where we were also all housed, and lasted some two or three days. Morarji and Shoaib seemed to get on very well socially, and after dinner Morarji, to our surprise, stayed up until long after the rest had gone to bed, playing bridge with Shoaib!

When the discussions between the two delegations ground to a halt, the Ministers met in private sessions to hammer out an agreement. At the end of their deliberations, Morarji recounted that, when he put forward India's demand, Shoaib challenged it by making a counter-claim. That was for Pakistan's share of uncollected arrears of income and other taxes and his figure exceeded India's original claim! The Pakistani counter-claim when questioned could not be proved, but neither could it be disproved. Shoaib finally said that even if Pakistan were to concede the Indian claim, it had, in any case, no foreign exchange with which to meet it, and even if it wanted to, it would ask for a long period of time, some forty years, in which to pay it in installments. Such minute amounts would hardly be worthwhile for India considering the magnitude of its economy.

Morarji confided that he saw the force of Shoaib's arguments and considered it idle to pursue the matter further. But he could not write if off either, as it would be politically unacceptable at home, especially in view of India's own financial difficulties. I suggested that if relations genuinely improved, we could consider, as a gesture of magnanimity and friendship, the formal waiver of the debt; this would have a good psychological effect not only in Pakistan but on world opinion as well. Morarji agreed that we could keep this tactic in mind for a more propitious time, which unfortunately has still eluded us.

This episode revealed Morarji Desai as a sound and pragmatic negotiator who was prepared not only to look facts in the face, but also to turn a reverse into an opportunity. Incidentally, it was Morarji's first and perhaps his last visit to Pakistan and he earned the respect of his hosts for his forthrightness, clarity of mind and openness in discussion, belying the image projected of him as inflexible and obdurate. After a visit to Peshawar where we went to meet Khan Abdul Ghaffar Khan, then under house arrest, and after seeing the crowds of rugged Pathans and armed tribesmen, Morarji remarked that with Partition we were well rid of such rough and unruly elements.

I was shuttling a good deal between the two capitals, and on my official visits to and from Dacca, I always broke journey in Delhi to report directly to the Prime Minister. Nehru seemed to approve of how things were progressing and would often say that, being the man on the spot, I would know how best to proceed. But while the Prime Minister encouraged me to pursue a search for solutions, my immediate superior in the Ministry, the Commonwealth Secretary, M.J. Desai, was less than cooperative and seemed to revel in raising pettifogging objections and irritants. Ayub Khan, who had rarely met him but had apparently sized him up, referred to him as 'that bullet-headed fellow'. V.K. Krishna Menon, variously Minister without Portfolio and Defence Minister, would point a warning finger at me whenever I ran into him in Delhi and say that I was on the wrong track and no good would come of whatever I was trying to do in Pakistan. At the time, Menon's influence with the Prime Minister was considerable and, because of this, he was regarded with a degree of awe in Delhi's official circles. Besides, his mercurial nature and rasping tongue made people avoid him. He could also be quite pleasant and even unctuous, but such occasions were rare. Fortunately, on Pakistan he was not able to deflect the course of developments as the Prime Minister was on a different track.

The decks had by now been sufficiently cleared to tackle a problem of crucial importance to both countries, viz., the division of the waters of the Indus river basin. This immense system of five mighty rivers took its birth in the upper Himalaya, mostly in India. Four of the rivers issued for the most part in the plains of Pakistan. These rivers with their extensive canal systems were the life-blood of the farmers in both countries. Without their life-giving waters and in view of the deficient rainfall in the respective areas, there would have been widespread distress and starvation. All the rivers joined the Indus in Pakistan, but the main canal headworks were at Suleimanki and Husseiniwala in India. The problem was how to determine and apportion a fair share of the combined waters between the two countries.

Under the auspices of the World Bank, negotiations had been going on for nine years with delegations commuting to and from Washington, accompanied by experts and engineers. Volumes of statistics had been produced and exchanged in support of the rival claims and technical data regarding river flows, present and future uses, crop patterns, climatic variations, etc. And there was much disputation about the rights of upper and lower-riparian states.

The protracted negotiations ultimately reached near finality, but one last obstacle was raised by Pakistan. This related to the construction in the Kashmir valley of a hydro-electric project on the Jhelum, this river being assigned wholly to Pakistan. The existing use in Kashmir of Jhelum water for irrigation which had existed since time immemorial had been conceded to the extent of its present utilisation. But it was now argued that its use for the generation of electric power was something different. Also, any more extensive use for irrigation would reduce the quantum available to Pakistan.

This unexpected impediment gave rise to much alarm and disappointment on both sides. Ayub Khan, at a meeting with me, warned that the great Rajasthan canal system was nearing completion, but 'rivers of blood', not water, flow, if the Washington talks should collapse. I tried to pacify him by urging that the remaining problem was comparatively minor in relation to the overall progress of the talks, and that with a little goodwill on both sides it could also be satisfactorily resolved. Ayub Khan remarked that if the matter could be fairly and equitably settled, he would be the first publicly to thank the Indian Prime Minister for making it possible.

I submitted to the President that the Kashmir valley was like a bowl and its fields were already fully irrigated, as they had been in the past, and that there was little scope for any substantial withdrawal of Jhelum water for the purpose. As regards the hydro-electric project, the water would merely flow to work the turbines, but its quantity would in no way be diminished nor its flow impeded. The Jhelum drained the whole valley and the surrounding mountainous region, and both the river and the rainfall had only one outlet, viz., to the plains of Pakistan. The final form of the Treaty would no doubt incorporate the required assurances to remove any shadow of doubt. Taking a practical view of the matter, Ayub Khan raised no further objection and the Treaty was soon ready for signature, thus successfully ending the nine-year long ordeal.

Ayub Khan, elated at this achievement which would redound to the credit of his regime, said that he would welcome a personal visit by Prime Minister Nehru for the signature of the historic Treaty or, alternatively, he would be glad to go to Delhi himself. Now that almost all the practical problems between us had been settled, only one issue which had generated much emotion on both sides remained. That was Kashmir. He said his predecessors had made certain promises to the people from which he could not resile, and India had adopted a contrary position which Pakistan, likewise, could not accept. 'Let us start talking and Inshallah something will come out of it', were his words. He added that Pandit Nehru was at the zenith of his power and popularity in India, and any decision taken by him would be unquestionably accepted, while he in Pakistan also had the necessary authority to ensure acceptance of any settlement to which he may agree.

I hurried to Delhi to report Ayub Khan's views and reactions to the Prime Minister and to arrange a mutually suitable date and programme for the visit and signature of the Treaty. Pandit Nehru was greatly relieved by the successful outcome of the negotiations; he gave his preference for Karachi as the venue of the signature ceremony and a date early in September 1960 was arranged. He was very keen to address a public meeting in Karachi on the occasion.

The Canal Waters' Treaty awarded the waters of the three western rivers, the Indus, Jhelum and Chenab to Pakistan in their entirety, while India received those of the Sutlej and Beas in their entirety. The arrangement about the fifth river, the Ravi, was a little complicated, involving an apportionment of its waters between the two countries, by far the greater volume going to India.

In the result, about 80 per cent of the waters of the Indus river basin fell to Pakistan's share, India receiving the balance of 20 per cent. Despite this statistical imbalance, India has had no reason for dissatisfaction with the Treaty, which has been registered with the United Nations and scrupulously respected by both sides despite two subsequent wars. The prosperity of Indian Punjab and Haryana, both heavily dependent upon canal irrigation, is due, in no small measure, to the settlement of this difficult problem.

I reported Ayub's proposal that, with the conclusion of almost all the unfinished business of Partition on a basis of mutual accommodation, the remaining problem, that of Kashmir, which was of a sensitive nature and clouded by emotion, could now be taken up. I submitted my view that talking about Kashmir would help drain it of its emotional content. To engage in talks did not imply conceding anything in advance. On the contrary, the strength of our position would be reinforced, while the weakness of Pakistan's claim would be exposed. Furthermore, as experience of the complicated negotiations on the canal waters' problems had shown, the very process of discussion could produce its own solution. The talks on the canal waters' problem which affected the very livelihood of millions on both sides of the border had gone on for nine years, yet their outcome was awaited with patience and without mutual recrimination. What is more, the final outcome was entirely unexpected, but had nevertheless been accepted without question.

It would, in the context of Kashmir, be of interest to recall the dispute between Italy and Yugoslavia in regard to the former Free Territory of Trieste which was settled by timely international intervention. That agreement, though provisional, has been more durable than many definitive treaties. It meets the felt needs of both sides while side-stepping the contentious question of sovereignty.

The manner in which Ayub Khan put his proposal implied that all he expected at that stage was that the process of discussion on Kashmir be initiated without precondition. He was too much of a realist to expect early results and he knew that the process would be long-drawn. The matter had not revived at the United Nations since 1956 when Krishna Menon made his marathon fourteen-hour speech at the Security Council. (That oration merely drew yawns and the wry comment of delegates that it must be a weak case that required such laboured presentation.) Significantly enough, the matter of Kashmir had not been raised earlier by President Ayub or his Foreign Minister. The process of talking about Kashmir would at least have given some assurance to Ayub Khan's constituency, the army, as well as to the people at large, that the regime was not neglectful of a problem which had excited such high emotions. Ayub Khan may possibly have realised that the best that could be expected was a settlement; along the cease-fire line, or perhaps something on the lines of the Trieste agreement. The talks could either have gone on for years, draining the issue of its emotional content, or the worst that could have happened was that the talks would run to ground.

With the easing of the Kashmir situation, trade could have opened up, helping to ease the financial burden on India while creating a new and profitable market in Pakistan for Kashmiri goods in Pakistan. Great quantities of Kashmir timber were lost to Pakistan, for which claims for compensation were annually presented and summarily rejected; these could be sold profitably instead of being confiscated. Similarly, tourism in Kashmir could be opened to Pakistanis in principle, the issue of visas being regulated and the activities of visitors closely monitored. Leaving aside the non-negotiable question of sovereignty, what Kashmir had to offer was its incomparable climate and scenery and trade in its superb silks, carpets and handicrafts and, of course, tourism. All this of course belonged to an unpredictable future and much depended upon how the talks progressed. At the time, however, the prospect did not seen improbable.

I placed these thoughts in some detail before the Prime Minister, just before I was to leave to take up the stewardship of the United Nations Mission in the Congo. The Prime Minister listened attentively and seemed particularly interested in the analogy of the Trieste agreement. The upshot was that Pandit Nehru agreed to the proposal to accompany Ayub Khan to the cool heights of Murree to the President's Lodge for a tete-a-tete, without formalities or advisers.

Ayub excelled in face-to-face encounters and felt confident that he could win the Indian Prime Ministers' confidence and persuade him to agree to the commencement of a wide-ranging dialogue on Kashmir. After some hesitation, he also deferred to Pandit Nehru's wish to address a public meeting in Karachi on signing the Canal Waters' Treaty. The Pakistani authorities' hesitation was given out as concern for their Indian guest's security; in reality, they feared Nehru's popularity with the Karachi population, especially the Urdu-speaking mohajirs, who had begun to wonder if they had indeed made the right choice in opting for Pakistan. The Pakistani authorities were not mistaken, as Pandit Nehru made an elegant figure and gave an eloquent address at the civic reception given in his honour on the lawns of the Town Hall and received a rousing ovation. A vast crowd had assembled to catch a glimpse of the famed Indian leader and to hear his words of friendship and goodwill spoken in fluent Urdu.

The details of the Prime Minister's visit to Pakistan being tied up, the time for my departure was fast approaching as the UN Secretary-General was pressing for my arrival in New York before the end of August 1960. I was to relieve UN Under Secretary-General, Ralph Bunche, a Nobel Laureate, who was suffering from extreme fatigue after heading the mission for some six tumultuous weeks. The Prime Minister said he expected my return in six months or so; meanwhile, the momentum generated in Indo-Pakistani relations would be maintained, and temporary arrangement made to carry on the work of the High Commission. I had wanted my Deputy in Karachi, Padmanabhan, who was fully conversant with every nuance of the several negotiations over the last two years and personally knew the Pakistani personalities involved, to carry on in my place as acting head of mission. But M.J. Desai had other plans, and Padmanabhan was arbitrarily transferred and my deputy in Dacca, Trivedi, who was totally unacquainted with the Karachi scene and the central government authorities, was sent as a replacement. Trivedi was an acolyte of Desai's and fully shared his negative perceptions, which he was to demonstrate during his brief tenure.

When I went to take leave of Ayub Khan he was less than pleased that I should be going away at that juncture even for a temporary period, as he strongly felt that I should be present for the crucial visit of the Prime Minister. I tried to explain that an envoy was but the agent of his government whose policies he tried to carry out. Ayub Khan, who believed strongly in personal contacts, demurred as he feared that the combined influence of Krishna Menon and Desai on Mr Nehru would now prevail. I tried to reassure him that the forward movement would continue as before, apparently without carrying much conviction.

Three ministers of the government with whom I had established close personal rapport very kindly hosted a private luncheon in my honour. Warming up to the theme of how close our two peoples were to each other, Manzur Qadir, who had always acknowledged our common origins, culture and history, said that his family were Hindu Kayastha converts. General Sheikh said his was Khatri, while Bhutto claimed to be a Rajput. Especially touching and flattering was Foreign Secretary

Ikramullah who, taking a leaf out of the *Ramayana*, told Susheela that they would place my sandals on my official seat to await my return!

We had reached a peak in relations between the two countries. At the official and personal levels we found that we had suddenly become popular. Even the normally hostile press spared us undue attention. The general public too responded to the new mood and our flagged car when passing in convoy was greeted with clapping instead of boos. Even when not in procession, there was the sound of applause from the passers-by, with occasional cries of 'Visa please!' Invitations to High Commission functions where eagerly sought, especially to Indian film shows in the auditorium of our fine new four-storeyed chancery building. There were frequent music recitals at the residence given by visiting Indian musicians, which were attended by highly appreciative, culture-starved audiences. The local notables no longer felt afraid or inhibited in inviting us to their functions. Some were even given in our honour. Our Urdu, and especially Susheela's impeccable Lucknow accent, was much admired. The migrants from UP, nostalgic for their old homes set amidst greenery, found our presence particularly reassuring. We were delighted to renew contacts with families and friends of long-standing who had migrated, some out of political conviction or religious sentiment, but most to improve their economic prospects. At national day functions we were sought out by friends and journalists, the latter eager for quotable asides. Since even a chance remark appearing in print could be misunderstood or twisted, extreme caution was necessary in word and deed. Any press conference was taboo and all that could safely be allowed was an off-the-record briefing to select, responsible pressmen.

Ayub Khan had never been happy with the national capital being at Karachi and wanted to shift to the north. He disliked the climate and the ambience of Karachi and detested having to share the capital with a centre of commerce, and its horde of venal businessmen, wheeler-dealers and favour-seekers. He wanted, for good reason, to be at army headquarters where he could keep an eye on the generals. And, as a military man, he found Karachi too exposed and vulnerable and situated far from the heartland of Pakistan. He therefore decided, as an interim measure, to shift the capital to Rawalpindi until a new site could be chosen. Meanwhile, in Rawalpindi he would find himself in familiar surroundings and could again occupy his old residence, that of the Commander-in-Chief.

The great migration of the central offices began first with a few less essential ministries, then with others and soon the President and his ministers too became more peripatetic. Foreign missions were invited to move north to the nearby hill-station of Murree as Rawalpindi could not accommodate them. The shuttling to and fro had caused much dislocation of government business and inconvenience all around and many missions, comfortably settled in Karachi, were loath to break up house and move to unfamiliar surroundings far from international air routes and with poor communications. We in the India High Commission fully shared their misgivings. When Ayub Khan tried to persuade me to migrate to the north, I protested that we had recently built a new chancery in Karachi and could hardly afford to duplicate our establishment; besides, we could not possibly compete with the more affluent Western missions who would take over the best of the limited accommodation available in Murree. But when Ayub offered to requisition any house that Susheela might fancy in Murree, one could hardly refuse. Accordingly, a fine residence-cum-office, Hoti House, was selected and duly requisitioned. We spent two very pleasant and useful months in summer and a month in autumn in the hills, a welcome respite from the humid heat of Karachi. We were also invited to select a site for our mission in the proposed new capital of Islamabad, and again the President was good enough to ensure that we got one of the best sites set on high ground.

Our relations were always cordial with the President and his family and few opportunities at receptions or other gatherings were lost without a friendly conversation with Ayub Khan. Begum Ayub, a simple, warm-hearted lady with no airs, seldom appeared in public, but she remembered and remained faithful to her old friendship with Susheela dating back to our days in Mathura. Addressing Susheela as 'Meri Jan' (beloved) she would recount to her daughters Susheela's Cambridge education and family background. Modestly saying that she herself was only a Risalder's daughter, she would exhort them to try to emulate Susheela's example.

In the relaxed atmosphere of the mountain resort of Murree, the President, on his arrival, would lose little time in inviting us over. At restricted functions for heads of missions and their spouses, Begum Ayub would insist on Susheela's company. The Begum never, to our knowledge, attended a function, even a formal dinner party, at any diplomatic mission; she, however, made an exception in our case when she came to dinner with the President and his principal ministers and their wives more than once. Our personal rapport with the President caused much surprise and bewilderment among our foreign colleagues as it went counter to their preconceived notions about relations between our two peoples, even at the personal level.

Ayub Khan, though true to his religion and devoted to his country, felt strongly that it stood in urgent need of reform and modernisation. He had little patience with the straight-jacket in which the Mullahs, to preserve their hold on the Umma, had tried to confine their religion and society. Soon after he assumed power, Ayub Khan introduced far-reaching reforms in Muslim personal law and practice, especially in regard to divorce and polygamy. These were naturally resented by the clergy and the orthodox, but there was little they could do about it. The reforms brought about a great improvement in the status of women in Pakistani Muslim society and correspondingly weakened the power of the Mullahs. It is ironical that what Ayub Khan was able to do practically by a stroke of the pen in Islamic Pakistan with hardly a whisper of protest, secular India is unable even to touch without raising a veritable hornet's nest.

By way of example of Ayub Khan's rather catholic approach to religious observance, one incident stands out prominently in memory. During the month of Ramzan when fasting was rigorously observed all over Pakistan and when even at social gatherings people vied with each other in proudly recounting the number of days they had fasted, I had occasion to call on the President on official business. I was given an appointment for around 7.00 p.m. I found Ayub Khan sitting on the lawn in a relaxed mood; soon a butler appeared and asked what I would like to drink. Being conscious of the austerities of Ramzan, I declined, but on Ayub Khan's insistence, I asked for a lemonade. At this, Ayub Khan asked why I was not having a whisky, and when I still hesitated, he exclaimed that it would be a good reason for him to have one too! Thereafter we had two drinks each and the official business was transacted in good humour.

How was it that Ayub Khan, who did not have a particularly distinguished military career and would hardly have risen much above brigade rank in the Indian army, rose to the commanding heights as an all-powerful Head of State, Field Marshal and Supreme Commander of the armed forces of Pakistan? Roundabout 1950, conditions in the new state were going from bad to worse, which made the military class turn an anxious eye towards the chaotic political scene. As crisis followed crisis, and the whole system began to totter, Ayub began to see himself as the one person who could still save the country. In fact, as early as 1951 after an assassin's bullet claimed the life of the first Prime Minister, Nawabzada Liaquat Ali Khan in 1951, Ayub was exhorted by no less a person than the Aga Khan and even Fatima

Jinnah, the Quaid-i-Azam's sister, to take over power. After his induction into the cabinet as Defence Minister he produced a paper setting out his ideas for the recovery of the country. He still seemed to believe in a democratic form of government. But with Iskander Mirza taking over as an autocratic President, he gave him his support in repudiating all pretensions to democracy and declaring Martial Law. That was Ayub's opportunity. As a cautious but shrewd man, he let the onus fall on Mirza and, enjoying virtually dictatorial power as Chief Martial Law Administrator, he soon converted a de facto situation into a de jure one as well, by overthrowing Mirza and assuming his place. His well-timed moves, while holding himself in the background until the crucial moment, won him popular acclaim, and even Martial Law, instead of inspiring dread, was regarded as a panacea for the country's ills.

In my very frequent dealings with him in Pakistan, especially in the earlier years, I found Ayub Khan frank, open-minded and cooperative. He was straightforward and quick in grasping the essentials of a problem and, once convinced, quick in decision. He often observed that it was senseless on the part of our two countries, which were destined to live together, to be in a constant state of confrontation. An armed conflict between them would be unthinkable as it would solve no problem; besides, neither country could hope to subdue the other. He betrayed not a trace of religious bigotry or narrow-mindedness, and whenever he mentioned Prime Minister Nehru, he was always did so in terms of respect.

It was not as though all the pulls and pressures, irritants and frustrations, almost endemic in Indo-Pak relations, had suddenly evaporated. They continued as usual, but with less virulence, and were handled at appropriate levels. Mohatta Palace, the ornate and ugly former residence of an evacuee Sindhi Hindu merchant housed the Pakistani Foreign Office in Karachi. There was the usual exchange of formal protests about atrocities against Hindus in East Pakistan or of communal riots in India. These were routinely rejected by either side. Charges of spying, followed by the expulsion of personnel in one mission, would be reciprocated by similar action against the other, to the accompaniment of angry letters of refutation. Cases of the citizens of one country going with valid visas to the other and merging with the local population were not infrequent.

There was an ugly incident when an Indian Air Force pilot on a surveillance mission in a Canberra, flying deep over Pakistani territory, was intercepted and shot down. Out of sheer bravado and rashness he was flying below the ceiling of Pakistani fighters and was taken prisoner after he parachuted down. A strong protest followed, to which Delhi replied rather lamely that the pilot had strayed inadvertently over Pakistani territory while on a routine flight. This incident, while causing surface ripples, did not do any permanent damage to relations, possibly because it was tacitly accepted that mutual spying was being freely indulged in. Little that happened in one country was unknown to the other, and one wondered what purpose expensive intelligence agencies, with their unlimited budgets and unaccountability, were fulfilling. The Canberra incident's comparatively mild aftermath was in sharp contrast to the vast upheaval caused in Soviet-American relations by the shooting down of an American spy plane piloted by Gary Powers over the Soviet Union. The great sense of outrage felt by Khrushchev led to the cancellation of a projected summit meeting with the American President.

We sometimes had to intercede on behalf of Indian businessmen whose industries still continued to function under their former Indian or Pakistani managers. There were problems about the repatriation of profits and the generally harsh treatment meted out to the Indian staff.

In one such incident concerning the Sutlej Textile Mills belonging to the Birla Group, our Home Minister requested our intercession to secure the release from prison, where he was serving a long sentence, of the Marwari General Manager, arrested for the violation of some rule. A personal appeal to Ayub Khan succeeded in bringing about the frightened official's release, followed by his quick flight home and to safety.

The Martial Law Administration looked with deep suspicion and distrust at businessmen generally. The President of the Pakistani Chamber of Commerce, Rangoonwala, was summarily arrested and imprisoned, as was the Parsi head of a leading firm of shipowners. There were not many of the entrepreneur class in Pakistan at the time; migrant Muslim businessmen from Bombay had set up some textile mills and other medium or small industries. The two leading Karachi hotels—the Metropole and Beach Luxury had been established by Parsi hoteliers, Minwala and Awari. Punjabi families had workshops assembling motor-cars, etc., while the Muslim Sehgals had become textile magnates. There were no heavy industries at the time.

For six or seven months I remained submerged in the depths of the Congo, trying to keep that newly-liberated country afloat and to prevent its precarious independence from becoming the victim of Cold War rivalries. Little news about the Indian sub-continent percolated through beyond occasional snippets in some Western papers which reached us erratically. It was only when I called on President Ayub Khan in London on my way to New York when he was attending a conference of Commonwealth Heads of Government that I learnt, to my intense disappointment, how wrong things had gone. Instead of greeting me with his usual warmth and cordiality, Ayub Khan was cold and distant. After initial formalities, he upbraided me for leaving my post in Pakistan at such a critical juncture, remarking caustically that Pandit Nehru seemed to think that the Congo was more important to India than Pakistan. When I once more pleaded that an envoy was not a prime mover but only a conveyor belt, Ayub Khan bristled. He soundly blamed Krishna Menon and M.J. Desai for their evil counsel and the Prime Minister for being influenced by them. Lapsing into Urdu, he said with much bitterness: 'Woh mujhe hiqarat ki nazar se dekhte hain', 'Mr Nehru looks down upon me with contempt.' I was flabbergasted and tried vainly to assuage his hurt feelings. He went on to say that he expected better of Pandit Nehru, adding that he too was the head of a large state and should not have been treated thus. I was dismayed at what I heard and daunted by the thought that the sisyphean task of trying to restore some degree of sanity and civility in our relations would have to be faced again.

As a military man, Ayub Khan naturally thought in military terms, first building up the country's defence before turning his attention to politics. His paranoia about India, which he shared with practically all Pakistani politicians but which was not evident earlier, developed gradually. Having been in the Indian army for a decade or so before Independence, he must surely have known of the sterling fighting qualities of the Indian jawans amongst whom he had served. Yet he later came to acquire such absurd perceptions and prejudices as to say to his commanders that 'the Hindu has no stomach for a fight', or that 'give the Hindu a couple of hard knocks' and he will cave in. He also thought that 'one Pakistani jawan was equal to ten Hindu soldiers'. It was such empty boastfulness that led to the folly of the 1965 war against India which had such disastrous results for Pakistan and led to Ayub Khan's eventual downfall in disgrace.

After the death of Nehru and at the instigation of Foreign Minister Bhutto and Chief of the Army Staff, General Yahya Khan, Ayub succumbed to the temptation to try and make a grab for Kashmir. Previously, he had always stressed that the use of force could never solve any problems between our two countries, nor could either one ever hope to overcome the other. This view he also repeated in public on several occasions.

On my return to Karachi I was to discover to my dismay how sharp was the decline in Indo-Pak relations. This was vividly reflected in the sad state of our chancery building. The elegant foyer was a complete wreck, its huge plate glass frontage had been smashed in. The built-in furniture was in splinters. Fortunately, the vandals had been prevented from storming up the staircase, or the ruin would have been complete. But most of the glass windows on the different floors had been shattered. All this destruction had been wrought by a mob in protest against some real or imaginary happening in India. In a Martial Law regime, where the slightest whisper of protest was firmly suppressed, the vandalisation of the Indian chancery by a mob was undoubtedly the administration's crude was of expressing its displeasure.

After the unremitting efforts of the last two years, it seemed a daunting task to make a fresh start. To face the task, there had to be some understanding of the reasons for this sharp reverse.

There was a change even in the Foreign Office as new faces appeared in the person of Mohammad Ali Bogra as Foreign Minister and Dehlavi as Foreign Secretary. Bogra was a rather shifty character who carried little weight with the military rulers or even with his native East Pakistanis. He was not overburdened with principles and was little more than a time-server. He could waffle endlessly without committing himself to anything. His Foreign Secretary was of a piece with him. Originally from Bombay, Dehlavi had developed all the complexes about India which he felt would advance him in his career. To make matters worse, he was also pompous and verbose. What a sad contrast these two presented to their distinguished predecessors! It was a frustrating exercise trying to do business with them. In Indo-Pakistani relations, experience has amply demonstrated that there can never be a state of stability or equilibrium; unless a forward movement, however imperceptible, can be sustained, there will inevitably be a slide backwards.

It was clear that the intimate talks between President Ayub and Prime Minister Nehru in the quiet of the pleasant Murree hills, from which Ayub had expected the commencement of a new chapter in relations had, instead, prove an unmitigated disaster. This was evident from Ayub's bitter remarks to me in London some months earlier. All that Ayub Khan revealed was that when he tried to open a conversation about Kashmir, Nehru simply stared out of the window at the scenery and 'shut up like a clam'. From that time the relations between the two countries, which had been built up brick by brick, suddenly collapsed in rubble.

While attitudes at governmental level began to harden, our personal relations with the President and his family continued to be cordial enough. Our social relations generally also continued as before. We took our daily walks, unaccompanied by securitymen, both in Karachi and in Murree. Our weekend excursions to Hawke's Bay, a pleasant beach within half an hour's drive from Karachi, provided a welcome change. The mission possessed a charming little beach house of three or four rooms which we had found in a state of total neglect as my predecessor had warned us about not venturing out to the beach for security reasons. Susheela had the house and the furniture repaired and painted and, with some curtaining and other conveniences, it became a great boon to members of the mission and their families. There one could also invite those of our colleagues, including the British, who did not posses a similar facility. We frequently met Pakistani friends and politicians, including H.S. Suhrawardy who had become a non-person. A thoroughly unscrupulous politician, but an interesting conversationalist, Suhrawardy was Chief Minister of undivided Bengal and responsible for the Calcutta killings; he had once dreamt of creating an independent state of Bengal under his leadership.

In 1959 when the Chinese had overrun Tibet, and were encroaching into Aksai Chin and clashes between them and Indian patrols were increasing in number and seriousness, Ayub

Khan gave expression to his concept of 'joint defence'. He had been obsessed by what he described as pressures from the north bearing down on the sub-continent which, in his view, could be fended off only if the armies of our two countries, instead of facing each other inwards, were to face together outwards. He had written and spoken on this theme and had perhaps also mentioned it in a general way to Nehru at their brief meeting at Palam. But it had never till then been spelt out or discussed in detail, as one would have expected of such a far-reaching proposal. When it did come out more formally, the Indian response was: 'Joint defence against whom?' Perhaps the response was rather brusque as an attempt could have been made in quiet exchanges to draw out the President into disclosing his idea more fully. The Pakistani reaction to the Indian rejoinder was one of disappointment, real or feigned. After further desultory exchanges, India suggested that, before one could even think of joint defence, it was necessary to take some confidence-building measures such as the disengagement of forces and at least their token reduction. To this the response was that pending differences must first be solved, such as Kashmir. That, of course, was begging the question and we was back to where we began.

Was the joint defence proposal genuine and intended to be taken up seriously? Or was it a piece of slick propaganda to show up India in a belligerent light and, at the same time, to impress the United States of Pakistan's fervent anti-communism? Was it a trap, as India could not have answered with a 'yes' or a 'no', in the light of the prevailing circumstances? Perhaps it was an amalgam of all three.

Had the proposal been really serious, it would not have come out in the rather slap-dash manner in which it did. Even on matters of far less import, careful soundings and preparations should first be made before serious negotiations are launched. Ayub Khan no doubt often voiced in the course of my talks with him his fear, which was almost obsessive, of the common danger from the communist powers to the north of both our countries. But in first giving expression to his views on joint defence to an American journal and at a press conference, he clearly intended to catch the eye of Washington rather than to evoke India's interest and support. India's close friendship with the Soviet Union was well-known, and India's relations with China were still friendly despite the occurrence of ugly incidents in Ladakh. These were increasing in aggressiveness in the Aksai Chin area as the Chinese continued their steady encroachments. But India did not then regard these skirmishes as a serious military provocation which could not be resolved by pacific means.

Pakistan's membership of what were western-dominated aggressive military pacts like CENTO and SEATO, part of the western policy of containment of the communist giants, was totally incompatible with India's policy of staunch non-alignment. Any kind of military association with Pakistan, given the prevailing atmosphere of mutual suspicion and mistrust, was totally out of the question.

If the proposal was intended as a trap or ruse, it betrayed naivete in expecting India to be so undiscerning as to fall into it. India could hardly have been so easily weaned away from its friendship towards the communist powers and, in the process, abandon its policy of non-alignment, of which it was the originator and leading exponent.

When the matter came up more formally between the two governments, I tried to ascertain from the Foreign Minister of Pakistan what precisely it entailed. It then transpired that the whole scheme was contingent on a prior settlement of the Kashmir question, no doubt on Pakistan's terms. We suggested a withdrawal of forces facing each other to a safer distance and even a mutual reduction, albeit only a token reduction, of forces. To this the response was that any disengagement could only follow a settlement of the Kashmir question. That, of course, was the end of the matter. It was clear that serious negotiations would not have produced any serious results. The only advantage could have been that the insincerity and propagandist nature of the proposal would have been exposed to the world. As it happened, it was Pakistan that secured the propaganda advantage. The more ill-informed or more ill-disposed of our critics, especially those abroad, did not conceal their view that, had some understanding on the subject been reached, or even if it had still been on the anvil, the subsequent Chinese attack in 1962 could have been pre-empted.

East Pakistan was an important part of the High Commissioner's bailiwick and a visit there a few times annually was essential to obtain a total picture of the situation. Scenically and in most other aspects, East Pakistan was very different from its western twin. The countryside was lush, and lavishly watered by enormous rivers. Its predominant colour was the emerald green of rice paddies. It was a glaring contrast to the stark and sandy countryside of Sindh. The people were much gentler and poorer and miserably clad as they struggled for a living by fishing with nets waist-deep in every pond or wayside pool, or laboured in flooded rice fields. Jute seemed to be the only industry, the factories being mostly owned by industrialists from the western wing while the jute trade continued largely in the hands of Marwari businessmen from their offices in the interior.

While money had been lavished on Karachi and other West Pakistan cities, Dacca wore the aspect of neglect. The governors and the top officials were mostly non-Bengalis and, instead of enjoying the status of an equal and more populous partner, East Pakistan was regarded more as a colony to be patronised and exploited. The West Pakistan officials and others disliked the place; they could not endure its climate, they could not speak its language, they could not stomach its food. Similar sentiments of aversion towards the westerners were volubly reciprocated by the

Bengalis who said that, if the westerners took pride in their brawn, they had the brain. The sense of separateness from the Bengalis was general among West Pakistanis who felt no affinity whatsoever with them and, in fact, regarded them as troublesome and cantankerous and slightly comic. Ayub Khan, who had served for many years in East Pakistan, was not immune from such sentiments. He often complained that he had done more for East Pakistan than any of his predecessors, yet it continued to whine and complain. He was interested to know how we in India managed to deal with the Bengalis and to keep them quiet. More than once he said half jokingly, but revealing his subconscious feelings, that we could have an exchange of East Pakistan with Kashmir. The reply, also half-joking, was that Kashmir was not up for barter.

The Hindus, who comprised some 15 per cent of the population at the time of Partition, were dispirited and orphaned, their leaders having fled to the safety of Calcutta, leaving the rest to their fate. The persecution and discrimination they suffered drove many to flee their homesteads, only to share the privations of the pavement-dwellers in Calcutta. Hindus counted for little or nothing in the political life of the country or in the provincial cabinet. They did, however, occupy positions in the judicial and administrative services as well as in the learned professions. The sole political leader who held fast to his convictions and his duty when all the rest had fled, was the redoubtable Sarat Chandra Chatterjee, the Grand Old Man of Bengal. Sarat Babu was fearless and outspoken; he had a commanding personality and was both feared and respected by the new masters of the country. What a shining contrast he was to the great Maharajas—of Cossim-bazar, of Mymensingh, the Tagores and other big landlords and notables who deserted their flock and fled forsaking their palaces, retainers and followers. From their sanctuaries in Calcutta they pestered the High Commission to salvage for them the abundance of valuables and heirlooms abandoned by them in the hurry of departure.

A Hindu businessman who had come to terms with the regime and had greatly flourished was Rai Bahadur Ranadi Prasad Shaha. He had become a boon companion of Ayub Khan when the General was Army Commander in the region and this connection, especially when his friend became President, stood him in good stead. He had a near monopoly of the import of coal from India and travelled freely to and fro between Delhi and Calcutta. A widower and reputedly a Tantrik, he had devoted his considerable wealth to charitable purposes. At his headquarters in the village of Mirzapur, some twenty-five miles from Dacca, he had built a magnificent, lavishly-equipped free hospital. It had excellent medical services and a trained nursing staff under a British matron. It had some 100 beds and patients were treated, fed and provided with medicines free. Near by, there was a girls' college, also built and funded by the Rai Bahadur, where the pupils were provided with uniforms, housed, fed and taught absolutely free. The donor was fanatical about cleanliness and both institutions were spotlessly clean while the extensive grounds were in keeping with the high standard of the whole complex. The Rai Bahadur himself lived in a modest mud-brick hutment across a narrow inlet, where he entertained his guests at trestle tables under shady trees, to simple Bengali fare. A temple to the goddess Kali presided over the scene. Tragically, despite his good works and his genuine popularity with the village folk far and wide, in the communal frenzy unleashed by Yahya Khan, the Rai Bahadur met a cruel death at the hands of the West Pakistani soldiery.

Praise is also due to the swamis of the Ramakrishna Mission who continued to minister to the spiritual needs of the people in their well-run institutions.

Work at the Dacca office of the High Commission was mostly of a consular nature. There was hardly any trade while the political work was handled in Karachi, the then federal capital. But its presence gave a sense of reassurance to the beleaguered Hindu community. It was expected to keep a finger on the pulse of things in that distant province and to keep the High Commission informed. It was daily besieged by a swarm of visa-seekers, including a smattering of Muslims, and had to lend ear to the tales of woe of Hindu families desperately seeking migration to India.

There was some trade in jute as the Calcutta mills had always drawn the bulk of their supplies from East Bengal. But with the increasing cultivation of the fibre in West Bengal, and especially in Assam, the need for Pakistani jute diminished greatly. A cement factory was coming up in Sylhet district for which sandstone was to be supplied from Assam across the border. Then there was the traditional trade in head-loads of fish and other rural products, mostly destined to meet the insatiable needs of Calcutta. In the absence of any formal agreement, this was mostly clandestine and continued practically unabated, surviving the vagaries of fluctuating political relations.

Pakistan's policy of shutting off practically all commercial relations with India was self-defeating as it was the greater loser, especially in East Pakistan. Undivided Bengal was an economic whole, as was freely admitted by Ghulam Farouqui, a former Governor and Commerce Minister. The great industries of West Bengal drew heavily on the produce of the eastern part, while the whole area was served by the vast network of waterways leading down to the bustling port of Calcutta. Cut off from its natural economic zone, East Bengal was now condemned to remain abjectly poor and isolated.

However precarious may have been East Pakistan's economy in comparison with the West's, politically the Bengalis were far more alert and conscious than their feudal partners. Volatile and somewhat unpredictable, their apparent submissiveness concealed the storms brewing within.

Like the famed 'nor' westers', the tropical storms endemic to the area, the calm and smiling landscape would suddenly be transformed. The great rivers Padma and Meghna, with their deep green waters flowing silently to the sea with a myriad sailing boats skimming their sparkling surfaces like butterflies, would suddenly become violently agitated, and great waves would begin lashing against the banks. With deafening peals of thunder, inky black clouds would advance with great rapidity, obscuring the sun and casting a pall of darkness over the scene. This would be accompanied by pelting rain and gales of alarming ferocity, carrying in their fury tin roofs and great branches of uprooted trees, while the stately palms would bow low before the wind as if in obeisance, their fronds brushing the ground. The dark sky would be filled with flying objects, posing a danger to man and beast. Human beings and animals would scamper to seek shelter from the raging elements. Soon, before one's unbelieving eyes, the storm would abate as suddenly as it came, leaving a trail of death and destruction behind.

During 1959, beneath the apparent quiescence imposed by the stern vigilance of the military rulers, rumblings of discontent were beginning to be audible. A marked way in which their resentment against West Pakistan was expressed was in their hostility towards the Urdu language. When a few words in Urdu were inadvertently addressed by me to a Bengali gentleman, promptly came a rebuke that if I was ignorant of the Bengali tongue I should use English instead. They were rightly proud of their rich language and of Bengali culture, regarding themselves as its true repositories and inheritors, whereas Indian Bengali culture had been infiltrated and corrupted by Hindi influences.

This dislike of Urdu was in notable contrast to the position in 1950, when I happened to pass through Sylhet on my way from Shillong to Karimgunj on a special mission. I was met unexpectedly by a large delegation comprising the mayor, local officials and notables and treated to a lavish luncheon in place of my frugal traveller's sandwiches. Having noticed from a large signboard in Urdu that the town had been rechristened 'Jalalabad' and the famous Harishchandra College sacrilegiously renamed 'Mohammad Ali Jinnah College', I asked the Mayor and his colleagues in Urdu how they liked the language. They shuffled around uneasily until the Mayor mustered the courage to answer in execrable Urdu, execrably pronounced, that they liked the language well enough but the pronunciation was very difficult, a sentiment with which I fully agreed. Incidentally, the Bengalis are often burdened with obscure and unpronounceable old-fashioned Arabic and Afghan names, real tongue twisters, full of guttural qs and khs, which not even the Punjabis are able to pronounce.

There had been language riots all over East Pakistan when Urdu was sought to be imposed as the sole national language of Pakistan. The central authorities had perforce to cave in and Bengali was conceded an equal place with Urdu. The ruling Muslim League, the architect of Pakistan, had been wiped out in the 1954 elections in East Pakistan, largely on the language issue and to emphasise East Bengal's sense of separateness from the west.

On my return to Dacca after almost a year's absence towards the end of 1961, the change in the political climate was immediately evident. The old reticences were no more, our invitations were readily accepted and conversations were no longer stilted and guarded. At receptions the new post-Independence Muslim middle-class—men and women— was very much in evidence and even Hindu invitees began to make an appearance. The women were not shy or diffident and comported themselves well and seemed to take pride in their 'modernity'. They were elegantly dressed in silks, and what was most surprising, wore a 'bindi', on their foreheads! We were informed that their coiffeur and dress were based on 'Calcutta fashions', the bindi being a necessary adjunct.

A still greater surprise lay in store. To our dinner invitations, to which we invited a dozen or so notables, there was a ready response. And what is more, the conversation was embarrassingly free and uninhibited, turning always to politics. Among the guests were Hamidul Haq Chowdhury, Ataur Rahman Khan, both former Ministers, the Chief Justice, Nurul Amin, and other prominent political personalities. They waxed loud and eloquent against their western military overlords of whom they spoke with contempt and disdain. They thought the Punjabis crude and aggressive, lacking in the finer things of life. They spoke of their own great poets and patriots like Rabindranath Tagore and Nazrul Islam, and of their revolutionary leaders, like Subhash Chandra Bose, Jatin Das, etc. They said they would not allow themselves to be exploited and treated as a colony any more and would assert their rights, if necessary, by force.

I listened fascinated as the guests gave free vent to their thoughts and feelings. Fearing that they were on dangerous ground, I tried unsuccessfully to divert the conversation to safer topics. I wondered what all this portended; was it just froth and effervescence or was it something more?

Future visits to Dacca resolved my doubts. The talk became even more agitated and strident and turned towards freeing the country from the 'Punjabi' yoke. With this all agreed and proclaimed that sooner or later when the time was ripe, they would overthrow their oppressors. By now I was quite alarmed and feared that if there was an informer among them they could get into deep trouble while the High Commissioner would be accused of being an accomplice to rebellion. I cautioned that I could not be a party to such conversation and wished to be kept out of it as it was both highly embarrassing and impolitic. The guests then demanded to know what would be India's attitude when they made their bid for freedom. I told them that it was entirely a matter between them and their western friends, and we

Din Dayal,
the author's father.

The author's mother.

At the UN, May 1951 :
the author in the
Delegates' Lounge
before a meeting of
the Security Council.

At the UN, October 1953 : the author addressing the
General Assembly Ad Hoc Political Committee.

Beirut, September 1956 : UN Secretary General Dag Hammarskjold being
seen off by UNOGIL. Left to right : Galo Plaza, Hammarskjold,
the author and Maj. Gen. Odd Bull.

President Ayub Khan being welcomed by Susheela at the
Indian High Commission : 26 January 1959.

The author and Susheela with President Ayub Khan : Karachi, 26 January 1959.

Morarji Desai (left) and the author : Karachi, February 1959.

February 1959, Karachi : The author, Z.A. Bhutto
(the Commerce Minister of Pakistan) and M.J. Desai.

Mr. Z. A. Bhutto and Mrs. Bhutto at a Reception hosted by the
author and Susheela, Murree, June 1960.

The author and Ralph Bunche : 2 September 1960, New York.

At the UN, April 1971 : the author at a meeting of the Committee on
the Elimination of Racial Discrimination.

January 1964 : five brothers. From left to right : Bhagwat, Kishen, Rajeshwar, Maheshwar and Harishwar. (Inset : Bishumber, the missing one.)

Family snap : January 1964.

could have no lot or part in it. They then pressed for a straight reply to the question whether India would help their 'enemies' or at least keep neutral. I could only reply that there could be no question of our intervention in an internal matter between them and their western link. As it was, we were being constantly accused of not being reconciled to Partition and losing no opportunity in trying to undo it.

The passion and persistence with which the visitors spoke left no further room for doubt as to the seriousness of their resolve. But between the intention and the deed there could be a wide gap. When and how it would be bridged, was the question. I had of course reported these conversations to the ministry, without, as usual, getting any reaction. Now I recounted the conversations which I had been hearing on repeated occasions, to the Prime Minister. Mr Nehru showed keen interest and did not question my conviction that an explosion was impending. He enquired when that could be. I said that that depended upon the resoluteness of the Bengali leadership and the blunders of the regime. No prediction was possible in regard to the timing as it all depended upon a conjunction of these two factors. I then expressed the view that from our point of view the breakaway of the east wing would not be an unmixed blessing. From the strategic angle the defence of East Pakistan imposed a drain on the resources of the military establishment composed almost entirely of Punjabis and some other westerners, which could then be concentrated in the west. While the loss of the east wing would be a severe psychological blow and could possible reduce Pakistani bravado, arrogance and aggressiveness, we would now have to deal with two difficult neighbours instead of one. Pandit Nehru did not disagree. However, he did not live to see the day when the Bengali leadership, with India's assistance, gave proof of their determination to achieve their freedom. It was surely the sword of nemesis that the Pakistan government, which had been crying itself hoarse over 'self-determination' for Jammu and

Kashmir, geographically, legally and historically an integral part of India, should itself have been struck down when the unnatural union with East Bengal—separated by 1,200 miles of territory—exercised by force its own right to self-determination and an independent existence. It also exploded the myth of the 'two nation theory', the very basis of Pakistan.

My term in Pakistan was drawing to a close when, after a farewell visit to the east wing, I arrived in Delhi on my way back to Karachi. At the airport I was met by an emissary from the Ministry of External Affairs with a letter marked 'Immediate'. It announced that the Defence Minister was holding an important conference at which my presence was urgently requested. Puzzled as to its purpose, I hurried to the Ministry to seek from those who should have known, some enlightenment about the topic of discussion. But they were completely in the dark about it.

When I presented myself at the Defence Minister's room at the appointed hour, Krishna Menon greeted me with what seemed like relief. Presently the three service chiefs trooped in, followed by the Commonwealth and Defence Secretaries, the Director of the Intelligence Bureau and sundry other officials. They all wore a look of puzzlement and concern, asking each other in whispers what it was all about. Seating himself at the head of the table, the Minister sat me to his right while the Army Chief, General P.N. Thapar, sat to his left, the rest, a dozen or so, took their respective places at the table.

Opening the meeting, the Minister observed that he was glad the High Commissioner was present to give a first-hand account of the vast preparations being made in Pakistan to launch a professedly non-violent massive infiltration of so-called volunteers across the ceasefire line into Kashmir. Taken aback, I said that I was not aware of any such plan when I left Karachi a week earlier; if something had developed since, the Intelligence Bureau and Military Intelligence would no doubt know. When pressed by the Minister, I said that advertisements had indeed been appearing in some papers calling for volunteers for Kashmir and offering a pittance as compensation. There had been no response, which was not surprising as no one would risk his neck for a song. These advertisements had not been taken seriously. The Minister, not satisfied, asked what the East European envoys were saying. I replied that they almost routinely used to talk in general terms about Pakistan's aggressive intentions. I did not think their sources of information were better than ours. This vague second-hand rumour seemed to be just what the Minister was driving at; he exclaimed that Pakistan's sinister designs were now evident. He asked the General what action he proposed to take to meet the imminent danger. General Thapar replied that he would have barbed-wire enclosures set up along the ceasefire line and would collar the infiltrators and herd them in the moment they transgressed the line. Approving of the plan, the Minister thereupon directed that all leave be cancelled and the armed forces put on alert.

Alarmed at such a far-reaching conclusion drawn, and the drastic measures ordered on the basis of flimsy hearsay, I interjected that the rumour could easily be pinned down by me personally on my return to Pakistan in a few days. I hurried back to Karachi and arranged to advance the date of our September sojourn in Murree, a hill resort strategically situated for observing any military movements towards Kashmir. It was now the end of August 1962, a significant date in view of what was to follow elsewhere a few weeks later.

On our arrival in Murree, the two officers posted at our camp office there expressed surprise at my enquiry whether any extraordinary movement of military traffic had been noticed. From our garden terrace the motor road passing by Murree from Rawalpindi to Baramula in Kashmir was clearly visible. A security man was posted there to keep a count of the military trucks passing up or down and another posted at the crossroads to observe the contents of the open military vehicles. The reports confirmed that the daily traffic was no more than normal and consisted of winter stores such as charcoal and kerosene, blankets and food, etc. A drive some twenty kilometers down the Baramula road with a picnic basket and the tricolour flying provided a pleasant and uneventful outing for my wife and myself, and further confirmed the absence of any hostile movement.

As was my custom, I telephoned the General commanding the region, General Shaukat Ali Shah; he was most cordial and immediately asked us over to tea with him and his charming family. He said he was under orders of transfer but had asked for them to be deferred to enable his daughter to take her final school-leaving examination. A few days later, I had an unusual visitor, General Jilani (serving military officers would normally never call on the Indian envoy). Jilani had rented a house of his to the mission and that excuse enabled him to obtain permission to call on me. He seemed to be a bitter and frustrated man. He said he had just been ordered to go on retirement from command of the crucial Sialkot military area. He added for emphasis that it was he who had conquered the entire northern territories of the state of Jammu and Kashmir in 1948 and, but for the unexpected appearance of General Thimayya's tanks across the impossible Zoji-la pass, he would have poured down into the Kashmir valley itself. He complained that his premature retirement was all the gratitude shown to him by the Punjabi rulers, who could not tolerate the presence of Pathans in senior positions in the army.

It was abundantly clear that what the Defence Minister had hastened to believe was pure fantasy, without a shred of supporting evidence. Added to the normal situation on the ground, was the important fact that two key generals who commanded the very areas through which the supposed infiltrators would have breached the cease-fire line, were to be transferred or retired. Reports on my personal observations were promptly transmitted to New Delhi. But they failed to evoke any reaction either from the Defence Minister or External Affairs. And no wonder, because in a few short weeks the Chinese attacked not only in the Aksai Chin bulge where a perilous game of chess between the Chinese and Indian military posts had been going on, but also along the central and eastern Himalaya. No wonder too that the Indian army was totally unprepared to meet the Chinese onslaught as the Defence Minister's sights were aligned in the wrong direction.

It is difficult to understand what Krishna Menon's arcane motives were in thus deluding himself and trying to delude others. Not that Pakistan would not be up to any mischief to cause embarrassment to India and to further its acquisitive ambitions in Kashmir. But at the time, no such plan or activity was contemplated. On the other hand, the Chinese menace was looming large along the Himalaya, but the Defence Minister had refused to acknowledge the overwhelming evidence of the impending peril. General Thimayya, when he was Chief of the Army Staff, repeatedly warned the Minister of the increasing aggressiveness of the Chinese in the Ladakh area, but the Minister had turned a deaf ear to his warnings. His successor, General Thapar, had likewise repeatedly reported on the gathering storm and had asked for the necessary arms and equipment which the army sadly lacked, but again, he met with stony indifference. The result of this obtuseness and refusal to face facts by the Minister responsible for the defence of the country, was to cost the country dear. Like an avalanche, the Chinese poured down from the Himalayan heights into Indian territory, and the Indian army was ill-prepared to repel them.

The conclusion of my mission in Pakistan was approaching and it was time to make a reckoning of the successes and failures of the four tumultuous years of anxious toil. Almost all the problems that constituted the unfinished business of Partition had been substantially solved. The question of Kashmir was broached at the personal talks between the Indian Prime Minister and the

Pakistani President in the cool of the Murree hills. But that encounter, from which much had been expected, had however turned out to be a fiasco.

The account of the Murree encounter, according to Manzur Qadir, was as follows: the President and the Prime Minister drove up to Murree in an open car with Manzur Qadir in the front seat. There was no conversation between the two leaders throughout the hour-long drive. Manzur Qadir made some attempts to start a conversation but met with deafening silence; thereupon he gave up the attempt.

Arrived at the President's Lodge, the host led his guest to the sitting room for a quiet tete-a-tete behind closed doors. The Foreign Minister and the Presidential staff waited outside. They did not, however, have very long to wait. When the doors opened, and the two leaders came out, instead of the smiles usual on such occasions, their expressions were serious. The return journey was as frigid as the drive uphill.

Manzur Qadir later recalled that he had tried to draw out the President about the meeting, but all that he could gather was that when the subject of Kashmir was broached, Pandit Nehru 'shut up like a clam' and gazed out of the open window at the panorama of the mountains of Kashmir.

Another version, that of Ayub Khan's biographer, Altaf Gauhar, is that Nehru merely repeated the old offer of the ceasefire line, with minor rectifications, as the international border. With this proposal, presumably on a 'take it or leave it' basis, the talks concluded.

A third version is contained in Ayub Khan's autobiography entitled *Friends Not Masters*. The rather jumbled account is hectoring in tone and reads like a homily. The opening gambit was in characteristic vein as Ayub Khan urged that, since both leaders enjoyed pre-eminence in their own countries, the present was the most propitious time to arrive at a settlement on Kashmir. In military fashion, he explained how vital Kashmir was to

Pakistan's economy and security. Nehru, in reply, stated that to rake up the Kashmir question again would cause much destabilisation, which would not only prejudice the position of the large Muslim community in India, but also divert attention from the pressing needs of economic development. Ayub Khan expatiated on the wisdom and far-sightedness of his own views about joint defence and for a settlement of the Kashmir question for the benefit of the peoples of both countries. At the same time he lamented the obtuseness of his guest for not being able to recognise their merit. But Ayub Khan has given no explanation as to why he took umbrage at Pandit Nehru's response, which was only a reiteration of the well-known Indian position.

Nehru was fully aware of Ayub Khan's expectations since they had been fully reported and discussed with him by me. Ayub Khan was a realist enough not to expect a sudden breakthrough in a problem that had defied solution all these years. He had freely acknowledged that the two countries held divergent views on the subject, which in Pakistan's case, he said, were inherited from his predecessors. What he had asked for was that talks be started, in the hope that, to use his own words, 'Inshallah, something will come out of them.' I had favoured the proposal as the mere opening of talks would have greatly helped in reducing the pressure on an issue heavily overcharged with emotion. Besides, from a substantive point of view, the thorough airing of the subject, greatly obfuscated in Pakistan by false assumptions and exaggerated expectations, would have helped in a more rational and realistic understanding of the issues at stake.

The agonising question is whether there was a failure of statesmanship on one or both sides which led to the loss of a valuable opportunity to commence a process of reconciliation. Assuredly, if Ayub Khan did deliver a lecture, as he claims to have done, Nehru's reaction, given his political pre-eminence and personal temperament, should have been foreseen. And if Nehru's final response was to reject outright the proposal to start talks on the ground that things should be left undisturbed, that could also have foreclosed any possibility of progress. In going all the way north to Murree, after the formal Karachi ceremony, the Prime Minister implicitly accepted the question of opening unconditional talks on Kashmir.

Pandit Nehru had previously discussed a solution to the Kashmir question with Pakistani leaders on more than one occasion and India's complaint against Pakistan was still on the agenda of the UN Security Council. Recently, however, Krishna Menon's thesis that there was nothing to discuss since Kashmir was an integral part of India, had been gaining currency. While this position may have been legally tenable, politically it could hardly withstand the pressure of events. The principle of a dialogue was conceded by Mrs Gandhi in the 1972 Simla Agreement. In spite of India holding no less than 93,000 Pakistani prisoners of war and the Indian army occupying a large tract in the heartland of Pakistan, she had agreed to discuss bilaterally all pending issues 'including Kashmir'. That commitment holds good to this day. If it is possible to discuss Kashmir in 1997, it could also have been possible thirty-seven years ago in 1960. A mere two years later when the Chinese attacked India, there was great danger of a Pakistani stab in the back. To ward off that menace, India came under heavy pressure from Britain and the United States to come to a final settlement with Pakistan on Kashmir and various quite unacceptable proposals involving extensive territorial concessions were thrust upon India. A series of meetings at ministerial level on Kashmir followed, ending in a stalemate.

All this points to the melancholy conclusion that at Murree in September 1960 a promising opportunity of improving relations between the estranged neighbours by engaging in a process of discussion on Kashmir, which could have lasted for years, was lost. At the same time, Pandit Nehru's whole purpose in going all the way for a face-to-face encounter with Ayub

Khan, presumably in the hope of finding some common ground, came to naught.

Had the outcome been different, the projected bilateral talks would have taken their familiar leisurely course as did the talks on canal waters. All this time a more relaxed atmosphere would have prevailed. What influence this could have had on China's decision in 1962 to attack India, cannot of course be gauged. At any rate, India's fears of a Pakistani stab in the back would have been allayed. As for the ultimate outcome of the talks, it would no doubt have fallen far short of Pakistan's inflated expectations. But Pakistan would have shot its bolt and forfeited any future possibility of raking up the issue and any military action would clearly have been an outright case of unabashed aggression.

Pakistan's irredentist ambitions in Kashmir have provided its government with a martyr complex which helps it to maintain a semblance of unity among its divided peoples. Also, the incessant anti-Indian propaganda and the vicious propaganda attacks on 'Hindus' are intended to keep the most fanatical and aggressive sectarian feelings on the boil. So long as Partition memories are kept alive by constant stoking of the fires of hatred, this propaganda will have effect. The only hope lies in the younger generation of the educated and more enlightened young men and women, who are becoming increasingly aware of the broad currents of thought and behaviour which are coursing through the world. They are more tolerant of people, and sceptical of official or sectarian propaganda; they wish to judge matters for themselves.

Now that the Indian tiger is freeing itself of its shackles, it is bound to advance rapidly towards economic progress and well-being and to become a world-class political and economic power in consonance with its size, human and material resources and global significance. If Pakistan continues on the path of irredentism, Islamic bigotry and blind hatred, it will be condemning itself to backwardness while the world marches on.

In retrospect, what has the creation of Pakistan really achieved? Has it fulfilled the hopes and promises of its architect, Mohammad Ali Jinnah? His 'two nation theory' had proclaimed that the Muslims of India, from one end of the country to the other, constituted a separate and distinctive nation that could not co-exist with Hindus. They therefore demanded a homeland of their own where they could live in accordance with their own customs, traditions and, presumably, the precepts of Islam.

Yet what Jinnah managed to achieve was what he himself described as a 'moth-eaten Pakistan', which embraced a smaller percentage of the Muslim population than that which remained in India. On the creation of Pakistan, Jinnah had proclaimed the secular character of the new state when he emphasised that all its citizens would be equal in every way regardless of their colour, caste or creed. Jinnah himself thus jettisoned his own 'two nation theory'. The coup de grace to it was administered most decisively by the secession of Bangladesh. It is, of course, another matter that the Congress leaders never accepted Jinnah's fictitious theory, conceding Pakistan only as a secessionist state and not on communal grounds.

To the hard-headed but realistic politician that Jinnah was, the expectations from Pakistan could not have been very dissimilar. He must surely have realised that his new country, over which he presided in fulfillment of his ambition to be its first Governor-General, was no match for India. While India, despite Partition, remained a going concern, Pakistan had to improvise practically from scratch. Comparatively poor in resources and with an impossible geography, its inherent weakness and contradictions were self-evident. Having exploited the 'two nation theory' to the hilt, Jinnah realised that it was of no further use to him and declared its demise, announcing that in the new state all communities would receive equal treatment. He must also have seen that Pakistan was hardly in a position to try military conclusions with India. It can of course be argued that the ill-fated adventure in Kashmir belies this assumption, but it was perhaps the result of the mistaken belief that a quick decision there would take the Indians by surprise and would not be seriously challenged, especially as the question of accession was still open due to the Maharaja's dithering.

Jinnah, the hard-headed politician, could not have intended that the new state would be permanently embroiled in an unequal struggle with its giant neighbour, or be engaged in a periodic test of arms with it. He must have hoped that at least a state of peaceful co-existence would prevail. He had, no doubt, attempted by force to take advantage of the situation of the state of Jammu and Kashmir which was still malleable at the time, with the Maharaja dithering between independence and accession to India or Pakistan. The Indian army balked Jinnah's plans, but not before he had seized one-third of the state's territories. Pakistan has, throughout its short life, been engaged in the hopeless endeavour to equal or even outstrip its neighbour, much to its own detriment.

Jinnah, himself a skilled parliamentarian, had envisioned the new state as being a parliamentary democracy and, indeed, in its early years under the Prime Ministership of Liaquat Ali Khan, it did try to follow that path. But for much of its uneasy existence since, it has been a military dictatorship. The political development of the country has therefore remained stunted as feudal attitudes and the dominance of oligarchies prevails.

Pakistan has now openly rejected Jinnah's concept of a secular democracy, and styles itself as an 'Islamic Republic'. This immediately relegates its tiny and dwindling minority communities to an inferior status. Because Pakistan is an overwhelmingly Sunni country, Ahmadiyas have been declared heretics while even Shias are under constant persecution. The Human Rights Commission of Pakistan has roundly condemned the oppression of the minorities and other Muslim sects. It has also strongly criticised the depressed status of women in the country.

In the economic field, some progress has no doubt been made in industry and commerce. Industrial construction has been largely in the medium- and small-scale sectors, mostly textiles. The broad masses have, however, benefited little from such developments and it is estimated that some two dozen families only are the main beneficiaries.

There has been a large inflow of funds remitted by migrant workers from abroad, but this can hardly be a stable source of national income. Much tainted money has also been raised by drug smugglers, Pakistan being one of the world centres of traffic in narcotic drugs. Also, large fortunes have been made, reputedly by high military officers, from the misappropriation and sale of vast quantities of American arms destined for the prosecution of the war in Afghanistan against the Soviets. An accretion of money by such tainted means in the hands of criminals and corrupt officials and politicians corrupts the entire social fabric.

In the social field, the record is lamentable. The status of women remains dismal. Little progress has been made in the spread of education and the literacy rate, especially among women, is one of the lowest in the world. Public health has not received the attention it deserves. Because of the huge drain on maintaining a highly inflated military establishment and pursuit of a clandestine nuclear programme, it is no wonder that sufficient resources are not available even for essential nation-building activities.

The nature and characteristics of an 'Islamic' state have defied definition despite the repeated efforts of conclaves of Mullahs and Muftis. But even the definition of the term 'Muslim' demanded by the Supreme Court of Pakistan has baffled the learned divines. All that the fundamentalists have been able to achieve has been to turn the clock back by forcing a change in the law on the offence of blasphemy which is now punishable by death, a provision which can be much abused for private vengeance. Furthermore, denying their great Indian heritage, international conferences have been convened to evolve an ethos for the new state; these too have been barren of results. Unlike older states which have recognisable characteristics, Pakistan has no distinctive traits, no history, no distinctive forms of artistic or literary expression, no language or customs that are not also 'Indian' to distinguish it. What is called Pakistani culture is a mix of many cultural traditions (as is Indian culture) that it shares with India. Pakistan's leitmotif of unrelenting hostility towards India and rejection of all things Indian is not sufficient ground for a new cultural identity to develop. No state can progress or be sustained on the basis of a permanent negation without condemning itself to stagnation.

Far from uniting the Muslims of undivided India under one flag, as Jinnah had promised, they have been divided between three countries with little communication between them. Families have been cruelly divided, millions have been uprooted from their ancestral homes for the illusory benefit of living on alien soil. Even in Pakistan itself, relations between its four constituent units are far from harmonious as the Punjabi Muslims, who comprise about two-thirds of the total population of the country and dominate the army and government, try to dominate the other three groups. In Sindh there is an endemic separatist movement. In the Frontier Province there has never been any love lost with the Punjabis, while in Baluchistan, a state of rebellion has prevailed for years, ruthlessly suppressed from time to time.

Most unhappy is the lot of the migrants from India, the 'Mujahirs', the leaders of the Pakistan movement or their descendants, as well as their dupes among the impressionable masses. They are concentrated in Sindh and dominate its principal cities of Karachi and Hyderabad. Because of their skills and higher motivation they have outclassed and ousted the native Sindhis who naturally resent the intrusion of these unwanted outsiders. The Punjabi establishment too resents them for their greater political awareness and industry. Another general cause is, ironically, the Urdu language, the mother-tongue of the Muhajirs, while the Pakistani provinces have their own local languages or dialects. The Urdu language which was adopted as the national language of Pakistan, instead of being a cementing factor, has only given rise to resentment and jealousy against the Urdu-speaking Muhajirs. Fifty years after independence, the migrants continue to be described as refugees and treated as such. What a sharp contrast to the Hindus and Sikhs evicted from Pakistan who are among the most prosperous citizens of India and whose migrant status has long since been forgotten. So strong has been the reaction in Pakistan on the part of the Muhajirs against their oppression, that the Pakistani army has been deployed to crush their spirit and their demand for equal treatment or a separate province of their own.

To contain these divisive tendencies, various Pakistani regimes of different hues have resorted to different methods. In the absence of any distinctive direction or national policies in the economic, social and political fields which would command general allegiance, the governments have been floundering. So acute have been the political divisions that the main preoccupation of governments has been sheer survival. The Mullahs, who had been put in their place by Ayub Khan, began to raise their heads after his fall, and were given full rein by President Zia-ul-Haq. Various reactionary laws were passed and practices enjoined in emulation of the Ayatollahs and Saudis. The Mullahs are now a rival centre of power in the land and the conversion of Pakistan into an 'Islamic state, in the narrowest sense of the term, is their recipe for national unification. The political establishment, for its part, tries to exploit the Mullahs for its own ends, but without allowing them to become too powerful. The Mullahs are convenient allies in inciting the masses over Kashmir and they are also useful in fending off their political foes.

In a situation replete with ironies, the fact stands out that the Pakistan of today was, before Partition, relatively free of communal dissension, unlike UP, Bihar and Bengal. The Punjab had a Unionist ministry until the very eve of Partition and the Muslim League carried little weight. That ministry, comprising Muslims, Hindus and Sikhs, functioned remarkably smoothly under the leadership of Sir Sikander Hyat Khan Tiwana. It was only when the prospect of Pakistan loomed near that the successor Ministry of Khizr Hyat Khan Tiwana was overthrown. Socially also, the three communities lived together peacefully, frequently acknowledging their common clan kinships, as their surnames still testify. The Frontier Province was a stronghold of the Congress under the leadership of the redoubtable Khan Abdul Ghaffar Khan, the 'Frontier Gandhi'. In Sindh the government was free from communal bias and the various communities there lived together in empathy and mutual cooperation. Yet today the Punjab is the most virulently bigoted and aggressively anti-Indian of the provinces of Pakistan.

With unstable governments, frequent military take-overs, little regard for democratic principles or human rights and limited economic progress, a mood of disillusionment is frequently encountered among the more enlightened Pakistanis. In fact, thinking people wonder what benefits the creation of Pakistan has really brought to the people. It has certainly not provided a homeland for all the Muslims of the Indian sub-continent or bettered their general lot. The sole beneficiaries of Pakistan are the Punjabis who dominate the others. This is a far cry from the country of Jinnah's dreams.

It may well be asked whether Partition, to which the Congress leaders were consenting parties, has brought any benefits to India. It is said that it was the price paid to secure Independence. Furthermore, Nehru has himself admitted that the Congress politicians were too weary to continue the struggle for an independent, unified India and to fill the jails again. A less charitable reason given is that the Congress leaders could hardly wait to seize the reins of power from the hands of the departing

British. The experience of working with the Muslim members in the 1946 central cabinet was so frustrating that the final decision to separate was taken. There was also the expectation that Partition would result in an amelioration of the communal problem and the end of the confrontation with the Muslim League. It was also feared that any delay in the transfer of power would have led to further bloodshed on the pattern of the terrible Calcutta killings. All these considerations are believed to have influenced the Congress leadership, with the exception of Mahatma Gandhi, to agree to Partition.

After the lapse of half a century, the results of Partition have belied many of the more optimistic expectations of the consenting parties. Far from avoiding any further bloodletting, Partition was accompanied by horrendous massacres of hundreds of thousands of innocents and a refugee problem of unparallelled dimensions involving millions on both sides of the border. While the old Muslim League may have been banished, the communal problem has in no whit lost its acerbity, while narrow sectarian movements have proliferated. Paradoxically, while separate electorates for Muslims, one of the political grievances against the colonial power, have been eliminated, the reservation of seats in the legislatures and government services for Scheduled Castes and Tribes has been institutionalised. And what is more, the reservation of government jobs for all kinds of categories of castes, sub-castes and social groups including Backward ones, has been made, reducing greatly the percentage of those qualifying by merit. What effect this will have on the already abysmal low efficiency of the public services can well be imagined.

The spate of Hindu-Muslim riots in which numbers formerly undreamt of are killed or made destitute, testifies to the dire state of Hindu-Muslim relations. Added to this, with the rise of Muslim fundamentalism in Pakistan and beyond, the evil has begun to spread to India. In reaction to it, the phenomenon of

Hindu fundamentalism has now raised its head and become a menacing political reality. Moreover, the consciousness of caste, which Mahatma Gandhi and the earlier generation of national leaders had tried to eradicate, has been officially reinstated, thanks to Mandal and his votaries, and has only served to further divide Hindu society on narrow sectarian lines.

The Muslim community in India, left leaderless, suffers from a sense both of insecurity and inferiority. Its nominal representation, despite its size, both in the legislatures and the services, deprives it of an effective and responsible voice in the governance of the country. It therefore takes to agitating on narrow sectarian issues, resisting even such reforms as would improve its social practices and raise the status of its women. Ayub Khan's reforms in this field are of a revolutionary nature and have, by and large, endured, despite the Mullahs. In India the Muslim resistance to change finds reflection in the resistance of the community to modern education with the inevitable result that it is getting hopelessly outstripped in the race for economic betterment and is becoming increasingly impoverished and backward.

The weakening of the morale of the Muslim community has led to a serious loss in the maintenance and development of the composite culture of the northern states, of which those states are justly proud, as well as to the elegant Urdu language. It is little consolation that, with the near total expulsion of the non-Muslim population from Pakistan, that country has become a cultural wilderness. The interaction of the two communities had much to offer to each and its loss makes both culturally poorer.

Had Partition been avoided, be it by acceptance of the Cabinet Mission Plan or by any other political arrangement, a united India would have emerged as a more powerful and prosperous country. True, there would have been serious rioting in the northern states at the time, but the loss of life would have borne little proportion to the holocaust that took place at Partition. The two communities, without an alien power between them, would have got the measure of each other. The Muslim community would have learnt that it would have to coexist peacefully with a far more numerous Hindu majority. The Hindus, for their part, would have realised that one cannot trifle with an enormous Muslim minority—in course of time both would have learnt to cooperate with each other. In Europe, the bitter wars between Catholics and Protestants, which lasted decades, are unthinkable today. In their millenium-old coexistence on the sub-continent, before the advent of the British, the two communities did live together in comparative peace and amity. In the Indian legislatures, the presence of a large representation of the minority community would have had a leavening effect, curbing the excesses that a single party drawn mainly from one community, long in power, inevitably develops.

Instead, India now has Pakistan as a hostile neighbour, determined to harm and obstruct India everywhere and in every possible way. In place of verbal arguments with the Muslim League, there are now periodic wars, both open and by proxy, as well as terrorist acts and conspiracies to destabilise and weaken the country. Pakistan's unwanted solicitude for the Indian Muslims only creates suspicion and resentment against them, while it further lowers their morale. The wars with Pakistan and the constant state of military preparedness have exacted a heavy toll in blood and treasure. Having been decisively repulsed in three wars, Pakistan now seeks international intervention to secure from India by political intrigue what it could not obtain by force. India could have clinched the Kashmir issue once and for all after the 1965 war and especially after the 1971 war, in which Pakistan was soundly defeated, by securing acceptance, as the price of peace, of the ceasefire line as the international boundary. In the Simla agreement of 1972, as an act of mistaken generosity or incomprehensible misjudgement, India agreed to keep the Kashmir question open to future dispute despite its commanding position. Pakistan is now attempting to resile even from that commitment. Such are the legacies of Partition.

The British had prided themselves on their rule, especially for having achieved the unification of the country and its general pacification under the rule of law. This much-vaunted claim was belied on their departure when the country was divided and, with the lapse of suzerainty, when the 565 odd princely states could legally also have declared their independence. This balkanisation of India was prevented by the statesmanship of Sardar Patel by securing the peaceful accession of the states to India. The boast about bestowing peace and order on India was belied by the communal holocaust at the time of Partition which they had lamentably failed to anticipate or prevent.

In sum, therefore, it must be said that there were tragic miscalculations on the part of all three parties concerned, for which the successor states are paying a heavy recurrent price.

# TEN

# Lebanon and the Sixth Fleet

In the summer of 1958 Lebanon erupted in a crisis threatening death and destruction. But before much damage could be done, the storm subsided as rapidly as it had arisen.

The cause of this turbulence was a political crisis in Lebanon which had led to a popular uprising against the policies and actions of an insensitive and unresponsive head of state. Departing from the country's traditional policy of non-involvement in the rivalries of the Cold War and between the Arab states themselves, President Chamoun had subscribed to the controversial 'Eisenhower Doctrine' and the Baghdad Pact. Not content with dragging his unwilling country away from its moorings, he also aspired to a second term in office in violation of accepted convention.

The President perceived the armed rebellion as being both inspired and then quelled by a foreign hand, that of the United Arab Republic of President Nasser. He was strongly backed by the United States and other western powers who feared the spread of Nasser's influence in the region. A complaint was filed in the UN Security Council against the United Arab Republic, which denied the charge. The Council decided to send a UN mission to Lebanon to ascertain the facts and inhibit the illegal entry of arms and soldiers.

While the unarmed UN peacekeeping mission was fulfilling its task, a spasm of revolutionary fervour in Iraq wiped out the royal family. Although events in the two countries were entirely unconnected, they were attributed to a sinister conspiracy. Without any forewarning, the formidable US Sixth Fleet descended upon Lebanon, off-loading its marines on the beaches. The proclaimed reason for this intervention was to protect the sovereignty and independence of Lebanon, as well as American lives and property, and to assist the United Nations in its peacekeeping task. The United Nations was taken completely by surprise. The Soviet Union reacted violently, threatening that it would not stand idly by in the face of such an act of aggression. A local disturbance in a tiny country now assumed the awesome proportions of a global upheaval.

The world was rescued from the brink by the issue being taken out of the context of super-power confrontation to that of oratory and debate at the UN General Assembly. The immediate problem was how to extricate the US Sixth Fleet from the dilemma of being marooned on the beaches without a function. The General Assembly, in its wisdom, passed on the responsibility to the fragile UN mission in Lebanon to pilot the mighty Sixth Fleet back to the waters from which it had come.

I found myself in the midst of these dramatic events in the role of a leader of the UN mission. On home leave on transfer from Yugoslavia to Pakistan, Susheela and I had gone to Kerala to pay homage, as we frequently did, to a great Advaitin sage, Sri Atmananda. To our surprise, Sri Atmananda would question us closely about the situation in Lebanon. He had never before spoken about secular or even personal matters, and we thought his interest was due to the involvement, as a key figure in the conflict, of a devoted disciple, the Druze chieftain, Kemal

Jumblatt. From Kerala we proceeded to Naini Tal; we had hardly reached Naini Tal when the Foreign Secretary called urgently from New Delhi. The United Nations Secretary-General, Dag Hammarskjold, had cabled to request my services for the UN mission in Lebanon. Mr Nehru wanted me to accept; the Karachi High Commission would be kept vacant until my return. I was required to join the UN mission immediately, so I left the very next day for New Delhi, where I tried to gather some information about the nature of the assignment.

In the Ministry I was disappointed to learn that the Defence Minister, V.K. Krishna Menon, had refused Hammarskjold's request for some Indian military officers to serve on the mission. I immediately went to see Menon, who, though most affable, was opposed to Indian officers being associated with the Group because of India's close friendship with President Nasser. When I pointed out that my participation had already deeply involved the country in the operation, Menon changed tack and said the army was 500 officers short of strength and so none could be spared. But I pleaded that a mere 15 to 20 officers for a few months would hardly make any difference to India's defence; besides, they would gain valuable experience in UN peacekeeping. Menon finally relented. But he reminded me that Nasser was our friend and that I should keep out of trouble. I replied that I had a long enough nose and could smell trouble from a distance!

The next day found me in Beirut where I was received by my two colleagues, Señor Galo Plaza, till recently President of Ecuador, and Major-General Odd Bull, Commander-in-Chief of the Norwegian air force, and various UN officials and representatives of the Lebanese government. Beirut, always pulsating with life, the financial and business capital of West Asia, was now a dead city. The normally bustling streets were empty, the shops shuttered, with hardly a vehicle or pedestrian in sight. A lone car or taxi would sometimes fly past and an occasional pedestrian would furtively hurry along. The deathly silence would be punctuated by the sharp crack of a sniper's rifle or the rattle of a machine gun or, more rarely, the boom of a mortar.

The impromptu headquarters of the United Nations' Group in Lebanon, or UNOGIL as it came to be called, had been hurriedly set up in a small requisitioned hotel named the Bierritz situated on the sea front. There was Andrew Cordier, the Secretary-General's Chief of Staff, who had been in continuous conference on the modus operandi and organisation of the mission with UNOGIL's Chief Secretary, David Blickenstaff, and other UN personnel. In the conference room, the large glass window showed a neat hole through which a bullet had crashed seconds after Cordier had moved off. His portly frame silhouetted against the light, smoking a cigar and peering at the seascape, had provided a tempting target. Thereafter all windows were kept shuttered and were prudently avoided. We learnt also that, a few days earlier, the correspondent of the Press Trust of India, Lazarus, had truly risen from the dead when a bullet burst in through the open window of his hotel room in the town square and hit the wall at the very spot where his head had been just a moment earlier, when he left for the toilet. Pitched battles seemed to be rare. The danger was stopping a sniper's bullet.

Soon after my arrival, the Secretary-General himself flew in from New York where he had been under pressure from some western countries to show early results. He looked fresh and buoyant and immediately got down to work. The very first problem discussed was to define our functions. Clearly, the Security Council mandate did not limit us merely to passive 'observation' or fact-finding, for we were enjoined 'to ensure' against any infiltration of arms or the illegal entry of armed men. It was also decided that our responsibilities as a group would commence only from the date that we started functioning, but did not require us to perform a post mortem since we could report only on what we observed ourselves. We further agreed that the Operation should be limited in numbers and that our military observers would be unarmed. But that notwithstanding, as a group we were agreed that the problem was to be settled peacefully, not by force. The group had been constituted under Chapter VI of the UN charter—peaceful settlement of disputes— and not Chapter VII, which authorises the use of force against threats or breaches of peace. There were some very practical reasons also for this decision. Since fighting was going on all over the country, controlling it by force would require more armed men than we had; further, physically sealing the open land frontier of some 280 kilometres would itself require a large number of men and materials, neither of which we had. The United Nations should rely only on its moral prestige and not offer unnecessary provocation by mounting an armed operation. It would require qualities of courage and dedication for unarmed military men to interpose themselves between warring factions, relying solely on their white jeeps and blue UN ensigns.

As the non-stop conference continued until well past midnight, with Hammarskjold showing no signs of flagging either in physical energy or mental dexterity, the rest of us found our endurance fast ebbing and our mental capacities becoming increasingly befuddled. We had had nothing to eat or drink since morning and were ravenously hungry. Hammarskjold grudgingly agreed to a brief respite and an emissary was sent down to the kitchen in search of something edible. To our disappointment, the kitchen, functioning erratically, had long since closed down, and not a hotel servant was anywhere in sight. Remembering that Air India had earlier delivered a wooden crate in my room, it was hurriedly sent for, and we found a dozen luscious Alphonso mangoes nestling in it. A bottle or two of beverage donated by some kind Samaritan completed the repast. Years later, Hammarskjold often reminded me of that unusual meal, which he had immensely enjoyed. We dispersed after an hour or two as we were in no condition to keep pace with Hammarskjold's intricate legal subtleties as he expatiated on the mandate, method and means of the operation. We resumed the conference early next morning.

Of the land frontier of some 280 kilometres, the government controlled a bare eighteen. The entire country was practically under the sway of the various warlords. The government's writ ran only in some segments of the capital and a little beyond. It was clear that the observers could not venture into the opposition-held areas, much less as far as the borders, without the consent of the chieftains. But the government had insisted that we should have no truck with them and deal solely with the legal authorities. While we were debating over the dilemma, I confided to Hammarskjold that one of the principal leaders of the revolt, the powerful Druze chief, Kemal Jumblatt, was a close friend of mine. If Jumblatt, who controlled a particularly sensitive part of the country, could be persuaded to allow our observers to set up a post in his territory, other opposition leaders might follow suit. Hammarskjold was intrigued by the suggestion, but warned that if the government got wind of it the consequences could be serious not only for me personally but also for the mission; but he would leave the matter to my discretion.

I told Hammarskjold that from New Delhi I had sent a personal message to Foreign Minister Mahmoud Fawzi who was another old friend of mine, to the effect that if there had been any UAR assistance to the Lebanese opposition, I would earnestly request that it cease before my arrival. The UAR Ambassador in Beirut had already visited me with the assurance on behalf of his government that my message had been taken to heart and that there would be no cause for complaint. Hammarskjold exclaimed that he too had made the same request to President Nasser when he visited him and had been assured 'on the word of a soldier' that compliance would be made, but

Nasser asked for a few days' time for his message to reach those concerned.

The Secretary-General called on President Chamoun in his embattled palace and found him in a mood of great depression. When we had called earlier we found the palace sand-bagged, with the shutters down and soldiers keeping guard. The President himself was cowering in the basement, looking pale and forlorn. He wished us to accept and act on the basis of information provided by his government. He expected the UN to have more personnel fully armed, in order to crush the rebels by force. He complained that he was the victim of a dark conspiracy; foreign elements led by the UAR had sent in massive quantities of arms and hordes of armed men to create violent disorder. He was scornful of General Chehab, his Army Chief, whom he blamed for doing nothing on the plea that the army's duty was to defend the country's borders and not to intervene in political strife. Chamoun was a pitiful sight. He had not ventured out for weeks and had cut himself off from contact with all but a chosen few. He had been making pathetic appeals to the United States, France and Britain for help. While we told him as politely as we could of the nature and limitations of our mission, the Secretary-General was more brutally frank in disabusing his mind of any illusions that UNOGIL's mandate was to save his regime by armed force.

The breakneck speed with which the UN operation had been launched was a masterpiece of organisation. On the very day—12 June 1958—that the Security Council had passed its resolution, the Chief Secretary, David Blickenstaff, had flown in from Paris and the first batch of military observers, seconded from the UN Truce Supervision Organisation, led by a swaggering Colonel Browne, had arrived from Jerusalem. Our Group of Three was in position within five or six days and the Secretary-General himself had undertaken a tour of five countries of the region as well as London in the space of less than a week. Hammarskjold's intellectual agility was matched only by his physical stamina. When he flew back to New York after his visit, to calm down the western powers who were clamouring for instant results, he looked as confident and energetic as when he first arrived.

A Liaison Group of some five senior Lebanese officials led by the Acting Foreign Minister, Dr Albert Moukhaiber, had been set up to deal with us. These meetings were rather contentious because of the conflicting views of our functions and our scepticism about the information supplied to us.

We paid a call on the Patriarch of the Maronite Church in his palace at Jounieh, some ten kilometres north of Beirut, and were received in a warm and kindly manner. He left us in no doubt about where his sympathies in the conflict lay. He was a fervent nationalist but he sent shivers down one's spine when he confided in a hushed voice that we should beware of Chamoun, the President, as he was a British spy! We had earlier been warned by the Prime Minister, Sami-el-Solh, to be careful of the military member of the Liaison Group, a Captain Ginadry, as he was a UAR spy! Ginadry in turn, had cautioned us against the Chief of Security, Emir Fuad Chehab, as he was a British spy! These weird confidences left us perplexed about whom to trust and whom not to. It was typical of the intricate and confused state of affairs in the country, where it was difficult to tell friend from foe. To gain some understanding of the causes of the conflict, we had to pick our way warily through the thicket of Lebanese politics. The immediate and ostensible cause was the President himself, whose policies, both domestic and foreign, had evoked a storm of protest.

But the genesis of the problem harked back to the very origin of the state of Lebanon. During the centuries of Ottoman rule and even earlier, the territory had been a formal part of Syria and indistinguishable from it. With the advent of Islam, the Christian and Jewish communities either accepted conversion to the new faith or fled westwards into the mountains and the Mediterranean littoral. The Druze and Shia communities also moved westwards to escape Sunni intolerance. The area of the Lebanon and Anti-Lebanon mountains thus came to be inhabited by the Christians, mostly Maronites and the Druzes. The Shias populated the south and the Baalbek area, Sunni Muslims much of the rest. Beirut had a very mixed population. The western powers, especially France, showed much concern for the safety and welfare of the small Christian community living in the midst of a sea of Islam and often intervened on its behalf with the Ottoman ruler.

The foundation of the state of Lebanon was laid under the Treaty of Versailles on the dismemberment of the Ottoman Empire after World War I. In carving out a country largely for the Christians, large tracts of the coastal plain north and south of Beirut as well as the plain of Akkar, which were inhabited mostly by Sunni Muslims, were detached from Syria to extend the territory of the new state. This was done at the insistence of the Maronite Patriarch who represented the community at the Conference. This proved to be a factor of acute division as the Muslim communities could never reconcile themselves to separation from their Muslim roots and to become a minority community. While the Maronites looked up to 'Mother France', the Muslims looked across the border towards their Arab brothers. The new state had been mandated to France as the administering power and, as the winds of nationalism swept across the dependent countries, Christians and Muslims, joined together to wrench their independence in 1943 from the mandatory power.

To reassure all sects and communities of their fair share of power and government employment, the leaders concluded what came to be known as the 'National Pact'. This enjoined that the ratio of members in the legislature would be six Christians to five Muslims, thus guaranteeing majority status to the Christians. The President would, accordingly, be a Maronite: the Prime Minister, a Sunni; the Speaker, a Shia; the Defence Minister, a Druze; the

Foreign Minister, Greek Orthodox, and so on. Fourteen different religious denominations were recognised and all offices, down to the meanest, distributed among them. To such absurd limits did the Pact go that, if a Greek Orthodox clerk or peon retired or went on leave, his replacement would have to be from the same community. The system was not intended to be permanent, but only until a true sentiment of national loyalty developed. As often happens, however, vested interests took root, which prevented any change, much less abrogation of the system, thus perpetuating separatism. The 1958 revolt, although sparked off by sharp political differences, was fanned by sectarian divisions. The opposition consisted mostly of non-Christian communities, although many Christians led by their Patriarch were also in opposition. But few non-Christians were with Chamoun and the few who were, were regarded as traitors by their fellows.

Britain and the United States were eager to intervene in response to Chamoun's pleas, and Ralph Bunche, who held the fort at UN Headquarters during Hammarskjold's lightning shuttle diplomacy, was doing all he could to cool them down. Our observers had been reporting that large numbers of armed men had, no doubt, been seen, but it was not possible to establish their identity. In our first observation report to the Security Council, we were in a position to state that we had succeeded in gaining access to some border areas and, although some suspicious movements had been observed, their origin could not be ascertained. We further reported that our very arrival had inhibited, or at least reduced to a trickle, whatever infiltration may have taken place in the past, and we concluded on a hopeful note regarding our future plans and capabilities.

Our report caused considerable rage and disappointment in Washington and London and scornful articles began to appear in the western press about the mission. The *Times* of London had even got wind of the fact that Jumblatt and I were friends, from which it deduced where my sympathies lay. Our report made

President Chamoun absolutely furious and he felt greatly let down. He even made bold to call a press conference, something which he had not done for months, to denounce us as 'tourists' and 'playboys' disporting themselves in clubs and on the beaches! Some papers likened us to the three legendary monkeys 'who saw nothing, heard nothing and spoke nothing'. The government and its agencies came to regard us almost as adversaries, but with customary Lebanese courtesy their manner remained scrupulously polite and correct.

Between Hammarskjold's fleeting visit to Cairo and his return to Beirut, I was able to pay a secret visit to Kemal Jumblatt in his mountain castle up in the mountains of the Chouf. It was the first and last 'cloak and dagger' experience in my life, and it fortunately passed off without disaster. I was to proceed in a white UN car with the blue ensign flying, to an assigned spot where I was to dismiss the driver and walk quickly through a maze of empty streets until I spotted a green Chevrolet. I did as arranged and, finding the green car, quickly entered it beside the driver, not a word being said on either side, and was driven off at high speed. The driver was saying his beads, and when he asked why I had not spoken I said I did not wish to disturb him at his prayers. No, they were 'worry beads', he said, introducing himself as Nessim Majdalani, a Deputy and friend of Kemal Jumblatt. There were government and opposition road-blocks on the way and, to avoid detection, I was told I must sit low, pull down my hat to cover my face and not utter a sound. We soon arrived at a bridge, heavily sand-bagged and manned by well-armed government troops. We were stopped and a long argument in Arabic ensued between my escort and the sergeant who was brandishing an automatic rifle at us. The tone of the exchanges began getting less urgent and menacing, the sergeant finally dissolved in smiles and, seeing my escort's identity card, waved us on. Majdalani heaved a sigh of relief, saying it was a close shave, and so did I. The sergeant had insisted on examining me but Majdalani had pleaded that I was a very sick friend and that it would be inhuman to harass me! As we sped along the coastal road, we soon came upon another road-block, where a similar tragi-comedy was enacted, but at a lower key. One more road-block and we began ascending the unmetalled track to the Chouf. After a stiff climb, further progress was blocked by enormous boulders. From behind them emerged ferocious-looking bearded men, resembling bandits, armed with weapons of all descriptions. A long and angry confrontation took place, with Majdalani trying to soothe the highly excited bearded men. Eventually they relented and one of them clambered down the steep hillside to a stone hut in the distance. My escort had told them that a visitor had come all the way from India to meet the Sheikh, and this had an emollient effect. A tall slim figure, elegantly dressed in a dark suit, emerged from the hut and began a slow climb towards us. After greeting me, we got into a waiting jeep and drove up the hill to a village and alighted at Jumblatt's house. Once inside, I handed Jumblatt some flowers sent by Susheela from the Ashram at Trivandrum, which he applied reverentially to his forehead. We then got down to business.

Jumblatt said he had at first wondered why India, as represented by me, should have got involved on behalf of the United Nations, but on reflection realised that it was due only to a genuine desire to help in a peaceful and equitable settlement of the problem. I said it would contribute to a just and peaceful settlement if UN observers could be allowed entry into areas controlled by the nationalists. After some discussion, Jumblatt agreed and asked for two days' time, after which UN observers would be able to come to the Chouf. I requested that word be sent to other opposition leaders as well, to which my host agreed. Our return journey was uneventful as the men at the barricades could now recognise us.

Following the meeting with Jumblatt, I was able to call on Saeb Salaam, the Sunni chieftain, in his fortified mansion in the heart of the Basta. From there he controlled a large part of the city, including the President's palace near by, into whose grounds he would occasionally lob mortar shells, to shock rather than to harm. Saeb Bey was a courtly gentleman, more like a Pasha than a revolutionary, and he was affability itself. He had received Jumblatt's message and would send necessary word to his fighters and other opposition leaders. Like Jumblatt, his main demand was for Chamoun's removal as he feared foreign intervention so long as he stayed in office.

When I reported to Hammarskjold on my undetected visits, he welcomed the outcome and felt more sanguine than ever about the success of our mission, given time. He was reassured enough to wire Bunche that 'of all the conflict situations that had arisen in the general area, the one in Lebanon offered the least excuse for any foreign intervention'.

We began establishing static posts at strategic centres and jeep patrols fanned out in different directions towards the frontier. Very little movement of armed men was now to be seen and it appeared that Nasser had been as good as his word. The opposition leaders, too, were more willing to accept our independent role and began to afford us increasing access to sensitive areas.

The artificial and unmarked boundary between Lebanon and Syria allowed unimpeded access to villages on either side, and it was impossible to tell a Syrian villager from his Lebanese counterpart. As for arms being infiltrated from Syria, it was common knowledge that Beirut was a flourishing market for almost everything, including weapons of all descriptions. To test the versatility of Lebanese merchants, we sent a decoy to pose as a buyer of heavy weapons. His report was amazing: he found on offer every type of armament, including mortars and a basement used as a rifle range!

There was hardly any need for Lebanese to go across the frontier to procure arms or ammunition. But there was a bizarre exception. The Belgian Consul in Damascus named de Sa, a bachelor and eccentric who lived like a Pasha, was a frequent visitor to Beirut and was able to cross the border without let or hindrance. One day, however, he was intercepted at the border post of Masnaa on the main highway linking the two capitals and his car was searched. The search revealed a huge assortment of a variety of arms and ammunition. He was expelled from his post and the arms confiscated, but we never got to know for whom they were destined.

Our operations were proceeding smoothly as our patrols stretched out deep and wide towards the borders. But in one area, the plain of Akkar to the north, observation posts had not yet been established. The area lay beyond the port city of Tripoli where artillery duels were taking place; it was controlled by Rashid Karami, a Sunni leader. Our Chief of Staff, General Odd Bull, had been sending out planes for nocturnal aerial observation of the area. The pilots were young Scandinavians fresh from training who were totally unfamiliar with the terrain, the people or their way of life. Their daily reports went to General Odd Bull, who was himself an airman, but he too was equally ignorant of the ways of the east. As a matter of routine he sent the undigested reports before their evaluation to New York.

Although the situation throughout the country had greatly improved, the aerial observation reports were in complete variance with the general trend. This glaring anomaly clearly called for clarification and correction.

The young pilots had been reporting in orchestrated fashion that they had observed convoys of trucks with their head-lights blazing converging towards Tripoli from the direction of Homs in Syria and other places in the north. They were guided by a powerful searchlight which was immediately switched off when the drone of the planes was heard and they concluded that it was the signal for the convoys to do the same. The inference was that it was guilty traffic and could be nothing other than the illegal entry of arms and fighting men. When these undigested copybook-perfect reports of remarkable verisimilititude were examined by us, their proper evaluation and verification was ordered. Our experts advised that aerial observations were a guide and had to be verified on the ground. Until that was done we made no reference to them in our own reports to New York.

To check these highly disturbing reports, Plaza and I decided to proceed to the north to confront the opposition leaders in order to obtain their clarifications and explanations of the real state of affairs. Plaza and I were to go north to meet Rashid Karami, while Bull was to visit Baalbek. But before we could complete our enquiries, sinister developments, unknown to us, were taking place elsewhere, When we visited Karami, he strongly denied receiving any help from across the border and was genuinely surprised at the reports and promised full access to the border. Bull also returned fully satisfied that no illegal movement of arms and men were taking place in the Baalbek area.

One of the pilots had, as later enquiries revealed, taken the bit between his teeth and given an interview to a British correspondent complaining that the observers were suppressing the aerial findings. There was little doubt that our messages to headquarters were being intercepted by certain western missions and the pilots' amateurish reports had reached their hands. The serious breach of discipline, almost of betrayal, had grave consequences.

Washington and London seized upon this misinformation to denounce UNOGIL loudly and to accuse it of suppression of reports inculpating the UAR. UNOGIL had incurred the displeasure of the British and United States governments since its findings belied their expectations. They had convinced themselves that the UAR was involved on a massive scale in the strife in Lebanon. Charles Malik, the Foreign Minister of Lebanon, who remained throughout the crisis in New York, was busily engaged in decanting wildly exaggerated tales of the continued presence of hordes of heavily-armed Syrians in Lebanon. The western powers were prepared to believe the worst of UNOGIL and charged it with partiality for attempting to suppress information damaging to the UAR. Armed men had no doubt been seen, but they were few in number and belonged to various local militias. Such Syrians as were apprehended and interrogated were found to be workmen and others in search of employment. It was the normal practice for Syrians to come in substantial numbers to Beirut in search of jobs as labourers, fishermen and the like. It was a highly significant fact that the Lebanese army had refused the President's repeated calls to suppress the insurrection.

UNOGIL had been repeatedly reporting that, with the comforting presence of the military observers in their white jeeps spread into the interior, the level of violence had palpably declined. In fact, the daily situation reports from the military staff showed hardly any casualties among the disputants. As confidence in the healing mission of UNOGIL increased among the leaders and their followers, UNOGIL's presence and efforts acted as a catalyst in promoting better understanding among the leaders. But the British and Americans were raring to go at Nasser, awaiting any provocation, any excuse, to deliver a body blow. The British were still smarting from the deep wounds their pride had suffered from the Suez fiasco. The Americans were infuriated at Nasser having successfully switched over to the Soviet Union for aid for his cherished Aswan Dam project after John Foster Dulles brusquely reneged on his promise to do so. Furthermore, they feared and resented the spread of his influence in the Arab world and the respect and admiration he received from the Arab people for standing up against western pressure by going to the Soviet Union for aid. It was assumed by the Americans that he had surrendered to 'international communism' and would spread the pernicious doctrine among the masses of the Arab world and destabilise their conservative regimes. Both powers had been making elaborate preparations for naval and military action in the area long before the Lebanese question even came up before the United Nations.

The London *Times* admonished UNOGIL, saying that 'it is no business of such a group to suppress evidence merely because it thinks the interests of peace will be best served thereby'. It went on to complain that while evidence of the convoys came from spotter planes, it had remained with the Group 'until disagreement in the Commission had leaked out the information'. In the British parliament, Prime Minister Macmillan emphatically asserted that convoys crossing from Syria into rebel-held Tripoli had been observed. The Foreign Secretary, Selwyn Lloyd, added that 'there was a feeling that the group was reluctant to report these movements'. Contrary to what the *Times* surmised, there was not the shadow of disagreement between the members of the Group on the issue. Indeed, throughout the duration of the mission, they worked together as a team in remarkable harmony.

Strong complaints were addressed to the Secretary-General, who was greatly disturbed by the accusations. He was extremely sensitive to any slur upon his integrity and that of his trusted representatives. Plaza and I had already been to clear up the matter with Rashid Karami. Our observers had already scoured the area and fully corroborated the statement of Karami, a man of honour. But we did not know until then the source of the 'leak', nor did the Secretary-General, who wired us as follows:

> After careful checking, we are convinced Bull's preliminary report to me Monday morning cannot have reached Selwyn Lloyd from here, although two members of US delegation were privately informed about it with precise explanation of its unevaluated nature. We have traced the leak down to Beirut. This particular leak is deplorable especially in view of the highly derogatory implications. Please check with all

your senior people to determine if anybody has had contact
with British or Lebanese...

An enquiry was duly held and Odd Bull reported that one of
the pilots had confessed to the misdeed. Thereafter, the team of
Scandinavians was replaced by a mixed group of pilots, whose
reports were much more reliable and accurate.

Our meeting with Rashid Karami had a highly dramatic side.
We were received at his fine residence on the hill above the city
of Tripoli, a temporary cessation of the artillery duel for the
duration of our visit having been previously arranged. The house
had a gaping hole in the front caused by a mortar shell and the
meeting was therefore prudently arranged in a rear room. Karami
was obsessed by fear of American intervention, which President
Chamoun's ouster alone could prevent. The armed struggle
would continue until that danger was removed, when the
country's internal differences could be resolved in the traditional
Arab way of negotiation and mutual accommodation.

The previous day when news came of the horrendous
assassination of young King Feisal and the entire royal family of
Iraq in a barbarous manner, President Chamoun had been
particularly panic-stricken and hysterical. He had sent for the
American, British and French envoys to whom he made a frantic
appeal to persuade their governments to grant immediate military
help on his behalf. The three envoys, on their return, conferred
together and agreed to send identical reports to their governments
emphasising that, in their considered opinion, there was no
justification at all for intervening to keep Chamoun in office.
They repeated that the conflict was essentially of a domestic
nature and would not be influenced by events in Baghdad.

This information was given by the American Ambassador,
McClintock, to Galo Plaza; they knew each other well since the
former had served in Ecuador, and they maintained frequent
contact in Beirut. McClintock was an able and fair-minded man

of a frank and open nature. What he had said was very reassuring and we all felt convinced, as he did, that there would be no American or British armed intervention. Armed with this positive information, Plaza and I had gone to seem Rashid Karami, confident that we could reassure him about his fears of an American invasion.

We had successfully bearded the last of the militia leaders in its own den and obtained satisfaction on all counts. The serious doubts about the nature of the nocturnal convoys had been cleared. The traffic was of an innocent nature: traditionally, the Akkar plain supplied the town of Homs and other places across the border with agricultural produce and, because of the heat of midsummer, the trucks moved with their loads of fresh fruit and vegetables at night. We had obtained permission to set up an observation post in the sensitive area and for our military observers to go on patrol right up to the northern border with Syria. And above all, we had laid to rest Karami's apprehensions about foreign intervention which was the basis on which Karami had accepted all our demands. We relaxed in a mood of exultation as we sped on our way back to Beirut.

We had not gone far when a racing UN jeep, hooting loudly, caught up with us, and the Burmese colonel in charge of the post gave us most disconcerting news. He had just heard on his radio that at that very moment the US Sixth Fleet had appeared off the coast of Lebanon and marines were already landing on the beaches of Beirut!

My first reaction was one of mortification at the fact that Rashid Karami, who had given us his trust, would feel betrayed at our having deceived him. Pondering over the reasons for the American intervention despite the Ambassador's firm advice and in disregard of the factual situation, it seemed that whatever motivations may have led to the landings, they had little to do with the prevailing situation in Lebanon.

Our periodical reports to the Security Council and the

Secretary-General's constant briefing of the impatient American and British envoys on UNOGIL's progress should have left no room for doubt that the situation was well in hand. Indeed, the level of violence had dwindled to a desultory exchange of firing, while free movement around the country had been restored, barring occasional check-posts marking the territory of militia leaders. Even these minor breaches were being rapidly corrected. The curfew which had paralysed Beirut for weeks had since been lifted and the city was bustling with life, its eager merchants avidly making up for lost time.

At the political level, confabulations between the contending politicians had superseded the language of the gun. The main obstacle to a settlement was Chamoun.

Like a coy maiden, he would say neither yes nor no. Instead, the Prime Minister, Sami-el-Solh, publicly announced that the President would not seek a second term. It had been made plain to him that while the United States would stand by its assurance to come to the aid of Lebanon to preserve its independence, it was not committed to maintaining any particular individual in the Presidency. Ultimately, in July, in an interview to a foreign correspondent, Chamoun disclosed that he would not seek a second term but would relinquish office only when his term came to an end in September. That immediately lowered the political temperature and opened the way towards national reconciliation. The search for a compromise candidate acceptable to all factions now began. He had to be a Maronite, but among the Maronite politicians there was none who would be acceptable to the opposition.

The only Maronite who stood outside the conflict and was universally respected was General Fuad Chehab, Commander of the National Army. Chehab was a man of sterling integrity and a fervent patriot, who had raised and trained the army and kept it out of politics. He was a modest and self-effacing person who lived unostentatiously in his small villa in Jounieh, a small town near Beirut. I used frequently to see him to discuss his country's problems and was impressed by his fair and objective views. Politicians of every hue had nothing but respect for him and he seemed to be the only person who could hold the country together. But Chehab had very definite views on the role of the armed forces in a nation's polity; their function was to guard the sovereignty and integrity of the country but they must not get involved in politics or governance as that was the responsibility of the civil power. Arguments were put forward by others to the effect that, while the doctrine was no doubt correct, such scruples should be set aside when the integrity and independence of a country were in peril. Gradually it began to dawn on Chehab that chaos in the country would almost certainly invite foreign intervention. Talk with the opposition as well as pro-government leaders also revealed a general consensus in the General's favour. This finally clinched matters and Chehab gave his grudging consent on the assurance of unanimity in Parliament in his favour. This brought the political crisis almost to an end.

We found UNOGIL headquarters agog with excitement on our return from Tripoli. The view from our seaside hotel was awesome; the black hulks of innumerable warships stretched across the horizon. There was the scream of warplanes as they swooped across they sky. The situation was full of foreboding and uncertainty. It was clear that UNOGIL, which was on a mission of peace and charged with ensuring against foreign armed intervention, had now become irrelevant. Before its very eyes a massive intervention of the military might of a superpower was taking place. It was more like an invasion; neither the United Nations nor the American Ambassador had any foreknowledge of this, nor did it have the consent of the Lebanese Cabinet. My own position had became highly anomalous and I had already taken my decision to leave UNOGIL—but more of that later.

There was, however, a lighter side to this grim scenario. It was a hot and sweltering midsummer afternoon and Beirut was enjoying its siesta behind shaded doors or at the beach. A rumour spread that naval movement had been observed south of the airport. Ever ready for whatever excitement came their way, curious onlookers rushed to the scene, among them the British correspondent of the Middle East News Agency. A somewhat rotund man given to the easy life of Beirut, he was at his favourite stand at the bar of St George's Hotel, finishing his last gin and tonic after a hearty lunch. He was just in time to see the first wave of marine landings. The following graphic account was given to us immediately on his return from his escapade by the correspondent.

The seven ships of Amphibious Squadron 6, consisting of the command ship, an attack transport, an attack cargo ship, and two landing craft were in position at 2.30 that afternoon. At 3 o'clock amphibian tractors were launched and they trundled off to the nearby airport. Next came the landing craft. Out into the waist-deep water jumped a burly sergeant followed by his men. Rushing on to the hot sands, they began scooping out fox-holes into which they jumped, their weapons at the ready.

Up to that moment the scene at the Khalde beach was serene and blissful, with young women and men disporting themselves in the water, children splashing about, making sand castles or taking donkey-rides. Ice-cream vendors with their bells tinkling and soft-drink hawkers were busily plying their trade. The holiday throng, swollen by curious onlookers and soon joined by peasants from the neigbhouring villages, were noisily speculating whether they were witnessing the screening of a film or a practice exercise. The enterprising Lebanese hawkers, avid for fresh custom, fell upon the sweating marines, steel-helmeted and laden with heavy loads, offering them ice-cream and soft drinks. The British correspondent, an ace in his profession, crouched beside the sergeant and pulled out his notebook.

The sergeant, satisfied that all his men were safely in position, barked out an order and the whole line of marines, at the double, raced across the airfield. The correspondent, puffing and panting and clinging close to the sergeant, did the same. The following breathless exchange ensued:

'What are you here for?'
'We are here at the invitation of the Lebanese government to protect the country's independence.'
'Who is threatening it?'
'The Communists.'
'Russian or Arab?'
'I don't care.'
'Where will you find them?'
'I don't know'
'Then why are you here?'
'Get the hell out of here.'

With that the correspondent fell behind; besides, he was in no condition to keep pace with the battle-hardened sergeant. At the end of the runway ran a drainage ditch, along the Beirut-Saida coastal road. The sergeant and his men, on gaining it, jumped in and took up battle positions, the correspondent, trailing along behind, tumbled limply into it. When he regained his breath—and his wits—he wondered how he would get out to more congenial surroundings and company. Busy traffic whizzed past until he was able to hail a passing taxi. Levering himself out of the ditch, he climbed exhausted into the taxi and made for the destination from which he had recently been separated. Duly revived after his unwonted exertions, he came over to us to recount his adventures and to gauge our reactions.

Blickenstaff from his desk at UNOGIL headquarter at the Riviera Hotel on the Corniche had been startled to see the first units of the Sixth Fleet sailing in. In the absence of the three members of the Group, he took some swift and prudent decisions, cabling New York as follows:

One destroyer and three troop transports on horizon outside our hotel. Obviously proceeding towards airport where they would arrive in about half an hour. We have withdrawn all personnel from airport. I do not exclude local trouble as result of any landings. All staff is being restricted to Riviera Hotel for the time being!

Blickenstaff was able to contact McClintock who assured him that he would arrange free access to the airport for UN personnel with the US Commander. But McClintock added that at that very moment the President's palace was under attack and that American troops would intervene 'to endeavour to save his life'. When our military observers were dispatched to scout around the city, they found an eerie silence, with shoppers hurriedly laying in stores for any unforeseen contingency; but there was no evidence of fighting anywhere. The misinformation about an attack on the palace was given to the American Ambassador by President Chamoun himself. The false report illustrated the jittery atmosphere that prevailed when a stray bullet or sudden panic could have started a major conflagration.

Our immediate anxieties concerned the safety of our own unarmed personnel, thinly spread over the country whose safety and daily needs depended on the goodwill and forbearance of the village folk. The distinction between the UN military observers, mostly white-skinned and in their national uniforms (although capped by blue berets), could not be evident to the rough hill dwellers. They had therefore been directed by wireless to return forthwith to headquarters.

Our next worry was how the opposition leaders would react and whether they would be able to maintain control over their excitable followers. And what if General Chehab and the Lebanese army offered opposition? We sent out emissaries to make as wide enquiries as possible. The opposition leaders were found to be in a state of shock and fuming with anger, loudly threatening to oppose force with force. The National Front called upon the people 'to kill the invader'. Saeb Salaam hurled threats against 'the aggressive American forces', calling upon them to withdraw for the sake of Lebanese freedom and independence. He proclaimed that Lebanon would ask for aid from 'all the free people of the world' against 'the crying aggression and gross violation of the United Nations Charter'. We strongly urged the opposition parties to be extremely wary and to refrain from any impulsive action for they would be pulverised were they to act rashly against the marines. General Chehab stayed in his villa, humiliated at the uninvited intrusion of a foreign force. He too strongly cautioned the opposition leaders to exercise the greatest restraint in the face of grave provocation.

The only note of jubilation came from President Chamoun when he was informed on the morning of the fateful day by the American Ambassador of the imminent landings. McClintock himself was kept in the dark until he was awakened early that morning to be told by the duty officer that a message had arrived from Washington giving the 'big news'. He thereupon informed the President and also General Chehab.

From the very moment of the sudden incursion of the marines we had been in continuous conference in UNOGIL about their possible motivations, actions and their consequences. Such a massive force could have laid the diminutive country low in a matter of days, if not hours. Would the marines spread out all over the country or limit themselves to taking over Beirut? Would they intervene in the politics of Lebanon to keep a conservative and subservient government in power? Or was their presence in Lebanon merely symbolic; if so, why did they come in such overwhelming strength? If they had come to the aid or spearhead the restoration of a conservative regime in Iraq, how would they leap-frog over Syria? Finally, had the presence and activities of UNOGIL been taken into account and a modus vivendi with it been thought of? We knew that the

Secretary-General had not been consulted or forewarned; Hammarskjold's efforts all along had been to ward off any possibility of foreign intervention. It was also evident that no reckoning had been made of the attitude of General Chehab and his army. Would the foreign force and the national army coexist together in a state of armed neutrality or get involved in active hostilities?

The coexistence of UNOGIL, which could exercise only moral force, with the brute force of the Sixth Fleet was wholly irreconcilable. My continued association with UNOGIL in the present circumstances was highly anomalous and embarrassing. I cabled the Secretary-General to the effect that in the vastly altered circumstances I should be allowed to make my own decision regarding my membership of UNOGIL. I also cabled Prime Minister Nehru in similar terms. I informed Plaza of my decision and his reaction was that, as a Latin American politician, he too could hardly stay on as he did not wish to be seen as collaborating with 'Yankee imperialism' or condoning 'gunboat diplomacy'.

Hammarskjold cabled back in most pressing terms with the request that he be allowed a few days time to try and sort out the muddied situation. At the same time came an urgent message from Nehru enjoining on me to stay on until the Secretary-General could find a way out. I later learnt that to reinforce his appeal to me, Hammarskjold had strongly pleaded with Nehru for his intervention.

Hammarskjold, in a superb exercise of diplomatic skill, showed my cable to Cabot Lodge, US Ambassador at the UN, adding that, if I pulled out in protest the whole UN operation would collapse and he would feel compelled to withdraw it and disclose the reason. Lodge threw up his hands in horror, saying that should never be allowed to happen as it would expose the US forces to grave danger. He rushed to see the Secretary of State, John Foster Dulles, who expressed equal alarm and addressed a most pressing message to Ambassador McClintock in Beirut to be passed on to us.

McClintock came to call on Plaza and me at UNOGIL headquarters, announcing that he had an urgent message to deliver from his Secretary of State. It would make matters easier, he said, if he were to read it out in its entirely. It began by asking him to see 'Dayal and Plaza' to reassure them that the US forces had been sent for the sole purpose of assisting the United Nations in its task of safeguarding the independence and integrity of Lebanon. To achieve that end, the Commander of the Sixth Fleet had been charged to work in close cooperation with UNOGIL and to render whatever assistance may be required. It went on to request UNOGIL to continue its work and offered assurances that US forces would not interfere with its activities in any way.

Our spontaneous reply to Mr Dulles's appeal was to state firmly and in unison that our functions and those of the Sixth Fleet were wholly incompatible and we could not entertain any relations, formal or informal, with its commanders. McClintock, a little shocked, asked if that was our final reply, to which we gave an emphatic reaffirmation. He seemed a little disappointed with Plaza who was known to be pro-western and expected him at least to show a little flexibility. He duly conveyed our negative response to Washington.

A few days later, the Commander-in-Chief of the Sixth Fleet, the four-star Admiral James Holloway, came to call on us at the Riviera. He was a man of impressive presence and courtly ways and fully deserved his sobriquet of 'Lord Jim'. He had come, he said, to offer the hand of friendship and cooperation to UNOGIL on behalf of his command. Blickenstaff and I replied almost simultaneously that there could be no fraternisation or official relations between us because of the basic incompatibility of our objectives. The Admiral, a gentleman to the core, took the rebuff in good part and withdrew. But we frequently ran into him at the beach when the situation began to ease or at McClintock's dinner table. We found him a charming and engaging personality and a man of his word. Ralph Bunche instructed us from New York to have no truck with the US forces; we were able to tell him that we had already made our position clear to the Admiral.

In the light of Mr Dulles's offer to abide by whatever conditions UNOGIL would prescribe for agreeing to US troops remaining in Lebanon and our refusal of cooperation with the US forces, Hammarskjold extracted an undertaking that, having landed on the beaches, US forces would on no account spread out into the interior or engage in any military action except in self-defence. Nor would US warplanes be permitted to violate the country's airspace. Furthermore, any entry of US troops into the city, even for recreation, would be regulated by prior arrangement with UNOGIL.

General Chehab complained to us that President Chamoun had neither consulted nor informed him about the landings and the late intimation allowed him little time to deal with his own uncertain army. He lamented that all his efforts to promote national reconciliation would be undermined. He greatly feared that foreign armed intervention in a domestic dispute would destroy the loyalty and cohesion of his army and lead to its disintegration. So as not to disturb the present uneasy equilibrium in the country, could not the marines remain on board their ships without disembarking? Alternatively, as a token, could not two or three tanks be unloaded and posted at the harbour? The Ambassador, who was himself ignorant of the operational plans and objective of the marines, thought the General's requests not unreasonable and promised to take them up with the Fleet Commander.

On the night of the landings, David Blickenstaff, in an admirable display of enterprise not unmixed with bravado, went reconnoitring through the empty streets to the airport to check up on UN supplies and aircraft. As an American national and a dutiful international official, he thought his presence would not be particularly resented. After assuring himself of the security of UN property, he accosted a marine officer and casually enquired which side the US forces were backing. The officer replied, almost by rote, that they had come at the invitation of the legal government of Lebanon for its protection. Thereupon, with seeming innocence, Blickenstaff asked if the US was sure it was backing the right side. That abruptly ended the conversation, Blickenstaff being told in strong and colourful language to take himself off. Prudently, he complied.

Our enquiries had revealed that neither the marines nor their commanders had any idea of the aims and objectives of the landings or even the faintest notion of operational plans. Having landed on the beaches, they awaited further orders but these never came. Instead, there were heated discussions with the Lebanese army, a political roadblock represented by the very presence of UNOGIL and fierce debates at the United Nations in distant New York. Meanwhile, the marines lay marooned in boredom and inactivity on the hot sands of the beaches of Beirut.

The entire US operation was based on a series of grave misconceptions and misreadings of the real situation in Iraq, Lebanon and, indeed, in the entire region. It was thought that in Iraq a loyal brigade was marching on Baghdad to restore what remained of the monarchy, which the American force would help achieve the desired end. But the whole concept was purely chimerical; there was no such brigade and not a trace remained of the Iraqi royal family. In Lebanon, likewise, there was no massive or even minor intervention by the UAR and the political differences had almost been resolved.

In their respective apologias, the principals in Washington and London have, with little regard for facts, given conflicting reasons for their interventions in Lebanon and Jordan and fanciful claims about the results. It is a daunting thought that great powers, on the basis of conjecture and suppositions, should have brought the world to the edge of catastrophe.

Beirut slept uneasily on the night of the landings, fearful of the morrow. Would the foreign force with its awesome might lay the country waste and set Beirut ablaze? Would Lebanon be drawn into a wider conflagration and lose its identity and independence? And would the opposition leaders be hunted down and shot? The possibility of such calamities wracked the citizens as they cowered in their homes awaiting their fate.

The morning after the landings began on an ominous note. The commander of the marines, General Wade, called early on Ambassador McClintock to inform him that a column of marines was ready to move into the city from the airport at half-past nine. At that moment, General Chehab, having got wind of the proposed entry in force of the marines, agitatedly contacted the Ambassador begging him to hold up the column as he feared his army might offer resistance. The Ambassador passed on the message to the eager General Wade, who ultimately agreed to a brief delay. The Ambassador, taking General Wade with him, called on President Chamoun for his intercession, but Chamoun insisted on the marines moving without delay into the city. He was fearful that any delay would encourage his opponents to break out of the Basta area and, with the help of his Lebanese army guard, kidnap or kill him. This would leave the United States in the embarrassing position of rallying to the support of a government that had ceased to exist.

By this time General Wade had received information that a detachment of Lebanese tanks had, in fact, set up a roadblock, cutting off the route from the airport into the city. The Ambassador, thereupon, rushed off to see General Chéhab while the marine General returned to his troops. There followed further confusion as to when the marine column would move. Meanwhile, Admiral Holloway had arrived to take command of the operation and he ordered the column to advance at 11 o'clock. The Admiral himself drove ahead to confer with the Ambassador whom he intercepted on the way; with him was

General Chehab. The column of American tanks led by Colonel Hadd, had halted at a roadblock set up by the Lebanese army one mile from the airport. A dozen Lebanese tanks and recoil guns blocked the road, the guns unlimbered and aimed menacingly at the advancing American tanks.

There in the middle of the road, between the guns of the opposing tank columns and within sight and hearing of assembled journalists and onlookers, took place an extraordinary conference in an extraordinary setting, which will long be remembered in Lebanon. On one side was Admiral Holloway, his deputy, Admiral Jaeger and General Wade, while on the other was General Chehab. Ambassador McClintock acted as mediator. General Wade, stamping impatiently, insisted that the column advance forthwith through the city and on to the dock area. General Chehab warned that if the column moved in formation, the Lebanese tanks would open fire, even if it meant suicide. In any case, the column must not enter the city or in formation as it would be regarded as an invading and not a friendly force. While the exchanges were going on, Admiral Holloway, tiring at the delay, declared that, come what may, the column would advance at 12 noon. The tanks had been lined up since early morning and the crews were getting tired and restive. General Chehab then suggested that the column be broken up with Lebanese army jeeps in between to give the impression of a friendly and not hostile force. The Ambassador finally resolved the issue by suggesting that General Chehab, Admiral Holloway and he drive together in the Ambassador's car, leading the procession of American tanks and Lebanese jeeps to the dock area, avoiding the city by taking the Corniche route. To this, Admiral Holloway agreed, but before the plan could be executed, Chehab insisted on informing his own headquarters to avoid any untoward incidents. In search of a nearby telephone, he disappeared from the scene. The inordinate delay in his return greatly irritated the Admiral. Chehab's long absence suggested that he had encountered considerable difficulty in dissuading his staff from offering resistance.

Eventually, after 12.30 p.m. and led by the Ambassador's car with the US and Lebanese flags fluttering, the column began to advance. On approaching the city, General Chehab forsook the company of the US Ambassador and Admiral, not wishing to be seen by his fellow-citizens as leading a foreign force whose unwelcome presence on his native soil he was powerless to prevent.

At UNOGIL headquarters in our sea-front headquarters at the Riviera Hotel we maintained an anxious vigil, awaiting developments. The approach of the column was heralded by a shattering noise. As the procession of steel thundered past our windows, the glass and concrete structure shook to its foundations and the screaming supersonic warplanes overhead contributed their own high decibel of sound. By 7 o'clock that evening, under the command of a four-star Admiral, the force had secured its uncontested objective.

Another marine landing took place later at Jounieh beach, a few miles north of Beirut in what the *Washington Evening Star* described as a picnic atmosphere. A couple of landing craft had to swerve to avoid some children playing in the water. There were some disagreements between the Lebanese and American commands over comparatively minor matters, which were almost invariably settled in favour of the Lebanese. A dispute arose about cordoning off the Basta area in the city by the marines to prevent a clash with the Sunni militia; General Chehab insisted that it was a Lebanese and not an American responsibility. There were differences about the guarding of coastal road bridges leading into Beirut. Protests were loudly voiced when US warplanes violated Lebanese and Syrian airspace. But, by and large, the American forces kept to their undertaking to confine themselves to the beaches and to refrain from any offensive or provocative action. It was an unusual situation for them to have to negotiate to establish their positions instead of just seizing them. Yet, despite having no function to perform, the US build-up of men and material continued apace.

It is of interest to recall the premises and perceptions on the basis of which such a vast undertaking was launched and the preparations that went into giving it shape. Thanks to the US Freedom of Information Act and the principle of accountability for executive actions, a wealth of material which throws light on the subject became available soon after. The autobiographies of the principal decision-makers, President Eisenhower, in his *Waging Peace*, and Prime Minister Harold Macmillan, in *Riding the Storm*, contain most revealing information regarding their plans and objectives. Among the material since available is a particularly valuable research paper entitled 'Marines in Lebanon' prepared by Jack Shulimson of the Historical Branch, G-3 Division, Headquarters, US Marine Corps, Washington, D.C. His detailed account is based on the records of the US departments concerned and on interviews with many of the key participants.

Although the landings had the appearance of a reflex action to the Iraqi revolution, they had no relevance to the Lebanese conflict which had been practically resolved. The preparations for such an elaborate undertaking had commenced no less than eight months previously. As early as November 1957, the US Joint Chiefs of Staff, on the assumption that there were definite possibilities of the overthrow of the Jordanian monarchy and the Lebanese government, directed the Commander-in-Chief of the US Naval Forces in the Eastern Atlantic and Mediterranean, Admiral James L Holloway, to prepare contingency plans for carrying out landings in the general area of the Middle East. The first stage was assigned to a Task Force at Camp Lejeune in North Carolina which began preparations for implementing a practice amphibious landing off the coast of Sardinia in combination with units of the British and Italian navies.

The contingency plans were related more to the Baghdad Pact or Middle East Treaty Organisation which had been foisted on the area and was deeply resented by the Arab people, who were anxious not to get embroiled in the Cold War. This Pact had as its aim 'the soft underbelly of the Soviet Union'. The Eisenhower Doctrine had also been promulgated, offering armed assistance to any state threatened by 'international communism'. This too was deeply unpopular with its intended beneficiaries. Ironically, the proposed intervention would, in fact, seek to protect such unpopular Arab regimes as subscribed to the hated Pact and Doctrine against their own peoples, rather than against any external danger.

The assurance of support to Chamoun was in patent contradiction to President Eisenhower's conviction that Chamoun 'had made a political error' in nursing the hope of enjoying a second term. Although the US Government and delegation had backed the UN Security Council's decision to establish UNOGIL, President Chamoun had been assured by Washington that its 'intentions had not changed basically as a result of a United Nations Observation team'. However, in early July the US administration believed that 'the crisis in Lebanon would pass without western military assistance'.

When the lightning Iraqi coup took place, Washington jumped to the conclusion that 'the situation in Lebanon which had seemed to be quieting, was now made critical by events in another land—Iraq'. Even before President Eisenhower called in his advisers on that fateful day, according to him, his 'mind was practically made up'. It was argued that an intervention in Lebanon would be far different from the British-French attack on Egypt, as it would be on invitation from the Lebanese government and in accordance with the Eisenhower Doctrine. When Dulles warned that 'many people would not get the difference', the President brushed him aside. The decision was taken for the United States to go it alone despite the fact that Macmillan's government was 'almost eager' to join in. A group of legislators was called in to be told of the decision, but they had serious misgivings about its legality and of the crisis being communist-provoked and not purely domestic. Some Senators cited UNOGIL's findings that the crisis had been practically resolved and all was calm in Lebanon. The President himself admitted that 'except for a very few ... none of the leaders was outspoken in his support of intervention in Lebanon'.

The above quotations from President Eisenhower's *Waging Peace* bear eloquent testimony to the arbitrary manner in which such a crucial decision was taken and the fallacious reasoning and false perceptions on which it was based. The precipitate manner in which the grave decision was taken is illustrated also by the testimony of Admiral Burke, the Chairman of the Joint Chiefs of Staff who recalls that, in several discussions with President Eisenhower when he was ordered to mobilise the Sixth Fleet for immediate action, he pleaded for at least forty-eight hours' notice, but in the end was granted only twelve hours. If the President had agreed, if would have become clear that any intervention in Iraq 'was pointless as there was no trace of the monarchy left to restore'; or in Lebanon, which had not reacted to the events in Iraq and where the political crisis had ended.

According to President Eisenhower, as recorded by him, a meeting was held at the White House on 13 May 1958 at which Secretary of State Dulles and others were present to discuss a message from President Chamoun enquiring how the US would react to a request from him for armed assistance. A few days earlier rioting had broken out in Beirut and Tripoli, caused by the murder of a pro-Chamoun journalist. The meeting was marked by impatience generated by the belief that Chamoun's woes were part of widespread Soviet plans to stir up trouble in different parts of the world. It was therefore agreed that the

United States could move into Lebanon confident that it would be in conformity with the government's wishes and in full accord with the Charter of the United Nations.

In the course of the discussion, Eisenhower recalls, John Foster Dulles raised some doubts about adverse political reactions in the Middle East, the danger of closure of the Suez Canal (only recently reopened after the Anglo-French-Israeli attack of 1956), and the cutting of the Iraqi pipeline across Syria. But the President dismissed the risk of a strong Soviet reaction as unlikely. Allan Dulles, the CIA Director, felt that the needs of caution would be met by deferring a decision by twenty-four hours. All these suggestions were briefly examined and overruled. Chamoun was, accordingly, informed that the United States 'would respond favourably and strongly' subject to certain conditions. These were that US troops would not be sent only to ensure Chamoun a second term as President; that the request for assistance would be backed by some other Arab country as well; that the mission would be for the protection of American lives and property and the assistance of the legal government. Orders were accordingly sent to General Wade of the US Marines to move his headquarters immediately into the Mediterranean area because of the situation in Lebanon.

Across the Atlantic, Prime Minister Harold Macmillan was on the same day discussing in Cabinet a similar enquiry from President Chamoun. But the perception of the problem in London was different. Nasser was seen as the main culprit, a man cast in a Hitler-like mould whose objective was to force an anschluss of Lebanon with his United Arab Republic. 'In other words, after Austria, the Sudetan Germans', as Macmillan noted in his diary, adding pessimistically: 'Poland (in this case Iraq) will be the next to go.' The mood in the Cabinet was bitter as Britain was still licking its Suez wounds while Nasser was riding high 'threatening the stability of the whole Middle East'. The Cabinet mused that while Britain's military position was much weaker than in 1956, 'the western world had learnt much in the last two years and we no longer stood alone', as the Prime Minister recorded. The Cabinet had little difficulty in agreeing that Britain would go fully along with the United States. Attention then turned to the necessary military plans and preparations, hopefully in conjunction with the Americans. But when Admiral Holloway, who had his headquarters in London, was contacted, it was learnt with intense disappointment and disbelief that the Admiral had received no instructions in the matter. Evidently the Americans had decided to go it alone and had no desire to carry their British ally with them. Nevertheless, British military planning went ahead, on a modest scale, but on somewhat parallel lines.

Elements of the Sixth Fleet began moving into the Eastern Mediterranean. On board the USS *Mount McKinley*, General Wade and Rear-Admiral Robert Cavenagh, the amphibian force's commander, began revising and completing a plan for a landing in Lebanon. They were joined off the coast of Cyprus on 21 May by the British Brigadier John Reed, the earlier contretemps about British participation having apparently been resolved, at least for the time being.

The operation, known as Bluebat, envisaged simultaneous landings by two US marine battalions, one north of Beirut and the other south, to secure the airport. A British brigade would then be flown in to relieve the marines who would strike across the city to gain control of the port. The military aim was to interdict any attempt at invasion by the Syrian First Army. The next few weeks passed without any further alarms or incidents and many ships of the Sixth Fleet dispersed for repairs or their normal routine duties. The crisis appeared to have passed.

With the suddenness of lightning the picture changed. The fall of the Iraqi monarchy and the loss of the central pillar of the Baghdad Pact, renewed the call for action. The US Chief of Naval Operations in Washington warned Admiral Holloway's headquarters of the imminent possibility of intervention in Lebanon in the next forty-eight hours.

President Eisenhower telephoned his loyal British ally, Prime Minister Macmillan, of his decision and found him 'completely in accord', 'almost eager'. Macmillan could not resist the comment (as he records in his *Riding the Storm*): 'You are doing a Suez on me.' He told the President that he had received a similar request for assistance from King Hussain of Jordan, and remembering Suez, insisted that the two countries would be 'in this together, all the way'. This assurance he was duly given. The Americans, however, had intended to go it alone and as Macmillan, feeling betrayed, wryly records: 'This was a strange reversal of the situation only nineteen months before.' If the Eisenhower Doctrine of 1957 represented a marked change in attitude from 1956, Macmillan mused, the active interpretation given to it in 1958 was nothing less than 'a recantation—an act of penance—unparalleled in history.' Present US policy, he notes could 'hardly be reconciled with the Administration's almost hysterical outbursts over Suez.'

Added to British concern about Jordan was anxiety about the future of Iraq and the Persian Gulf and, above all, of the drying up of 'sterling oil'. It was feared that the oil installations at Tripoli in Lebanon would be destroyed, the pipeline through Syria cut, and attacks made on oil installations in the whole area. But these concerns seemed to bother the Americans not at all. Macmillan tried to impress upon the President that 'an operation confined to Lebanon entailed much greater risk to us than to the Americans'. It was also clear that 'neither the President nor Dulles had given full consideration to the position in Jordan'. During the next twenty-four hours, while a decision about dispatching British troops to Jordan was being debated and American support was being eagerly sought, 'American responses were indeed confusing and even alarming'. Without the assurance of full moral and material support from the United

States, Macmillan greatly feared that Britain would be 'first exposed and then abandoned ... only to find that the United States forces had left Lebanon and handed over to some shadowy and insufficient United Nations groups'.

The Foreign Secretary, Selwyn Lloyd, was dispatched to Washington on an urgent mission to plead with John Foster Dulles for American support. But despite Lloyd's best efforts, Dulles prevaricated and, while patronisingly describing British intentions as 'praiseworthy', feared they were 'rash'. He pleaded Congressional opposition to any operational support, but eventually agreed to provide logistical assistance. The British government nevertheless decided to embark on the Jordanian 'adventure' as Macmillan describes it, regarding it as 'a quixotic but honourable undertaking'. The 'adventure' was ill-prepared and it nearly collapsed at the outset. Macmillan records that 'it nearly led to a terrible disaster which would ... have resulted in the collapse of all our policies and the fall of the government'. The Israelis, over whose territory the transport planes carrying British troops were to fly, had not been informed nor had their permission been obtained. But for last-minute American intercession after the first wave had streaked across, further flights would have been prevented.

In the fast-moving situation, policies were changing with ever-increasing velocity. Macmillan had spoken scornfully of UNOGIL as a nebulous and ineffective UN authority, yet a fortnight later he was to muse that if serious trouble broke out in Jordan, the small British force would be gravely endangered and would be difficult to extricate. 'So it is—and will be—until we can get a UN force in their place', he was to say. Again, some three weeks later, the Prime Minister expressed the hope that he would 'at some point in the near future be able to use the United Nations ... to allow our forces to withdraw'. Indeed, he was soon to approach the United Nations Secretary-General for that very purpose and UNOGIL did, in fact, lend its services to organise the extrication of the marooned British battalion from an impossible situation.

This was not the last of the amiable thoughts and actions of the two allies towards each other as well as the UN. When the Americans found themselves in a similar untenable position in Lebanon and were compelled to turn to UNOGIL to bail them out, Macmillan could not help chuckling at the irony of their predicament.

The American landing had stirred up a supersonic storm of titanic proportions—Chairman Khrushchev fired a broadside from Moscow which reverberated around the world and set off an answering echo from Washington. In an angry message he stated that it was 'one of the most momentous periods of history when the world is standing on the brink of catastrophe', and that 'the armed interventions in Lebanon and Jordan and the threat to Iraq may lead to highly dangerous and incalculable consequences; they may initiate a chain reaction which no one will be able to stop'. He warned that 'if the United States has atomic and hydrogen bombs, so has the Soviet Union', and that it would not 'stand aside at a time when the question of war or peace is being decided'. Charging the United States and United Kingdom with 'violating international law and striking a blow at the UN, Khrushchev demanded the immediate withdrawal of the forces of intervention. He proposed an urgent summit meeting on 22 July of the leaders of the Soviet Union, the United States, the United Kingdom, France and India, with the participation of the UN Secretary-General to find a solution which would ensure the sovereign rights and interests of the states in the area and restore peace and security there. Similar messages were addressed to Prime Minister Macmillan and President de Gaulle.

Khrushchev's message to Prime Minister Nehru was in restrained but no less imperative terms. Describing the crisis as being 'one of the most crucial moments in the history of mankind, a moment when the slightest careless step may result in the greatest possible catastrophe for the world', Khrushchev said that 'any local war may rapidly develop into a world conflagration'. He likened the military interventions to colonial wars, of which India had itself been a victim. He urged the early holding of a summit conference, as 'a single hour of delay may mean a serious danger to peace'; and further, that all peace-loving forces must be mobilised and used to avert the 'awful peril threatening the world'. Nehru, agreeing with the proposal, expressed firm opposition to armed intervention in other countries and urged the US and UK governments to withdraw their forces. He warned that the world was 'living through one of the most serious crises in the history of mankind, and that, at this moment of peril it is the duty of governments as well as others to approach those questions with wisdom and calmness and not to take any action which might worsen this situation and provoke a world conflagration'. He therefore advised that it should not be 'through military strength and pressure but by calm negotiations and firm determination that peace must be maintained'.

President Eisenhower responded to Khrushchev in kind, indignantly refuting the charges and innuendoes and levelling counter-accusations. He sought to justify the interventions as being 'fully in accord with the accepted principles of international law and the Charter of the United Nations'. Khrushchev's proposal, on the other hand, was not in conformity with the principles of the Charter as it would derogate from the authority of the United Nations and reduce it to a 'rubber stamp'. Besides, on what authority could five states decide the fate of smaller states over their heads, he argued. Instead, he proposed that the Security Council, which was already seized of the matter, take up the question.

Macmillan, in line with Washington, echoed Eisenhower's suggestion. President de Gaulle refused to follow the Anglo-American line and supported the summit proposal, but with its venue in Geneva and not in New York. The three powers viewed the problem from the standpoint of their respective and, sometimes, conflicting interests. Dulles could not reconcile himself to sitting at the same table facing Mr Khrushchev; he was also strongly allergic to India's participation. Macmillan, while equally against India's inclusion, could not openly oppose the participation of a leading member of the Commonwealth. General de Gaulle, while pleased at the recognition of France among the big powers, wished to prevent American dominance at the conference by proposing Geneva as the venue and supporting India's inclusion. Nehru was gratified at the implied recognition of India's importance and as a leader of the non-aligned states.

The world which had been on tenterhooks fearing the worst, breathed a sigh of relief that, instead of bombs and missiles, verbal darts flew across the oceans. The sense of relief was equally felt at United Nations Headquarters, and especially by us in Lebanon who were caught in the very eye of the storm.

Various proposals and counter-proposals in highly polemical and pugnacious terms flew between the principal protagonists, each suggestion being shot down on ingeniously contrived grounds. The upshot was a compromise agreement to convene an emergency session of the General Assembly, the item already being on the agenda of the Security Council. It was like a mountain in violent labour producing a mouse, but a mouse that roared. The session was convened soon thereafter, yet the military and naval build-up in Lebanon continued at a furious pace.

A brief survey of the operational arrangements that went into the launching of the Bluebat enterprise and its objectives is of interest in the context of the furious international storm it raised. Its objectives were nebulous and variously defined and unclear even to the commanding Admiral. Its vast scale, which involved no less than seventy warships of the Sixth Fleet, almost 15,000 fighting men, enormous numbers of tanks, guns and war-planes were hardly required to deal with a local uprising in a diminutive country. If it had a wider purpose, it was never spelt out and was perhaps vague even to its principals. It may have been feared that the Iraqi revolution would, in accordance with the fanciful 'domino theory' of John Foster Dulles, trigger similar revolutions elsewhere, toppling conservative Arab regimes one after another. But when the Eisenhower Doctrine was offered to an unreceptive Arab world, even kingdoms like Saudi Arabia and Jordan had publicly proclaimed their opposition to it.

When the operation was launched, President Eisenhower himself drafted and issued a press note in its justification giving five reasons: the intervention was in response to an appeal from the government of Lebanon; it would demonstrate the concern of the United States for the independence and integrity of Lebanon which were vital both to the United States and to world peace; the very presence of US forces would encourage the Lebanese government to take measures in defence of its sovereignty and independence; and finally, to protect American citizens' lives and property. These reasons were specious on their very face. Apart from the Lebanese President, not even his cabinet or army commander had asked for American armed assistance, while the American Ambassador was informed only at the last moment. There was no threat to the sovereignty and independence of Lebanon as UNOGIL's observations had clearly established, and none whatsoever to American lives and property.

We at UNOGIL were deeply concerned that the intervention would violently disturb the peace process. The dilemma which faced General Chehab was most awkward, but it was worse for the marines themselves. The marines had been told that they were to fight the communists at the invitation of a friendly government. Prepared for combat, neither the friendly government nor the hated foe were anywhere in evidence. Even the commandos of the force were at a loss about what they were expected to do. The confusion was worse confounded when different signals of American intentions came from New York as the heated debates continued at the United Nations. The US delegate, Cabot Lodge, first cited article 51 of the Charter which provides for collective self-defence, later the controversial 'Uniting for Peace' resolution. He finally asserted that the purpose was to assist UNOGIL in the peacekeeping role. But what could 15,000 American troops and seventy warships do which UNOGIL, with its ninety-four unarmed observers could not do and, indeed, had already done? The assurance was nevertheless offered, that US Forces would be withdrawn as soon as UNOGIL could take over the task. The UN Secretary-General had not been consulted nor informed and his efforts all along had been to ward off any pretext for US intervention. It did not take long for Admiral Holloway, the Force Commander, to realise that the intervention lacked a real purpose. Meanwhile, the tough troops who expected to be engaged in active combat, broiled in their dug-outs and bunkers in the hot sands and in heated tanks in the summer sun. With nothing to do and confined for weeks to a narrow strip of beach, morale began to sag out of sheer boredom and ennui. The problem now was how to extricate the force from its sorry predicament. A sledgehammer had been used to swat a non-existent gnat.

Although Presidential orders allowed only some twelve hours for the Bluebat operation to be mounted, it had been in preparation since November 1957 when the situation in the area was no more agitated than usual. The only new factors were Soviet aid to Nasser to enable the Aswan dam to be built after the revocation of the American offer.

Following the initial landings, plans went ahead to provide for the assignment of the entire 2nd Marine division at Camp Lejeune and the 2nd Marine Aircraft Wing at Cherry Point, North Carolina, to the Mediterranean area. From the Far East at Okinawa, an amphibious squadron was ordered to proceed to the

Persian Gulf, prepared to land in Iran or Saudi Arabia in the event of the crisis spreading. The 24th Airborne Brigade of the US Army, based in Europe was flown into Beirut to take the place of the British Army Brigade, which was to have participated in the landings but was kept out at the last minute. The US Army in Europe had prepared plans for the commitment of two airborne battle groups, reinforced with support elements, in the Middle East. The US Air Force in Europe had also been kept at the ready for a Mediterranean operation. On 16 July 1958 a Composite Air Strike Force had been flown from the United States to the Adana Air Force base in Turkey. The marine corps had its own airlift. A second battalion of marines was flown from Camp Lejeune in twenty-six transport planes.

Soon US Army Units began to reinforce the original battle group from Germany and Southern France. The Strategic Air Command, with more than eleven hundred aircraft and their guns at the ready, was put on an increased level of alertness.

Although there was a hold-up of sixteen hours since the first landings in unloading essential supplies and ammunition, the subsequent movement was on a massive scale, no less than 10,000 tons being unloaded. In addition to the sea-borne cargo, ammunition and other critical items were flown in day and night. The problem of storage became most acute; the dock area and sheds having been filled to overflowing, the railway marshalling yards were requisitioned, but these too proved inadequate.

The total strength on land attained by the US forces was 8,508 army troops and 5,790 marines, i.e., 14,498 effectives. They were supported by large numbers of tanks, armoured personnel carriers and innumerable trucks and jeeps. The artillery consisted of 8-inch howitzers, 4.2 inch mortars, and 105 mm howitzer batteries, and, ominously, an 'Honest John' rocket battery with atomic capability.

Offshore lay some seventy warships of the Sixth Fleet whose supersonic jets screamed over the Lebanese skies and whose helicopters whizzed constantly over Beirut. The ships included the heavy cruiser *Des Moines*, the guided missile ship *Boston*, the super-carrier *Essex*, twenty-eight destroyers, some oilers and transporters and a submarine hunter-killer group. Neither we in UNOGIL nor the Lebanese had ever seen such a mighty array before.

The only military task of this vast armada was keeping watch over a perimeter of a mere twenty miles around Beirut. According to Shulimson, 'the main problems for the American force were the avoidance of conflict with the local Lebanese irregulars and the provision of the necessary staff and logistical and combat support....' The operation had acquired a momentum of its own, the dimensions of which there seemed no effective means of controlling. There was indeed a danger of the Force being ground down by its own weight. As Horace has said: 'Force without mind falls by its own weight.'

The problem now was of finding a way for the armada to leave in peace without the feeling that the vast effort, the tremendous risks undertaken, the two hundred million dollars spent, had all been in vain. No country, and certainly not a super power, would easily concede that it had over-reacted to a situation or lacked a real sense of purpose in an undertaking of such vast and incalculable dimensions. For then it might be tempted to create a purpose, if only to justify its actions. Even while the US forces were being physically augmented, the search began to discover means for extricating them from the maze into which they had so precipitately thrust themselves. The scene therefore shifted to the United Nations in New York.

The emergency session of the UN General Assembly opened on a stormy note and generated much sound and fury. Opening the debate, Cabot Lodge on behalf of the United States sought to justify the intervention by asserting that it was fully in consonance with the principles of the Charter; he cited various articles which enjoined respect for the sovereignty and integrity of states and interdicted threats or acts of aggression against them. He concluded with the assurance that the US forces would be withdrawn when the United Nations was able to ensure the independence of the country. The representatives of France and the United Kingdom, as was to be expected, supported the American position. What was particularly noteworthy was that the earlier scorn that used to be poured on UNOGIL by these powers now gave place to fulsome praise and a unanimous demand that it continue its beneficient activities. Indeed, Ambassador Lodge went so far as to lavish high praise on its leaders, mentioning each of them by name. Delegates, in turn, began to tear American claims to pieces; the articles of the Charter cited did not apply, as UNOGIL's reports had conclusively proved; there was no threat to the sovereignty or independence of Lebanon; American armed intervention was not authorised by the United Nations; the item on the agenda as inscribed under Chapter VI related to the peaceful settlement of disputes, whereas the use of armed force came under the punitive provisions of Chapter VII; the United Nations was already in Lebanon dealing successfully with the situation, etc.

The Soviet delegate, Ambassador Sokoliev, was more scathing in his attack. He condemned the landings in no uncertain terms as 'an act of aggression against the people of the Arab world and a case of gross intervention in the domestic affairs of the peoples of that area'. He too tore the American arguments to shreds, quoting extensively from UNOGIL reports with evident approval.

Secretary-General Dag Hammarskjold, trying to pour oil on troubled waters, gave a bland dissertation on the legal interpretation of the mandate and the relevant articles of the Charter, thus impliedly demolishing the American case. He administered a further shock by announcing that on that very day the UN observers had secured full freedom of movement and access to every part of the country. To forestall a western demand for the conversion of UNOGIL into an armed police force, he argued that the right to use force fell under Chapter VII of the Charter, whereas the mandate was under Chapter VI.

In the Security Council four draft resolutions were submitted but all four failed to be adopted. The American proposal 'invited UNOGIL to continue to develop its activities' and called for the 'immediate elimination of all illegal infiltration of arms and other material across the Lebanese borders'. The resolution was vetoed by the Soviet Union on the ground that it was otiose and was silent on the main issue. The Soviet proposal described the US and UK interventions as 'a serious threat to international peace and security' and called for their immediate withdrawal. It was, in turn, rejected for lack of support. A Japanese compromise proposal asking the Secretary-General 'to take such additional measures as he may consider necessary in the light of developments so as to fulfil the purposes of the Council's mandate' to UNOGIL and make possible the withdrawal of US forces from Lebanon also fell through. It received a Soviet veto on the ground that it did not call for the immediate withdrawal of US forces. The Swedish representative, Ambassador Jarring, reflecting his government's strong disapproval of the landings and their incompatibility with the principles of the United Nations, tabled a resolution calling for the suspension of UNOGIL's activities in the context of the changed circumstances. This resolution too was defeated.

In view of the complete deadlock in the Security Council, Hammarskjold tried to find a way out from the wreckage. The Japanese proposal did embody the views of the overwhelming majority of members and was, in fact, inspired by Hammarskjold himself. He therefore decided that he was entitled to take guidance from it and to develop UNOGIL's activities accordingly. What emerged from the high-level pyrotechnics was a UNOGIL with its prestige greatly enhanced and with added authority. Those who until the other day had treated it with derision, now looked upon it as a saviour. To it fell the task of retrieval of the forces of intervention from their predicament, and salvaging the prestige of the big powers concerned. The choice of timing and means was left to UNOGIL's discretion. It was the triumph of the voice of peace with justice over the arrogance of overwhelming power.

Between the Secretary-General and UNOGIL there was a continuous dialogue to keep each other fully informed and to coordinate their respective actions and tactics. In view of the larger tasks which had fallen to UNOGIL, measures had to be concerted to carry them out while remaining within the limits of the mandate. The Secretary-General cabled his suggestions as follows:

> I now turn to you with urgent appeal to consider possibility of presenting a report ... which sets out fully how you would envisage future of UNOGIL, irrespective of complications introduced by landings ... and without reference to them—with a view to give UNOGIL scope which would provide it a basis to press for US withdrawal.

Continuing the dialogue, the Secretary-General enquired if it would be feasible to double the strength of UNOGIL to about two hundred, supported by troops for ground reconnaissance, which would give it the appearance of a 'force' without any change of task or authority. Such a cosmetic process would provide him with a good political argument. The legal justification for establishing posts in the interior would be that, since some infiltration of illegal arms, etc. could have penetrated through the border, it could be intercepted when in the interior. Anxious to provide a pretext, however flimsy, for the US forces to leave the country, we readily agreed to the suggestion and, to give the process greater credibility, proposed an increase from the present strength of 94 to 364, including unarmed foot soldiers.

Agreeing with our assessment, Ralph Bunche informed us that 'inevitably UNOGIL must play the role of token, symbol and cover. In this context, it must be visible and go through motions which, nevertheless, serve an indispensable purpose'. The addition to UNOGIL's numbers began with much fanfare and publicity, but they were very gradual and calibrated, the final total being neither achieved nor required. But they provided what the US administration accepted as sufficient cover to enable their forces to commence their withdrawal.

Hammarskjold advised that when UNOGIL officers were 'sprinkled over the country ... it is bound to have a psychological effect on the population. They will, in fact, act as a kind of police, although they have no police duties.' They could thus help in 'stabilising the country although this in no way is explicitly our task. Therefore the members of the Group while firmly holding on to their observation hat could now assume more boldly their invisible diplomatic and political hats as well.'

I had been paying numerous visits to General Chehab to try and persuade him to forsake his soldierly scruples and, as a matter of patriotic duty, save his country from worse perils by agreeing to stand for election to the Presidency. Most political parties had chosen him as a consensus candidate and finally he agreed. The election was due on 21 July. All the candidates had withdrawn on the announcement of Chehab's candidature except one, and he was defeated. With Chehab's election, the political crisis was conclusively settled, and with it there was a marked improvement in the general atmosphere.

The Third Special Emergency Session of the General Assembly lurched ponderously into slow motion. It was attended by President Eisenhower himself and a large assortment of Foreign Ministers. The Secretary-General in his opening statement tried to lift the debate out of the dead centre of mutual recrimination to the wider context of problems of the area as a whole. He expatiated on the need to promote overall economic relations between all the states of the region for their mutual benefit and development. In that context, the political problems within and between them would lose much of their acerbity and facilitate all-round settlements. He referred to the admirable principles enunciated in the Pact of the Arab League which could provide the basis for such cooperation and from which a fruitful harvest could be gathered, instead of the Dead Sea fruit of mutual rivalry and suspicion. These proposals excited much interest, the Arab delegations taking seriously the suggestion to adopt a joint declaration reaffirming their adherence to the principles embodied in their Pact.

President Eisenhower, in his address, administered only a mild reproof of Soviet policies and actions before proceeding to justify his own intervention in the affairs of Lebanon. He blamed 'indirect aggression' for breaking the fragile peace of the area. Taking his stand on the United Nations Charter, he offered an assurance to withdraw US forces if requested by the government or whenever 'through action by the United Nations or otherwise, Lebanon was no longer exposed to danger'. To ensure peace and political order in the Middle East and to prevent the danger of 'indirect aggression' and an arms race, he proposed a plan for the area. Its main ingredients were support for the measures taken by the United Nations for ensuring the safety and integrity of Lebanon and Jordan, setting up a regional economic development plan and the establishment of a United Nations peace force. Recognising Arab nationalism as a valid force, he urged the Arab states to take the initiative in improving their economic condition, for which he promised substantial assistance, both financial and technological.

The President's speech was conciliatory and showed that in the short space of less than a month his administration's perceptions about Arab nationalism being a disruptive communist-inspired force, and the ineffectiveness of the United

Nations, had been completely reversed. Now the United Nations was the peg on which the President's proposals were to hang.

The Soviet Foreign Minister, the unflappable Andrei Gromyko, after castigating the United States and British governments for violating the Charter, refuted the charges against the United Arab Republic by reference to UNOGIL's reports. He pointed to the illogicality of armed intervention in one country in order to deal with events in another. Referring to the inapplicability of article 51 of the Charter, he argued that the right of collective self-defence could be invoked only 'if an armed attack occured against a member of the United Nations', but no such attack had occured against either Lebanon or Jordan. Even the term 'aggression' had eluded definition all these years at the United Nations. He scoffed at the solicitude now being shown for the welfare of the Arab states; such interest was confined to exploiting their oil reserves. The immediate issue was the withdrawal of foreign troops from Lebanon and Jordan, and he asked the Assembly to adopt a resolution to this effect.

Mahmoud Fawzi, the shrewd and experienced Foreign Minister of the UAR, astutely welcomed President Eisenhower's assurances about the withdrawal of American forces from the area and the offer of economic aid. He skipped over all contentious issues and read a homily on world peace and human brotherhood. Selwyn Lloyd followed the American cue in defending British landings in Jordan. He suggested that the presence of so many Foreign Ministers should be availed of for informal consultations on the Eisenhower proposals.

As the debate droned on, punctuated by occasional bursts of excited rhetoric, some positive elements began to emerge. The concept of mutual cooperation and development caught the imagination of the Arab states, but that of setting up a standing UN peace force received general criticism. The latter proposal was impracticable for several reasons: how would such a force be constituted and financed; where would it be located and what would it do in peacetime; who would lead it and when would it be called into action? UNOGIL's endeavours for the restoration of peace and the settlement of the internal political problems in Lebanon received universal and generous praise.

With the Secretary-General's prompting, seven powers tabled a resolution embodying many of the positive suggestions which had emerged from the debate, especially those proposed by the Secretary-General himself and the President of the United States. But it was criticised for slurring over controversial issues and for being vague and inadequate. The Soviet delegate opposed it tooth and nail for not condemning the US and UK interventions and demanding their immediate withdrawal. Even the Asian and Arab states were divided on the issue, the latter being opposed to their fate and future being decided over their heads.

The Arab delegations, alarmed at the prospect of their fate being decided as pawns in the Cold War, set aside their differences for once, and joined in a common endeavour to seize the initiative. The prime mover in the effort was Mahmoud Fawzi of the UAR, a skilled negotiator who was thoroughly at home with the intricacies of United Nations politics. The resolution took its stand on the pious principles enunciated in the Charter of the League of Arab States on which much oratory had been expanded. The central question of withdrawal of US and UK forces was relegated, almost as an aside, to the preamble. The first operative paragraph called upon all member states to practice tolerance and retrain from fomenting civil strife or impairing the freedom and integrity of any state. It requested the Secretary-General, at his discretion, to make such arrangements as he thought necessary to enable the withdrawal of US and UK forces from Lebanon and Jordan. The question of setting up an Arab development organisation, as suggested by President Eisenhower, would be examined as well as the proposal to establish a stand-by UN force.

When the Arab resolution was presented to the Assembly, all

others were withdrawn and it was adopted with acclamation. Little now remained to be done by the Assembly, which duly concluded its session. There was a universal sense of relief that the crisis which appeared so ominous when the Assembly convened had passed in a mood of euphoria. Many countries, including former critics, paid fulsome tribute to the work of UNOGIL.

The remarkable success of the United Nations in Lebanon illustrated how smaller powers could, with an adroit mixture of diplomacy and peacefully conducted field operations, bail out big powers from dangerous predicaments into which they had blundered. What a contrast to the fiasco of the UN's 1996 efforts in Somalia, where big powers in the guise of UN peacemakers engaged in active warfare against those whom they had ostensibly gone to assist. And what made matters worse was that American forces, acting independently of the mandate and authority of the United Nations, waged a parallel war against the Somali people. The inevitable result of this double-pronged belligerence was to antagonise the people against the United Nations. Peace can be brought about only by peaceful means and cannot be imposed by force. And the peacekeeper must be prepared to pay the price by suffering without retaliation, and persevering in his task. In Somalia, the casualties suffered by US troops led them to abandon ship, leaving others to carry on. The UN operation in Somalia had all the ingredients of disaster. Then there is the case of Bosnia, where no less than 60,000 well-armed NATO troops, amply provided with fire-power and .fully supported by air and naval power, are to supervise the cease-fire in Bosnia, supplanting the United Nations peacekeeping mission. There was no unified command of the NATO force as the Americans and French insisted on operating only under their own command. It is difficult to comprehend how NATO and the UN, whose basic objectives and philosophy are different, can operate together as a peacekeeping force.

At UNOGIL we felt enormously elated at the resounding success achieved in New York. Our efforts had been lauded and our labour borne fruit. The initiative had passed to the United Nations and the Secretary-General and we, acting together, could now call the tune. The political crisis in Lebanon had been conclusively solved and the civil war had sputtered out. Beirut lost no time in returning to its habitual bustling self: the shops, bursting with piled-up goods, reopened and busy shoppers swarmed the streets. The hotels, dance halls and nightclubs were soon festive with guests and music, and the gregarious Lebanese abandoned themselves to hectic social pursuits combined with busy trade and business activity. The interior of the country, too, opened up and the picnic spots again came to life.

Meanwhile, UNOGIL's proposal to increase its strength having been accepted, additional observers began arriving slowly but with much publicity. This increase, functionally unnecessary but psychologically and politically expedient, provided just the pretext for the Sixth Fleet to commence its withdrawal. At the peak, we had no more than some 250 observers sprinkled over the countryside. The crucial stage of our task was over, but we had to stay on to see the last of the marines depart. The new government of General Chehab insisted on our continued presence until it was able to consolidate itself. The blue berets and white jeeps were everywhere welcomed as saviours and guardians of the peace, and even village disputes began to be referred to UN observers as impartial arbitrators.

The situation was relaxed enough for Susheela, who had been marking time anxiously, to join me, Plaza's and Bull's families soon following suit. We found ourselves greatly sought after and received much warm hospitality. We spent more than one pleasant afternoon with Kemal Jumblatt at his fortress palace up in the mountains. Set among terraced orchards was a delightful pavilion through which passed a water channel. A damask-covered tablecloth was spread over a dining table which straddled the water course, and on a hot afternoon it was pleasant to dangle one's feet in its cool waters while partaking of the lavish hospitality of the Sheikh. Our host, so gentle and cultivated, contrasted strangely with his wild and ferocious-looking followers, bearded and festooned with bandoliers and hand grenades and carrying lethal weapons of every description.

We spent one afternoon at Baalbek where, after visiting the famous Roman ruins, we were entertained to lunch by the Speaker of the Assembly, Sabre Hamade and local Sheikhs. On arrival, a fusillade of shots rang out which made us duck to the floor of the car; it happened to be the traditional form of greeting for honoured guests! Susheela was ushered into the ladies' quarter where she sat exchanging wordless smiles and nods with the assembled Shia ladies, not one of whom knew a word of anything but Arabic. I sat with the Sheikhs on a long divan alongside the wall, with occasional words of English or French, punctuated by appreciative smiles or grunts, passing between us. Susheela joined the male company for lunch where the main dish was a whole roast lamb sitting on a mountain of rice full of nuts, with spinach in its mouth, roast hens in its stomach, boiled eggs inside the hens, while its glazed eyes stared reproachfully at the diners. The guests of honour were obliged to accept the eyes, which they had a problem in discreetly disposing of under the table!

We watched with much satisfaction the departure of the marines, a process which seemed more difficult of accomplishment than the landing. It was evident that the gallant Admiral Holloway, sceptical from the start about the wisdom of the whole exercise, felt an infinite sense of relief at the prospect of an early departure. At a dinner at Ambassador McClintock's, Susheela found herself at table next to the Admiral who asked her opinion on whether the Sixth Fleet should have come at all. Susheela asked if the Admiral wanted her frank opinion and when he said he did, she replied: 'Certainly not!' The Admiral took it in good heart, remarking that she was frank indeed.

With the induction of General Chehab into the Presidential office and the appointment of the suave Rashid Karami of Tripoli as the Prime Minister, another big step was taken towards the restoration of normalcy. In a statesman-like proclamation, the General stated his priorities. The first was the early completion of the withdrawal of foreign forces, the restoration of peace and security, and political reconciliation, followed by reform of the administration and review of the political system to ensure that political representation and official patronage would not be based on sect or denomination, but on merit. In the field of foreign policy, the country would revert to its traditional role of non-involvement in big-power rivalries and inter-Arab disputes. The President valiantly began the process of implementing the more immediate goals. He was particularly interested on being advised on India's experience in dealing with somewhat similar problems. We frequently found ourselves in conference with the Prime Minister or President about matters not strictly within UNOGIL's purview.

With the departure of the last of the foreign forces, it was time for us also to leave, but neither the Lebanese government nor the Secretary-General would hear of it. We were pressed to stay on until the new government was able to consolidate itself. But that could take an indefinite time. I was anxious to take up my post in Pakistan, having been delayed much beyond the time originally anticipated by Hammarskjold and agreed to by Nehru. Besides, I was convinced that UNOGIL should fold up its tent and withdraw while still at the height of its popularity, and well before the law of diminishing returns began to operate. Reluctantly, Hammarskjold agreed and the operation was wound up on 15 December 1958, almost six months since it was launched.

General Chehab did much to solve or ameliorate some of the

more damaging among the plethora of problems plaguing his country. But in his term he was unable to prepare the ground sufficiently to reform or abolish the obsolete and divisive National Pact. His successors lacked the will or capability, or were too involved in the game of Levantine politics, to attend to the matter. The social and political structures as a consequence remained weak and fragile and invited a recurrence of conflict. The situation was further complicated by the increase in the population of unruly Palestinian refugees on their expulsion from Jordan, who had virtually set up a state within the state and were forcibly indulging in armed provocations against Israel. This brought about Israeli retaliation which was countered by Syria, while the weak Lebanese government was powerless to act. The stage was set for a bitter three-cornered war over the prostrate body of Lebanon, which lasted ten years, and wrought havoc on the once prosperous country, almost leading to its extinction.

# ELEVEN

# The Congo Cauldron

At a time when relations with Pakistan were at last on the ascendant and were soon to attain the summit of a visit by Prime Minister Nehru as the guest of President Ayub Khan, I least expected to be suddenly called away from my post as High Commissioner to head another United Nations peacekeeping mission, this time in Africa. What occasioned the abrupt change was an importunate message from the UN Secretary-General to Prime Minister Nehru, as follows:

> I am certain that you have followed the phases of the Congo crisis which has engaged us in the first full-scale effort of the United Nations to save a country and forestall a war.…
>
> I have in this connection one overriding problem, and that is who would be the head of the whole operation in the Congo.… I thus must seek [a person]… combining great diplomatic tact, real understanding of the problems of a people like the Congolese, the highest intelligence and the highest integrity. You will certainly in no way be surprised—you may even have guessed who I have in

mind.... [There] is one name that stands out and that is Rajeshwar Dayal.

Once before, you have kindly permitted us to use him in another crucial assignment, where he performed his exacting duties with all the skill of which he is capable. I was hesitant to come back to you requesting him to be made free once again, but he is so obviously the right choice that I feel I have to do it....

I was accordingly urgently recalled to New Delhi from Dacca where I was on tour. When I called on Mr Nehru I found that his mind was already set on acceding to the Secretary-General's appeal. He seemed pleased that the services of a member of the diplomatic cadre which he had created, should have been sought for so crucial an assignment. I tried vainly to argue that an interruption in Karachi at that stage would be undesirable in view of his forthcoming visit. But Nehru only said that the post would await my return and an acting arrangement made.

The moment I arrived in New York, I was plunged into an endless round of discussions. The Secretary-General carried about him an air of supreme confidence, the immensity of his task seeming only to exhilarate him. He had launched on a new and uncharted course of international action which would greatly enlarge the scope of the Organisation's capabilities. For the first time, every specialised agency was functioning in the Operation under the leadership of the Secretary-General. And for the first time such a massive international military force would be deployed in a peacekeeping role under the blue ensign of the United Nations.

Hammarskjold had a highly personal style of dealing with his vast responsibilities and was himself able in an emergency to work literally around the clock with very little rest. The 'Congo Club' appeared to be in continuous session, luncheons and dinners being generously provided by the Secretary-General. Late every evening, when the lights in the building had been turned off and the last of the delegates had departed, Hammarskjold's suite would come to renewed life. The faithful would reassemble after a long and tiring day when there would be a review of the fast-changing panorama of events in the Congo and in the conference rooms. Messages and instructions would be discussed and dispatched and the following day's strategies planned. On days of exceptional crisis the team would remain together until well past midnight, and Hammarskjold himself would remain at his desk on the 38th floor.

When I met Ralph Bunche on his return from the Congo, I was shocked at his physical appearance. A man of robust physique, the gruelling time in the Congo had greatly affected his health and normal equanimity. Bunche described at length the highly complex nature of the task and the many and varied difficulties encountered. He had found the Congolese leaders to be suspicious, and unpredictable and most difficult to deal with. He had fallen foul of the Prime Minister, Patrice Lumumba, because the latter had totally misconceived notions of what the United Nations' functions and capabilities in the situation were. The UN Force Commander, Major General Karl von Horn was an irascible old man, whose exaggerated ideas about himself were not matched by his competence. With the Prime Minister and his own Force Commander not even on speaking terms with him, it was difficult for Bunche to function effectively. Nor had he got on with the American Ambassador, Clare Timberlake, or his British counterpart, Ian Scott. Both thought that, as their countries made substantial contributions to the UN budget, they had a prescriptive right to expect compliance by the UN with their wishes. Bunche had gone to the Congo to represent the UN on the occasion of the country's independence from Belgian rule and to offer the fledgling state any technical assistance which it needed to help put it on its feet. But with the outbreak of a mutiny in the Congolese army and the consequent return of the Belgians, a totally new situation had arisen. The Congolese government had appealed to the United Nations for help in restoring its independence and integrity and the Security Council, on the initiative of the Secretary-General, had agreed to provide the necessary assistance. Bunche had accordingly to prolong his stay in order to organise the vast amount of international assistance, civil and military, that would now be required. Within days, the nucleus of the mission was established and expanded rapidly to meet the needs of the situation.

Because the big powers, embroiled in the Cold War, could not be expected to work together harmoniously in a peacekeeping operation, Hammarskjold relied almost exclusively on the middle and smaller powers not involved in military blocs—African countries and neutral states like Sweden and Ireland; he was particularly appreciative of the consistent support which India had unhesitatingly given whenever requested, both in civilian and military personnel.

The vast territory of the Congo, three-quarters the size of India, had fallen to Belgium's share during the loot of Africa by the European powers in the eighties of the nineteenth century. Little had been known about it until the unexpected granting of independence to it on 30 June 1960. Official propaganda had made out that Belgian colonial rule was beneficent and impressive statistics were produced to support this impression. In the UN Trusteeship Council loud was the praise of Belgium's enlightened policy and even the discerning Indian representative, Shiva Rao, was not wanting in praise of Belgium's performance. But when the clamour for independence swept through all of Africa, Belgium panicked and decided to bow to the popular mood.

The natural wealth of the Congo is so great that it has been described as a 'geological scandal'. Its extensive mineral deposits had been exploited first by King Leopold for himself and then by the great Belgian corporations; and in 1960, at the time of independence, it produced some seventy-five per cent of the world's industrial diamonds and cobalt and half its uranium (reportedly used for the Hiroshima and Nagasaki atomic bombs). There are other rare metals, including huge reserves of copper and tin. Its extensive forests and agricultural produce add to its wealth. All this abundance made the Congo the richest country of the continent after South Africa.

In this country of almost one million square miles and a population of some fourteen million at independence, there was not one Congolese judge or magistrate, not one qualified doctor, not one engineer, only one lawyer and not even a dozen university graduates. Every office, institution and organisation was headed by a Belgian; the highest that the Congolese could aspire to were subordinate positions as clerks, hospital assistants, low-grade teachers, petty officials and the like. There were no elective bodies, not even local self-government ones. The army, known as the Force Publique—which was extensively used to quell any sign of dissent by draconian means—was officed entirely by Belgians. Independence came to the Congo when it was totally unprepared to assume the functions of government. A constitution—the Loi Fundamentale—based on a parliamentary form of government, was bestowed on the country, with a constitutional President, an Assembly and Senate, and an elected Prime Minister. Joseph Kasavubu and Patrice Lumumba, who had conducted the negotiations for independence and had led the political agitation, were appointed President and Prime Minister respectively.

The Belgian government and vested interests, failing to recognise the growing temper of the African peoples, had hoped that, while granting the form of independence, real military, administrative and economic power would remain in their hands. The army continued under Belgian command, ministries retained their former Belgian heads under new designations, the great commercial houses and mining companies continued as Belgian monopolies.

With independence, great were the expectations of the people. The common man expected some tangible improvement in his lot, a little more pay, better living conditions, greater promotion prospects. He saw with envy the newly appointed ministers, men of unknown origin and doubtful credentials, riding about in luxurious cars, occupying the splendid garden villas vacated by their Belgian overlords and enjoying a newly-found affluence. But the realisation soon dawned on the people that such privileges were not for them. The euphoria of independence rapidly evaporated as discontent grew apace. The people returned to their daily toil with no hope of improvement in their hard lot.

In the army, the same Belgian officers continued in command. There was no improvement in living standards of the Congolese soldiery, no pay increases, no promotions. To their insistent demands, the only response of their Belgian Commander was that things would continue as before. To drive home the point, General Janssens, the Army Commander, wrote provocatively on a blackboard: 'Before Independence = After Independence'. This was all that was needed to set off an explosion of anger among the rank and file. The mutiny that followed spread like a contagion throughout the country to the accompaniment of much violence against the Belgian officers and their families, who, thoroughly alarmed, began fleeing across the Congo river to the safety of French Brazzaville. There was a complete breakdown of any semblance of public order, and in the ensuing chaos the Congolese soldiery rampaged through the country spreading terror all around. Only the province of Katanga which, under Belgian auspices, had declared its independence, was able to curb the mutinous rabble with the help of Belgian troops still manning military bases there. The leaders of the fledgling Congolese state, unused to the responsibilities suddenly thrust upon them, tried valiantly but vainly to stem the tide of disorder. But their attempts to restrain the soldiery from its orgy of rapine and loot were unavailing.

In Belgium there was shock and indignation at the catastrophic turn of events in its former colony. Unasked by the Congolese authorities, troops were dispatched, ostensibly to protect Belgian life and property. The troops fanned out over the country quelling the mutinous soldiers, but thereafter showed no disposition to leave. Fearful lest their newly-acquired freedom be forfeited, the Congolese leaders, President Kasavubu and Prime Minister Lumumba, sought assistance to restore and safeguard the nation's sovereignty and independence and to assist in its rehabilitation.

An appeal was first addressed to the United States, but on its rejection it was made to the United Nations. The Secretary-General, in exercise of his special powers, called a meeting of the Security Council which adopted a resolution on 14 July 1960 for the provision of military aid to enable the Congolese government to restore order; it also called upon the Belgian interventionist troops to leave the country forthwith. The United Nations would also provide technical assistance to enable the restoration of normal conditions. The United States and the Soviet Union voted affirmatively for the resolution, while France and Britain abstained. The Secretary-General lost no time in organising military assistance, his first choice falling on the African countries. Bunche had already been organising a civilian assistance programme and he was then entrusted with the formidable task of setting up the whole United Nations operation in conditions of exceptional difficulty.

The airports and river and rail transport were re-activated, civic services restored, hospitals brought into function, customs and tax collection agencies reorganised, the administration revived. All this was done through the UN experts from the specialised agencies. In the government offices, there was a UN expert assisting in every ministry and a banking expert trying to restore some financial sanity and discipline. The country was being gradually rescued from the brink of total collapse and financial bankruptcy.

Before the arrival of United Nations experts, many Congolese had tried valiantly to keep the country afloat. Credit must be given to them for performing what they conceived to be their patriotic duty, though with little success. Court clerks had occupied the benches vacated by the fleeing Belgian judges and magistrates, office assistants took charge as district administrators, while medical orderlies and assistants tried to keep patients alive, even performing serious operations, generally with fatal results.

The problem of assisting in the restoration of public order and security also presented formidable difficulties. The main danger came from the *Armé Nationale Congolaise* (the ANC) as the army had been rechristened. Wild and uncontrollable, it had not been paid for months. Unless the ANC was disarmed or trained, it could not be checked in its destructive course. To that daunting task the newly arrived contingents of the United Nations force began to apply themselves.

To add to the numerous problems was the seemingly intractable one of the secession of the province of Katanga. It was by far the richest province in the country, accounting for 75 per cent of the country's mining production estimated at 11.8 billion Belgian francs (in 1960 fifty Belgian francs equalled one US dollar). Its contribution to the national exchequer was about 50 per cent; it also accounted for 75 per cent of the country's foreign exchange earnings. It was extravagantly endowed with precious and rare metals. The loss of Katanga would have resulted in the virtual bankruptcy of the Congo.

The Security Council had not recognised the legality or the finality of the secession; its decisions required that Katanga be dealt with it on a par with the other provinces. The entry of UN troops in the other five provinces was achieved without difficulty, but in Katanga it was strongly opposed by the provincial President, Moise Tshombe. The Central Government regarded the speedy liquidation of the secession as one of its primary tasks, to be achieved, if necessary, by force. The Secretary-General, however, was of the view that the purpose could be achieved by a judicious blend of political pressure with a show of force. Katanga's pretensions were solely dependent upon Belgian political, financial and military support and their denial would effectively undermine the secession.

The question of Katanga became one of primordial importance to the future of the Congo and the success of the United Nations. The Belgian government insisted that its troops were serving legitimately in Katanga as they had been invited by the Katanga government which had declared its independence. The western powers held that Katanga was entitled to determine its own political destiny and that its incorporation in the Republic of the Congo would only spread the area of disorder. They therefore strongly opposed the use of force to end secession. Such reasoning, especially on the part of the United States, betrayed a disregard for its own history and principles. It had fought a biter civil war to end the secession of the southern states during the Civil War, but in the case of Katanga it chose to adopt a different standard. It also failed to take into account the limitations of the doctrine of self-determination which, if indiscriminately applied, could disrupt many existing nation states the world over.

The Soviet Union pressed for firm measures against Katanga, including the use of whatever degree of force would be required. This view ignored the Security Council's mandate and the stated purpose of the UN Force: it was not a fighting force but a deterrent one, and was not equipped to take offensive action. The African and Asian states urged the speedy end of secession by all available means, but they did not insist on the use of force, leaving the means to the decision of the Secretary-General. The

Congolese leaders, however, were emphatic in their conviction that political means were totally inadequate with one as obdurate as Tshombe, and thought that only the immediate application of military sanctions would bring him to heel.

The Secretary-General's interpretation of the mandate remained unchallenged in the Security Council—that the function of the UN Force was to assist the national government in the maintenance of law and order, but that any intervention by it to bring about a political result which would favour one party or another was beyond its domain. The question of Katanga was essentially a political one, to be solved by diplomacy and political pressure, backed up by a show, but not application, of force. Such an attitude, however, was anathema to the impatient Congolese leaders who seemed to imagine that the UN Force was a subordinate body functioning under their orders, rather than an independent entity under its own command, assigned to assist them in the maintenance of law and order.

The secession of Katanga and the means to end it, therefore, became the touchstone whereby the fidelity of member states to the aims of the United Nations in the Congo came to be judged. It was also the principal cause of the serious difference between Prime Minister Lumumba and Ralph Bunche, and subsequently of others with Dag Hammarskjold himself. This lack of mutual understanding and comprehension was to sow the seeds of suspicion in the minds of the Congolese leaders, and to their an attitude of confrontation with the UN mission.

The Secretary-General wished to establish a United Nations presence of a symbolic nature in Katanga by sending in a token contingent of UN troops. As the problem of Katanga was intertwined with domestic politics, and in view of the anxiety of the Congolese government to retain the initiative in its own hands, the Secretary-General felt that any UN move in the diplomatic and military fields should be related to the efforts of the Central authorities themselves. Hammarskjold therefore hoped that Kasavubu could be persuaded to take up the matter with Tshombe directly. Kasavubu typically prevaricated. To force the issue, armed with the authority of the Security Council, the Secretary-General flew into Katanga on 12 August 1960 with four plane-loads of UN Swedish troops, compelling Tshombe to agree to their stationing in his capital of Elizabethville. Tshombe shrewdly calculated that the UN troops would be useful to him in holding the ring, while he built up a force of his own—a Foreign Legion composed largely of foreign mercenaries, which could repel any attack by forces of the Central Government.

The Secretary-General's tour de force in installing UN troops in Katanga, instead of receiving accolades, raised a hurricane of protest. Prime Minister Lumumba, who had been bypassed, was seething with rage at what he construed as a personal insult and a deep-rooted Western conspiracy. He was supported by the Soviet Union and several African states. The Congolese showed their anger against the UN by wanton arrests of UN personnel, beatings and threats of all kinds and it became even more difficult to deal with the government in a rational and cooperative manner.

The UN had won the first round in Katanga, but the subsequent stages were to be far more tortuous. Thus, while Tshombe was bolstered politically, materially and militarily by Belgium and its western allies, the United Nations was denied the political support of those on whom it had counted and without which its efforts in the field would be ineffective. At the United Nations, sharp polarisation developed on the issue. Hammarskjold's bold Katanga strategy may well have succeeded had he received even minimal support from the United States and its allies. But under Belgian influence and because of their own financial interests in Katanga, they had foiled every UN move to deal with the problem. The United States, obsessed by its anti-communist phobia, was opposed to lending its support since it would strengthen the Congolese Central Government under

Lumumba, whom they had anathematised as a communist. The problem of Katanga was to remain a running sore for two and a half years until it was finally resolved by the gallant efforts of the Indian UN Brigade.

Despite all that I had been told about Lumumba, I was not unhopeful that, with patience and understanding, one could do business with him. I believed that at least one clue to the problem was understanding the psychology of nationalist leaders emerging from colonialism; in the Congo the treatment of the people by their colonial masters had been particularly harsh and humiliating.

On my arrival in New York I expected that I would take over from Bunche. But, to my surprise, I learnt that the Secretary-General had sent his own Executive Assistant (later to be called Chef-de-Cabinet), Andrew Cordier, to the Congo to hold the fort during the brief interregnum. Cordier was a dour, high-powered American who kept a firm grip on things and could deal sternly with importunate or erring delegates. He seemed to be on easy terms with the US administration.

The moment I set foot on Congolese soil on 5 September 1960, I felt an oppressive sense of tension as before a tropical storm. At Le Royal, the glass and concrete apartment house where ONUC (Organisation des Nations Unies au Congo) had its headquarters, there was a palpable air of restlessness and anticipation. Elaborate security precautions were evident around the premises. To my puzzled enquiries, Cordier revealed that President Kasavubu had decided to remove the Prime Minister and would be making an announcement on the radio shortly. Cordier seemed mainly concerned about gearing ONUC to meet the shock and to ensure that there would be no rioting or intervention by Congolese troops loyal to the Prime Minister. UN troops had already been alerted and Cordier, who was in a mood of confidence, felt assured that they could hold the ring.

These ominous developments were totally unexpected and there was not the faintest inkling in New York about the sudden turn of events. I found myself caught in a situation from which it was impossible either to retreat or to advance. ONUC would now be forced to adjust to events beyond its control, instead of shaping them.

Kasavubu and Lumumba had a very uneasy equation; the former was devious and slow-moving, 'like a water buffalo', as Hammarskjold described him, while Lumumba was impatient, mercurial and erratic. When Cordier saw Kasavubu he heard a litany of complaints against Lumumba, charging him with ignoring him and his ministers, behaving in a dictatorial and arbitrary manner, striking terror among his opponents, starting a fratricidal war and bringing ruin to the country. Kasavubu had, therefore, in exercise of his constitutional prerogative, decided to remove him.

Kasavubu disclosed his mind to Cordier at successive meetings, apparently to gauge his reactions. But Cordier said nothing to dissuade him or take any action to deter him. All that he said was that he hoped the President had weighed the consequences of his action and made sure of his ground. Kasavubu was left with the impression that, while ONUC would not acquiesce in the action, neither would it oppose it.

On the appointed day, Kasavubu sent for Cordier and informed him of the time of his announcement on the radio. He asked for United Nations protection for himself and the radio station. This Cordier promised, but his demand for UN assistance in the arrest of Lumumba was refused. Kasavubu had hoped that as Head of State he would receive the full backing of the United Nations. The serious differences between the UN and Lumumba were common knowledge and there were rumours that a change of government would not be unwelcome to the harried UN officials. The western embassies had been insistently urging Kasavubu to overthrow Lumumba.

As the hour of the President's broadcast approached, the senior ONUC officials gathered around the radio expectantly. In a monotonous drone Kasavubu said that Lumumba had betrayed his trust. He repeated his list of charges and announced that he had dismissed him and was appointing Joseph Ileo in his place. Simultaneously, a Belgian adviser had called on Cordier with a letter from Kasavubu making more demands, including the closure of the airfields and radio station.

There was much discussion among ONUC officials as to whether the President was not exceeding his constitutional authority in removing a Prime Minister who continued to enjoy a parliamentary majority, without giving him a chance to test his strength in parliament, as enjoined by the *Loi Fundamentale*. The Presidential prerogative could be exercised if there was vote of censure or if important legislation was turned down. But the Prime Minister would still continue in office in a caretaker capacity until a new government had obtained a vote of confidence in parliament. These procedures had not been observed. Cordier, however, in a mood of confidence, was not unduly concerned about these constitutional matters as he seemed to attach greater weight to the President's powers of removal than to the limitations on their exercise. In any case, he did not think it was ONUC's business to interpret the *Loi Fundamentale*. His main anxiety was the maintenance of law and order and he was prepared to take whatever action he considered necessary to that end.

Lumumba had clearly been taken by surprise, but he lost no time in making his response in a broadcast challenging the President's authority to remove a government enjoying the confidence of the people. The government would continue in office to fulfil its appointed tasks, he asserted. The statement was moderate and well-reasoned. An hour later, Lumumba returned to the radio with a much stronger and accusatory statement, full of vituperation. It was evident that Lumumba would fight back with all the force and energy at his command. His parliamentary strength and popular appeal could be rallied to turn the tables upon Kasavubu.

There was no indication of what, if anything Kasavubu proposed to do. Cordier now became alarmed that Lumumba's incendiary broadcasts would stir up the populace to militant action, leading even to civil war. He was particularly worried about the possibility of Soviet planes being used to ferry troops to Leopoldville to try conclusions with Kasavubu and his supporters.

To prevent the Leopoldville ANC from going on the rampage, Cordier wired New York for a million dollars to pay off the starving soldiers. To head off a civil war which he feared, he ordered the closure of all airfields except for UN traffic. Another concern of his was the verbal skirmishing on the radio which he feared would incite the populace, so the radio station was ordered to be closed. These decisions suited Kasavubu's interests in the trial of strength, for while his influence was largely tribal and local, Lumumba had great popular appeal, not only in Leopoldville, but practically throughout the country. Cordier's actions were enthusiastically applauded by the Americans and their allies, but caused intense indignation among Lumumba's partisans, and strong criticism and dismay among the African and Asian nations and the Soviet block.

The Secretary-General's instructions to Cordier were that ONUC must maintain an attitude of strict non-intervention and not take or appear to take sides in any political conflict, only reserving to itself the right to take necessary action for the preservation of peace. He also emphasised the symbolic nature of the UN force as a strong moral factor in peacekeeping. He expressed considerable disquiet at the closure of the airports and radio station and the likely consequences.

The western countries urged ONUC to follow up with the arrest of the Prime Minister and his supporters. The Soviet Union charged ONUC with conspiracy and collusion with the western powers, sharply accused the Secretary-General as an accomplice, and demanded the immediate revocation of Cordier's orders. At one stroke, ONUC had fallen headlong into the vortex of the Cold War and the Secretary-General into direct confrontation with the Soviet Union. A chain of events followed, leading the Operation deeper and deeper into trouble.

Lumumba followed up his counter-attack after a long cabinet meeting with a well-reasoned communique. Refuting each of Kasavubu's accusations, he declared the President a traitor and deprived him of his functions. Both houses of parliament were convened in an emergency session when Lumumba made an eloquent and constructive speech. He received a convincing majority in his favour; a resolution was adopted revoking both orders of removal of the President and the Prime Minister and setting up a Commission of National Reconciliation. So far Lumumba had won on all points and there seemed some hope of a retrieval of the situation. But other and deeply sinister forces who were at work determined to prevent such a peaceful denouement.

Early on the morning of 6 September 1960, Cordier asked when I wished to take over. I told him that he had taken certain initiatives and should now see them through, to which he agreed with some alacrity. The kaleidoscopic sequence of events which followed each other in such bewildering rapidity was beyond the control or comprehension even of the participants. After a long and tiring flight, I had been thrust on the very afternoon of that fateful day into the heart of the mess. But I felt deep disquiet about all that was going on, with ONUC getting ever more deeply enmeshed in a very murky situation.

Although acute fear and tension gripped the city, none of the disasters anticipated by Cordier had occurred. Le Royal was inundated with irate or panicky Congolese and Belgians, either angrily denouncing ONUC or pathetically pleading for protection.

So pervasive was the fear and panic that Colonel Joseph Desiree Mobutu, a former clerk who had been designated Commander of the Camp Leopold garrison, sought shelter from his own troops at the residence of General Kettani of the Moroccan UN Brigade.

The Secretary-General, who had initially welcomed Lumumba's ouster, began to feel alarmed and ONUC seemed to be slipping deep into the mire. My own position in Leopoldville—physically present but without authority—was becoming increasingly untenable. I accordingly decided, come what may, to take over from Cordier on 8 September, barely two and a half days after my arrival.

My first task was to bring about some degree of order and sanity to the situation. The reopening of the radio station and airports was a necessary condition. ONUC should also work for reconciliation of the opposing factions and to tame the unruly ANC. But at the same time ONUC had to put its own house in order as it was evident that the operation was going to be long and arduous. On the sixth floor of Le Royal, the nerve-centre of the operation, all the senior officials sat clustered together, night and day, around a large table heaped with papers of all descriptions. The heap kept piling up as more and more cables and papers came pouring in. Separate rooms were now allotted to all senior officials. Regular meetings were held every morning and duty officers appointed for night duty. The morning meetings, which included the top military brass, came to be known as 'prayer meetings', and the informal evening meetings were a round-up of each troubled day's events.

The disbandment of the 'snake pit' as ONUC's earlier office was called by some of its members came as a relief to all as it allowed time for some rest and, if possible, recreation. To relieve the strain, everyone was encouraged to take some exercise; I set the example by patronising an abandoned riding club. Energetic walks along the Congo river promenade also provided a welcome break from the nervous tension.

In the absence of any eating arrangements, everyone was subsisting on tinned 'K' rations. One day, to my surprise, a group of Pakistani UN soldiers led by their sergeant-major, turned up with salvers of pilaf, kababs and chicken, as they had learnt of our spartan diet. Thereafter my colleagues and I fed sumptuously on Pakistani hospitality until other arrangements, including a commissariat, could be organised.

The next task to be tackled was the question of finding adequate accommodation. An apartment building housed many of the staff and I searched for accommodation for myself. In their headlong flight, the Belgians had abandoned their beautiful homes, with their extensive gardens and swimming pools. As evidence of their precipitate flight, food was still in the refrigerators, clothes still hung in cupboards, and drying flowers filled vases, as if the occupants had just stepped out. The faithful Congolese guardians had protected the houses from marauders; only the motor cars were missing. These were frequently found abandoned on roads when the petrol ran out or smashed against roadside trees or upturned in ditches as their Congolese thieves drove them madly and inexpertly. I could not bear to take over one of these abandoned homes and found the guest house of the great mining company, Union Miniere, located by the river, more suitable. Surprisingly, it was economically furnished and rather austere, but it afforded space and privacy. With these arrangements ONUC could now brace itself for the long haul.

The UN Operation in the Congo struck a new path in many respects. For the first time it involved armed military units in a peacekeeping role. In the name of 'non-intervention' it involved the assumption—by proxy—of all the functions of government. It sought to bring back to life a country which was only a breath away from total collapse. It was a forbidding task even in the best of circumstances. But the circumstances were far from propitious in the prevailing international atmosphere.

The mission was on a scale commensurate with the vast extent and complexity of its responsibilities and the size of the country. There were over 20,000 troops from about fifteen countries, and supporting services from another half a dozen states. Some 1,100 international personnel were engaged in carrying out the civil assistance programme. We also had forty aircraft and hundreds of trucks and jeeps.

In Leopoldville the political turbulence continued unabated and every day and every hour produced its own crop of new and complex problems. Lumumba was fighting back, employing his histrionic talents to the full and mobilising his supporters. He used the instrumentality of parliament where he commanded a convincing majority, and mostly constitutional means to overcome his opponents. Kasavubu remained invisible, confining himself to statements on the radio and having warrants of arrest issued through the Belgian Prosecutor-General.

All day long, irate Congolese from one faction or another would troop in demanding the active intervention of ONUC on their behalf.

Far more difficult than these, however, were some of the western ambassadors, who kept up a constant barrage of telephone calls and visits, urging ONUC to jump into the fray against the parliamentarians and to support Kasavubu. A typical example was a panicky visit by the British envoy, Scott, to ONUC. Bursting into the room of Brian Urquhart, one of my senior political assistants, he demanded to know what the UN was doing when riotous Congolese soldiers were about to break out of their barracks. Surprised, Urquhart enquired how Scott knew. Prompt came the answer: 'My military attaché' heard of it as he moved around inconspicuously in the ANC camp.' 'Oh, I see', said Urquhart as he returned to contemplation of his papers. The said inconspicuous attaché, Colonel Sinclair, was over six feet tall, ginger haired, and habitually wore a kilt!

There were some half a dozen African envoys whose advocacy of Lumumba's cause, however ardent, was not overbearing. Their countries had contributed troops to the Operation and they were naturally distressed at the catastrophic turn of events in a sister African country. As the crisis deepened, they engaged themselves actively as mediators in a sincere attempt to bring about reconciliation. I gave their praiseworthy endeavours every encouragement as they shuttled between one group and another. The parliamentarians and other Congolese leaders of goodwill strongly backed their efforts, which complemented their own. Lumumba was persuaded to consider a negotiated settlement, but Kasavubu remained evasive and procrastinating.

It became increasingly clear that in the imbroglio the Congolese leaders alone were not involved. Kasavubu had a string of Belgian advisers and was subject to constant incitement and pressure from the western embassies. Lumumba was surrounded by a motley group of disreputable characters of no particular nationality. But more sinister were the efforts of foreign secret agencies in suborning vulnerable Congolese politicians with lavish funding and other enticements.

I made my first official calls on the President and Prime Minister soon after taking charge. Kasavubu, courteous but taciturn, raised no controversial issues while I assured him of the United Nations' help in safeguarding the country's integrity and independence.

The call on Lumumba was of a very different order. Arriving late from a public meeting, the Prime Minister straightaway burst into a tirade against ONUC for the closure of the radio station and airports and peremptorily demanded their reopening on that very day. He complained against the Prime Minister being denied the means of reaching out to his own people. He also excoriated his political opponents and went on in this fashion in an excited monologue. Interrupting him, I tried to assure him that the closures were only a temporary measure and I was taking steps, in consultation with the Secretary-General, for their earliest possible withdrawal. Not satisfied with my assurance, Lumumba kept repeating: 'Not tomorrow, today.' I could only ask for a day's respite for practical reasons, but he would have none of it, and even threatened the use of force. I was then obliged to say that in that case ONUC would be compelled to repel force with force and I hoped that such a contingency would not be allowed to arise. In conclusion, I said that I had come to pay a courtesy call and to introduce myself; in reply Lumumba wished me a warm welcome. I could not resist saying that I had received not only a warm welcome, but indeed, a hot one! At this, Lumumba dissolved into laughter in which I too heartily joined. The interview concluded on a cordial, if not a constructive, note.

Lumumba had an arresting personality. Tall and lean, his eyes burning with passion through his thick lenses, he seemed to be seized by an almost messianic sense of mission. Highly intelligent and articulate, he was most excitable and impatient. Unlike most Congolese politicians whose horizons were confined to their tribal loyalties, Lumumba's vision embraced not only his own country, but extended to the whole of Africa. His faults, and they were manifest, were those of inexperience and his earlier conditioning. Persecuted when he was a humble postal clerk for his nationalist activities and discriminated against because of his race, he had developed certain complexes which often blurred his vision. But in the midst of the deep international intrigues which engulfed him, his very virtues proved to be his undoing.

Unfortunately, Lumumba tried to carry out his threat the following day to seize the radio station by force. This could not possibly be allowed and the Ghanaian soldiers guarding the radio station had no difficulty in pushing back the intruders. The next day, having received the concurrence of the Secretary-General, the restrictions over the radio station and airports were removed, thus ending a highly contentious issue.

Efforts to resolve the political tangle and the restoration of public order continued on different fronts. An appeal was addressed by a joint session of parliament to Kasavubu and Lumumba 'to put an end to their quarrels and to reunite in a spirit of patriotism, sacrifice and mutual concession'. Full powers were voted to the government to deal with the 'alarming situation'. Lumumba readily accepted the appeal. But Kasavubu's reaction was typically mean and ungenerous. In a communique, he summarily rejected the appeal and declared parliament's decision null and void on the ground that the joint session itself was illegal. Fearing that the Ileo government would never get a vote of confidence, Kasavubu issued an ordinance, countersigned by Ileo, adjourning parliament for one month. This in turn was declared inoperative by parliament as Ileo had not appeared before it for confirmation!

Hidden behind these constitutional exchanges and verbal skirmishes, malign forces were at work to undermine every constructive effort to end the conflict. The expelled Belgian Embassy continued to function from across the river in Brazzaville; their agents would slip across to Leopoldville every day to foment trouble and then return to their safe haven, while the secret services of the major powers were ceaselessly at work.

The political struggle was so far confined to statements and counter-statements. It had not yet spread to the streets or army barracks. The parliamentarians held endless rounds of conferences and the peacemakers, singly or in groups, pursued their efforts. Relays of bewildered politicians trekked to Le Royal seeking our advice, which though given in abundance was monotonously uniform. It was to seek national reconciliation, a responsibility which no outside authority could discharge. Our good offices would always be available if sought.

One of my visitors was Joseph Okito, Vice-President of the

Senate, a elderly man by Congolese standards, who came in a highly emotional state. To my embarrassment, he suddenly fell at my feet and with tears coursing down his cheeks, begged me to help the country to overcome its travails. I tried to comfort him and encouraged him to persevere in his patriotic efforts to solve the crisis by compromise. Expressing deep gratitude and full agreement, he promised to return with the President of the House of Representatives for further discussion. He returned with his colleague, Kasongo, who was in a furious mood and began berating me for 'interfering' in his country's internal affairs; I was completely flabbergasted at this strange encounter and was forced to the realisation that, at the level of mutual comprehension, much had yet to be learnt.

Kasavubu remained as obdurate and obstructive as ever, rejecting every proposal, however reasonable. His nominee, Ileo, had announced the formation of a government, but he remained a disembodied spirit and his ministers invisible.

But politics, like nature, abhors a vacuum. And into the vacuum created by Kasavubu, stepped young Colonel Joseph Mobutu. Mobutu had been appointed Chief of Staff of the Congolese National Army by Kasavubu in place of the mature General Lundula. The army was little better than an armed rabble and Mobutu trembled before the incendiary force under his uneasy command. He had been very unhappy at the turn of events and had earlier threatened to resign. He was a regular visitor at Le Royal where he sought comfort and advice. He had been Lumumba's protege and still professed loyalty to him. He was yet modest and diffident, obviously overwhelmed by his new and unfamiliar responsibilities and the transition from a clerk to the commander of an unruly national army. He would sit in Le Royal in his uniform and dark glasses, copiously imbibing whisky to build up his spirits.

Late one evening, Mobutu was ushered into my room looking more nervous than usual. He talked randomly and seemed preoccupied. When asked what was on his mind he began a lament, after much fidgeting, against Kasavubu and Lumumba who, by their quarrels, had led the country to the verge of ruin. Affirming his devotion to Lumumba, he said that neither he nor Kasavubu could govern. In the circumstance, he had decided 'to neutralise' both President and Prime Minister 'as a temporary measure'. Taken aback and not quite comprehending his meaning, I asked Mobutu what he proposed to do. He replied hesitatingly that he would be making a radio announcement at half-past eight that evening, only a few minutes later. Thoroughly alarmed in case it should be thought that ONUC was colluding in what was a military coup, I had Mobutu quickly bundled out of the room.

A new and highly dangerous element had now arisen. The unruly army, which we had tried to keep out of political interference, would now occupy the centre of the political arena. What had caused the sudden transformation of the weak and vacillating Mobutu into a would-be military dictator? We did not know, but had our suspicions which, as events unfolded, were fully confirmed.

A few days later, Mobutu arrived, the picture of misery and despair, pleading that as he had not slept for days, could we provide him with shelter at Le Royal for a brief stay? After some discussion we reluctantly agreed. He then asked if he could bring his wife and children over. So abject and downcast was our visitor that we could not refuse, and hurriedly improvised some arrangements. The next request was whether his sister-in-law could also join the party! From 'a few days' our unwanted guests stayed on for eight or ten, until we were forced to ask them to leave. As the Indian proverb says, a tree does not deny its shade to the woodcutter.

Lumumba and Kasavubu were taken completely by surprise by Mobutu's coup. Lumumba issued an angry denunciation of his erstwhile follower, while Kasavubu reacted mildly, describing the action as 'senseless'. The western embassies and press hailed the military takeover enthusiastically, glorifying Mobutu as the 'strong man of the Congo'. When asked by the western media for my perception of the 'strong man', I could not help saying that he was the weakest 'strong man' I knew, a remark widely reported and resented by those who had prompted his deed.

The ANC, prime cause of the country's woes, had been so far kept in check. But now the genie had been let out of the bottle and it would not be easy to control or neutralise it.

At ONUC we anxiously deliberated on how to deal with the situation, and to fathom the forces which had brought it about. It was obvious that Mobutu by himself lacked the determination to overthrow the political structure. Even after his coup he lacked the courage to face his own troops on whom his military regime was dependent.

In the midst of these grave developments, an event occurred which could have had disastrous consequences. Colonel Joseph Ankrah, Commander of the Ghana Battalion in Leopoldville, rushed into my office one afternoon with a strange tale. Lumumba had gone into Camp Leopold to address the troops, when he was attacked by a group of angry soldiers of the Baluba tribe. He fled to the Ghana officers' mess near by, followed by the irate soldiers who laid siege, demanding his blood for an earlier massacre of their tribesmen by troops from Leopoldville. The Ghanaians were under great pressure and could not hold out much longer to prevent the storming of the glass-fronted building. The best hope was to persuade Kasavubu to call upon the soldiers to withdraw as they would respect his word.

I rushed to the President's residence accompanied by the Colonel and a highly excited Baluba soldier whom he had brought with him. Kasavubu appeared after much delay and in answer to our joint pleas began offering one excuse after another for inaction. Even the explosive mood of the Baluba soldier failed to move him. Night began falling and we were informed by wireless that the situation at the mess was becoming increasingly parlous and there was no further time to lose. After wasting three hours in fruitless parleys with Kasavubu who kept asking that we arrest Lumumba, I stamped out threatening to withdraw the UN guard from the President's residence. He ran out after us begging me not to leave him unprotected, but on the Lumumba issue he still would not relent.

Around the Ghana officers mess, the soldiers, wild with rage, had lit torches and were beginning to dig in. We forced our way through the howling mob and rushed up the stairs to where Lumumba was cowering in the corner of a room and a number of soldiers in ugly mood were being held back by UN guards from bursting in. Lumumba hailed me as a saviour and expressed much gratitude for my arrival; he pledged he would cooperate fully with the UN in future. I lectured him on the imperative need for compromise and moderation. But his attitude abruptly changed towards the gallant Colonel when the Ghanaian Ambassador, a Mr Djinn, suddenly appeared: he began now to charge the Ghanaians with abducting him and denied that he had sought protection, much to the disgust of the Colonel who had risked his life to save the fugitive. I too lost patience and ordered the Ambassador, who joined in accusing Ankrah, to leave. We then arranged for Lumumba to be quietly spirited away by the kitchen door in a UN jeep under cover of darkness. I made my way out by the front door with much noise and ceremony to distract the attention of the besiegers. Fortunately, the ruse worked and we were able to extricate Lumumba and ourselves from a perilous situation. Thereafter, we mounted a strong UN guard around Lumumba's official residence.

Mobutu's visits to Le Royal were becoming infrequent and he began to display a new self-confidence. He had announced wholesale promotions in the ANC and a doubling of salaries. No longer did he depend on ONUC for funds or supplies of whisky. Sensitive to the reality of power, the western envoys had begun flocking to pay court to him. ONUC's liaison officers with Mobutu reported frequent visits to him by western military attachés with bulging briefcases, from which they would deposit large paper packets on Mobutu's table.

These bizarre events which crowded in on each other caused stupefaction among the feuding Congolese politicians. The Afro-Asian envoys, reflecting their governments' reactions, were furious with Mobutu and deeply apprehensive of the future. We at ONUC were now to face an even more tangled situation. It was difficult enough with two pretender governments stridently claiming recognition. But now there was a third and wholly illegal one. It was obvious that ONUC could have no truck with a regime whose only sanction was force.

Mobutu lost no time, no doubt at the behest of his hidden patrons, his *conseilleurs occultes*, to declare the Soviet and Czech Ambassadors personae non grata and to demand their expulsion within forty-eight hours. The expulsions were a move in the Cold War, in which the Congo was a mere pawn, and which was being waged through the instrumentality of the benighted and venal Congolese leaders duped into betraying their own national interests.

On receiving the peremptory order, the Soviet Ambassador approached me with a request for UN protection at his departure, but he refused my offer of intercession on his behalf. He said he would also withdraw the Soviet 'technicians' in Stanleyville along with the ten Soviet transport planes with their medical supplies. The Soviet personnel in Stanleyville, often mistaken for the hated Belgians had had an unhappy time there and were glad to leave.

I was able to prevail upon the Soviet Ambassador to leave at least the crates of medicines behind; these, on being opened, were found to contain generous quantities of vodka! This was to give much comfort to our hard-pressed Ethiopian troops.

## TWELVE

# *Cloak and Dagger Diplomacy*

E arlier works on the Congo, including my own book entitled *Mission for Hammarskjold: The Congo Crisis* (published in 1976 by the Oxford and Princeton University Presses), were not in possession of authentic information on how every positive initiative by the United Nations to help the Congo floundered, making the task one of sisyphean difficulty. That information has since been made available, and in ample measure, in the archives of the Eisenhower-Kennedy libraries since opened to researchers under the US Freedom of Information Act. Secret cables exchanged between Washington and the US embassies in Leopoldville and elsewhere, as well as cables sent to or from CIA agents and the minutes of closed door meetings are readily available in those libraries. On these primary sources, the later writings are largely based and their authenticity is beyond question. I am greatly indebted to their American authors for what their patient research into the archives and their extensive enquiries have so convincingly revealed.

Andrew Tully in his *CIA: The Inside Story* states categorically that the Central Intelligence Agency had long spotted Mobutu as 'their man' and had been fully supporting him, a statement confirmed by Catherine Hoskyns in her authoritative book *The Congo Since Independence*. Tshombe's biographer, Ian Colvin, who was witness to the events in the Congo, states with conviction that Mobutu had the backing of Colonel Devlin, the CIA agent in Leopoldville. Two later scholars, in particular, in their carefully researched books drawing extensively from and frequently quoting from the wealth of new material, are *The Congo Cables* by Madeleine Kalb and Robert Mahoney's *JFK: Ordeal in Africa*. What has been described as 'one of the most shocking documents in American government history' is the published report of the Senate Select Committee, presided over by Senator Frank Church on 'Alleged Plots to Assassinate Foreign Leaders'. The Committee heard over one hundred witnesses, studied thousands of documents and assessed ten thousand pages of sworn testimony. I have drawn heavily on these sources in this chapter to reveal the almost impossible odds that the United Nations was facing in the Congo, especially during the Eisenhower era. The facts as now revealed surpass even the wildest conjecture made at the time.

We at ONUC were trying to labour disinterestedly in an open and transparent manner with the UN mandate as our guide and the principles of the Charter as our inspiration. All our decisions were promptly reported to New York for confirmation or correction by the Secretary-General. The Security Council, which had the ultimate responsibility, was kept fully informed and instructions sought from it as the Operation progressed. Striving for what to us was a noble cause, we implicitly believed that, despite all obstacles and misrepresentations, truth would ultimately prevail. This may have been rather idealistic, but the United Nations itself was founded on the highest idealism—that of world peace and the universal brotherhood of man.

While we were thus trying to follow a straight path, powerful forces were engaged in secretly undermining the very principles which they publicly professed for narrow partisan and dubious ends. The UN had no secret sources of information and even its cypher was not unbreakable. The large volume of published works that has appeared on the subject of the Congo reveals the distressing fact that ONUC was facing not only the perils of the Congolese situation, but the cloak and dagger activities of a great power, fully backed by its western allies. Therefore, every life-saving measure, every carefully-planned move to help the benighted country, was sabotaged by a deep conspiracy. At the same time, those very powers were demanding that ONUC should have taken certain actions while denying it the means to do so. This narrative should therefore be read in juxtaposition with the activities of the underground operations as now revealed. What the other western countries were doing under cover has not been revealed.

A central fact of which neither the UN Secretary-General nor his Special Representative were aware was that a crucial decision had been taken in Washington, a bare six or seven weeks after the country's independence, to remove the elected Prime Minister, Patrice Lumumba, from the scene. As head of the United Nations mission, I laboured for the first few months of my stewardship of the operation unaware of the minefield sown under our feet which was blasting all our efforts and hopes.

The startling decision concerning Lumumba's fate was taken at the highest level of the American administration. At a meeting of the National Security Council in the White House at Newport on 17 August 1960, President Eisenhower declared Lumumba to be a very dangerous man, a threat to world peace, who must be eliminated by all possible means. The meeting was attended by a large number of important officials, from the President's White House staff, National Security Council, State Department, CIA and Pentagon. The understanding of practically all of them was that the President had authorised, if he did not actually so direct, the physical elimination of Lumumba. The CIA Director, Allen Dulles, construed the President's statement as a directive to the Agency to carry out the assassination itself, if not through local assassins. He therefore set about to implement it in a carefully planned and scientific manner.

The CIA had long been concerned about Lumumba's political tendencies. Allen Dulles had, in fact, reported to the President that Lumumba had a 'harrowing past' and that he was 'another Castro and a danger to the United States and to world peace'. The CIA agent in Leopoldville had been plotting with disgruntled or venal politicians to eliminate Lumumba, or inciting potential assassins to action. Substantial funds had been sanctioned by CIA headquarters for the purpose. These sinister activities continued throughout, until Lumumba's assassination was accomplished by other means.

The US administration was obsessed by fear of communist penetration of Africa and what it termed as a 'Soviet takeover' of the Congo. It viewed control of the Congo and its riches as a critical factor in the Cold War. The protection of the vast financial interests of Belgium and its allies was another pressing concern. Unfortunately, the welfare of the long-suffering Congolese people, their progress and enlightenment, the strengthening of their newly-won independence and territorial integrity, were not among their concerns. The Congo was not seen as an end in itself but as a mere pawn in the exercise of power politics.

The Western powers, led by the United States in support of its NATO partners, had been resolutely opposing efforts at decolonisation. They also opposed the elimination of racial discrimination in South Africa and regarded the non-aligned policy of the African countries as inimical to their interests. The doctrine of the United Nations was entirely different and the purpose of its mission in the Congo was far removed from the interests, objectives and activities of the western powers. That the United Nations would run into a collision course with these powerful forces was therefore almost inherent in the situation.

How was it that the United States should have been thrown so far off-balance by fear of a young, half-educated and untried African leader whom a turn in the wheel of history had thrown up as a natural leader of his people? True, Lumumba was impulsive and impatient, rough of manner and sometimes threatening or boastful. He was no doubt distrustful of the Europeans, for, as he said, he and his likes had for generations been treated with insults and brutality and exploited by them. But, most leaders of independence movements in colonial countries had little reason to trust their former overlords, and Lumumba was no exception.

The CIA, however, decided that Lumumba was a communist and a 'stalking horse' for Soviet penetration into Africa. But not a shred of evidence is available for this assumption. At a press conference in New York, Lumumba had stoutly denied that he was a communist; he declared that he was a nationalist and subscribed to no ideology and believed in a policy of 'active neutralism' for his country. While thanking the United States, he said he would take help for his country from any quarter, even the Soviet Union. In fact, the US embassy in Leopoldville had reported as follows: 'Lumumba is an opportunist, not a communist, his final decision as to which camp he will eventually belong to will not be made by him but rather will be imposed upon him by outside forces.' The real conflict in Africa was not between capitalism and communism, but between nationalism and tribalism, a basic fact which the western powers failed to grasp. In fact, the only ideology of the newly-independent African states at the time was one of sheer survival.

Both Kasavubu and Lumumba had appealed jointly to the United Nations for help, fearing that their newly-won independence would again be lost to the Belgians. To follow up the appeal, Lumumba proceeded to London, Washington, New York and Ottawa for help. The secession of Katanga and the diamond-rich Bakwanga, the loss of which would have bankrupted and fragmented the new state, was another pressing problem. The Congolese leaders had convinced themselves that it could be solved only by military means. Failing to get the help asked for, they turned to the Soviet Union which did provide ten aircraft, a hundred trucks and 'technicians'. The plans of the Congolese leadership, however misconceived they may have been, did not point to a sudden defection to the Soviet Union or any communist proclivities. As Lumumba had said, he would accept help for his country from any quarter, 'even from the devil'. This was no different from the attitude of many countries emerging from colonialism.

It was not because of solicitude for the United Nations in its difficulties in dealing with Lumumba that the US administration had decided to eliminate him. His very qualities of leadership, his eloquence, patriotic fervour, and fierce independence went against him. The western powers in reality wanted only a willing accessory who would be amenable to their influence and watchful of their interests.

The Belgian government had, at independence, recognised that, for all his faults, Lumumba was an essential element in the Congo's political spectrum. This the Americans too had accepted. The Congo had been given a constitution based upon a parliamentary form of government. It was therefore for the parliamentarians to keep Prime Minister Lumumba in check and to oppose his excesses. His faults were due to sheer inexperience of the world outside and ignorance of the principles of governance. But he was not likely to surrender his country's freedom from one form of colonialism for another, that of the Soviet Union or any other foreign power. He, however, had no chance of survival as a decision about his fate had already been taken thousands of miles away and the sands of time were running out for him.

The top scientist of the CIA, Sydney Gottleib, had been commissioned to prepare a deadly toxin which would cause certain death or permanent incapacitation. As events in Leopoldville appeared to be moving in a direction favourable to Lumumba, a 'most secret' cable was sent to the CIA operative, Colonel Devlin, in Leopoldville that 'Joe from Paris' would be arriving on an important mission and must be given all possible help. But he was not informed of the nature of the secret mission, while the embassy was kept completely in the dark. Gottleib arrived in Leopoldville on 26 September 1960. When he disclosed the plan to Devlin, the latter, hardened operative though he was, confessed to an 'emotional shock', not because he had any moral qualms, but because he felt it would be safer for a third party, and not the US administration itself, to get directly involved in the matter. But as a loyal secret agent, he complied with the instructions. The toxic substance was so lethal that special precautions were needed to handle it. Gottleib's deadly poison was to be administered orally, either in Lumumba's food or his toothpaste. In order to carry out the task, a house was hired for Gottleib facing the Prime Minister's house. As a precaution against Mobutu's threats, however, concentric rings of UN, Ghanaian, Tunisian and Moroccan troops were put on guard around Lumumba's house. Because of the unceasing vigilance of these guards, the would-be assassin was foiled in his attempt to gain access to his intended victim. After some frustrating weeks, Gottleib returned to Washington, having thrown the poison into the river. But he left some of it with Devlin for use when opportunity arose. This remained in Devlin's safe until after Lumumba's capture and death, when it was no longer needed.

With the battle-lines between the Congolese President and Prime Minister sharpened, Kasavubu and his backers used every device to eliminate Lumumba from the political scene. The closure of parliament led to verbal skirmishing, giving place to violence in street and barrack. The Leopoldville garrison became increasingly unruly and arbitrary arrests and beatings were commonplace. As already noted, Lumumba had to be freed by UN troops when he went to harangue the ANC and was detained there. Mobutu himself was threatened by the troops and fled from the barracks to Le Royal for protection. ONUC was inundated with politicians and others of all shades and conditions begging for UN protection, which was generally provided at their residences. The best we could do was to mount a holding operation until order was restored.

The upheavals had resulted in a bizarre lining up of forces. When some degree of fluidity had been brought about, the peacemakers returned to their mission with renewed hope. From the safety of his UN-protected residence, Lumumba plied us with messages of gratitude for UN help to the Congo with assurances of his full cooperation. Even Mobutu now advocated reconciliation and pledged he would demit power before long. But Kasavubu's attitude remained enigmatic. While he gave encouragement to the peace makers, he would commit himself to nothing.

The American establishment was getting increasingly frustrated and angered by Kasavubu's vacillation and failure to take decisive action. Anxious to humour Mobutu, by confering on the Commissioners the cloak of spurious legitimacy, Kasavubu administered the oath of office to them. But this infuriated Mobutu who regarded the Commissioners as his own proteges. The Afro-Asian ambassadors had, after much skilful footwork, obtained broad agreement to a practical and entirely workable plan for reconciliation. It involved a political truce, release of political prisoners and the reopening of parliament. Even Kasavubu had given his verbal agreement, perhaps for fear of Mobutu's growing power and aggressiveness. But at the last minute, he reneged on his promise. Those who were determined to prevent a return to parliamentary government and the rule of law, had again prevailed.

At one point when Mobutu faced a mutiny of his troops he approached me with a plan for reconciliation. It proposed a meeting between Kasavubu and Lumumba under UN auspices, followed by a round-table conference. While Lumumba agreed to the proposal with some minor conditions, Kasavubu was uncooperative.

To frustrate these hopeful developments it was given out that some letters of a highly incriminatory nature had been seized from Lumumba's briefcase when he was waylaid at the Ghana officers' mess. They were evident forgeries, as close examination by our experts proved. One purported to be a letter from Lumumba to President Nkrumah of Ghana with a plan to expel the UN, to replace it with Soviet aid and to carry out a large number of arrests and executions—in short, to set up a reign of terror. These forgeries and a minor incident about the beating up of a Commissioner by some youths provided the excuse for Mobutu to back down on his own plan to demit power. The hidden hand operating vicariously had again triumphed over our well-planned efforts to apply the healing touch.

At ONUC our spirits rose and fell in tune with the ever-changing situation. Our moods were fully reflected in New York, as the daily exchange of personal cables between the Secretary-General and me fully revealed. At the end of each weary day, we would both open out our hearts and minds in our cables. They show us working together in remarkable harmony, at 'the same wave length' as Hammarskjold observed. The Secretary-General was engaged in battling pressures and attacks from both ends of the international political spectrum, relying heavily on his principal constituency, the Afro-Asian group. We at ONUC, were engaged in a sort of *dance macabre* with Congolese protagonists of various hues and at the same time trying to avoid the deep-laid traps and pitfalls set by the moles of the secret agencies. The delegates in the elegant refinement of UN Headquarters at New York offered various theoretical nostrums based on finely chiselled political theories. But they were far removed from the harsh and primitive realities of the Congo. In order to bring the delegations down to earth from their lofty perches, I suggested to the Secretary-General that I send 'Progress Reports', for circulation among member states. These helped greatly in easing the pressures on the Secretary-General and directing some of their virulence towards us. The Secretary-General and the Special Representative thus came to be engaged in a sort of balancing see-saw act, and it was essential to ensure that one or the other did not go down.

The historic fifteenth session of the General Assembly, attended by a glittering array of captains and kings from all corners of the globe, commenced on 20 September 1960. The most significant item on the agenda was the granting of independence to no less than sixteen African countries. And, as the problem of the Congo dominated the agenda, the fifteenth session virtually became an African session.

The Cold War was at its height and much was expected from the session to lower tensions and reduce the threats to world peace. The meetings therefore began in an atmosphere of hope mixed with apprehension. Unfortunately, it soon became apparent that differences would be exacerbated and made more irreconcilable and the modest consensus on the Congo achieved earlier would be dissipated. The first to take the floor was President Eisenhower; to woo the African leaders and to whet their cupidity, he announced a programme of aid to their countries. Turning to the Congo, ignoring the directions given by him to the CIA about Lumumba just one month earlier, he exhorted all countries to give their full support to the United Nations mission and to refrain from any acts of interference in the country's affairs. He then warned member states not to 'incite its leaders and peoples to violence against each other'. These stern warnings were followed, just six days later on 26 September, by the arrival in Leopoldville in great secrecy of the CIA's arch poisoner, Sidney Gottlieb, with his murder kit!

Krushchev launched an abusive and vitriolic attack on the Secretary-General and all his works. He also blasted American policy in the Congo and, to outbid Eisenhower, proposed the immediate granting of independence to the remaining African and all other colonies. He then sprung a surprise with his 'troika' proposal, a 'three-headed God' as Nehru described it. It met with a frigid response from all sides. The violence of his attack on the Secretary-General alienated the Afro-Asians whom he had sought to woo and his 'shoe-banging' episode capped his discomfiture.

The Secretary-General counted heavily on the great non-aligned leaders: Nehru, Nasser, Sukarno, Nkrumah. They did not fail him, although they had their misgivings about certain aspects of his Congo policy. In particular, they pressed for the over 20,000 strong UN force to play a more active role in preventing arbitrary arrests and lawlessness and in crushing Katanga's. secession and activating the political process. They could not understand Hammarskjold's fine philosophical distinction between the doctrine of intervention and non-intervention in the Congo's internal affairs. After all, the UN mission itself was a massive form of intervention. This accorded fully with my views as I had been pressing for authority for ONUC to play a more active role. We had the force and the will to use it effectively, but were hedged in by restrictions and restraints which deprived us of the possibility of acting in a mediatory or preventive capacity. High on my agenda was the reconvening of the Congolese parliament to solve the political tangle, the restoration of peace and security being a necessary precondition.

The great of the earth departed from New York leaving behind a trail of blasted hopes and the echoes of noisy debate. The Secretary-General set to work, in consultation with me, on a plan of action based on the reconvening of the whole parliament with the participation of Katanga. This would need a massive diplomatic effort and, if well synchronised, could not only restore the situation to normal in the Congo, but also go a long way towards the solution of the vexed problem of Katanga. The key to Tshombe's participation was the prior expulsion of his Belgian advisers and mercenaries. This would necessitate not only a direct appeal to Tshombe by the Secretary-General but also steady pressure by the United States on Belgium. Tshombe received the Secretary-General's appeal with feigned enthusiasm. But the Americans were cool to the idea, while the Belgians exploded in anger. They called for a meeting of the NATO council to rally their supporters—the United States, Britain and France—to oppose the plan. Tshombe followed up with a tough and unbending reply drafted by his Belgian advisers, for 'the mouth was the mouth of Esau but the hand was the hand of Jacob'. Thus ended another attempt to bring peace and sanity to the Congo.

When the resumed session of the General Assembly met in November 1960, Hammarskjold asked me for another report to help in focusing the debates so that they would not follow the same desultory course as at the main session. This was a rather outspoken document, squarely blaming the Belgians for persistent defiance of UN resolutions. It pointed to the continuing dilemma of ONUC in dealing with three pretender governments, besides three secessionist ones. Committed to the principles of neutrality and legality, it could not give recognition to a regime founded on force, but in order to maintain contact with the ministries it was compelled to deal with whoever was found in occupation of the ministerial chairs. The continued lawlessness and the disruptive role of the ANC as well as administrative collapse and financial bankruptcy were highlighted. The report was warmly welcomed by the African and Asian countries but strongly criticised by the western powers. It raised a veritable storm in Brussels.

To assist him in his diplomatic efforts, the Secretary-General invited me to New York during the discussion of my report. After being submerged in the murky and turbulent waters of the Congo, it was a welcome relief to find myself in different surroundings. Hammarskjold exclaimed on seeing me that I looked 'disgustingly well' (unlike Bunche who had returned shattered from the Congo), as indeed I felt, working for a cause without passion or prejudice. There was, however, no reprieve from toil. I was always surprised at the degree of ignorance that prevailed among delegates about the stark realities of the situation in the Congo and the limited mandate of the Organisation to deal with them.

Among my numerous interviews, my meetings with Averell Harriman were of particular interest. He had visited us in Leopoldville and seemed sympathetic to what we were doing. He had no illusions about the Congolese politicians or the role of the Belgians. He arranged a luncheon at his residence for me to meet the Belgian Ambassador in Washington and Count Dhani, whose forebears had collaborated with King Leopold II in exploiting the Congo and who still owned vast interests there. The Belgians at first eyed me suspiciously but, thereafter, the conversation proceeded pleasantly enough until they asked why I hated Belgians so much. Startled, I tried to reassure them that I was merely trying to carry out an assigned task without any emotional involvement whatsoever, and was anxious for its completion to resume my post in Pakistan. The duration of the task would be in inverse proportion to the degree of cooperation received from Belgium.

Soviet Ambassador Zorin came to see me and gave me a grilling for two hours, at the end of which he exclaimed that he believed I was an honest man, but my views were far removed from those of the Secretary-General. I retorted that, if I differed from the Secretary-General, I would myself quit, and if he disagreed with me, he could ask me to leave.

I had meetings with the Congo Advisory Committee comprising representatives of countries contributing troops to the Operation. To Dean Rusk, still in academia, I tried to stress the importance of building stable political institutions in a shifting situation and not fostering venal and unreliable individuals at the cost of principles. To all who would care to listen, I tried to explain the hard facts of the situation.

When the General Assembly again took up the question of the Congo it became abundantly clear that, while the African and Asian countries strongly supported efforts at national reconciliation and the recall of parliament, the western powers led by the United States were even more firmly opposed to it. To them a return to constitutional rule meant only one thing—the return of Lumumba. However, they could not openly oppose reconciliation or the restoration of legality; nor could they brazenly support Mobutu's dictatorship. A UN Conciliation Commission had been set up which was to assist in the efforts of ONUC and other peace-makers in Leopoldville to bring about peace among the warring politicians. The Chairman of the Commission was Jaja Wachuku from Nigeria. India's representative on the Commission was Rameshwar Rao, a Member of Parliament and a former member of India's Foreign Service.

To undercut these efforts, the western powers deftly introduced a procedural manoeuvre using Kasavubu as a willing pawn. The contentious issue of the recognition of rival claimants to the Congo's seat at the UN had earlier been deferred in order not to muddy the waters further and to give a fair opportunity to the Conciliation Commission to do its work. To block a parliamentary solution, Kasavubu was brought over to New York to attend the session. Lumumba's efforts to follow him to counter the move were frustrated by the ANC but he would not, in any case, have been granted a visa by the US embassy. Even the previously accredited Congolese government's official representative had been denied a visa on the ground that his passport had been impounded by the Commissioners. The field was thus cleared for Kasavubu who, as Head of State, would automatically be entitled to address the Assembly and demand the seating of his delegation.

In one of the most sordid episodes in the history of the United Nations, many delegations were bribed or bullied into reversing their votes. So disreputable were the methods used that Hammarskjold felt 'extreme disgust', while *Le Monde*, among other journals, commented that the manoeuvre was a 'success of the American big stick'.

The result of the forced vote would immeasurably increase our problems. It would now be more difficult to keep the scales even, as western pressure would mount for ONUC to lend active support to Kasavubu and the illegal regime which he had fathered. It would also impose a strain on ONUC'c troops, drawn from the non-aligned states, to carry out policies of which their governments so strongly disapproved. The only fading hope now lay in sending out the UN Conciliation Commission as early as possible. Kasavubu was now riding high, and the Secretary-General's efforts to come to an understanding about ONUC's future role found him totally unresponsive. My own meeting with Kasavubu in his sumptuous hotel suite where he was surrounded by American and Belgian advisers, was equally unproductive.

At the United Nations, various draft resolutions were offered from different parts of the political spectrum. An anodyne one sponsored by eight non-aligned powers which represented the lowest common multiple of agreement, provided no positive guidance to ONUC. Differences were further sharpened all around and even the Afro-Asian group was splintered by pulls and pressures.

At this point of the narrative it would be pertinent to recall that, while constitutional issues were being discussed and political positions adopted in the conference rooms of the United

Nations, much more down-to-earth and indeed, portentous, activities were going on in Leopoldville. As already noted, the CIA Director, Allen Dulles himself had recommended (on 26 August) the liquidation of Lumumba, and plans were afoot towards that end.

A day after President Eisenhower's admonitory address to the UN General Assembly, i.e., on 21 September, he was briefed on the Congo situation by Allen Dulles, who pointed out that the danger of Soviet influence was still there and feared that a reconciliation might take place between Lumumba and his opponents. He added that although Mobutu was in effective power, a grave danger remained so long as Lumumba was 'not disposed of'. To make assurance doubly sure, Allen Dulles sent another personally signed cable to Devlin on 27 September:

> We wish give every possible support for eliminating Lumumba from any possibility resuming governmental position or if he fails in Leopoldville setting himself up in Stanleyville or elsewhere.

Devlin meanwhile had not been idle. On 15 September he reported to headquarters that he was serving as an adviser to a Congolese effort to 'eliminate' Lumumba. On 17 September another CIA agent met a Congolese Senator who agreed 'reluctantly that Lumumba must go permanently'; and requested a 'clandestine supply of small arms' to accomplish the task.

It is abundantly clear in the light of these damaging disclosures that the United States, behind its posturing about support for the United Nations, was pursuing aims in the Congo totally antithetical to those of the Organisation, the Charter principles, and indeed the demands of common morality. Belgium, Britain and France were making their own contributions individually and in combination to scuttle the Operation. No wonder that, in the face of such powerful forces, the United Nations, that 'fragile instrument in men's hands' as Hammarskjold described it, found itself baulked at every step.

I had assumed charge of ONUC on 8 September, but a decision had been taken three weeks before in Washington to liquidate the Prime Minister of the country which had invited the UN there. Barely eleven days later, when the preparations for murder were complete, the CIA man in Leopoldville was alerted; the would-be assassin arrived a week later. These dates provide eloquent proof of why all our labours were of little avail, for we were, indeed, 'beating our wings in the void in vain'. While we could have dealt with the Congolese politicians and established a measure of order and legality, we were powerless to contend with these hidden foes with their immense power and resources. Had we at ONUC or at UN headquarters the slightest inkling of what deep conspiracies were afoot, there is little doubt that the UN mission would have been withdrawn. Many valuable lives of UN civilians and soldiers including the Secretary-General's, and much toil and heartache would have been saved.

Susheela had been fretting at home reading the daily newspaper stories of mayhem and violence in the Congo. She now insisted on sharing the perils and difficulties which faced me. Accordingly, on my way back from New York, she joined me in Paris, from where we flew down to French Brazzaville. We were met by Brigadier Rikhye who had been left to hold the fort during my brief absence. He and other UN officials who had come to receive us all looked rather worried and absorbed. Flying across the Congo river by helicopter, we did not land at the Leopoldville airport or at the residence where I was quartered, but on to Le Royal. There, temporary arrangements had been made for our stay. My earlier residence, I was told, had become unsafe since it was exposed to attack from all sides. The reason for this unexpected burst of hostility of exceptional virulence was a fire-fight between UN troops protecting the Ghana Embassy and its Ambassador who had been declared persona non grata but was refusing to leave, and an ANC force. Unfortunately, firing broke out and the garrison Commander Colonel Kokolo, who was leading his troops, was killed. Mobutu thereafter practically declared war on the United Nations.

I was in New York when these dire events took place. Instructions had been sent to ONUC to give protection only against bodily harm to the errant Ghanaian envoy, but not to interfere in the matter of expulsion and, above all, on no account to get involved in armed conflict with the ANC. Palavers had been taking place but tempers had been rising when the Congolese tried to force the issue. As a result, ONUC got involved in the very situation it had been strictly enjoined to avoid.

Le Royal was in a state of siege and ONUC personnel had to be provided armed protection at their residences and when they went about their business. It was a stormy 'homecoming' for Susheela, but she took it with exemplary courage and patience, giving heart to our harried colleagues. Mobutu was cock-a-hoop with Kasavubu's success in New York and his own in Leopoldville where he had managed to put the UN on the defensive. Arbitrary arrests were the order of the day and politicians began fleeing the city or begging us for protection. Many of Lumumba's followers had fled to Stanleyville and he himself was seized with panic at the increased prospect of his own arrest. In fact, Mobutu's soldiers had appeared at Le Royal time and again with warrants for Lumumba's arrest, but they were turned back on the ground that political arrests were not permissible. This greatly infuriated Mobutu and his western patrons, but the Secretary-General fully supported our actions. Mobutu had tightened the ring around Lumumba's residence, but he could not penetrate our stout UN triple cordon. Lumumba had begun complaining of claustrophobia and was fretting at being unable to go to Stanleyville for the burial of his infant daughter who had died in Switzerland. We counselled patience, assuring him full protection so long as he remained within the protected premises, but we could not follow him around if he chose to leave of his own volition. Unfortunately, he was to disregard our advice, inviting tragedy on himself, bringing disaster to the country and discord to the United Nations.

To relieve the pressure on ONUC and to reduce the dangerous tensions in Leopoldville, Hammarskjold took energetic diplomatic action with member states. His efforts had a sobering effect for a while as the excitable western envoys who kept up a chorus of protest at ONUC's refusal to permit Lumumba's and other arbitrary arrests, now simmered down. The overheated atmosphere in Leopoldville also began to cool down somewhat. The Supreme Commander of the UN force, Major General Karl von Horn, had made himself scarce during the stormy interludes of the past few weeks, obviously unable to cope with the situation. I therefore had to ask the Secretary-General for his replacement by the Irish Chief of the Army Staff, Major-General Sean McKeown, who had visited the Irish contingent serving with us and had created a favourable impression.

Reports had began appearing in the international press about the physical danger in which Susheela and I stood, which evoked anxious enquiries from Hammarskjold. In reply I sent him a copy of a report which had been received from the Colonel of the UN Tunisian Brigade to the effect that ANC troops in two boats armed with machine guns and mortars had been trying to land behind our house with a view to storming it, but had been repulsed by the UN guards. Another threatened danger was from Captain Pongo, ANC Security Officer (later the captor of Lumumba), a frequent visitor to our Command headquarters, who would brandish a loaded revolver, bragging that it was for use against the Special Representative. There was no way of silencing him as ONUC lacked the power of arrest. But worse were Pongo's telephone calls to Susheela, which she later stopped taking. These dangers did not demoralise Susheela and we took them stoically.

Susheela's presence and fearlessness were a great morale booster for our staff, especially the civilian and female personnel. To encourage our people we attended receptions given by our various military contingents in honour of their national days and held frequent receptions ourselves. We also entertained, as best as local conditions would permit, the steady stream of official visitors who came from abroad. These included Edward Kennedy, Averell Harriman, Mennen Williams, Senator Frank Church, etc.

At the end of November 1960, Kasavubu returned from his pyrrhic victory in New York. The diplomatic corps and I were lined up at his red carpet airport reception. After much delay the tubby Kasavubu emerged from the aircraft, an incongruous figure in a white Field Marshal's uniform, complete with gold epaulettes and dangling sword. That night, while a great storm raged outside, there was a banquet at the President's house to celebrate his return. The next afternoon we learnt to our consternation that Lumumba had fled from his sanctuary. No doubt taking advantage of the storm, he was able to elude both the UN protective cordon and the hostile ANC outer ring. When the news got around, I received a summons from a highly annoyed Kasavubu, who, along with his advisers, charged the UN with complicity in the escape and refused to accept any explanation.

At ONUC we got sporadic news of the fugitive's progress. He appeared to be making for Luluabourg where his wife had arrived from Switzerland with the body of their infant daughter for burial. In consultation with the Secretary-General and in conformity with our repeated warnings to Lumumba, we announced that ONUC would give no assistance to either pursuer or pursued. We refused to provide a plane to Mobutu to track down Lumumba, much to his annoyance. Meanwhile, Lumumba had reached a river crossing on the other side of which lay Orientale province and safety. He had moved at a leisurely pace, addressing large crowds when he could have easily made it to safety. To help in Lumumba's capture, the US Ambassador, Timberlake, himself went across the river to French Brazzaville and obtained from Kasavubu's kinsman, President Youlo, the loan of a helicopter. It was in this helicopter that Captain Pongo flew in pursuit of Lumumba, whom he succeeded in intercepting at the river crossing. Why Lumumba did not accompany his colleagues across the river is not clear. One account has it that he awaited the arrival of his wife, another that he had such strong conviction about his hold on the masses and the inviolability of his own person that he felt confident no harm would befall him. Pongo triumphantly brought back Lumumba as prisoner to Mobutu, who supervised his merciless beating before he was incarcerated.

But Lumumba, even in captivity, was seen by his antagonists to be too dangerous to be held in Leopoldville; he was therefore transferred to the military camp at Thysville, down the river, for safer custody as the garrison there was regarded as more dependable than that in Leopoldville. Soon, however, news spread that Lumumba had won over the garrison there and imbued it with strong nationalistic feelings. This set alarm bells ringing in Leopoldville. The CIA man, who had been master-minding the whole affair, informed Washington that Lumumba in captivity was no less dangerous than in freedom. Among the peacemakers, fading hopes began to revive. At last the fact even began to dawn on the State Department that Lumumba was a vital factor in Congolese politics and could not easily be set aside. Talk was revived of the formation of a government of national unity with the possibility of Lumumba's return to power. The convening of parliament and a return to legality were no longer thought to be dangerous or subversive heresies.

But not by the CIA chief in Leopoldville. His inflexible objective, towards the achievement of which his energies were bent, was still to encompass the physical elimination of Lumumba. By protecting Lumumba at his house, ONUC had frustrated the poisoning conspiracy, and had repeatedly prevented Lumumba's arrest. It was the CIA man who was responsible for the issue of arrest warrants against Lumumba, and it was he who had organised what came to be known as the 'Binza' group, comprising Foreign Minister Bomboko, Security Chief Nendaka, Mobutu, etc. This group got its instructions from Colonel Devlin and was supplied lavishly with funds.

The extensive CIA establishment in the Congo, with its wide ramifications among Congolese politicians and its close association with the Belgians and other western secret agencies, had overshadowed the US embassy. Timberlake, because of his erratic behaviour, fluctuating views and hysterical reporting, had waning influence and his views carried little respect in Washington. It was the CIA therefore, which, in effect, made US policy in the Congo.

Lumumba's sway over the Thysville garrison had so inflamed it against his captors that a serious mutiny broke out. The officers were attacked, their wives raped. Rumours spread in Leopoldville that Lumumba had been freed and was making for the capital. Panic gripped Kasavubu, Mobutu and their adherents while the Belgians, who had been returning in large numbers, again began fleeing across the river.

Great was the agitation over these developments in New York where the Security Council was called in session to discuss the rapidly changing situation. The UN was falsely attacked for having tried to rescue Lumumba from arrest by force. Others attacked it for doing nothing to prevent his capture. All that emerged from the heated debates was a stern warning to Kasavubu from the Secretary-General, demanding humane treatment and a fair trial for the prisoner.

In the Congo we were battling not merely the feuds and follies of the Congolese. We were up against the power politics of countries, great and small, being played out in the Congolese context. The Congolese themselves were shrewd enough to realise that, having various powers backing them, it would suit their purpose to draw them deeper into their commitments. Great countries therefore got enmeshed in the primitive politics of the Congo. Big powers became hostage to the fortunes of ephemeral Congolese politicians, the Congolese finally reversing roles and turning their patrons into clients. Thus, if Lumumba fell, it became a rebuff for the Soviet Union; if Mobutu was held in check, the United Kingdom felt offended; if Kasavubu was not seated at the UN, the United States would be affronted; if Tshombe was pressured, Belgium would be infuriated. It was like a three-legged race in which a great power was linked to a Congolese politician, with the diverting quality that if the pigmy fell, he brought his giant partner down with him.

We had come to another perilous crossroads in the tortuous course of the mission. There were now four pretender sovereignties: the shadowy Ileo 'government', Lumumba's 'legal' government, the Commissioners in ministerial chairs, and now a Lumumbist 'government' in Stanleyville. Lumumba's followers had been gathering in Orientale province and, on his capture, declared themselves as the legitimate government under the absent leader, and Gizenga as the regent. In addition, there were two rebel regions: Tshombe's in Katanga and Albert Kalongi's in South Kasai, the latter having declared himself the 'Mulopure or king of the "diamond state".'

With rival armies proliferating, the stage was being set for civil war. The writ of the Kasavubu-Mobutu combine now ran over only one-third of the country. To buttress Mobutu's waning strength, his patrons began plying him with arms, which he began turning on the UN force, threatening to expel it from the country. With the departure of several contingents in protest against

ONUC's failure to prevent Lumumba's arrest, there was danger of the UN force being worsted in a trial of strength with the ANC.

Hope lay in a possible change in US policy as the Kennedy administration was due to take over shortly. In his election campaign, Kennedy had strongly criticised Eisenhower's policy that had alienated the countries of Asia and Africa. He also opposed the line pursued in the Congo of favouring a military dictatorship, and advocated a return to parliamentary democracy with a broad-based government. He appealed for non-interference in the Congo's affairs and demanded full support for the UN effort. The president-elect's view corresponded to what we had been consistently urging.

As this point, the UN Conciliation Commission arrived in Leopoldville. Its Chairman was the Foreign Minister of newly-independent Nigeria, Jaja Wachuku, who turned out to be an unfortunate choice. Clad in flamboyant robes and a tinselly cap, he behaved like a tribal potentate, regarding his colleagues, all prominent representatives of their countries, as his subjects. He was irascible, capricious and obtuse and had fallen foul of his colleagues from the start. He had insisted on being provided with a suite of rooms in Le Royal, spurning the hotel where his colleagues were comfortably accommodated. Commission meetings would degenerate into angry polemics and I had frequently to intervene to restore order. Rameshwar Rao, a distinguished member of the Commission, was indefatigable in his daily efforts to bring its unruly Chairman to heel. The Commission passed a few weeks in making desultory contacts and did some aimless wandering without achieving any result beyond earning the scorn of the Congolese.

Fearful of Lumumba's release from custody and possible return to power, the Kasavubu-Mobutu faction tried to placate him by throwing out feelers of working together for the restoration of civilian rule. An approach was reportedly made to offer Lumumba a place in Ileo's cabinet, which he summarily refused. But he was not averse to a peaceful settlement of differences. While these exchanges were in progress, Mobuto's hostility towards ONUC began tapering down. We hoped that we could sustain a holding operation until the new American President took over, when we might be able to reverse the tide.

Meanwhile, in a trial of strength with Mobutu's ANC, the Stanleyville regime showed remarkable intrepidity. It seized Kivu province and a part of Kasai as well as north Katanga by carrying out practically bloodless, lighting raids. European planters and residents were threatened and they flocked to the headquarters of the UN Ethiopian Brigade for protection. The European envoys began demanding UN protection for the far flung factories and plantations of their nationals. These events, betokening the growing power of the Stanleyville regime, again set alarm bells ringing in Leopoldville.

In South Kasai a tragic situation had developed which called for immediate attention. A quarter of a million tribals who had been evicted from North Kasai as a result of tribal warfare had sought refuge in Kalongi's realm. They were starving and disease-stricken and dying at the rate of about two hundred a day. I set off for the refugee camp with a team of journalists. We had not gone far when we ran into a roadblock manned by several heavily-armed men in uniform. A sergeant thrust the muzzle of an automatic weapon through the window of my car and asked brusquely who we were and what was our business. Disregarding my explanation, we were told we could not proceed without the express orders of the 'Mulopure'. The argument of the loaded weapon with a quivering finger on the trigger proved conclusive, and bowing to the threat, the whole convoy reversed its tracks. I had tried to avoid meeting the 'Mulopure' who was regarded as an outlaw, but was compelled to give in. The said gentleman, who had been enjoying himself drinking champagne with his cronies, was all courtesy and, apologising profusely, deputed one of his 'ministers' to accompany me.

The scene at the camp was one of utter desolation. All around lay the sick and dying, being ministered to by our gallant Indian nursing sisters who had volunteered for the heart-breaking task from the Leopoldville hospital so efficiently run by an Indian medical contingent. The cruel irony of the tragedy was that thousands were dying literally atop a mountain of diamonds, for the rich diamond mines of the Belgian company Forminiere stretched for miles alongside, protected by barbed wire. My fervent appeal for international help, broadcast far and wide by the accompanying journalists, evoked an immediate response. Plane-loads of food, medicines and other supplies began arriving in a steady stream and in a few weeks the suffering was eased. But what a sad commentary it provided on the cupidity and heartlessness of men that the opulent Belgian diamond company could not persuade itself to extend a helping hand to ease such appalling human suffering.

It was at this time that the Secretary-General arrived to see things for himself and to try and prevent a dangerous drift towards civil war by promoting efforts to bring the quarrelling factions together. The Conciliation Commission was still floundering about in Leopoldville and its activities needed to be correctly focused. Contact had also to be made with Ileo's new government, which had suddenly materialised, the youthful Commissioners having been got rid of because of their incompetence and self-indulgence. Mobutu, under pressure from the western envoys, was engaged in a quixotic enterprise in an effort to subdue the rival Stanleyville regime. He had first tried to impose an economic blockage of Orientale province reportedly on the advice of the British Ambassador, but that only boomeranged against western vested interests as their newly-harvested cotton crop and other exportable goods were left to rot in the open. Mobutu had then taken a flotilla of rafts on the river to make a frontal attack, but his troops had no stomach for a fight and were easily held back at the border. ONUC then established a broad neutral zone to inhibit any further hostile contact between the opposing forces. The whole episode thus ended farcically.

Hammarskjold reviewed the difficult situation that the UN was up against both in New York and in the Congo. If the Kasavubu-Mobutu line-up could be held in check and political processes reactivated, there could be hope of a breakthrough. Well-cordinated moves by ONUC in the field and by the Secretary-General by diplomatic means with the western and neutral powers were required. Nehru had been approached with urgent requests for a larger number of Indian troops to replace those which had departed or were about to do so. Nehru laid down certain conditions. There should be a moratorium between the two super-powers against bringing the Cold War into the Congo; political prisoners must be released and the ANC prevented from interfering in politics; parliament should be convened and a coalition government installed. Hammarskjold was in broad agreement with our approach to the problem based on these principles. The presence of Rameshwar Rao on the Conciliation Commission, and his persistance, helped in no small measure to persuade the Government of India and Prime Minister Nehru in agreeing to Hammarskjold's request for Indian troops being sent to the Congo.

I asked the Secretary-General to tell me frankly what mistakes ONUC had made. Hammarskjold replied that the only mistakes were the closure of the airports and radio stations, for which I was not responsible. He said he found ONUC well organised and functioning smoothly and fully capable of meeting its tasks. I finally asked what difference he found in ONUC since his last visit five months earlier. He replied: 'There we were all full of confidence in New York, but things here were panicky. Now, we are panicky in New York, but here in ONUC I find a mood of confidence.'

Hammarskjold's meetings with Kasavubu and other

Congolese leaders were a dialogue with the deaf. To his finely chiselled arguments advocating political means for the solution of political problems, the answer in chorus was for the forcible suppression of the Stanleyville regime. When Hammarskjold stressed the importance of principles over personalities, the others could only pour venom on their enemies by name. The argument made no sense to Kasavubu that, if the use of force against Katanga to end secession, on the one hand, was not permissible, it was equally out of the question against the Stanleyville regime. Instead, he accused ONUC of preventing the arrest of his political foes. The trump card of the President's men was to accuse ONUC of deliberately causing the various conflicts and fomenting civil war. The talks took place in this vein, leaving Hammarskjold utterly baffled. His razor-sharp mind and exquisitely civilised way contrasted strangely with the wooden-headedness and crude behaviour of his interlocutors. The realisation again came forcefully to Hammarskjold of how difficult it was to negotiate with people of whom Gustavo Duran had said, somewhat crudely perhaps, that Belgian haberdashery could not conceal their primitive jungle mentality.

Such a mentality was perhaps infectious, but as yet no one in ONUC had succumbed to it. In this context, a midnight call on Hammarskjold by the British Ambassador, Scott, was revealing. Scott, in a state of great agitation, stated that an intercepted cable from Gizinga to Khrushchev had carried an appeal for help to meet an attack by Belgian troops against Stanleyville. Hammarskjold tried to calm the distraught envoy and, referring him to a map, explained the impossibility of such a contingency occurring. He afterwards made the wry comment that the Leopoldville air had a strange effect on some people.

I must here pay a sincere tribute to my colleagues, civil and military. I was always struck by the complete objectivity and impartiality of my principal political advisers who betrayed not a trace of national bias in their views and work. All worked devotedly for the cause of the United Nations in a true international spirit. The military units and their commanders, drawn from many countries, worked together as a team under the directives of our military headquarters, often performing tasks in disregard of the policies of their governments, as a well-knit international force. There was never an occasion to take disciplinary or corrective action against any national contingent.

In a strange way, Lumumba's capture and transfer to Camp Hardy in Thysville, had brought about a sharp change in the situation. So long as he was cocooned in his UN-protected sanctuary, he had been out of the political calculus of his foes. But he came to occupy centre-stage from the moment of his break-out from the sanctuary of the Prime Minister's house and it came to be recognised that he was a factor to be reckoned with. It was thus a time of both hope and of hazard—hope that saner counsel leading to a search for peaceful settlements would prevail; hazard that, in their desperation, the guilty men might bring about Lumumba's demise.

As John F. Kennedy's inauguration as President approached, he and his advisers became much preoccupied with the problem of the Congo. As a Senator, Kennedy had earlier set up a Task Force to give body and substance to his ideas on the Congo, the general thrust of which reached the ears of the Congolese politicians. They gave heart to the Lumumbists and to the peace-makers, but caused consternation among Kasavubu, Mobutu and the 'Binza' group. The European powers took alarm while the Belgians redoubled their efforts to build up Tshombe's forces and, with the help of Timberlake and Devlin in Leopoldville, to have foreign military aircraft delivered to the rebel Katanga regime in an American carrier plane.

Hammarskjold had taken a strong antipathy to Lumumba—a rather surprising attitude in one so urbane—because of the latter's earlier uncivil behaviour towards him. But now, bowing to the inevitable, he was fully prepared to accept Lumumba as an essential factor in the political situation. Even the erratic Timberlake had to acknowledge for once that Lumumba was the only Congolese with the qualities of leadership to hold the country together. But the next moment he shared the CIA view that there was no time to lose in removing Lumumba from the political scene. Kennedy's advisers generally took a relaxed view and favoured the recall of parliament, the freeing of political prisoners and the disciplining of the ANC as the best means for ending the chaos in the country.

Whatever may have been the perceptions of the incoming administration, the CIA operatives in Leopoldville were to follow an agenda of their own. They were a power unto themselves, accountable to none. They still had left-over allies in the US administration, chief among whom was Allen Dulles who continued as CIA Director. They were appalled by the weakness of Mobutu and Kasavubu in trying to entice back Lumumba with offers of a cabinet post or their inability to deal decisively with their inconvenient prisoner. They now conspired with Kasavubu, Mobutu, the 'Binza group' and their Belgian advisers to lay a trap for their quarry. Using an erstwhile follower of Lumumba's, now ready to betray his patron as a decoy, Lumumba was lured out of the relative safety of his prison at Camp Hardy. The pretext was that the Leopoldville garrison had risen in his favour and the ground had been fully prepared for his resumption of power.

President Kennedy was to be installed on 20 January 1961 and it was common knowledge that he would reverse Eisenhower's hard-line policies towards the Congo. He would not be averse to a coalition government to include Lumumba and to the disciplining of the ANC. The CIA, determined to foreclose any such eventuality, decided that there was no time to lose and Lumumba must be delivered forthwith into the hands of his mortal enemies, Tshombe or Kalongi. Just two days before Kennedy's inauguration, Lumumba was dispatched to

Elizabethville in a plane piloted by Belgians. Lumumba and two of his companions were treated with such brutality during the flight that one of the Belgians vomitted and the crew locked themselves up in their cabin. Half-dead on arrival, Lumumba and his companions were flung into a jeep and taken to a nearby building. There Munongo, Tshombe's dreaded 'Home Minister', plunged a bayonet into Lumumba while a Belgian mercenary administered the coup de grace about which he later bragged. The bodies were secretly buried. To celebrate the event, the local CIA man sent an ecstatic cable to his chief.

These dastardly activities were carried out in the utmost secrecy and even the new American President and his administration were kept completely in the dark. Timberlake, playing second fiddle to the CIA man in Leopoldville, was equally an accessory to the murder. The irony was that Munongo, the direct descendant of Msiri, the last tribal chief whom the Belgians killed to seize the rich prize of the Congo, was the murderer of the very man—Lumumba—whose mission it was to avenge Msiri's assassination.

The Kennedy administration had been going ahead with what came to be known as the Kennedy Plan, unaware of the fact the Lumumba was already dead. The plan was, in effect, what the Secretary-General and I had been advocating all along. It also corresponded to what Prime Minister Nehru had insisted on as a condition for the provision of the sorely-needed Indian troops. There were endless confidential discussions in Washington at which Timberlake was present on the plan's implementation, and garbled information about these discussions leaked out to the press, reaching the ears of the Congolese in exaggerated and distorted form. Fearing that it could lead to the return of the Lumumbists to power and the disarming of the ANC and their own overthrow, Kasavubu, Mobutu and their coterie reacted violently and viciously towards the United Nations. No amount of explanation had any effect, and outrages against UN personnel continued and every kind of obstruction to ONUC's work was offered. The western missions did their best to incite the Congolese further while their governments were strident in their criticism of the United Nations and of Kennedy's apparent receptivity to Hammarskjold's proposals.

Taken aback by the virulence of the reaction in the western capitals, the American administration set about trying to mollify its NATO partners by retreating from its more enlightened position. The spectre of McCarthyism had not yet been laid, while Cold War compulsions still dominated American policies. The brave intentions to reorient American foreign policy by showing greater understanding of the urges and interest of the countries of Africa and Asia and sympathy towards the force of nationalism were now submerged by the overriding concern of maintaining NATO solidarity. The inevitable outcome was that only halting approaches were made to Belgium to cease its mischief in the Congo and to withdraw its aid to Katanga. The backtracking also undid the previous advocacy of all political prisoners, including Lumumba, and bringing the ANC under control.

While the Kennedy administration was locked in endless debate about Congo policy and what to do about Lumumba, the subject of their concern had, weeks earlier, already been liquidated. The Secretary-General and I sent endless messages to Tshombe urging humane treatment and a fair trial for their prisoner, but the replies were both evasive and insolent, warning us to 'mind our own business'. At last, on 13 February 1961, four weeks after the murder, the story was given out that Lumumba and his companions had escaped from their place of detention and been captured and killed by villagers. All my attempts to enquire about the bodies so that they could be properly buried, met with rude rejoinders.

The cold-blooded murder of the Congo's first Prime Minister sent shock-waves throughout the world. At the United Nations in

New York, it raised a veritable storm. The African and Asian countries were aghast and roundly blamed the United Nations for its passivity in allowing such a horrendous crime to be committed without using all the means at its disposal. The Soviet Union reacted violently, charging the Secretary-General with direct responsibility for the murder.

The Congo now entered upon a new and perilous phase in its violent infancy as the politics of murder displaced the politics of persuasion and discourse. All constraints now removed, the stage was set for renewed violence and even fratricidal war.

The political aftermath was a complete rupture between the United States and the Soviet Union on Congo policy. The Soviets promised full support to the Stanleyville regime, which it recognised as the legitimate government of the Congo. Gizenga's government also received the recognition of a large number of African and other countries. Belgian embassies were stoned in various capitals, and Europeans attacked. In the United States, violent race riots broke out, the administration being charged with complicity in the murder. At CIA headquarters there was private exultation, from Dulles down to the station chief, Devlin, all of whom were committed to the liquidation of Lumumba by fair means or foul.

In the Congo, among the people at large there was a sense of deep shock and stupefaction. But to the guilty men in Leopoldville the feeling of relief at the removal of an indomitable foe was tempered by fear of retribution. The Stanleyville regime had been steadily widening its sway over the country and gaining in military strength, while the Leopoldville regime's writ ran only in the city and lower Congo regions. Mobutu's ill-advised 'blockade and invasion' of Stanleyville—the brainwave of Ambassador Scott—was an unmitigated disaster. Mobutu lost both men and morale in the brief encounters with Stanleyville before the UN imposed a neutral zone between them. The European farm and factory owners lost their produce which lay exposed in the open and the Leopoldville authorities lost their customs revenue.

In sheer frustration the Kasavubu-Mobutu clique sent a group of Lumumba's followers imprisoned in Leopoldville to their certain deaths in Bakwanga. In retaliation, Stanleyville followed suit by putting to death a group of men from Leopoldville. Fortunately, Stanleyville had hitherto remained remarkably quiet, few Belgians and Europeans being threatened and none killed. The scared foreigners were collected by UN troops from all parts of Orientale province and kept under their protection in Stanleyville and arrangements made for their repatriation. But the western missions kept insisting on protection for Europeans at their scattered farms and factories and guarantees of free movement. They also demanded that the UN suppress by force the Stanleyville regime. This was in sharp contrast to their strenuous opposition to the use of even the threat of force against the Katanga secessionists.

At the United Nations in New York, there was horror and incredulity at the renewed round of barbarism in the Congo. Spurred to action after much debate and acrimony, a resolution proposed by three African and Asian countries was eventually adopted by the Security Council on 21 February. It permitted ONUC to use force, if necessary, for the expulsion of Belgian and other foreign military personnel. It also called for the convening of Parliament under UN auspices. Washington at first demurred because of the wider implications of the resolution but, along with its allies, finally voted for it. It would be highly questionable for countries professing democracy to openly oppose a proposal for the return of legitimacy, or the expulsion of foreign military elements, or the disciplining of the unruly ANC. However, to them, the reconvening of parliament meant only one thing—the seizure of power by Gizenga and his followers, which they were determined to prevent at all costs. Indeed, the Pentagon had already prepared contingency plans to send a force of some 80,000 to prevent any such eventuality. The line adopted, therefore, was to sabotage on the ground what had perforce to be acceded to in the Security Council. The local representatives of those governments incited the Congolese leaders, already fearful of losing their power, to violence against the United Nations.

Washington feared that since both Hammarskjold and I were too close in our stance to the Afro-Asian group, they could not be relied upon to neutralise the ANC or to reconvene parliament in a manner favourable to the US and Belgian plans. Timberlake had gone even further when he reported that the UN had moved 'measurably closer to the Soviet line' and, therefore, must be bypassed. The CIA station simply ignored Washington's concerns and pursued its own line.

Kasavubu, Mobutu and their followers reacted to the 21 February resolution as to the sting of a viper. Kasavubu went on the air and, charging the UN with betrayal, called upon the ANC to wage war against it. A new and most virulent reign of terror followed: UN civilian personnel were arrested in large numbers, while beatings, brutalities and threats of murder became common. The UN force, depleted by the withdrawal in protest of several contingents, was outnumbered and outgunned by the ANC in Leopoldville.

Greatly emboldened by the support and encouragement of the western missions and secret agencies, the Congolese tried to throttle ONUC by cutting off its lifeline to the sea. They expelled the UN from the port of Matadi, and forebade the Belgian rail and river transport agencies from carrying UN stores and the airline from accepting UN traffic. The hands of the CIA chief, Devlin and of the US mission were very evident behind all these hostile actions. There was a concerted plan to drive the UN out so that the Congo could again revert to being a virtual colony behind the facade of independence. The Secretary-General, on the other hand, was convinced that the departure of the UN would

453 • A Life Of Our Times

precipitate a frightful civil war, and with outside powers joining in, this would become a threat to world peace.

At ONUC we braced ourselves to withstand the attacks being made against us. With our depleted military strength, we regrouped our forces, while carrying on with our civilian aid programmes as best we could. Among our more noteworthy efforts was the training of large numbers of young Congolese in district administration and in running the various departments of government. Particularly successful was the progamme to send promising Congolese abroad for training in various fields. Yet ironically ONUC was declared an enemy.

To discredit the leadership of ONUC, a shocking fabrication was floated that India's very substantial contribution to the UN's effort was in return for a secret pact between Nehru and Lumumba for the settlement of two million Indians in the country. A searching enquiry produced incontrovertible proof that the rumour originated at the British Embassy and was given circulation by the British Vice-Consul. I made a strong protest to Ambassador Scott and sent a detailed report to the Secretary-General, who demanded an explanation from the British government. The offending Vice-Consul was recalled. This disgraceful episode involving a fellow member of the Commonwealth, illustrates the depths to which our detractors had resorted in order to malign us.

While ONUC could deal with the machinations of the Congolese, it was powerless to counter the powerful forces inciting them. The United States, still suffering acutely from communist-phobia, saw the danger of a 'communist takeover' in all kinds of improbable situations. It habitually equated nationalism with communism; from this arose its predilection for subservient military dictators the world over. Mobutu was therefore favoured over a democratically elected Prime Minister, the ANC over parliament, the rule of the gun over the rule of law.

Along with the attempt to throttle ONUC, a parallel scenario was developing. Kasavubu asked the Secretary-General for my recall, blaming ONUC for all the mayhem and mischief which was overtaking the country. He accused me of refusing to help in crushing Stanleyville by force. This demand came as a surprise as only the previous day Kasavubu had said that he would like to invite Susheela and me to a dinner in our honour! The Secretary-General rejected the demand outright, pointing out that the Special Representative was not accredited to the Congolese government but was a senior UN official under the special authority of the Secretary-General. He enjoyed the fullest confidence of the Secretary-General and had carried out his duties with meticulous care according to the rules and the mandate. Kasavubu returned to the charge a fortnight later and was again rebuffed by the Secretary-General in even stronger terms.

Kasavubu then tried another tack. His personal secretary called with a confidential message from his chief requesting that if only I were to give the word, the UN force could be deployed against Stanleyville and all would be well again. The President wished to assure me that he had nothing against me personally but was acting under 'heavy compulsions.' I had to explain again that what could not be done against Katanga could equally not be done against Stanleyville. This episode confirmed the suspicion that behind Kasavubu's unusual burst of epistolary energy, there were other forces goading him on. We at ONUC did not take these petulant complaints too seriously, as it was a not uncommon phenomenon for the Congolese to suddenly break off relations and then to resume them again.

The resumed session of the General Assembly was to meet in March and the Secretary-General was anxious for me to be present for it in order to press for more powers for ONUC. But before leaving I wished to ease the high tension that had built up. The reopening of the port of Matadi, where a UN Sudanese company had to surrender after an unequal battle forced on it by a much larger and heavily-armed ANC force, was a matter of top priority. After a series of meetings with the Ileo government, the blockade was eased and tension in Leopoldville palpably diminished.

I had been pressing Hammarskjold for an African deputy to relieve my heavy load. Just before my departure for New York a senior Sudanese official, Mekki Abbas arrived, and I felt I could safely leave him in charge. I had been requested by Hammarskjold to make a stopover in London to meet the Commonwealth Heads of State and governments there to attend a conference and to tell them about the Congo, which was hot news at the time. Accordingly, in London, I dutifully made my rounds. Nkrumah was in a hopeful mood, Tafewa Balewa of Nigeria somewhat critical; Diefenbaker of Canada helpful; Tunku Abdur Rahman of Malaysia most cooperative; Ayub Khan reproachful at my absence from Pakistan; Srimavo Bandarmayake interested in Congolese cannibalism; Edward Heath concerned only about the Belgians and strongly pro-Tshombe. But I did manage to get promises of much-needed troops and aircraft.

The long evening with Prime Minister Nehru at 'Broadlands', Lord Mountbatten's estate, was particularly significant. Susheela and I had been asked over to tea by Mountbatten—we actually stayed for dinner as well!—when I recounted my story to eager ears. Nehru questioned me closely about the situation. At the end he said the Operation must not be allowed to fail and the UN must be fully supported. He asked my opinion about Hammarskjold's pressing request for Indian troops; this I strongly backed. He agreed to send the troops but insisted that he would not allow them to be pushed around and further insisted on their being used effectively and given the requisite powers to do so. I could now carry with me to New York assurances of continued support of the Commonwealth countries and Nehru's agreement to the provision of a sorely-needed Indian brigade.

On the 38th floor at UN Headquarters the pace of frenzied activity continued unabated, the Secretary-General sparing neither himself nor his associates. The round of meetings and conferences continued relentlessly. Wherever I moved around in the building or even outside, I was accosted by eager delegates, journalists and others avid for information from the man at the epicentre of the turmoil. Submerged in Leopoldville, the brief cabled press summaries provided the most fragmentary idea of the world-wide storm brewing over our heads. Its full intensity and fury therefore came to me as a rude shock. It seemed inconceivable that so exacting a task being carried out in such difficult circumstances with a scrupulous regard for impartiality and fidelity to the Mandate and the Charter should be so misrepresented and represented and maligned. I therefore embarked on a round of interviews to try and dispel the miasma of prejudice and falsehood which was obscuring a correct understanding of the harsh reality.

My first interview was with Adlai Stevenson, widely reputed to be liberal-minded and intellectually honest. My meeting turned out to be a bitter disappointment and an insult both to his intelligence and to mine. After keeping me waiting for half an hour, the first question he put was about my health; he then asked if I was not finding the strain too great. I replied with due modesty that although the burden was no doubt heavy, it was not unbearable. Feigning continued solicitude for my health, the next question was whether I did not feel the need for a holiday. Changing tone, Stevenson feared that my long absence from Pakistan could not be good for Indo-Pakistani relations. The interview continued for a while in this puerile vein, not a question being asked about the Congo. Not only was I treated as a moron, but the reputed statesman, Stevenson, had exposed himself as a mountebank. I voiced my indignation to Hammarskjold who said that Stevenson, disappointed politician that he was, had obviously lost his bearings. He conveyed my feelings to Stevenson who soon thereafter invited me to lunch at the Waldorf along with his deputy and behaved in a civil and serious manner, discussing the Congo problem rationally and at length. This strange encounter gave me the measure of the prejudice and ignorance in high quarters that one was up against.

Mrs Eleanor Roosevelt, with whom I had served on the Human Rights Commission, was very sympathetic in a motherly kind of way and arranged a tea in her apartment with the Belgian Ambassador in Washington and a Belgian count who had extensive economic interests in the Congo. The Belgians were initially rather suspicious as the Belgian press and propaganda had portrayed me as a rather satanic character. I tried to reassure them that the UN had no sinister designs in their former colony and in fact would protect their legitimate interests. Averell Harriman was friendly as usual, but his influence in Washington seemed to be on the wane. I also addressed a meeting of the influential Foreign Policy Association where the response was not unfriendly.

What appalled me was the daily newspaper barrage on the Congo mission and the unprincipled attacks on me. It was clearly an orchestrated campaign of slander. The articles appearing daily were wholly divorced from the truth and full of innuendoes and fabrications. Many of the correspondents had been to the Congo to interview me and had probed around to find something damaging or sensational about the functioning of the mission. Finding nothing, they were reduced to personal attacks, slander and inventions. I was dubbed a cypto-communist, and even the celebrated cartoonist Herblock carried a cartoon in the *Washington Post* depicting me driving a jeep in the African jungle, blazing a trail for Khrushchev, in a bulldozer. Marguerite Higgins had a column in the *New York Herald Tribune* of the most vicious kind, while Joe Allsop, another well-known journalist, was also doing a hatchet job. It was almost reminiscent of the national hysteria of the McCarthy era, except that the full venom of the attacks was directed at one lone individual. While I could have fought back or persuaded face to face, I felt helpless against these invisible adversaries. It was profoundly depressing that hard and disinterested work performed in such perilous circumstances in the cause of peace and humanity, instead of receiving support, if not approbation, should be so maligned. But, all my colleagues, both in the Congo and in New York, stood by me to a man; the Secretary-General was unshakeable as a rock.

Continuing my efforts to educate our critics, I went down to Washington to meet as many people as I could. I first called on Chester Bowles, then Under Secretary of State, a former greatly-liked Ambassador to India and an old friend. He was most understanding and believed that 'no none could have done better', but he confided that it would be best for me to leave. He later disclosed that Kennedy had declared, at the end of one of his interminable and frustrating Congo sessions in reply to those of his advisers who were standing up for me: 'I don't care how good he is, but he must go.' For want of a coherent policy, the President had decided 'to make a clean sweep' of everyone, especially his own blundering Ambassador, Timberlake. My meeting with Dean Rusk, Secretary of State, was very different to the one before he took office. Rusk was cool and unreceptive and obviously had a closed mind. At a press conference I was plied with captious questions intended to ensnare me. Even the supreme pontiff of American journalism, Walter Lippman, showed less than his famed objectivity. Everyone seemed more obsessed with the phantom of communism than the fate of the UN or of the Congolese people. Although lip service was paid to the concept of parliament, in reality the aim was to ensure the supremacy of those subservient to western interests. Personalities meant more than principles.

In the midst of the depressing scenario, one event stands out in pleasant contrast—an invitation to a luncheon meeting in the Capitol with the Senate Foreign Affairs Sub-Committee on Africa. The Chairman, Senator Gore and twelve of his colleagues received Susheela and me warmly in the private dining room of the Senate. Influential Senators such as Hubert Humphrey, Stuart Symington, and Frank Church were present. I spoke about our plans for the reconvening of parliament and a return to legality, our programme of training and education and economic development. The Senators were most friendly and gave their hearty approval to what we were doing. Led by the Chairman, many of them made speeches of fulsome praise about our work for peace. Not a doubt was expressed, not a word of criticism uttered.

I also called on John Kenneth Galbraith, one of President Kennedy's inner circle, who had just been designated Ambassador to India—he was later to become a close and dear friend of a lifetime. From him I received coffee and much sympathy, but little else. My round of visits had left me no wiser as to the administration's policy towards the Congo mission. Not a word was said in support of the United Nations and the Secretary-General, while the attitude towards me was rather cool and equivocal. The only encouragement came from the Senators, but one did not know how much weight they would carry.

At New York a stream of cables passed up and down as I continued my vicarious stewardship of the mission. My deputy, Abbas, had run into difficulties both with Kasavubu and with ONUC staff. The Matadi affair, which seemed on the point of solution when I left, had encountered a series of road-blocks. To every proposal for the restoration of the port to UN control, Kasavubu countered with one puerile objection after another. Despite Hammarskjold's efforts at high levels to persuade the American and British envoys to use their influence with Kasavubu to fulfil his obligations, the envoys continued to sabotage the UN's efforts by backing Kasavubu's outrageous demands. At one point, Timberlake, in sheer panic and without any reference to Washington, ordered the American naval task force cruising along the West African coast to reverse course and sail to the mouth of the Congo river! President Kennedy blew up when he learnt from a press leak of this whimsical exploit, so typical of his unpredictable envoy. UN troops were finally able to return to Matadi after weeks of effort on the part of the Secretary-General.

Meanwhile, I had been working on a plan for the reconvening of parliament, which won general support among the delegates assembled for the resumed session of the General Assembly; the Congolese leadership too had already been prevailed upon to accept it.

Earlier, Kasavubu had conspired with Tshombe in an effort to undermine the UN, by calling a conference of Congolese factions in Tanarive, Madagascar. Under Tshombe's influence, it decided to break up the country into a couple of dozen autonomous states, loosely linked together as a confederation. On his return to Leopoldville, the belated realisation dawned on Kasavubu that, instead of undermining the UN, he had only succeeded in undermining himself. From being the President of the whole of the Congo, he would be reduced to becoming President of a tiny segment of the lower Congo region. To undo the shameful surrender to Tshombe, Kasavubu had at last agreed to the convening of parliament under certain safeguards.

At the resumed session of the General Assembly, after much debate and argumentation, two resolutions were adopted; one was proposed by twenty-one countries of Africa and Asia along with Yugoslavia, and the next by seventeen others. They called upon Belgium to withdraw military personnel and political advisers from the Congo, the release of all political prisoners, the recall of parliament and the appointment of another Conciliation Commission of seven members.

The Kennedy administration had been wobbling badly over

evolving a coherent Congo policy. Its initial brave intentions had been abandoned because of pressures from its allies and its own internal Congo lobbies and financial interests, as well as by the insidious voice of the CIA raised in alarm at any move towards a more liberal line. Abandoning principle and respect for the UN Charter and mandate, it succumbed to the malady of personalising what was essentially a political problem. American policy now boiled down to a change in the leadership of the UN mission and keeping out the Gizengists at all costs.

The Mobutu-Kasavubu clique warned that it would step up its attack on the UN unless 'the communist Dayal' was withdrawn. The western missions in Leopoldville endorsed the demand, even blaming me for provoking the fighting between the ANC and UN troops. Further, Timberlake gave a racist slant to the matter by imputing that I had a high-caste disdain for blacks.

President Kennedy was being briefed daily on the Congo situation. The State Department, now reconciled to the inevitability of the recall of parliament, determined to prevent a Lumumbist majority by fair means or foul. In a policy paper submitted to the President, it urged as a necessary condition that, 'we must intensify our efforts to prevent the return of Dayal, by direct representation with Nehru'. 'The Affaire Dayal' came to occupy much of the time and attention of the White House.

At the other end of the political spectrum, the countries of Asia and Africa supported me with equal vehemence, insisting that I stay and cautioning the Secretary-General against bowing to western pressures. In India, public support was unwavering and great was the indignation against the United States and its allies over the issue.

In the middle of this turmoil stood the Secretary-General, pulled from one side and pushed from the other. Adlai Stevenson was instructed to take up the mater urgently with him. When he did so, Hammarskjold reacted sharply, telling Stevenson that the 'over-the-table' attacks on him by the Soviets were no worse than the 'under-the-table attacks on Dayal.... Who would replace Dayal?' the Secretary-General asked; 'there were very few UN officials equally qualified or available'. He had declared earlier that he would not make a 'sacrificial offering' of one of his collaborators, either as 'an act of atonement or of appeasement'. The Secretary-General was also under intense pressure from Nehru, who insisted that the Special Representative must stay if the UN was to get the much-needed Indian Brigade.

The convening of the Congolese parliament was imminent, but a pro-western majority could not be ensured without the UN actively participating in suborning or intimidating the parliamentarians. The US administration was convinced—and rightly so—that I would never be a party to this. Dean Rusk, the Secretary of State, was therefore urgently flown to New Delhi to persuade Prime Minister Nehru. He began by explaining that 'the principal source of the difficulty had been an uncertain UN mandate' which prevented the Secretary-General himself from giving clear guidelines to his civil and military representatives. It was not surprising, Rusk remarked, that 'tempers, had worn thin ... that impatience and frustration had led to remarks which might have been later regretted....' Perhaps the Prime Minister 'might wish to suggest someone else'. Nehru had nothing to suggest except to reiterate that he was 'entirely opposed' to my recall. Rusk however chose to trivalise this by declaring that the issue had become a matter of prestige both for Prime Minister Nehru and Secretary-General Hammarskjold.

While the world-wide storm raged, I was torn between two extremes—whether to stay on doggedly or to leave with dignity. It went against the grain to give in to bullying or to run away from the post of duty. On the other hand, the unprincipled attacks filled me with revulsion. I had often discussed the issue with Hammarskjold, who would not hear of my leaving as he insisted that it would undermine his own position.

My six months' deputation to the UN was over, and it was

finally agreed with the Secretary-General that I should return to the Congo for a brief period to put the UN house in order and set arrangements in train for the convening of parliament. During my absence, Abbas had been caving in to the Kasavubu-Mobutu clique, showing subservience to the British Embassy and disregarding the Secretary-General's directive. Furthermore, he was losing control over the large UN civilian staff which was offended by his unseemly behaviour and style. Accordingly, the Secretary-General decided that Abbas' services would now be terminated. He was asked to pay his farewell calls and to present to Kasavubu the Secretary-General's letter informing him of my return for a limited period.

Kasavubu reacted hysterically to the message and threatened he would abrogate every agreement with the United Nations and obstruct its activities at every step. Mobutu was even more violent, and with threats and imprecations said he would turn his soldiers on all UN personnel and impose a state of war with the Organisation. Both said they would stop at nothing to prevent my setting foot on Congolese soil, Mobutu even threatening assassination.

Abbas' message arrived late at night and I was hurriedly summoned from a dinner party to a midnight conference with the Secretary-General and his principal advisers. There was a long minute of silence while I read the message. I could see from Hammarskjold's expression that he felt defeated; his detractors had played their trump card. I said it was no longer a question of political pressures in New York, but of basic considerations about the sheer physical survival of ONUC and the safety of its personnel. While I understood the Secretary-General's reluctance to relieve me in the face of political intrigues motivated by Cold War considerations, the situation now was one of jeopardising the lives and honour of all UN officials in the Congo. I could never forgive myself for killings or outrages against UN personnel as the price others would have to pay for my return.

Nor could I be party to the collapse of the Operation to which so much toil had been devoted by the Secretary-General and his colleagues. While I was grateful to the Secretary-General for his steadfast support he would surely not wish to jeopardise the future of the mission and the lives of its personnel.

Now that a decision had been taken, there was a palpable reduction in the tension that had been building up over the last several weeks. Hammarskjold said he felt deep revulsion at the intrigues which had led to my decision. I cabled Prime Minister Nehru about my resignation and the circumstances which necessitated it. I also urged that the Indian brigade should nevertheless not be withdrawn. In reply, Mr Nehru acquiesced in my decision but deeply regretted the circumstances. He agreed to retain the Indian troops in the Congo.

In a press note, the Secretary-General expressed his 'full gratitude' for my service to the Organisation and announced that no new Special Representative would be appointed. The work of ONUC would henceforth be the direct responsibility of UN Headquarters, while an Officer-in-Charge would look after the day-do-day affairs of the mission.

My mission in the Congo ended on 27 May 1961. News of my resignation created a sensation and made headlines throughout the world. In most African and Asian countries the western powers were roundly blamed for imposing their will on the Secretary-General. In India there was an outburst of anger and a deep sense of outrage. There was a torrent of questions in Parliament which reflected the popular mood. To reassure the nation of his government's support of the mission and its leadership, Nehru replied:

So far as Shri Rajeshwar Dayal is concerned, he left his mark wherever he worked as a very able person and he is respected in the UN and in the Congo in spite of many people criticising him there, and he came away with great dignity.

Announcing my resignation, the UN Secretary-General in a statement said:

> It is with reluctance and great regret that I have to accept his resignation for it is my firm conviction that he has carried out his United Nations responsibilities with the highest ability, equalled by loyalty to the purposes of the UN and unfailing integrity.

The Secretary-General tried to persuade me to accept a senior advisery position in the Organisation, but I was anxious to resume my interrupted work in Pakistan.

My critics, having found nothing concrete to go by, tried to ferret out something disparaging from the UN staff in the Congo. In this connection, Brian Urquhart (later Sir), who was one of my principal political assistants in the Congo, notes as follows in his celebrated biography of Hammarskjold:

> The accusations against Dayal were greatly exaggerated and painful. It was said that he was arrogant and high-handed and did not sympathise sufficiently with the Congolese ... Hammarskjold shared the unanimous view of Dayal's Secretariat colleagues that he was an immensely able, high-minded and dedicated man of rare integrity and courage. Dayal's plight was largely the result of having served loyally and unswervingly the Secretary-General's directives and policies, and Hammarskjold was determined to support him to the ultimate possible limit.

My decision to leave was received with much relief by our many American friends who had been greatly worried about our personal safety as they had no illusions about the capacity of the Congolese to carry out their threats. They had worked indefatigably with the press and politicians on our behalf. The President of the UN General Assembly, Frederick Boland of Ireland, told us that he felt greatly alarmed as our return to the

Congo would have meant 'certain death'. Most touching was Hammarskjold's concern. A man of indomitable courage himself, he never worried about his personal safety or that of his colleagues. But he now said that he had been very anxious and would never have forgiven himself if any harm had befallen us.

Yet, I can say in all honesty that the physical danger of returning to the Congo never crossed my mind or influenced my decision to resign. This was not because of some blind fatalism or sheer foolhardiness, as sceptics may be inclined to think. I was conscious of a deep sense of protection, of a 'presence' in whose aura I lived and breathed. There was a sense of guidance which helped me to overcome crisis after crisis. Susheela shared this conviction with me. She insisted on sharing my lot, and her cheerful presence put heart into many a wavering spirit. We would often take an evening walk along the river, accompanied by a single UN security guard. We drove around freely to receptions and functions. My timings for going to office and back, and the route I took were common knowledge. We did not alter our routine throughout our stay in Leopoldville. Susheela's unshakeable courage, a manifestation of her deep faith, never ceased to win the respect and admiration of my colleagues, many of whom were breaking down under the strain. Susheela's faith and my conviction about the purity of my motives and action gave us the courage to stand up in defence of principles over expediency, and never sacrificing means to meet a desired end. How else, but for this faith, could a mere individual have stood up to the sustained pressure and intrigues of great powers and the daily fare of threats and crises? This may be thought too idealistic an attitude, but the United Nations is itself founded on principles of the highest idealism, and those called upon to serve under it should work in the spirit of the organisation and uphold to the best of their capacity its high principles and objectives.

Some two weeks after my departure, when the moral issue was still being fiercely debated, Hammarskjold composed a poem dated 18 June 1961, evidently inspired by the imagery of recent events which led to his musing on their impact on his own fate. The Americans and British, the prime movers in my case, were known to be hostile to Hammarskjold as well, for they could not bend him to their will. While their fire was concentrated against me, they could not, at the same time, attack Hammarskjold, a fellow Westerner. That task was being performed by the Soviets. But four months later, Hammarskjold was driven to his death in the jungles of Central Africa by similar compulsions. He wrote:

> He will come out
> Between two warders
> Lean and sunburnt,
> A little bent,
> As if apologising
> For his strength,
> His features tense,
> But looking quite calm.

> He will take off his jacket
> And with shirt torn open,
> Stand up against the wall
> To be executed.

> He has not betrayed us,
> He will meet his end
> Without weakness.
> When I feel anxious,
> It is not for him.
> Do I feel a compulsion in me
> To be so destroyed?
> Or is there someone
> In the depths of my being
> Awaiting for permission
> To pull the trigger?

It had been put out in some western circles that Hammarskjold had insisted on the removal of the American and British Ambassadors in the Congo as the price for my simultaneous recall. The fact, however, is that the Secretary-General had himself frequently complained to their governments about their envoys' obstructive attitudes. In Timberlake's case, President Kennedy too wanted to get rid of him. Nehru had also complained to the British government against the calumny spread by the British Embassy in Leopoldville about a secret pact between Nehru and Lumumba for the emigration of two million Indians to the Congo.

On my departure, Hammarskjold put the senior civilian official in Leopoldville, Sture Linner, in charge of the mission, even though earlier, when someone had been needed to hold the fort during my ten days' absence in New York, Linner had been passed over as too weak and indecisive. Linner soon came under the spell of his deputy, Mahmoud Khiari, a scheming and forceful Tunisian, and was virtually reduced to playing second-fiddle to him.

The plan drawn up by me for convening parliament in a safe venue—the campus of Lovanium University—where the deputies would be insulated from blandishments and threats by UN troops and an electrified wire fence, was soon set in motion. But with a difference, for Linner had made himself such a pliant tool of the US Embassy that the US Chargé d'Affaires reported him as being 'extremely cooperative' and, indeed, 'pro-United States in outlook', maintaining 'day-to-day and hour-to-hour' communications with the Embassy.

I had been recommending Cyrille Adoula as the most mature and moderate Congolese politician who could command general acceptance, a recommendation which the Kennedy administration had accepted. When parliament met, Gizenga and the Stanleyville deputies attended in force, but Tshombe kept away, despite western pressures. It soon became evident that the Gizengists would command a majority, an outcome which the Americans were determined to prevent by all possible means, even by overthrowing the entire parliamentary process and getting Mobutu to install a military dictatorship. The ingenious Colonel Devlin again came to the rescue by discovering a sewer which ran from the campus to beyond the boundary fence. Through this sewer, the CIA, aided by Linner and Khiari, who had free access to the campus, siphoned large funds to bribe the waverers and the greedy among the Congolese politicians. The strategem worked and Adoula was elected. It was hailed in America and Europe as a great triumph for democracy and a signal victory over communism! Indeed, a senior White House adviser, George Ball, declared: 'It was an act of faith in the democratic process.' So much for democracy!

Much praise was lavished upon Linner for his full participation in the strategem, one high American official declaring in his enthusiasm that Linner 'was a natural candidate for the 1961 Nobel Peace Prize'. Such exuberant encomiums served only to fire exaggerated ambitions, which led to disastrous consequences for ONUC and tragedy for the United Nations.

Enthused by their performance in cobbling together the Adoula government, ONUC's leadership contrived by a daring stroke and somewhat fancifully to try ending the secession of Katanga, a task that had hitherto baffled all efforts by the Secretary-General and ONUC. Khiari was flown across the country to Elizabethville to organise, under cover of the 21 February resolution, the expulsion of all foreign mercenaries by the use of force. The UN representative in Katanga, Connor Cruise O'Brien, was falsely given to understood that the operation had the sanction of the. Secretary-General. The operation, code-name 'Morthor', met fierce resistance from the start, with heavy casualties on both sides. Continued fighting found the UN troops greatly outmatched and badly prepared. An Irish UN company suffered heavy casualties and was forced to surrender. The whole rash enterprise had resulted in unmitigated disaster.

On the very day on which the military adventure had been launched, 13 September 1961, the Secretary-General had emplaned for Leopoldville in accordance with an earlier plan to bolster Adoula's shaky coalition and to inspect ONUC's work under the new arrangement. It was only on arrival that he learnt with alarm the facts of the situation. The action was totally unauthorised and was in flagrant violation of the Secretary-General's express directions. The expulsion of foreign military personnel had to be effected peacefully, if possible, or with the minimum use of force, and only in self-defence. Furthermore, any initiative in the use of force was expressly prohibited, it could not be used to effect a political solution.

Hammarskjold's immediate concern was to put a stop to the fighting and avoid further bloodshed. He sent urgent pleas to Tshombe, suggesting an immediate ceasefire and negotiations, but Tshombe, flushed with victory, was not listening. Belgium and its western allies were in full cry, denouncing the UN for committing 'aggression'. On the question of responsibility for the disaster, O'Brien in Elizabethville said action had been taken under Khiari's explicit instructions, Khiari said he had been authorised by Linner. But Linner, straining credulity, denied all responsibility. Even the Force Commander, General McKeowan, had been kept totally in the dark.

The British government accused Hammarskjold of a breach of faith in resorting to offensive military action to subdue Katanga instead of employing political means, as promised. It also threatened to withdraw all support from ONUC if it did not receive satisfaction. Dean Rusk, on behalf of the US government, expressed dismay and joined in demanding an end to the fighting. The Secretary-General was peremptorily called upon to enter into direct negotiations for a ceasefire and to stay in the Congo until it was achieved. Hammarskjold was well aware that, with

Tshombe riding high, he would be at a grave disadvantage. He therefore cabled Ralph Bunche in New York to arrange for a couple of jet fighters from Ethiopia which could be used to ground Tshombe's Fouga aircraft which were pounding UN positions. The British government, however, declined to give permission for their overflight. Word arrived that Lord Lansdowne, a junior minister in the Foreign Office, was arriving in Leopoldville, obviously to keep up pressure on the Secretary-General.

Hammarskjold had been put in an impossible position and he knew that both his future and that of the United Nations was at stake. He therefore embarked on the desperate venture to negotiate with the outlaw, Tshombe, in the unfriendly territory of Rhodesia, with Lansdowne breathing down his neck. His plane crashed in the jungle as he was nearing his destination in circumstances that have never been discovered or revealed. Thus ended the life of one who had dedicated himself unreservedly to the service of peace and whose unique contribution to the cause of international understanding will be a landmark in mankind's march towards a better world.

Adoula's ramshackle government lasted less than two uneasy years. Adoula was followd by Tshombe, to whom Kasavubu had surrendered the reins of power. But that government proved to be even more unstable and collapsed under the weight of its own dissensions. Once again, Mobutu seized power quite unbashedly and clamped a military dictatorship on the country. The magic of Lumumba's name was still potent and with brazen hypocricy Mobutu seized upon it to endow his ussurpation of power with a pretence of legitimacy. Proclaiming his former patron, whom he had consigned to a cruel death, a 'national hero', Mobutu declared: 'Glory and Honour to that illustrious Congolese, that great African, the first martyr of our economic independence ....'
He has since erected a great statue, which has become a national icon, to the man he had martyred. Mobutu's ruthless dictatorship

has lasted over twenty-five years and may continue as long as he does. To proclaim his own nationalist credentials, he styles himself as Field Marshal President Sesen Seko Mobutu. He had forbidden the Catholic clergy by decree from baptising any child with a European name under pain of five years' imprisonment. As further proof of his nationalism, the name of the country and the name of all the towns have been changed.

Whatever may have been Mobutu's contribution in winning the Cold War for the west, only those who had nurtured him would know the truth. But so far as the unfortunate Congolese people and the outside world are concerned, the results are there for all to see. Mobutu, from being a penniless ex-clerk in 1960, is today reputed to be one of the richest men in the world. His ill-gotten fortune is computed at over three billion US dollars, and he owns palatial residences in Belgium, France, Switzerland and elsewhere, besides palaces in the Congo (since re-named Zaire, after a Portuguese coin).

And what of the people? The Congo, one of the richest countries of Africa at the time of independence, is today one of the poorest. It is estimated that real wages have fallen to a bare ten per cent of the 1960 level. Every year thousands of children die of malnutrition. All foreign-owned plantations and small businesses were nationalised and handed over to inexpert Congolese favourites, with the result that the system of production and distribution has collapsed. The great Union Miniere and other mining companies were nationalised, but as the Congolese could not run them they were handed back to foreign engineers. All schools were nationalised, displacing the Catholic missionaries, but as there were not enough teachers the educational system too has collapsed. The International Monetary Fund was called upon to rescue the country: its experts found that the all-pervasive corruption was one of the prime causes of the country's bankruptcy. Mobutu and his cronies were helping themselves to no less than forty per cent of the national revenue.

Corruption extends to every corner of the country and affects the life of every citizen. In the bloated army, the officers pocketed the pay of the soldiers and the soldiers, in turn, extorted money from the people.

All political activity has been ruthlessly suppressed and politicians eliminated by one means or another, never to be seen or heard of again. The dictator's word is the law of the land. The country has become a personal fiefdom of Mobutu, no less absolute than that of Leopold II.

It was not the aim of the United Nations to make the country safe for dictatorship. It sought to ensure the unity, integrity and stability of the country, to instil respect for the constitution and rule of law, to strengthen democratic institutions, to restore the administrative structure, to rehabilitate the economy and to train the Congolese in the arts of governance. In four years of unremitting toil the United Nations managed not only to prevent civil war but a wider conflagration. The parliamentary process was revived and the reins of government handed over to an elected ministry. But this was accomplished at great cost in blood, toil and treasure. The task was performed with a tenacity that defined the machinations of the power blocks and the mindless hostility of the beneficiaries themselves. Sadly, all this was overturned at one blow by the usurpation of power by a ruthless western-promoted dictator.

Contrast ONUC's efforts with the failed United Nations mission in Somalia. It was led by an American Admiral who commanded a larger force than did ONUC, and which had awesome fire-power, including helicopter gunships and all manner of armoured vehicles. It enjoyed the unquestioned political support of the entire membership of the United Nations and its task was a purely humanitarian one: to bring an end to the prevailing famine. The UN Force included large American and European contingents, besides those from Asia and Africa. An extraordinary feature was that the UN was supported by a heavily armed American force, not under UN command but functioning on its own. Yet, after the first American UN casualties, the whole nature of the operation was transformed; instead of a peace-making humanitarian mission, it became a military expedition to wage war on those whom it had come to serve. And the war aim was reduced to a single issue: the personalised one of capturing, dead or alive, General Aidid, one of the faction leaders. That aim was never accomplished and, as further casualties occurred, the Americans and Europeans withdrew from the operation, leaving others to carry on. So unrewarding and exacting did Washington discover its first experience of UN peace-keeping to be, that no US contribution of ground troops to the UN is likely in the future. Even though the Indian contingent suffered heavy casualties, it held fast to the very end.

The fact that the United Nations mission in the Congo, bereft of political support, denied adequate funds and beset with difficulties on all sides, hung on tenaciously for over four tumultuous years, is little short of a miracle of endurance. But it called for even more than moral and physical courage. It demanded blood sacrifices. The first to be sacrificed was that African patriot, Patrice Lumumba. The next was the foremost servant of humanity, the apostle of peace, Dag Hammarskjold. But many people, Congolese and in the United Nations, have shared their fate. Ralph Bunche barely managed to escape with his life: Brian Urquhart, though viciously injured, was rescued in the nick of time. And if the author, although unbroken in body but scarred in spirit, was spared a similar fate, it was not because of any solicitude on the part of the Congolese or their foreign mentors, but because destiny had willed otherwise.

# THIRTEEN

# Midwifery in Zimbabwe

In December 1979, an envoy arrived from London with an urgent message from the Commonwealth Secretary-General, Sir Sridath Ramphal. It was a request to me to accept the Chairmanship of a group of 'independent and experienced' persons to observe and monitor the Independence elections shortly to be held in the rebel colony of Southern Rhodesia.

The problem of the liberation of Southern Rhodesia was an exceptionally difficult and obstinate one. The colony had been founded by that arch-imperialist, Cecil Rhodes, who by a mixture of force and fraud, had appropriated one vast territory after another from the chiefs and tribes in the latter part of the nineteenth century during the great land grab of Africa by the European powers. The colony soon attracted immigrants from Britain because of its equable climate, vast open spaces, fertile soil and abundant opportunities. By dint of their labour and enterprise, in the space of some seventy years the colony was endowed with a network of roads, railways, electricity, well-planned cities, etc. Huge farms, expertly run, modern factories, trade and business, flourished. But the local population of some seven million remained poor, backward, and under-privileged, while the two hundred and twenty thousand settlers prospered greatly. When the winds of change swept over Africa in the early 60s, the British colony of southern Rhodesia stood out as an exception. A group of white settlers usurped power from the faltering British colonial authority and made a unilateral declaration of independence. This flagrant act of rebellion received only mild reproof from the British government, but it aroused world-wide indignation. In the colony itself, the nationalist parties took to arms and in the ensuing conflict no quarter was given by either side. The situation in Southern Rhodesia was hotly debated year after year at the United Nations and at gatherings of Commonwealth leaders, where it became a sharply divisive and acrimonious issue.

The British government, unwilling to take any action against the white settlers pleaded that it no longer had any control or jurisdiction over its former colony. This plea was almost unanimously rejected by the international community as legally and factually untenable. But the only corrective or punitive action which the United Nations could take was to impose sanctions on the recalcitrant colony.

While the Labour governments made some infructuous attempts to bring around Ian Smith, the self-styled 'prime minister', the Conservative Party backed the usurper regime, and Prime Minister Margaret Thatcher made little attempt to conceal her sympathy for Smith.

The civil war, which had been raging with ever-increasing ferocity for seven years, was going badly for the Smith regime. The nationalist guerrilla fighters were within bombing distance of the capital, Salisbury, and had blown up oil and petrol tanks in the outskirts. In an attempt to give the regime a less blatantly racist colour, a constitution was devised in which the legislature contained some Africans, mostly tribal chiefs, and some of the more humiliating aspects of racial discrimination were modified.

Ian Smith co-opted a pliant cleric, Bishop Abel Muzorewa, into the administration and renamed the territory Zimbabwe Rhodesia. This 'internal settlement' of March 1978 settled nothing, and the war continued with undiminished virulence.

It was against this sombre background that the Commonwealth leaders met in Lusaka, Zambia, in August 1979, almost within earshot of the fighting in the adjacent territory. While Thatcher still tried to cling to the spurious Smith-Muzorewa combine, her Foreign Secretary, Lord Carrington, had a greater sense of realism and urgency. Under pressure from Kenneth Kaunda, President of the host country, the full backing of Malcome Fraser, Prime Minister of Australia, the persuasive powers of Lord Carrington and the deft diplomacy of Sridath Ramphal, Mrs Thatcher was ultimately compelled to come to terms with reality. The Lusaka Accord recognised the principle of independence on the basis of majority rule following free and fair elections. It set in train processes that brought the major protagonists to Lancaster House in London, where they engaged in what was perhaps one of the longest unbroken conferences on the constitutional future of a country. Meanwhile, the war continued with unabated intensity even as the belligerents faced each other at the conference table in endless argument. The final agreement covered the terms of an independence constitution, a ceasefire, and detailed pre-independence arrangements, including elections.

The British government ultimately accepted responsibility as the colonial power, and a British Governor with full legal, legislative and executive powers assumed office in the middle of December 1979. The Governor was Lord Soames, the son-in-law of Winston Churchill, a junior minister in the Thatcher government.

Elections preceding independence had been the normal pattern in the evolution of former colonies to full nationhood. But the circumstances attending the Zimbabwe elections on the basis of 'One man, one vote', were far from normal. The elections were to take to place in the immediate aftermath of the long civil war which only eight weeks before had spluttered to a cease-fire. Effective observance of the cease-fire was, however doubtful. The armies had not been disarmed, nor had their deep mistrust of each other been dispelled. Martial law was in force, but over large parts of the country the writ of the authorities had ceased to run. Conditions for the holding of elections would be far from normal. It was, therefore, with considerable misgiving that I had accepted the assignment against which the odds were so heavily loaded.

I arrived in London in the middle of January 1980. My first meeting was with Shridath Ramphal. Ramphal was most articulate, a diplomat to his fingertips and possessed of great energy and ability. From his extensive briefing, it was clear that the functions of the mission would be far more extensive than what its rather anodyne title of 'Commonwealth Observer Group' might suggest. The next morning I was received at the vast and gloomy Foreign Office by Lord Carrington who emphasised that our mission was integral to the Lancaster House Agreement and offered assurances of the full cooperation of the British government.

Soon my ten colleagues began to assemble from different quarters of the globe. As Chairman, I had been invited in my personal capacity, but all the others had been appointed by their governments. They were a very varied group drawn from different walks of life, but all were men of distinction and experience—a Cabinet Minister, two senior Ambassadors, Chief Election Commissioners, Supreme and High Court Judges, etc. All were very conscious of the seriousness of the task which lay ahead.

The British press, by and large, was very sceptical and caustic about our Group, commenting that a body whose members were drawn from countries with wholly different political systems could hardly be expected to arrive at coherent findings, far less unanimity, on the forthcoming election. The secretarial staff had preceded us to Salisbury and the full Group was in position by 21 January.

My first call was on the Governor, Lord Soames, who received me rather pompously, and with much ceremony. He thanked me for my message sent to him from New Delhi and assured me that we would receive full cooperation from him and the administration in our work. After the formal exchanges he said he would like to have a word in private, without the presence of our assistants. He began in a confidential manner to emphasise that much depended upon the success of the enterprise for the future of the country and its people. It would be disastrous if a one-party Marxist regime were to emerge as the winner; the best hope lay in a Smith-Muzorewa government which alone could lead the country to prosperity in freedom, and he very much hoped that such a result could be ensured. Rather surprised at this not-so-suitable suggestion, I replied that everything would depend upon the result of the poll and one could not anticipate it. We were both committed to the goal of free and fair elections and I was sure we would both work in harmony to achieve it. I greatly hoped also that everything would be done to hold the scales even and the occasion would never arise for me to be compelled to declare the election as not having been free and fair. This greatly alarmed Soames, who pleaded that it should never be allowed to happen as it would ruin his career as a politician. I pointed out that if that unfortunate contingency were to arise, which heaven forbid, the consequences to the country would be disastrous. The civil war would be resumed with even greater virulence and he would be compelled to flee by the first aircraft, with me following close on his heels as we would both be fair game!

From this strange interview I came away with the uneasy feeling that Prime Minister Thatcher and her chosen Governor were not really reconciled to the agreement reached at Lancaster House. We needed therefore to be doubly vigilant.

In our briefing by the Secretary-General on our terms of reference, he had laid great stress on the fact that we were an integral part of the Lusaka Accord, in the absence of which there would have been no Lancaster House Agreement at all. We were the representatives of the Commonwealth as a whole, which would rely exclusively on our judgement about the integrity of the poll. We would be performing a good-offices function, and by the very process of observing and bringing shortcomings to the notice of the administering power, we would be performing a custodial role on behalf of the Commonwealth. In that sense, ours would be a constraining and corrective influence. The election was being held in the most unusual circumstances; the weapons of war had not yet cooled; the air was loud with angry accusations; the cease-fire was precarious and uncertain; large numbers of refugees were yet to return; in short, the situation was teetering on a razor's edge. The task would therefore be heavily fraught with difficulty and danger.

From start to finish, the Group functioned with great harmony. It was decided that we should fan out across the country in attempting to fulfil our task. Each member could take with him an assistant of his own nationality; otherwise all the teams would be mixed to avoid any suspicion of national bias. But we would all interview leaders of political parties, officials and concerned citizens, etc. together. The Group decided unanimously that to avoid questioning at cross-purposes, only the Chairman would interrogate visitors. After the members had dispersed to their posts, the Group as a whole would re-assemble at week-ends to share its experiences.

We interviewed the leaders of all political parties, big and small, except Bishop Muzorewa who had decided to keep away. The ablest and most articulate was Robert Mugabe, who made a very favourable impression on us. In reply to my very first and pointed question as to whether he was a communist by conviction, as depicted by the western press, he replied in measured terms that his sole aim was the improvement of the condition of his people. He was prepared to borrow from any 'ism', without being an adherent of any, even from Catholicism, a faith to which he belonged. His replies to all other questions were equally thoughtful, well-reasoned and moderate.

Joshua Nkomo's ZIPRA warriors had fought in collaboration with Mugabe's ZANLA fighters, but the two leaders had already begun to drift apart. Nkomo complained about Mugabe's men setting upon his followers and beating them up. He seemed to nurture the hope of coming out on top in the contest for leadership of the country after independence. Later, when we saw him after the election, he sat slumped in his vast armchair like a deflated balloon, his great frame wracked by sobs. The British regarded him somewhat indulgently, and when Mrs Thatcher was reported to have observed that she could just about stomach him, it was presumed she would find Mugabe too indigestible!

The other leaders were also quite well-educated and stated their cases well, but all were lost causes. We never met Ian Smith, who had retired to his vast and prosperous farm. But the spokesman of the European Rhodesian Front was much less rabid than might have been expected. The church groups were well-informed and liberal in their outlook.

Of special interest was our interview with General Peter Walls, Commander of Combined Military Operations. There had been ugly rumours that should the election result be adverse, he would stage a coup and call in South African forces to reinstate white supremacy. To my pointed question on this matter, the General emphatically denied any such unworthy intention. He was a professional soldier, he said, and had no political ambitions. He gave his word as a soldier that he would serve loyally under any government that came to power. This unsolicited oath of loyalty startled and impressed us. But the oath was soon to be broken. The General was defeated and fled to South Africa, where he spoke out strongly against the new regime in Zimbabwe, threatening its overthrow. Other Rhodesian officials were, however, more honest and forthright.

My first impressions about our surroundings, despite the smouldering, and often erupting, hatreds, were of a very pleasant and salubrious country. The wide tree-lined avenues, the orderly and prosperous-looking commercial area, the vast, well-tended parks, the elegant bungalows with their fine gardens and swimming pools, could be the envy of any country. We were all put up in fine hotels and provided with excellent transport. There did not seen to be any particular shortages despite fears of sanctions; there was an abundance in the shops and restaurants. As I travelled around the country on my tours of inspection, I initially marvelled at how much had been accomplished in the short span of some seventy years of colonial rule. Most of the main roads were tarred and, despite the highly disturbed conditions, still in fairly good condition. The small towns which dotted the countryside were well-planned and well-endowed with shops, restaurants, comfortable hotels and good housing. The 'commercial' farms, as they were called, owned by the European settlers, were meticulously maintained, and produced an annual surplus of a million tons of grain, mostly maize, for export.

But on the other hand, African workers lived in barracks on the estates, while the 'tribal trust lands', inhabited by the indigenous inhabitants, were little more than unkempt bush, with indifferent plantings of maize and thatched one-room huts which looked poor and wretched. No wonder the opulent neighbouring farms excited the cupidity of the latter and led to occasional murders of the white farmers. The segregation of the indigenous people from the white population and racial discrimination were as rampant as in South Africa. Nowhere were Africans to be seen in the hotels or other establishments, except in menial occupations. By nightfall, all had to make themselves scarce from the city and return to their own township, located miles away. Black Africans seen loitering around after dark found themselves in the lock-up. As a result, social entertainment by the whites was done in daylight hours when the servants were available; for dinner parties, special permits had to be obtained from the police for the servants to remain after dark. The African township was crowded and its housing basic. The appearance of African and Asian guests comprising our Group in the still racially-exclusive hotels excited a good deal of disapproving attention.

The fairly considerable Indian community, almost all Gujaratis and among Gujaratis, almost all Patels, fell into neither category. The Indian township lay beyond the confines of the main city. They were an opulent community and had built an opulent township to match, with ornate and ostentatious houses, garishly furnished. They had set up a big school named 'The Gujarati School'. They held a well-attended reception for me, with speeches. The Indians were rather ambivalent about their prospects after independence, being well content with the present dispensation. Unlike their brethren in neighbouring South Africa, they had kept aloof from any political activity, confining themselves with single-minded devotion to the safer business of money-making.

The world of make-believe in which the ruling class lived was vividly illustrated by the media—the press, radio and television. One never saw an African face on the television screen, never heard an African name on radio or saw mention of any African in the press. It was as though Africans did not exist at all. The television showed elegant garden parties, reminiscent of the Victorian era, with ladies in picture hats and gloves being served tea on manicured lawns by liveried servants. Or there would be long shots of gymkhanas, horse-races, other sports and similar frivolities. There was never a mention of the impending elections which would inevitably overturn this topsy-turvy world. The media, including the newspapers, were largely owned by

South African interests, the Argus Press in particular. The three nationalist newspapers had long since been banned. But beneath this facade of a good life, lay a deep sense of insecurity. Everyone, including women, carried a weapon. Hotels had check-in counters for arms rather than for valuables. Women wheeling infants or going to swimming pools were observed carrying arms. Military service was compulsory for young and old. It was an embattled society of some two hundred and twenty thousand trying to hold back the tide of a discontented seven million who surrounded them.

The practice originated by western nations of categorising human beings, nations and even whole civilisations on the basis of their supposed colour must be deplored. To label human beings, who, according to Christian doctrine are cast in the image of God, on the basis of pigmentation offends both religion and our common humanity. Nor are racist descriptions valid as there are no 'pure' races, only admixtures. Another pernicious usage is to compartmentalise the world as First, Second and Third, again revealing the same attitude of inherent superiority. At a time when in the United Nations and among enlightened people the world over, the concept of 'One World' and 'World Brotherhood' is a guiding principle, it is a reactionary and backward-looking attitude that tries to divide the globe into segments. Unfortunately, it is a trap into which the 'developing' countries have themselves unthinkingly fallen.

I had been invited to hold a press conference and, after introducing my colleagues and giving a resume of our status and functions, questions were invited. The hall was packed with journalists, mostly from abroad. All was going smoothly until a rather belligerent questioner raised captious questions regarding the private armies maintained by most politicians. Obviously a Muzorewa adherent, he took umbrage at an innocent remark concerning the Bishop's private army, the so-called 'auxiliaries'.

We invited all the leading politicians and a large number of officials, concerned individuals and organisations to meet us. All except Bishop Murzorewa replied in the affirmative. Charging us with partiality and partisanship, he refused to meet us except towards the end when things were going badly for him; he then threw out feelers, but by then, we were not interested. Through these interviews we gathered a large cross-section of opinion, but the real insights came from our personal observations and extensive tours throughout the country.

Although Britain had assumed constitutional responsibility for the country, its control of the administration was only notional. The same District Officers remained in position, the Secretariat was run by the same civil servants, the laws and regulations underwent only token amendment, command of the army continued as before. The Governor's authority was dependent on the compliance of an administration which had loyally served the previous regime. Even the former ministers were not given their quietus; they retained their designations, official residences, pay and perquisites; in return they surrendered their powers. The Governor had an assortment of British advisers and other functionaries, some from the Foreign Office, who were to assist in the task of overseeing the all-Rhodesian administration.

The entire election process was to be telescoped within the space of some two and a half months from the date of the ceasefire, in accordance with a time-table laying down the different stages. The question of primordial importance underlying all these arrangements was how effective the cease-fire would be and how long it would hold. In this respect the Monitoring Force did a remarkable job. There was to be no disarming of the nationalist forces, and on the call of their leaders they were to assemble at designated camps. After independence they would be absorbed in the national security services. Each of these camps was supervised by a handful of officers who kept the sullen and suspicious guerrillas occupied with games and sports to ensure that they did not riot or break out. However, there remained many armed bands in the field and skirmishes with the security forces were frequent. Country roads were often strewn with mines and lurking snipers were not uncommon. The newspapers continued to publish communiques from 'Combined Operations' giving lurid details of the daily head count of those killed or captured.

Our multi-national supporting staff was drawn from the Commonwealth Secretariat and was headed by Manmohan Malhoutra. It included legal, media, editorial and security advisers. Half a dozen assistants and stenographers completed the team. Malhoutra was a man of considerable ability and resource and his hand-picked team gave an excellent account of itself. The eleven observers were each accompanied by several assistants, one or two of their own nationality. I had selected Girish Mehra, a very able and energetic officer, competent and devoted, who rose to be a Secretary to the Government of India and retired as High Commissioner to Canada. The other assistant was a senior official of the intelligence services, Keki Daruwalla, a sensitive poet, a man of grit, determination and sense of humour, who functioned cheerfully and effectively in outlying places.

As the election drew near, we added another thirty assistants to our number. We were able to cover all but one of the fifty-five districts in the country. At four provincial headquarters we set up offices under senior observers, almost all of whom remained in the field. The Chairman stayed in Salisbury to maintain contact with the Governor and to coordinate the work of the mission.

I frequently went out on inspection tours by road; sometimes I travelled by a tiny plane, which seemed to have been held together by sheer will-power alone! My most adventurous trips were into the tribal trust territories which lacked proper roads and were heavily mined. The mode of transport was by a fearsome-looking contraption. The wheels were slung on a very long chassis and there was a capsule in the middle where the driver and a passenger or two sat strapped in tandem with steel helmets on, the lid being clamped down on them. One felt like a sardine sealed in a tin. It heated up like an oven in the burning sun, the noise was deafening, and one was soon coated from head to foot by a thick layer of red dust which filled the capsule to suffocation. This contraption was considered to afford some protection from exploding mines: when the front wheels struck a mine, the mine would blow up, flinging the capsule a good distance away. One hoped thus to escape with one's life, though not without a fractured skull! Although I led the convoy of three such vehicles, there was fortunately no occasion to put its qualities to the test! One of our colleagues was less lucky but his experience resulted only in shock, deafness and bruises.

On inspection trips we normally met the District Officers, all of British origin, whose official residences and offices were on a much more modest scale than ours in India. The young officers received us correctly, but not with much enthusiasm. Considering they would soon be facing an uncertain future, they were remarkably self-possessed, stoically performing their duties to the last.

The nationalist leaders had trickled back from exile after the cease-fire; of the principal leaders, while Joshua Nkomo returned in good time, Robert Mugabe, who commanded a much larger force, was not able to do so until just a fortnight or so before polling day. The opposition leaders charged that South African troops continued to remain in the country in flagrant violation of the Lancaster House Agreement; that the whole weight of the official machinery and of laws designed for other purposes, was being used to neutralise their political campaign.

Although the Lancaster House Agreement envisaged the lifting of martial law before the election, this was not done and the election was held under martial law on the plea that conditions were still disturbed. Moreover, a state of emergency which had been in force since before the Unilateral Declaration of Independence, was extended by the Governor for a further period of six months. A draconian piece of legislation, the 'Law and Order Maintenance Act' of 1960 was regarded as so severe that it led to the resignation of the Chief Justice in protest. Its provisions had been greatly extended since, and it clothed the administration and security forces with the most arbitrary and far-reaching powers. Among other things, it provided for strict control of public processions and meetings; it empowered the administration to ban newspapers, and imposed restrictions on a wide variety of activities to the extent of penalising persons who were regarded as 'undermining legal authority' by exposing any public officer to 'ridicule or disesteem'. Severe penalties, up to five years' imprisonment, could be imposed under the Act. Non-violent political agitation or civil disobedience had also been outlawed; there was a penalty of up to twenty years for any such activity. Under an Emergency regulation, a person could be arbitrarily placed under indefinite detention; this power could be exercised even by a police officer.

With such an extensive range of extraordinary powers, it was evident that the administration could exercise control over every facet of political activity. Freedom of expression was liable to marked restrictions, freedom of assembly was subject to licence and control; freedom of movement was subject to restraint by arbitrary detention, and in many parts of the country, movement was curbed by curfew. It was therefore of the utmost importance to monitor the manner in which this battery of laws was enforced, as they had the potential to erode the essential democratic elements of the election process.

The law, governing meetings was complex, and required the permission of the local police, and provision of a list of speakers at no less than forty-eight hours notice. The law against 'unlawful gathering' could be quite inadvertently breached as it could apply to as few as three people and could even be extended against people meeting in private homes. Although complaints against the application of the laws governing meetings were fairly general, they were applied with particular severity against the nationalist parties. Police permits were often difficult to obtain and meetings were broken up on one pretext or another.

The exercise of the right of arbitrary detention without trial or court appearance was a matter of special concern to us. We learnt with considerable surprise that there was no central record of persons who had forfeited their liberty in this peremptory fashion. After pursuing our enquiry at all levels, we ultimately learnt that over 700 persons were arbitrarily held, but their party affiliations were not known except that twelve of them were polling agents of a certain political party. In addition, there were 1,240 men and 40 women held under martial law. A spate of complaints had poured in from the nationalist parties that a large number of their party workers were under arbitrary arrest, including some candidates. We took up the matter with the authorities, emphasising that party workers, and especially candidates, should as a matter of principle not be subject to arbitrary arrest, but only if there was a definite criminal charge against them. However, the administration, for reasons of its own, failed to respond, and arbitrary arrests continued, polling agents being detained only hours before the poll.

The misuse, and often abuse, of executive power to the detriment of the Patriotic Front became clear in several respects. The powerful instrument of the media was initially allowed to be used selectively in favour of Muzorewa's party. The administration was reluctant to allow equal time to all the political parties on radio and television, but this was later corrected. The ban on newspapers was ultimately withdrawn, but the problem of obtaining newsprint remained. This also affected significantly the printing of party propaganda. ZANY (PF) encountered difficulties in hiring accommodation for its offices while telephone connections were long denied. There was also the problem of refugees numbering some 228,000—exceeding the settler population—being repatriated from their exile in Mozambique and Zambia. As the date of the election approached, the Governor passed a string of ordinances of a most arbitrary nature empowering disenfranchisement of individuals, parties or regions merely on suspicion of intimidation of voters. Complaints continued to pour in of various types of harassment and excesses against political workers.

Throughout the electoral process, I went frequently to Government House for talks with Lord Soames. The Governor seemed clearly disappointed that my offer of cooperation did not extend to ensuring a Smith-Muzorewa victory. Minor irritants and pinpricks to us, in which the official functionaries seemed to delight, were often corrected on reference to Government House. But on major issues, it was often found that our information and the results of our on-the-spot investigations, often varied, sometimes widely, from official perceptions. We were not an investigating agency, but we were required to produce almost judicial proof before the administration would admit that a matter called for rectification. As the date of the election approached, our differences with the British administration became sharper; on some major issues, however, which would have seriously vitiated the fairness and freedom of the poll, we were able to obtain some satisfaction, possibly as a result of timely reminders that in the ultimate reckoning our judgement on the issue, publicly expressed, would be the deciding factor. It must be said, however, that in respect of the physical arrangements at polling booths, the able British Election Commissioner, Sir John Boynton, who had much experience of the scrupulous conduct of British elections, kept strictly aloof from any malpractice and tried to assure a fair and equal field for all parties.

Our intrusiveness in insisting on enquiring into every aspect of the electoral process was not only unwelcome to the administration but also unexpected. It may have been thought that because of difficulties of terrain and extent and the complicated nature of the situation, we would be content to skim the surface and be guided by the administration in submitting a positive, if not laudatory, report. A large number of observer groups had been invited from various countries and many did appear, but only from Europe and the old Commonwealth. Efforts were constantly made to downgrade our unique status as an integral part of the Lancaster House Agreement and to bracket us with various non-official groups. As these groups were total strangers to Africa and lacked any secretarial or logistical arrangements worth the name, they had perforce to confine themselves to the guided tours arranged by the administration. But the more perceptive among them, bewildered by the scene, repaired to us for enlightenment; this we were glad to give and their concerns and final reports reflected our own views and observations.

Among our most significant callers was a delegation from the United Nations led by a senior Under Secretary-General, in response to a demand from a sceptical Security Council about the progress and reliability of the electoral process. The emissary was no less a person than Perez de Cuellar, who later became Secretary-General of the United Nations. He had come with a letter of introduction from my nephew, Virendra, who rose to become a distinguished Chef-de-Cabinet and Under Secretary-General at the United Nations. My visitor was obviously in a state of exhaustion after his long flight from New York and utterly perplexed by the complexity of the situation. He was at a loss about how to submit a report, as demanded by the Security Council, in a matter of a few days. After giving him a brief resume, I suggested that while he took some rest, my staff would assist his associates with their report; this offer was accepted with much relief and gratitude. The Security Council thus vicariously voiced our concerns and findings.

The conduct and complexion of the civil service were matters of considerable relevance to the electoral process. It was contemplated by the Lancaster House Agreement that the Governor would organise and conduct the elections through the existing official machinery. The civil service, which also ran the day-to-day administration, was therefore in a position to condition the environment in which the election campaign was conducted and to influence the manner in which votes were to be cast. Therefore much depended on the civil servants' impartiality and lack of political involvement. The senior official cadre was composed entirely of persons of British origin while Africans occupied only subordinate positions. This was reminiscent of the state of affairs in the Congo, but unlike the Congo, the level of education and enlightenment among the African people in Rhodesia was far higher. Yet, educated young Africans were excluded from recruitment to senior posts for 'security reasons' as their loyalty to the regime was suspect. During the years of armed conflict the civil servants had been conditioned to regard the PF and ZANU(PF) as mortal enemies to be exterminated and, indeed, many civil servants had taken to arms themselves. Among some we found a strong element of bias, but many had reconciled themselves to the inevitable and showed commendable objectivity. But all were understandably anxious about their future and their pensions under an independent majority-rule government.

Among the problems was the return of some 228,000 refugees which was being arranged in stages to facilitate their rehabilitation. The largest number was in Mozambique, then in Zambia, and a sprinkling in Botswana. The Rhodesian administration managed the entry while the UN High Commissioner for Refugees coordinated the repatriation. But snags had developed which obstructed the process. There had been unconscionable delays in setting up entry points; an arbitrary numerical limitation of numbers had been imposed on the doubtful ground that military personnel were returning; police ill-treatment often frightened refugees away.

I personally undertook a visit to one of the main crossings from Mozambique to assess the situation. There were large numbers of men, women and children on the other side of the barrier eager to return. However the assumption seemed to be that any middle-aged or young man was a guerrilla in disguise; they were all pushed back on the specious plea that the Lancaster House Agreement had required all movement of military personnel to cease after the December cease-fire dateline. It was also abundantly clear that the centre could have taken in very many more refugees. Our protests with the Governor produced little effect as he evidently had a closed mind on the issue. As a result, a large number of entitled voters were unfairly disenfranchised.

Another contentious issue was the continued and highly objectionable presence of South African troops in the country, despite the fact that the African participants at the Lancaster House Conference had insisted on their expulsion as a condition for their acceptance of the cease-fire. When we raised the matter with the Governor, he admitted the presence of South African troops at the Beit Bridge, straddling a river dividing the two countries. This admission of a blatant violation of assurances greatly incensed the Patriotic Front and cast serious doubts on the good faith of the British authorities. It was only at the end of January that the unwelcome intruders were finally withdrawn.

Yet another infraction was the liberty and, indeed, licence accorded to the security forces to operate freely in the country when they, like other armed forces, should have been restricted to their bases. Throughout the election campaign they remained very much in evidence, their previous belligerent role hardly qualifying them as impartial guardians of the law. The Monitoring Force, some 1,500 strong, was insufficient to cover all the assembly points as well as to monitor the behaviour of the security forces, but did a remarkable job despite the odds. In terms of the Agreement, if a breach of the ceasefire occurred, or to curb armed bands, joint action was to be taken by the security forces and Patriotic Front military personnel. Later, the two forces were to be incorporated. This process was taken up very tardily and not seriously carried out until after independence.

Another problem was the intimidation of people. This, in turn, was linked to the problem of the functions and activities of Bishop Muzorewa's 'auxiliaries' and other private armies on the one hand, and the guerrillas who had failed to report at assembly points, on the other. The Popular Front charged that the auxiliaries were terrorising the people on behalf of the UANC and had moved into areas previously controlled by the guerrillas. A large number of complaints regarding the misdeeds and lawlessness of the auxiliaries were referred to us by leaders of the Patriotic Front. Many of them were enquired into by our own personnel and some verified. They were taken up with the Governor, who strenuously denied them and asserted that the auxiliaries were, in fact, performing an important function in assisting the hard-pressed police force in the maintenance of law and order. He charged, on the other hand, that guerrilla bands and other armed elements of the Patriotic Front were brutalising and intimidating the people, and preventing any election campaigning by other parties in many parts of the country, notably in the east and south-east. The upshot was that little or no action was taken to rectify even genuine grievances. It was evident that the Governor was relying implicitly on the tailored and slanted information served up to him by the Rhodesian security forces and administration, with no independent attempt by him at verification, although he had the means to do so.

Our conclusion after detailed enquires was that, while there certainly was some intimidation, its extent was not nearly as great as was alleged, nor was it only one-sided. Besides, the number of guerrillas outside the assembly points was nothing like the figure stated by the Governor. The fact was that during the war large parts of the country had passed under the control of the nationalist forces, where the writ of the government had long ceased to run. The population was clearly in sympathy with the guerrillas who could not have maintained and expanded the area of armed struggle for so long without the support and sympathy of the local people. In many cases, our observations were fully endorsed by the British supervisers. The fact that the Governor and his staff saw things otherwise, revealed their refusal to face facts.

A serious consequence of such an attitude, which threatened to subvert the whole election, was the Governor's ill-advised decision on the very eve of the election to issue two ordinances in quick succession to deal with his exaggerated notions of the extent and nature of intimidation of voters. These empowered him to debar any person from taking part in the election on allegations of indulging in 'disruptive activities'. He could also declare a whole area as subject to disruption and effectively disenfranchise all the inhabitants thereof. These sweeping and arbitrary powers, if exercised, would have had disastrous consequences. In response to our protests, the Governor provided us with maps showing areas marked in red and blue where the level of intimidation, charged exclusively to the nationalist forces, was said to be particularly high. These areas were closely investigated by us through personal visits and enquiries and we found that the allegations were highly coloured if not downright false. Here again, the British supervisers supported our findings. But nothing would move Lord Soames. Then came Robert Mugabe's stern warning that, if action was taken under the ordinances, the war would be resumed with full intensity. Other observer groups also made known their strong disapproval of any capricious exercise by the Governor of such sweeping powers. Because of the universal condemnation of the ordinances, the Governor offered the rather unconvincing explanation that he had considered them necessary to avoid blame if any party were to repudiate the election on the ground that he had failed to curb intimidation. In the end wiser counsels prevailed and, but for some token action, the impugned ordinances were allowed to lapse.

Mugabe's return from enforced exile had been prevented by the authorities until days before the election. To my repeated protests, the Governor made the unacceptable excuse that Mugabe's return would cause great turmoil and violence and he could not possibly abdicate his responsibility for the maintenance of peace and order. Mugabe had been branded a communist by the British press, one who, if he came to power, would bathe the country in blood, persecute his opponents and enslave the people under a rigid dictatorship.

Two deliberate and carefully-planned attempts were made on the life of Robert Mugabe. In one instance, Mugabe narrowly escaped being blown up by a remote-controlled land mine while out campaigning; it had been planted at a spot over which his car had just passed. Although a large police contingent was camped in the close vicinity, the would-be assassins were never apprehended nor their identity established. In the second incident three persons attacked Mugabe's house with lethal weapons but fled on detection before they could do much harm. Again, the miscreants escaped arrest and identification.

In another shocking incident, a powerful bomb explosion took place right in front of the entrance to the hotel where I and some members of the Group were staying. It was a little after eleven at night when I, accompanied by Girish Mehra, had just come in from dinner with Arthur Sulzberger and A.M. Rosenthal, publisher and executive editor of the *New York Times*, at their hotel. As I entered my room, there was a deafening sound as of a thunderclap. At first we thought it was the precursor of one of the fierce African storms, but on looking out of the window, the sky was sparkling with stars, with not a cloud in sight. I then asked Girish to go down to the lobby to make enquiries; he returned breathless with the report that a time-bomb had been set off which had blown up the entire glass frontage and windows on several floors. When I went down to see for myself, the spacious hall was found littered with broken glass. Fortunately, there were no guests around and the receptionist had escaped decapitation from a sheet of flying plate glass by ducking behind the counter. It was like shrapnel and would have caused heavy casualties had the lobby been full. I was a familiar sight, walking or on television, and the South African radio and press had been routinely maligning me as the man of Congo repute who was instrumental in expelling the Belgians from there.

The same night, another large bomb exploded in a church, while still another failed to explode. The third explosion occurred in a parked car belonging to a member of the so-called Selous Scouts, a secret adjunct of the security forces, in which the two occupants, one a European, were killed. First reports blamed anti-religious elements for the outrages until the identities of the occupants of the car were revealed. The whole truth never came out, but it was evident that the aim was to disrupt the election process.

On a matter of administrative detail involving the observation functions of our mission, the Governor quite gratuitously provoked a sharp controversy. It had been envisaged at the outset that to cover all the fifty-five districts we would need that number of extra assistants. All that we asked was they be accorded observer status. Soames, however, took alarm at the simple request, insisting that our present complement should be enough. On it being pointed out that that was a matter for our decision, he changed tack. No accommodation or transport would be available; young and untried officials would hardly be competent to do the job; it would appear that there was a rival governmental authority; there would be obstruction of the work of the regular polling staff, etc. All these points were rebutted; we would make our own arrangements for accommodation and transport; the assistants would work alongside the British supervisers; they were experienced in election duties; budgetary provision had already been made, etc. But Soames was impervious to argument and totally unprepared even to concede a lower figure. Commonwealth governments had already earmarked officials experienced in election duties who were awaiting orders until the dispute was resolved. I was constrained to invoke the intercession of the Commonwealth Secretary-General in this senseless dispute; he, in turn, took up the matter with the British Foreign Secretary. The upshot was that we got our additional assistants, their number however being reduced by agreement to thirty.

The election campaign proceeded smoothly. Large crowds turned out at election meetings, especially of the Patriotic Front. Bishop Muzorewa moved about in a helicopter, lavishly provided with funds, and holding expensive jamborees where all kinds of inducements were offered to the audience. The elections were to be conducted over three days to enable adequate security arrangements to be made. There was much excitement among the populace as the time of the election approached. The Independence Constitution provided for a President, a Parliament consisting of a Senate and a House of Assembly. The Assembly comprised 100 elected members; 20 seats were reserved for Europeans elected on a separate roll.

As the election was being held under extraordinary conditions, a special procedure had been prescribed. For the eighty non-reserved seats, there were no constituencies, no registration of voters and therefore no common roll. Instead, a party list system was adopted, according to which every party submitted a list of candidates provincewise. The ballot papers contained the names of only the political parties and their election symbols, and each voter was to indicate his choice of party. The number of seats was then distributed in proportion to the votes each party had received in each province in relation to the total votes cast. The standard of literacy was low—33 per cent among African adult males and 41 per cent among females; they were helped in marking their choice. There was no recent census of the population: the last census gave a count of 7.2 million and it was estimated that some 2.9 million were potential voters. Indelible dye was used to identify those who had already voted. Arrangements at polling booths followed the usual pattern, including provision for secrecy.

There was a festive atmosphere on election day and the two successive days of the poll, when all controversies of the past were laid to rest. Our observers and assistants were in position all over the country. I visited a large number of polling stations in Salisbury and a wide swathe of country within a radius of several miles. Nowhere were there any disorderly scenes; the voters, men and women, festively clad, were in good humour as they moved slowly in long queues. The indelible and invisible dye, which could be seen only by ultra-violet light, served its purpose well. At one stage there was considerable commotion as the rumour spread that multiple voting had been taking place as the dye was removable by Coca-Cola! But a demonstration by Sir John Boynton proved that it was not possible.

An imaginative innovation which caused much wonder and delight among the voters was the sight of London 'bobbies' at polling stations. Nothing like it had ever been seen, as the bobbies in their high helmets, towering above the crowd, good-naturedly watched over the scene, occasionally lending a helping hand to move the voters forward.

Everywhere we went there were sounds of crowing among the voters; they were adherents of Mugabe whose election symbol was a cock. The election staff manning the booths comprised both communities and was doing its job impartially and well. Each day the ballot boxes were sealed and collected for dispatch to Salisbury for the counting.

The scene in the counting halls was extraordinary; the tellers, almost entirely European men and women, were performing their duties with scrupulous efficiency and fairness. The pile of ballot papers in favour of the ZANU (PF) and the PF kept rising higher and higher, while that of Muzorewa's UANC lay flat. Many of the European women were in tears but they continued with their work, aware that their old familiar world was collapsing before their eyes. I felt sorry for them, but admired their courage and fortitude in carrying on with their jobs to the last, and I hoped that under the new dispensation they would still find a place for their talents.

Before the counting was done, it was imperative that we express an opinion as regards the freedom and fairness of the election, otherwise it would be thought that our judgement was influenced by its result. The whole Group discussed its impressions based on personal observation and we arrived unanimously at a common conclusion. An interim report was carefully drafted in which the shortcomings and aberrations were duly indicated, but were balanced against the positive aspects of the entire exercise. Our conclusion therefore was that, taking all aspects of the electoral process into consideration and despite many inadequacies, it was our considered opinion that the result of the poll would, by and large, reflect the opinion of the people regarding their future governance. This conclusion we wired to the Commonwealth Secretary-General. I called a press conference to announce it to the international and national press and public.

The press conference was attended by over six hundred correspondents from many countries who awaited, with bated breath, the result of our findings. Its opening had to be repeatedly delayed, which increased the excitement and tension among the correspondents. The Nigerian observer had suddenly developed cold feet after having subscribed to our conclusions; he had signed the interim report which had already been cabled to the Commonwealth Office in London. He had meanwhile been brainwashed by his more radical colleagues and journalists who had come determined to question the whole election process.

When the Group took its place on the dais, I read out our interim report and had copies distributed. There was a volley of questions which were easily disposed of by reference to our stated conclusions. The Nigerian journalists questioned our unanimity by pointing to the absence of our Nigerian colleague, who had quietly vanished before we entered the conference hall. I feigned surprise at his absence, and pointing to his signature on the report, said he probably had some more pressing engagement, a remark that raised his ire and that of his fellow Nigerians!

When the results of the poll were announced, there was much concern in Government House. It seems unrealistic for anyone to have imagined that people who had suffered three quarters of a century of colonial subjection and the travails of civil war, could possibly have opted in favour of a continuance of the old dispensation under a Smith-Muzorewa regime. But the British, adept at cutting their losses soon came to terms with the fait accompli. Lord Soames, who until the very end, had done all he could to load the dice against Mugabe, began to ingratiate himself with him. Mugabe himself, in statesmanlike manner, spoke out loud and clear, urging national reconciliation and the forgiveness of old wrongs. He invited the European settlers to stay on in peace in their farms and factories as equal citizens of the new Republic of Zimbabwe. Those who did not heed the call, hastily sold their assets and drove away to South Africa. But most stayed, reassured by Mugabe's invitation, and Lord Soames' continuance as Governor General. The presence of Europeans in the Cabinet and the absence of any African backlash provided additional reassurance. Among those who stayed was Ian Smith, now a common citizen, who retained his vast and highly lucrative farm. All controversies were suddenly stilled and the settler community, which began shedding its complexes of superiority, and the indigenous people, now masters of their own fate, came to share as equals a common fealty.

The African people, by and large, received the result of the poll with much satisfaction, although there were disgruntled elements. Chief of these was Joshua Nkomo who had taken part in the armed struggle side-by-side with Mugabe and had vainly imagined that he would come out on top. The voting had in the main followed a tribal pattern; Mugabe's tribe, the Mahona, was far more numerous than Nkomo's Matabele and he gathered correspondingly more votes than his rival. Nkomo was a pathetic figure when we saw him last, completely deflated and bitter, and fulminating against his former companion-at-arms. Mugabe was fully aware of the sustained attempts by the administering power to influence the outcome of the poll against him and was full of gratitude for our vigilance and persistence in defeating them. In thanking me warmly he emphasised that but for our efforts he would have returned to the bush to resume the armed struggle.

Our task having been done, it remained for us to complete our detailed report. We flew back to London to receive the thanks of the Commonwealth Secretary-General, Sridath Ramphal, who was highly elated at the success of the first field experience of the Commonwealth in bringing peace to a war-torn country and leading it to independence. Lord Carrington also received us warmly and was most appreciative of the successful implementation of the Lancaster House Accord in such difficult circumstances. Finally, we were received by Queen Elizabeth II and the Duke of Edinburgh who, in thanking us individually, showed that they had kept in touch with developments in the country and our contribution to the final result.

When I returned to New Delhi, I sent word through Protocol to the Prime Minister, Mrs Gandhi, and the Foreign Minister, P.V. Narasimha Rao, that I was at their disposal to report on the mission in Zimbabwe, but neither showed any interest in the matter. The Prime Minister had taken a prominent part at Commonwealth meetings and other international gatherings in condemning the Smith regime in Rhodesia and the British government for abdicating its responsibility for its rebel colony.

Indian delegations at the United Nations and elsewhere had also, year after year, taken a lead in pressing for an end to the racist rengime. The Indian press, too, spared no ink in joining in the general condemnation. Yet, when it came to the final act nobody showed the slightest interest in being informed of the facts.

When the ceremony of the formal transfer of power from British to Zimbabwean hands took place, a great and festive gathering of heads of state and governments assembled in Salisbury, since renamed Harare. Mrs Gandhi, who was prominent among the guests, was accompanied by a large delegation. She graciously acknowledged the gratitude of the hosts for her signal contribution to the final achievement of independence by Zimbabwe. The Chairman of the Commonwealth Observer Group was, however, a noticeable absentee among his colleagues, all of whom had been invited to join their countries' delegations.

*FOURTEEN*

# Farewell to South Block

L ooking back over the years from the perspective of a life
that has spanned the best part of the century, the changes
that have taken place in this ancient land are truly
stupendous. Growing up in the small town of Naini Tal in the
early years of the century, it seemed to me that everything was
stable and secure, and everyone and everything had a place and
function. It was when I moved to Allahabad during my years at
the university that I first became aware of the ferment in the
country and the stir among the students.

Then, as a recruit to the ICS for fourteen years I plodded
away at the various jobs that came my way. That too was a secure
life, but with enough opportunities and challenges to make it
interesting and to widen my horizons. In 1946, when I found
myself in the demanding position of Home Secretary of the
Government of UP (the United Provinces), I became closely
involved with the impact of the national movement. With the
advent of Independence the following year my responsibilities
increased greatly.

Our most pressing tasks were dealing with the outbursts of

communal frenzy, and rehabilitating the vast influx of enraged and bitter refugees, straggling survivors of the holocaust, witness to the brutal annihilation of whole communities. But along with these tasks the everyday business of administration, the collection of land and water revenues, customs and excise dues, the running of hospitals, courts of law etc. had also to go on.

Exacting enough as these tasks were, what demanded a special measure of tact and forbearance was that of gaining the confidence and trust of the new and untried ministers, and without being presumptuous, educating them regarding the enormous and complex responsibilities which they had undertaken. These were political personalities, many of whom had spent long years in the Independence movement at the sacrifice of other careers. We officials fully realised that they had to keep a balance between their political compulsions and their administrative duties and we hoped that the balance would not tilt unduly in favour of the former.

The working habits of the ministers were highly varied and irregular and one could never be certain when and whether they would be at work. When they did turn up, they would be surrounded by a motley group of party functionaries and hangers-on, in whose presence serious official business was difficult, and confidential work impossible. They would sometimes hang around in their offices well after nightfall, mostly engaged in conversation with their own constituents, occasionally casting a casual eye on an official file.

How different all this was to the business-like ways to which we were accustomed, when matters were promptly attended to or when discussion, when required, took place in a purposeful and decisive manner. There was a sharp distinction between leisure and working hours and attitudes. Now such distinctions were blurred and leisure and conversation intruded into offices and work into the domestic ambience. As a result of this rather lackadaisical manner, a due sense of priority and proportion tended to be lost, inconsequential matters claiming much time and talk, while matters of far greater moment were lost sight of in the prevailing confusion.

To counteract these distracting tendencies at a time of such peril, some half a dozen of us at the nerve-centre of the UP Secretariat, made it a habit to meet daily to confer on each troubled day's problems and trials and to devise a common line of action to meet future contingencies. We could thus offer coherent and consistent advice to the ministers and steer them towards taking the right decisions.

Gradually, the convulsions which had rocked the province began to settle down and the administration fell into a more orderly and purposeful routine. But every now and then one minister or another would be seized by a sudden brainwave which, after much discussion, would be found to be chimerical and totally impractical. But by now, what had at first seemed to us as abnormal, had become the normal.

In regard to public expenditure, certain disturbing trends had begun to manifest themselves. Without doubt British imperial policy was highly exploitative of the Indian economy, as was only to be expected of a colonial power; it had kept the country impoverished and impeded development and progress. But at the provincial level, the British administration observed strict financial rectitude while in the districts it was downright parsimonious. The Collectorate buildings were mean and primitive, but kept in working condition by carefully-supervised annual repairs. The District Officers were housed either in existing buildings inherited from former rulers or in mud and brick bungalows roofed with thatch or tiles. All items of government property, however small, had to be properly recorded and accounted for. Accounting of public expenditure was double-checked, while the skimpy budgets were meticulously adhered to.

Not a single official was provided with transport at public

expense, apart from the Governor. The former ministers and high officials had to maintain their own vehicles. Touring officers were paid mileage and daily allowances for travel in their own cars. Corruption was unthinkable and unheard of at higher levels. At the lowest level of the revenue administration, there was some corruption on a modest scale but among the all-India services one never heard of a single case of corrupt practice. The provincial services too were relatively clean and any aberrant officer was severely taken to task.

Even during the War, when there was much frenetic activity to feed the voracious war-machine and simultaneously to curb the rising tide of popular discontent, the administration, which had taken the whole economy under its control, remained clean. Vast contracts and permits were given and there was never any question, certainly not in the Lucknow Secretariat, of any under-the-counter deal. In fact, even the thought of such a possibility never crossed anyone's mind and the entire government functioned with perfect confidence.

The Governor's Advisers who had replaced ministers, had no armed guards or official cars and were treated like all other officials in this respect. They rode to work on bicycles accompanied only by liveried peons carrying their files behind them. Even at the centre, members of the Viceroy's Executive Council enjoyed not a single perquisite beyond their official salaries. They paid the prescribed house rent and met their own electricity and water charges as well as charges for private telephone calls. They were not provided with any armed guards. They moved about in privately-owned cars with a small blue triangular flag with the letters 'E.C.' embroidered on it, unaccompanied by any pilot car or escort. From the Viceroy's Councillors down to the most junior official, all they received was a salary and nothing else, and while ICS officials in the senior scale could live on their salaries with some dignity and comfort, an opulent life-style was impossible, nor could they make any savings beyond their provident fund, except at the most senior levels. It surprised and dismayed one, when the Congress government took over, that, in accordance with their Gandhian principles, they would take a salary of no more than Rs 500 a month. This seemed both incongruous and unrealistic when even junior Secretaries to Government were receiving some Rs 2,000 and their seniors Rs 3,000 a month. We imagined that a regime of austerity, consonant with the homespun peasant dress which the new rulers affected, would now be ushered in. But we were wrong. The new ministers made a grab for the most sumptuous houses, mopped up the new American limousines which were beginning to appear in the market, and surrounded themselves with liveried chaprasis and armed guards. No house rent was paid, the houses were elaborately furnished and the gardens maintained at government expense. Electricity, water and telephone charges were also met from the public exchequer. We were disconcerted to discover that many ministerial households were maintained by sundry businessmen, who also financed the ministers' lavish ways and took care of the hordes of followers and petitioners who daily crowded their residences and expected to be fed.

What seems highly incongruous is that republican India, which professes Gandhian values, should have maintained and elaborated upon the pomp and panoply of its British imperial past. The former Viceroy's House—rechristened Rashtrapati Bhawan—was built with the ostensible purpose of emphasising the might and glory of the British Raj. It is the largest palace in the world still in occupation and is undoubtedly awe-inspiring in its magnificence. The banqueting hall can seat one hundred guests under glittering crystal chandeliers. The protocol at state banquets and ceremonial occasions is more elaborate than during the viceregal epoch or in any European or Asian capital. The bodyguard, splendid lancers, superbly accoutred, who line the grand staircase on state occasions, make an unforgettable sight as they and their officers go on escort duty on their prancing chargers. But all this pomp and circumstance goes ill in a country which has one of the lowest per-capita incomes in the world and forty per cent of whose population exists below the poverty line and an equal percentage of villages have no potable water.

The Mahatma was right when he said that the head of state of independent India should observe a simpler life-style and that Viceroy's House should be put to other public purposes. But his followers, those that had ears to hear, would not hear.

Obsessive concern with security has converted nearly every ministerial house into a veritable fortress, protected by barbed wire, searchlights and armed guards against the very people whom their occupants pretend to represent. Half the police force of Delhi is detailed for the protection of ministers while over ten million citizens in the city are left to the mercy of dacoits and assassins. An entire once-busy road has been closed for the protection of the Prime Minister's residence, to the great inconvenience of law-abiding citizens. Traffic on busy highways is dislocated for half an hour or more to allow a prime ministerial cavalcade to sally past through empty streets while traffic piles up on side roads. Such disregard of the rights of the citizen was not to be found even in Stalin's Moscow or other dictatorships as is the daily travail of the citizens of the capital city of the world's biggest democracy. The same pattern of insensitive behaviour is followed, though in a lower key, in the state capitals.

During the Nehru era, the country moved forward steadily and unitedly, with a clear sense of purpose and direction. Not only had the country successfully surmounted the trauma of Partition, but it firmly established a democratic polity and evolved a strategy for economic progress and development. The world over, India received high praise for its achievements and was held up as a model for other developing nations to emulate. The country basked in the aura of the Mahatma from whom it derived its unique moral authority. India's voice was heard with attention and respect at the United Nations and in world capitals, weak though the country was in economic and military strength. In contrast with that of other developing countries, the political structure was surprisingly free of the canker of corruption while the administration continued, by and large, to maintain the standards of efficiency and cleanliness inherited from the British. There was, therefore, every reason to feel confident that within a measurable space of time, India would rank among the foremost powers in the world.

The people of India had every reason to be proud of their country and to be grateful to Nehru, who consolidated our independence and brought stability and security to a fractured land. He helped to build an industrial and economic infrastructure and to develop modern scientific and technological institutions. And weak as it was in comparison with the big powers, India commanded universal respect as the foremost developing nation of the world.

Nehru took the first giant step towards the country's progress and development. It fell to Lal Bahadur Shastri to take his great work to the countryside, to raise the villages, where the heart of India beats, from their poverty and backwardness. Raised in the villages himself, he was fully in tune with rural India's interests and urges. He could have given a new orientation to the country's policies, more in consonance with the Mahatma's concepts and advice. It was a cruel misfortune that this man of peace was forced into a war, and sacrificed his own life in the quest for peace. Had he lived to serve the nation, how different might its subsequent history have been!

Indira Gandhi's accession to power was almost fortuitous. Shastri's sudden disappearance from the political scene and the conduct of rival contenders to the succession, led them to enthrone an as yet uncontroversial figure, one outside the coterie of power brokers who, it was thought, could be easily manipulated by them. But they had not counted on the power of the office or the manipulative skills of their young and untried nominee. The outward traits of Indira's character, her sense of insecurity and diffidence, concealed an iron will and ruthlessness, and a determination to thwart or circumvent any challenge to her supremacy. She fought back any suspected attempt to challenge or dislodge her with the greatest tenacity, even at the cost of breaking up the historic Congress party. The party had traditionally embraced with rare catholicity every type of opinion in the political spectrum, from the left to the extreme right. Indira Gandhi, by splitting the party, sharpened political differences and set in train the lamentable practice of parties splitting up and being distinguished by the initials of their faction leaders.

To sustain the myth of disguising what was essentially a power struggle as a clash of irreconcilable ideologies, she resorted to leftist slogans and ill-conceived populist measures; a reckless course of state capitalism and indiscriminate nationalisation was embarked upon so as to dominate 'the commanding heights' of the economy. Banks and insurance were nationalised at a stroke of the pen, the government made forays into all kinds of industries including hotels, flour mills, and textiles—the list is endless. But wherever the government's heavy hand fell, the result was little short of disastrous. The control of the economy bred the notorious 'permit-licence raj' which opened the floodgates of corruption at every level and in every public office. And in a cynical act of spitefulness, the solemn pledges given to the princes as the price for their accession to the Union, were broken without any qualms of conscience.

Indira Gandhi's obsessive suspicion of her senior colleagues and exaggerated fears of being ousted led her to functioning in a conspiratorial manner behind the backs of her cabinet colleagues and official advisers, relying almost exclusively on the notorious 'kitchen cabinet', a coterie of left-leaning pseudo-intellectuals. When this group was dissolved, she turned increasingly to a miscellaneous set of Kashmiri advisers, whom critics referred to as the 'Kashmiri mafia' or the 'Panj Piaras'. The pernicious practice of miscellaneous persons wielding authority without responsibility was carried to dangerous limits when Indira Gandhi's half-educated mechanic son, Sanjay, began to wield unbridled, almost dictatorial power both over the emasculated Congress (Indira) and over national policies and government. Sycophancy and grovelling, which Nehru had spurned, began to flourish unabashedly, reaching its abject climax in the slogan coined by the puppet Congress (Indira) President, Dev Kanta Barooah, 'India is Indira, Indira is India'.

Consumed by the passion to consolidate her power and that of her progeny beyond any challenges, Mrs Gandhi needed subservient Congress (I) ministries in all the states. Thus began the practice of toppling non-Congress (I) governments by every possible means. Even Chief Ministers of her own party who showed any signs of independence or assumed any stature, were cut down and replaced by nominees of the centre. The Governors of states, who were required under the Constitution to be politically neutral and independent, were reduced to becoming agents of the party and the centre. The Supreme Court was packed with compliant judges. The civil services were corrupted by being required to be 'committed'—but to whom or to what? Not to the nation, the people or their true vocation, but to the Congress (I) and its supreme leader. Thus, institution after institution was systematically destroyed, or allowed to atrophy.

The fount of unbridled power had to have an abundance of resources to maintain it. Vast funds now began to be collected from commissions and bribes on government contracts and purchases made at home or abroad; these could be deployed to entice or suborn legislators of other parties and, at election time, as a lever to finance compliant candidates. The permit-licence raj continued in full force to augment the illicit hoard.

The near-dictatorship provided circuses but no bread. Empty

sloganeering and 'twenty-point programmes' took the place of any real economic policy, except to tighten government's stranglehold on economic activity. While the government was far too intrusive in matters affecting the economy, it was indifferent to the glaring problems where its intervention was essential, viz., in education, public health, social reform. Instead, a fascist type of compulsory family-limitation programme was imposed and enforced by methods which created an angry nation-wide reaction, setting back any attempt—however well conceived—to deal with the urgent need to control population growth.

Indira Gandhi had come to believe that she and her sons had been ordained by divine right to rule over the country. Her choice as successor had fallen on her younger son who believed that political power flowed from the ruthless exercise of muscle power buttressed by money. Not for him the restraints of democracy or the rule of law. He had contempt for public opinion and is said to have exclaimed that if the people rose in opposition, they should be 'kicked in the teeth and would come crawling'.

A nation of such size and diversity as India cannot be dragooned into sullen obedience. A groundswell of discontent and disaffection rose and swept through the country. It was given voice by the great patriot and true Gandhian, Jayaprakash Narayan. The Indian people have, by belief and tradition, always responded to one who, spurning power and wealth, has been ready to make any sacrifice in the service of a noble cause. In their eyes, Jayaprakash Narayan was such a man.

The response of an uncaring government to the people's woes was to suppress the movement by draconian means. In defiance of the Allahabad High Court's judgement disqualifying her from membership of Parliament for six years following an election petition, Mrs Gandhi declared a fraudulent state of 'emergency', imposing unabashed fascist rule on the country. The Constitution was amended and Parliament dissolved. Thousands were cast into prison, civil liberties were suppressed, even the right to life was denied, and a reign of fear and terror imposed. It was the darkest chapter in the history of India since Independence. The memory of the shameless outrage on democracy can never be erased from the consciousness of the Indian people.

But the Emergency could not last. In the general election, Mrs Gandhi, confident of success, mistaking the people's sullen mood for acquiescence, was roundly defeated. After an interregnum when a succession of coalition governments, riven by factions, had fallen under their own inner contradictions, Mrs Gandhi had a second chance to start on a clean slate. Unfortunately, she was quite unregenerate and committed one mistake after another which not only cost the nation dear but also cost her own life.

One may well ask how a shy, reclusive woman like Indira Gandhi came to be possessed by such an overweening will to power. Her character was no doubt conditioned by her early life of loneliness, with her mother ill and her father ceaselessly engaged in political struggle or absent in prison. The estimate of her psychology attributed to one of her senior cabinet colleagues, P.V. Narasimha Rao (later Prime Minister), provides an explanation. Observing that Mrs Gandhi could never get over her many complexes, he goes on to say that they consisted of 'a feeling of inferiority, and an admission of inadequacy inside; and a nagging awareness of deathlessness, coupled, above all, with the consuming ambition to attain immortal fame, eclipsing her great father'.

Indira Gandhi had a frustrated and unhappy private life from childhood to marriage, which made her cheerless and withdrawn. In her father's household, it was her aunt, Vijayalakshmi Pandit, sparkling and extrovert, who shone, while Indira maintained a sullen and resentful silence. The lack of a regular education and failure to make the grade at Oxford must have rankled. Indira insisted, on her official travels abroad, on meetings being arranged with intellectuals while at home she consorted with those who preened themselves as such. Unlike her father, who described himself as agnostic in his philosophical beliefs, she was highly superstitious. She made it a habit to visit shrines and temples and to pay homage to all manner of spiritual pretenders, not for enlightenment but for worldly power and fame.

After the overwhelming victory of Indian arms in the Indo-Pakistan war of 1971, Mrs Gandhi was apotheosised by her acolytes and devotees as the goddess Durga. But the moment of her greatest ascendancy also signalled the beginning of her downfall. The arrogance and intolerance which resulted, frequently led to egregious, often calamitous decisions.

One of Mrs Gandhi's biggest mistakes was her handling of the Punjab problem. The troubles in the Punjab and disaffection in the Sikh community were nothing but a result of underhand manoeuvres to break the hold of the Akali party in the state and to establish the ascendancy of the Congress. A prime mover in this plot was Giani Zail Sigh, who had his personal scores to settle. He was rewarded by being elevated to the Presidency of the Republic. So loyal a follower he proved to be that he publicly proclaimed his willingness even to sweep the streets at the behest of his leader! The man chosen for the job of breaking the Akalis was one Jarnail Singh Bhindranwale, who was given a very long rope. But Bhindranwale developed into a bloodthirsty monster who turned on his own creators and plunged the state in blood. Having released the genie, Mrs Gandhi and the Giani had no way of enticing it back into the bottle. Meanwhile, Bhindranwale sought sanctuary from the consequences of his innumerable crimes by holing himself up in the sacred precints of the Golden Temple, which he began converting into an armed citadel. He continued with his evil deeds from this privileged sanctuary, organising and directing his gangs of thugs on their murderous forays. So monstrous were his crimes that there was deep outrage and anger throughout the country at the government's powerlessness to protect the lives of innocent citizens. The moment for action came when a senior Sikh police officer, who had entered the portals of the Temple for worship, was gunned down to the horror even of the Sikh community, who would have acquiesced in the criminals then defiling the temple being flushed out.

But Mrs Gandhi prevaricated despite the advice of even those of her cabinet colleagues who were not noted for their valour or decisiveness. The reason for her inaction, according to her principal adviser, was her concern about the effect of any action on the large Sikh element in the armed forces. Bhindranwale, emboldened by the government's pusillanimity, increased his depredations and fortified the Temple to withstand a siege. Months later Mrs Gandhi chose to act. But the moment was ill-timed and the dramatis personae ill-prepared. The miscreant was by then fully prepared to meet the army's onslaught and exacted a heavy toll of killed and wounded before forfeiting his own life. In the process, the Temple was heavily bombed and damaged. This sent a wave of shock and resentment throughout the Sikh community in the country and abroad. The memory of Operation Blue Star, as it was called, still causes deep anguish. Wrong means can only lead to wrong ends. The policy followed in the Punjab was morally wrong and politically unwise. A loyal and gallant community had been deeply hurt and alienated. Mrs Gandhi had to pay a terrible price when she herself was assassinated by her own Sikh security guards.

The aftermath of the assassination was so cowardly and brutal that it makes every decent-minded citizen squirm with shame. Organised bands of hooligans armed with iron rods and tins of kerosene or petrol scoured the city in trucks and systematically attacked Sikh houses. Dragging out their inmates, they hacked them to death or burnt them alive while setting their houses alight after looting them. In less than forty-eight hours some 3,500 innocent Sikh citizens of the capital city had been murdered in broad daylight and within sight of the guardians of the law or even with their active connivance and participation. While such horrors were being committed in their very midst, the central government abandoned the city to the murderous mobs, to rampage at will in their orgy of death and destruction.

On getting news of the assassination of the Prime Minister, I took the first plane back from France where I had been attending a meeting. Susheela, who had been in India alone with our domestic staff, watched incredulously as lorry-load after lorry-load of miscreants, shouting slogans of hate and brandishing their weapons, passed in front of the house. On my arrival, Susheela and I hurried to the house of a friend, Patwant Singh, to enquire about his welfare. There was a group of people there, dazed and silent. I proposed that the authorities at all levels must be pressed to restore order and make restitution for what had happened. It was agreed that we should individually do all we could to influence those in power to do whatever they could to restore order and take remedial action without delay. The mob leaders who had organised and led the mobs were well-known politicians. They and their followers should be promptly arrested and tried. The families of the victims must be given immediate relief.

Accordingly, I saw the Vice-President, Shri R. Venkataraman, a man of honour and integrity, whom I had the privilege of knowing well. I urged that action be taken immediately to arrest and punish the ringleaders, to compensate the widows and orphans and arrange for their housing and rehabilitation, and to take all necessary measures to reassure the stricken community and bring succour to the bereaved. I warned that if immediate action was not taken against the evil-doers, who were well-known and identifiable, vengeance would be exacted on the streets. I spoke with all the passion and earnestness of which I was capable. But to my disappointment, Shri Venkataraman, while expressing regret for what had happened, said he could do nothing as he did not know the new men in power. Such abdication of moral, if not strictly official responsibility and such passive acceptance of monumental evil deeply shocked and angered me. I left after giving a further warning that if the government failed to do its manifest duty, the citizens of Delhi would hold an enquiry themselves which would amount to an impeachment of the government for its indifference and culpability.

A delegation of eminent Sikh citizens led by Air Chief-Marshal Arjan Singh went to appeal to the President, Giani Zail Singh. The Giani, professedly a man of wisdom and religion (as the designation 'Giani' proclaims) threw up his hands, pleading complete powerlessness. He was totally unprepared to come to the relief of the suffering widows and children who happened to belong to his own community. He said he had no influence or authority in the matter, although barely a couple of days earlier he had, by what can only be described as a constitutional coup, installed Indira Gandhi's son as Prime Minister. Rajiv Gandhi was at the time not even a Member of Parliament, nor had he ever exercised ministerial responsibility or held any administrative office. He was moreover only a recent entrant into the Congress. Yet, the Giani was afraid to exercise his constitutional prerogative even to advise in a matter involving such a massive violation of human rights and dereliction of duty as the massacre of thousands of innocent citizens.

Approaches to Arun Nehru, who was riding high as the novice Prime Minister's 'Man Friday', produced nothing but evasions and a tissue of falsehoods. The Lieutenant-Governor sat like a dummy, more attached to his chair than faithful to his conscience. As for the Home Minister, who was directly responsible, he was immobile and unapproachable, seeing nothing, hearing nothing and saying nothing.

Faced with such a gross betrayal of trust by these high functionaries, a meeting of concerned citizens was held to consider the situation. On being asked to open the proceedings,

I described our unavailing attempts to persuade the authorities to live up to their constitutional pledges and sense of morality. I said that we, the citizens of Delhi, must therefore take the initiative by setting up a Citizens' Commission to make a detailed enquiry into the horrendous events; to reveal the facts to the public; to identify the ringleaders and culprits; to expose the authorities' culpable failure to do their duty or to make amends. The proposal found unanimous favour and a group of five members was suggested by me whom I forthwith telephoned to obtain their acceptance. Declining the Chairmanship, I said that the committee should be one of equals. To give it a judicial colour moreover, it should include a high judicial personality. Former Chief Justice of India, Mitra Sikri, despite his poor health, readily accepted our request. The other members were Badruddin Tyabji, a senior retired diplomat; Govind Narain, a former Governor of a state and a former Home Secretary, and Gurbachan Singh, who ably served as Secretary. We spent hours visiting most of the affected areas, meeting hundreds of victims' families and survivors, and interviewing a large cross-section of people. It was a heart-rending experience listening to the tales of horror of the stricken widows and children and seeing with our own eyes the blood-spattered walls and burnt homes. The police officers whom we confronted at their stations were generally truculent and defiant, resentful of our questioning. Everywhere we heard the same names of the principal ringleaders who had organised the mobs, arranged for their transport, provided steel rods and kerosene and dispatched them to various localities to loot and destroy members of the Sikh community. It was all diabolically organised and brutally executed. The evildoers, it must be said to their eternal shame, were leading lights of the Delhi Congress party.

Barbarous and outrageous as the attitude and behaviour of the Congress government and party was, it was compounded by an uncaring and foolish statement made by the newly inducted

Prime Minister, Rajiv Gandhi. Instead of expressing remorse and sympathy for the victims, all that he could say was that when a great tree falls, the earth will shudder.

Before compiling our report on our findings, we made repeated attempts to contact the authorities to inform them of the facts and to seek explanations. We sent letters to the Home Minister requesting answers to direct questions, but were not vouchsafed so much as an acknowledgement, which betrayed a strong sense of guilt. Our report, carefully prepared, was categorical in its findings though it refrained from mentioning the names of the guilty. That was left to the report of the People's Union for Civil Liberties which had also carried out extensive enquiries and whose findings corroborated our own.

Our report received very wide notice in the country and abroad, but nothing could move an impassive and obdurate government. Many years have elapsed and not one of the ringleaders has been jailed, while the hundreds of known and identifiable rioters move around free and unfettered. Only now, the former President of the Delhi Congress Committee has been proceeded against on a complaint made to a conscientious magistrate by a courageous woman whose husband, son and brother were dragged out of their house and beaten and burnt to death before her very eyes. Her attempts over the years, like those of a host of other sufferers, to have their complaint recorded at police stations, had been consistently refused. Another ringleader has defied attempts for an arrest warrant to be served on him and continued to strut about as a Member of Parliament for several years. Two others, believed to have been implicated in inciting the killings, met their deaths at the hands of aggrieved persons.

The wanton and barbaric killings incited and organised by Congress netas have left a deep scar on the hearts and minds not only of the Sikh community but also of all decent-minded citizens. But even more than the massacres, what rankles was the complete insensitivity of the Congress government and its reluctance to show any remorse or make some amends. The politically and morally wrong action of raising the monster of Bhindranwale for unworthy political and personal ends led to the storming of the Golden Temple, for which Mrs Gandhi had to pay with her own life. That became a signal for the massacre of innocents which has ultimately resulted in breeding hatreds which, in turn, led to disaffection and militancy in Punjab.

As in Punjab, so in Kashmir. Political manoeuvring and high-handedness by the Centre in the affairs of the state of Jammu and Kashmir, while neglecting the real concerns of the people, threatens the country's integrity. As in Punjab, Indira Gandhi was fired by the sole aim of overthrowing a non-Congress government by whatever means, and installing a government under a compliant tool of her choice. The state was under a National Conference government, led by Dr Farouque Abdullah, son of the 'Lion of Kashmir'. He had begun promisingly, though his methods were unorthodox. He was a patriotic Indian and popular with the people. But as time went by he began to be regarded as a playboy. His administration too had become increasingly lax. Adverse reports about him began reaching Mrs Gandhi which encouraged her to feel that they provided adequate grounds for his removal and the installation of a Congress government. The Governor, B.K. Nehru, was summoned for consultations and, according to him, he strongly advised against Abdullah's removal. Whatever Abdullah's inadequacies, the Governor felt convinced that it would be a mistake to oust him as his successor would only be worse. At this, Mrs Gandhi, whose mind seemed to have been already made up, flared up, exclaiming that her information was very different. The Governor stuck to his guns and offered his resignation since the Prime Minister seemed to have lost confidence in him. Though this made Mrs Gandhi pause, she nevertheless transferred Nehru to Gujarat and adhered to her decision to remove Abdullah.

A Congress government under G.M. Shah was installed. Under this most venal and corrupt character, the administration went to pieces. Bribery and peculation flourished. There was acute public discontent, and the central government was forced to act and impose its rule. All that people yearned for was a moderately honest and efficient government and some improvement in their lot. But for years they had been denied the satisfaction of their basic needs and control over their destiny. Militancy and sessionism began to fester which provided just the opportunity for Pakistan, ever casting a rapacious eye on the valley, to stoke the fires of discontent. The insurgency in Kashmir, aided and abetted by Pakistan, has kept the Indian security forces engaged for years and will continue to do so until a political solution is found. Pakistan has seized upon the opportunity to reactivate a dead issue and to internationalise it. India has been charged with the violation of human rights in Kashmir, and the region provides one of the most unfortunate legacies of Mrs Gandhi's mistaken policies of imposing Congress governments, however corrupt and inefficient, upon non-compliant states.

The saga of Kashmir is full of lost opportunities, mistaken policies and corrupt and uncaring governments. The original Indian complaint to the United Nations Security Council against Pakistani aggression, made against the advice of Sardar Patel who had a greater sense of realism, was inspired by a spirit of idealism and faith in the impartiality and integrity of the United Nations. But its poor presentation in the Council could not stand up to the wiles of Zafrullah Khan of Pakistan and the machinations of the western powers. Britain had never forgiven the Congress for encompassing the dissolution of the Empire 'over which the sun never set', and it managed to carry its American ally with it. Treating the aggressor and his victim alike and the state as *tabula rasa*, the fact was disregarded that the Instrument of Accession signed by the Maharaja was in similar form to the over five hundred executed with other princes. It had been accepted by the British Governor-General, Lord Mountbatten, cousin of the Queen of England.

Zafrullah Khan charged that India had secured the accession by 'force and fraud'. The timely arrival of Indian troops in an airlift organised by the Governor-General, a renowned military strategist, succeeded in stemming the orgy of murder, arson and loot of the tribesmen, armed and incited by the Pakistani government and led by its officers. The action of the Maharaja (who had harboured dreams of independence and had long dithered over the question of accession) in acceding to the Indian Union after making a desperate appeal for help was decried as 'fraudulent'. It is noteworthy that Pakistan has not dared to challenge the accession in the International Court of Justice at the Hague as it knows that its case would be summarily dismissed. Pakistan's own seizure of no less than one-third of the territory of the state was an act of unabashed aggression, totally devoid of the slightest colour of legitimacy. These hard facts cannot be over-stressed and must be dinned into the ears of those western powers who now presume to sit in judgement on the issue.

The Security Council, giving a twist to Nehru's unilateral offer to ascertain the wishes of the people of Kashmir when the soil was cleared of the invader and the situation restored to normal, adopted a resolution calling for a plebiscite. In a tacit recognition of Indian sovereignty over the state, Indian administration was to be restored in the areas usurped by Pakistan, from which the invading bands had to withdraw. The Indian government could maintain sufficient forces in the state to ensure its security. These conditions did not suit Pakistan as it knew that the inhabitants of the area which it held and who had suffered at the hands of the marauders, would flock behind their leader, Sheikh Mohammad Abdullah. Without the coercion of its regular and irregular forces, Pakistan could not hold down the people of the area it had seized. It therefore tried every subterfuge to evade fulfilling its side of the prescribed conditions. The argument has revolved around the question of the 'quality and quantum' of the so-called 'Azad Kashmir forces'. These, Pakistan claims, are only local militias raised by the people themselves and are no part of the armed forces of Pakistan. India holds that these forces are nothing other than Pakistani irregulars in disguise, raised, armed and officered by Pakistan. This argument has never been resolved and never can be. A UN Plebiscite Administrator, Admiral Nimitz, appointed at the time, idled in the wings until he faded away into oblivion.

The Soviet Union had initially shown complete lack of interest in the matter as Stalin believed it to be a domestic quarrel between two states of the Commonwealth, still under British tutelage. But it woke up with a start when it dawned on it that Pakistan had allowed itself to become a link in the American global plan to ring in the Soviet Union and threaten its 'soft under-belly'. The discovery that the Pakistani air-base of Kahuta had become a taking-off point for American spy-planes to overfly the Soviet Union finally clinched matters. Thereafter, whenever the western powers tried to push through a resolution which India opposed, the Soviet delegate, Ambassador Jakob Malik, threatened to use his veto. Fear of a Soviet veto kept the western powers at bay thereafter and no resolution inimical to India has been attempted or passed. True, after the Suez fiasco, Britain initiated another Security Council debate out of spite against Krishna Menon for his harsh attack on Britain over that affair, but apart from providing an opportunity to Menon to make a marathon speech, it produced nothing.

In 1965 Pakistan launched a vicious attack on Kashmir in the mistaken belief that the time was ripe as the new Shastri government was weak and divided. It believed that the appearance in the valley of three converging columns of Pakistani troops in accordance with the infamous 'Operation Gibraltar' plan would spontaneously arouse the people to revolt. This was to be followed by 'Operation Grand Slam', a large-scale invasion of India to preempt the Indian army from crushing the revolt. This foolhardy plan was concocted by Z.A. Bhutto and Aziz Ahmed against the better judgement of President Ayub Khan and his army command. It met with an ignominious end as the intruding columns in the valley were decimated and beaten back while the armoured division of Patton tanks was annihilated. Indian troops pushed back the intruders from salient points in Pakistan-occupied Kashmir and, what is more, seized a vast tract of territory in the Pakistani heartland right up to the gates of Lahore. Bhutto's diabolical plan, instead of winning him glory, resulted in ignominious defeat and humiliation.

At the UN Security Council meeting which followed, Bhutto excelled himself in vituperation and hysterical abuse of India. Threatening 'a thousand years of war' he referred to the Indian delegation as 'Indian dogs'. The hardened delegates at the Council table were shocked at the vulgarity and venom of Bhutto's outburst. The Council called upon the parties to observe a cease-fire and abjure the use of force and to settle their differences only by peaceful means.

The Soviet Union stepped in as a peacemaker and invited the parties to meet under its good offices at Tashkent. Shastri agreed to vacate the Pakistani territory which Indian forces had captured and Ayub Khan agreed to withdraw from the desert areas which had been infiltrated. Shastri, in a further display of generosity, agreed to vacate some strategic areas in Kashmir which Indian forces had captured, notably the Haji Pir Pass which overlooked the valley. Pakistan was desperate to get the Indian forces off its neck in the vicinity of Lahore from where the inhabitants were fleeing in panic. Ayub Khan got back all that he had lost; Shastri got no reparations and no political or territorial advantage from his resounding victory. This generosity proved to be mistaken and was attributed to weakness, as six years later, Pakistan again resorted to the use of force.

After the Bangladesh war, Indira Gandhi, in a fit of almost unbelievable credulity, accepted the signature of a perfidious foe on a scrap of paper—the Shimla Agreement—in exchange for the captured Pakistan army in the east and a large tract of territory in the west, while throwing wide open for future discussion India's sovereign rights in its own territory in the state of Jammu and Kashmir. This question is of such moment that it needs a separate short chapter of its own.

# FIFTEEN

# The Shimla Agreement—
# Victory into Defeat

fter India's signal victory in the 1971 Bangladesh war, the Indian army took as prisoners the 93,000 strong Pakistani army in the east, along with its commanders, and seized some 5,000 square kilometres of Pakistani Punjab, within artillery range of Lahore. Yet, despite the overwhelming victory of Indian arms, the fruits of victory eluded India. Bhutto returned from the Shimla Conference triumphant, having fully secured his aims, while Indira Gandhi returned to New Delhi nursing a scrap of paper.

At Lahore airport on his return from Shimla, Bhutto proudly proclaimed that he had recovered all the prisoners-of-war and the lost territory, and had conceded nothing. He swore 'as a Muslim before Almighty Allah' that there was no secret clause to the Agreement and Pakistan was not bound in any way on the Kashmir issue or any other. He had also succeeded in making India agree to a time-table for the withdrawal of Indian forces.

How did Bhutto carry off this sleight of hand?

The Indian delegation at Shimla, led by Prime Minister Indira Gandhi, included three Cabinet Ministers—Jagjivan Ram, Y.B. Chavan and Swaran Singh. The official team was led by D.P. Dhar who occupied the nebulous position of Chairman of the Policy-Planning Committee in the Ministry of External Affairs; P.N. Haksar, Principal Secretary to the Prime Minister; P.N. Dhar, of the Prime Minister's Office; T.N. Kaul, Foreign Secretary, and R.N. Kao, Director of the Research and Analysis Wing. The Home and Defence Secretaries were conspicuous by their absence. From all accounts, both Indian and Pakistani, the Ministers had little part in the actual negotiations. The above-named favoured officials alone seemed to enjoy the Prime Minister's trust and confidence. D.P. Dhar, who, had conducted the preparatory negotiations at Murree, fell ill at Shimla on the day of arrival. P.N. Haksar then took over as the chief negotiator.

On the Pakistani side, President Zulfiqar Ali Bhutto's principal negotiator was Aziz Ahmed, Secretary-General in the Pakistan Foreign Ministry who carried the rank of Minister of State. Ahmed had the usual supporting cast of a clutch of officials. As proof of his democratic credentials after fourteen years of military rule, Bhutto had included in his delegation leaders of opposition political parties. To add a touch of allure to his entourage, he had brought the young Benazir with him. Bhutto was well-known to anyone who had dealt with him or had served in Pakistan as an extremely wily, unscrupulous and untrustworthy man. He had betrayed his own patron, Ayub Khan, and his accomplice, Yahya Khan, to climb to power. Aziz Ahmed, sharp and haughty, harboured a consuming hatred of India and invariably misused his undoubted dexterity and guile to vent his malice.

There has been a pall of silence over what happened at Shimla until twenty-two years later, when Professor P.N. Dhar chose hesitantly to lift the curtain, though not fully, in a newspaper article; he has promised to reveal all but only after his own demise. The younger officers who attended the conference have a vivid recollection of events within their purview. The Pakistani version has been given in considerable detail in a series of newspaper articles by Abdul Sattar in a rejoinder to Professor Dhar's account. Abdul Sattar was part of his country's delegation and rose to become a Minister of State.

At the conference table the two sides came with very different objectives. In the words of Professor Dhar, 'the overriding consideration for India was to put an end to its adversarial relations with Pakistan and to forge an instrument that would help to build a structure of durable peace'. According to him, the Indian side, ever mindful of the lessons of the Treaty of Versailles, was anxious not to appear to be imposing harsh terms as by a victor in war. In fact, D.P. Dhar, even in his discussions at the Murree preparatory meeting to lay down general principles for the Conference, waxed eloquent, according to Sattar, in disclaiming any intention 'to use the occupation of territory and prisoners-of-war as levers of pressure'. Whatever Bhutto may have confided to Mrs Gandhi in private about his willingness ultimately to accept the status quo in Kashmir, at the Conference Aziz Ahmed adamantly refused to discuss the issue at all. According to Dhar the Indian side relented as it did not wish to appear harsh. By this act of self-abnegation the Indian negotiators renounced the overwhelming advantage which they held in their hands and left the vital issue of Kashmir wide open for future contention.

Pakistan, with a much greater sense of realism, and with all the cards stacked against it, came with the one-pointed aim of recovering occupied territory and the release of its prisoners-of-war with as little cost to itself as possible. Taking the fullest advantage of Indian assurances, it played its hand adroitly, achieving fully its set objectives, while conceding little, except some empty verbiage. The only price it could have paid, and which India could have demanded, was in regard to its claims in Kashmir. Pakistan had always insisted and the Shimla

Agreement had, indeed, affirmed that Kashmir had 'bedevilled relations' between the two countries over the previous twenty five years. Yet, despite India's stated intention finally to end the state of confrontation, this vital question was side-stepped.

The question of the agenda could not be resolved at the Murree meeting as Aziz Ahmed insisted on restricting it to immediate post-war issues. D.P. Dhar wanted to widen its scope by removing all sources of conflict coming in the way of the establishment of a durable peace.

At the main Conference, the two leaders left the wrangling over the drafts to their officials. To establish good-neighbourly relations, the Pakistani side proposed an approach which was diametrically opposed to that which they had adamantly adopted before the Conference and to which they have reverted since. They demanded a step-by-step approach to improve relations in order to clear the atmosphere for the settlement of the 'basic issues'—their euphemism for 'Kashmir', which they currently describe as the 'core issue'. They now insist on its settlement first before anything else, and by 'settlement' they mean settlement on their terms.

In Shimla the two sides excelled each other in sophistry and legerdemain. The problem of priorities was glossed over and the forbidden word 'Kashmir' was omitted until the final paragraph of the draft. It was then slipped in among all pending issues for future settlement. The Pakistanis, like a well-drilled team, strove hard to attain their single objective, viz., recovering their crippling losses in war and saving themselves from future danger and humiliation. Their attitude was not that of supplicants in defeat but of equals, for had they not been assured by the Indians that there would be no victor, no vanquished, at the talks?

P.N. Dhar states that at a preliminary meeting with Indira Gandhi, Bhutto disclosed that he was personally prepared to consider a settlement of the Kashmir question along the ceasefire line. But his political enemies and military bosses would denounce him for what they would consider as the surrender of a vital interest. That would endanger Pakistan's fragile democracy after fourteen years of military rule. Furthermore, he was anxious to carry the support of all political parties who were represented on his delegation. He emphasised that he particularly wanted the support of Aziz Ahmed and, through him, of the powerful bureaucracy.

Aziz Ahmed, however, was strongly opposed to any discussion on Kashmir but, according to Dhar, relented when it was explained that the Indian side 'was not insisting on the immediate and formal acceptance of the status quo which they believed could be looked upon as the imposition of harsh terms by the victor in war'. Leaning over backwards to mollify the obdurate Aziz Ahmed, the Indian side again 'reminded themselves of the Treaty of Versailles as it might nurture a revanchist sentiment in Pakistan and lead to another war'. From Dhar's account, it seems that the Indian side was almost apologetic for having been victorious and it went out of its way to placate the adversary, instead of pressing home its advantage. There was an evident contradiction between acceptance of the view that friendly and harmonious relations could not be established, unless the 'basic issues' (i.e., Kashmir) which had 'bedevilled relations' were resolved, and the complete lack of willingness to discuss those issues at the Conference.

The Indian side 'put their proposal in a low key and in an indirect manner', according to Dhar, by proposing that the description of the ceasefire line be changed to the 'line of control'. Some deep esoteric significance seemed to be attached to the proposal which the Indian side considered to be the 'core' of the Indian solution to the Kashmir problem. But on close examination, it really amounts to little more than a distinction without a difference; in actual fact it has made little or no difference to the ground situation. But even this change in nomenclature was vehemently opposed by Aziz Ahmed. The

Indian hope was that by some alchemy the change in description of the line would 'graduate it to the level of the de jure border'. On this issue, after five days of wrangling, the Shimla Conference was declared to have failed. The Pakistanis began making preparations for departure on the following morning.

But then a dramatic turn of events occurred. Bhutto asked for an appointment with Mrs Gandhi to say farewell. This was a well-known and often practised ploy to seize success from failure. Bhutto breezed in at Mrs. Gandhi's residence for a tête-à-tête; outside the closed door Haksar and P.N. Dhar posted themselves like dwarpals. Within an hour, Bhutto emerged, all smiles, and told the waiting officials that they would have work to do that night. Mrs Gandhi disclosed that Bhutto, in a great show of reasonableness, had agreed to the use of the offending words 'line of control' which had been the stumbling block. But he added the phrase 'without prejudice to the recognised position of either side'. He explained that this was necessary to placate the likes of Aziz Ahmed and other hard-liners. In the Pakistani perception, however—as disclosed by Sattar—these words nullified the first part of the sentence which called for respect for the line of control. As a further bait, Bhutto dangled the prospect of the ultimate recognition of the line as an international frontier. But, he explained, this could only be done gradually as he had to carry the people with him and especially the army and the Opposition. He therefore pleaded that no reference to his pledge be incorporated in the final document. Mrs Gandhi was persuaded or cajoled into accepting Bhutto's plea, who assured her on leaving: 'Aap mujhpe bharosa keejiye' ('You must trust me'). And she put her trust in him.

Professor Dhar reminds us that the most important clause was 4(1) which called for respect for the line of control, to which two clever sentences were added by him and Haksar. These state that 'both sides shall refrain from the threat or the use of force in violation of the line'. The Professor derives comfort from the belief that the adroit Bhutto would thus be bound firmly to his oral promise. The subtlety of the wording obscured its presumed intention, but had no impact on Pakistan's irredentist ambitions. This is evident from the patent fact that these interpolations have not made an iota of difference to the harsh ground realities.

Equally astonishing is Professor Dhar's revelation that Mrs Gandhi had confided to Bhutto that 'she would hate to appear to be dictating terms to a defeated adversary'. She had therefore readily agreed to the 'earliest possible' withdrawal of troops from occupied territory. She had also accepted Bhutto's pretexts for not incorporating his pledge regarding Kashmir in the document. To this she added her own fear that 'the formal withdrawal of the Indian claim on Pak-occupied Kashmir could create political trouble for her'. But most astonishing of all was her ready agreement to not insist on a secret protocol, since, according to P.N. Dhar, 'it was considered inconsistent with the desire to build a structure of durable peace'. As far as is known, Mrs Gandhi also made no record of her secret conversation with Bhutto. Nor is there any tape-recording of so crucial a meeting. So much for the democratic principle of accountability!

It was a most remarkable confidence trick performed on Mrs Gandhi, a woman who was not the most trusting of persons; she did not trust even her own Cabinet colleagues. It made even the Pakistanis wonder how she could have caved in so readily. Writes Abdul Sattar, reflecting the Pakistani reaction:

> Why did Indira Gandhi decide to concede the vital changes Bhutto sought in India's final Draft? Was she under pressure from the great powers to conclude a peace treaty? Did she feel that India, having already cut Pakistan into two, should legitimise the gain by securing Pakistan's agreement? Was she influenced by the thought that the elected leaders of Pakistan should not return empty-handed? Or was she beguiled by Bhutto's eloquence and promises?

The answer to Sattar is to be found in his last question; the astute Bhutto had inveigled Mrs Gandhi into unquestioning acceptance of his 'good faith'.

Whatever satisfaction Mrs Gandhi's advisers may have derived from their illusion that they had managed to entrap Bhutto in a web of words, the fact remains that, having achieved his objective of recovering lost territory and prisoners-of-war, Bhutto did not consider himself bound by anything else in the Agreement. Indeed, from the moment he returned to Pakistan, in public speeches and private statements, he made the point that he had conceded nothing. As evidence of Pakistan's bad faith, in 1973, the very year after the Shimla Agreement—Pakistan went to the International Court of Justice charging India with violation of the Geneva Convention on prisoners-of-war.

In his newspaper articles Abdul Sattar, spells out the Pakistani official version and rebuts the assertions of Professor Dhar about the understandings reached at the Conference, and controverts the Indian interpretation of practically every article of the Agreement. He has poured scorn on the principle of 'bilateralism', by which India laid great store, pointing out that the very first substantive paragraph of the Agreement ('both sides have undertaken to abide by the principles and purposes of the Charter of the United Nations', thereby accepting the various methods spelt out therein for the pacific settlement of disputes) ignores 'bilateralism'. Even on the question of the prisoners-of-war, on which India had shown such mistaken generosity by delinking it from Kashmir, Sattar senses that India tried linking it with the question of the recognition of Bangladesh and the latter's demand for the return of some prisoners for trial as war criminals. The Indians, from Sattar's account, were almost apologetic for raising the issue, which the Pakistanis indignantly rejected. Sattar contends that Pakistan was totally unwilling to pay any price for the return of the prisoners, for that would be against 'an obligation' under 'international humanitarian law'.

Actually, it was largely a matter of tactical importance to Pakistan.

On the question of returning captured territory, Pakistan accused India of not complying with a Security Council resolution calling for the status quo ante bellum since the line of control deviated marginally from the ceasefire line. He reveals that the vacation of the captured territory by India would enable one million displaced persons to return to their homes, and that fear of the territory being taken over permanently by India would be dispelled.

Sattar strenuously denies that Bhutto had made any commitment to Indira Gandhi accepting the subsequent conversion of the line of control into an international frontier. There was only Professor Dhar's assertion in this regard without any supporting evidence whatsoever.

Despite India's easy surrender of the fruits of victory, Sattar complains that the Agreement was made 'under duress', and, citing the Treaty of Versailles, argues that because of Pakistan's position of disadvantage, this Agreement too could be similarly repudiated. But he expresses satisfaction at the fact that Pakistan had successfully averted the danger which it had greatly feared, of Kashmir being brought into the discussions.

It is difficult to understand why the Indian negotiators should have been at pains to persuade a reluctant Pakistan to consent formally to the annexing of one-third of the territory in Jammu and Kashmir forcibly seized by it by aggression in 1947. This ran counter to India's legal and principled stand at the United Nations throughout the long and troubled history of the Kashmir problem, that Pakistan must first vacate those territories seized by aggression. It legitimised Pakistani occupation of the territory without affecting the status of the line-of-control. What recondite purpose this manoeuvre served is known only to its authors.

Another curious feature of the negotiations was the advocacy on behalf of Pakistan—which should have been left to fight its own political battles with its formers partner—to dissuade Sheikh Mujibur Rahman from demanding the return of Pakistani war criminals for trial. Sattar says that such a trial would have greatly embittered Pakistan's relations with Bangladesh. It was hardly in India's interest to go out of its way to prevent such an eventuality.

Taken all in all, the Shimla Agreement was a lamentable case of the squandering away of a unique opportunity to resolve the Kashmir problem once and for all. The result is there for all to see: India's position is far worse today both internally and externally than it has ever been since the problem arose.

The Indian side seemed to have bowed deferentially to the Churchillian dictum: 'In victory, magnanimity; in defeat, defiance'. Their naive belief was that soft words would soften Pakistani hearts. It had been forgotten that the same Zulfiqar Ali Bhutto, representing Pakistan, had come to India during the Chinese aggression and, with the arrogance of a victor, demanded the surrender of the whole of Jammu and Kashmir, barring a sliver of territory in Kathua tahsil, as the price for not stabbing India in the back. Earlier, after the 1965 war, he had threatened India at the United Nations with a 'thousand year war'. Yet, at Shimla the Indian negotiators felt they would be overstepping the bounds of delicacy were they even to press for a discussion on Kashmir, much less insist on its prior settlement before agreeing to hand over the fruits of victory to the vanquished. Truly it was a case of defeat in victory and victory in defeat.

# SIXTEEN

# Three Prime Ministers

The first three Prime Ministers of independent India could hardly have been more disparate. In presence, character, attributes, ideas and ideals and ways of functioning, they were far removed from each other. Nehru was welded in the harsh discipline of a British public school—Harrow—which spawned empire-builders and rulers. Then followed Cambridge where social class and scholarship were the passport for entry. After eating his dinners at the inns of court to become a Barrister, he returned to India after many years, an accomplished 'English' gentleman of high degree. But it was galling to his pride and spirited nature to find himself in his own country in a position of inferiority to the ruling class with which he had freely associated abroad. Revolt against this order of things, therefore, came almost naturally to him.

Nehru was a true patrician: he wielded power and authority as to the manner born. He was drawn to Mahatma Gandhi, whose passion for the freedom of the country and the regeneration of the people he shared. The Mahatma's unique thoughts and actions in the classical Indian spirit, his indomitable faith and invincible courage, fascinated him. But Nehru himself had different ideas and a different pattern of behaviour, moulded by his training and education no less than by his impatient nature and imperious temperament. In spite of, or perhaps because of, these differences, a bond of deep affection and respect was forged between the Mahatma and his acolyte. But Nehru was no unquestioning disciple; he never hesitated to differ from his mentor until he was persuaded to the contrary.

When Nehru assumed office, the British felt quite comfortable with him, which they never did with the Mahatma whose unexpected ways and seemingly strange manoeuvres they never understood. No wonder that the British press never tired of taking delight in referring to Nehru as 'the last of the Viceroys'. Not one for dissimulation, Nehru never hesitated to speak out his mind, but always in a restrained manner without causing unnecessary umbrage. Although unquestioned as a leader, democratic values were ingrained in him. He detested the fawning and flattery which seemed to come so naturally to Congress politicians and any attempt to touch his feet would be sharply rebuffed.

When Independence came, Nehru as the 'favourite son' of the Mahatma assumed the reins of power almost as a birthright. There were, however, many who favoured Sardar Vallabbhai Patel, whose organisational and administrative skills, resoluteness and indomitable will, were legendary. But the down-to-earth Sardar lacked Nehru's glamour or the degree of affection that the Mahatma had for the latter. While Nehru endowed the new government with style and distinction and projected it on to the international stage, the Sardar quietly and determinedly brought about the unification of the country by the merger of the five hundred odd princely states. He also suppressed disruptive forces with a stern hand and restored the fractured administration, enabling it to meet its daunting responsibilities. Nehru was strongly allergic to the Indian Civil Service and many would have taken premature retirement, but the Sardar, with his sturdy realism, recognised the imperative need to retain a band of experienced and dedicated administrators without whom the whole structure would face collapse. Had his advice on Kashmir—to hold what we have—been heeded, the story of that state would have been different.

Nehru, with his world view and socialist orientation, thought and functioned on a different wave-length to most of his cabinet colleagues. One of the areas where Nehru thought differently and was far ahead of his colleagues, as well as most of his countrymen, was foreign affairs; most people regarded this as a fad or fancy of the Prime Minister, failing to recognise their relevance to the country.

Throughout his Prime Ministership, Nehru retained the portfolio of foreign affairs, to which he devoted much thought and attention. As the agency through whose instrumentality effect could be given to policy, it was necessary to have a diplomatic service. Little time was lost in creating such a service and an obvious source was the Indian Civil Service.

For almost the entire seventeen years of Nehru's Prime Ministership, I worked under his shadow abroad and at home. At first only a few diplomatic missions were set up, on a selective basis, by the newly-inducted ICS officers, most of whom headed them or were second-in-command. Ambassadorships of some missions regarded as of special interest were generally given to second-rank Congress politicians who were not elected to Parliament or were not considered for cabinet appointments. But before long, many of them proved to be liabilities and some even disasters. Thereafter, the exclusion of permanent officials from such posts became less rigid. To fill the lower diplomatic ranks, a selection committee of three senior officials made ad hoc selections, and in the process a good deal of chaff came in with the grain.

How closely the Prime Minister followed events around the

globe became evident when I took up my first assignment as the deputy to Vijayalakshmi Pandit, our Ambassador in Moscow. Our reports, some of which in retrospect must have been rather amateurish, elicited comments and sometimes long minutes from the Prime Minister.

It was at the United Nations that Nehru's guiding hand was most evident. I arrived there in the midst of a raging controversy over the Korean war. The United States delegation was using every means to get an endorsement for its policy to extend the war to the north. The newly-independent countries of Asia and Africa were divided and uncertain and were being dragooned into voting with the United States. But under Nehru's firm instructions, the Indian delegation stood out against all pressures and blandishments. It was a lonely position, for many had sought safety in numbers. Soon some other states began to take an independent line more in consonance with their national interests.

No specific directive enunciating India's overall foreign policy had been issued, but its broad parameters could be discerned from the Prime Minister's statements and directives on particular issues as they arose. We refused to be aligned with any power blocs but would judge every question on its merits. We would struggle relentlessly against colonialism and racism; we would work for the promotion of peace and the lowering of international tensions and take a firm stand against the arms race. Such were the general principles which gradually evolved. It was at the United Nations that one had to take an open position on all current issues, which in one form or another were on the agenda. While in the chancelleries one need not disclose one's hand and muffle it in diplomatic verbiage, at the United Nations where 'open disagreements were openly arrived at', the voting pattern spoke for itself.

Nehru took considerable personal interest in the debates in the UN Security Council—of which India was a member at the time—and in the General Assembly. Moreover, when instructions from South Block arrived which appeared to be out of context, an appeal to the Prime Minister would generally result in an immediate corrective.

The Prime Minister took a hand in the posting of heads of sensitive missions: for these he chose persons he knew and in whom he had confidence. A sort of dialogue was continuously in progress, the missions supplying information and ideas with the help of which overall policy began to take shape. At the United Nations where the nations of the world met, one experienced with pride the degree of respect and admiration which the young Republic of India under Jawaharlal Nehru's stewardship was held. This was all the more remarkable as the country was at that time battling with daunting problems of every description. The economy was weak, there was little industry and there was a chronic food shortage. There were problems of internal disorder and national integration; and the defence establishment was hardly worth the name. Yet, no important decision was taken at the United Nations without India's views and if possible concurrence being sought. There was no Non-Aligned Group at the time and even the Afro-Asian Group, such as it was, had yet to take shape. What a contrast to today. India is the world's biggest democracy and has the third largest army in the world. It has a burgeoning economy, galloping industrialisation, a fast-expanding middle-class and it is one of the big emerging markets. Yet our international standing, especially as revealed at the United Nations, has greatly declined.

I was always surprised and gratified at the amount of time the Prime Minister gave me when I came home for consultations or on leave from postings abroad. Invariably, I would be asked to stay to lunch, to continue a conversation. Vijayalakshmi Pandit was often at Teen Murti House. Occasionally Padmaja Naidu and Krishna Menon would be present, while Indira Gandhi was a constant fixture. In such mixed company, the conversation was always entertaining but little business was done. It was only when Nehru—albeit with the silent Indira—was 'alone' that business could be discussed.

From several small incidents and the general attitude of the two towards each other, I got the feeling that Nehru stood in some awe of his daughter, while she seemed to exercise a sort of guardianship over him. There was none of that warm and affectionate relationship that was so evident between Nehru and Vijayalakshmi. With Indira there was a sort of holding back, of cautious restraint. I remember a time when Nehru, against the advice of his doctors, helped himself to ice-cream and Indira reacted sharply, reproaching him for not controlling himself: he pleaded defensively that just a little would do no harm!

On another occasion at Brioni while I was hurrying from the guest house to the waiting horse-drawn phaeton to join the Prime Minister who was already seated with Indira, I heard her stridently upbraiding him for some minor indiscretion. It was only when I caught up that the tirade quietened down, leaving Indira fuming within. Nehru, very much on the defensive was making placatory noises.

Nehru used to send out detailed letters periodically to all Chief Ministers and Indian envoys abroad, among others, which revealed his thoughts and hopes for the country. Foreign affairs occupied a prominent place in those letters. They put one in touch with the various plans and programmes under way and contained broad guidelines for the benefit of the states. These communications were of an educative nature, intended to draw state-level politicians out of their limited grooves and to point to wider horizons. In Parliament Nehru continued this educative process, particularly evident in the case of foreign affairs when he would expatiate at length on global developments to an unresponsive, and sometimes bored audience.

In retrospect, it is remarkable with what intrepidity India embarked on the turbulent and totally unfamiliar waters of international affairs. The pioneers of the diplomatic service were drawn from administrative or secretariat posts and they had to educate themselves on the job. The ease and aplomb with which India was able to conduct itself among the nations of the world never ceased to surprise foreign countries. It was Nehru's inspiration and guiding hand that gave reassurance to India's envoys abroad. In the ministry, the Prime Minister had wisely placed Sir Girija Shankar Bajpai in charge as Secretary-General. Bajpai, an outstanding former civil servant had earlier also held the high office of Member in the Viceroy's Executive Council. He shared Nehru's style and flair, and lent tone and quality to the new service. The policies fashioned in the hard school of experience have guided Indian governments ever since and have stood the test of time and circumstance. Now, however, the standards of performance have fallen lamentably over the years and the service, now greatly expanded, has become flabby and otiose.

Nehru observed regular working hours in the ministry. He met the senior officers regularly at an appointed time, allowing them first to study the cables as they poured in through the night. He was always receptive to new ideas and avid for the latest information about international developments. He was sharp in picking upon weaknesses in a proposal and would readily offer a better solution. He prided himself on his fitness and would take two steps at a time going up to his office in South Block. It was only when his policy towards China lay in ruins and a rapid decline in his health set in that a small elevator had to be installed for his use. His drowsiness as he sat at his desk became more and more marked. When reporting to him, he would at first listen intently but gradually his eyelids would droop and then close altogether. He would try and jerk himself out of his weariness but it was evident that he could take no more. This growing weakness became rather embarrassing when foreign personages came to call on him. On one occasion when King Husain of Jordan called on him at Teen Murti House, the visitor began by saying how honoured he felt to be meeting the Prime Minister whom he regarded as an 'elder brother' whose advice and blessings he had come to seek. The King continued in that vein; the Prime Minister listened wearily and then shut his eyes without saying a word. I tried to break the embarrassing silence. What really began to worry one was the change in Nehru's complexion which used to be bright and clear; it began to lose its lustre and to turn a murky yellow. Nehru, however, kept his work routine although his noting on files became brief and he now preferred to deal orally with matters. One felt a sense of foreboding as one daily watched the relentless decline in the Prime Minister's condition.

Nehru inspired great loyalty and respect. Senior officials, who are often critical of their ministers and of politicians generally, could hardly fault Nehru. They felt secure in the knowledge that the Prime Minister would not let them down and would accept full ministerial responsibility for decisions taken. What a contrast to the lamentable state of affairs nowadays when officials are treated as lackeys and made scapegoats to shield ministerial culpability, corruption and ineptitude. Nehru functioned openly and transparently, without a shadow of underhand dealing. He worked through the responsible officials and would never bypass them or deal surreptitiously with their subordinates.

The sensitive manner in which he expressed his appreciation of an official's work was to quietly walk unannounced into his room and ask a few questions while looking out of the window; after a few minutes, he would quietly walk out. We would sometimes be caught unawares, pipe in mouth and shoeless feet on the table, while going through papers.

Nehru was compassionate and considerate and would pay heed to the human aspect of a problem. As Secretary in charge of personnel, I had occasion to take hardship cases to him, particularly those in which other ministries or senior colleagues had taken what seemed a rather harsh stand.

In one particular case, a young officer had applied for permission to marry a foreign girl. He was refused, and left with the hard choise of either following the dictates of the heart or the stern path of duty. There was a rule in the ministry prohibiting marriage with foreigners on pain of removal from service. The reason was that the wife of a diplomat represented the culture of her country and Indian diplomats could therefore have only Indian wives. Whatever may have been the justification for the rule, which, incidentally, was not unique to India, the question was how rigidly or humanely it should be enforced. In India there were many senior officers, both civil and military, who had foreign wives. The head of our ministry had a foreign wife as did the Vice-Chief of the Army Staff. There were also officials in the finance and other ministries who had foreign wives and one or two such officials had even been given important diplomatic assignments. Nehru agreed that the First Secretary's case should be given a second thought; the young officer was transferred to another post to enable him to overcome what could have been merely a passing infatuation, but if he remained constant in his affection his case could be reconsidered. After a few months of separation from the object of his love, the young man made an appeal for reconsideration, otherwise he would be compelled to resign. It did not need much persuasion with the Prime Minister for permission to be accorded to the young man who rendered a creditable account of himself in the service.

Another case worth mentioning concerned a student who had graduated from Cambridge and successfully taken the competitive examination for entry into the Foreign Service held in London. As a matter of routine, the character and antecedents of a candidate have to be verified before appointment to any government job, however humble. In India it is normally done through the police. The Indian High Commission referred the case to Scotland Yard which sent a strongly adverse report stating categorically that the candidate was a communist and subversive and totally unfit for any employment in government, let alone the Foreign Service. This report was endorsed by the Education Adviser to the High Commissioner without further enquiry and then by the High Commissioner himself, and transmitted to New Delhi. The Home Ministry and the Intelligence Bureau, for their part, expressed full agreement with Scotland Yard. The papers then came to the External Affairs Ministry where the Committee of Secretaries, of which I was a member, endorsed the negative recommendation and overruled my reservations. It then fell to me as Secretary Personnel to get the final orders of the Prime Minister.

In reporting to the Prime Minister, I said I was much troubled by the handling of a matter on which the future life and career of a promising young man depended. In the first place, when we had an Educational Adviser in London whose business it was to keep an eye on Indian students in England, why was it necessary to refer the matter to Scotland Yard and to accept its report blindly? It also seemed infra dig and subservient to refer the case to a foreign police agency when we had our own means of verification as there was also a Security Adviser in the High Commission. The Cold War was then at its height; in the west there was an obsession about communists and it was easy to brand anyone a communist if he showed any leftist leanings. The young man in question had the gift of the gab and had taken a prominent part in debates at the Cambridge Union. It was normal for young people to be rebels, at least verbally, for as Bernard Shaw had said, if a man until he was thirty was not a communist, he was wrong in the heart; but if he remained a communist after thirty, he was even more wrong in the head. My wife, Susheela, had herself as an undergraduate at Cambridge, moved in leftist circles and sold the *Daily Worker* at street corners.

The Prime Minister had no hesitation in deciding that a

second and less perfunctory look at the matter was called for. He asked how I intended to proceed. I said an enquiry could be addressed to the candidate's Moral Tutor at his Cambridge College who would be in the best position to testify. The unique institution of Moral Tutor provides every undergraduate with a guide, mentor and friend to whom he can turn for advice, support or sympathy and who keeps an avuncular eye over his ward, discreetly watching his progress in his varied activities.

The report of the Moral Tutor on the young man over whom the sword of Democles hung, was most eulogistic; it praised his debating skills and his general behaviour without a word of disparagement or reference to any subversive views. It strongly favoured his suitability for the Foreign Service. That clinched matters and the Prime Minister, overruling the whole array of negative reports, ordered the candidate's entry into the service. The man did well in the service and would have gone far had he stayed the course. But his ambition took a quantum leap, landing him in the murky world of party politics—not, however, as a communist or leftist.

Foreign Service officers coming home from distant postings around the globe were hard put to find even the most rudimentary accommodation. Thanks to the foresight of my predecessor, a fine hostel building to meet this need had come up and was awaiting occupation. It caught the acquisitive eyes of other ministries who wanted it to be made available for general use. When the matter was referred to the Prime Minister for adjudication by the Works and Housing Ministry, which strongly backed the other claimants, the Prime Minister asked me to settle it with the minister concerned. As expected, there was a sharp division of opinion, which the Prime Minister decided in favour of the Foreign Service. The hostel has been a great boon to the members of that peripatetic service.

Nehru would often ask whenever a senior official of the service was retiring, if he had anything on hand. When told that there was nothing, he would ask if something could be found for him to help tide over a difficult period of adjustment.

An incident which was long remembered in the Ministry concerned my younger brother, Harishwar, who had been seconded from the ICS to what was known in British days as the Foreign and Political Service, recruitment to which was made by interview by the Viceroy himself. At Independence Harishwar found himself in the department now renamed the Ministry of External affairs. The Prime Minister chose him as his Private Secretary to look after his External Affairs portfolio. Harishwar was a man of outstanding intellect and ability, with a quiet and lovable but independent nature. Nehru had greatly taken to him for his sterling qualities. One day as Harishwar walked into the Prime Minister's office, as was his wont, Nehru in a tantrum, flung a fat file at him. Harishwar, who had nothing whatsoever to do with the file, promptly turned on his heel and made for the door, leaving the file where it lay. Nehru quickly got up from his desk, picked up the file himself and intercepted Harishwar at the door. Bringing Harishwar back, he discussed other matters as though nothing had happened. Fifteen years later when Harishwar, then Ambassador in Nepal, suddenly passed away at age of 49 while climbing the Everest glacier, Nehru sent a most moving personal message of sympathy. Himself a dying man, he praised Harishwar warmly as a 'jewel' of a man, who was 'an ornament of the service which he adorned'. Nine days later, Jawaharlal Nehru himself passed away.

The Prime Minister's interest in world affairs did not flag until the last. I last saw him when he was mortally ill at Teen Murti House. I had gone to enquire after his health, but was ushered up to his bedroom. There he sat in front of an open door, his legs wrapped in a blanket in the heat of May, looking wanly out at the garden. He had difficulty in turning around or in breathing, and his colour was frightening. He asked: 'Rajeshwar, what is the state of the world today?' just as he often did when at his desk. When I said I did not wish to tire him, he insisted that I proceed. When I came down the stairs I was filled with sorrow mixed with admiration for the titan of a man that Nehru was. That was the last I saw of him: three days later he was gone.

For all his greatness, Nehru was not a paragon of all the virtues. It would not be fair to expect him to be exempt from all the ills that man is heir to. His critics of today fault him on a multitude of counts, some real, many imaginary. A balanced and impartial appraisal would unquestionably arrive at the conclusion that Nehru served the country truly well. He held the country together after the havoc and trauma of Partition. What is more, he raised a weak and fractured nation to the heights of world eminence. He enabled it to regain its pride and self-respect after two and a half centuries of foreign domination. This alone entitled him to the nation's eternal gratitude.

True, Nehru was much criticised by some for what was regarded as excessive pontificating about peace and tolerance among nations. Perhaps this was carried to a fault, but the message of peace could not but strike a sympathetic chord in a world that had suffered the horrors of war, and even those who thought mainly in terms of force and might could not be entirely deaf to it.

Nehru is also being criticised by the high priests of liberalisation for the economic policies pursued by his government. At the time, the accepted wisdom was that poor countries which had enormous economic and social problems but woefully inadequate resources, had no option but to resort to some form of planning. This approach was intrinsically not unsound, but much depended on its implementation. Nehru was much influenced by Socialist theoreticians of the London School of Economics persuasion. In some ways the Soviet pattern, duly adopted, was accepted as a model; undue emphasis was placed on industrialisation to the neglect of agriculture on which an overwhelming proportion of the Indian people depended. It was mistakenly imagined that the setting up of industries would have a 'trickledown effect' and help to regenerate the countryside. Also, in theory, it was believed that the expected profitability of the state-owned industries would finance the wider development plans without casting an extra burden of taxation on the people. In result, however, state enterprises, far from generating the huge surpluses expected, produced only huge losses and became a drain on the country's slender resources. Nehru at least restricted himself to heavy industry; it was left to his successors to pile failure upon failure by carrying the process of nationalisation even to consumer industries, hotel-keeping and the likes, with disastrous results.

Nehru often spoke of the 'scientific temper' which he was anxious to instil in his countrymen. He wanted to bring them out of their traditional backward-looking grooves of thought and behaviour. To this end, he set up a chain of scientific research institutes all over the country. Unfortunately, the results have generally belied expectations. A distinguished former revolutionary of the Ghadar Party, Dr Gobind Behari Lal, regarded as the father of American scientific journalism and one of the earliest winners of the Pulitzer prize, was invited to visit India to write in the international press about India's progress in science and technology. His report of his tour was most depressing; at practically every institute, instead of finding any scientific discoveries or original research, he was treated to what he described as a lot of 'gobbledegook'. The distinguished scientists could wax eloquent only about the inadequacy of their pay scales, accommodation, poor promotion prospects, transgressions of their rivals and so on. Dr Lal, a proud and patriotic Indian, returned with nothing for the foreign press, a sorely disappointed man.

The experience of the Indian Institutes of Technology has, however, been more encouraging. They have contributed towards endowing the country with one of the biggest pools of

well-qualified technicians and engineers in the world.
Unfortunately however, as the Indian government and industry
have been unable to absorb them gainfully, there has been a
heavy haemorrhaging of skilled personnel trained at heavy cost
by India and then migrating to other countries able to put their
talents to use.

Nehru, by his sheer force of personality and unchallenged
authority and prestige, was able to keep the Congress party,
composed of widely disparate elements, more or less in line. At
cabinet meetings, this was very evident. It was only Sardar Patel
and Maulana Azad, and occasionally Rafi Ahmad Kidwai, who
had the courage to voice a contrary opinion. After them, cabinet
meetings became a monologue. Ministers had seldom read the
papers and were inclined to find relief from boredom in slumber.
On one occasion, when the Prime Minister went around the table
asking for opinions on a matter of some importance, one minister,
jerked out of his somnolence, exclaimed that he fully shared the
Prime Minister's opinion. Nehru calmly reminded him that he
had not expressed any opinion so far!

While Nehru passionately loved the people of India and felt
greatly exhilarated by the adoring crowds, he did not seem to
love individual Indians, except for a very select few. He was not
a good judge of men and sometimes harboured vipers to his
bosom. One such was M.O. Mathai. This ingrate, who was raised
from the dust by his patron as his personal assistant and
stenographer, usurped much influence, besides enriching himself,
and finally wrote a scurrilous account about Nehru after his
death.

At another level, Nehru's blindness about Krishna Menon
constantly raised eyebrows and baffled his colleagues and
aroused their jealousy. Nehru had little in common with most of
his ministerial and party colleagues whose vision did not extend
beyond the confines of their home states or, sometimes, the
borders of the country. Menon, on the contrary, had spent much

of his life in England. He had numerous British friends—mostly of the left—and was at home with foreigners and revelled in international politics. He was a stimulating talker with a wry, sometimes biting, sense of humour and was scornful of most of his ministerial colleagues and more so of civil servants. He was thought to be somewhat of a misanthrope.

Menon had a razor-sharp mind, but he functioned in a conspiratorial sort of way. At the United Nations he immersed himself in intrigues. Despite his skill at semantic jugglery, he failed to carry much conviction largely because of his manner. His abrasive tongue and haughty ways were not calculated to win friends or influence people. He undoubtedly made a strong but rather negative impact in the council chambers of the United Nations, but he was more feared than respected, more suspected than trusted, more disliked than favoured. The former image of the Indian delegation as 'the conscience of mankind' and the apostles of peace and friendship among nations, gave way to a strident and much sharper contour. Menon's long-winded and convoluted speeches, while they received much applause at home, carried little weight among delegates. His marathon oration on Kashmir lasting fourteen weary hours merely left delegates yawning, but in India it was acclaimed as a sheer tour de force which had sent the Pakistanis scurrying for cover. The reaction among Council members was that it must be a weak case that needed such lengthy and elaborate pleading. The prisoner-of-war issue in Korea and one or two other successes caught the public eye, but Menons' more numerous failures went unnoticed.

Nehru overlooked Menon's failures, the most catastrophic being India's defeat at the hands of China in 1962. Menon was most unsuited to be the Minister of Defence, a portfolio which required an accurate assessment of the security threats to the country, and tact and circumspection in dealing with the commanders of the defence services. It was the duty of the minister, to keep the armed services in a constant state of readiness to defend the borders of the country. Menon failed lamentably in perceiving the real threats to the country with the tragic result that the army was caught totally unprepared; he failed to ensure that the services were adequately equipped with the most modern weapons; he failed to inspire the loyalty and trust of the general staff by constantly interfering in matters of personnel; he failed in qualities of leadership. Yet, Nehru clung on to him against the unanimous opinions of his own hitherto subservient colleagues and the nation-wide clamour for Menon's head. It was only when Nehru's own position was imperilled, that he was forced to give in.

Menon's forays, as Minister Without Portfolio, in matters of foreign policy were often very ill-conceived. He viewed indulgently the brutal suppression by the Soviet Union of the 1956 uprising in Hungary. At a time when India needed Western support and assistance, Menon seemed almost to go out of his way to needle the Western countries, especially the hyper-sensitive United States. Towards the Soviet Union and other Communist states, he was always prepared to bend over backwards. Menon's preferences and prejudices had nothing to do with the national interest but were based solely on personal factors. Such an attitude frequently led to a distorted view of foreign policy issues which ultimately cost the country dear.

Menon had an almost pathological aversion towards Pakistan. Yet Pakistan was a fact—however inconvenient—that one had to live with. One cannot write off a next-door neighbour, obtuse and wrong-headed though it be. The only course, if one wishes to live at peace in one's own house, is to try and achieve some form of modus vivendi. But even this, Menon was not prepared to accept, preferring instead, to shut his eyes to the patent facts. Only some weeks before the Chinese attack, his sights were trained towards Pakistan as he feared it was about to launch a massive campaign and infiltration into Kashmir. Of this there was no evidence whatsoever apart from the scare stories routinely put out by some Communist missions of Eastern Europe. Because of this fixation, the army commanders were ordered by Menon to take immediate steps to meet the imagined onslaught from the wrong direction. This was at a time when Indian and Chinese patrols were playing hide and seek with each other, sometimes bloodily, in Ladakh, and the Chinese were making menacing moves along the central and eastern sectors of the Himalayan frontier. When the Chinese struck like a hurricane, the Indian army, which in World war II had won many accolades, found itself totally unprepared. Menon had even broken the morale of the army by indulging in his penchant for intrigue among the general staff, pushing up his favourites and down-grading able and independent officers.

At Independence, Menon was rewarded by being appointed High Commissioner for India in London for his work for independence as founder and all-in-all of the India League. That was perhaps the first regular job that he had ever held and in that exalted office he allowed his eccentricities full play. He made a great pretence of austere living by occupying the ante-room of his office in India House and, spurning the great mansion which had been purchased by the government for the High Commissioner's residence. Menon ate from the office canteen. He also took no pay. But he rode about in a Rolls-Royce and later collected all his accumulated arrears of pay! The staff he moved around like pawns on a chess-board, creating dissatisfaction all around. He had greatly increased the staff by patronage and it took years to pare it down somewhat; it still continues to be bloated.

Menon's complex nature was a constant matter both of fascination and frustration. To most he presented a forbidding image of hauteur and offensiveness. But there were other traits to his character. He made entertaining company when he chose to be sociable. He had a caustic sense of homour and loved to shoot barbs at others, but could not take a joke against himself. In the company of women—especially beautiful women—he could be most charming and agreeable, attracting much attention to himself. Impeccably clad, lean with sharp aquiline features and a mane of curly greying hair, he made an arresting figure. In a curious way, women were often attracted to him, especially western women, and though some women did hang around him, he was not known to have any mistresses. When down-and-out, as he was when he first appeared at the United Nations after his removal from his London post, he was meek and almost supplicating. His ultimate fall from power was as precipitate as his rise had been meteoric. When out of office, those who had fawned on him turned their backs on him. In his declining years, he would, like a lost soul, haunt the corridors of South Block calling on officials whom he had once despised. I used to feel rather sorry for him and would welcome him with a cup of tea and a pleasant chat, all previous differences forgotten. When Menon died, there was no national mourning. But curiously enough, Menon's fame and reputation, after several year's of eclipse, began to grow after his death. A leading avenue in South Delhi came to be named after him, his death anniversary is fairly widely remembered, especially in his native Kerala and he has come to occupy a niche in the Valhalla of the great. 'The evil that men do lives after them but the good is oft interred with their bones' said Mark Anthony in his funeral oration to Caesar. In Menon's case, the opposite is true.

The yawning chasm that Nehru's passing had left could never be fully bridged. After his death the Congress bosses were lost for a while in dithering and disputatious argument over his successor. There were whispered rumours of Nehru's own preference, but he had not named an heir-apparent and there were many contenders. Shastri had been brought in as Minister Without Portfolio to assist the ailing Prime Minister, especially with party and other miscellaneous work. But this was only after

Nehru had suffered a stroke at the Bhubaneshwar Party Congress. When Shastri was asked about the late Prime Minister's wishes, he replied in Hindi: 'I think it was she whom he wanted.' This was interpreted as a reference to Indira Gandhi, but was not taken seriously at the time by the power brokers.

A couple of days after Nehru's death, when the whole nation was in mourning, and we in the External Affairs Ministry felt orphaned, I was in my office as usual when the telephone rang. It was the familiar voice of Khanna, Nehru's Private Secretary, saying as he always did in Hindi: 'The Prime Minister is remembering you'. Greatly startled, I proceeded to the Prime Minister's room a few doors away, where my surprise turned to stupefaction. There, seated in Nehru's chair was another figure, that of Gulzarilal Nanda, the Home Minister, looking very pleased with himself. Nanda, though perhaps next in the pecking order, was a clownish character known for his fads, who consorted with wandering sadhus and the like. He was as incompetent as he was vain and self-opinionated. He had jumped into Nehru's vacant seat with alacrity and resented being referred to, during his few days of assumed glory, as 'Acting' Prime Minister'. It was a relief when we saw the last of him, and the mantle fell on Lal Bhadur Shastri, a man known for his integrity, ability and genuine humility.

The very first thing that Shastri did on assuming his heavy burden was to ask that the Prime Minister's office room in South Block be completely rearranged. How could he possibly sit in the chair that 'Panditji' had occupied, he said, a new chair had to be provided. The office table by the main window had to be shifted and all the furniture rearranged. The next problem was of the Prime Minister's residence. No, he would absolutely not occupy Teen Murti House which suited 'Panditji' who was a regal personality. He himself was used to far more modest surroundings. 'Indiraji' he said had told him with tears in her eyes that she could not bear to think of anyone else occupying

Teen Murti House, with which so many of her memories were wrapped up and with whose every tree she was familiar. Shastri said he had assured her that he could not even think of moving into that grand house; his needs were simple and he was content where he was.

I happened to be the only one in the Ministry with whom Shastri was familiar and I also happened to be the Secretary in charge of Administration. Shastri felt that he could confide in me and take advice in regard to personal matters. He had known me since 1946 when he was a Parliamentary Secretary to the UP Chief Minister, Pandit Gobind Ballabh Pant, and I was the Home Secretary. (Incidentally, Chaudhury Charan Singh was another Parliamentary Secretary to the Chief Minister but Pant had more trust in Shastri.) When Rafi Ahmed Kidwai, the Home Minister, moved to the Centre, Shastri was allotted his portfolio. I had then much to do with him and found him an admirable minister—thoughtful, compassionate and decisive.

The question of a suitable residence for the Prime Minister then arose, and many suggestions were made. But Shastri insisted on staying on at 1 Akbar Road, a pleasant bungalow, originally built for Joint Secretaries but since appropriated by ministers. Shastri said his wife thought it was auspicious for them and absolutely refused a change. When it was pointed out that as Head of Government he would receive calls from eminent foreign dignitaries and would need a larger reception room and appropriate catering arrangements, he said he personally was content with his wife's cooking on a charcoal stove. Eventually, he was persuaded, while continuing to reside in 1 Akbar Road himself, to use the adjacent house at 10 Janpath for official purposes, with suitable catering arrangements and staff provided from the surplus at Rashtrapati Bhawan. We then had to persuade the reluctant High Commissioner of New Zealand, who was occupying 10 Janpath, to move to another residence. The two houses were then connected by a rather ungainly covered corridor, the boundary walls raised, and adequate security arrangements provided. No.10 Janpath later became the residence of Rajiv Gandhi on his relinquishing the Prime Ministership and, since his death, continues to be a magnet for Congress Politicians eager to be associated with the surviving mystique of his family.

The next problem concerned the Prime Minister's sartorial arrangements. Shastri said he could not possibly get into the sort of tight pajamas that Nehru wore as his legs were too thin and he felt very 'awkward' when he once tried them on! 'Panditji' was the soul of elegance and he could not hope to emulate him, so could he continue to wear his habitual kurta-dhoti? I said that for official banquets for visiting Presidents and Prime Ministers the regulation dress was a black achkan, adding that a pair of socks would be necessary even if the Prime Minister wore a dhoti. For formal luncheons a grey achkan would be appropriate. Nehru's excellent tailor was summoned and the new Prime Minister, who possessed only a single tin trunk for his entire wardrobe, was adequately sartorially equipped.

Attention next turned to the rather more serious business of the late Prime Minister's External Affairs portfolio. Shastri said with disarming candour that he knew nothing about foreign affairs, and that he had never been beyond the country's borders. When I said that the Prime Minister had a special responsibility for the formulation and conduct of foreign policy, Shastri expressed confidence that the 'able and experienced' senior officers would carry things through. Nevertheless, he wished to divest himself of the portfolio; moreover, because of his short stature, he felt 'awkward' talking to the generally tall foreigners! He asked for suggestions about who would be the most suitable person to take over the portfolio. The choice lay entirely with the Prime Minister, he was reminded. Eventually, the tallest in height among his ministers was chosen, viz., Sardar Swaran Singh. He held the office until Mrs Gandhi's 'Emergency'. Sardar Sahib was a most durable politician; a small town lawyer, he had been a minister in the pre-Partition government of the Punjab and continued in the national government uninterruptedly until he was ousted by Mrs Gandhi. He had wisely advised her to step down in deference to the Allahabad High Court judgement out of respect for judicial authority and democratic principles, suggesting too, that she could return to power after an interregnum with greatly enhanced prestige. But Mrs Gandhi could not countenance such advice or even the person who offered it, so the Sardar had to pay the price.

As Foreign Minister, Sardar Sahib left much to the senior officers without interference or adventurousness on his part. Realising his own lack of familiarity with a subject, he preferred discussing it rather than expressing any views on paper. This worked well enough, although we missed Nehru's sure guiding hand and comforting presence. At international gatherings or in discussions with foreign visitors, especially on contentious issues, Sardar Sahib was unequalled, he could talk endlessly in his broad Punjabi brogue without really saying anything, leaving the others bewildered. In the Ministry, he proceeded cautiously in feeling his way around the intricacies of foreign policy matters. The story put out about him by a colleague known for his wit—that he had enquired how far Aksai Chin was from Ho-Chi-Minh—did him less than justice. But when he came to Paris from Rome he did ask if the Seine was the Tiber!

There was an unfortunate contretemps which ruffled the otherwise calm waters of the Ministry. It had been decided to bring out a periodical on foreign affairs for wide circulation, especially abroad. In its very first number, which was otherwise quite admirable, there was an introductory article on the new Foreign Minister which contained a most unfortunate printer's devil. In a reference to the Sardar's long experience of public affairs, the article appeared in print with the letter '1' missing from the word 'public'. When discovered, there was consternation in the Ministry and long cables were despatched to all the missions to recall all copies forthwith. Even the Sardar's proverbial equanimity was understandably disturbed.

It was not easy for Shastri to fill Nehru's place, nor did he attempt to do so. He retained his individuality and courageously shouldered great responsibilities in his own way. He was very accessible and responsive not only to his own party's views but to the opinions of the opposition, as well as the voice of the public. He believed in the method of consensus in the pristine spirit of the Congress which had tried to carry all shades of opinion with it. Shastri's was the 'still, small voice' of reason and persuasion, and when he spoke in Parliament he was listened to with respect. In dealing with issues, however complicated, he showed a sturdy common sense, getting to the heart of the matter without circumlocution. He arrived at decisions after careful thought and deliberation, weighing all options carefully. This method did sometimes occasion delays, but it was perhaps better to hasten slowly than to act in haste and repent at leisure. Those who were impatient and wanted quick action were critical, and Mrs Pandit dubbed Shastri and his government as 'prisoners of indecision'. But when the chips were down, Shastri could indeed take firm and decisive action without flinching; this he did to repel Pakistani aggression in Kashmir in 1965.

Shastri was a true Gandhian. He genuinely believed in simple living and his life-style was austere. He spurned riches and had little craving for power. He believed in Gandhian values in other respects too. While by no mean opposed to industrialisation, he was perceptive enough to dispute the then accepted wisdom that the setting up of industries in the countryside would automatically have a 'trickle-down' effect, spreading employment and prosperity among the village-folk around, Shastri wanted much more to be done directly for village uplift and the deployment of far more resources for the purpose. With his own rural background, he was deeply aware of the problems and hopes of the rural masses to whom the government's economic policies had so far brought little benefit.

By his own example, Shastri gave a new tone to the administration. Ministers no longer looked up to a father-figure to take decisions for them but were expected to take responsibility themselves. For the accountability of ministers, Shastri had himself set the example earlier by resigning as Minister for Railways when a serious accident costing many lives had occured somewhere in the vast railway network. How different was his behaviour to that of a much later minister who held on to his office when a particularly appalling accident occurred of a train falling into a river, causing many casualties. A senior railway official of impeccable credentials at headquarters two thousand miles away was unfairly made a scapegoat. The minister had himself to admit that the accident was in fact caused by a sudden squall and was therefore an act of nature.

One episode illustrates Shastri's attitude towards the services. He had invited many Secretaries to dinner at his residence, where we were warmly received by him on the lawn on a hot summer night. As we sat around having been served vegetarian food, we were astonished to see the Prime Minister himself coming around serving puris. When we remonstrated with him, he said we were his honoured guests who carried a heavy burden of responsibility and it was a pleasure to serve us. That spontaneous gesture won our hearts and filled us with a sense of admiration and loyalty towards our host. That act of humility bespoke Shastri's own bigness.

By his own example, Shastri had set a pattern of rectitude, accountability and high purpose which he expected others to follow, but there were exceptions. Until then the canker of corruption had nevertheless not invaded high places. Nehru had no doubt turned a blind eye to some notorious aberrations among some of his associates and provincial satraps, but India had the reputation the world over of having a clean and caring administration, in striking contrast to the state of affairs in most Asian and Latin American countries at the time. Indian envoys abroad felt proud at the encomiums showered on India for adhering to the high principles enjoined by the Mahatma and for being torch-bearers of democracy and the rule of law. What a sorry state our country has fallen into today!

On foreign-policy issues, Shastri displayed sturdy common sense and a down-to-earth attitude. Not for him the Nehruvian forays into distant lands and intractable global problems. He set his sights much nearer home. He declared India's primary aim was to seek and establish sound, peaceful and cooperative relations with all the neighbouring countries.

Shastri's decision in a trade negotiation with Afghanistan reveals his vision and quick grasp of essentials. The import of fresh and dried fruits from Afghanistan has been going on for ages and certain types of green raisins are produced exclusively for the Indian market. Afghanistan depended heavily on this traditional export trade which was a form of barter, and in exchange it imported practically all its requirements of cloth and various manufactured goods. A stalemate had developed in the trade talks, as representatives of the Commerce and Finance Ministries bargained hard and long like usurious traders in a market, to beat down the Afghans and, what is more, to reduce the annual import into India in weight and value. Nothing would move them and all efforts to persuade them to take a broader view fell on deaf ears. I then took the matter to the Prime Minister, explaining how dependent the impoverished Afghans were on their traditional trade with India and what loyal friends they had been. Shastri said our imports were very beneficial and nourishing and we must show generosity to our Afghan friends. He immediately increased the quota of imports and sanctioned a generous price for them. The Afghan delegation returned full of respect and gratitude towards the Prime Minister.

Shastri abhorred war and violence and passionately believed in peace. He settled a long-standing problem with Ceylon (as Sri Lanka was then called) on the question of Indians in that country, arriving at a formula which envisaged a large number being accorded Ceylonese citizenship and the rest repatriated to India in stages. It removed a long-standing grievance of the government of Ceylon and paved the way for the strengthening of relations. With Nepal, likewise, he took a new approach to disarm Nepalese suspicions of any Indian hegemonistic ambitions. Pakistan was the most intractable problem and he sought an opportunity to start a dialogue with that difficult neighbour.

The Cairo Summit Conference of the non-aligned nations was due only a few months after Shastri's coming to power in 1964. That was also to be Shastri's debut on the international stage. Nehru, with his great prestige, dominated such conferences and set the pace. Now that he was no longer there and India's position had, after the 1962 debacle at the hands of China, suffered greatly, it would be an uphill task to regain lost ground. As leader of the official team, I spent long hours in working out our strategy and tactics on the various issues on the agenda and to plan how best to counter the machinations of our adversaries and detractors.

At the Conference, Shastri comported himself with great wisdom and understanding, soon winning general respect and acclaim by his constructive interventions. He had been requested by general consent to deliver the valedictory address. The draft had been prepared by me and my colleagues, summing up the achievements of the Conference and its hopes for the future. As is usual with such formal utterances, it was couched in appropriate language with a ringing peroration. The draft had much earlier been submitted to the Prime Minister and nothing more had been heard about it. But barely an hour before nine o'clock at night when the final session was due, I was called to

Shastri's room a few doors away from mine in the Hilton Hotel where our whole delegation was housed. Shastri was pacing up and down while his Private Secretary and the Commerce Secretary sat, obviously discussing the draft. Shastri said that he was being urged to add a caveat in the body of the speech or at least in a footnote, keeping in mind the question of Kashmir, that it would not apply to a part of an existing state. Shastri asked for my frank opinion whether I agreed, or not to the addition. I objected strongly. I said that the Prime Minister of a great country should not be seen to be pettifogging about a matter which had been discussed in detail and on which our position had been made amply clear. His address should be inspiring and uplifting as it called for peace and cooperation in a distracted world. Shastri said he fully agreed and requested me to rewrite the speech which had been much mangled meanwhile. This seemed a difficult feat in the very limited time available. Asking the Prime Minister to have his dinner and to proceed to the place of the meeting in time, I hurried to my room and, calling my colleague Azim Husain over and finding two stenographers who had already packed their typewriters in preparation for next morning's departure, we got down to work. By the time the speech was rewritten, the typewritten copy checked and errors corrected by hand, the time for the session was almost upon us. Snatching a sandwich we sped to the meeting to find the delegates assembled. As we reached the Prime Minister's seat, he was invited to the podium to make his address. Taking the typed pages from my hand, he walked up and began his speech without even a glance at the papers. It was a faultless performance and was greeted with warm applause. At the conclusion, the Prime Minister received a standing ovation. When he returned, his first act was to thank us generously for our hard work.

Thanks to Shastri's leadership, India had regained at the Cairo Conference much of the prestige lost after the 1962

Chinese invasion. He had very successful meetings with President Nasser and other heads of states and governments. The only reverse we suffered was a result of an ill-conceived proposal of doubtful provenance. China had exploded a nuclear device, the shockwaves of which reverberated far and wide, but especially in India and other states in its neighbourhood. A proposal was therefore hawked from our side for the Conference to deplore the event and, in a show of solidarity, to urge that Asia remain a nuclear-free area. Sardar Swaran Singh, who should have fought it out in the Committee, kept away and was content to watch from the sidelines. Even in the lobby I could find no takers, our friends, one and all, deserting us on one pretext or another. Nobody was prepared to antagonise China in our support, and the proposal floundered ignominiously.

Shastri had expressed a wish to seek an early opportunity to meet President Ayub Khan of Pakistan. Since we would be overflying Pakistan on our return from Cairo, would it not be appropriate to meet him en route, as Ayub had met Nehru at Palam earlier? I heartily agreed, and a stop-over in Karachi was arranged through our respective embassies. On arrival at the Karachi airport, there were Ayub Khan and his ministers lined up. As Shastri inspected the guard of honour, a sudden squall swept the airfield and his dhoti was blown about, sending a titter through the assembled Pakistanis. The two heads of government travelled together into town and their dialogue continued at the guest house. After an elaborate luncheon, the principals continued their talk, at the end of which the Pakistani Foreign Secretary and I were called in. Aziz Ahmed, a hard-liner, full of hate and venom, objected to the words of the draft communique, but he was overruled by Ayub Khan who had got the measure of his visitor and seemed much pleased and impressed. Shastri was no push-over and, while conciliatory, could be very firm. When we departed for New Delhi, the dignitaries at the airport were more respectful as they had discovered that it did not take a hulking, moustachioed frame to be strong, and that a frail body could house an indomitable spirit.

Shastri's initiative in starting a dialogue with Pakistan in a spirit of accommodation unhappily came to nought. The evil triumvirate—Bhutto, Aziz Ahmed and General Yahya Khan—had other designs. They were convinced that after Nehru there was division and weakness in the government in New Delhi, and the Indian army weak and demoralised after its defeat in the Himalaya. Now was the time, they thought, to put matters to the test, with an ultimate eye on Kashmir.

In the 1959 boundary settlement with Pakistan, one area, that of Kutch, had been left out for 'later settlement' on the insistence of the then Commonwealth Secretary, M.J. Desai. The reasons for its deferment were, however, not disclosed. I was convinced that in the atmosphere of goodwill generated by the general settlement of the boundary question, this segment could also have been similarly settled in a spirit of give and take. The Kutch area became for the Pakistan hawks a testing ground of India's resolve in the confident hope that India's weakness would thus be exposed.

The Kutch area is low-lying and gets inundated at high tide, only the 'ranns' or higher projections of land remaining above sea level. These 'ranns' provide good grazing and herds of sheep and goats are raised there. Before Partition the herds moved freely up and down, but now disputes began to occur between the herdsmen on both sides of the undemarcated border. The Pakistani claims were first backed by their rangers, but later by army personnel, and serious clashes began to occur. Then tanks appeared on the high ground and, it became necessary to repel this unprovoked use of force. The problem of risking a minor war greatly troubled Shastri, but he was compelled to accept that there was no option but to counter force with force. He was tearful when be gave the necessary orders to the army.

The Indian army found itself having to fight at the wrong

place and at the wrong time. The terrain in which it had to operate was marshy and low-lying, while its adversary was on high ground and not far from its Karachi base. Steel strips had to be laid to prevent the tanks from being bogged down, while reinforcements had to be called in from distant locations. The clash found its echoes in the United Nations Security Council which called for a cease-fire and arbitration of the dispute. India accepted the call and agreed to arbitration. After lengthy hearings, the Arbitrator, the Swede Gunnar Jarring, gave an award which Shastri accepted although it fell short of Indian expectations. The critics fretted at what they thought had been lost, but the discerning accepted what had been gained. It was not merely grazing rights that were the bone of contention; it was believed that the area was rich in oil and gas.

About this time the Paris embassy had fallen vacant and I opted for it. My brother Harishwar's untimely death had been a crushing blow from which I had not yet recovered, and I felt that a change of scene would help restore me. The personal reason apart, I had advised the Prime Minister of the advantage of developing close relations with a leading western European country. Our ties with Britain were inevitably somewhat conditioned by memories of the past. Besides, Britain was tethered to the policies of the United States, whose interests in the Cold War it fully echoed. France under de Gaulle was one country which, though a member of NATO, boldly chose to follow an independent line. It had refused to participate in NATO's military activities and had expelled the NATO headquarters from Paris. Disregarding all pressures, and under the inspiration of André Malraux, the great savant who was also Minister for Culture, de Gaulle 'opened a window to the East.' What could be more natural, therefore, than to turn to India, a country for whose civilisation and culture Malraux had the greatest respect? Shastri had welcomed my suggestion, seeing its evident advantages, not only in political but also in economic and technological terms.

Thanks to this conjunction of interests, when I took up my post I found all doors open. Never was a country more conscious of India's ancient culture and civilisation than France, itself a seminal influence on European civilisation. The high dignitaries on whom I called would almost invariably refer to India's ancient heritage, and even so prosaic a functionary as the Governor of the Bank of France could talk of little else. I soon realised that this indeed was the bond which could link us together. At the level of policy, more than one minister expressed appreciation for India's independent foreign policy. France, some said, would take a non-aligned stand itself but for its membership of NATO. At the Quai d'Orsay the redoubtable Foreign Minister, who was reputed to be aloof and inaccessible, readily gave me appointments and was generous with his time. There was hardly any occasion for a direct meeting with the Olympian President, but I discovered that messages could be passed on to him through his Secretary-General, Burin de Rosieres, who happened to be at New College, Oxford in my time.

André Malraux greatly befriended me from the outset. Susheela had got to know him well during her previous visits to France, and his lovely and talented wife, Madeleine, became one of her closest friends who came over almost daily to visit her. Soon after my arrival, Malraux telephoned to say that a state funeral would be given to Le Corbusier and only two persons would be invited to pay tribute to the great architect, viz., his foremost associate and disciple, a Greek, and the Indian Ambassador, because Chandigarh was one of the greatest expressions of Le Corbusier's genius. The Greek would offer earth from the Acropolis and I should offer homage in the traditional Indian manner with water from the holy Ganga. A bit startled, I replied that we had no Ganga water with us, but Malraux insisted, adding that someone in the mission was bound to have a bottle and even a few drops mixed with tap water would do! Thereupon Susheela got busy and a few drops of the precious liquid were procured, as Malraux had rightly guessed. On the appointed morning I set out for the Great Court of the Louvre. It was packed with an array of notables and the diplomatic corps when I arrived in Indian costume holding an ornate Banarsi silver tray and jar decorated with marigolds. The catafalque was brought in by the Garde National to the accompaniment of mournful music and placed at the far end of the vast court. After the Greek, the Master of Ceremonies led me across to the catafalque where I dutifully poured my libation. Then began Malraux's funeral oration. In a solemn voice, after paying homage to the great departed, he proclaimed that the deceased had been honoured with ancient earth from the Acropolis and with Ganga water in the manner in which Hindu widows have honoured their dead for centuries! Malraux called up the next day to ask if I realised that the event had been televised and fifty million people seen it and could now recognise the Indian Ambassador!

The sophistication that one encountered in ministries and bureaus in France was impressive in its professionalism and competence. Our expectations of finding a reciprocal desire to develop a special relationship were not mistaken. French officials were ready to share views on political and other matters and to offer whatever help they could in our own development efforts.

India had long been anxious to find a market in Europe for its hand-made silks and textiles but could make little headway. In collaboration with my colleague, Maharaja Yadvendra Singh of Patiala, who was Ambassador in Italy, I had been trying to get European fashion houses interested. With Susheela's help we jointly arranged a reception for *haute couturiers* from both countries in our magnificient reception room. Susheela hung the walls with whatever materials were at hand, but mostly the pick of her own saris. The reception was a great success as the big fashion houses were all represented by their heads who showed much interest in what was on display. The reception over, one guest stayed on—Pierre Cardin—who was greatly fascinated by the Chanderi saris, and it was arranged that he should visit India to see things for himself. That, I believe, was the beginning of the now flourishing garment and fabric export trade of today.

We were convinced that the only way to make Indian handloom skills and textiles acceptable in Europe was to marry them to French and Italian fashions, and not to peddle bolts of cloth from warehouses. With Cardin himself undertaking the promotional task, the opening could be exploited by starting a showroom in Paris. I tried to sell these ideas to the ladies in Delhi who seemed to exercise dominion over the products of the loom and, after much delay, the sanction arrived. We had found a fine site on the Rue St Honore which was done up in Indian style, arches and all. I had pleaded that it be run as a commercial venture with the minimum of staff who should all be employed on a commission basis and paid according to the sales they made. On no account should there be the paraphernalia of a government office consisting of second to fourth division clerks and chaprasis, staff cars and the rest, as it must at least pay its way. But that was not to be, and the usual top-heavy paraphernalia arrived from India, not a bit interested in pushing sales but in agitating for more amenities for themselves. The result was inevitable: a white elephant.

It was during the 1965 war that Pakistan waged against India that the French government demonstrated its friendship towards India. When India's supply of arms and stores dried up, it was France that kept up the supply. Close cooperation had developed between the defence services of the two countries; Mirage fighters and Alouette helicopters were obtained from France, among other military stores. Our atomic energy agencies were in close association with each other, and many of our scientists were sent to Saclay for training. It was when on a visit to Saclay that the famed Homi Bhabha met his untimely death in a plane crash in the Alps. That was a great blow to the country and to us personally; Homi, an old friend, was to have stayed with us.

Work in Paris was very rewarding. To be functioning in that entrancing capital was indeed a privilege and a delight. Although I had visited France fairly often in the past, my sojourns had generally been brief; but now I had the time and the opportunity to get to know the country a little better. One must walk in Paris to get acquainted with the city, to feel the air, to admire the fine buildings, the broad boulevards and ancient streets, the Seine flowing serenely through the heart of the city, to breathe the air and to admire the golden light. Its very stones are eloquent of its turbulent history, and the names of its streets evoke memories of stirring events of the past. Yet the city pulsates with life; it is a place for artists, poets and musicians, for all the finer things of life. The great edifice of Notre Dame standing witness to the ebb and flow of human destiny, the domes, spires and cupolas which punctuate the skyline, add glory to the city. The urban landscape, whether viewed from the great arch of L'Etoile down Champs Elysee', past the Place de la Concorde with its great obelisk, the gardens of the Tuileries, on to the vast and stately Louvre and the twin towers of Notre Dame, is indeed an unforgettable sight. The great museums and art galleries seem inexhaustable with their treasures from all over the world. And everywhere one encounters such intelligence and such elegance.

The even tenor of our lives was rudely shattered by the 1965 war thrust upon India. Pakistan launched the infamous and ill-fated 'Operation Gibraltar' in Kashmir and breached the international frontier subsequently in the hope of making a lightning putsch deep into India. The conflict in Kutch had been peacefully resolved by international arbitration, but it was only a trial balloon to test the resolve of the Indian government and the preparedness of the Indian defence forces. The full details of this sordid affair have been disclosed in an authoritative biography of

Ayub Khan by his *alter ego*, Altaf Gauhar, the ghost writer of
his autobiography. Altaf had in his possession the President's
diaries and papers as well as his own extensive notes taken at all
the meetings attended by his patron. The biography is remarkably
candid and revealing, particularly on Zulfiquar Ali Bhutto's
intrigues and machinations, the bellicosity of Yahya Khan and
the malevolence of the Chief Secretary, Aziz Ahmed. No wonder
that Benazir Bhutto suppressed its circulation in Pakistan.

This is not the place to write about Pakistan's shameful folly
in forcing that war, except to say that having served in Pakistan
for almost four years and been involved in its affairs for many
more I could not but watch the rapid march of events with
considerable concern. Ayub Khan, who had often and with
evident sincerity expatiated to me on the utter futility of war
between our two countries, had been prevailed upon against his
better judgement by Bhutto and his fellow conspirators to embark
on the ill-fated adventure in the belief that, with a supposedly
weak India, Kashmir was now ripe for the taking. Their folly had
been compounded by the myth disseminated by the blustering
and bragging Pakistani military that one Pakistani soldier was
more than a match for ten 'Hindu' (not Indian) jawans and that
'one hard knock' would send the 'Hindu' scurrying away in
fright. This lunatic belief seemed to have seized the conspirators,
and even Ayub Khan had succumbed to it.

It was not long before the aggressors learnt their lesson. The
dimunitive and soft-spoken Shastri showed that he had a will of
steel when it came to a question of defending his country. Not
only did 'Operation Gibraltar' prove a costly fiasco, but the
blitzkreig which was meant to follow it and administer the *coup
de grace* to the Indian army, was blunted and the vast array of
Patton tanks, the spearhead of the aggressor, was wiped out at
Khem Karan. Their hulks, which still lie where they were
destroyed, bear testimony to that epic victory of Indian arms and
generalship. That, however, was not all, for the Indian army had

advanced to the very gates of Lahore, causing the panic-stricken flight of its inhabitants across the Ravi. There the army stopped in its victorious tracks to avoid causing the death of civilians and damage to Lahore's historic buildings. India accepted the cease-fire demanded by the United Nations and withdrew behind its borders; India also agreed to the Soviet offer of assistance in bringing about peace. India's generosity of spirit was met by Bhutto's demented fulminations at the UN Security Council when, in his impotent rage, he threatened to fight a thousand-year war against those whom he described as 'Indian dogs'.

Prime Minister Shastri, ever anxious to seek peace and reconciliation, chose the path of magnanimity by going to Tashkent to negotiate peace with Ayub Khan with the Soviet Prime Minister, Alexei Kosygin, acting as an honest broker. After long and arduous negotiations, Shastri accepted a formula to end the state of hostilities. But the effort proved too demanding for his frail body and he died in the service of peace.

Shastri's sudden death at the very moment of his triumph sent shock waves around the world. The courage and wisdom with which Shastri had filled the gap caused by Nehru's death, the decisiveness with which the 1965 war had been fought and peace restored, had won world-wide acclaim. In India, the people's grief was mixed with anxiety about the future. Just when Shastri's government had been firmly established and was pursuing a steady course, the helmsman had been removed and the prospect of uncertainty and dissension had again clouded the horizon.

One may well speculate on the course India would have taken had Shastri lived longer. Shastri had himself set the example of simplicity, honesty and transparency which would inevitably have made an impact on the functioning of the central and state governments. What is more, the Congress politicians in government and outside may have been shamed into conforming, in however limited degree, to the Gandhian ideals of integrity, humility and service which they never ceased to profess. What a profound difference it would have made to the Indian polity had politicians become true servants of the people instead of their exploiters. And how rapidly would the country have progressed had the rulers been true to their vocation. In the international sphere, if India had been known and seen to be following in the Mahatma's footsteps, its prestige would have increased immeasurably and its voice heard with greater respect.

If Shastri could have successfully pursued his goal of peace and conciliation with India's neighbours and settled all pending problems on a basis of give and take, new vistas of cooperation among the nations of South Asia would have opened. With China the border problem would have been greatly eased and better understanding reached. Even with recalcitrant Pakistan, it would not have been impossible to establish a sort of *modus vivendi*; at any rate, the acuity of relations might well have been blunted. With Sri Lanka, the only outstanding issue of Indian settlers had already been resolved. With easier relationships all round, the need for elaborate defence preparations would have been obviated and the resources so saved could have been devoted to productive purposes.

On the country's economic policies and development, there would have been the greatest impact. The fascination with the Soviet model of planning and state control which had afflicted most newly-independent countries, would have given place to greater adherence to the Mahatma's ideas. Emphasis on state-owned heavy industry to the virtual neglect of agriculture would have been reversed. The aim would have been to build from the ground upwards, rather than from the top downwards. The regeneration and awakening of the impoverished countryside—where the backbone of our society lives, would have had a profound effect on the economy and society, as well as on the polity. The ignorance and backwardness of the rural masses which are exploited by politicians for their personal aggrandisement would have given place to an alert and responsible citizenry. The process of industrialisation may have slowed down initially, but with greater prosperity in the villages, living standards would have risen, creating an increasing demand for goods and services. That would have stimulated all-round productivity, including industrial, to meet the burgeoning demand.

All this is, of course, purely conjectural, but most thinking Indians look back nostalgically to the Shastri era, which, though brief, seemed to hold out much promise and to reflect true 'Indianness'. The country was destined, however, to be taken in a very different direction.

After Shastri there was again the question of succession. It was feared that the country would be thrown into turmoil as the Congress chieftains would once again battle against each other for primacy. Chief among them were those known as the Syndicate, virtual kingmakers, viz., Atulya Ghosh, S.K. Patil and Kamaraj. They worked out a strategy for blocking Morarji Desai, the most experienced and senior member of the cabinet who was a serious contender. But because of his unbending nature and rigid views he was not popular with the power brokers. They wanted someone more malleable through whom they could manipulate the levers of power. Evoking the name of Nehru which none dare oppose, their choice fell on Indira Gandhi. Although she had not been a Member of Parliament at the time, Shastri appointed her as Minister for Information. With Morarji Desai effectively bypassed, Indira Gandhi was catapulted to the Prime Ministerial gaddi.

That Mrs Gandhi would be no marionette dancing to the Syndicate's tune, soon became clear. She quickly revealed a mind of her own. Power breeds its own strength and, as time passed, she developed increasing confidence. The Syndicate was soon sidelined. When Vijayalakshmi Pandit publicly expressed sympathy for her niece because of the 'heavy burden which had fallen on her frail shoulders', the niece greatly resented the insinuation of weakness. There was never any love lost between the two and when Mrs Pandit went to offer what help she could, Indira, with tears in her eyes, said: 'But Aunt, I don't trust you.' This episode was recounted to us more than once by Mrs Pandit herself with much amusement and has been subsequently recorded in her autobiography.

Soon Indira Gandhi felt secure enough to undertake a tour abroad. She first came to Paris, accompanied by her two sons and a lady attendant. Susheela and I had know her fairly well over the years when she was just her father's daughter, but one could never pierce through her reticences. On this occasion she was much more relaxed and expansive. On the drive from the airport to our residence where she was to stay, she spoke quite openly of her hopes and fears. To my surprise, since I did not consider myself one of her confidantes, she said she felt reasonably secure although there were some disgruntled elements in her cabinet. There was Morarji Desai, but she felt she could manage him. There were, however, two ministers whom she would like to get rid of, viz., the Home Minister and the Finance Minister. About the Home Minister, Gulzarilal Nanda, I was not surprised as he was a known eccentric, quite misplaced in his high office. But the other name, that of Sachin Choudhuri, the Finance Minister, greatly startled me, but I kept my peace. We had long known Sachin who was a very close friend; he had only recently told us on a visit to Paris how well he got on with the young Prime Minister, who addressed him as 'Dada' (elder brother) and how he gave her friendly advice on all kinds of matters and how much she relied on his. Sachin, who had been appointed to his post by Shastri, was soon to be made a scapegoat for the unpopular decision of devaluation taken by the Cabinet as a whole. We later learnt from Sachin that when he had gone to see her in her office, she remarked, almost casually, how she would like him to take over the Embassy in Washington! Sachin, a gentleman to the core and one who did not hanker after office, took the hint, but not the embassy. This episode, while showing commendable decisiveness on the part of the as yet untried Prime Minister, also revealed a ruthless and underhand trait to her character.

President de Gaulle gave a private luncheon for Mrs Gandhi at which Susheela and I were also present. The General was very considerate, almost avuncular towards his guest, who maintained a shy dignity. At one point the General asked what he could do for India; Mrs Gandhi replied that she would ask only for his understanding. It was an apt reply which seemed to have made an impression on our host.

Mrs Gandhi was quite relaxed during her three or four days in Paris, doing the things that tourists did. Her first request on arrival was for a baguette, the French bread which has no equal anywhere—elongated, and with a crunchy shell enclosing a cotton-soft interior. We found her a pleasant and informal guest, and, to our surprise, she even told some risqué jokes! She pressed me to return to New Delhi as Foreign Secretary and it was agreed that, after a decent interval, I would; my departure now after so short a stay would be frowned upon by the host government.

On arrival in Delhi, I was disappointed to find that M.C. Chagla, the Foreign Minister, and a close friend of mine, had just resigned in disagreement over the government's language policy. Chagla had been a distinguished Chief Justice of the Bombay High Court and our envoy to Washington and London. Mrs Gandhi, like her father, had now assumed the foreign affairs portfolio, but, unlike her father, was not at that time particularly interested in her new charge. She appointed a Minister of State who dealt mostly with routine matters, leaving the Foreign Secretary very much to himself. But certain important matters, such as those concerning policy, had to be referred to the Prime Minister; these I discussed briefly with her for her assent. She seldom raised any matter herself, nor did she pen a well-reasoned minute on any question of particular concern or to propose a new line of policy. She discontinued her father's practice of daily discussion on current regional and global issues.

In other respects too, South Block had become a rather different place. Nehru had tried to build up institutions and to work through them. Although he enjoyed untrammelled power, he used power with restraint. He had ICS officers as his Private Secretaries, but they had no independent authority of their own. Their job was largely as monitors to ensure the smooth movement of official papers and to chivvy laggard ministries.

Shastri was rather diffident on assuming Nehru's outsized mantle and he felt the need for supporting staff. This included, apart from an ICS Private Secretary, a Public Relations Officer who was also a competent speech-writer, and sundry other officials. A sizeable Prime Ministerial office thus came into being. Nehru used to take his own decisions and prepare his own speeches, but Shastri began to involve his office more closely in assisting him.

Under Mrs Gandhi, the Prime Minister's Office became greatly bloated. A middle-rank Foreign Service officer was brought in and elevated as Principal Secretary. An Economic Adviser was added, while a Joint Secretary dealt with parliamentary affairs; several lesser functionaries were added to the office.

Indira Gandhi had little experience of government or even of parliament and began to rely heavily on her personal staff. This was an ideal situation for an ambitious private secretary to build up his own power, invoking the name and authority of the Prime Minister. Also, Mrs Gandhi was, at the time, much concerned with the problem of survival as she feared that many of her senior colleagues who had been baulked in their ambitions were conspiring to oust her. This, to some extent, distracted her attention from the business of governance. The Congress party had lost much ground in elections in several states, while at the centre it enjoyed only a precarious majority. The officials were not so fearful of the government falling on a snap vote, but Mrs Gandhi no doubt had more sensitive political antennae.

We would spend much time during parliamentary sessions with the Prime Minister in her chamber in Parliament House, drafting replies to starred questions and to their supplementaries. Every possible question that could be raised was conjured up and rejoinders prepared. Often the exercise would go on through the lunch break, all sharing a frugal lunch with Indira Gandhi at her table. Much of this proved to be love's labour lost as most of the ingeniously thought-out supplementaries never came up.

Mrs Gandhi's habit—or was it a cultivated practice?—of not saying a word when confronted with a problem on which a decision was to be taken, did not particularly irk me as I took silence for consent. But visitors found it most disconcerting. Among the eminent personalities who used to call regularly on Nehru and Shastri was the celebrated J.R.D. Tata whose views were listened to with respect. After some infructuous visits to Mrs Gandhi who kept silent throughout, J.R.D. said that he had given up any further attempt to draw a word out of the Prime Minister. Similar was the experience of Sachin Choudhuri, who had been Mrs Gandhi's and Shastri's Finance Minister and an eminent lawyer and public figure. Sachin felt particularly hurt at what he perceived as her cold-shouldering of him and he too then kept away.

Mrs Gandhi seemed to be cutting herself off from even the most responsible and well-informed outside opinion. In its place what came popularly to be known as her 'Kitchen Cabinet' was taking shape. This consisted of a miscellaneous coterie of people, some self-styled intellectuals, some busy-bodies, some without roots, and some without any ostensible means of livelihood, but all with strongly leftist pretensions. Leftist also was the colouring of her personal office. Ministers with leftist views came into favour and permanent officials, sensing the prevailing wind, began to profess 'progressive' views as a passport to preferment. Even appointments to posts falling within the government's discretionary powers began to be filled by persons otherwise obscure or unsuitable, but with known leftist leanings.

The new catchword was 'commitment', but commitment to what was never defined. Was it to the country, the Congress party, to some favoured ideology or to the person of the Prime Minister? Officials soon became aware that to get on they must get along. The democratic concept of an impartial and apolitical bureaucracy, serving each government loyally regardless of its political complexion, with fearlessness and integrity, went by the board. This marked the beginning of the decline in the morale, efficiency and integrity of the bureaucracy and its growing subservience to the partisan interests of the political bosses. Honestly expressed views that went counter to the prevailing political perceptions were frowned upon. Officers who were not prepared to be false to their vocation or to barter their consciences for political favour soon found themselves in the wilderness. The result was that, by a process of osmosis, the most venal and incompetent rose to the top. This malaise which afflicted the centre soon spread to the states in virulent form. The politician-bureaucrat nexus about which there is much concern today became an established fact, and it was not long before a third and still more venomous element was added, that of criminality.

It is a curious fact that, while the Prime Minister had in practice absolute discretionary power in the appointment of ambassadors, there is no such power in the rather inconsequential matter of appointing even a humble clerk without observing the set rules and procedures. How this power came to be exercised under the new password of 'commitment' is illustrated by appointments to two key diplomatic posts, Peking and London. After the 1962 war, India and China had withdrawn their ambassadors, but now, after the lapse of some five years, it was decided to restore full diplomatic relations. The name of a suitable person to fill the post was not discussed in the Ministry, but it was expected that one who would carry some weight with the hardheaded men in Peking would be selected. The choice that came to me from the Prime minister's office, however, was that of an undistinguished individual, a free-lance journalist with an English wife, whose political orientation was leftist. His reports from Peking were journalistic while his wife's demands for additional amenities and allowances were insatiable. What impression he made on Premier Zhou-en-lai or the 'great Helmsman', Mao Zedong, one never knew.

The appointment of a High Commissioner to London was another eye-opener and required a good deal of sophistication and finesse. I was greatly startled when I received a two-line note from the Prime Minister's Office that it had been decided to appoint one S.S. Dhawan to the post and asking that the necessary formalities be taken in hand. Dhawan had arrived in Allahabad from his distant home in the Frontier province to practice law, but found the going very tough. The galaxy of legal talent for which Allahabad was celebrated, led by Sir Tej Bahadur Sapru, a great patriot, a Privy Councillor and former Member of the Viceroy's cabinet, regarded Dhawan with amused indulgence because of his leftist posturing and bizarre ways. When a large number of vacancies on the Allahabad High Court bench had to be filled, Dhawan found himself occupying one of them; but he had since retired. I wondered how his name for the London post came out of the blue, but I had my suspicions.

I queried P.N. Haksar, Principal Secretary to the Prime Minister, but he pleaded total ignorance, saying that it was the Prime Minister's choice. I thereupon walked over to the Prime Minister's room and asked if she really meant to post Dhawan to London. She said she did not know the man but had been told that he had a roaring legal practice and the right political views. This confirmed my suspicion abut the source of the proposal.

Then Mrs Gandhi asked if I knew him and was surprised to hear
the details, especially my conviction that he would not last out
six months because of his abrasive and outlandish nature; he
would carry little weight with the host country, and would even
have the High Commission staff feeling upset and disgruntled.
Mrs Gandhi asked me if I could suggest any other names as the
post had been long vacant and there was much criticism about
that in Parliament.

The next morning I suggested two names of eminent persons
who would have brought honour to the office and the country.
The first was that of C.K. Daphtary, leader of the Supreme Court
bar, a former Attorney-General of India, the epitome of culture
and who, incidentally, was a brilliant Cambridge scholar of
Greek and Latin which he was still fluent with. Mrs Gandhi
turned him down out of hand, as he was too old in her opinion.
True, Mr Daphtary was in his late seventies, but he enjoyed
vigorous health. My next suggestion was J.R.D. Tata, the doyen
of Indian industry and a man of international repute and great
integrity. He was later conferred the highest honour that the
government could offer. But he too was turned down on the
ground that he was 'not in tune' with the government's policies.
Besides, added Mrs Gandhi, she wanted someone who could
reach out to the people over the head of the government. This
seemed a peculiar requirement as we would certainly take it ill
if any foreign envoy were to do the same in India. The original
proposal therefore remained.

When the High Commissioner-designate called on me for
instructions, it did not take long to discover that he had not
matured with the years. He was hopelessly out of touch with the
outside world, which he had not visited for nearly forty years
since he returned from England. His questions startled me, but
what really appalled me was his total misconception about the
relationship between a sovereign independent India with the
United Kingdom. Dhawan asked how he should expect to be

treated in England, and before I could reply he wondered if the treatment would be similar to that which he had meted out to his sweeper's son who had come up in the world and to whom he felt compelled to offer a chair when he came to call on him. The question betrayed a lamentable inferiority complex and made one wonder how the questioner, nearing seventy years of life, could make the necessary mental and psychological adjustment as behoved the representative of a great nation.

Reports from London about the new High Commissioner soon began justifying our worst fears. There were mumblings of discontent among the staff of India House and the British government did not take kindly to the new incumbent. This was confided to us by the wife of Lord Gore-Booth, the top official at the Foreign Office, who had been a very popular and sympathetic High Commissioner in India. Dhawan also did little official entertaining for which he was paid a lavish allowance, and when he did, it was shoddy. But what really caused dismay was this shabby episode.

The statue of Mahatma Gandhi was to be installed at a solemn ceremony on Tavistock Square by Lord Attlee. A galaxy of British notables from public life and industry, including Lord Mountbatten, was present on the occasion on the appointed date and hour. But the official host, the Indian High Commissioner, was missing. After waiting for some time in vain, Lord Attlee commenced his speech and was almost halfway through when he had to interrupt it to welcome the just-arrived host and repeat some of the speech for his benefit. This scandalous episode which was meant to bring honour to India brought only disgrace. It received wide publicity in the Indian press and caused intense indignation all around.

A spate of angry questions in the Indian Parliament followed, to which replies were sought from the High Commissioner. The explanations, when they arrived, would have shamed even a delinquent schoolboy. In language of indignation Dhawan began by berating the ignorance of the questioners. It was incorrect that he was fifteen minutes late; it was only twelve minutes. The parliamentarians were obviously unaware of the traffic conditions of a large metropolis like London where traffic jams were frequent, and he happened to have been caught in one of them. Furthermore, he was so engrossed in the Mahatma's works that he had lost count of the time. Other replies were in the same vein and it was our painful task to try and put a gloss on them as best we could in order to try and appease the enraged parliamentarians. The replies, however, carried little conviction and there were insistent cries for the errant envoy's head.

The High Commissioner's foibles and antics had, of course, duly come to the notice of the Prime Minister who, however, continued to show supreme unconcern. But sometime later, she said that she had heard adverse reports about the High Commissioner; he had made no impact on the Indian community in Britain or on the student community. But what particularly displeased her was that the official residence was badly maintained and there was little official entertainment, and that too was very inferior. A change should therefore be made. One could not but wonder at this belated realisation until we learnt from a mutual lady friend recently returned from a visit to London of how badly our High Commissioner was doing and how poorly the tea had been served at the residence. The lady's testimony had clinched matters, which all the official reports had failed to do! The errant envoy was soon replaced, but promoted as Governor of West Bengal. This episode is worth mention as it contrasted with Nehru's method in making even ad hoc appointments which he first discussed with the Secretaries. When he proposed Dr Jivraj Mehta, a prominent Congress politician for the London post, he himself summed up all the pros and cons, including the prospective envoy's age of 74 years which he felt should not stand in the way as he was in good health. We could hardly demur and Dr Mehta duly went to London. But his heart was not in the job. He returned after a time to become Chief Minister of Gujarat, only to meet his end by being shot down by a Pakistani fighter while flying on a tour of inspection along the Kutch border.

Indira Gandhi was initially a non-interfering Prime Minister who seemed content to let the professionals soldier along. But after a time, typewritten notes began to appear on files and one wondered where this sudden burst of interest came from. The mystery was solved when a typed note by the P.M.'s secretary was found pinned to the note sheet; it had been duly copied on the file and signed 'I.G.' When I protested against this vicarious noting, there was a let up for a time, but it seemed to have become an established procedure in regard to papers coming up from other ministries also. This gradual assumption of supervisory power in anonymity conferred authority without responsibility and violated the established procedures and damaged institutions.

One Sunday morning I was summoned to the Prime Minister's residence. As it was the first such summons, I wondered what crisis had occurred. When I arrived at 1 Safdarjang Road, there was the usual crowd of hangers-on and visitors and I was immediately ushered into the dining room. Then Mrs Gandhi sailed in, all smiles, and I waited to hear what the problem was. To my surprise she said almost casually that papers were being much delayed in the Ministry: when I protested that that was the first I was hearing of it, she dropped the matter. Then she said that she had heard that the Foreign Secretary was inaccessible to foreign envoys. This took my breath away, as much of my time was taken up meeting a daily procession of diplomatic visitors. This too was not pursued and, after a little miscellaneous talk, I took my leave. This extraordinary visit left me with the uneasy feeling that intrigues were afoot, whose epicentre was not far distant.

Coming to foreign-policy matters, our consistent policy since

Independence had been to pursue a steady and even course between the two poles in the Cold War. But now a gradual change of track began to be perceptible. It was a comparatively tranquil period and India's relations with both camps were fairly equable. The American Ambassador, Chester Bowles, was an acknowledged friend of India's. Chester Bowles was also a leading figure in the Democratic party. He had occupied the second position in the State De⌐ ⌐tment and had now returned to India for a second term. He and his wife were very popular and did their best to strengthen relations between our two countries. The Soviet Ambassador was a senior apparatchik who tried to ingratiate himself with the centre of power, especially those operating behind the scenes.

While there was constant competition between the two countries for India's favour, on one issue both were united. The Nuclear Non-Proliferation Treaty was open for signature and both were anxious to obtain India's accession to it. The Americans played their hand with some finesse, using argument and persuasion to press the point. The Soviets, however, were rather maladroit. When the Americans realised that India could not be pressured or persuaded to sign the treaty, they laid off. But not the Soviets; day after day, the Soviet Ambassador would be at my door using the same tried arguments and the same tactics ad nauseum and receiving the same reply. India's position was that the treaty was discriminatory as between the nuclear haves and have-nots, and was not really a step towards genuine disarmament.

On the question of Vietnam, American and Indian perceptions differed widely. The US administration was still suffering from the dementia of the Dullesian 'domino theory' which held that the 'fall' of one country to 'godless communism' would automatically lead to the fall of the rest of South-east Asia and further. India had urged that the phenomenon of Vietnam was the expression of a powerful nationalistic upsurge which had recently overthrown French colonialism and should not be mistaken for any other 'ism'. But the Americans laboured under the almost pathological delusion of equating nationalism with communism, an error which they repeatedly made and which cost them dear, and brought untold suffering to distant peoples. The Soviets, for their part, were content to let the Americans bleed to death in the rice-paddies and marshes of Vietnam, fighting an unwinnable war in pursuit of no discernible American interest.

The President, Dr Zakir Husain, was due to leave in a couple of days on a ten-day state visit to the Soviet Union when I received an urgent summons from the Prime Minister late in the evening. The urgency was this. The Soviet Chargéd Affaires had phoned to say that he had an urgent message to deliver from Prime Minister Kosygin. At 9.30 in the evening the Soviet emissary arrived and, taking out some handwritten papers from his pocket, asked if he could deliver an oral message from his Prime Minister through a hurried translation. The gist of the message was that the Soviet government had decided, in reversal of its policy, to deliver arms to Pakistan. The decision should not be misunderstood by India as there would be a strict injunction that the arms must not be used against India. The motive behind this policy was to wean Pakistan away from excessive dependence on the United States and to build up Soviet influence with the Pakistani leadership.

Mrs Gandhi was taken aback by this message and asked the Soviet envoy if she could read the message herself in her study where the light was better. The notes were reluctantly handed over to her and she disappeared from the room. I tried to remonstrate with the envoy, pointing out that his justification was a precise echo of American arguments. Mrs Gandhi soon returned and handed back the notes and the visitor took his leave. Very deftly she had had the 'oral' message photocopied.

It was a serious situation. The Prime Minister was clearly taken aback, and hurt at having been let down. I said there was no way of reversing the Soviet decision; what we should do was to decide how best to live with it, but it was important to take the cabinet into confidence. Unfortunately, between the envoy's nocturnal visit and the President's departure for Moscow, the week-end supervened. Nevertheless, whoever among the ministers was within reach, should be rounded up. Mrs Gandhi agreed, and asked me to see if Dinesh Singh, then Minister for Commerce, was in the anteroom, while she went over to instruct her Personal Secretary to try locating members of the cabinet committee on Foreign Affairs. I found Dinesh Singh idling in a side room, looking absently at an old newspaper. He came into the sitting room and I apprised him of the situation. His immediate reaction was to suggest that, to show our displeasure, the President's visit should be immediately cancelled. Besides, he added, there would be much criticism of the President, both personally and officially, if the impression were to be created that the end result of his visit was the supply of Soviet arms to Pakistan. I was aghast at the idea, as it would betray gross over-reaction on our part and cause serious offence to the Soviet Union. I objected strongly to any such reflex action as the scandal would reverberate around the world and forfeit our friendship with a powerful country. Instead, I said we should hold the Soviets to their undertaking to build up their influence with Pakistan to persuade it to be more cooperative and peaceful. A paper would be prepared setting out our position for the consideration of the cabinet committee, which should be convened as soon as possible. Mrs Gandhi agreed to this line of action.

The ministers had been wandering around, some within reach by air, others in their bailiwicks and a few in New Delhi. Some half a dozen turned up for the meeting held at Mrs Gandhi's dining table. I had prepared a detailed paper on the subject which was promptly distributed to help in focusing the discussion. It would also help to deflect any criticism regarding failure of a policy, about which Mrs Gandhi felt rather sensitive. Mrs Gandhi said little, referring any question to the paper and there was little discussion. The upshot was that the proposed line of action was agreed upon and I was charged with taking up the issue personally with the Soviet Foreign Minister, Andrei Gromyko. At the end, Mrs Gandhi felt a sense of relief at the quiet denouement of what could have been an explosive issue. A couple of days later, I duly took up the matter at a long meeting with Gromyko, using the full battery of arguments against the Soviet decision. In return, I received repeated announcements of Soviet good intentions and renewed asseverations of eternal friendship towards India. At the end, Gromyko agreed to use prospective Soviet influence with Pakistan to cooperate in moving Indo-Pakistani relations from total immobility ever since the 1965 war, to constructive channels. Every endeavour on our part to persuade Pakistan to agree to talks even at a technical level on matters such as reopening communications, transport links and trade and commerce had been infructuous. Let the Soviets help to break the log-jam; in our eyes that would be a test of the efficacy or otherwise of their change of policy. Needless to say, while the Pakistanis avidly accepted Soviet arms, they adamantly refused to accept Soviet advice.

The renowned Homi Bhabha was the pioneer of nuclear research in India and between him and Prime Minister Nehru nuclear policy had been decided. But with their disappearance from the scene, there was a vacuum, especially as Bhabha's successor, Vikram Sarabhai, was more interested in astrophysics and missile technology than in nuclear science. There were no policy papers nor had there been any discussion on this crucial matter in the External Affairs Ministry. It therefore seemed appropriate to have studies made on different aspects of nuclear policy. Such studies would be intended to provide government with some basic data on which to frame future policy. Clearly, the background papers could not be, nor were intended to be, a formulator of policy. I put these considerations to Mrs Gandhi suggesting that studies on the political, strategic, financial and technological aspects of nuclear policy be made and submitted for consideration. Mrs Gandhi gave her assent and work was taken in hand by the respective ministries to prepare the confidential studies. On their completion, a meeting of the Cabinet Committee on Foreign Affairs was convened.

On the appointed day, when we entered the Cabinet Room, the papers lay on the table, apparently unread. Mrs Gandhi glowered at us and asked who had authorised their preparation. I tried vainly to refresh her memory, but she would have none of it. She said something about a 'national decision', but we were not aware of any national decision or even debate in Parliament on the sensitive issue. The studies had intended to introduce some order and clarity on the subject and were not an act of supererogation on our part. When the 'national decision' had been taken was not clear. The External Affairs, Defence and Finance Ministries had an interest in the matter, but they had been kept in the dark. The Department of Science and Technology had been created by Prime Minister Nehru and remained under his wing and was now under Mrs Gandhi. Sarabhai had provided a paper, but it was a purely political document, the phrase 'national decision' recurring frequently. Because of the lack of information it contained, the Finance Secretary was hardly in a position to make any but the most haphazard cost projections. At least three of us were greatly puzzled at our summary and inexplicable rebuff for carrying out what we conceived to be our assigned duty.

I had occasion to accompany Mrs Gandhi on two long official tours abroad as her principal adviser, the first to a number of East European countries and Egypt, and the second to eight Latin American and Caribbean countries and the United Nations. Indira Gandhi greatly enjoyed these trips, unaffected by the gruelling schedule. She remained relaxed, no doubt welcoming a respite from the daily toil of governance and party politics. She cut an elegant figure in her colourful silk saris, frequently changed in the course of the day, and she revelled in the adulation of the crowds and the admiration and wonderment of foreign heads of government that so frail a figure should carry so heavy a burden as the governance of a vast country like India. The two tours were in the nature of goodwill visits without any serious business being done, with joint communiques being issued at each capital, replete with vapid platitudes.

The usual method of talks in those visits was for the two heads first to meet in private and to follow up with a full meeting of both delegations; but Mrs Gandhi generally skipped the latter meeting. She also left it to the Foreign Secretary to conduct the talks with the host country's Foreign Minister and to negotiate the joint communique which she seldom saw. Her speeches at banquets and other occasions were carefully prepared by her speech writer in English and she would begin by speaking a few sentences in Hindi and passing on the body of the speech to an interpreter, herself concluding with a couple of sentences in Hindi. This delighted the correspondents of Hindi newspapers and their patrons who could report home about the spread of the language to distant continents!

On such visits, it is usual to exchange gifts between governments. Our gifts consisted mostly of fine carpets, carved ivory, or bronzes or inlaid sandalwood objects and the like. In some Latin American countries the return gifts were often of a personal nature; thus, for example, in Brazil and Argentina the President presented gold and diamond necklaces, and in Colombia a huge emerald of impeccable colour in its natural setting. Such gifts were to be deposited in the *toshakhana* maintained by the Ministry for subsequent public display.

The tour had its lighter moments. In Buenos Aires, where the military dictator observed rigorous protocol, the delegation was lined up at an assigned place while the Prime Minister inspected the guard of honour. After the national anthem and speeches, we were to follow the host and chief guest in procession to the terminal building. It was a hot day and the tarmac had been freshly laid for the occasion. As we tried to join the procession in marching order, we found that during the long wait our shoes had stuck fast to the tarmac. There followed the ungainly spectacle of the entire Indian delegation tugging at their feet, and then limping along, crestfallen, some on only one shoe, squelching tar, others holding their knees, yet other abandoning their shoes altogether. Instead of making a grand entry, we were more like a bedraggled and routed army. On reaching town the first thing that many of us did was to invest in a pair of shoes!

From Argentina we flew over the Andes to Santiago de Chile, just catching a glimpse through the clouds of the highest volcanic pinnacle in that vast mountain chain, Aconcagua. After two interesting days in Chile we were to have flown to Lima, Peru as Mrs Gandhi was anxious to see the great ruins of Machu-pichu. But on the eve of our departure, news came that the democratic government of President Belrunda had been overthrown in a military coup. We held a hurried consultation with Chilean President Frei as we felt it would not be proper for a distant country like ours to accord recognition to a usurper regime when its Latin American neighbours were holding back. President Frei was very distressed at the fall of one among the group of what were known as the 'Andean democracies', viz., Chile, Peru, Bolivia and Venezuela, the rest being military dictatorships. He invited us to accompany him to Vina del Mar, a delightful coastal resort on the Pacific while an urgent message was dispatched to the Peruvian junta cancelling the visit on the ground that the Prime Minister had suddenly fallen ill. The junta, for its part, kept sending messages through the night imploring the Prime Minister to adhere to her programme.

It was a long flight due north between the Pacific coast and the Andes. Chile is like a beanstalk with much length and no breadth. Our commercial flight had to stop to refuel at Lima before it could make it to Bogota, the capital of Colombia, our next port of call. Mrs Gandhi was expected to keep up a charade of illness and on no account was she to disembark from the plane. As we approached Lima, I saw with dismay a guard of honour lined up, a red carpet laid and official-looking figures moving around. When the plane taxied to a halt, a welcoming party entered, but making excuses on the Prime Minister's behalf, I accompanied them down instead, followed by some of our party, into the waiting lounge. Outside the lounge, there was an attractive display of handicrafts for which Peru is famous and we made modest purchases of copper vases and Llama and Vicuna wool scarves and ponchos. When we turned around, there was Mrs Gandhi and her entourage laden with shopping bags and brown paper packets! She looked a bit sheepish when she saw our mildly reproving looks.

Throughout the gruelling trip up and down the vast South American continent covering nine countries in eleven days with innumerable functions to attend, Mrs Gandhi never showed the slightest signs of fatigue or ennui. The rest of us were distinctly frayed and travel worn. She changed two or three times a day into one splendid sari after another and had her hair coiffured almost daily. She was enjoying the trip and took the formal meetings with the heads of state in her stride. At meetings and press conferences, Mrs Gandhi would pass on inconvenient or obscure questions to me to answer. At these encounters she was cautious and even a trifle coy, which seemed to attract the Spanish sense of gallantry of her interlocutors. I was sometimes able to catch remarks by high dignitaries addressed to each other in astonishment, such as 'Que mujer' ('What a woman').

The Prime Minister travelled abroad much more modestly than is the case now. We had flown to New York by a regular Air India flight. The only chartered Air India flight was from

New York to Rio de Janeiro. The numerous flights in between were by commercial aircraft of the countries traversed or by their official aircraft for internal trips. There was little or no dislocation of Air India schedules, unlike today when no fewer than three Boeing 747s are taken off their regular routes for days, badly disrupting the regular services.

Mrs Gandhi was to address the United Nations General Assembly and a speech had been prepared for her by her speech writer. She had asked me to revise it and fill in gaps, which I did. In New York I was told by a friend on our delegation that he was busy working on the Prime Minister's speech! Who else may have had a go at it, remained unclear. But when the speech was actually delivered a number of people caught phrases and ideas of their contribution and all were left wondering where the rest came from.

On our return a matter of considerable importance arose in a rather novel way. The Ministry had a Director of Security whose job in those relaxed times was not very exacting. It largely concerned ensuring that no unauthorised persons entered the Ministry premises, that papers from trash baskets were duly destroyed every evening and did not find their way to *paan* venders and hawkers, that suitable security personnel were posted to our neighbouring missions, etc. One day the Director of Security, R.N. Kao, came to me with a brief typewritten note and asked for my signature thereon. The request was made casually, as though it was a matter of minor routine. But one glance at the paper took me aback. It said that it had been decided to create a service for external intelligence and that External Affairs should include the names of the operatives to ensure their cover on its list of diplomatic officers. When I asked when the decision was taken I was blandly told that it had been taken by the Prime Minister! It seemed extraordinary that a far-reaching decision which so obviously and intimately concerned External Affairs should have been taken without a word of consultation with that

Ministry. Furthermore, how could any cover be preserved if the names of the one hundred or so operatives to be appointed were added to the one hundred and fifty or so Foreign Service officers? Besides, there would be one hundred and fifty letters of protest landing on the Foreign Secretary's desk from the entire Foreign Service cadre, whose members would at one fell swoop find themselves down scores of notches in the list; and they would wish to know who the new incumbents were. The point would not be lost on the foreign missions in India either.

I took the paper from Mr Kao and appended a long note to the Prime Minister setting out my view. Recalling that I had had close field experience in Lebanon and the Congo of the functioning of the espionage agencies of the big powers as well as in the four Communist countries where I had served and in which they abounded, besides the United Nations and Pakistan where too they were rather active, I would like to record my views for what they were worth. The need of a spy organisation abroad was clearly contingent upon our foreign policy objectives. The big powers had global ideological and strategic interests which they sought to promote, often against each other, especially in the context of the Cold War, by any means possible, overt or covert. They therefore had old and experienced secret agencies such as the British M15 and M16, the French Deuxieme Bureau, the Soviet KGB, and in the United States, the post World War II CIA. By contrast, India's policy was open and transparent, that of non-alignment, and it had no global ambitions, no clandestine interests. That policy had served the country well and called for no secret dealings. In certain neighbouring countries where we had special problems or interests, there were already members of our Intelligence Bureau who were more than adequate for our needs. The creation of an organisation for foreign espionage would therefore be both redundant and wasteful of foreign exchange. The present tendency elsewhere was to reduce the number of agencies doing intelligence work, and we too should avoid their proliferation. Spying, because of its extreme sensitivity, needs extensive training for specific tasks and the most effective spies have not carried diplomatic rank but wormed their way into humble and obscure occupations, such as street hawkers, chauffeurs, window-cleaners and the like. What good could an Indian police officer, pulled out from some jungle district of Madhya Pradesh or Orissa, do in, say, Buenos Aires and Belgrade? He would in all probability never have stepped out of the country and would certainly not know a word of any foreign language.

Nothing more was heard about the matter during my remaining months in service before retirement. But some time thereafter a 'Research and Analysis Wing' was created, functioning directly under the Prime Minister and undercutting our old established Intelligence Bureau which was in the Home Ministry. RAW functionaries soon proliferated far and wide, without a discernible function, in many capitals. Everywhere I travelled, our Ambassadors complained bitterly about these privileged supernumeraries thrust upon them, who were outside their operational control and seemed lavishly endowed with funds without accountability. Totally ignorant of any worthwhile knowledge of the country they were sent to, they seemed to be mostly engaged in shopping for gadgets or spying on their comrades in the Embassy. In the time that has elapsed since, they may have acquired some familiarity with certain of the skills of espionage, but since our policy of non-alignment remains basically unchanged, their functions must still be greatly circumscribed. As an indication of their redundancy in many capitals, I was asked by the Yugoslav Foreign Office when on a visit to that country, as to why it was necessary to post an intelligence agent there when there were no secrets between our two countries and whatever information we wanted would be readily available. On many crucial matters, especially relating to a next-door neighbour, intelligence has been lamentably poor and we have often been caught on the wrong foot.

As a free-wheeling spy agency under the Prime Minister's direct control, RAW was readily available to undertake any tasks assigned to it even within the country. It was known to have been very active during Mrs Gandhi's 'emergency' rule in keeping a watch on her opponents and even on her Cabinet colleagues and, generally, in bypassing the Intelligence Bureau which functioned under established rules. In the troubled states of Jammu and Kashmir, Punjab and the north-east, it is ineffective, if not actually at fault. For example, when there were rumblings of trouble in Kashmir, the Governor had strongly urged the retention of the Chief Minister, Farouq Abdullah, but Mrs Gandhi overruled him as her information—no doubt from RAW—was different. A most corrupt, unpopular and inefficient Congress ministry was foisted on the state by underhand means. That was the spark that, in effect, set the state aflame.

One of my last acts in the Ministry was to prepare a comprehensive paper on a subject with which I was only marginally concerned: the perennial problem of sharing the waters of the Bhagirathi, a tributory of the Ganga, with East Pakistan (now Bangladesh). From New York, I had gone up to Harvard to spend a day with our close friends, Professor and Mrs John Kenneth Galbraith. There were several erudite professors there at dinner who were very knowledgeable about the problems of the subcontinent. After dinner, one of them, Professor Ravel, persuaded me to accompany him to his office where he said he had made the Ganga and Brahmaputra and their tributaries flow through his computers. What I saw and heard astonished me as the Professor had the most detailed and precise figures of river flows at different seasons, the various crops and their growth patterns, etc., and had worked out every kind of permutation and combination of what could be achieved by way of enhanced production if the waters were more fully and scientifically utilised. In brief, as during certain seasons the Brahmaputra was in flood while the Ganga ran dry, the whole situation could be transformed if the two systems were linked. To achieve this, a system of canals and tunnels could be built over a period of years linking the two great rivers at the point where they both turned south. This would be supplemented by a series of barrages, dams and hydro-electric installations. The project cost would be spread out over years and the Professor was confident that international funding would be forthcoming. From being a disaster area, Bengal would become the rice bowl not only of the whole Indian subcontinent but of a much wider area. Funding could be arranged, as in the case of the division of the Indus basin waters. On my return I discussed the question with our Minister for Irrigation, a distinguished engineer himself, but he dismissed the whole proposal as chimerical. Later studies have, however, shown that it is perfectly feasible if the political will is there; modern engineering skills and technology are perfectly competent to meet the challenge. Some twenty-five years have elapsed since Ravel's study, but typically, nothing was done until 1997 to tackle the problem, which still remains a source of tension between India and Bangladesh despite a recent Treaty.

In the ICS there was a thirty-five year retirement rule, so that one knew from the very day one joined the Service the exact date of one's retirement. One my last date in office I went to say farewell to the Prime Minister. I found her dawdling over papers and announced that I had come to take her leave. She looked up and said I should feel proud at having completed my years in service. I made some deprecatory noises in reply, feeling that it was hardly for me to feel proud or otherwise, but for others to judge whether I had served the nation well or ill. Then Mrs Gandhi numbled something about going to Pakistan and I asked if she meant that I should go there on a goodwill-fact-finding mission. She replied: 'My Secretary said you should go to

Pakistan.' This shook me and I said I had already served there and a return would not be appropriate or fruitful. She asked me to reconsider, to which I repeated my refusal, adding that it should not be thought that government owed me a living all my life. That concluded the rather ungracious leave-taking.

I came away smarting at the indignity and gracelessness of it all and the offhand manner in which the offer of the Pakistan post had been made—like throwing a scrap at an abject supplicant. It as humiliating to be offered a job at the behest of the Private Secretary and on the basis of grace and favour. It seemed almost like a trap or strategem which would have ruined whatever reputation I may have acquired in Pakistan or elsewhere. One could see that the situation in Pakistan was hurtling towards a crash, relations with India were daily worsening and nothing that any envoy could do would have stemmed the rot.

It had become painfully evident that intrigues were afoot to undermine confidence in the Foreign Secretary; crucial decisions were being taken in a clandestine manner and insidious centres of power and influence were coming into being, rendering the responsible ministries almost redundant. The 'kitchen cabinet', an extra-constitutional coterie enjoying power without responsibility, had been gaining the Prime Minister's ear. Another group also began coalescing around the Prime Minister which came to be known as the 'Kashmiri mafia'.

The Prime Minister was becoming increasingly intolerant of independent official advice, especially that which went counter to her own prejudices and predilections. Sycophancy, servility and submissiveness were becoming the passport to official preferment and in the prevailing atmosphere others would atrophy and decline.

Emissaries from the Ministry came to persuade Susheela and me to reconsider my decision to retire from government, offering minor sops as alternatives. But my mind had been made up. To make amends, I was awarded the distinction of the Padma Vibhushan in recognition of my services, and was later elected as the first Chairman of the United Nations Committee on the Elimination of all Forms and Manifestations of Racial Discrimination, a quasi-judicial body established to administer an international convention which had the force of international law. Thus ended my thirty-five years of association with the governance of the country.

# SEVENTEEN

# *Freedom Regained*

When I walked out of the Ministry on that November day of 1968, I had completed thirty-five years of public service to the day. Dag Hammarskjold used to say that a civil servant, whether international or national, dedicates his life to the service of humanity with little thought of self, if true to his vocation. For a pittance of what he could earn elsewhere, he carries a heavy load of responsibility. He works anonymously without hope of reward; the credit goes to his political master, the blame alone is his.

The politician too often works for himself, for power and glory and for the wealth that he can acquire. True, he lacks the job security of the civil servant, but that makes him all the more eager to provide amply for himself should he lose at the next election. He is thus under the constant temptation of playing to the gallery, of making promises which he cannot keep, and of acquiring assets which he can salt away.

Unlike a job in business, public service gives one a sense of vocation. One makes much more money as a business executive, particularly in a multinational, and one can retire in comfort with ample assets and a munificent pension. In government service there is always the problem of retirement, with no work and no money. A business executive, however high he may reach, would still be selling soaps and boot polish and on retirement would hardly miss not being obliged to sell more. But a government servant retires at the peak of his official responsibility when he may be heading a great department charged with the most momentous affairs of state affecting the lives and future of countless millions. The responsibility cast on him demands every ounce of his intellectual, moral and physical ability, and at the age of retirement, fifty-eight in India, he is full of ideas and initiative, rich in experience, a power house of drive and energy. But when the day of retirement dawns, there is an abrupt full-stop and all this ability and experience is lost to the nation. As for me, I knew I had many years of work yet in me, though what that work might be, I had no idea. I was determined, come what may, to face the future boldly. But now I had a feeling of relief, of having given of my best and I looked forward to enjoying a spell of unaccustomed leisure.

The Delhi winter is delightful. I could now enjoy my beautiful garden with its flowers and birds and trees, and bask in the winter sunshine on the lawn. I could also now catch up with family and friends, read, listen to music and attend concerts. Our annual week in the lovely forests of the Terai and Bhabar could now stretch to a fortnight without any qualms of conscience, we could now savour fully the delight of spending long days on elephant-back wandering through the forests, returning in the great silence of the twilight, watching the sun dip and the stars appear, listening to the sounds of the evening—the call of birds nesting, the purr and roar of the great felines, and the cautionary bark of deer, and seeing in the distance the welcoming flicker of our camp fire.

In summer, when the sun beat down in ever-increasing fury, our thoughts turned to cooler climes. Now we were free to go where we liked, and for as long as we wished. So to Kashmir we went, staying with friends and family in their charming villa in the midst of an apple orchard near the Nagin Lake and Nishaat Bagh. How we revelled in the sheer loveliness of the surroundings. We went for treks along the pine-clad valleys, through meadows carpeted with multicoloured flowers, along rivers tumbling over rocks as they issued from the snow-clad peaks which, like deities, presided over the valley.

In the company of my good friend, the eminent journalist, Sri Mulgaonkar and the Area Commander, General Umrao Singh, both accomplished anglers, I spent many delightful days at fishing camps in different river valleys. Early every morning we could be at the stream with rod and line. A good angler has to be in tune with the river's many moods; and it seemed to me that a rod and line brought about a closer communion with nature and sharpened one's awareness of its beauty and bounty.

Our return to Delhi after almost two months of this idyllic existence coincided with the end of the six-month period when I could still occupy my official bungalow. There was now the problem of winding up our establishment and storing away our things until our own house was built, which was almost two years away. And now also, the state of idleness and the absence of any exacting intellectual activity began to pall.

I knew that my break with Mrs Gandhi and her dispensation was final. I had refused the offer of vegetating in a minor Raj Bhavan. I had turned down job offers from business houses. I had even refused the Vice Chancellorship of my alma mater, the University of Allahabad, which had fallen sadly from its high esteem. Worthwhile occupation I greatly needed, but there was little or no field of choice.

But heaven tempers the wind to the shorn lamb. Ralph Bunche, on a visit to India as an official guest of the government, asked what I intended to do, and when I replied that I had no plans, he suggested I go to Princeton to write about the United

Nations and peacekeeping. As it happened, the President of that distinguished University, Professor Goheen, was in India. Bunche said he would arrange for him to receive me. Goheen, a most agreeable and distinguished personality, offered me a visiting senior fellowship and within a week of his return to Princeton came his formal cable of invitation.

Meanwhile, my name had been sent to the United Nations for election to the new body in the human rights field which was just being constituted. I was duly elected with a maximum number of votes. This Committee on the Elimination of all Forms and Manifestations of Racial Discrimination was the first United Nations body which had powers of implementation. Two other similar Committees followed in the fields of economic and political, and social and cultural rights. At the first meeting of my Committee, I was unanimously elected Chairman.

Arriving in New York, we visited President Goheen in Princeton, where he and our old friend, the celebrated historian and Gandhian, Louis Fischer, showed us round the campus. We then gave our final assent and were allotted a simple but comfortable University residence. That was to be our base for the best part of the year except when I was in New York to attend meetings at the United Nations. I was allotted a fine room stacked with books in the Woodrow Wilson Institute for International Studies. I also had the services of a secretary-cum-typist and, what was most welcome, a Research Assistant. The University Library, enormous in dimension and superb in efficiency, left one wonder-struck. Any book asked for would be produced in minutes from the library itself and within a day or two from any other library in the country. Working conditions could not have been better and in the six months or so which I spent there, I wrote most of my book on UN peacekeeping with special reference to the Congo. Ralph Bunche had very kindly provided me with a room on the 38th floor of the UN building and had made available the famous secret 'Congo Cables' from which I was able to quote extensively.

The surroundings of the university town were attractive; the architecture was modelled on the ancient styles of Oxford and Cambridge, but the teaching and living conditions were altogether different. Those were the days of the 'flower people' and hippies and living styles and dress were lax and outlandish. The teachers led a more familiar existence; the faculty club served superb and elegant luncheons, the town abounded in fine restaurants and shops of quality and the town and campus were impeccably maintained. New York was about an hour's drive away.

It felt rather strange after almost two decades of living in embassies to find oneself in a simple cottage with no transport, no domestic help and no assigned functions. For days I would lie fallow with a blank sheet of paper in front of me, glancing listlessly at the books on the table, without writing a word. And then, in a burst of energy and inspiration, I would scribble away, working late into the night, returning through the empty snow-covered streets to my lonely den. It was a rather spartan and ascetic existence during the winter months when Susheela was away in India. But it helped in coming to terms with myself after the artificial and sheltered life of the past.

My visits to New York provided a welcome respite from my reclusive existence in Princeton. My UN Committee met twice a year for about five weeks at a time, and in between, too, I would frequently return to New York to gather material for my writing.

As the Committee had the powers of implementation, it was far more effective in promoting the observance of human rights in general than the Human Rights Commission which could only make recommendations without any powers of implementation. The international convention obliged all states to observe its provisions and to report in detail on the action taken.

The Committee was a restricted body of some dozen

members, elected in their own right, as experts. It had a formidable membership of legal and judicial luminaries and some very senior former officials. There was Professor Rénée Cassin, President of the Coéscil d' Etat of France, who was known as the 'Father of Human Rights', having been the principal force behind the Universal Declaration of Human Rights (adopted in 1948) and Convention on the Crime of Genocide. Professor Partsch, Rector of Bown University, was an eminent academic, as was Professor Sayegh from Kuwait, who served as Rapporteur for at least ten years. Ambassador Morozov was well-versed in Soviet legal principles and Sir John Marchand in British practice. I felt quite inadequate presiding over such a gallery of talent.

Our first task was to draw up our own rules of procedure, but far more complex was the task of interpretation of the Convention. There was, for instance, a prolonged debate over a clause enjoining the outlawing of any organisation propagating doctrines of racial hatred or superiority and penalising those giving it financial or practical support. The National Front and a neo-Nazi organisation had made their ugly appearance in British and Germany respectively. The provisions of the clause were mandatory and admitted of no exceptions.

Yet the British argued that any proscription of the National Front would violate the cherished principle of freedom of expression. The German objection was that any ban on the incipient neo-Nazi movement would only give it undue prominence and it should instead be left to atrophy through neglect or ridicule. These views were totally unacceptable to the Committee, which ruled that any national legislation or practice repugnant to the mandatory provisions of the international Convention must be abrogated and new legislation, in line with the obligations imposed by the Convention, adopted.

At the end of the debate on each article, it fell to me as Chairman to sum up the conclusions, to announce the majority view or consensus and to formulate it as the Committee's decision. It was gratifying that not a single vote had to be taken throughout my stewardship of the Committee.

The main means of enforcement was public exposure of aberrant or delinquent governments, as no government would wish to be publicly pilloried for mistreating a section of its own citizens or condoning their maltreatment. The Committee could itself receive complaints of violations which it would normally refer to the governments concerned for enquiry and rectification, as necessary. If the aggrieved party still remained dissatisfied, it could revert to the Committee. States sent senior law officers to offer explanations regarding their government's reports.

There was hardly a state among the sixty or seventy who had acceded to the Convention at the time, where some form or other of discrimination did not exist. Many states began abrogating existing laws found to be incompatible with their obligations under the Convention, and enacting new laws. Governments began setting up vigilance bodies to deal with the problem in a meaningful way. We found that the Netherlands was handling the problem of immigrants from its former colonies in the most intelligent and humane way. But the British record was, regretfully, about the worst. At the time a new law on immigration had come out which was too intricate even for lawyers to comprehend and impossible for intending immigrants.

The Convention could come into force only after a certain minimum number of states had acceded to it, but every year a number of states were added to the list so that most members of the United Nations are now parties to it. One notable exception until very recently was the United States of America. That such an ardent present-day crusader for human rights should have so persistently refused to subscribe to any of the instruments adopted by the United Nations, including the Convention on the Crime of Genocide, was a cause both for surprise and dismay. The reason offered was that as the subject of human rights pertained to its [states], the Federal government of the USA was powerless to act. The counter-argument, that numerous other federal polities had no such problem as an international instrument overrode national and state legislation, proved unavailing. It was thought that this reluctance was because of the massive and persistent violation of the human rights of the black and hispanic minorities and of the land rights of its dwindling indigenous peoples within its own borders. The United States government has now overcome its federalist qualms and acceded belatedly to many of the international instruments.

A pleasant digression from my life of academic seclusion was when I received an invitation to attend a conference on the energy policy of the United States at the Aspen Institute for Humanistic Studies. The Aspen Institute was one of America's premier think tanks. I found myself one of the assemblage of persons of eminence in the field of the production and use of all kinds of energy. These were physicists (including a couple of Nobel laureates), representatives of great oil companies, and of massive consumers like New York City, etc. Presumably I had been asked because of my association with human rights matters and as a representative of a developing country. But what I heard at the conference astounded me: the United States, with the world's most gargantuan appetite for energy, had no energy policy to speak of and, such as there was, it was predicated on the assumption that the country had unlimited reserves of natural oil and gas. There was shock and surprise when some experts revealed that US reserves on land were running down fast, there was already need for imports, and that within the first few decades of the next century, the United States would be largely dependent on imported oil. The world's biggest reserves were in Saudi Arabia, the Soviet Union and, possibly, China. There was some discussion about developing renewable sources of energy in place of fossil fuels, but with no concrete results.

In my intervention, I pointed out that it was highly inequitable that the United States and other affluent societies should be squandering a non-renewable natural resource in such a profligate manner, depriving the developing nations of an essential resource for their progress and development. What was the justification for the gas-guzzling behemoths which cluttered the streets, the vast sky-scrapers hermetically sealed against the weather and dependent, night and day, on artificial lighting and ventilation, and for every home to be a veritable factory run on machines of every description?

The upshot of the conference was to raise a general alert as to the seriousness and urgency of the problem. But before its conclusion, I was invited to attend a seminar on problems of the environment. A byproduct of the conference was concern about pollution and its impact on the environment.

When I returned to Aspen a few weeks later, this time accompanied by Susheela, there was a different gathering of concerned citizens, experts and scientists. The discussions centered on the pollution caused by industries and emissions from transport vehicles which were threatening the ozone layer. I protested against this narrow and western-centred conception of the problem. The environment was global and not confined to national or continental limits, and unless the developing countries which occupied two-thirds of the land cover and the same percentage of population were involved, no programme could succeed. The problem of pollution as narrowly defined, was regarded as a rich man's disease. The poor countries were concerned with development and what they yearned for—factories and modern transport—were the opposite of what the industrialised countries regarded as the root of the problem. The environment was under threat in various ways—by the pollution of rivers, by poor land-use, over-grazing, destruction of forests, etc. All these problems were the result of poverty and technological backwardness. I pressed for the need to bracket development with the environment. This view ultimately prevailed and the newly created body was named International

Institute for Environment and Development. I was designated a member of the governing council, a position which I held for two decades.

A new convert myself, when I returned to India I tried to interest the authorities, the press and the public in the problem and to recognise its relevance to our conditions. I addressed some gatherings and wrote a number of newspaper articles. But nobody paid any attention and I failed to muster any interest or support. It was only when the United Nations Stockholm Conference on Environment and Development took place that Indira Gandhi, sensing the global publicity value of her appearance, addressed the gathering as a champion and saviour of the world's environment. Ironically, the documentation for the conference was prepared by the Institute for Environment and Development, and when the United Nations set up an agency to deal with the subject, one of our members, Maurice Strong, was appointed its head.

Before completing my assignment at Princeton, I received a telephone call from Ben Read, speaking from the prestigious Smithsonian Institution in Washington, requesting an appointment. When Ben arrived on the following day, he explained that he was the Director of a new institute set up by a resolution of the United States Congress as a living memorial to President Woodrow Wilson. It was inviting scholars from different parts of the world to be able to meet each other under a common roof, but to be free to work at their own disciplines. The main interest would be on studies in politics and international affairs, with special emphasis on international cooperation, since Woodrow Wilson was the inspiration behind the concept which led to the creation of the League of Nations and now the United Nations. Ben said I was the first to be invited because of my long association with the United Nations in various capacities.

I did not wish to be drawn ever deeper into academia and I

told Ben that I would have to think matters over. When I sought Louis Fischer's advice, he was enthusiastic, and urged me to accept. I still prevaricated, but when on my return to India I received a cabled reminder to send in a resume of my bio data, I finally wrote accepting the assignment.

Our life in Washington was almost sybaritic after the austerities of Princeton. The Director of the Centre, Ben Read, and his wife could not have been more friendly and helpful. We were sumptuously housed in a suite at the Park Sheraton Hotel at a subsidised rate and there we stayed throughout our two terms at the Centre. With the acquisition of a car, we were well set for work and pleasure.

At the Centre, the facilities surpassed even those at Princeton. The Fellows hailed from different parts of the globe, with a preponderance of Anglo-Saxons. A wide spectrum of disciplines was represented and animated discussions took place in the Common Room and at luncheon meetings. It was a stimulating experience to rub shoulders with those who were renowned authorities in their own fields. Some came to study, others to write, others to listen and to learn, while still others came for some respite from the rough-and-tumble of politics. Along with my work at the United Nations, I was able to complete the writing I was engaged in at Princeton.

During one of my visits to Aspen, the trustees invited me to join the Institute as a Scholar-in-Residence. Susheela and I had been entranced by the place and we had no difficulty in accepting for the following summer. Nestling between high mountains at a height of 9,000 feet in the Colorado Rockies, Aspen is a fashionable summer resort and an even more fashionable winter resort. In summer, its life revolves around the Institute with its numerous literary, artistic and cultural activities. At one end of a vast meadow lie a cluster of buildings housing the Institute, its library, seminar rooms, guest houses and restaurant. At its centre is an open amphitheatre, known as the 'Tent', which can be roofed over like a pyramid in cold or inclement weather. We were housed in a charming cottage in the meadow, fully equipped with books and gadgets and everything of daily use down to the last spoon and duster, and, what is more, ample maid-service. A car had been hired on our behalf although everything was within walking distance. A great joy were the almost daily concerts by the Baltimore Symphony Orchestra in the 'Tent' where seats in a whole row reserved for the Centre's scholars were always available for a nominal amount. When we did not go the 'Tent', strains of symphonies would waft in through the open windows.

There was a very mixed group of participants at the Centre. At the apex were the scholars, limited in number; among our colleagues were the musical composer, Nabikov; Saul Bellow, the Nobel laureate novelist; and Roy Jenkins, the British politician. There was a group of very bright and lively young students—the Danforth Fellows—who could brighten up any discussion. But most surprisingly, there were many totally unexpected types—senior businessmen, serving military officers and civil servants, retired stockbrokers and even a clergyman or two. The idea seemed to be for them to detach themselves temporarily from their intense but limited activities and widen their horizons through an exposure to cultural and intellectual influences.

The Scholars-in-Residence were expected to devote a couple of hours or so daily as 'resource persons' to lead and guide discussions. The subjects of the seminars had been chosen in advance and a great deal of reading matter on each was provided to the participants. The subjects ranged from 'The Nature of Man', 'The Quality of Life', 'Comparative Religions', to 'Forms of Government'. Many of the businessmen and others had never even heard of some of the authors and were quite overwhelmed by the scope of the prescribed reading. But all were most earnest and anxious to learn. Susheela showed keen interest in the discussions and the Director requested her to lead the seminar on

Comparative Religion as the resource person. Her group included, among others, Henry Ford II, a Catholic Bishop, an air force General and an angry but highly intelligent and articulate black student. Sparks would fly between the young man and the establishment figures, and Susheela would have to step in to cool things down. At the end of their six weeks of daily reading and discussion, those who had come with closed or vacuous minds did indeed benefit from their unusual experience and felt they could return to their respective activities more creatively and with a freshness of outlook. I doubt if in any other country multi-millionaires, top executives, military brass and others at the apex of their professions, would bother to descend from their pedestals to undergo a course of study and self-correction as simple students.

The following year found us again in Washington as Ben Read had come to Aspen to persuade us to return with an offer to join the Centre permanently to lead studies in international relations. I accepted to return for three years but declined a permanent appointment. In these three years or so we had become quite attuned to the varied and somewhat vagrant pattern of our existence and I had sloughed off the shades of what may still have clung to me of my previous official existence. If my life lacked the certainty and inevitability of official existence, it was at least not subject to remote control by some hidden hand in South Block. After they have been working at maximum pressure in positions of great responsibility, officials at the moment of retirement are like deep-sea creatures, suddenly brought up to the surface—or like long-term prisoners, inured to prison routine and its certainties, on the day of release when they feel completely at a loss without their fetters. I had fortunately escaped the worst aspects of the change of life-style and occupation. And with abundant freedom of choice, our sights now turned towards Oxford.

During our passing visits to Oxford and Cambridge to renew

old memories, Susheela and I often thought how delightful it would be to return to those hallowed places as faculty members. The lives of university dons in those entrancing surroundings, far removed from the noise and frenzy of the cities, seemed civilised and cultivated and we hoped to be able to savour it. On one of our visits to Oxford, I met Dr Albert Hourani, a University Reader and Fellow of St Antony's College, a renowned scholar and authority on Arab affairs also met the Warden of St. Antony's, Sir Raymond Carr. They put me up for election and I was duly made a Visiting Fellow. With the help of a Rockefeller Foundation grant, it became possible for us to spend many summers in Oxford, pleasurably and usefully.

To be in Oxford in the summer is an experience never to be forgotten. The University Park and college gardens are at their glorious best. The shady chestnut trees were laden with blossoms and the air was fragrant with the mixed scent of flowers from trees, hedges and bushes. We awoke to bird song and all day long there was the twittering of birds and the murmuring of innumerable bees. From the distance the breeze carried the sound of church bells. The river, as it meanders through the parks and gardens, shaded by overhanging willows, is unspoilt and inviting. Wandering along the familiar old streets, some of them still cobbled, wandering into college quadrangles and passing by groups of eager undergraduates, one was carried back decades in time. The place seemed timeless—the same old buildings, grey with age, contrasting with the youth and liveliness of those whom they nurtured. Suffusing everything was an atmosphere of scholarship and study, search and enquiry, seriousness and frivolity, leisure and laughter.

Living and working conditions in Oxford, so different from those at the youthful American universities, were in keeping with its venerable past. The accent was on tradition and continuity rather than on comfort and movement. The same old facilities, the same old procedures, were made to serve modern needs. Such changes as occurred were conceded grudgingly, more out of compulsion than need. Yet the inconveniences and shortcomings were forgotten for the sheer delight of being part of the scene.

St Antony's College, established by a Frenchman, was initially cradled in an old convent. A new building was set up on the grounds and the various faculties dispersed wherever accommodation could be found. My work took me to the Middle-East Centre which had adequate material for study and research. We were provided with a newly-furnished flat in a rather tumbledown house in a shady lane. It was a glorious summer and, with the acquisition of a car, we were able to roam the lovely Cotswolds. The Cherwell river was ever-inviting and I was gratified to discover that my skill at punting remained undiminished.

The War and inflation had greatly impoverished most colleges and the salaries of faculty members had not kept pace with the times. The fine Victorian villas of North Oxford, once inhabited by single academic families with uniformed maidservants, were now broken into apartments and domestic help was practically non-existent. The great colleges, however, still maintained their style at high table which would be aglitter with shining silver-ware and crystal. Five-course meals, elegantly served, were followed by a port and coffee session in the Senior Common Room, enlivened by pinches of snuff and lively conversation. My reputation—totally meretricious—as a scholar was firmly, and to me unexpectedly, established when the *Times Literary Supplement*—the ultimate arbiter of scholarly and literary reputations—came out with a half-page review, most flattering to my ego, on my book on UN peacekeeping. As a further affirmation, there appeared soon thereafter a long signed centre-page article by Philip Howard in the London *Times* entitled: 'A New Insight into the UN in its Finest Hour' on the basis of an interview with me.

There was always an attractive variety of cultural and

intellectual activities in Oxford. Oxford was host to a conference on the Commonwealth convened by the Commonwealth Office, attended by a Minister of State and the heads of a large number of Commonwealth organisations, diplomats and a smattering of Oxford dons in whose company I found myself. I had no idea that there was such a plethora of Commonwealth organisations of which I had never heard before, nor did I have any ideas of what, if anything, they did. They were represented by superannuated knighted gentlemen who showered panegyrics on themselves and presented glowing accounts of the benefits which they had heaped on Commonwealth countries. As the speeches droned on in this fashion, my exasperation mounted until I was forced to intervene. I pointed out that not a single word had been uttered to address the real concerns of the Commonwealth countries. These concerns, I pointed out, had been given full expression in the recently concluded conference of the non-aligned nations—racial discrimination, colonialism and neo-colonialism, economic and cultural backwardness and a determination to overcome the legacy of centuries of foreign domination. Unless these problems were recognised and addressed, the Commonwealth would be devoid of meaning and relevance. I also said that the link of the English language had been greatly weakened by the narrow policy of requiring Commonwealth students to pay exorbitant fees while those from the affluent European community enjoyed concessional benefits. The Commonwealth could not subsist merely on sentiment or as a talking shop; it must have a solid and pragmatic foundation on which alone could it thrive. This outburst was greeted with a long silence and, although many of the participants said in private that they were in agreement, not one took up the cue in open debate. The conference did not appear to have had any particular objective and it ended in futility. But I felt like a spoil-sport to have introduced an honest but discordant note.

After Oxford, it was Canberra. Thanks to our friends,

Ambassador and Mrs Peter Curtis, I was invited as a Visiting Fellow to the Australian National University. During my wanderings around the globe, I had never been to Australia, as from the point of view of foreign policy it had been an appendage of Britain and toed the British line. But now, after Prime Minister Whitlam, a change had set in and Australia had begun to come to terms with the geo-political realities of its situation. Immigration from Asian countries, though on a limited scale, had been opened up and towns like Sydney were becoming more cosmopolitan.

The campus of the University was large and attractive and the standard of scholarship impressive. The library was well-stocked and the work facilities excellent. New South Wales is said to be the most populous state in the country, yet it seemed strangely empty. One could drive miles from Canberra without encountering a dozen passing vehicles. And all one saw were undulating pastures with herds of sheep, but not a single human being. The few roadside villages had the aspect of having been hurriedly put up, all of similar pattern, with nondescript clapboard buildings, a small inn, a few meagre stores, a travellers' lodge, a tiny church, all reminiscent of the past century. The flora and fauna were unique to the country. Our pleasant Australian experience concluded my incursion into academia.

I now found myself involved in philanthropic work. His Highness Prince Karim, Aga Khan, whose friendship I was privileged to enjoy, had pressed me to set up a branch of his charitable foundation in India and to be its Chairman. I found the task of absorbing interest. We secured excellent office accommodation in New Delhi and had it set up artistically and functionally and built an Aga Khan auditorium alongside the building. The Chief Executive was a dedicated man, a barrister with a Cambridge degree. We appointed highly qualified and experienced field officers along with office staff. The philanthropic work extended to needy persons, irrespective of community or religion and covered a wide spectrum of activities in the fields of health, education, environment, irrigation and agriculture. Apart from some projects directly set up by us, the Foundation was essentially a funding organisation. The accent was on investment in human beings, on developing and providing training, not on brick and mortar. Projects were selected with meticulous care to ensure their viability and continuity, the aim being to make them self-supporting within a reasonable time. Preference was given to those that were innovative, catalytic and replicative; these became our catch-words in the selection of projects.

The funds for the growing number of projects flowed in from the Aga Khan's ample cornucopia, not a penny being raised until then in India except from rents from properties standing in the name of His Highness. These properties were in enormous number, several hundreds of them, and varied from opulent office blocks and residential apartments in cities to humble village hamlets, all registered in the name of, and without the knowledge of, their Imam. To maintain these far-flung properties we had a fully qualified engineer and set up a procedure for collecting rents which were added to our budget. We confined our activities to four states where we could count on the voluntary help of the Ismaili community, who worked with rare dedication.

The programmes sponsored by us sought to apply new techniques to old problems. For example, the ponderous efforts of government agencies at afforestation produced meagre results, the vana mahotsava programmes often ending up with photographs of netas planting saplings which were soon devoured by passing cows or goats. We took up a forest area denuded by tribals and set them to work on wages to plant nurseries, dig wells and tanks and plant saplings. In three years, the forest of useful fruit, fuelwood and timber-bearing trees was rehabilitated and the tribals were able to benefit from it while conserving it at the same time. Another project concerned irrigation in an arid area. Inexpensive polythene lining of shallow tanks dug in dry watercourses, were found to conserve monsoon water for irrigation. Such tanks in Gujarat helped to save thousands of cattle in the great drought. Our work included pre-primary education as well. We found that children, given a little instruction in balwadis, did better than others when they went to primary school. Their cognitive faculties and curiosity would have been aroused, and they would not drop out of school later. We also assisted many highly-motivated individuals who had abandoned their city jobs and professions to live and work among tribals and backward communities in remote areas. In the field of public health, on the principle that prevention is better than cure, we set up extensive programmes for immunisation of children. Large numbers of hand-pumps to provide clean water were provided. Many village dispensaries were established. Midwives and nurses were given training. It was very satisfying to be the instrument through which the lot of suffering human beings could be relieved in however limited a degree. It inspired Susheela and me to set up our own charitable trust in gratitude for what life may have bestowed on us, and as our own offering to it.

## EIGHTEEN

# *Looking Back*

A survey of the national scene half a century after Independence makes one alternate between feelings of despair and hope. Recovering from the trauma of Partition with its security and a measure of stability ensured, the country looked forward with hope and confidence to a better future. Under a galaxy of leaders imbued with the ideas and ideals of the Mahatma, India won the plaudits of the world for its democratic structure, tolerance, respect for law and justice, and the probity and efficiency of its administration. It enjoyed a high standing despite its lack of the conventional attributes of power: the economy was weak; there were few industries and a heavy dependence on foreign food aid; the defence services were rudimentary. The enlightened policies and actions followed at home for the reconstruction of the country, and also the principled and fearless advocacy of noble causes abroad, gave India its position of pre-eminence among the developing nations of the world.

Today, the country is infinitely stronger; it has a rapidly expanding and increasingly sophisticated industrial network; the foreign exchange resources have fluctuated, but are currently substantial; there is more than self-sufficiency of food: the middle-class is estimated to number some two hundred and fifty million and increasing at ten per cent annually; the pool of qualified technicians is numerically about the third largest in the world; an already large entrepreneurial class is expanding; the defence establishment is the third or fourth largest in the world. And yet, despite all these considerable assets, India's position has greatly slumped abroad, and at home discontent and discord are rampant. While the small countries of South-east Asia are surging ahead and China, the only Asian country of comparable size, is being eagerly sought after and hailed as an emerging super-power, India is limping unsteadily along. But for the change of direction and consequent loosening up of the economy, prompted by the World Bank as the price of bailing the country out of incipient bankruptcy, the country might still have been entangled in a web of outdated and discredited populist slogans and sterile policies.

Indira Gandhi gave the country a firm government during her eventful rule of fourteen years. The turmoil around India did not shake the country. India's independence and integrity remained inviolable, and her voice, though more strident, still found a hearing around the world.

Within the country, however, the traditional way of politics by consensus was being supplanted by the politics of contention. The new and untried leader felt the imperative to build up her power and image beyond challenge. She feared and distrusted her own ministers of the old guard, men of experience who had taken part in the freedom struggle, and who enjoyed national acclaim. Lacking any real ideological moorings herself, Mrs Gandhi was swayed by a coterie of advisers into taking one populist measure after another. A sharp departure from the traditional laissez-faire policies of the Congress, it led to the breakaway of old stalwarts like Morarji Desai and to the splintering of the venerable party, which, for all its faults, had served the country well through its difficult infancy. Then began the pernicious practice of designating dissident factions by the initials of their leaders, a practice which has infected many other political parties since. All this ushered in an era of manipulative politics, floor-crossing, and the suborning and bribing of legislators.

The wholesale nationalisation of industries, proliferation of inefficient state capitalism, shackling of industry by permits and licences, wasteful expenditure on populist schemes, all brought little tangible benefit to the people. While other Asian countries were moving forward, allowing adequate scope for the productive capacities of their peoples, in India economic power and initiative were being increasingly concentrated in the hands of the central bureaucracy. Near absolute political power came to be combined with supreme economic powers. As if this was not enough, it had to be buttressed by comparable money power. The permit-licence regime provided the ideal means for this purpose.

The regime of corruption in high places in the guise of collecting 'party funds' began to take root. As there was no accounting of these cash collections, there was no way of determining what, if any, went into the party's coffers and how much stuck to the collector's fingers. Party leaders came to be judged by the amount of money they were able to collect. In the process, many enriched themselves greatly and quite openly, buying lands and properties and affecting extravagant life-styles. So blatant did fund collection become that at election time a high party functionary would turn up in the country's most affluent city, Bombay, for the purpose. According to a leading industrialist, the said gentleman would call up all the industrialists, great and small, and on the basis of a roster, demand the assessed amount in cash from each, and woe betide any who demurred. The compliant industrialist would, in return, expect favours from the authorities.

But since the collection of funds through a miscellany of party functionaries was diffuse and leaky, the bulk of the collections were to be concentrated in 1 Safdarjung Road under the personal supervision and control of Indira Gandhi. All contracts, government purchases, foreign-exchange transactions, etc., were to pass through the Prime Minister's personal staff. This device for gathering in the bulk of the booty in a single pair of hands, was generally attributed to the fertile brain of Sanjay Gandhi. Those of Mrs Gandhi's ministers who were in the habit of helping themselves, far from being put off, felt encouraged to continue in their ways. A corrupt minister needs a corrupt supporting official staff, so that the virus spread all down the line. Those unwilling to comply were eased out. The administration was thus thoroughly corrupted and honest and principled officers who refused to succumb to the spreading malaise were fobbed off with inconsequential jobs, or simply denigrated as cranks or eccentrics. In most of the states the situation was worse.

Since politics had become such a profitable occupation, loaded with wealth and privilege and little work, it attracted those seeking a quick fortune in the shortest possible time. No longer were the criteria for election the esteem and respect that a candidate enjoyed, or his distinction and public-spiritedness. What began to count now was the money and muscle-power that a candidate commanded, with which he could bribe or bully the voters. As a result, the character and quality of legislators has steadily eroded not only in the state assemblies but even in the central legislature.

Instead of striving to promote unity in a country riven by diversities, the politics of division was pursued, creating new conflicts. By dividing caste from caste, community from community and fixing quotas and reservations, dissatisfaction has spread all around. The traditional systems of relationships which made for stability have been disrupted, giving rise to caste wars in the countryside. The lessons of the partition of the country have been forgotten in the reckless pursuit of egregious policies. The purpose of empowerment of the under-privileged could have been better served by raising their standard of enlightenment by special subsidised programmes instead of by lowering the general standard.

Legislators begin their political lives in sin by giving false certificates regarding their election expenditures. The vast sums deployed to bribe or bamboozle voters have to be recovered manifold, and the so-called tribunes of the people, false to their vocation, have become their exploiters and money-grabbers.

An unholy alliance took shape between corrupt politicians, venal officials, drug mafias and gangsters. As the President of India warned the nation, the evils of corruption, criminality, communalism and casteism are poisoning the body politic. Scandal after scandal of increasingly monstrous proportions involving corruption in high places, has rocked the nation. Corruption has come to be regarded by a tolerant and long-suffering people almost as a way of life.

The saddest consequence of corruption has been the breakdown of values. This has brought to the surface all the weaknesses of our ancient society. The injunctions of dharma, violated by the ruling elite, no longer govern behaviour patterns and relationships. Social consciousness has gone by the board and it is now 'each for himself and the devil take the hindmost'. Contempt for the law has reached almost endemic proportions.

The destruction of values and the attempt to attain power for self-aggrandisement has been accompanied by an assault on the nation's democratic institutions. These had been nurtured and respected by the early leaders of the Republic. It was Indira Gandhi, avid for untrammelled power, who was largely responsible for the subversion of institutions. This reached its outrageous climax during her 'Emergency'. An attempt had then been made even to sully the very fountain-head of justice by packing the Supreme Court with so-called 'committed' or

624 • *A Life Of Our Times*

compliant judges. The very excesses set in motion a reverse process. A vigilant and independent Supreme Court later stepped into the breach and in public interest litigation, despite what the purists might say, took firm action against corruption in high places. The Election Commission, too, despite occasional excesses, took positive steps to prevent the more blatant forms of capturing votes and, by cutting down election expenditures, helped cleanse the political process.

It is part of the Indian psyche that everything revolves in cycles of good and evil. Even the aeons alternate between the good and the bad. There can be no light without shade, no knowledge without ignorance; no virtue without vice; no joy without sorrow. Rulers can alternate between the benign and the benighted; years of plenty are followed by years of scarcity; periods of peace by those of turmoil. And so the wheel of life keeps turning. But there is always hope. When evil becomes too dominant or unbearable, an avatar arises in divine human form to destroy it, ushering in a time of peace and plenty. Every year, in town and village throughout the length and breadth of the country, the triumph of good over evil is celebrated at the festival of Dussehra. At its conclusion, men and women return to their daily toil, refreshed and renewed, to face life with new hope and confidence. Thus does Mother India meet and overcome all her tribulations.

One can be reasonably confident that the awakened peoples with their roots going back to the dawn of civilisation and with their extraordinary resilience and powers of survival, will triumph over their present ills and confidently march forward towards a future of promise and fulfilment. India will then fulfil its proud destiny and shine with refulgence as a beacon of peace and harmony in a distracted world.

# Index